Public Law
in Scotland

The authors and publisher gratefully acknowledge the generous support of the Clark Foundation for Legal Education without which it would not have been possible to publish this book.

Public Law in Scotland

Editors

Aileen McHarg

Tom Mullen

Avizandum Publishing Ltd
Edinburgh
2006

Published by
Avizandum Publishing Ltd
58 Candlemaker Row
Edinburgh EH1 2QE

First published 2006

© The authors 2006

ISBN 1–904968–08–2
    978–1–904968–08–5

British Library Cataloguing in Publication Data
A catalogue record for this book is available from the British Library

Typeset by Waverley Typesetters
Printed and bound by Bell & Bain Ltd, Glasgow

Contents

Foreword

The title of this book implicitly asserts a proposition which might, at least until recently, have been regarded as controversial: that Scotland possesses a body of law which can aptly be described as public law. Although writers on Scots law have distinguished for centuries between public rights and private rights (indeed, a distinction between *publicum ius* and *privatum ius* can be traced back to Ulpian), the concept of public law has been slow to win acceptance in Scotland. Whereas the concept came to be accepted in English law, despite its Diceyean heritage, in the 1970s and 1980s (notably through the intellectual leadership of Lord Diplock), Scottish writers continued to express doubts about the soundness of the distinction. It was thought by some to have been authoritatively rejected in *West v Secretary of State for Scotland* 1992 SC 385; but it was employed in the more recent case of *Davidson v Scottish Ministers* 2006 SC (HL) 41. Although, as was observed in that case, there are difficulties in defining the exact scope of the concepts of public law and private law, it is clear today, even if it was not in Dicey's time, that the legal relations between government (in the broadest sense) and the governed often raise issues, in Scotland as elsewhere, which differ from those raised by relations between individuals, and which require distinct consideration in terms of both procedural and substantive law.

Those who, like myself, consider that Scotland possesses a body of law which can aptly be described as public law might however find it more difficult to describe that system and the respects in which it differs from the public law of the other parts of the United Kingdom, or to undertake a critical evaluation of it. This book undertakes that task of description and evaluation.

Discussion of public law issues in Scotland in recent years has not infrequently been influenced by nationalism, and by a related concern to assert and protect the distinctiveness of Scots private law. There has therefore been particular interest in the pre-1707 constitution of Scotland (in, for example, the presence or absence of a doctrine of parliamentary supremacy) and in the legal consequences of the Union. The distinctiveness of public law in Scotland did not however end in 1707. Scotland continued after the Union to have a distinctive system of government, at both a national and a local level. In terms also of legal concepts and principles, Scots law remained distinct in some respects: in particular, it differed from English law in drawing fewer distinctions between public and private law (for example, in having no special forms of procedure for public law disputes, at least following the abolition of advocation as a civil procedure in 1868; in applying private law rules of standing even in public law contexts; and in according the Crown no immunity from delictual liability). Some of these differences have been elided, over time, by legislation (such as the Crown Proceedings Act 1947), or by judicial decisions, in order to establish throughout the United Kingdom a broadly consistent approach to public law, which reflects the thinking of the time about how legal relations between government and the governed should be regulated. Other differences in legal doctrine nevertheless remain: not always, as it seems to me, to the advantage of Scots law.

Devolution has added to the distinctiveness of public law in Scotland. The establishment of a Scottish Parliament and Executive whose powers are limited by law has already resulted in issues of a novel kind (such as legislative review) coming before the courts. In addition, initiatives taken by the Parliament and the Executive have resulted in the creation of new public institutions in Scotland (such as the Judicial Appointments Board for Scotland and the Scottish Public Services Ombudsman), giving rise to a further range of issues. The arrangements which have been established as a consequence of devolution (for example, as to the involvement of the devolved institutions in the adoption and implementation of EU law and policy, or as to accountability in areas where executive power has been devolved but legislative competence is reserved to Westminster) are not however always widely known, and merit description and appraisal.

In the daily practice of the law, public law is of the greatest importance. Yet it is a subject with which many practitioners are relatively unfamiliar, reflecting its lack of prominence in the syllabuses of the universities, at least in the past. Although public law in Scotland has a long history, reflected in the establishment of chairs of public law at Edinburgh and Glasgow Universities, it has until recently been the subject of only limited attention by academic lawyers (with some exceptions, notably the late Professor J D B Mitchell, several of whose pupils have been active as counsel and judges in the development of Scottish public law). Nor has the subject received much attention from the Scottish Law Commission. In the area of judicial review, in particular, the judiciary have been primarily responsible for developments in the law, with the House of Lords, aware of developments in English law, providing the principal impetus for change.

The catalyst for the introduction of a modern procedure for applications for judicial review, for example, was the speech of Lord Fraser of Tullybelton in *Brown v Hamilton District Council* 1983 SC (HL) 1, itself inspired by the earlier introduction of a modernised procedure in England and Wales. Lord Fraser (who was sitting in a committee chaired by Lord Diplock) suggested that there might be 'advantages in developing special procedure in Scotland for dealing with questions in the public law area, comparable to the English prerogative orders': possibly the first example of the use of the expression 'public law' in a Scottish case. The unfamiliarity of some practitioners with public law was illustrated, following the introduction of the new procedure, by uncertainty as to its proper scope. That uncertainty was resolved to a considerable extent by *West v Secretary of State for Scotland,* but the decision in that case has given rise to other questions. It may, for example, be a matter for consideration whether the approach adopted in the decision was entirely coherent, in so far as it rejected a test of jurisdiction based on the existence of a public law element, but accepted that the grounds of review should be the same as those developed in English law specifically for resolving public law disputes.

That is not the only area of Scots public law which might benefit from critical appraisal. The rules of standing, for example, might be thought to be ill-adapted to public law: they are derived from private law, and can be satisfied by non-governmental organisations only in limited circumstances. Partly at least as a consequence, some public law cases relating wholly or mainly to Scotland have been brought before the English courts, where the rules of standing are more generous. In practice, the government and the Scottish Executive do not normally take an objection to the standing of non-governmental organisations. Nevertheless, a reappraisal of the traditional Scottish approach to standing might be thought to be overdue.

One of the major difficulties faced by anyone wishing to research or reflect on issues of public law in Scotland is the absence of an extensive and systematic academic literature. The present book makes an important contribution towards filling that gap, not only describing the relevant law but also undertaking a critical evaluation of it. A series of essays addresses all the issues which I have mentioned, together with many others.

I have enjoyed reading the essays in this book. Several provide an explanation and assessment of institutional arrangements (particularly those introduced since devolution) which I have not seen explained as clearly, if at all, elsewhere. Other essays contain stimulating analyses and criticisms of aspects of substantive or procedural law. Considered as a whole, the book provides a valuable contribution to debate on the issues which it covers, with a high level of discussion being maintained. It is to be hoped that the book will stimulate debate: a debate which, with the help of this book, should be better informed.

The book will be of interest to students, academics and practitioners at all levels, and should be welcomed in all quarters.

Robert Reed
Senator of the College of Justice in Scotland

Preface

The idea for this book was born out of the frustration we experienced as teachers of public law in Scotland, especially at advanced level, as a consequence of the relative paucity of literature on public law from a Scottish perspective. Although there is now a choice of textbooks on Scots constitutional law, they are not exclusively focused on the Scottish aspects of our constitutional order, and most of the wider theoretical or contextual literature on public law tends to be written against a background of the detail of English law. In areas where Scots public law differs from other parts of the United Kingdom, therefore, students and teachers in Scotland have had to work much harder than in other areas both to discover what those differences are and to evaluate their significance. As the extent of those differences has grown post-devolution, this situation has become increasingly unsatisfactory.

No doubt some of the blame for this absence of a specifically Scottish body of public law literature is to be laid at the door of Scots public law teachers – although, despite the historical and contemporary strength of public law teaching in Scottish universities, we are still a small band. However, as we discovered when trying to find a publisher for this book, the reason is also partly attributable to the economics of the legal publishing industry. The Scottish legal market is simply too small to sustain an extensive critical literature, for which neither extensive student nor practitioner sales can be guaranteed. Accordingly, we are extremely grateful to the Clark Foundation for providing a grant with which to underwrite the publication costs of this book, without which it would not have seen the light of day, and also to Avizandum Publishing for agreeing to undertake a slightly unusual publishing project (what one contributor to the book cruelly described as a form of vanity publishing).

The primary aim of this book is thus to examine, in a reasonably systematic manner, the areas where Scots public law differs from the rest of the UK, and to discuss the significance of these differences in the light of relevant theoretical and policy debates, in a way that is accessible to a student audience. However, in addition to its pedagogic aim, the project acquired a larger ambition, namely to stimulate debate amongst academics and public law practitioners in Scotland about the scope for and desirability of a distinctively Scottish approach to public law questions. It is therefore our hope that the book will be a useful resource for both academics seeking to make sense of Scots public law as a whole, and for practitioners of law and government, whether engaged in case work or in institutional and law reform. It goes without saying that neither of these aims could be fulfilled without the efforts of our contributors, and we are, finally, also very grateful to them for both their insightful treatment of the various issues covered by the book, and for their patience with our editorial demands.

Aileen McHarg
Tom Mullen
University of Glasgow
November 2006

Contributors

Gavin Anderson is Senior Lecturer in Public Law at the University of Glasgow

Noreen Burrows is Jean Monnet Professor of European Law at the University of Glasgow and Dean of the Faculty of Law, Business and Social Sciences

Sarah Craig is Lecturer in Law at the University of Glasgow

Chris Himsworth is Professor of Administrative Law at the University of Edinburgh

Heather Lardy is Senior Lecturer in Law at the University of Aberdeen

Aileen McHarg is Senior Lecturer in Public Law at the University of Glasgow

Tom Mullen is Professor of Law at the University of Glasgow

Jim Murdoch is Professor of Law at the University of Glasgow

Aidan O'Neill QC is an advocate, a practising member of both the Scottish Bar and the English Bar and an associate of Matrix Chambers, Gray's Inn, London

Alan Page is Professor of Public Law at the University of Dundee

Scott C Styles is Senior Lecturer in Law at the University of Aberdeen

Brian Thompson is Senior Lecturer in Law at the University of Liverpool

Stephen Tierney is Reader in Law at the University of Edinburgh

Adam Tomkins is John Millar Professor of Public Law at the University of Glasgow

Barry K Winetrobe is Reader in Law at Napier University

INTRODUCTION

1

Chapter 1

Public Law in Scotland: Difference and Distinction

Aileen McHarg

THE PARADOX OF SCOTS PUBLIC LAW

Writing about the prospects for judicial review of Acts of the Scottish Parliament, Alan Page comments that '[d]evolution … has once more made it meaningful to talk of a Scottish constitution'.[1] However, from this perspective, devolution is not really such a ground-breaking event as it might appear. Elements of a distinct body of Scots public law have persisted ever since the Union with England in 1707. Although the Union legislation abolished Scotland's separate Parliament and, by Article XVIII, provided that 'the laws which concern public right, policy and civil government may be made the same throughout the whole United Kingdom', it did not actually *require* assimilation of Scots and English public law, and in fact guaranteed the continued existence of certain important Scottish institutions – the royal burghs, the Church of Scotland and, above all, the separate court system.

Following the Union, very little assimilation was imposed on Scotland by the Westminster Parliament.[2] As had been foreshadowed in the Union agreement, the Scottish Privy Council was abolished in 1708. However, '[i]ts disappearance left a void. Scotland could not then – or indeed since – be governed simply by being absorbed by existing English institutions'.[3] During the eighteenth century, 'the British state … was always mediated through … "native Scottish surrogates"'[4] – the so-called Scottish 'managers'[5] or the Lord Advocate, acting as adviser to the British Home Secretary. With the expansion of government functions in the nineteenth century, a number of separate Scottish boards were set up to carry out administrative and regulatory functions and, in 1885, the system of administrative devolution was formalised with the establishment of the Scottish Office as a separate territorial, rather than functional, department of state, reinforced in 1926 when the responsible minister was upgraded to the status of Secretary of State for Scotland. During the twentieth century, the practice continued of creating, or maintaining, separate Scottish institutions of intermediate government. For instance, there remained important differences in the organisation and regulation of the police. And, although substantially reformed, the Scottish system of local government was still distinct from that elsewhere in the UK (see Chapter 8).

Separate executive institutions were accompanied by some recognition of Scottish difference at the Westminster Parliament. Until the Great Reform Act

---

1 In L Farmer and S Veitch (eds), *The State of Scots Law* (2001), p 11.
2 J D B Mitchell in J A Andrews (ed), *Welsh Studies in Public Law* (1970), p 70.
3 R Sutherland in J P Grant (ed), *Independence and Devolution: the Legal Implications for Scotland* (1976), p 19.
4 L Paterson, *The Autonomy of Modern Scotland* (1994), p 34.
5 See Paterson, above n 4, pp 32–34.

of 1832, Scottish MPs were elected by a unique system carried over from the old Scottish Parliament,[6] and, from 1707 until as late as 2005, the Scottish electorate was substantially over-represented at Westminster in terms of the number of MPs it returned. According to Robert Sutherland, this was a deliberate, albeit slight, measure of compensation for Scotland's loss of sovereignty,[7] and it continued to be defended as such[8] until devolution made it untenable. In addition, in many areas, Westminster continued to pass separate legislation for Scotland and, by the time of devolution, special procedures were well established for handling Scottish legislative business.[9]

Finally, the maintenance of separate judicial institutions has meant separate arrangements for appointing judges and judicial tenure in Scotland (see Chapter 9). It has also further contributed to the distinctiveness of Scottish government – in the nineteenth century, sheriffs acquired extensive administrative functions, elements of which they retain to this day[10] – and, more importantly, has permitted the preservation or development of separate Scottish public law doctrines. Although considerable doctrinal assimilation has taken place since the Union – perhaps inevitably, given the greater weight of English precedent – much of this has been at the instance of Scottish judges themselves, rather than being imposed by the English-dominated House of Lords.[11] Moreover, significant differences have persisted, for example, in the law relating to judicial review (see Chapters 11 and 12), Crown privileges and liability (see Chapter 13), civil liberties and police powers (see Chapter 16) and, above all, as to the status of the Union legislation itself as a limitation on the sovereignty of the Westminster Parliament (see Chapter 2).

Taking these distinctively Scottish governance arrangements as a whole, Lindsay Paterson argues that, even before devolution, Scotland enjoyed a level of autonomy comparable to that of other small European nations with greater formal independence.[12] Even if that autonomy was sometimes used to assimilate to its larger neighbour, Scotland retained a sense of distinct national identity, as an equal partner in the Union.[13] Moreover, that sense of national identity was largely based upon *institutional* distinctiveness (with the separate Scottish legal system being regarded as particularly significant),[14] more than on distinctions of language, religion or ethnicity.[15] Thus, Neil Walker argues that, whether or not the Union legislation places legally enforceable limits on Westminster's legislative sovereignty, it can properly be described as fundamental law, since it is 'one of

6 Sutherland, above n 3, pp 20–21. In addition, until the 1960s, peers who held only pre-Union Scottish titles would assemble at Westminster to elect which of their number would sit in the House of Lords – in effect, the continuing convocation of the First Estait of the Scottish Parliament. I am grateful to Aidan O'Neill for this point.
7 Sutherland, above n 3, p 21.
8 See M Keating, *Plurinational Democracy: Stateless Nations in a Post Sovereignty Era* (2001), p 120.
9 See C M G Himsworth, 'The Scottish Grand Committee as an instrument of government' (1997) 1 EdinLR 79.
10 See G Little in W Finnie, C M G Himsworth and N C Walker (eds), *Edinburgh Essays in Public Law* (1991).
11 Mitchell in *Welsh Studies*, above n 2, p 71; M Loughlin, 'Sitting on a fence at Carter Bar: in praise of J D B Mitchell' 1991 JR 135 at 147.
12 Paterson, above n 4, p 4.
13 Paterson, above n 4, pp 14, 43; see also T Nairn, *After Britain* (2000), p 13.
14 Paterson, above n 4, pp 12, 169; Keating, *Plurinational Democracy*, above n 8, p 37.
15 S Tierney, *Constitutional Law and National Pluralism* (2004), p 71.

the fundamental generative influences of the contemporary Scottish legal and political system'.[16]

Rather than seeing devolution as the catalyst for a renewed constitutional distinctiveness in Scotland, therefore, it is perhaps more accurate to regard this pre-existing level of distinctiveness as the catalyst for devolution; the lack of a separate legislature and national political representation increasingly being seen as anomalous in the light of these other differences. Nevertheless, devolution does undeniably add to Scotland's constitutional distinctiveness, producing, according to Michael Keating, an unprecedented combination of, on the one hand, a high degree of symbolic recognition of Scotland's separate national identity with, on the other, a large amount of functional decentralisation.[17] Thus, it creates new sites of constitutional inquiry – the Scottish Parliament and Executive (see Chapters 5 to 7) – and raises new constitutional issues – a quasi-federal division of competences and the possibility of legislative review (see Chapter 10) – which, thanks to the asymmetric nature of devolution, have no exact parallels in other parts of the UK.[18] In addition, devolution itself generates further opportunities for constitutional differentiation. Although much of the constitutional framework, including the terms of the Scotland Act 1998 itself, is reserved to Westminster[19] – thereby acting as a written constitution for the Scottish Parliament and Executive and creating a further point of differentiation from Westminster – this is not true in all cases. Indeed, some constitutional development, in relation to arrangements for investigating maladministration (see Chapter 14) and financial audit, was explicitly foreshadowed in the Scotland Act, while issues such as local government and the court system are within the competence of the devolved institutions, and some important changes have already taken place (see Chapters 8 and 9). Hence, Walker contends, the Scotland Act can also make undoubted claims to fundamental status in terms of its generative capacity.[20]

Where devolution does perhaps represent a break with the past, however, is in terms of a heightened *awareness*, or at least acknowledgment, of the possibility of Scottish constitutional difference. The devolution policy was developed during the 1980s and 1990s by the Scottish Constitutional Convention in a conscious process of constitution-making which was explicitly premised on a rejection of the British doctrine of parliamentary sovereignty in favour of an alternative Scottish tradition of popular sovereignty.[21] This sense of an indigenous and continuing constitutional

---

16 'Fundamental Law' in title on 'Constitutional Law', *Stair Memorial Encyclopaedia* (Reissue, 2002), para 66.

17 Keating, *Plurinational Democracy*, above n 8, p 123.

18 This is, therefore, now true of all parts of the UK, including England. Eg, there is an emerging tier of functional (ie, non-elected) regional government in England which does not apply elsewhere: see R Hazell (ed), *The English Question* (2006); and Adam Tomkins argues that, properly understood, the West Lothian Question is an issue for the English constitution (or, more accurately, the English and Welsh constitution) rather than for the UK constitution as a whole: A Tomkins in A Tomkins (ed), *Devolution and the British Constitution* (1998), p 101.

19 See Scotland Act 1998, Sch 4. However, reservation of matters to Westminster does not necessarily imply that there should be uniformity of provision across the UK: C M G Himsworth, 'Devolution and the mixed legal system of Scotland' 2002 JR 115 at 124.

20 'Fundamental Law', above n 16, para 72. Whether it might also be regarded as fundamental in the sense of being (to some degree) protected against repeal or revision by the Westminster Parliament is considered in Chapter 2.

21 See the *Claim of Right for Scotland*, adopted at the Convention's inaugural meeting on 30 March 1989. The historical authenticity of this alternative tradition is, however, debatable: see C Kidd, 'Sovereignty and the Scottish constitution before 1707' 2004 JR 225.

tradition was also invoked by Winnie Ewing MSP at the opening ceremony for the Scottish Parliament, when she declared that the Scottish Parliament 'is hereby reconvened'. In so doing, she implicitly challenged the assertion in the Scotland Act (section 28(7)) that Westminster's sovereignty was unaffected, and hence that devolution should be understood as a concession by the British state, rather than the fulfilment of the rights of the Scottish people.[22]

By contrast, prior to devolution, notwithstanding the substantial differences outlined above, there was very little academic interest in public law from Scots lawyers. Any distinctively Scottish theoretical tradition in constitutional law[23] appeared to have been cut off at the Union and, although Scottish legal writing in general was marked by a notable legal nationalism, this was almost entirely devoted to the preservation of the Scottish legal tradition as a body of *private* law. For example, according to Andrew Dewar Gibb, one of the foremost legal nationalists: '[t]oday there is no Scottish constitution. Whatever was written [on that subject] would of necessity be pure history.... To write at length on this subject in a book of Scots Law would be something of an absurdity'.[24] Similarly, according to Lord Anderson, in *Macgregor v Lord Advocate*, 'the constitution of Scotland has been the same as that of England since 1707 [and] there is a presumption that the same constitutional principles apply in both countries'.[25] And even today, Gloag and Henderson's encyclopaedic work, *The Law of Scotland*, is exclusively concerned with private law.[26] To the limited extent that legal nationalists have been interested in public law matters at all – namely concerning the status of the Union legislation as fundamental law[27] – this too can be seen as largely motivated by the desire to protect Scots private law against outside interference. Thus, in *MacCormick v Lord Advocate*,[28] although Lord President Cooper was prepared to accept in principle that the Union legislation constituted a binding limitation on the Westminster Parliament, it was only in extreme cases, such as an attempt to replace the whole body of Scots private law or to abolish the Court of Session, that, he suggested, the Scottish courts would be willing to strike down Acts of Parliament.[29]

This lack of interest in Scots public law appears doubly paradoxical. In the first place, as noted above, institutional and doctrinal differences have been important in sustaining a separate Scottish national identity, yet there has been little attempt to explore the nature of these differences and their practical or theoretical implications. Secondly, comparative lawyers have traditionally regarded public law as more nationally specific than private law, yet in Scotland it has been private law that has been the focus of (legal) nationalist activity.

A number of explanations for this may be suggested. Chris Himsworth notes that the civilian inheritance of Scots law, which is what mainly distinguishes it from

22 On this distinction, see Keating, *Plurinational Democracy*, above n 8, p 11.
23 See further Chapter 2.
24 *A Preface to Scots Law* (1964), p 2.
25 1921 SC 847 at 848. Other judges, in extra-judicial writings, have also tended to stress the fundamental similarity of the basics of the constitutional order, even when writing about the subject from an explicitly Scottish perspective: see, eg, W I R Fraser (later to become Lord Fraser of Tullybelton), *An Outline of Constitutional Law* (2nd edn, 1948); the Rt Hon Lord Clyde, 'Introduction' in title on 'Constitutional Law', *Stair Memorial Encyclopaedia* (Reissue, 2002).
26 L J Dunlop et al (eds), 11th edn, 2001.
27 See, in particular, T B Smith, 'The Union of 1707 as fundamental law' [1957] PL 99.
28 1953 SC 396.
29 See also *Gibson v Lord Advocate* 1975 SLT 134.

English law, has very little to say about public law.[30] In addition, the priority given
to private law reflects the terms of the Union legislation itself. Colin Kidd points
out that the Scottish constitution of 1706 was not a venerable historic entity, but
dated only from the Revolution settlement of 1689–90.[31] It can therefore be argued
that, at the time of the Union, governance arrangements were far less important as
markers of Scots identity than institutions of civil society, in particular the Church
of Scotland.[32] Further, there is no necessary connection between legal nationalism
and political nationalism. On the contrary, the former has frequently been deeply
unionist in character,[33] and this in fact reflects a widespread commitment to the
Union, from the eighteenth century onwards, as the best means of promoting and
protecting Scotland's national interests.[34] Paterson argues that:

> '[T]he really important lesson that would have been drawn from [a] survey of other
> small nations by a nineteenth-century liberal would have been a reinforcement of
> the belief that state forms mattered less than the scope which the state gave to the
> autonomous operation of civil society. [European] nationalist movements ... pursued
> national autonomy because it was a vehicle for liberalism. A Scottish liberal would
> have been more inclined to celebrate the common liberal framework of Britain as a
> whole than to detail the institutional autonomy which Scotland enjoyed. Scotland
> had freedom mainly because the UK state let civil society function autonomously.
> Thus Scottish autonomy was a by-product of something that was regarded as much
> deeper.'[35]

Finally, this commitment to the Union was reinforced in Scotland by the legacy of
Enlightenment thinking. This stressed the virtues of rationalism and universalism,[36]
and was therefore prepared to abandon historic Scottish constitutional practices
in favour of their English counterparts, since the latter were regarded as more
advanced.[37]

But if Scots lawyers neglected the distinctive aspects of Scots public law because
they assumed that these were, and should be, UK-wide matters, English lawyers
have all too frequently made the opposite assumption: that the UK constitution is
essentially the same as the English constitution. Typically, this is an unconscious,
or at least unacknowledged, process, whereby theoretical or contextual discussions
are conducted from the point of view of English law, even though Scots law on the
subject may be different. At times, though, it is explicit and overtly antipathetic
to Scots law. For instance, Himsworth claims that the House of Lords in the
nineteenth century exhibited a hostile and offensive attitude towards Scots law
which made a deep impression on public as well as private law, and which reflected
the specific assumption that one necessary effect of the Union was to dissolve
differences between Scotland and England.[38] But even as recently as 1976, the
English historian Hugh Trevor-Roper wrote that:

30   In B Hadfield (ed), *Judicial Review: a Thematic Approach* (1995), p 288.
31   Kidd, above n 21, p 229.
32   See Paterson, above n 4, p 31.
33   See L Farmer in *The State of Scots Law*, above n 1, pp 151–152.
34   Paterson, above n 4, pp 19, 60.
35   Paterson, above n 4, pp 99–100.
36   Paterson, above n 4, p 65.
37   Keating, *Plurinational Democracy*, above n 8, pp 36–37. Although, according to J D B Mitchell,
     the pre-Union Scots public law displayed a rationalism that was later displaced in important fields
     by the 'false historicism' of English law: *Welsh Studies*, above n 2, pp 69, 72.
38   In H L MacQueen (ed), *Scots Law into the 21st Century* (1996), p 225.

'We speak of "the British constitution", whereas we ought to speak of the English constitution; for the Scots had no part in making it. The Scotch [sic] political system and political tradition, which they surrendered in 1707, was quite different.

'In fact, it was a system of political banditry. Groups of men, organised into factions, competed for power and, once they had got it, held it by force and corruption until they were overthrown by stronger force, which was afterwards sustained by continued corruption.... There was no neutral administration, no effective parliament, no political institutions recognisable by us or contiguous with our own.

'All this was ended in 1707. After that date, intelligent Scotchmen rejoiced in the removal of their national politics to London.'[39]

At other times still, the motivation for Anglo-centrism is more benign. For instance, in justifying his decision to write a book, published in 2003, about *English* public law, Adam Tomkins cites, first, reasons of modesty: 'English lawyers ... should be wary of continuing the lazy (not to say arrogant, even imperialist) assumption that the English can with authority equate themselves with and speak for the British.' Secondly, he argues that many of the central and most important pillars of public law (particularly the relationship between the Crown and Parliament) were erected before 1707 and are therefore, historically, aspects of English, not British, public law,[40] which may not be applicable in Scotland.[41] However, important though the constitutional upheavals of the seventeenth century undoubtedly were, this does not make it impossible to speak of a British/UK constitution, nor does it mean that Scots and English constitutional histories are entirely unconnected. For instance, the relationship between Crown and Parliament has no necessary implications for that between Parliament and the courts or between the courts and the executive. Both would appear to owe their contemporary roots to the post-Union period[42] and both have been subject to significant change in the late twentieth century.[43] Other highly significant aspects of our constitutional arrangements – such as the system of cabinet government, professionalisation of the civil service, electoral reform and the extension of the franchise, or the creation of the welfare state – also developed after the Union, and there is no obvious reason to think that they are peculiarly English in origin. Indeed, important reforms were sometimes directly motivated by concerns about the relationship between constituent parts of the Union. For example, the Parliament Act 1911 was enacted in part to facilitate home rule for Ireland and disestablishment of the Welsh church.[44]

In any case, whatever the reason for constitutional Anglo-centrism, the effect is the same: to ignore the diversity of constitutional tradition and practice

---

39 'Scotching the myths of devolution', *The Times*, 28 April 1976.
40 *Public Law* (2003), pp 2–3.
41 A Tomkins, 'The constitutional law in *MacCormick v Lord Advocate*' 2004 JR 213 at 220–221.
42 Eg, the doctrine of parliamentary sovereignty was not firmly established until the nineteenth century: see A V Dicey, *The Law of the Constitution* (1885); and the principle that executive actors must be able to show specific legal authority for their actions, and hence are subject to control by the courts, is usually traced to *Entick v Carrington* (1765) 19 St Tr 1030, followed in Scotland by *Bell v Black & Morrison* (1865) 5 Irv 57.
43 Eg, parliamentary sovereignty has been qualified as a consequence of Britain's membership of the EU: *R v Secretary of State for Transport, ex parte Factortame Ltd (No 2)* [1991] 1 AC 603; judicial control over the executive has been significantly extended by the expansion of judicial review and the enactment of the Human Rights Act 1998.
44 Government of Ireland Act 1914; Welsh Church Disestablishment Act 1914.

within the UK where differences do exist. Thus there are considerable gaps in our knowledge about the significance of the specifically Scottish aspects of our public law – about their practical implications, whether they constitute better or worse solutions to common constitutional problems, or even whether they suggest fundamentally different answers to the basic questions which must be addressed in any system of public law, about the appropriate constitution, distribution and regulation of governmental power, or the relationship between citizen and state.

The aim of this book is therefore to attempt to fill some of these gaps. Instead of providing a comprehensive account of public law in Scotland, the contributions focus on areas where there are potentially significant differences between Scotland and the rest of the UK, dealing with the general aspects of public law, concerning institutions of government (Chapters 5 to 9) and mechanisms for controlling public power (Chapters 10 to 16),[45] rather than specific, functional areas, such as planning, social work or water services. The object in each case is to examine the nature of, reasons for and appropriateness of the differences to be found in Scotland, in the light of wider debates in the relevant area of public law. In addition, the book is concerned with broader questions about the scope for different approaches to public law issues in Scotland, given its status as a nation within a larger, unitary state, and in a world in which governmental authority is increasingly shared with supranational organisations such as the European Union (EU), and disciplined by the forces of globalisation. Hence, Chapters 2 to 4 examine the various contextual factors which shape and constrain Scots public law.

The remainder of this chapter seeks to draw together some of the threads running through the later essays regarding the extent of constitutional difference and to pursue the general theme about the scope that exists for such difference to occur. It therefore considers three issues. First, it sets out a conceptual framework for understanding the various types of constitutional difference that we might expect to find. Secondly, it discusses the extent to which constitutional diversity can be accommodated within a unitary state. Finally, it assesses what, if anything, is truly distinctive about public law in Scotland.

CLASSIFYING CONSTITUTIONAL DIFFERENCE

Whether one can sensibly talk of a diversity of 'systems' of public law within the same state, or merely about diversity within the same system,[46] and the extent to which such diversity is acceptable, are controversial questions which will be discussed in the following section. The prior issue to be discussed here, though, concerns how the types of difference that can be found between public law rules in Scotland and those in the rest of the UK *might potentially* be understood. Clearly, these may have varying degrees of significance, whether in practical or theoretical terms, and they may arise for a range of different reasons. The categories suggested here are not necessarily exhaustive, and there may well be disagreement as to how particular instances of difference should be classified.

45 Nb, it is not exhaustive in its coverage; important areas of difference, such as policing, freedom of information, financial audit and the relationship between church and state are not discussed in detail.
46 Himsworth in *Scots Law into the 21st Century*, above n 38, pp 224–225.

Trivial difference

Many of the differences that arise between public law in Scotland and elsewhere in the UK are likely to be relatively trivial in the sense that, although the details of particular rules or institutional arrangements may vary, these are not intended to alter fundamentally the underlying objectives being pursued. Prior to devolution, such differences often arose simply from the practice of enacting separate legislation for Scotland to implement substantially uniform policies.[47] Post-devolution, where responsibility for particular aspects of public law is now divided between the UK and Scottish Parliaments, we might expect the differences in the detailed content of legislation to be greater, but again this does not necessarily mean that the two Parliaments will pursue radically different policy goals. For example, the Freedom of Information (Scotland) Act 2002, enacted by the Scottish Parliament, is structurally identical to the UK-wide Freedom of Information Act 2000, although differences of detail, such as variations in the wording of certain exemptions, the higher threshold for withholding information covered by non-absolute exemptions in Scotland,[48] and the more limited ability of Scottish Ministers, compared with their UK counterparts, to override disclosure orders, may make a significant difference to the operation of the two Acts in practice.

As this suggests, differences of detail are not necessarily to be regarded as unimportant. They may well represent considerably better or worse means of pursuing particular goals, or dealing with particular problems. For instance, Brian Thompson (in Chapter 14) argues that the one-stop-shop ombudsman model set up by the Scottish Public Services Ombudsman Act 2002 represents a substantial improvement on the arrangements which existed at the time of devolution, and which still apply in England. However, in terms of its objectives, it constitutes a recognisable evolution from the previous system, rather than a fundamentally different approach to dealing with complaints against administrative bodies.

Indeed, it could be argued that devolution itself is in reality no more than an example of trivial difference; simply a pragmatic attempt to better govern the Scottish people within the existing constitutional framework, akin to local government reform, rather than being intended to bring about any fundamental constitutional change. During the 1997 general election campaign, for example, Tony Blair (in)famously compared the proposed Scottish Parliament to an English parish council.[49] Within Scotland itself, there was support for devolution on both instrumental grounds – as a means of bringing about more effective government – and on affective grounds – because a devolved Parliament would better symbolise Scotland's national identity – and there has been some dispute about their relative importance.[50]

Contextual difference

A second set of differences might also be regarded as relatively trivial in the sense that they are contingent upon the existence of other differences. In other words,

---

47 Himsworth in *Scots Law into the 21st Century*, above n 38, p 227.
48 Ie, the need to prove 'substantial prejudice' to the interest in question, rather than merely simple prejudice.
49 *The Scotsman*, 4 April 1997.
50 See J Curtice in *The English Question*, above n 18, pp 120–121.

public law doctrines and institutions might have to be adapted in Scotland because of the different legal and governance context in which they apply, or issues may arise which have no direct parallels elsewhere in the UK. Once again, this does not mean that they are unimportant in practice, but rather that they do not represent deliberate attempts, in themselves, to set Scots public law apart from the rest of the UK.

One key reason for the existence of such contextual differences is the distinctive nature of the Scottish legal system. Thus, for example, Sarah Craig (in Chapter 15) shows how the organisation and operation of certain UK-wide tribunals have been adapted to fit with Scottish legal practice. Similarly, the distinctive Scottish approach to judicial procedure and remedies has produced important divergences between Scots and English law in relation to judicial review (see Chapters 11 and 12).

The fact of devolution is an even more significant source of contextual differences. For instance, as noted above, it necessitates a quasi-federal division of legislative competences which must be respected when legislating for Scotland, but which does not apply in relation to English legislation. Another difference relates to rules on government formation. At Westminster, this is governed by a mixture of royal prerogative and convention, and the rules are notoriously unclear. By contrast, because the use of a system of proportional representation for elections to the Scottish Parliament makes coalition or minority governments much more likely than single party majorities, this led to the codification in the Scotland Act of a set of rules and procedures for formation of the Scottish Executive, which were designed to avoid the need for the Queen to exercise any personal discretion. In addition, the existence of an extra layer of government in Scotland adds new complications to relations with other government institutions, such as local government or the EU. For instance, Chris Himsworth argues (in Chapter 8) that devolution has reinforced in Scotland a pre-existing (and UK-wide) trend towards the depoliticisation of local government, while Noreen Burrows (in Chapter 3) shows that, despite the apparent reservation of EU policy-making to the UK level, a range of European and domestic structures has developed which allows for a specifically Scottish input.

Finally, Scots public law may be affected in its practical operation by less formal contextual differences, such as the size of the jurisdiction. For instance, the inevitably closer relationship between governors and the governed in a small country like Scotland may produce more intensive scrutiny of official action (see Chapter 7) or, as Scott Styles argues, make it more difficult scrupulously to maintain the appearance of judicial impartiality (see Chapter 9). Gavin Anderson also argues that the impact of globalisation may be felt differently in a small, sub-state unit like Scotland, compared with its impact at the state (UK) level (see Chapter 4).

Difference through conservatism

A third set of differences is more substantive, in that it does seem to embody alternative value judgments about the appropriate constitution, regulation or scope of governmental power. However, such differences may arise, not from positive and/or defensible decisions to be different, but merely from inertia or a conservative attitude to change. Thus difference may simply be a question of clinging to old ways, rather than defending peculiarly Scottish (or English) traditions.

In terms of common law doctrines, a small jurisdiction like Scotland, with relatively low litigation levels and limited judicial specialisation, may be particularly prone to the perpetuation of outmoded ideas. Judicial review is a case in point here. Aileen McHarg argues (in Chapter 11) that the rejection of the public/private distinction as the basis for determining the scope of judicial review in Scotland reflects a discredited view of the constitutional basis of judicial review rather than a rationally defensible alternative to the English law approach. Similarly, Tom Mullen (in Chapter 12) is critical of the Scottish courts' failure to follow the example of their English counterparts in liberalising the law of standing, and he points to the low number of judicial review cases reaching the Inner House in recent years as one reason for the persistence of the traditional approach. Jim Murdoch also points out (in Chapter 16) the relative backwardness of the Scottish courts in taking into account the European Convention on Human Rights (ECHR) prior to its legislative incorporation, which resulted in a number of successful challenges to Scottish laws and practices before the European Court of Human Rights. On the other hand, Adam Tomkins claims that Scots law relating to Crown liability and privileges has often been *more* progressive than English law, and has suffered from pressures to assimilate (see Chapter 13).

As far as legislative reform is concerned, a frequent complaint prior to devolution was that modernising initiatives were often delayed in Scotland compared to England. Post-devolution, the situation may well be reversed; the Scottish Parliament may be better able to find legislative time for measures that are sidelined by more pressing matters at Westminster. In fact, the entire devolution settlement has been imbued with a modernising spirit which affected the basic design of the devolved institutions in relation to matters such as the electoral system (see Chapter 5) and the protection of human rights (see Chapter 16), as well as their own policy agendas. For instance, the Scottish Executive set up an independent Judicial Appointments Board well in advance of similar reforms in England (see Chapter 9).

Nevertheless, it should be borne in mind that people may disagree about what should be regarded as outdated and undesirable, and what is progressive and beneficial. The merits of proportional representation and strong judicial protection of human rights, for example, are still highly contested issues. Thus, Heather Lardy (in Chapter 5) discusses criticisms of the Additional Member System used for elections to the Scottish Parliament. And Anderson (in Chapter 4) is critical of the fundamental rights provisions in the Scotland Act for their potential to stifle redistributive policies, although both Aidan O'Neill (in Chapter 10) and Murdoch (in Chapter 16) are more positive in their appraisal. Styles also suggests (in Chapter 9) that the Judicial Appointments Board has not significantly improved the transparency and accountability of the judicial appointments process.

Moreover, the complex division of legislative competences between the Scottish and UK Parliaments, combined with different political priorities, may well produce differences in approach in areas where some degree of uniformity would be appropriate. Tribunals again provide a good example, where the UK government has pursued a programme of reform which affects UK-wide tribunals in Scotland, but the Scottish Executive has shown no interest in adopting similar reforms for devolved tribunals although they exhibit much the same problems that the reforms are intended to address (see Chapter 15). Conversely, both Alan Page (in Chapter 6) and Barry Winetrobe (in Chapter 7) point out that, in areas reserved to the

Westminster Parliament, arrangements for scrutiny of legislation and executive action affecting Scotland have been neglected, and seem increasingly inadequate compared with arrangements at Holyrood.

Symbolic difference

The fourth class of differences is also substantive, but remains largely symbolic – a matter of constitutional 'folklore' or rhetoric – rather than having any major practical effects on the operation of particular institutions or on the way in which cases are decided by the courts. The best example of symbolic difference in Scots public law is probably Lord Cooper's dictum in *MacCormick v Lord Advocate* that 'the principle of the unlimited sovereignty of Parliament is a distinctively English principle which has no counterpart in Scots constitutional law'.[51] This suggests a radical distinction between Scots and English public law. Yet, as Tomkins points out, in all respects other than in relation to the status of the Union legislation, the Scottish courts have accepted and applied the doctrine of parliamentary sovereignty. Moreover, even in that limited respect, no statute, despite several challenges, has ever been struck down as being contrary to the Union legislation. As already noted, it is only in very extreme, and very unlikely, cases that Scottish judges have suggested that they might refuse to accept the validity of Westminster legislation, and even then it is far from clear that the Court of Session would have any suitable remedy at its disposal.[52]

It might be objected that to focus on the *legal* implications of Lord Cooper's dictum underestimates its *political* significance in sustaining the notion that the Scottish constitutional tradition rests upon a principle of popular sovereignty which played an important part in justifying calls for devolution. Again, though, as argued above, this is not the only way in which devolution can be understood, and it can be easily accommodated within the orthodox theory of parliamentary sovereignty. Similarly, devolution was accompanied by a rhetoric that it would lead to a new, and more participatory style of politics, distinct from the elitist and adversarial modes practised at Westminster. However, as Lardy, Page and Winetrobe note (in Chapters 5, 6 and 7 respectively), notwithstanding some innovations in the Scottish Parliament's working practices, the evidence so far suggests that the 'New Politics' has not had as much impact in practice as was hoped.

Nevertheless, it would be a mistake to discount the importance of symbolic difference. Much of constitutional discourse operates on the symbolic plane – perhaps especially in the UK, where Walter Bagehot's distinction between the 'dignified' and the 'efficient' constitution continues to have resonance[53] – and constitutional reality often falls far short of constitutional ideals. More fundamentally, as Walker points out, there is a reflexive relationship between constitutional discourse and constitutional reality:

> 'Constitutional law and discourse ... is no mere reflection of a prior political order or process, but as one of the deepest and most pervasive "structures through which we experience the meaning of our political lives" is recursively implicated in the (re)framing, elaboration and consolidation of that order. Just as there can be no

51 [1953] SC 396 at 411.
52 See Tomkins, above n 41, pp 216–220.
53 See *The English Constitution* (1867).

constitutional discourse in the absence of a referent polity or political process
– achieved or aspired to – so there can be no polity or other constitutional process
in the absence of its constitutional *representation* as such, and it is precisely that
"discourse of conceptualisation and imagination" which has the capacity to invest the
authoritative claims, the institutions and the principles associated with the putative
polity or constitutional process with polity-affirming or process-affirming, and thus
constitutional status. In this intensely reflexive process, constitutionalism is not, or
not simply, about observing appropriate types of data "out there [in the] constitutional
landscape," but is necessarily itself a constitutive endeavour.'[54]

In other words, by conceiving Scotland as having a distinctive constitutional
identity, this may itself help to bring about the reality of such distinctiveness. Thus,
for example, Neil MacCormick argues that it is a sign of the importance of the
MacCormick case that questions about whether Scots law can generate a distinctive
conception of the UK constitution remain live to this day.[55]

Genuine distinctiveness

Examples of the final category of difference are the hardest to identify, requiring
not only genuinely different answers to fundamental public law questions, but
also that those differences should have been consciously chosen or defended, and
that they have some real practical significance. In previous times, the position of
the Crown in Scots law might have been placed in this category since, as Tomkins
argues (in Chapter 13), Scottish judges historically displayed a much less
deferential attitude than their English brethren to claims for special treatment on
the part of the Crown.[56] Today, however, much of that distinctiveness has been
eroded by a process of mutual assimilation. Similarly, the relationship between
church and state in Scotland[57] might once have been regarded as an area of
fundamental constitutional distinction.[58] In fact, it was the perceived erosion of
the constitutional independence of the Church of Scotland, as guaranteed by the
Union legislation, that led to the issuing of a previous 'Claim of Right' on behalf
of the Scottish people in 1842.[59] Nevertheless, the relationship between church
and state is no longer generally regarded (at least in the UK) as a central issue in
constitutional law.

Other potential candidates for inclusion in this category are more difficult to
classify with confidence. Thus, as we have seen, devolution might be regarded
as the expression of a right to political self-determination on the part of the
Scottish people, or merely a concession by the British state, in the interests of

---

54 N Walker, 'The idea of constitutional pluralism' (2002) 65 MLR 317 at 343 (references
    omitted).
55 N McCormick, 'Doubts about the "Supreme Court" and reflections on *MacCormick v Lord
    Advocate*' 2004 JR 237 at 250.
56 See also Chapter 2.
57 On which see S C Styles, 'Church and State' in title on 'Constitutional Law', *Stair Memorial
    Encyclopaedia* (Reissue, 2002).
58 Indeed, this relationship differs in all four parts of the UK.
59 See Paterson, above n 4, pp 56–57. The issue at stake was the right of congregations to appoint
    their own ministers. The failure of the UK Parliament to heed the demands in the Claim of Right
    led, in 1843, to the Disruption in the Church of Scotland, when some ministers and congregations
    broke away to form the Free Church of Scotland – an event often regarded as a form of national
    assertion.

efficient government. The existence of strong protection for human rights against the Scottish Parliament, but not Westminster, could be seen as evidence of a fundamentally different approach to the relationship between the state and the individual. Alternatively, it could be read simply as reinforcing the constitutionally subordinate status of the Scottish Parliament. More generally, it could be argued, as does O'Neill (in Chapter 10), that Scotland's constitutional distinctiveness in this respect is more apparent than real because the doctrine of parliamentary sovereignty is gradually being eroded throughout the UK. Perhaps the most promising candidate for identification as an area of genuine constitutional distinctiveness is the apparent rejection of a 'winner-takes-all' style of electoral politics in favour of the adoption of proportional representation both for elections to the Scottish Parliament and, from 2007, for local government elections (see Chapter 8). But even here these developments might more accurately be seen as merely the results of pragmatic political calculations,[60] or alternatively as part of a growing UK-wide trend away from first-past-the-post elections.[61]

If, therefore, we struggle to identify clear examples of genuine distinctiveness in Scots public law, the question that now arises is why that should be so. Is it because of the limits on constitutional diversity imposed by membership of a unitary state? Or are we looking in the wrong place when trying to identify what is truly distinctive about Scots public law?

CONSTITUTIONAL DIVERSITY IN A UNITARY STATE

According to Tomkins, there is not necessarily any difficulty in having different rules of public law in different parts of the UK, even regarding the fundamental rules of the constitution, and hence no objection to talking about the English constitution or the Scottish constitution as separate and potentially distinct systems of law.[62] For others, though, this is problematic because constitutions have traditionally been associated with states.[63] Although we sometimes talk, for example, about the constitutions of clubs or associations, and these to some extent perform similar functions to state constitutions,[64] Himsworth claims that the two are conceptually distinct, and, moreover, that traditional discussions of the principles and values which inform constitutional law can only be understood against the backdrop of the state.[65] Admittedly, the 'state-centredness' of constitutional law has come under challenge in recent years from the constitutionalisation of other sites of political

---

60 It is often claimed that the adoption of proportional representation for Scottish Parliament elections was intended to prevent the Scottish National Party from gaining an overall majority at Holyrood, while electoral reform for local government was the price of continuing coalition between the Labour and Liberal Democratic parties after the 2003 election.

61 Various systems of proportional representation have also been adopted for European Parliament, Welsh Assembly, Northern Ireland Assembly and Greater London Assembly elections since 1997, and the single transferable vote system has been used for local government elections in Northern Ireland since 1973.

62 Above n 41, pp 220–221.

63 See C M G Himsworth, 'In a state no longer: the end of constitutionalism' [1996] PL 639 at 648–651; N MacCormick, *Questioning Sovereignty* (1999), p 22.

64 Eg, for Karl Llewellyn the allocation of power and authority was one of the 'law-jobs' that has to be performed in any social grouping: 'The normative, the legal and the law-jobs' (1940) 49 Yale LJ 1355.

65 Himsworth, above n 63, p 648.

authority, particularly at the supranational level.[66] However, this does not mean that the state level is no longer important and can therefore be ignored in discussions about constitutional law. On the contrary, Walker points out that the existence of rival claims to constitutional authority does not undermine the exclusive right of each constitutional order to determine, from its own internal point of view, what is constitutionally acceptable.[67] In other words, from this perspective, because neither Scotland nor England is an independent state, but rather both are members of the same state – the UK – the degree of autonomy and diversity which each may be permitted is a question for the UK constitution, and not for Scots or English law alone.

This association of constitutional law with the state, and the fact, moreover, that the UK is a unitary state – that is, the same rules regarding ultimate legal authority apply throughout the state, and there is no division of sovereignty between the centre and sub-state levels, as in a federal state – helps to explain the assumption, noted above, that, since the Union, it is no longer appropriate to talk about a separate body of Scots public law. It also explains why Unionists have claimed to have fewer problems with secession by constituent parts of the state than with asymmetrical devolution, which undermines the uniform application of constitutional rules.[68] Hence, prior to 1997, the (traditionally Unionist) Conservative party opposed devolution to Scotland as involving an inherently unstable constitutional settlement which would create a slippery slope to outright independence.

However, Walker has argued that the unitary conception of the constitution is actually a much more flexible notion than has often been assumed, capable of embracing a wide range of constitutional structures and visions.[69] There is, he claims, 'arguably … only the loosest of coupling between a unitary political discourse and the unitary legal theory of the state'.[70] Although the fundamental rule of the constitution – the sovereignty of the Westminster Parliament – precludes the *entrenchment* of other governmental institutions and values, and hence the adoption of a federal division of competences between the UK level and sub-state levels, it is nevertheless compatible with considerable diversity and asymmetry in our governance arrangements.[71] Thus, as already noted, devolution has, so far, had no formal effect on the status of the UK as a unitary state.

In addition, Walker argues, the unitary conception, as a statement of the legal character of the state, 'has always been a less eloquent and influential statement of the overall character of the constitution than has been assumed or credited by man'.[72] As we have already seen, it has in fact co-existed with considerable symbolic recognition and institutional autonomy for constituent parts of the state, Scotland in particular. This has led some people to assert that the UK is more accurately described as a 'union state' than a unitary state – that is, one in which, because of the way the state emerged historically, heterogeneity of governance arrangements between constituent regions or nations has become a normal and persistent

---

66 See Himsworth, above n 63; Walker, above n 54; and Chapters 3 and 4 in this volume.
67 Walker, above n 54, p 349.
68 Keating, *Plurinational Democracy*, above n 8, p 108.
69 'Beyond the unitary conception of the United Kingdom constitution?' [2000] PL 384.
70 Walker, above n 69, p 394.
71 Walker, above n 69, pp 394–398.
72 Walker, above n 69, p 389.

feature.[73] Union states may be either unitary or federal in formal terms,[74] but lack the symmetry that is associated with both constitutional models. However, whereas in a federal state, the (varying) rights of the sub-state units are legally entrenched, in a unitary state such diversity can only be politically entrenched.

Nevertheless, matters are complicated by the fact that constitutions are not merely related to states, but are also related to legal systems. As well as allocating and regulating power within the state, the constitution sits at the apex of the legal system, determining the hierarchy of norms within that system and identifying sources of legislative, executive and judicial authority. Further, in so far as they have legal effect (that is, they are not merely conventions), constitutional rules have to be interpreted within the legal system. Accordingly, because the UK contains more than one legal system, this creates the possibility that there might be more than one *interpretation* of what the UK constitution requires or permits.[75] This is so notwithstanding that, at least in civil matters, we have a UK-wide final court of appeal (the House of Lords/Privy Council, soon to be replaced by the Supreme Court). Simply because of the 'pull' that precedent, whatever its formal authority, normally exerts in practice, as well as for more obviously 'political' reasons, it is suggested that the House of Lords/Supreme Court would nowadays find it difficult to override a clear line of Scottish authority when deciding a Scottish case in favour of a conflicting approach based on English case law.

The existence of different interpretations of the UK constitution in Scots and English law is not necessarily problematic in so far as the issues to which they relate are geographically separate. For instance, the persistence of differing interpretations in Scots and English law as to the status of the Union legislation may be explained by the fact that it does not have the same practical significance for England as for Scotland because most of its guarantees were directed towards preservation of Scots law and Scots institutions, and because, in any case, England has always been the numerically dominant force in the UK Parliament. Similarly, the question whether Acts of the Scottish Parliament should be regarded as a species of primary or secondary legislation[76] is, in practical terms, an issue which affects Scots law only. More fundamentally, as Daniel Elazar reminded us, in the context of federal systems, 'it is a mistake to present unity and diversity as opposites. Unity should be contrasted with disunity and diversity with homogeneity'.[77] Thus, for example, it is conceivable that Scots and English law could maintain differing interpretations as to the basis of the Union without necessarily threatening their mutual commitment to that Union.

However, Stephen Tierney argues that such interpretative conflicts *are* potentially a more serious threat to the survival of 'plurinational' states[78] like the UK than constitutional asymmetry per se, or even conflicting views as to the fairness of existing constitutional arrangements and the need for constitutional reform.[79] This is because, he claims, proper constitutional accommodation of the aspirations

---

73 Walker, above n 69, p 398. See further Chapter 2.
74 Walker, above n 69, p 398.
75 N MacCormick, 'Is there a constitutional path to Scottish independence?' (2000) 53 Parl Affairs 721 at 727. See also D Feldman, 'None, one or several? Perspectives on the UK's constitution(s)' (2005) 64 CLJ 329 at 346–351.
76 On which see A McHarg, 'What is delegated legislation?' [2006] PL 538.
77 *Exploring Federalism* (1987), p 64.
78 Ie, containing more than one national grouping.
79 Tierney, above n 15, pp 100–101.

of sub-state national groupings, such as the Scots, within the host state requires its plurinational nature to be recognised within the overall tenor or spirit of the constitution.[80] Such mutual recognition of the legitimacy of other constitutional visions is by no means impossible.[81] Thus, David Feldman has criticised the House of Lords for failing to recognise that differing interpretations of the requirements of the ECHR may be equally valid in different parts of the UK. Not only did the House of Lords refuse to follow a decision of the Privy Council in a Scottish case, with a majority of Scottish judges, as to the effect of Article 6 ECHR in cases of undue delay in criminal prosecutions, but it expressly emphasised that its decision was irreconcilable with that of the Privy Council.[82] However, in so far as such interpretative dissonance relates to the fundamental rules of the constitution – the location of sovereignty within the state (parliamentary versus popular sovereignty) – then mutual recognition may not be possible without changing the unitary nature of the constitution itself. It should not be forgotten, though, that, especially in an unwritten constitution like that of the UK, fundamental constitutional rules are not set in stone, and hence, as Tierney points out (in Chapter 2), alternative (political) readings of the constitution do have the potential to displace previously dominant (legal) understandings. Indeed, Tierney argues, devolution does appear to be contributing to the gradual erosion of the doctrine of parliamentary sovereignty throughout the UK. Accordingly, this may create an opportunity for greater recognition of divergent constitutional visions in the constituent parts of the UK.

If, therefore, there are fewer formal objections than might have been expected to the co-existence of different public law rules and values within the same overarching constitutional order the issue becomes simply a question of political judgment as to what degree of homogeneity is desirable or what degree of diversity tolerable: judgments, moreover, that are both contestable and contextual. Thus, for example, it might be difficult to defend differences between Scots and English public law where these relate merely to matters of detail, or where they rest on historically-based justifications which have lost their contemporary force.[83] Such differences might appear simply to involve unnecessary complexity, especially in the face of external pressures for homogeneity, such as those arising from the impact of EC law or the ECHR.[84] For instance, Burrows shows (in Chapter 3) how the requirement placed on the UK state to ensure compliance with EC law may limit the degree of autonomy which may be afforded in practice to the devolved institutions. McHarg also suggests (in Chapter 11) that the adoption of a public/private distinction for the purposes of determining the scope of the duty to comply with Convention rights under section 6 of the Human Rights Act 1998 might eventually persuade the Scottish courts to adopt such a test for determining the scope of judicial review more generally. Against such arguments, though, it could be claimed that the scope for learning offered by divergent public law rules is valuable in itself.[85] In addition, alternative narratives may be invoked to justify

80 Tierney, above n 15, pp 125–126.
81 Walker, above n 54, p 354.
82 Feldman, above n 75, pp 348–350. On this issue, see further Chapter 16.
83 Himsworth in *Scots Law into the 21st Century*, above n 38, p 231.
84 Tomkins argues that these now represent a far greater threat to the distinctiveness of Scots public law than does English law: above n 41, pp 223–224. See also Himsworth, *Scots Law into the 21st Century*, above n 38, pp 231–235.
85 See J D B Mitchell, 'The merits of disharmony' [1956] PL 6 at 7–8.

continued diversity. For example, in the context of a union state, the existence of historical differences might be relied upon not as a literal guide to what is now permissible, but as providing a general justification for sub-state units to develop their own solutions to problems.[86] Similarly, the EC doctrine of subsidiarity could be invoked to justify decentralisation within Member States, as well as between the EC institutions and state-level governments.

More importantly, though, it might be argued that, for reasons of territorial equity, there must be at least a minimum level of common citizenship within a single state. Perhaps for this reason, many aspects of the general constitutional framework of the UK are, as already noted, outwith the competence of the Scottish Parliament and, from this perspective, we might also see the simultaneous incorporation of the ECHR into domestic law as a necessary counterbalance to devolution. However, the differences in the way in which the ECHR has been incorporated at the Scottish and UK levels (see Chapters 10 and 16) mean that such common citizenship is not guaranteed, since the UK Parliament and (if permitted by primary legislation) UK executive institutions may flout the Convention whereas the Scottish Parliament and Executive may not. It has been suggested, therefore, that this simply reflects greater distrust of the ability of the devolved institutions to respect human rights compared to their UK counterparts.[87] It was apparently always intended that the former would be bound by the ECHR regardless of what happened elsewhere in the UK,[88] and Himsworth notes the parallel with the process of decolonisation, where British governments felt it necessary to incorporate fundamental rights guarantees into post-colonial constitutions, although this had never been seen as necessary under British rule.[89]

In any case, Keating argues, ensuring a minimum degree of respect for fundamental constitutional values does not require exact state-wide uniformity in the way in which those values are protected.[90] Hence the European Court of Human Rights recognises that states have a margin of appreciation (albeit varying in scope depending upon the right in question) to decide how best to strike the balance between Convention rights and other important objectives where these come into conflict. In federal states, we also find considerable variation in the distribution of competences between central and federal levels as regards citizenship rights. For example, in Canada, Quebec has substantial control over immigration, whilst in the USA, electoral qualifications are a matter for the states rather than the federal government, although both of these are reserved matters within the UK.[91] Further, the narrative of the union state might once again be invoked to argue that to override historically-based differences in the name of a unitary model of citizenship would itself involve a violation of rights,[92] and the example of the EU can also be

---

86 See Keating, *Plurinational Democracy*, above n 8, p 54.
87 MacCormick, above n 75, p 724. See also Keating, *Plurinational Democracy*, above n 8, p 127.
88 Page in *The State of Scots Law*, above n 1, pp 14–15.
89 In T Campbell, K D Ewing and A Tomkins (eds), *Sceptical Essays on Human Rights* (2001), pp 146–147. However, an alternative reading might be that the disparity simply reflects the desire of the UK government to retain control over the process of compliance with international obligations, and to ensure that only it can take the decision to depart from such obligations.
90 Keating, *Plurinational Democracy*, above n 8, p 127.
91 The First Minister, Jack McConnell, has, however, called for immigration rules to be applied differently in Scotland, arguing that Scotland's population needs differ from the rest of the UK.
92 Keating, *Plurinational Democracy*, above n 8, p 123.

relied upon to demonstrate that a plurality of conceptions of citizenship is mutually sustainable in practice.[93]

DISTINCTIVENESS OF SCOTS PUBLIC LAW

Clearly, then, the constitutional framework of the UK can potentially accommodate considerable – and not merely trivial – diversity of public law rules in the constituent parts of the state. So the question still arises why there appear to be few unequivocal examples of genuine distinctiveness in Scots public law.

One possible explanation is that, despite the institutional autonomy enjoyed by Scotland since the Union, and further enhanced by devolution, this has not been, and is not yet, sufficient to allow genuine distinctiveness to emerge in relation to constitutional matters. Thus, writing before devolution, J D B Mitchell argued that: '[i]t is as impossible for one part of a political union to stand apart from the general pattern of thought of that union, as it is for part of an economic union to insulate its own economy'.[94] On the eve of devolution, Walker also identified a deep structural coherence between the various elements of the UK constitution which, he claimed, tended towards centralisation and was not easily amenable to piecemeal reform. Hence, he predicted that, without complementary reforms, such as the possibility of constitutional review of Westminster legislation, reconstitution of the House of Lords as a federal chamber, or greater symmetry in the devolution arrangements, the deep structural connections embedded within the traditional constitution would 'provide obstacles to the realisation of this latest attempt at radical decentralisation' via devolution.[95] In fact, as Page points out (in Chapter 6), the expectation at the time of devolution that the Westminster Parliament would more or less cease to legislate in the devolved areas has not been borne out in reality. Moreover, as already noted, the working practices of the devolved institutions have largely involved modifications of pre-existing Westminster practices, rather than a completely new approach.

Tom Nairn argues that it is unlikely that a radically different democratic vision for Scotland could ever be created without a national state – that is, without becoming independent.[96] However, as far as the Scottish National Party is concerned, while independence, or 'independence in Europe', would expand the powers exercised by the existing Scottish governmental authorities, it need not involve substantial other change to the constitutional framework in which they are exercised.[97] This may perhaps be a reflection of the homogenising pressures exerted by European integration and globalisation. For example, Anderson (in Chapter 4) argues that the fundamental rights provisions in the Scotland Act should be seen as part of a global trend towards the adoption of judicially enforceable constitutional rights and, more generally, Esin Örücü claims that it is now in the area of public law rather than private law that we see the most fundamental cross-fertilisation between different legal systems.[98]

---

93 See Tierney, above n 15, p 330.
94 *Welsh Studies in Public Law*, above n 2, p 72.
95 In *Devolution and the British Constitution*, above n 18, pp 80–83.
96 'Sovereignty after the election' (1997) 224 *New Left Review* 3 at 15.
97 See MacCormick, above n 75, p 723. Although the draft SNP constitution is explicitly based on the principle of popular sovereignty: MacCormick, p 730.
98 'Approaching public law as a "mixed system"' 2002 JR 131.

In this context, we might question whether there is any point in stateless nations such as Scotland seeking greater constitutional autonomy if they will have only limited scope to develop their own approaches to fundamental constitutional issues. Indeed, James Tully claims that the trend towards devolution or dispersion of governmental authority is positively *un*desirable because smaller political units are weaker and therefore less able to resist the forces of globalisation: '[t]he trend ... thus tends, to a significant degree, to support rather than challenge the trend towards global juridification and so is of questionable legitimacy for the same reason'.[99] By contrast, Tierney argues that 'sub-state nationalism can ... be presented as a powerful democratic force in a world where globalisation seems to be reducing the effectiveness of popular decision-making'.[100]

More fundamentally, though, it might also be suggested that claims to a distinct Scottish national identity are themselves undermined if we cannot identify any distinctively Scottish values or approaches to political matters. There is a widespread assumption that claims to national identity are only authentic if they are based on some sort of cultural uniqueness. However, this sort of 'ethnic nationalism' is challenged by 'civic nationalists',[101] who argue that national identity need not be bound up in cultural distinctiveness, but rather in the fact that people see themselves as a nation and wish to determine their future as a collectivity.[102] In other words, according to Tierney, stateless nations such as the Scots

> 'position themselves in a relational way to the state not as internal "minorities", but rather as polities which are in fact comparable to the state in the way they offer, or have the potential to offer, an effective site for many if not all of those functional and identificatory roles which the state plays in the life of the citizen'.[103]

Thus:

> '[A]lthough sub-state nationalist movements argue for the specific institutional accommodation of their respective sub-state national society, this does not in any way suggest that they hold different political values from other territorial spaces within the state, or that their search for discrete institutional accommodation is in any way geared towards the institutionalisation of different values.'[104]

From a civic nationalist perspective, therefore, a sense of common societal identity may remain stable despite changes in the culture of the society, and can accommodate both cultural similarities with other groups and deep cultural diversity within the group itself.[105]

The conclusion that may be drawn from this is that, given that, as noted earlier, Scots national identity has been primarily institutional and civic, rather than cultural or ethnic in character, there is no reason to expect any fundamental variation between the basic values or objectives of Scots public law and the rules applied in other parts of the UK. Indeed, since the British constitution has

---

99 'The unfreedom of the Moderns in comparison to their ideals of constitutional democracy' (2002) 65 MLR 204 at 213.
100 Tierney, above n 15, p 339.
101 See Tierney, above n 15, pp 21–31 for discussion of these positions.
102 Keating, *Plurinational Democracy*, above n 8, pp 3–4.
103 Tierney, above n 15, pp 4–5. See also Keating, above n 8, p 17.
104 Tierney, above n 15, p 31 (reference omitted).
105 Tierney, above n 15, pp 37, 43.

traditionally been regarded as a political constitution, with legal constraints on public power historically of limited significance, it should not be surprising that the Scots' constitutional aspirations should be manifested primarily in a desire for separate political representation. However, what does mark Scotland out as distinct, certainly from England, and arguably also from Wales and Northern Ireland, is that the sense of Scotland as a distinct polity does *not* also entail a rejection of the wider UK polity. In other words, most Scots maintain a *dual* national identity[106] and hence plural political bonds with the different levels of governance which affect their lives.[107]

It is therefore in this commitment to institutional pluralism, whether or not it is accompanied by a claim to political self-determination or to legally divided sovereignty,[108] that we arguably find the true distinctiveness of Scots public law. Admittedly, this may be a temporary phenomenon only. It may be eroded either by a move towards independence by the Scots or by developments elsewhere in the Union, as the Northern Irish, Welsh or English seek the same level of autonomy as is currently enjoyed in Scotland.[109] Alternatively, it may in time be supplemented with other points of distinction, as devolution provides the institutional context within which fresh ideas about how to govern may develop. For the time being, however, it is in the detailed and contextual differences that flow from and sustain institutional pluralism, rather than in any grand constitutional theorising, that the reality of the distinctive nature of Scots public law can most clearly be found.

---

106 Paterson, above n 4, p 65; Keating, above n 8, p 100.
107 Tierney, above n 15, p 14.
108 Tierney argues that a pluralisation of the concept of sovereignty is logically and normatively required to accommodate the plural political bonds between peoples and modes of governance: above n 15, p 17.
109 Hazell points out that in Spain asymmetric devolution, which was originally confined to Catalonia and the Basque country, has spread to other regions which initially showed no interest: *The English Question*, above n 18, p 4. There is currently no significant support in England for either an English Parliament or regional devolution (see Curtice in *The English Question*, above n 50). However, in Wales, the Richard Commission recommended that the competences of the National Assembly for Wales should be enhanced to include primary legislative power (Commission on the Powers and Electoral Arrangements of the National Assembly for Wales, *Report* (2004)). In response, the Government of Wales Act 2006 gives it increased secondary legislative power, and the UK Government has accepted in principle that it should have primary legislative powers if there is support for this in a further referendum: Wales Office, *Better Governance for Wales* (Cm 6582, 2005). The fate of devolution in Northern Ireland is bound up with the wider peace process, and complicated by the desire of a substantial minority of the population to leave the UK altogether and join with the Republic of Ireland.

PART I:
SCOTLAND'S CONSTITUTIONAL CONTEXT

Chapter 2

Scotland and the Union State

Stephen Tierney

INTRODUCTION

The foundational characteristic of the British state and the enduring principle which underpins its constitutional framework is that of union. This is evident in the very name of the state – the United Kingdom of Great Britain and Northern Ireland – which reflects the fact that the UK is composed of a plurality of nations. England, Scotland and Wales are each discrete national societies with distinctive histories and traditions, while Northern Ireland, with its more complex demography, comprises two distinctive national groups – British unionist and Irish nationalist. The concept of union is particularly fundamental to the constitutional historiography of the UK because the constituent nations of the state came together, at least formally, in processes of legal union. Even the conjunction of England and Wales, although in political terms more an instance of conquest than voluntary marriage, was given legal recognition by an Act of the English Parliament.[1] In the modern era, however, the British state as it exists today was created by the more constitutionally significant unions between England and Scotland to form Great Britain in 1707,[2] and that between Great Britain and Ireland (of which Northern Ireland's presence in the UK is the remaining legacy) in 1800.[3] This self-conscious process of creating a multinational union has not been untroubled by political upheaval, most evident in the Irish campaign for independence which led to the partition of Ireland in the 1920s and the ensuing dispute over the constitutional status of Northern Ireland. Relations in other parts of the UK have been more amicable but, even so, since the 1950s there has been a revival in Scottish and Welsh nationalism[4] which has led in the late 1990s to the creation of devolved government in each of these three territories. These developments represent a degree of constitutional change and recognition of the UK's national diversity unprecedented since the very processes of union themselves. And today, therefore, devolution to Scotland, Wales and Northern Ireland (the latter presently in abeyance) serves to institutionalise further than ever before the national pluralism of these islands, adding a sophisticated governmental apparatus to the sociological reality of the UK as a 'union state'.[5]

---

1 27 Hen VIII, c 26. This is traditionally titled in England, the Laws in Wales Act 1535 and, in Wales, the Act of Union 1536.
2 Union with Scotland Act 1706 (6 Anne c 11); and the Union with England Act 1707 (APS XI, 406, c 7).
3 Union with Ireland Act 1800.
4 T M Devine, *The Scottish Nation, 1700–2000* (1999), pp 574–617; K O Morgan, *Rebirth of a Nation: A History of Modern Wales* (1982).
5 S Rokkan and D Urwin in S Rokkan and D Urwin (eds), *The Politics of Territorial Identity: Studies in European Regionalism* (1982), p 11; S Tierney, *Constitutional Law and National Pluralism* (2004), pp 6–8 and 110–117.

Although the idea of the UK as a union state embraces also the status of Wales, Northern Ireland and other island territories, for the purposes of this chapter we are primarily concerned with the Anglo-Scottish Union which in the eyes of many remains the foundational constitutional moment in the creation of the British state. The marriage of Scotland and England was completed by the union of the Parliaments of these two countries in 1707; an event that followed a lengthy courtship, which included, if one might extend the marital metaphor, an engagement through the union of the crowns in 1603. This chapter will review the constitutional significance of 1707, considering inter alia: the historical evolution of the Union; how different constitutional traditions in England and Scotland came together in 1707, shaping the state's fundamental constitutional doctrines and leaving as their legacy different visions of what union should mean; and the recent reconfiguration of the Union brought about by the devolution of government to Scotland through the Scotland Act 1998 with the implications this might have for dominant constitutional doctrines, most particularly that of the legislative supremacy of the Westminster Parliament.

THE LONG ENGAGEMENT: 1603–1707

Scotland's union with England was a gradual affair which took over a century to complete. In constitutional terms the first step was taken with the unification of the crowns of the two states in 1603; but, even though James VI of Scotland (1567–1625) assumed also the title James I of Great Britain and Ireland (1603–25), this regal union did not bring with it the creation of one state. Scotland and England continued to function as separate countries on the international stage, with independently functioning Parliaments until 1707. The union of crowns did, however, draw the two countries closer together at a time of savage internal strife unique in the history of the British and Irish islands. Rebellions against the Stuart monarchy characterised the seventeenth century, and separate but often linked processes of revolt occurred in Scotland and England which in turn spilled over into related periods of turmoil in Ireland.[6] The symbolic event which marked the commencement of open revolt against King Charles I (1625–49) was the signing in 1638 of the National Covenant at Greyfriars Kirk in Edinburgh by Presbyterians rebelling against the attempt by Charles to impose a modified form of the Episcopalian English Prayer Book in Scotland.[7] This was an open rejection of the authority of the monarch in religious matters, and, as it involved the ordinary people as well as political elites, it was in many ways a remarkable act of popular revolt in an age when many still espoused the doctrine of the untrammelled prerogative of kings to rule by divine right.[8]

Throughout the ensuing period of civil wars in Scotland, England and Ireland which ended with the execution of Charles on 30 January 1649, Scottish and English revolutionaries found common cause, most notably in the Solemn League and Covenant signed in 1643 and ratified by Act of the Scottish Parliament the

---

6 P Gaunt, *The British Wars, 1637–1651* (1997); T Royle, *The War of the Three Kingdoms 1638–1660* (2003).

7 J Morrill (ed), *The Scottish National Covenant in its British Context, 1638–51* (1990).

8 James VI, 'True Law of Free Monarchies', in J R Tanner, *Constitutional Documents of the Reign of James I 1602–1625* (1961).

following year. By this Act, Parliament allied itself with the rebellious parliamentary forces in England which were by then at war with the King.[9] However, throughout this period of civil war and on through both the resulting interregnum in which the throne of Scotland remained unoccupied from 1649–60 and the restoration of the monarchy marked by the accession of Charles II (1660–85) to the thrones of England and Scotland, both countries continued to function as independent states.[10]

Once again, however, as the century drew to a close, rebellion against the sovereign was to draw Scottish revolutionaries into close alliance with their counterparts in England. The Catholic King James VII (1685–88), the younger son of Charles I and brother of Charles II, eventually found his rule over the predominantly Protestant kingdoms of Scotland and England to be untenable, and in 1688 he abandoned his throne in the face of an insurgency which resulted in the arrival of an invading army from the Netherlands led by William of Orange. It was this development and the constitutional settlements in England and Scotland of 1688–89 which finally set in train the process towards the full parliamentary union of the two countries.

THE SCOTTISH CONSTITUTION: FROM CLAIM OF RIGHT TO UNION

The rebellion of 1688–89 resulted in William and his wife Mary (the daughter of James VII) acceding to the thrones of the two states (William III 1689–1702 and Mary II 1689–94). The revolution not only hastened the road towards full union, but also served to highlight how Scotland and England would each come into this union bringing with them very different constitutional traditions. In light of the lengthy struggle earlier in the century between the English Parliament and Charles I, an uneasy relationship was established between that Parliament and the Crown following the Restoration of 1660, with neither party clearly supreme at the time of the revolt against James in 1688.[11] In respect of Scotland there is still much debate about the relationship between Parliament and Crown before 1707.[12] What seems clear is that there was a strong sense, different from that in England, that a monarch who abused his or her power could be deposed by subjects either acting independently or through the Scottish Parliament. This tradition finds expression in the Declaration of Arbroath in 1320. This document, following the victory by King Robert I (1306–29) at Bannockburn in 1314, was an appeal to the Pope for recognition and protection of Scottish independence from England, and declared

9 *Act anent the Ratification of the calling of the Convention, Ratification of the League and Covenant, Articles of Treaty betwixt the Kingdoms of Scotland and England, and remanent Acts of the Convention of Estates, and Committee thereof*: at Edinburgh, 15 July 1644, Charles I. Parl 3. Sess 1. Act 5.

10 During the Interregnum, constitutions of the Commonwealth and the Protectorate were established under Oliver Cromwell and there was briefly a single Parliament for Scotland, England and Ireland. But this arrangement ended at the time of the Restoration in 1660 and the Scottish and English Parliaments were re-established.

11 G L Cherry, 'The role of the Convention Parliament (1688–89) in parliamentary supremacy' (1956) *Journal of the History of Ideas* 390.

12 J Goodare, *State and Society in Early Modern Scotland* (1999); *The Government of Scotland 1560–1625* (2004); C Kidd, 'Sovereignty and the Scottish constitution before 1707' 2004 JR 225; K M Brown and A J Mann (eds), *Parliament and Politics in Scotland: 1567–1707* (2006) and *The Scottish Parliament: A Thematic History, 1286–1707* (2006).

that although the subjects of the king were bound to him 'both by law and by his merits', this was a form of contract the ultimate aim of which was the maintenance of the subjects' freedom. If the king betrayed his obligations, it declared: 'we should exert ourselves at once to drive him out as our enemy and a subverter of his own rights and ours, and make some other man who was well able to defend us our King'.

This tradition is also evident in the deposition of Queen Mary (1542–67) in 1567. Angered by her reign and opposed to her Catholic faith, the Protestant Lords of Scotland rose against her, resulting in a civil war in which she was defeated. Mary was captured, imprisoned and forced to abdicate in favour of her infant son (James VI). This Scottish tradition of limited monarchy also found theoretical articulation in the work of one of the greatest political philosophers of the late middle ages, George Buchanan (1506–82), whose radical argument that monarchs were not omnipotent[13] provided both an influential political justification for the overthrow of Mary and more generally a sophisticated philosophical framework for the Scottish constitutional tradition of legitimate revolt *in extremis* against a monarch who was deemed to be in serious breach of his or her contract with the people.[14]

Some have argued that these documents, theories and events are evidence of a tradition of popular sovereignty in late medieval Scotland whereby ultimate sovereignty within Scotland rested with 'the people' whose will would be expressed through Parliament.[15] It would seem, however, to be difficult to sustain such an argument in respect of an age before modern political theory had formulated a notion of 'the people' as a political agent,[16] and generally contemporary historians deny the viability of the popular sovereignty argument.[17] Nonetheless, it is clear that even in the absence of such a doctrine, different traditions concerning the authority of the monarch prevailed in Scotland and England.[18] The National Covenant of 1638 is an example of how both political elites and ordinary people in Scotland thought it legitimate to rebel against an unpopular king, crucially questioning his *lawful* authority as well as his political capacity to impose his own religious confession upon the state, and even taking up arms against him; and in this respect the process differed significantly from the more protracted, elite-driven and legally ambivalent dispute between Charles I and the English Parliament in the early 1640s.[19]

---

13 G Buchanan, *De Iure Regni Apud Scotos* (1579); *Historia Rerum Scoticarum*, 20 vols (1582). See also I D McFarlane, *George Buchanan* (1981).

14 G Buchanan, *De Maria Scotorum Regina* (1571) and published in Scots as *Ane detectioun of the doingis of Marie Quene of Scottis.*

15 N MacCormick, *Questioning Sovereignty: Law, State and Nation in the European Commonwealth* (1999), p 55.

16 E-J Sieyès, *Qu'est-ce Que le Tiers Etat* (R Zapperi, ed, 1970) (original pamphlet, 1789).

17 Kidd, 'Sovereignty', above n 12; J Robertson in J Robertson (ed), *A Union for Empire: Political Thought and the British Union of 1707* (1995), p 218; M Goldie in B Bradshaw and J Morrill (eds), *The British Problem c 1534–1707: State Formation in the Atlantic Archipelago* (1996); and D Hayton in S Ellis and S Barber (eds), *Conquest and Union: Fashioning a British State 1485–1725* (1995).

18 Modern historians are even sceptical of the very idea of 'traditions' (Kidd, 'Sovereignty', above n 12, at 226), but the term is used here to denote a discrete constitutional system which evolved over time.

19 Although there are also examples of the late seventeenth century Scots Parliament seemingly accepting the doctrine of divine right of kings (see eg the Excise Act 1685), there were various documents published at the time of the union of the Parliaments which challenged the monarch's supremacy: C Kidd, *Subverting Scotland's Past: Scottish Whig Historians and the Creation of an Anglo-British Identity 1689–1830* (2003).

In the revolution of 1688–89 the distinction between these two traditions in terms of their respective conceptions of the monarch's legal position would again manifest itself. In particular, the Claim of Right of 1689[20] offers an interesting contrast to the Bill of Rights passed by the English Convention Parliament in 1688 and formally ratified in 1689. In England, former members of the English Parliament summoned a Convention Parliament which was by definition an irregular meeting of the legislature since by this time the king had deserted the throne (by constitutional law the English Parliament could not convene without the king). The Convention declared that the throne was vacant and offered it to William and Mary. In turn William and Mary, in assuming the throne subject to conditions, had to accede to a Declaration of Right which accepted both that the monarchy's powers were limited, and in particular that the monarch could only govern and make law with the consent of the Parliament. The Convention Parliament then passed the Crown and Parliament Recognition Act 1689 and the new English Parliament, convened with its new monarchy, duly enacted the Bill of Rights which incorporated the Declaration of Right.

A similar process led to William and Mary being offered the Scottish Crown by the Scottish Parliament through the Claim of Right in 1689. However, in its presuppositions concerning the constitutional status of the monarch it is a more radical document. Notably the Claim does not suggest that James had left the throne vacant. This somewhat disingenuous argument was advanced by the English Convention Parliament and found articulation in the Bill of Rights.[21] This permitted the Convention Parliament to create the legal fiction that there had been no revolution against James but that in fact the throne had passed seamlessly, through James' 'abdication', within the same constitutional order to William and Mary. In other words, since by 1688, as has been noted, there was still no clear answer to where ultimate legal authority lay in the relationship between the king and the English Parliament, a revolt against the king would have been unconstitutional, and therefore the Convention Parliament backed away from declaring that it had in fact forced the king from his throne. In Scotland the situation was different however. Since there was a strong constitutional tradition of limited monarchy, including the widely held understanding that a king could be ejected from the throne as the Declaration of Arbroath and the deposition of Queen Mary had shown, then rather than argue that James had left the throne vacant in 1688, the Claim of Right stated explicitly that James had forfeited the throne of Scotland. It declared that since he had invaded 'the fundamentall Constitution of this Kingdome And altered it from a legall limited monarchy to ane Arbitrary Despotick power because of his inversion of the ends of government', he had 'forfaulted the right to the Croune'. This unambiguous declaration that the Scottish Parliament could depose a king who acted in a grossly unconstitutional way gave new impetus to a freshly invigorated Parliament in the seventeen years between the Claim of Right and the Treaty of Union. And in consequence, as Munro notes, in this period 'the Scottish Parliament displayed a greater authority than it had ever before possessed'.[22]

20 *The Declaration of the Estates of the Kingdom of Scotland containing the Claim of Right and the offer of the Croune to the King and Queen of England* (1689).
21 '[W]hereas the said late King James the Second [his title in England] haveing Abdicated the Government and the Throne being thereby Vacant': Bill of Rights (I Will & Mar Sess 2 c 2), Preamble.
22 C R Munro, *Studies in Constitutional Law* (2nd edn, 1999), p 22.

1707 AND FUNDAMENTAL LAW

The Union of 1707 was largely instigated by the English state, and the political pressure which it brought to bear met with considerable support within the Scottish elite, particularly at a time when Scotland was itself economically weak.[23] The Parliaments of England and Scotland established negotiations between two groups of commissioners representing each Parliament and appointed by Queen Anne (1702–14). They reached agreement on a 'Treaty of Union' which was then passed into law as an Act of each Parliament whereby the two existing Parliaments of England and Scotland were abolished and a new Parliament of Great Britain was created.

The Acts of Union or Treaty of Union (these terms are often used interchangeably) recognised important institutions of Scottish life and sought to guarantee their continued existence into the future, guarantees which made the Scottish union with England a more consensual and more conditional process than the union of Great Britain with Ireland, which was in many ways more a process of conquest than union.[24] In terms of the Treaty the two kingdoms of England and Scotland became Great Britain and provision was also made for the descent of the Crown after the death of Queen Anne, providing that it would pass down the Hanoverian line to secure a Protestant succession and hence prevent any future succession of the Pretender, James Stuart (son of James VII, now living in exile in France). Representation for Scotland in the House of Lords and House of Commons was also guaranteed, as was the continuance of Scottish private law;[25] the distinctive Scottish legal system;[26] and the royal burghs in Scotland. A separate Act was also passed maintaining the established Presbyterian Church in Scotland, and this Act was incorporated into the Treaty.

Against the backdrop of the different constitutional traditions which prevailed in England and Scotland by 1707, one important constitutional question which emerged from this process and which continues to be raised from time to time is the extent to which the Acts of Union constitute a form of 'fundamental law' for the new state of the Kingdom of Great Britain.[27] In other words, in founding this new state did these Acts of Union represent some form of written constitution, superior in normative importance to the later Acts of the institution which they created, the new Parliament of Great Britain? And as such, are the most important provisions contained within these Acts, which guarantee the continuing operation of important institutions of Scottish civil society, protected from repeal or amendment by this Parliament? In other words, as this question is often framed: was the Parliament of the United Kingdom born unfree?[28]

In the intervening centuries it is indeed the case that different visions within the legal systems of England and Scotland as to the status of the Acts of Union

---

23   An account of the background to the Union is provided by Munro, above n 22, pp 23–25.
24   Although, at least in formal terms, in the case of Ireland's unification with Great Britain in 1800 a similar model to that used to unify Scotland and England (Acts passed by each Parliament containing certain constitutional guarantees) was adopted.
25   Union with England Act 1707, art XVIII.
26   Union with England Act 1707, art XIX.
27   T B Smith, 'The Union of 1707 as fundamental law' [1957] PL 99; N MacCormick, 'Does the United Kingdom have a constitution?' (1978) 29 NILQ 1; N Walker, 'Fundamental Law', in 'Constitutional Law', *Stair Memorial Encyclopaedia*, vol 5 (Reissue, 2002), paras 29–82.
28   J B D Mitchell, *Constitutional Law* (2nd edn, 1968), pp 93–98.

have occasionally appeared. Beginning with the approach taken by English law, the dominant story of the union of Parliaments in English constitutional historiography is that the Acts of Union do not constitute fundamental law. The Union of Scotland and England was in fact an incorporating marriage similar in reality to a conquest of Scotland by the English constitutional system; the normative structure of the English constitution subsumed that of Scotland, and thereby the English Parliament in effect continued in existence, surviving the Union of Parliaments despite the formula contained in the Acts of Union which provided for a new Parliament.[29] Therefore, the English Parliament survived the transition to the new state of Great Britain and brought with it into the new state the emerging principle of legislative supremacy which was set to become the dominant norm of the constitution of Great Britain. Thus, the modern story of English constitutional history is one which tells of a unitary constitution, born of an incorporating union, and concluding with a single and easily identifiable source of ultimate legal authority: the legislative supremacy of the Parliament of Great Britain composed of monarch, House of Commons and House of Lords, each of which plays an essential role in the law-making process. This doctrine of parliamentary supremacy which was already emerging within English law at the end of the seventeenth century thereafter crystallised within English constitutional thinking, receiving its most famous articulation in the work of the constitutional scholar Dicey, who wrote between 1885 and 1915. For Dicey the legislative supremacy of the Crown in Parliament was indeed unlimited; as such it was possessed of both a positive and a negative aspect: in a positive sense Parliament had the power to make or unmake any law for the UK, and in its negative manifestation no other body could make law for the UK; and it is this doctrine which continues to dominate debate about the power of the UK Parliament to this day.[30]

Many Scots at the time of the Union held a different conception of what union would mean,[31] and occasionally in the twentieth century the Scottish courts did suggest that the Scottish legal system retained a different vision both of the nature of the Union and perhaps also of the powers of the UK Parliament in the post-Union period.[32] This alternative reading of the Union sees it not as an incorporating marriage whereby Scotland and her legal and constitutional traditions were replaced by those of England, but rather as a compact within which the two sets of traditions survived. The new Parliament was therefore the creation of two equal, constituent nations, each of which endowed it with its own constitutional traditions, and neither of which should necessarily take

---

29 G M Trevelyan, *History of England* (1926), p 481. See also Devine, above n 4, pp 3–30.

30 A V Dicey, *An Introduction to the Study of the Law of the Constitution* (8th edn, 1927), p 38. See also Blackstone: 'what the parliament doth, no authority upon earth can undo': *Commentaries on the Laws of England*, Book 1 (1870), p 160. A judicial restatement of the doctrine can be found in *Madzimbamuto v Lardner-Burke* [1969] 1 AC 645 at 723A per Lord Reid who confirmed that the Westminster Parliament may even, by way of legislation, do things that are 'unconstitutional'. See also *British Railways Board v Pickin* [1974] AC 765 at 782, again per Lord Reid.

31 The Scottish delegates who negotiated the Union Agreement favoured an early form of federal agreement: MacCormick, above n 15, pp 55–60; C Munro in S Tierney (ed), *Accommodating National Identity: New Approaches in International and Domestic Law* (2000), p 138.

32 A W Bradley and K D Ewing, *Constitutional and Administrative Law* (13th edn, 2003), pp 71–74; and E Wicks, 'A new constitution for a new state? The 1707 Union of England and Scotland' (2001) 117 LQR 109.

precedence over the other.[33] Furthermore, according to this line of argument, the foundational documents of this Parliament were the Acts of Union which remain of higher constitutional value than subsequent 'ordinary' Acts of the new Parliament, and as such certain aspects of the Acts of Union are not open to repeal by the new Parliament.

It is due to Scotland's separate and distinctive legal system that this question has remained alive even in the most abstract sense. As MacCormick puts it: 'the state as a law-state, a "Rechtstaat", is recognised within two at least partly distinct systems of law.... There is no doubt that we have a single state, but it is at least possible that we have two interpretations, two conceptions, two understandings, of the constitution of that state.'[34] The notion of the Acts of Union as fundamental law received its most prominent articulation in *MacCormick v Lord Advocate*.[35] This case involved a challenge before the Court of Session in 1953 to the new monarch, Queen Elizabeth, who had assumed the title Queen Elizabeth II of Great Britain. The petitioners, who were Scottish nationalists, contended that, because there had never been a Queen Elizabeth of Scotland but only a Queen Elizabeth of England (1533–1603), this title was unconstitutional and in violation of Article I of the Acts of Union of 1707. The case was unsuccessful on the ground of relevance since the Acts of Union were held to be silent on the issue of royal title; but the case is more notable now for the obiter comments of Lord President Cooper in which he gave his view of parliamentary sovereignty within the Scottish constitutional tradition:

> 'The principle of the unlimited sovereignty of Parliament is a distinctively English principle which has no counterpart in Scottish Constitutional Law.... Considering that the Union legislation extinguished the Parliaments of Scotland and England and replaced them by a new Parliament, I have difficulty in seeing why it should be supposed that the new Parliament of Great Britain must inherit all the peculiar characteristics of the English Parliament but none of the Scottish Parliament, as if all that happened was that Scottish representatives were admitted to the Parliament of England. This is not what was done.... I have not found in the Union legislation any provision that the parliament of Great Britain should be free to alter the treaty at will.'[36]

There have, however, been few such allusions by the Scottish courts to the survival of a Scottish constitutional tradition which might draw upon the Acts of Union as a more fundamental source of constitutional authority than the Westminster Parliament. For instance, it is important to note that despite Lord President Cooper's remarks, no Act of Parliament has ever been found to be invalid on the grounds that it was incompatible with the Acts of Union. Since *MacCormick* other

---

33 According to Jim Wallace MP (later to become an MSP and Deputy First Minister of Scotland): 'the concept of parliamentary sovereignty was alien to the history of Scotland ... what was established in 1707 and augmented in 1801 when Ireland came into the Union was a Parliament of the United Kingdom. It was not a Parliament of England, of Scotland or of Ireland.... There is no earthly reason why the constitutional theories of a Parliament of England should take precedence over the constitutional theories of any other part of what was an equal Union' (HC Deb, vol 305, col 369 (28 Jan 1998)).

34 N MacCormick, 'Is there a constitutional path to Scottish independence?' (2000) 53 *Parl Affairs* 721 at 727. See also C Himsworth, 'Devolution and the mixed legal system of Scotland' 2002 JR 115.

35 1953 SC 396.

36 1953 SC at 411.

cases which have dealt with the issue have tended to suggest that except in the most extreme cases such a challenge to an Act of Parliament is unlikely to be justiciable.[37] This conclusion was in fact seemingly reached by Lord President Cooper himself in *MacCormick*.[38] It seems, therefore, from these cases that the only legislation which might be successfully challenged before a Scots court on the grounds of constitutionality would be an Act purporting to abolish the Court of Session or the Church of Scotland, or to substitute English law for the whole body of Scots private law;[39] and of course the prospect of Parliament passing such legislation is to say the least unlikely.

These circumstances have together led many to argue that the Acts of Union do not survive in any real legal sense as fundamental constitutional texts, particularly given the numerous repeals and modifications to which they have been subjected,[40] not the least of which is section 37 of the Scotland Act 1998 which, in implementing the devolution settlement, provides that the two Acts of Union are to 'have effect subject to this Act'. However, the status of the Acts of Union as fundamental law continues to be raised from time to time. In respect of the new Supreme Court for the United Kingdom, for example, the Faculty of Advocates argued:

> 'a Supreme Court which is created must be consistent with the Claim of Right of 1689 and the Act of Union of 1707. These instruments are fundamental parts of the constitution of the United Kingdom of Great Britain and Northern Ireland, and ... any proposal for a Supreme Court which contravened any provision of these instruments would be unlawful'.[41]

THE ROAD TO DEVOLVED GOVERNMENT

Turning to the devolution settlement encapsulated in the Scotland Act 1998, this chapter now considers how this has altered the nature of the Union from a unitary constitutional system to a decentralised system, asking whether it has

---

37 In one exceptional case, *Gibson v Lord Advocate* 1975 SLT 134, which concerned the UK's accession to the European Communities, Lord Keith stated that the courts could not adjudicate on the question whether an Act of the UK Parliament altering a particular aspect of Scottish private law violated the 1707 agreement, but he reserved his opinion on the legal position of an Act of the UK Parliament which purported to abolish the Court of Session or the Church of Scotland. Other unsuccessful attempts to raise this issue before the courts have occurred from time to time: eg *Pringle, Petitioner* 1991 SLT 330; *Sillars v Smith* 1982 SLT 539. See also N Walker and C M G Himsworth, 'The poll tax and fundamental law' 1991 JR 45.

38 *MacCormick v Lord Advocate* 1953 SC 396 at 411. Justiciability problems could arise in terms of jurisdiction, what a suitable remedy might be, and the title and interest of any party wishing to challenge such an Act: A Tomkins, 'The constitutional law in *MacCormick v the Lord Advocate*' 2004 JR 213.

39 *Gibson v Lord Advocate* 1975 SLT 134.

40 Munro in *Accommodating National Identity*, above n 31, pp 137–142; J Robertson in H T Dickinson and M Lynch (eds), *The Challenge to Westminster; Sovereignty, Devolution, and Independence* (2000), pp 198–227. For the alternative view that the Acts of Union retain special legal significance see Smith, above n 27; Mitchell, *Constitutional Law*, above n 28; and MacCormick, *UK Constitution?*, above n 27. See also Lord Bingham, 'Dicey revisited' [2002] PL 39 at 45 and M Upton, 'Marriage vows of the elephant: the constitution of 1707' (1989) 105 LQR 79.

41 Faculty of Advocates, *Response to the Consultation Paper by the Secretary of State for Constitutional Affairs and Lord Chancellor: Constitutional Reform: a Supreme Court for the United Kingdom* (Nov 2003).

also provided the institutional potential for the re-emergence of a distinctive Scottish constitutional tradition through the new, devolved institutions of Scottish government and the Scottish legal system.

Although legislative devolution was not introduced in Scotland until the creation of the Scottish Parliament in 1999, the century preceding this was characterised by a system of administrative devolution.[42] This system was established with the founding of the Scottish Office in 1885 headed by the Secretary for Scotland as a separate ministry within the UK executive; and this office was elevated to the status of Secretary of State for Scotland and thereby a Cabinet position in 1926.[43] Under the Scottish Office the Secretary of State and a group of junior ministers were empowered to administer a block grant for Scotland which was issued by the UK government each year. This enabled Scotland to be run with a degree of administrative independence allowing the Secretary of State to identify and respond to the different priorities and aspirations of the Scottish people. Although there has been an ongoing debate amongst scholars as to the strength of Scotland's administrative autonomy under the Scottish Office regime, retrospectively it does seem that the existence of this important Cabinet department helped consolidate the institutions of Scottish social and political life which had survived the Union and thereby worked to foster a flourishing and distinctive civil society in Scotland.[44]

Nonetheless, in the latter part of the twentieth century many critics of the Scottish Office regime argued that for various reasons it did not go far enough in giving Scotland autonomy. First, since the UK government is constituted by the party with an overall majority of seats in the House of Commons, it often happened that this would be a party which had in fact performed poorly in elections in Scotland, and so there was often a sense that Scotland was being governed by a party which did not really represent the wishes of the Scottish people. Also the Secretary of State, as a member of the UK Cabinet, was required by the doctrine of collective ministerial responsibility to abide by the collective policy of the Cabinet, even when this policy was, in his opinion, contrary to the best interests of Scotland. And furthermore, since the UK government determined the annual budget for the UK and as the Scottish grant was a percentage of this, Scottish funding would fluctuate in line with priorities elsewhere in the UK.[45]

A related phenomenon was the growth in Scottish nationalism from the 1950s onwards, a phenomenon to be found across a range of sub-state national societies in the developed world including also Wales in the UK, Catalonia and the Basque Country in Spain, Flanders in Belgium, and Quebec in Canada.[46] In Scotland this had resulted in the development of a strong, separatist Scottish National Party which won eleven seats in the House of Commons in the general election of October 1974. Growth in nationalist sentiment was also evident within the

---

42 Mitchell, *Constitutional Law*, above n 28, p 209; Munro, above n 22, pp 37–39.
43 R Brazier, *Ministers of the Crown* (1997), p 9.
44 Paterson argues that in this period Scotland's civil society was highly autonomous and that the effects of 'Anglicisation' were not great: L Paterson, *The Autonomy of Modern Scotland* (1994). See also R Brazier, 'The constitution of the United Kingdom' (1999) 58 CLJ 96 at 98.
45 Eg, O'Neill described the office of Secretary of State for Scotland as more 'London's viceroy than Scotland's consul': M O'Neill, 'Great Britain' (2000) 53 *Parl Affairs* 69 at 70. See also Chapter 7 in this volume.
46 Tierney, above n 5.

Scottish branches of traditionally unionist parties such as Labour and the Liberals, and although the new Scottish nationalism of these two parties was generally not separatist in outlook it did move them towards strong support for devolution. A further impetus for the growth in nationalism across the Scottish body politic was a reaction to the Conservative government of the 1980s and 1990s. Disillusionment with the neo-liberal policies of this period manifested itself in demands not simply for different economic policies but most volubly for 'home rule': for a system of devolved government which would give Scotland the opportunity to govern itself and set its own economic and social agenda.

This change in political climate is illustrated by the stark contrast in the level of support for devolution in the referendum held in 1997 compared to a previous referendum proposing devolution in 1979. In 1979, support for the creation of a Scottish Assembly was lukewarm, and ultimately the proposal failed.[47] However, by 1997 conditions had changed radically. What occurred in the intervening period was the emergence of an extra-parliamentary campaign for constitutional change which involved a broad range of political and civic actors – many of them political opponents of the Conservative government – which was initially embodied in the Campaign for a Scottish Assembly (CSA) launched in 1985. This campaign resulted in a document, *A Claim of Right for Scotland*, issued in 1988 and declaring the inherent right of the Scots to self-government. This document aired the grievance that the 'union state' pact stemming from 1707 had been undermined by subsequent UK constitutional practice.[48] Furthermore, it asserted that 'sovereignty' in Scotland rested with the Scottish people and as such they had the right to initiate changes to Scotland's constitutional position.

The *Claim* of 1988 recommended the establishment of a cross-party Scottish Constitutional Convention (SCC), which would draw up a scheme for home rule, mobilise the people behind it, and 'assert the right of the Scottish people to secure the implementation of that scheme'.[49] This was inaugurated on 30 March 1989 and over the next seven years it embraced much of Scotland's political elite, involving inter alia the Labour and Liberal Democratic parties, local authorities, churches and the Scottish Trades Union Congress.[50] Although not established by any official route, it was composed of fifty-nine of Scotland's seventy-two Westminster MPs and all six of its Members of the European Parliament. This resulted in a series of publications, the most important of which, *Scotland's Claim, Scotland's Right*,[51] set out a detailed blueprint for devolution which proved to be very influential, the eventual model of devolution enacted through the Scotland Act 1998 being remarkably similar to it.

The momentum for devolution created by this extra-parliamentary campaign meant that the process by which legislation was passed after Labour came to power in the UK in 1997 was very speedy. The political climate in 1997–98 was highly conducive to devolution; a Labour administration elected with a large majority was committed to devolution, and so, heavily influenced by Scottish Labour MPs, the

---

47 Only 52 per cent voted for devolution on a 64 per cent turnout, but the Scotland Act 1978 required that at least 40 per cent of the total electorate should vote in favour.
48 *A Claim of Right for Scotland* (1988), p 19. Its title was of course intended to echo the radical spirit of the pre-Union Scottish Parliament's revolutionary Claim of Right of 1689.
49 *A Claim of Right for Scotland* (1988).
50 J McFadden, 'The Scottish Constitutional Convention' [1995] PL 215.
51 1995.

government drove the devolution settlement through the first session of the new Parliament. The fact that the extra-parliamentary campaign had already developed a sophisticated model which could then be adapted by Parliament quite easily was of considerable assistance in streamlining the route to devolved government.

The process was as follows: shortly after assuming office, and building upon *Scotland's Claim, Scotland's Right*, the government issued a White Paper, *Scotland's Parliament*, which contained a fully worked-out model of devolution. This proposal was then put to a referendum in Scotland in November 1997[52] in which a large majority voted yes to the principal proposal.[53] In this sense the background to the Scotland Act takes on, at least by one construction, a strongly organic, and to some extent popular, dimension: the former because the devolution model stemmed heavily from a pre-parliamentary political initiative within the Scottish body politic, and the latter because of the strong popular endorsement of the devolution settlement in the referendum.[54] Although some minor changes were made by Parliament to the devolution proposal after the referendum, the model finally enacted was in substantive terms the same as that voted for in the referendum.

DEVOLUTION IN THE UK: A UNIQUE MODEL

The establishment of devolution certainly represents the most dramatic constitutional change to the nature of the Union since 1707. However, there remain questions as to how we should characterise the new arrangements. It is clear that the UK has not established a fully federal model. Federalism is a system of government in which final legal authority is divided between a central authority and constituent, territorially-based political units. The structure of devolution differs from classical conceptions of federalism in a number of ways. First, although the powers of the Scottish Parliament are limited, there has been no concomitant, express restriction on the powers of the Westminster Parliament; in other words, in the view of Westminster, its final legal authority has not been divided.[55] This serves to emphasise that devolution has been introduced in the context of an unwritten constitution within which the powers of the central parliament are assumed by that parliament to be unlimited; whereas in federal systems around the world, a written constitution provides that the powers of both the territorial and central institutions of government are limited.

Another structural feature of most federal systems is that as well as autonomy, sub-state territories receive constitutional guarantees of representation at the centre. For example, there is often a second chamber of the central legislature which is composed of an equal number of members from each of the federal

---

52 Referendums (Scotland and Wales) Act 1997.
53 On the first question: 'I agree that there should be a Scottish Parliament', 74% voted Yes; and on the second: 'I agree that a Scottish Parliament should have tax-varying powers', 63.5% voted Yes.
54 J Mitchell in *The Challenge to Westminster*, above n 40, p 161.
55 The Scottish Parliament has competence across a range of important areas. However, there are two important qualifications to this. First, the UK Parliament has a general residual power to make laws for Scotland (Scotland Act 1998, s 28(7)). Secondly, the Scotland Act also enumerates specific limitations upon the Scottish Parliament's competence (s 29).

entities such as the Senate of the American Congress which has 100 members, two from each state with the Vice-President of the United States possessing a casting vote in the event of deadlock.[56] Devolution was introduced into the UK without any such realignment of the central legislature; in other words, there has been no move to reconstitute the House of Lords as a 'territorial' chamber.

Given the seemingly unrestricted power of the Westminster Parliament, therefore, there remains the controversial question as to whether the UK Parliament will ever enact law on devolved matters without the consent of the Scottish Parliament. For now, a constitutional convention has emerged whereby this will not occur (the Sewel convention discussed below), but the issue serves to highlight how, in the absence of a fully federal system, according to the orthodox story of Westminster supremacy, there seems to be no legal mechanism which would prevent such encroachment by Westminster upon the prerogatives of the Scottish Parliament.

Another feature which distinguishes the 'untidy'[57] or, 'haphazard'[58] model of devolution in the UK from most federal models is its 'asymmetrical' structure.[59] A common feature of federal systems is that each sub-state territory has the same powers. The UK differs from this in that each of the devolution models for Scotland, Wales and Northern Ireland diverge greatly from one another, emphasising the union nature of the state and the differing nature of each of the national societies which it contains.[60] Furthermore, the largest nation of the UK, England, does not have devolved government at all, and continues to be governed exclusively by the central government of the UK state and legislated for exclusively by Westminster. This anomaly has created another tension for the Union in the post-devolution period. One consequence of ad hoc devolution, whereby Scotland achieved autonomy without any similar process for England, is that certain matters which are devolved to the competence of the Scottish Parliament are dealt with for England and other parts of the UK by Westminster. Therefore, MPs are returned to Westminster from Scotland where they can vote on matters which affect other parts of the UK but not Scotland. This has become known as the 'West Lothian question',[61] and it has become somewhat controversial particularly where the UK Government has relied upon Scottish MPs to secure a majority for legislation which will not affect Scotland. This has the potential to put a strain on the Union if it leads to increased resentment among English voters.[62]

---

56 Constitution of the United States of America, art I, s 3.
57 O'Neill, above n 45, at 78.
58 N Burrows, *Devolution* (2000), p 27.
59 C D Tarlton, 'Symmetry and asymmetry as elements of federalism: a theoretical speculation' (1965) 27 *The Journal of Politics* 86.
60 As Walker observes: 'The union state … provides a key historical pathway towards a more general model of asymmetrical government, in which a heterogeneity of governance arrangements between regions becomes a normal and persistent feature of the state': N Walker 'Beyond the unitary conception of the UK constitution?' [2000] PL 384 at 398.
61 Thus called because this anomaly was anticipated when devolution was first proposed in the late 1970s by Tam Dalyell, MP for West Lothian.
62 For a recent failed attempt to remove the right of Scottish and Welsh MPs to vote at Westminster on matters devolved to their respective countries, see the Parliament (Participation of Members of the House of Commons) Bill, HL Bill 61, 2005–06.

DEVOLUTION AND PARLIAMENTARY SOVEREIGNTY

Having reviewed the institutional structure of devolution it is now possible to consider how it is shaping and is likely to shape further the relationship between Scotland and the rest of the UK, in particular by way of relations between the Scottish Parliament and Westminster. Here two issues are of particular interest. The first concerns the power of the Westminster Parliament, referred to above, to make law in devolved areas without the consent of the Scottish Parliament. However, since the Scotland Act came into force a new constitutional convention has developed – the Sewel convention – which serves to limit this power at least in practice. The possibility of such a convention developing was articulated by Lord Sewel on behalf of the government in parliamentary debate on the Scotland Bill, thus: 'as happened in Northern Ireland earlier in the century [during devolution to Stormont from 1920–69], we would expect a convention to be established that Westminster would not normally legislate with regard to devolved matters in Scotland without the consent of the Scottish Parliament'.[63] This has indeed been the case, and when legislation has been passed by Westminster in devolved areas, when for practical purposes it has been felt that this was a more efficient process than two separate pieces of legislation, Westminster has first obtained the assent of the Scottish Parliament.[64]

The passage of legislation by Westminster in a devolved area without the consent of the Scottish Parliament would, therefore, be very controversial. It would not, however, in itself amend the Scotland Act; the powers of the Scottish Parliament would remain unaffected unless they were expressly amended by Westminster legislation. Although the Sewel convention seems to guarantee that this will not occur without the consent of the Scottish Parliament, that does not mean that the courts would attempt to restrain Westminster's power to legislate in devolved areas in the absence of such consent.[65]

A second issue concerns the status of the devolution settlement itself as set out in the Scotland Act. By the dominant doctrine of parliamentary supremacy the Scotland Act is simply an Act of Parliament like any other and is open to express or implied repeal by a later inconsistent Act of the UK Parliament. It has been observed above that, according to Dicey, the UK Parliament has the power to make or unmake any law. Therefore, it would seem to follow logically that the UK Parliament's legislative supremacy is unaffected by devolution to Scotland. The White Paper which preceded the Scotland Bill certainly took this view, stating plainly: 'the UK Parliament is, and will remain, sovereign in all matters', and 'Westminster will be choosing to exercise that sovereignty in devolving legislative responsibilities to a Scottish Parliament without in any way diminishing its own powers. The Government recognise that no UK Parliament can bind its successors'.[66] However, we have also observed that despite the overwhelming weight given to Diceyan orthodoxy within English constitutional presuppositions,

---

63 HL Deb, vol 592, col 791 (21 July 1998).
64 On the operation of the Sewel procedure see B K Winetrobe, 'Counter-devolution? The Sewel convention on devolved legislation at Westminster' (2001) 6 SLPQ 286; A Page and A Batey, 'Scotland's other Parliament: Westminster legislation in the devolved areas since devolution' [2002] PL 501.
65 *Whaley v Lord Watson of Invergowrie* 2000 SC 340; *Adams, Petitioner* 2002 SCLR 881. But see also the discussion below of *Jackson v Attorney-General* [2005] UKHL 56.
66 *Scotland's Parliament* (Cm 3658, 1997), para 4.2.

there has persisted a discrete Scottish constitutional tradition, voiced by the Court of Session in *MacCormick* and by prominent political actors through the SCC, that Westminster's self-assumed supremacy is not untrammelled, at least in the context of the Acts of Union. A question which remains therefore is whether, as devolution settles down, it will provide the institutional infrastructure within which this Scottish tradition might revive and, if so, whether the Scotland Act itself will be seen as a mechanism whereby Westminster's absolute supremacy might be modified.[67]

Already in English law some doubt has been cast on the traditional Diceyan doctrine at least as far as implied repeal is concerned.[68] In the English Court of Appeal, Laws LJ took the view that there is a set of particularly important statutes, including the Scotland Act 1998, that he termed 'constitutional statutes'. These, he suggested, cannot be repealed simply by a later, inconsistent Act of the Westminster Parliament. Instead the amendment of these statutes would require the express intention of the UK Parliament. This does not mean that a challenge to Westminster's *express* intention to amend or abolish the Scotland Act, even if such an Act went expressly against the will of the Scottish Parliament, would be upheld by either the Scottish or English courts. However there is another argument which asserts that in political terms at least the Scotland Act cannot be repealed or significantly amended without the consent of the Scottish people. This argument finds its energy in modern democratic theory which asserts that constitutional legitimacy is to be found in the will of the people. This was earlier articulated through the SCC and its related fora, and contends that the Scotland Act embodies a new popular agreement between Scotland and the rest of the UK which is built upon, from the Scottish perspective, an expression of self-determination by the Scottish people, manifest in the result of the referendum of 1997. As a result, it is assumed that the Act's important terms may only be changed with the consent of the Scottish Parliament or the people directly.[69]

In this context we should return to the extra-parliamentary process which preceded the devolution settlement. What is particularly interesting about *Scotland's Claim, Scotland's Right*, bearing in mind the strong involvement of the Scottish Labour Party in the SCC, is that the Convention shared the earlier commitment of the CSA to the idea of popular sovereignty. As the SCC declared: 'we, gathered as the Scottish Constitutional Convention, do hereby acknowledge the sovereign right of the Scottish people to determine the form of Government best suited to their needs'.[70] Rather than a rejection of the Union constitution, *Scotland's Claim,*

---

67 Some consider that Westminster's absolute supremacy is now open to question more than at any time since the Union of Parliaments in 1707: Walker, 'Fundamental Law', above n 27, p 50.

68 *Thoburn v Sunderland City Council* [2003] QB 151, para 63.

69 The SCC's understanding of Scottish devolution was as 'a constitutional settlement in which the Scottish people, being sovereign, agree to the exercise of specified powers by Westminster but retain their sovereignty over all other matters': *Scotland's Claim, Scotland's Right.* Jones discusses the earlier assertion of popular sovereignty in the Claim of Right and concludes: 'it does not matter what view the UK Parliament takes of its own powers; as far as Scotland is concerned, the powers of Westminster would be limited to those agreed to by the Scottish Parliament.... The ultimate logic of this approach is that actions of the Westminster Parliament could be declared ultra vires the constitutional settlement': T H Jones, 'Scottish devolution and demarcation disputes' [1997] PL 283 at 293.

70 *Scotland's Claim, Scotland's Right.*

Scotland's Right can in fact be seen as a reaffirmation of the UK constitution – the constitution of a union state.[71] It contended that this constitutional pact was being broken by the central authority of the state, particularly in the 1980s as a result of the UK government's process of constitutional centralisation; more radically it also seems to suggest that this process of 'unconstitutional' behaviour entitled Scots to revise the Union, if need be, unilaterally.[72] Indeed the 1988 *Claim* openly accused the UK constitution, or at least the dominant interpretation of it, of betraying the 1707 agreement: 'the Scots are a minority which cannot ever feel secure under a constitution which, in effect, renders the Treaty of Union a contradiction in terms'.[73] In doing so, as was noted above, it asserted that 'sovereignty' in Scotland rests with the Scottish people.

This campaign and these declarations highlight that one strong assumption which informed the extra-parliamentary campaign was that Scotland retained a distinctive constitutional tradition in which the sovereignty of the Westminster Parliament was not a universally shared assumption.[74] It might be argued that the notion of popular sovereignty in Scotland is simply a political principle, distinguishable from a legal conception of sovereignty (sovereignty in the domestic sense meaning the source of ultimate legal power). There is a tradition within legal theory, which we might call the 'strong positivist tradition', which asserts that legal rules are a discrete set of norms of an entirely different normative order from political rules and constraints which also operate upon political actors. In other words, legal rules are so free-standing that we can conceive of them as operating in a zone which in conceptual terms is wholly separate from the political realm. This is important when we turn as constitutional scholars to the notion of 'fundamental law'. This is the idea of the source of law within a constitutional order; in other words, a model of higher law – typically to be found in the constitutional text of those states with written constitutions – which operates above and gives legitimacy to 'ordinary' law made by parliaments. Within the strong positivist tradition once again we see that such fundamental law is conceptually separable from political rules and constraints. Therefore, although some might say that the Scottish people are sovereign, according to strong positivists this is simply a political principle which does not modify in any way the free-standing fundamental law of the UK which is that Parliament is legislatively supreme. The political principle of sovereignty is entirely distinct from and normatively subordinate to the legal principle of sovereignty which is to be found in the Westminster Parliament's untrammelled law-making power. Parliament retains the authority to make or unmake any law and therefore can entirely override ideas of popular sovereignty, for example by repealing the Scotland Act even without the consent of the Scottish Parliament or the Scottish people in a referendum.

71 Mitchell in *The Challenge to Westminster*, above n 40, p 161.
72 As Keating puts it, the governmental centralisation of this period was 'widely seen as an abuse of Parliamentary sovereignty and therefore a violation of the unwritten norms of the constitution. This sentiment was especially strong in Scotland, where the union is still seen as a compact': M Keating in T C Salmon and M Keating (eds), *The Dynamics of Decentralisation: Canadian Federalism and British Devolution* (2001), pp 26–27.
73 *A Claim of Right for Scotland*, p 19.
74 'This concept of sovereignty [the Westminster model] has always been unacceptable to the Scottish constitutional tradition of limited government or popular sovereignty': *Scotland's Claim, Scotland's Right*.

However, the coherence of this very distinction between law and politics has recently been called into question. Loughlin argues that legal sovereignty is an essentially relational phenomenon in two senses. On the one hand it encapsulates the relationship between law and politics. In this sense Loughlin identifies two elements of sovereignty: competence and capacity; the former representing authority in a legal sense, and the latter power in a political sense. Whereas many legal positivists would see these two phenomena operating discretely within the modern state, Loughlin argues that both combine inseparably to explain the modern conception of sovereignty:

> 'Sovereignty is both an expression of official power and is the product of a political relationship. The former, focusing on the institutional and public, depicts the legal conception of sovereignty; the latter expresses the political conception. These legal and political conceptions of sovereignty in turn reflect concerns about the issues of competence and capacity, of authority and power.'[75]

In particular, the competence of law is not free-standing and must always be understood in relation to capacity: 'the issue of capacity must be drawn into an appropriate relation to that of competence; the political aspects of sovereignty must not be suppressed'.[76]

There is a second relational dimension to sovereignty and that is the bond between people and state which emerges from the birth of the state itself. For Loughlin, sovereignty 'is a function of the institutional arrangements established as a consequence of the formation of the modern state'.[77] The important aspect of this second relational idea is that sovereignty does not have a fixed locus as positivists suggest; in other words it does not make sense to talk of sovereignty as belonging to Parliament as an institution. Instead its essence is encapsulated in the relationship between 'sovereignty' and 'the people';[78] and as such sovereignty is dependent upon the essentially political interaction between a people and its form of government.[79] Both of these relational components co-exist and interact making sovereignty both a more political concept than legal positivists accept, and also one that is fluid, thereby leaving the power structures of the polity open to change as the relationship between people and government changes.

What makes a union state like the United Kingdom distinctive is that in the process of union there emerged a plurality of relationships between people and government. A distinctive sense of peoplehood existed within both Scotland and England in 1707, and this was given added civic dimensions by the survival of different civic institutions, and an added legal dimension by the survival of the distinctive legal systems, in each country. In this sense, adapting Loughlin's relational concept, sovereignty within the UK has always been a contested concept as the different peoples of the state – and this also embraces Wales and Northern Ireland – with their specific experiences of union, envisage their relationship to the state in different ways.[80]

75 M Loughlin, *The Idea of Public Law* (2003), p 84.
76 Loughlin, above n 75, p 91.
77 Loughlin, above n 75, p 80.
78 Loughlin, above n 75, p 81. See also pp 72–73.
79 Loughlin, above n 75, p 83.
80 As Tomkins argues (above n 38, pp 220–221): 'it is indeed appropriate to have different rules of legislative supremacy in Scotland from those which pertain in England…. the explanation as to why English law vests Acts of the Crown-in-Parliament with legal supremacy is one that might

The political expression of difference which was manifested in the SCC and the referendum, and which now has an institutional platform in the form of devolved government, has helped invigorate the idea that in the UK the competence and capacity of Westminster's sovereignty are changing. It is already widely considered that the Westminster Parliament has surrendered both legal and political power to the EU,[81] and with these cracks in the monolithic structure the question now being raised is whether or not Westminster's absolute supremacy is also being challenged internally through devolution to Scotland. Indeed Loughlin believes that devolution may even pose a stronger challenge to this supremacy than the EU itself:

> '[S]overeignty, at its most basic, is an expression of a political relationship between the people and the state…. In this sense, the "devolutionary" arrangements of the Scotland Act 1998, which establish a Scottish parliament able to give institutional expression to Scots political identity, potentially provide the more radical challenge to the sovereignty of the United Kingdom state.'[82]

Whether the Scotland Act will come to be considered of such constitutional importance that in future a Scottish or English court would seek to protect its most central provisions from express as well as implied repeal, for example resisting any move by Westminster to abolish the Scottish Parliament, seems for the present at least to be very unlikely. But this is a question also raised recently by Loughlin. Despite the fact that the Scotland Act 1998 takes the form of a devolution of legislative authority to a subordinate body, he asks whether it is inconceivable that the courts would rule that powers conferred on the Scottish Parliament cannot lawfully be withdrawn without the consent of that institution.[83] His answer:

> 'To apply a Hobbesean metaphor, it might be said that the (legal) skeleton of sovereignty has, for the moment, been retained but in order to retain the life of the concept, the (political) nerves, arteries and vital organs must continue to work effectively. The prognosis does not look good.'[84]

In other words the assumption within the narrow positivist tradition that an absolute separation of law and politics can be found within any constitutional system seems overly simplistic.[85] As Loughlin's sophisticated analysis high-

---

not apply to Scotland. Whether Scots constitutional law is driven by the same dynamic between the Crown and Parliament as drives the English constitution is a question which would merit further research, but, on first sight, it seems doubtful, to say the least, that the Scots-law position is identical to the English.'

81 *R v Secretary of State for Transport ex parte Factortame Ltd (No 1)* [1989] 2 WLR 997 (HL); *(No 2)* [1990] 3 WLR 818 (HL).

82 Loughlin, above n 75, p 95.

83 M Loughlin, *Sword and Scales: An Examination of the Relationship between Law and Politics* (2000), p 154.

84 Loughlin, above n 83, p 154. In a related way Walker in 'Beyond the unitary conception' (above n 60) has asked whether the Scotland Act represents a move 'beyond a unitary conception of the UK constitution'.

85 For an analogous situation in which the Supreme Court of Canada showed itself prepared to extend its vision of the Canadian constitution beyond narrow formalism see *Reference re Secession of Quebec* [1998] 2 SCR 217.

lights, the very essence of a norm's legal validity cannot survive its political marginalisation.[86]

In the era of Scottish devolution, there have been few signs that the courts consider the new devolved settlement to be in any tension with parliamentary supremacy, and this may well be how things continue, particularly when political relations between London and Edinburgh are generally very amicable. However, from one recent case, which involved the ban on fox hunting in England, it seems that among certain House of Lords judges there is a sense that the traditional doctrine of parliamentary sovereignty may be weakening in the face of various challenges, including devolution to Scotland.[87] In *Jackson* Lord Steyn commented:

> 'We do not in the United Kingdom have an uncontrolled constitution.... The settlement contained in the Scotland Act 1998 ... points to a divided sovereignty.... The classic account given by Dicey of the doctrine of the supremacy of Parliament, pure and absolute as it was, can now be seen to be out of place in the modern United Kingdom.'[88]

Equally radically, Lord Hope, formerly Lord President of the Court of Session and now the more senior Scots judge on the Appellate Committee, argued:

> 'Our constitution is dominated by the sovereignty of Parliament. But parliamentary sovereignty is no longer, if it ever was, absolute.... It is no longer right to say that its freedom to legislate admits of no qualification whatever. Step by step, gradually but surely, the English principle of the absolute legislative sovereignty of Parliament which Dicey derived from Coke and Blackstone is being qualified.'[89]

While it is important to note that these sentiments were expressed obiter and were not expressly shared by a majority of judges in the case, they do represent significant breaches in what has traditionally been a monolithic acceptance by senior judges of Westminster's untrammelled legislative power. It is also significant that Lord Steyn's reference to divided sovereignty in respect of the Scotland Act came in a case which did not even involve devolution. These judgments may be seen to set down a marker to the effect that the different common law courts of England and Scotland may at some time in the future declare the doctrine of parliamentary supremacy to be significantly modified, and as such we may even see a divergence between Scots and English courts on this issue given that each has jurisdiction to consider devolution issues arising from the Scotland Act. As Lord Steyn also argued in the context of the English common law:

> '[T]he supremacy of Parliament ... is a construct of the common law. The judges created this principle. If that is so, it is not unthinkable that circumstances could arise where the courts may have to qualify a principle established on a different hypothesis of constitutionalism. In exceptional circumstances involving an attempt to abolish judicial review or the ordinary role of the courts, the Appellate Committee of the House of Lords or a new Supreme Court may have to consider whether this is a

---

86 An idea which also finds endorsement in Ackerman's idea of 'constitutional moments', whereby even written constitutions can change radically through informal channels as well as formal processes of constitutional amendment: B Ackerman, *We the People: Transformations* (1998).

87 *Jackson v Attorney-General* [2005] UKHL 56.

88 *Jackson*, para 102 per Lord Steyn.

89 *Jackson*, para 104.

constitutional fundamental which even a sovereign Parliament acting at the behest of a complaisant House of Commons cannot abolish.'[90]

It may also be that the courts are becoming aware in the context of the devolution settlement encapsulated in the Scotland Act, a settlement which most Scots consider should not be subjected to fundamental change or repeal without the consent of the Scottish Parliament or the Scottish people expressed in a referendum, that adherence by way of a narrow conception of legalism to an out-moded vision of an absolutely supreme Parliament in Westminster in the face of constitutionally unacceptable behaviour by that Parliament would be to cut the constitution off from the political legitimacy upon which it depends. As Lord Hope observed in *Jackson*: 'Parliamentary sovereignty is an empty principle if legislation is passed which is so absurd or so unacceptable that the populace at large refuses to recognise it as law.'[91] It is in this context that the question must be asked whether the devolution settlement, having transformed the Union in a way unprecedented since 1707, now offers the prospect of a revived Scottish constitutional tradition which might in time challenge the absolute nature of Westminster's self-ascribed supremacy.

90 *Jackson*, para 102.
91 *Jackson*, para 120 per Lord Hope.

Chapter 3

Scotland in Europe: Empowerment or Disempowerment?

Noreen Burrows

INTRODUCTION

The European Union is a union of states. It is created by treaties concluded between states in the context of public international law. Only European states may become parties to the Treaty establishing the European Union (TEU) and the Treaty establishing the European Community (EC) since only European states which respect 'the principles set out in Article 6(1) TEU may apply to become a member of the Union'.[1] Article 1 EC and Article 1 TEU provide that the High Contracting Parties create respectively a European Community and a European Union. Article 299 EC provides that the Treaty shall apply, amongst other Contracting Parties, to 'the United Kingdom of Great Britain and Northern Ireland'. The treaties are replete with references to the obligations imposed on the Member States and the Court is charged in Articles 226 to 228 EC with ensuring that the Member States fulfil their obligations. It is the United Kingdom of Great Britain and Northern Ireland, therefore, that is a party to the Treaties and it is by virtue of its constitutional position within the UK that Scotland is affected by the workings of the European institutions of governance.

The case law of the European Court of Justice reinforces the exclusive role of the Member States in the constitutional structure of the EU. The Court has consistently held that the term 'Member State', for the purposes of the institutional provisions of the Treaty, 'refers only to the government authorities of the Member States of the European Communities and cannot include the governments of regions or autonomous communities irrespective of the powers they have'. The Court argues that any other interpretation would undermine the institutional balance of the Communities. Therefore, according to the Court, 'it is not possible for the European Communities to comprise a greater number of Member States than the number of States between which they were established'.[2]

Thus a Member State cannot rely on the failure of a regional government to defend its own failure to ensure that directives are implemented fully and on time.[3] The responsibility of the Member State towards the Community exists even where the organs of the central government, according to the state's own constitutional law, are not empowered to compel the regions to implement Community legislation 'or to substitute itself for them and directly implement the directives in the event of persistent delay on their part'.[4] Neither can a Member State refuse to provide

---

1 Art 49 TEU.
2 Case C–87/02 *Commission v Italy* [2004] ECR I–5975.
3 Case C–33/90 *Commission v Italy* [1991] ECR I–5987, para 24; also, to that effect, the order in Case C–180/97 *Regione Toscana v Commission* [1997] ECR I–5245, para 7.
4 Joined cases 227, 228 and 229/85 *Commission v Belgium* [1988] ECR 1.

information to the Commission on the implementation and enforcement of Community legislation by local authorities even where the responsibility for failure to comply with Community law lies with the local authority.[5] This approach of the Court reflects its 'idea that the Community concept of the state is legally indivisible, as in international law', an approach that the Court has consistently held in relation both to infraction proceedings and in cases relating to state liability.[6]

Kottmann argues that this 'blindness towards the internal distribution of competences within the Member States' is a result of the original design of the European Communities which were conceived within the framework of the foreign policies of the Member States. He argues that this has resulted in an 'indirect skewing of intra-state authority in favour of central state institutions'.[7] In other words, the impact of increasing Europeanisation of policy has led to the diminution of the autonomous powers of regional governments in Europe within their own states and constitutional orders. Thus at the same time as there are movements within the Member States towards devolution or decentralisation of power there is an opposing tension requiring the central government to maintain overall control of policy so as to meet European imperatives.

Other academic writers have criticised the 'nation-centric' conceptual base of the European Union. Hopkins argues that it ignores the importance of regions and territorial governments in Europe. He argues that the EU does not lend itself to regional participation and that regional autonomy can be diminished by EU actions.[8] Others, however, have argued that the state can act as a bulwark against the encroachment on local autonomy in the face of global actors.[9] Nevertheless, even in this analysis the need for enhanced local autonomy is recognised as an element of democracy in a globalised world.

There is therefore a potential tension between the centralising tendencies within the European project and the desire for decentralisation within some Member States, including the UK, with the consequent need for appropriate mechanisms through which that tension is mediated. However, the EU does not have a coherent view of the role of the regions within the EU constitutional order and, therefore, the formal mechanisms to mediate potential conflicts are relatively weak and undeveloped. As discussed below, the hard-won concessions to the treaty structures themselves, such as the creation of the Committee of the Regions, have not proved sufficiently robust as a suitable mechanism to mediate tension between the EU, the Member States and regional government. The draft Treaty establishing a Constitution for Europe[10] would have gone some way to recognising the legitimate role of regional government in so far as it would have ensured that the Union shall

---

5 Case C–494/01 *Commission v Ireland* [2005] ECR I–3331. Ireland had failed to respond to a request for information in relation to waste operations in Fermoy, County Cork and was held therefore to have breached its obligations under the Treaty.

6 R W Davis, 'Liability in damages for a breach of Community law' (2006) 31 EL Rev 69.

7 J Kottmann, 'Europe and the regions: sub-national entity representation at Community level' (2001) 26 EL Rev 159. Kottmann quotes Ipsen on 'Länder-Blindheit'. See also S Weatherhill in S Weatherhill and U Bernitz (eds), *The Role of Regions and Sub-Regional Actors in Europe* (2005).

8 J Hopkins, *Devolution in Context: Regional, Federal and Devolved Government* (2002).

9 S Tierney, 'Reframing sovereignty? Sub-state national societies and contemporary challenges to the nation-state' (2005) 54 ICLQ 161.

10 The draft treaty establishing a constitution for Europe was rejected in referenda in the Netherlands and France. A period of reflection followed. Certain aspects of the constitutional treaty may be restored although the future of the entire document is currently uncertain.

'respect the equality of Member States before the constitution as well as their national identities, inherent in their fundamental structures, political and constitutional, inclusive of regional and local self-government' (Art I –5).

The principle of subsidiarity, policed both by the national parliaments and the Committee of the Regions, would also have been extended to ensure that the Union would only take action where the 'objectives of the proposed action cannot be sufficiently achieved by the Member States, either at central level or at regional and local level' (Art I–11). These provisions represent a vision of the European project that is not only based on the relationship between the Member States and the EU itself but reflects the reality of the variety of constitutional orders within those States.

Thus, in terms of European constitutional law, the regions within the Member States have little recognition but, in terms of practice, the regions in Europe play a major role in the European project in particular in implementing and observing Community law and policy. This is because many of the competences exercised at the European level are shared not only with the Member States but are often shared between the EU and the regional level of government, particularly regions with legislative powers. Within several of the Member States, regional governments have devolved powers in these same areas. Competence to act is therefore shared between the regional level of government and the EU institutions yet the power to legislate at the European level is shared between the European Council which, by and large, represents the central governments of the Member States, and the European Parliament which is composed of elected members from European political parties rather than European regions. In the UK context, for example, the Scottish Parliament has devolved powers in matters of fishing in Scottish coastal waters but the Parliament is constrained in the exercise of these powers by the fact that fishing is governed by a Common Fisheries Policy operating Europe-wide. This pattern is replicated across the vast majority of the Scottish Parliament's powers, for example in environment, aspects of economic development and, with the rapidly evolving policing agenda at the European level, in criminal law and procedure, an area which traditionally has not fallen within the competence of either central or European governance. Devolution means in this context, therefore, the ability of regional governments to operate across as wide a spectrum of policy areas as are devolved to them within the national constitutional order but acting within the constraints of European policy that is largely determined by the national-level governments: hence the use of the term multi-level governance to describe these complex arrangements.

What recognition and visibility the regions have within the EU is largely the result of some of the most powerful regions reacting to the effect described by Kottmann and others of Europe skewing powers in favour of central government. The German Länder were instrumental in forcing some, albeit limited, changes to the treaties precisely in recognition of the incomplete constitutional design of the treaties. The regions themselves have sought ways to maximise their influence and to ensure that they become more effective participants in devising and implementing common European policies. However, the regions appear to be fighting a continuing battle for recognition. For example, Scott argues that the regional dimension is the missing dimension in the Lisbon strategy and the absence of the regions is one of the reasons for the failure of the EU to meet its goals for 2010.[11] If Scott is correct in his analysis of the need for regional participation in meeting the economic agenda of the EU then the EU is doomed to policy failure wherever the regional dimension is lost or ignored.

One reason why the EU finds it difficult to accommodate the regional dimension is because no two Member States of the European Union share the same internal constitutional design. Germany is a classic federal model. Spain, Italy and the UK have devolved powers to territorial units, although the extent of devolution differs as between these countries. For example, devolution of taxation is a feature of the Italian scheme whereas the devolution settlement in the UK gives only some limited tax-raising powers to the Scottish Parliament and none to the Northern Ireland Assembly or the National Assembly for Wales. In some Member States the present constitutional structure predates their membership of the EU (Germany) whereas in others devolution is a more recent phenomenon (UK). In other Member States, either because of constitutional history or as a function of size, devolution is not a constitutional feature. Therefore, although there are a number of bodies that bring regional governments together in a European context, such as Regleg, discussed below, and although there has been extensive discussion of the regional element in the European polity, there is no definition of what constitutes a region in the European context. Currently there are more than 280 regions in the EU which have organised themselves in the Assembly of European Regions (AER) but they share no common defining feature. Furthermore, although some regions in Europe can be equated in some way with a sense of national identity or boundaries, examples being Catalonia or Scotland, this is not a feature of all regional governments. There is not and cannot be, therefore, a definition of a sub-national entity or region in the context of the European Union. However, all sub-national entities or regions share the same problem which is that the constitutional design of the European project remains in the hands of the central governments of the Member States. Each region must, therefore, strive to deal with European issues in a way which reflects the internal distribution of powers within the Member State of which it forms part and to devise appropriate mechanisms for influencing and reacting to European policy and law.

This chapter examines the European and domestic constitutional arrangements which provide the framework within which Scotland, as a region of Europe, can become an active participant in the European project. It examines in turn the ways in which Scotland has the opportunity and the obligation to shape, observe, and implement Community law and policy. It also examines the extent to which Community law and policy constrain the choices open to Scottish Ministers in deciding policy for Scotland and examines the very limited ways in which the Scottish institutions of governance might challenge Community law which impacts on Scotland.[12]

---

11 A Scott, 'The [Missing] Regional Dimension to the Lisbon Process' (Scotland Europa Discussion Paper, 13 Sept 2005) *www.scotlandeuropa.com*. Scott defines the Lisbon Strategy as follows: 'the Lisbon Strategy represents the central plank in on-going efforts to revitalise the economic performance of the major Member States. Originating with the Lisbon European Council of March, 2000, the Lisbon Strategy sets out a strategic goal for the EU such that by 2010 it would be "the most competitive and dynamic knowledge-based economy in the world, capable of sustainable economic growth with more and better jobs and greater social cohesion"'.

12 For a comparison with Wales see R Rawlings, *Delineating Wales* (2002).

SHAPING COMMUNITY LAW AND POLICY

As Kottmann has argued, the European project was conceived within a foreign policy framework. This approach is echoed within the Scotland Act 1998 (henceforth 'the Scotland Act') which provides that foreign affairs, including the European Communities (and their institutions) are reserved matters.[13] This means that 'although some of the policy areas with a European dimension are devolved, in the sense that they are not reserved by name (for example, agriculture, environment and so forth), nevertheless negotiation of them at European Community level is reserved to the United Kingdom government'.[14] However, these statements require a certain degree of clarification. On paper it would seem that Scotland could have no influence at all on the outcome of Community negotiations and no input into the UK position. This is not the case. Scotland has several routes into the European law and policy processes, either directly by way of European institutional structures or indirectly by way of intra-governmental structures within the UK constitutional order. The latter is by far the more effective of these routes simply because, at the European level, the institutional structures for direct participation are so weak. The UK can therefore be conceived as the gatekeeper with a constitutional responsibility for mediating between the Scottish and the European levels of government, reinforcing the intergovernmental paradigm of the EU where business is conducted by a series of bargains between the Member States.[15]

Scottish interests can be directly represented in Brussels in one of two ways: formally by way of the constitutional design of the European institutions and informally by way of lobbying either as a single region or by interacting with other regions. It is not axiomatic that Scottish and UK interests diverge and, in fact, having Scotland in Europe as a powerful region is beneficial to the UK as a whole. In conducting its 'paradiplomacy' with other regions, in the sense of developing region to region diplomacy, Scotland interacts with other regions in a way that the UK could not interact with the foreign regions themselves.[16] For example, the UK government could not engage in discussions on areas of European policy directly with the regional level of government in any other Member State. However, it is important not to overstate any independent foreign policy role of regions in a European Union context. According to Jeffery, even the use of the term paradiplomacy

> 'implies a form of sub-national "foreign policy" unmediated by the traditional foreign policy institutions of the state, and in the EU context would equate to the extra-state access by sub-national entities to European decision-making ... little evidence would exist for a North American style paradiplomacy within the EU'.[17]

To date there is no evidence that Scottish activities at the European level have undermined the UK but rather that Scotland is an additional, and distinct, voice reinforcing the UK as a key actor in Europe.

---

13   Scotland Act 1998, Sch 5, para 7(1).
14   C Carter, 'Democratic governance beyond the nation state: third-level assemblies and scrutiny of European legislation' (2000) 6 EPL 429.
15   A Bourne in M Cini (ed), *European Union Politics* (2003).
16   House of Lords Select Committee on the Constitution, *Devolution: Interinstitutional Relations in the United Kingdom* (2nd Report, 2002–03) HL 28, para 176.
17   C Jeffery, *The Regional Dimension of the EU: Towards a Third Level in Europe?* (1997), p 213.

Direct route to Brussels – 1

It is widely acknowledged that it was the German Länder which pioneered the debate about 'third level' governance within the EU, and the 1990s witnessed a new intensity in the debate about regional and sub-regional actors.[18] Meeting in the context of a Conference of a Europe of the Regions, the Minister Presidents of the Länder argued, in the run-up to the Maastricht Treaty, for four key amendments to the Treaty:

- the insertion of the principle of subsidiarity;
- the opening of the Council of Ministers to representatives of the regional level;
- the creation of a consultative 'regional council' as part of the institutional structure which would become, over time, a Chamber of the Regions with powers of co-decision;
- the creation of a right of action before the Court of Justice for the proposed Chamber of the Regions.[19]

The principle of subsidiarity was written into the Treaty, now Article 5 EC, although it is limited to establishing the boundary between the competences of the Community and the Member States and is silent on the competences of regions. Nonetheless, at the time, it was believed that the inclusion of the principle of subsidiarity would put a brake on the Europeanisation of further policy areas and, hence, would secure the powers of regional governments.

The membership of the Council of Ministers was amended by the Treaty of Maastricht. In its original formulation the Council was to consist of 'representatives of the Member States. Each government shall delegate to it one of its members'.[20] The Maastricht Treaty amended this and the Council is now composed of 'a representative of each Member State at ministerial level authorised to commit the government of that Member State'.[21] According to this formula, any person holding ministerial rank may represent her Member State within the Council and cast the votes of that Member State. However, if such a minister is a member of a regional government there must be prior agreement to her committing the entire Member State to a course of action and not just the region from which she derives her ministerial power. A Scottish Minister is therefore entitled to represent the UK within the Council of Ministers but, in doing so, she must represent the UK's interests and vote accordingly. Hence the key issue is to achieve agreement on the UK 'line'.[22] How this is achieved is not a matter for Community law but is a purely internal matter. Thus even when Scottish Ministers sit at the top table within the European institutions, they do so as a representative of the UK as a whole, including Scotland. The decision as to whether a Scottish Minister will attend a meeting of the Council is taken 'on

18 Jeffery, above n 17, p 204
19 Kottmann, 'Europe and the regions', above n 7, p 163.
20 Art 146 EC.
21 Art 203 EC.
22 *Memorandum of Understanding and Supplementary Agreements Between the United Kingdom Government, Scottish Ministers and the Cabinet of the National Assembly of Wales* (Cm 4806, 2000). See below for a discussion of the internal mechanisms by which the line is agreed.

a case by case basis'. However, it is the lead minister, who is always a minister of the Crown, who has the final decision on the composition of the UK delegation. In making that decision she must take into consideration the importance of the issue to the devolved administration.[23]

Scottish Ministers have attended meetings of the Council of Ministers some seventy-one times since 1 July 1999.[24] Although ministers have attended a variety of sectoral Council meetings, by far the most frequently attended Council is Agriculture and Fisheries, which reflects the importance of these matters to the Scottish economy, particularly fishing. Ministers have also attended the Justice and Home Affairs Council and are likely to continue to attend this Council due to the rapid development of Community law in both criminal and civil matters.

The Committee of the Regions was also created by the Maastricht Treaty. It is not one of the principal institutions of the Community; in other words, it is not mandated to carry out the tasks entrusted to the Community as are the Council, Commission, Parliament, the Court of Justice and the Court of Auditors. Instead, it is, like the Economic and Social Council, an advisory body to the Council and the Commission.[25] The Committee of the Regions is composed of representatives of 'regional and local bodies who either hold a regional or local authority electoral mandate or are politically accountable to an elected assembly'.[26] The UK has twenty-four members of the Committee of the Regions of whom four are from Scotland with four alternates. The First Minister is responsible for co-ordinating the appointment of the Scottish nominees. The Scottish Parliament and the Scottish Executive each nominate four individuals and the Convention of Scottish Local Authorities (COSLA) nominates a further four. All nominations are forwarded to the UK government for adoption and approval. Prior to the creation of the Scottish Parliament these representatives were all chosen from local authorities as their English counterparts still are.[27]

The Treaty requires that the Committee of the Regions be consulted in some key policy areas such as the environment,[28] public health,[29] and economic and social cohesion.[30] However, in the core areas of Community law such as the four freedoms, the approximation of laws or state aid there is no requirement to consult the Committee of the Regions.

Most research to date indicates that the Committee of the Regions is a weak body whose very composition militates against its success. The Committee comprises representatives of small local authorities as well as some of the biggest and most powerful regions in Europe such as Bavaria. It is difficult therefore to find a common approach to European policy. According to Nergelius, it may so far

'after ten years of existence, be said to suffer from a kind of identity crisis, since it may be very clearly asked if it is in fact able to represent the interests of the many different

---

23 *Concordat on Co-ordination of European Union Issues*, B3.13: *http://www.scotland.gov.uk/library2/ memorandum/mous–06.htm*
24 See *http://www.scotland.gov.uk/Topics/Government/International-Relations/Euope/Page6* (as of 6 Jan 2006).
25 Art 7 EC.
26 Art 262 EC.
27 See *http://www.cor.eu.int/documents/presentation/selection_en.pdf.*
28 Art 175 EC.
29 Art 152 EC.
30 Art 161 EC.

regions at the EU level and within the work of the EU institutions in an efficient way'.[31]

It falls short of the original conception of a Council of the Regions and is not perceived as having influence within the European institutional structure.[32] The Constitutional Treaty would have strengthened the role of the Committee of the Regions by providing it with access to the Court of Justice as a device to provide a legal safeguard against the infringement of the principle of subsidiarity. This may be one aspect of that Treaty which could be rescued.[33]

The European Parliament has seen an increase in the scope of its powers since the Maastricht Treaty. In a number of areas, Community legislation is now adopted following the co-decision procedure which places the European Parliament on a par with the Council of Ministers in the Community legislative process. The European Parliament is composed of 732 directly elected Members (MEPs). The MEPs sit in political groups that reflect their overall political orientation rather than regional or national groups. Seventy-eight MEPs are elected from the UK, of whom seven are from Scotland. For the purposes of the European parliamentary elections Scotland is one constituency. Scottish MEPs face a difficult challenge. They represent Scottish as well as party interests. On matters such as agriculture and fishing it appears that MEPs will work together to lobby for Scottish interests which are seen to transcend the party. However, there are areas where party interests transcend the regional priorities and where there are differences of views.

The Court of Justice is not a political institution but it shapes policy by interpreting existing Community legal rules. Judges in the Court of Justice, the Court of First Instance and Advocates General do not represent national interests but are independent of the governments of the Member States.[34] It is important, however, that there is representation of the different legal orders, partly because of the need to ensure that judgments of the Court are recognisable within the legal orders of the Member States but also as a means of finding common legal solutions. The Scottish legal order has, in the past, been well represented in the Community judiciary. It was a Scottish judge, Lord MacKenzie Stuart, who became the first British judge in the European Court of Justice (1973–88 and President of the Court from 1984–88). Judge David Edward was the UK's first judge in the Court of First Instance (1989–92) before becoming judge in the Court of Justice (1992–2004). This compares favourably with other large Member States. Bengoetxea, for example, points out that 'Spain has never adopted a policy of balanced representation of its

31 J Nergelius in *The Role of Regions*, above n 7, p 129.
32 Initially there was a flurry of research on the Committee of the Regions. See, eg, R E McCarthy, 'The Committee of the Regions; an advisory body on the tortuous path to influence' (1997) *Journal of European Public Policy* 439; T Christiansen, 'Second thoughts on Europe's third level: the European Union's Committee of the Regions' (1996) *Publius – The Journal of Federalism* 93; H Vos, 'Regions in the EU decision-making process' (1999*) Studia Diplomatica* Vol LII 19; J L de Castro, 'The other dimension of third level politics in Europe; the Congress of Local and Regional Powers of the Council of Europe' (1999) *Regional and Federal Studies* 95; A Reilly, 'The Committee of the Regions, sub-national governments and the IGC' (1997) *Regional and Federal Studies* 134; J Jones, 'The Committee of the Regions, subsidiarity and a warning' (1997) 22 EL Rev 312; G Clark, 'Scottish devolution and the European Union' [1999] PL 504.
33 S Weatherill in *The Role of Regions*, above n 7.
34 Arts 221–224 EC.

different legal systems or of its historic nationalities in its appointment of members of the Court'.[35]

The institutional design of the European institutions does not easily lend itself to direct participation in the Community method of working. There have been some limited changes to the structure of the institutions to accommodate the demands of the regions and those changes have been the result of powerful lobbying at both the European and the national level by the regions themselves. These changes provide only limited opportunities for direct involvement in the work of the institutions of the EU by regional governments or parliaments.

Direct route to Brussels 2 – influencing and lobbying

Precisely because of the weakness of the formal European constitutional design, regions have developed for themselves a series of networks, some more formalised than others, to influence policy processes, to seek improvements in the status of regions within the EU, but also to network amongst themselves as a means of learning best practice and exchanging knowledge and expertise on EU matters. In addition, both the Scottish Executive and the Scottish Parliament have established offices in Brussels to gather intelligence, to lobby and to market Scotland as a key player in Europe.[36]

Scotland is a member of one of the most influential of the regional lobby groups, Regleg. This is an informal grouping of some twenty of the most powerful regions in the EU, including Bavaria, Catalonia, the Basque country, Flanders and Piedmont, all of which are regions with legislative powers.[37] Regleg was established in 2000 to respond to the Inter-Governmental Conference (IGC) leading to the amendment of the treaties by the Treaty of Nice. Its aim is to lobby for a greater role for regions in the European processes at key constitutional moments such as the IGC or in the Constitutional Convention. The term 'regions with legislative powers' is significant in two respects. First, it reflects the constitutional reality that regional governments often have the responsibility for implementing and transposing European legislation. Second, it is a term that these regions themselves devised in order to gain recognition within the EU constitutional order. The Laeken Declaration of the European Council which established the Convention on the Future of Europe was the first official document to use the term.[38] In setting up the Convention, provision was made for representation of regions with legislative powers as a special category of members of the Committee of Regions. Of the six regional representatives on the Convention, five were from regions with legislative powers.

Rawlings uses the term 'constitutional region' to describe these territories, with Regleg acting as a means 'to underscore as a political phenomenon ... the evident tension between the classical conception of the EU as a constitutional order of states and the rise of meso-government across Europe'.[39] Jones sees

---

35 J Bengoetxea in *The Role of Regions*, above n 7, p 59.
36 In addition, Scottish Enterprise, along with other partner organisations such as local authorities, trade unions and universities established Scotland Europa as a means of providing a link between themselves and the European institutions.
37 For information on Regleg and its role see *http://www.regleg.org*. Wales is also a member despite the (current) absence of fully fledged legislative powers.
38 The Laeken Declaration can be found at: *http://europa.eu.int/constitution/futurum/documents/offtext/doc151201_em.htm.*
39 Rawlings, *Delineating Wales*, above n 12, p 453.

Regleg as an alternative structure to the Committee of the Regions which, for reasons discussed above, cannot capture the needs of very powerful regional governments.[40] What is interesting about Regleg, which distinguishes it from other networks, is the language that it uses to describe its own activities. Within Regleg, Scotland's First Minister becomes a 'President' attending annual meetings described as 'summits'. This is the language of statehood and reflects the sense of ambition for regions in the EU. It emphasises the constitutional status of these regions and their self-belief as important actors on the European stage and seeks to distinguish them from other forms of local democracy such as local authorities or municipalities.

Scotland has played an active role in Regleg, with the First Minister, Jack McConnell, holding the Presidency in 2003–04 and Scotland hosting the summit in 2004. However, whilst the Scottish Ministers endorse the general approach of Regleg, including supporting demands for greater regional involvement in Europe, they have been reluctant to engage fully in some of the debates. For example, it is not clear if McConnell supports the demands of Regleg for direct access for regions to the Court of Justice. Furthermore, he was reluctant to appear before the European and External Affairs Committee of the Scottish Parliament to discuss his Presidency. His view of the constitutional position was that

> 'the Chair of Regleg is a role I fulfil as First Minister ... I do so in light of Scotland's participation in the group ... the Minister for Finance and Public Service has portfolio responsibility for external relations and is therefore well placed to address the Committee on the work of Regleg'.[41]

Thus there is no direct accountability for the role that the First Minister as President plays within Regleg.

A number of other networks exists to enable regional government or local authorities to network and to attempt to influence policy. The Scottish Executive and some Scottish local authorities participate in the Conference of Peripheral Maritime Regions (CPMR) which aims to tackle some of the disadvantages faced by the regions situated on the geographical periphery of Europe. Within the EU wealth tends to be concentrated in the regions at the geographical centre of Europe, the so-called 'European Pentagon effect'. The CPMR campaigns for investment in development of the periphery of Europe and in maritime industries. Like Regleg, it also campaigns for the involvement of regions in European policy-making.[42] Fife Council, although not the Scottish Executive, participates in the Assembly of European Regions. Established in 1985, under the auspices of the Council of Europe, the Assembly's goal is to promote the concept of subsidiarity and regional democracy. With some 250 members, it is a vehicle whereby local authorities and regions can network to respond to Community policies which impact on them, such as the Lisbon Strategy and the review of the financial perspective, the latter being of particular importance since so much Community finance is channelled through the structural funds to regional governments for regional, agricultural or social development.

---

40 Jones, 'The Committee of the Regions', above n 32, p 313.
41 European and External Relations Committee, Agenda, meeting of Tuesday, 25 May 2004, 12th meeting 2004 (Session 2).
42 *http://www.erpm.org.*

The Scottish Executive has maintained a physical presence in Brussels since July 1999. The Scottish Executive EU Office supports the EU-related work of the Executive in attempting to boost Scottish influence in Europe. It provides operational support for the Executive in the sense of information gathering, assisting in influencing EU policies, raising Scotland's profile in the EU and developing regional links with other regions. It works closely with UKRep which is responsible for representing the views of the UK as a whole to the European institutions.[43] Because of this link with UKRep it has been said that Scotland and Wales are

> 'uniquely well-placed in Brussels because they are treated as separate units within the UK Representation to the EU. This gives them a diplomatic status and a much higher level of access to the EU institutions than is enjoyed by most other regional representations, including the German Länder offices.'[44]

The Scottish Parliament has also established a network of regional alliances. These alliances are not so much to influence policy design but to learn best practice as to how regional parliamentary processes can be improved. In 2002, the European Committee launched the Network of Regional Parliamentary European Committees (NORPEC) as a vehicle to discuss matters of common interest.[45] Elected members from the Flemish, Catalan and Scottish Parliament are represented in NORPEC. The Presiding Officer also attends the Conference of Legislative Regional Assemblies of Europe as a means of understanding the implications of Europeanisation for regional parliaments.

The response of the Commission to the rise in regional level lobbying can perhaps be described as unsystematic. Recently it has attempted to create a systematic dialogue with regions as part of its Better Regulation Strategy.[46] However, given the difficulties in engaging with the wide range of regional governments in Europe and the need for the Commission to engage with civil society more generally it is not easy to imagine a mechanism for such interaction that would be considered successful. This emphasises the need for regions to be pro-active in developing the dialogue with the Commission and the kind of networking described above is one way of ensuring that such effective consultation can take place.

Indirect route to Brussels – via the UK government

Given that Scotland does not have an automatic right to sit at the top table in Brussels and to vote for its own interests, it is rational that Scotland needs to maximise its influence in Brussels via the UK government. To do this the devolved administration must be provided with the opportunity to influence the UK 'line' on any proposed European developments. Mechanisms for information exchange and consultation have been developed to facilitate involvement by the Scottish

43 UKRep is the diplomatic representation of the UK to the European Institutions. Sir John Grant is the current UK Ambassador or Permanent Representative to the European Institutions and represents the UK in meetings of COREPER: see *http://www.ukrep.be/representatives.html* for details.

44 *Monitor*, The Constitution Unit Bulletin, Sept 2005, p 10.

45 A McLeod, *The Scottish Parliament and Europe* (The Scottish Parliament, SPICe briefing, June 2003), p 16: see *http://www.scottish.parliament.uk/business/committees/europe/norpec.htm*.

46 N Burrows, C Carter, M Fletcher and A Scott, 'The Better Regulation Strategy' (2004) at *http://www.scotland.gov.uk/Resource/Doc/1071/0006390.pdf*.

Ministers and officials from the Scottish Executive. These arrangements are set down in the Memorandum of Understanding and Concordat on Co-ordination of European Union Policy Issues.[47]

The mechanisms outlined in the concordats reflect pre-devolution practice in involving the former Scottish Office in discussions on European matters,[48] the difference being, of course, that prior to devolution the Scottish Office was a department within Whitehall and is no longer so post-devolution. What is made explicit in the Memorandum of Understanding and the Concordat are the principles governing interdepartmental discussions, in particular the requirement for early exchange of 'full and comprehensive information' (Concordat B3.2) and the need for confidentiality in the exchange of such intelligence. Departments within the Scottish Executive are therefore kept informed of European developments by their counterparts in Whitehall and are routinely involved in discussions, particularly in areas which are sensitive for Scotland such as fisheries matters. In return, they maintain confidentiality over the detail of such discussions.

Research suggests that, to date, these arrangements have worked well both at the level of officials and at the political level. Officials from Scottish Executive departments are still involved in developing EU policy. For example,

'agricultural policy officials from the Scottish Executive Environment and Rural Affairs Department (SEERAD) continue to have a very close involvement with counterpart officials in the Department for Environment Food and Rural Affairs (DEFRA) – this being the lead department on EU agricultural policies'.

Officials from Scottish Executive departments are welcome in the weekly meetings at which UKRep briefs 'both the Cabinet Office and other Whitehall departments'.[49]

There has been some restructuring of arrangements for policy co-ordination at the political level. A ministerial level committee (MINECOR) was established to 'provide a forum for discussion' of EU policy.[50] MINECOR was chaired by the Europe Minister in the UK government and was attended by ministers in the devolved administrations with responsibility for EU matters. At the same time, the Ministerial Committee on European Policy (the EP Cabinet Committee) continued to meet, chaired by the Foreign Secretary, although ministers from the devolved administrations were only copied into its discussions. A new body, the Joint Ministerial Committee in European format (JMC (Europe)) had been established under the Memorandum of Understanding and that also became a forum for discussion of European Union policy. The JMC (Europe) existed to seek 'to resolve differences between the UK government and the devolved administrations' (Concordat B3.7). More recently, the JMC (Europe) 'has virtually replaced the EP Cabinet Committee' and MINECOR has been abolished. Thus, although there has been a 'withering away' of the JMC in other formations, the JMC (Europe) meets regularly.[51]

47 *Concordat on Co-ordination of European Union Issues*, above n 23.
48 C Reid and G Ruiz-Rico Ruiz, 'Scotland and Spain: the division of environmental competences' (2003) 52 ICLQ 209; Carter et al, *Scotland and the European Union* (ESRC Briefing No 27, March 2005).
49 Carter et al, *Scotland and the European Union*, above n 48.
50 *Scotland and the European Union*, above n 48.
51 A Trench, 'Devolution: the withering away of the Joint Ministerial Committee' [2004] PL 513.

JMC (Europe) has never had to resort to dispute settlement mode.[52] As a consultative forum it appears to function smoothly and the phrase 'co-operative governance' has been used to define the working relationships within it.[53] That this has been possible is largely down to the shared political culture between the UK government and the Scottish Executive on European matters and, indeed, the dominance of the Labour party on both sides of the border. This shared political culture meant that in the course of the UK Presidency (July to December 2005) Scottish Ministers worked closely with the UK government and, for example, the Scottish First Minister attended the visit of the College of Commissioners in July 'to discuss presidency business'.[54] Such close working relationships are unlikely when the devolved administration and the central government are drawn from different political traditions and parties. Evidence from elsewhere suggests that the number of disputes over the handling of European matters rises and falls quite sharply as the political links between the centre and the regions diverge or converge.[55]

The need for confidentiality within the JMC (Europe) is well understood. Negotiations within the Council of Ministers are often difficult. A divided UK line would lead to a weakening of the UK position within the Council. However, the need to maintain confidentiality raises problems of accountability of ministers both at the devolved and the UK level, particularly given that the obligation of confidentiality is 'more stringent' than is generally applicable under the Memorandum of Understanding.[56] Neither Westminster nor Holyrood parliamentarians have the opportunity to question ministers about European matters discussed within the JMC (Europe). Lack of openness to the public may be the price that the devolved administrations have to pay if they are to be closely involved in European policy-making. The Welsh First Minister reported that the situation of the devolved administrations in the UK was more favourable than regional counterparts in Spain or in Germany. In the latter case, the German regional governments were able to attend meetings of the Council of Ministers but their influence on German EU policy is limited.[57] The House of Lords concluded that 'whatever the shortcomings of the ability of the devolved administrations to affect UK policy at EU level ... there is no doubt that the devolved administrations have better access to EU institutions, both formally and informally, than their counterparts elsewhere in Europe'.[58]

Accountability of Scottish Ministers on European matters has been extensively discussed within the European and External Relations Committee of the Scottish Parliament. Originally named the European Committee, this committee struggled to interpret its own scrutiny role in the first parliamentary session.[59] Faced with an overwhelming volume of paper including all proposals for EC and EU legislation,

---

52 Trench, 'Devolution', above n 51.
53 C Carter and A McLeod in *The Role of Regions*, above n 7.
54 *Monitor*, above n 44.
55 Eg, the number of constitutional disputes in Spain dropped dramatically in the 1990s as compared to the 1980s with the change of government: paper presented by E Aja to the ESRC Seminar on Learning From Overseas About Intergovernmental Disputes, University of Edinburgh, 23 Jan 2006.
56 House of Lords, *Devolution*, above n 16.
57 House of Lords, *Devolution*, above n 16.
58 House of Lords, *Devolution*, above n 16.
59 A McLeod, *The Scottish Parliament*, above n 45; C Carter and A McLeod in *The Role of Regions*, above n 7.

amounting to over 1,200 proposals per year, the Committee sought to redefine its role. Learning the lessons from its own inquiry into European governance, the Committee effectively renegotiated its relations with the Executive with the emphasis on transparency.[60] Since 2003, the Committee has concentrated on scrutiny of matters arising within Council meetings. It receives the agendas of the meetings and any briefings or reports prepared by the Scottish Executive and these are published on its web site. Although this level of scrutiny does not penetrate into the heart of the intergovernmental negotiations taking place within the JMC (Europe) it does at least allow MSPs the opportunity to see what is under discussion and to frame questions accordingly.

OBSERVING COMMUNITY LAW

The Scotland Act does not reserve the obligation to observe Community law. In Community law, responsibility for observing the obligations imposed by the treaties and secondary Community law lies with the Member State. It alone is responsible to the Community under Article 226 EC.[61] Thus a Member State is free to allocate internal competence in any way that it sees fit but it must retain overall legal responsibility for failure to comply with Community law. The reasoning of the European Court of Justice is set out in *Commission v Italy*:[62]

> 'First of all, it should be recalled that the fact that a Member State has conferred on its regions the responsibility for giving effect to directives cannot have any bearing on the application of Article 226 EC. The Court has consistently held that a Member State cannot plead conditions existing within its own legal system in order to justify its failure to comply with obligations and time-limits resulting from Community directives. While each Member State may freely allocate areas of internal legal competence as it sees fit, the fact remains that it alone is responsible towards the Community under Article 226 EC for compliance with obligations arising under Community law. Therefore, it is not relevant in the present case that the infringement results from a decision by the Abruzzo Region.'

Some 80 per cent of the devolved competences have a strong EU dimension. To avoid the possibility of the Scottish Parliament or the Scottish Executive either deliberately or accidentally failing to observe a Community obligation in the exercise of their devolved competences, the Scotland Act provides for a series of safeguards. Section 29 provides that an Act of the Scottish Parliament is not law so far as any of its provisions is incompatible with Community law. It is one of the functions of the Lord Advocate's Department to ensure that none of the provisions of a Bill presented to the Scottish Parliament is contrary to Community law.[63] However, an additional check is provided in section 35 which gives the power to the Secretary of State, a minister in the UK government, to make an order preventing the submission of a Scottish Bill for royal assent if she has reasonable grounds to

60 Carter and McLeod in *The Role of Regions*, above n 7.
61 Case C–33/90 *Re Toxic Waste, Commission v Italy* [1991] 1 ECR 5987; Case C–180/97 *Regione Toscana v Commission*, Order of the Court of Justice , 1 Oct 1997, unreported.
62 Case C–33/90 *Commission v Italy* [1991] ECR I–5987.
63 A Page in R Hazell and R Rawlings (eds), *Devolution, Law Making and the Constitution* (2005), p 25.

consider it incompatible with any international obligation or with any reserved matter.

If a matter is not within the legislative competence of Parliament it is not within the executive/administrative competence of a Scottish Minister either.[64] Thus, the Scottish Ministers are obliged to comply with Community law in all their actings.[65] That this sense of obligation is felt quite profoundly was apparent in the way in which the Scottish Executive handled the tendering for shipping contracts in August 2005. Faced with tenders from shipbuilders on the Clyde and from Poland, the contract was awarded to the Polish bidder on price. Ross Finnie MSP stated that Scotland 'was uniquely bound by the Scotland Act to abide by EU law – even more so than most Member States'.[66] It is true that the Scottish Ministers are bound to observe Community law by the Scotland Act but this is merely the UK interpretation of the more general Community obligation on the Member States to comply with Community law. Scotland is no more or less obliged to comply with Community law than any other region.

The consequences of the failure on the part of the devolved administrations to observe Community law are spelled out in the Concordat. Where the Commission instigates the procedure under Article 226 EC, the Cabinet Office is responsible for co-ordinating the UK response. Where the matter is the responsibility of the devolved administration, the draft reply to the Commission will be prepared by it and thereafter agreed with UK-level officials and ministers. If a matter is referred to the European Court of Justice, and it is a matter within the responsibility of the devolved administration, the devolved administration assumes responsibility for the preparation of submissions to the Court but these are co-ordinated by the Cabinet Office and the Treasury Solicitors' Department. Where the UK is found to have breached its obligations under Community law, but the responsibility lies with the devolved administration, and any costs or financial penalties are imposed on the UK, responsibility for meeting any such penalties lies with the devolved administration (Concordat B3.22–25).

The provisions in the Scotland Act and the Concordat are draconian measures to police the observance by the devolved administration of Community law by the UK government. They reflect the case law of the Court of Justice in so far as a Member State is held liable for breaches of Community law by any regional or local government but they are a measure of how far the Westminster Parliament was afraid to allow the devolved institutions freedom of action even within devolved powers. Each potential slip is documented in the Concordat; so much so that the Scottish Ministers are disciplined to avoid any potential breach of Community law, as witnessed in the Ross Finnie statement quoted above. Either because of the stringency of these provisions or because there have been few disagreements on the need to observe Community law by the devolved institutions, the Commission has had occasion to raise a potential violation of Community law by the regional governments of the UK only twice. The first was in relation to Wales.[67] Secondly, the Commission is investigating a potential breach of the procurement rules by the Scottish Parliament Corporate Body and the Scottish Executive in tendering for the building of the Parliament. If such a breach is found, any action brought by the

---

64 Scotland Act, s 54.
65 Scotland Act, ss 54, 57(2).
66 *The Herald*, 30 Aug 2005.
67 Rawlings, *Delineating Wales*, above n 12.

Commission in the European Court of Justice will be against the UK, as required by Community law, but the Scottish Executive will be required to answer for the breach internally.

TRANSPOSING AND IMPLEMENTING COMMUNITY LAW

As has been noted European Union matters are, in general, reserved matters. The duty to observe and implement Community law is, however, not reserved. Given the overlapping competences of the European institutions and the Scottish devolved competences there are many occasions on which the Scottish Parliament or the Scottish Executive will be responsible for implementing Community law in Scotland. Very often this may take the form of transposing the provisions of directives into law in Scotland. Within the UK it was routine, prior to devolution, that the transposition of directives into law was done by way of delegated legislation under section 2(2) of the European Communities Act 1972 and the Scotland Act provides that this approach can continue post-devolution. Section 53 of the Scotland Act transfers functions which are within devolved competence from a minister of the Crown to the Scottish Ministers under any pre-commencement enactment, including the European Communities Act. Thus the Scottish Ministers may transpose directives into law in Scotland by way of Scottish delegated legislation. Section 53 must be read in light of section 57 which relates specifically to Community law and Convention rights. Section 57(4) provides:

> 'Despite the transfer to the Scottish Ministers by virtue of section 53 of functions in relation to observing and implementing obligations under Community law, any function of a Minister of the Crown in relation to any matter shall continue to be exercisable by him as regards Scotland for the purposes specified in section 2(2) of the European Communities Act 1972.'

This provision ensures that the UK can continue to fulfil its obligations under Community law in two ways. First it allows the UK government to ensure that, in the absence of accurate and timely transposition of Community directives by Scottish Ministers, a minister of the Crown is enabled to transpose a directive within Scotland even in devolved matters. Second, it enables a UK-wide transposition of Community directives where this is considered appropriate.

The mechanism for deciding how Community law is to be transposed in Scotland is governed by the Concordat on European Union Policy Issues. The Concordat sets out a series of responsibilities (B3.16–B3.20) which effectively provide that a Whitehall department will always take the lead in establishing, in consultation with the devolved administrations, how directives are to be transposed. Where the decision is taken to transpose Community obligations separately the Scottish Ministers may choose to do so either by an Act of the Scottish Parliament, for example, the Water Environment and Water Services (Scotland) Act 2003 implemented the Water Framework Directive, or, more normally, by delegated legislation. The Parliament's Subordinate Legislation Committee considers the compatibility of any Scottish statutory instrument with Community legislation and reports to Parliament any issues of incorrect or late implementation.[68] It appears

---

68 McLeod, *The Scottish Parliament*, above n 45, p 10.

that devolution did create some difficulties in transposing Community directives correctly within the UK.[69] These were due to lack of expertise within the devolved administrations but it seems that such difficulties have now been overcome following assistance being provided by the UK government.[70] To date there are no examples of disagreements between the Scottish Ministers and their Whitehall counterparts over how and when Community obligations are to be transposed within Scotland. However, should such disagreements arise they would be dealt with within the framework of 'co-operative governance' outlined above. It is perhaps fair to say that disagreements are likely to be managed rather than resolved since the lead Whitehall department is always going to have the final word on implementation of Community obligations throughout the UK.

CHALLENGING COMMUNITY LAW

Given that regional governments are affected in their day-to-day operation by decisions made at the EU level, they have sought to establish a right to challenge the validity of those decisions in the European Court. They have sought to establish this right independently of the right of the central government to raise an action on their behalf on the grounds that they have a distinct interest in certain legal acts which is independent, and indeed may be inimical to, the interests of the Member States of which they form part.

Any challenge to the legality of a Community legal act takes place in the European Court of Justice or the Court of First Instance. The Court of Justice hears actions for annulment brought by Member States or by a Community institution and the Court of First Instance hears actions brought by a natural or legal person.[71] It is established case law that a regional government cannot be equated with the Member State of which it forms a part for the purposes of challenging the legality of a Community act before the Court of Justice under Article 230 EC. The rationale given by the Court is that 'it is not possible for the European Communities to comprise a greater number of Member States than the number of states between which they were established'.[72] The Court also reasons that the right to challenge the validity of a Community act mirrors the scheme of infraction procedures whereby it is the Member State which is alone responsible before the Court for a breach of Community law by a regional government or local authority. Thus, even where the national constitutional order devolves authority to a regional government to implement or uphold Community law in a defined area of competence or where a Community act encroaches on the competence of a region, that region does not have standing to challenge the Community act before the Court of Justice.

However, Article 230 EC recognises the right of a natural or legal person to challenge the validity of a '[d]ecision addressed to that person or a decision which,

---

69 McLeod, *The Scottish Parliament*, above n 45, p 10.
70 House of Lords, *Devolution*, above n 16.
71 Council Decision 94/149/ECSC, EC of 7 March 1994, OJ 1994 No L66/29.
72 Cases 227, 228, 229/95 *Commission v Belgium* [1988] ECR 1. For a discussion of the case law see
    N Burrows, 'Nemo me impune lacessit: the Scottish right of access to the European courts' (2002)
    6 EPL 45; J Wakefield, 'The plight of the regions in a multi-layered Europe' (2005) 30 EL Rev
    406.

although in the form of a regulation or a decision addressed to another person, is of direct and individual concern to' that person. A regional government which has legal personality under the law of its Member State may therefore bring an action for annulment in the Court of First Instance provided it can show an interest in bringing proceedings under the terms of Article 230 EC. The Scottish Ministers collectively have legal personality. They therefore have the opportunity to bring an action for annulment of a Community act in the Court of First Instance.[73] However, to do so, they must demonstrate direct and individual concern in the contested measure.

A regional government may not, under the terms of Article 230 EC, challenge a measure having general application. Thus, showing a general economic interest in contesting a regulation is insufficient to show the level of direct and individual concern which is required by Article 230 EC. For example, a regulation empowering the Commission to adopt decisions directed at the governments of Spain, Germany and Greece authorising payment of aid to shipbuilding could not be challenged by the Spanish autonomous community of Cantabria, even though the decision in question would impact adversely upon Cantabria. The Court stated:

> 'Reliance by a regional authority of a Member State on the fact that an application or implementation of a Community measure is capable generally of affecting socio-economic conditions within its territorial jurisdiction is not sufficient to render an action brought by that authority admissible.'[74]

The strict application of the tests of direct and, particularly, individual. concern continue to be applied by the Court of First Instance in cases where a regional government seeks to challenge the validity of Community regulations. For example, in a case brought by the Azores challenging the validity of a regulation which deprived it of the ability to legislate on fisheries matters which, from the point of view of Portuguese constitutional law accorded competence to the regional government of the Azores, the Court held that having responsibility for fisheries matters did not create individual concern under Article 230 EC.[75]

The Court of First Instance has had occasion to rule on the admissibility of actions brought by regional governments challenging the legality of decisions addressed to the Member State of which they form part. All these cases refer to decisions relating to state aid.[76] In each, it was the action or the legislation of the regional government in the first place that caused the Commission to adopt the contested decision. The Court, recognising that the decisions in question affected the way in which the regions themselves could exercise their autonomous powers, held that the regional government had an interest in the validity or otherwise of the decision that was separate from that of the Member State. The Court's approach in these cases is to examine whether the contested decision affects the way in which the regions can exercise their autonomous powers. If so, then the Court is willing

---

73 Burrows, 'Nemo me impune lacessit', above n 72.
74 Case T–238/97 *Communidad Autonoma de Cantabria v Council* [1998] ECR II–2271.
75 Neither could an explicit reference in Art 299(2) EC to the need to take into consideration the specific needs of the outermost regions of the Community create individual concern in the contested regulation since that would mean that specific regions were being accorded 'rights to bring legal proceedings akin to the rights of the Member States'. This case is extensively analysed by Wakefield, 'Plight of the regions', above n 72.
76 The cases are discussed in Burrows, above n 72, pp 61–65.

to accord direct and individual concern to the regional government and to proceed to the merits of the case.

Regional governments therefore have a limited right of audience before the Court of First Instance under Article 230 EC. However, it is clear that they do not have the right to raise an action for annulment in the Court of Justice on the same basis as the Member States, despite the devolution of legislative competence within the Member States. In actions before the Court of First Instance, regional governments must meet other tests of direct and individual concern where they seek to challenge Community regulations. The test of individual concern is almost impossible to meet and it is clear that general socio-economic concerns do not equate to individual concern. Neither can they challenge the validity of regulations, even where those regulations affect the way in which they may exercise their legislative powers to the extent of denying them that possibility. Regional governments have been able to challenge state aid decisions which affect the way in which they exercise their autonomous powers and where these decisions are directed at the state of which they form part.

These limitations have caused the regions, on several occasions, to lobby for a change in Article 230 EC. In November 2000 the Belgian government sought an amendment which would grant the Court of Justice jurisdiction to hear cases brought by an 'entity' of a Member State 'to the extent that it has its own law-making powers'. Regions with legislative powers would therefore be included in the formula. The amendment was not accepted although Regleg pushed for amendment to Article 230 EC as part of the debate on the Future of Europe following the Nice Treaty. The constitutional regions wanted the right to refer directly to the Court where their prerogatives were harmed by Community law or action. Similar proposals were put to the Convention on the Future of Europe alongside the proposal to create a right of access to the Court by the Committee of the Regions. The draft Constitution would not afford any new rights to regional governments but it would have provided the Committee of the Regions a right of action in the Court of Justice for the purpose of protecting its prerogatives (Article III–365).

As an alternative way of questioning the legality of a Community act other than by way of a direct action, questions relating to the legality of a Community act might arise in the context of an action raised in the national court. As the European Court of Justice has sole jurisdiction to rule on matters of legality of Community acts, the national court should refer such cases to the European Court of Justice for a preliminary ruling under Article 234 EC. The regional government of Friuli Venezia Giulia brought an action in the regional administrative court of Lazio against the Italian Ministry for Agriculture and Forestry which had prohibited the use of the words 'Tocai friuliano' to describe a variety of regionally produced wine. The national rule in question was introduced on the basis of Community rules adopted following the ratification of the Europe Agreement with Hungary.[77] By this means the validity of the relevant Community law could be decided by the European Court of Justice. The possibility therefore arises that the Scottish Ministers could seek judicial review of UK implementing measures of a Community act questioning the validity of the act. If the national judge is in doubt as to the

---

77 Case C–347/03 *Regione Autonoma Friuli Venezia Giulia and ERSA v Ministero per le Politiche Agricole e Forestali and Regione Veneto* [2005] ECR I–3785.

validity of the Community act on which the UK measures were based, the question would need to be referred to the Court of Justice for a ruling. In this way, regional governments could have access to the European Court of Justice in an attempt to protect regional interests. However, it is unlikely that such actions would be raised in the UK at the present time given the political alignments north and south of the border, as this would be perceived as a challenge to the UK government.

SCOTLAND IN EUROPE – EMPOWERED OR DISEMPOWERED?

It has been said that the process of European integration both empowers and disempowers sub-state actors or regions. Whilst the European integration process creates new opportunities for participation in transnational activities, it simultaneously appears to centralise power and authority in the hands of the central governments who participate in the European decision-making processes at the expense of the regional tier of government.[78] For Scotland the truth appears to lie somewhere between empowerment and disempowerment. Since the earliest days of devolution, the Scottish devolved institutions have recognised the importance of the EU and the need to understand and engage in the European project. Establishing a regional office in Brussels was one of the first steps in the European strategy of the newly created Scottish Executive. Establishing a European Committee and forging a role for it was an early preoccupation of the Scottish Parliament. Europe was therefore seen as an essential element of the devolution settlement. It was taken for granted that there would need to be an engagement at the European level just as there would need to be an engagement with the UK agenda. Scotland is part of Europe as well as part of the UK.

As part of its European strategy, the Scottish Executive has worked, in a form of co-operative governance, with the UK government. It has been, by definition, a junior partner. The Concordats that govern inter-governmental relations in the UK provide that the lead on European matters always lies with Whitehall and that participation and involvement in European affairs depends on respecting the working arrangements, including the need for confidentiality, set out there. On EU matters, this close co-operation appears to have functioned well, as much because of a shared political culture as for any other reason. It may not have a longer term future if Labour loses its political dominance either north or south of the border. The junior partner might have to struggle not just to have its voice heard but to be involved at all.

It seems too that the provisions of the Scotland Act have disciplined the devolved administration, perhaps to the extent that they would never knowingly gamble with a potential breach of Community law. Scotland is unlikely therefore to be a wild card in Europe; it is more likely to be a model citizen, respecting and complying with Community obligations. Given the number of constraints under which Scottish Ministers work – the case law of the Court of Justice, the domestic legal provisions and the informal working agreements – it is not surprising that the Scottish Ministers have not tried to develop an independent policy line even where

---

78 The point is made in a discussion paper for the Edinburgh-Rennes workshops: C Carter and R Pasquier, 'European Integration and Regional Governance: Testing the Analytical Purchase of "Europeanisation"' (2006).

Scottish interests were at stake. Thus they have attempted to get a good deal for Scottish fishermen in the negotiations around the Common Fisheries Policy by first negotiating a UK line and then participating in the meetings of the Council of Ministers. Whether they could have got a better deal using different tactics is, of course, impossible to tell.

Scotland, as a region, commands respect in Europe. It participates in a series of networks independently of the UK government. Via networks such as Regleg, Scotland has developed an independent 'foreign' policy despite the reservation of foreign affairs in the Scotland Act. It has networked where it can and has attempted to seize opportunities for engagement at the European level. It is however difficult to discern whether there are any aspects of the Scottish Executive strategy in Europe which can be differentiated from a more general UK policy. Thus when Jack McConnell acted as President of Regleg, the theme of his presidency, better regulation, happened to dovetail with one of the themes of the UK presidency, the Better Regulation Strategy. All of this suggests that the need to co-operate closely with the UK government is the price to pay for being given a limited degree of licence in European affairs.

The degree of active participation in European matters seems to belie the argument that European integration is inevitably a process of centralisation at the domestic level. It appears in the UK to be at least a process of negotiation. The JMC (Europe) meets frequently and there is interchange of information at both official and political levels. Where negotiation can be effective then it does not matter so much who sits at the top table in the Council. Therefore, although the constitutional design of the EU is flawed in that it fails to recognise a real role for the regional tier of government, this is not a fatal flaw if a regional government can tap into alternative frameworks and networks.

Chapter 4

Scottish Public Law in an Age of Constitutional Globalisation

Gavin W Anderson

INTRODUCTION

It may appear counter-intuitive to discuss globalisation in a collection of essays on public law in Scotland. While globalisation denotes the reduced importance of national borders, public law is most strongly associated with the nation state. Most teaching and writing on public law focuses on national institutions, and constitutions in particular have been closely related to each state's culture and history. In the Scottish context, as this collection underscores, there is now even greater emphasis on the local. Throughout the 1980s and 1990s, the 'constitutional issue' became shorthand for whether some measure of home rule should be restored to Scotland. With the establishment of the new devolved institutions, attention is turning to whether Scotland is now developing a distinct constitutional identity. These developments seem to confirm the view that constitutional law is globalisation's 'last frontier'.[1]

From another perspective though, globalisation challenges the basic assumption of the traditional approach that public law provides the framework for national 'communities of fate' to decide their own political destiny.[2] According to the sociologist Ulrich Beck, globalisation entails the 'escape [of politics] from the categories of the national state'.[3] On this view, many important decisions affecting citizens' lives are no longer taken by domestic institutions, but at the supranational and global level. Moreover, with the rise of the global economy, it is argued that nation states now have less room to manoeuvre in setting the domestic policy agenda. In this connection, some critics suggest there is now a global neoliberal economic consensus which has seen national policies narrow around practices such as privatisation, lower taxation, free trade, fiscal restraint and deregulation.[4]

It is important to consider this discussion against recent Scottish political history. The clamour for devolution began to intensify during the premiership of Margaret Thatcher in the 1980s in response to the imposition of monetarist policies which had been consistently rejected by large majorities in Scotland at general elections. It was envisaged that devolution would bring government closer to the wishes of the people of Scotland, and that public policy would reflect their attachment to more social democratic political values which accord an active role to the state and its agencies in reducing inequality. However, if the global economy signals the ascendancy of neoliberal values which favour greater

---

1 R Treitel, 'Comparative constitutional law in a global age' (2004) 117 HarvLRev 2570 at 2572.
2 See C M G Himsworth, 'In a state no longer: the end of constitutionalism?' [1996] PL 639.
3 U Beck, *What is Globalization?* (2000), p 1.
4 B de Sousa Santos, *Toward a New Legal Common Sense* (2002), pp 314–315.

reliance on the market and a reduced role for the state, this raises some important questions about the prospects for devolution. Does globalisation compromise the ambition that the Scottish Parliament would give Scotland greater capacity to determine her own affairs? Or are the devolved institutions in a better position than national ones to develop innovative strategies in response to the forces of globalisation?

This chapter focuses on the impact of globalisation upon Scotland's nascent constitutional autonomy. It will be argued that globalisation is increasingly relevant for students and practitioners of Scottish public law in two important, and related, respects. First, that traditional constitutional questions concerning the location, structure and accountability of political power can no longer be answered exclusively, or even primarily, by reference to domestic institutions and processes. In other words, globalisation means that we cannot regard constitutions as nationally-contained systems in isolation from what happens elsewhere. Second, that as a consequence our understanding of the nature of constitutions and constitutional law is being transformed. A number of writers now talk of supranational and global forms of constitutionalism and, as a result, some core constitutional concepts are being substantially redesigned in the process. Accordingly, the operation of public law in Scotland has to be considered against these new understandings. It will be argued that while both these developments do not prevent Scottish constitutional innovation, the latter takes place within limits which make it unlikely that Scotland will deviate significantly from global constitutional norms. Before elaborating these points, this chapter considers what is meant by globalisation in more general terms.

CONSTITUTIONAL LAW IN GLOBAL CONTEXT

While legal scholarship has only recently begun to engage with globalisation, in other subjects – whether politics, economics or cultural studies – debates about the nature, extent and implications of globalisation have been joined for some time.[5] Indeed, the literature on globalisation can appear quite daunting, both in terms of its range, and the complexity of the arguments canvassed. However, the globalisation thesis argues that this vast literature is worth taking seriously, as we are living through epoch-changing times which we would do well to try to comprehend. For most who subscribe to this argument, globalisation is not proved by the existence of a set of global political institutions or a single global culture. Nor does it mean that the state becomes wholly unimportant. Rather, they emphasise the greater degree of interconnection in the contemporary world. As Tony Giddens famously put it, globalisation brings about:

'the intensification of world-wide social relations which link distant localities in such a way that local happenings are shaped by events occurring many miles away and vice versa'.[6]

This greater interconnectedness can be demonstrated in various ways: by showing that domestic economies are more intertwined with and open to each other than

---

5   See D Held and A McGrew, *The Global Transformations Reader: An Introduction to the Globalization Debate* (2000), pp 1–50.
6   A Giddens, *The Consequences of Modernity* (1990), p 64.

at any previous stage in history; by highlighting changing social practices such as accelerating patterns of migration or the spread of western popular culture; or by pointing to the emergence of problems whose ramifications spread across borders, such as climate change or terrorism. While this is not the only era characterised by greater social interchange, it is argued that there is a qualitative difference to the present, not least because of technological advances. Thus, for example, the digitalisation of financial markets has facilitated an unprecedented increase in foreign exchange transactions which by 2004 had risen to a daily global turnover of $US 1.9 trillion.[7]

While the state does not disappear in this more interconnected world – for one thing, state private law is required to give effect to contracts made in the global economy – questions arise as to whether it can remain the primary reference point for understanding society. David Held argues that we are witnessing a 'reconfiguration of political power'[8] in which the nation state becomes simply one of a series of important actors on the world stage. An important part of this reshaping of political power is the emergence of supranational bodies, such as the European Union (EU) or World Trade Organisation (WTO), which exercise often extensive regulatory powers over member states, and also transnational legal regimes, such as international human rights law which may authorise intervention in states' internal affairs. The role of private actors is also emphasised, with multinational corporations being described as 'functioning like governments',[9] reflecting the extent of their influence over the quality of peoples' lives. The nature of political activism is also changing with the emergence of forms of politics which transcend national borders, such as environmentalism.[10] This produces a multifaceted system of governance which national governments can 'barely monitor, let alone ... command'.[11]

It is also important to bear in mind that globalisation unfolds in a highly uneven fashion. This is captured by Boaventura de Sousa Santos's insight that globalisation is a process whereby a particular local condition attains worldwide salience, and, having become global, is able to label its rivals as merely local.[12] It follows that there is no genuine globalisation: all supposed global phenomena have local origins, and so we could equally well speak about localisation. However, that we do not reflects that some, but only some, localisms are promoted to the global level, the key question being which ones. Here, Santos makes a further distinction between globalised localisms, which occur when a local phenomenon is successfully exported, and localised globalisms, where local practices are restructured in response to global pressures.[13] According to Santos, the West specialises in the former, the most prominent example being the presentation of liberal capitalism

7 Bank for International Settlements, *Triennial Central Bank Survey* (2005).
8 M Guibernau, 'Globalization, cosmopolitanism, and democracy: an interview with David Held' (2001) 8 *Constellations* 427 at 429.
9 A C Cutler in R B Hall and T J Biersteker (eds), *The Emergence of Private Authority in Global Governance* (2002), p 33.
10 See B Rajagopal, *International Law from Below: Development, Social Movements and Third World Resistance* (2003).
11 Held and McGrew, *The Global Transformation Reader*, above n 5, p 12.
12 Santos, *New Legal Common Sense*, above n 4, p 178.
13 Santos, *New Legal Common Sense*, above n 4, p 179. Santos gives the adoption of English as a global *lingua franca* and the spread of US fast food as examples of globalised localisms, and ecological dumping and the creation of free trade zones as examples of localised globalisms.

as the only possible form of societal organisation. When accepted by developing countries, this operates as a localised globalism as they reorder their economies under structural adjustment programmes.

Globalisation and constitutionalism

This evolving relationship between the local and the global is of potentially enormous significance for constitutional law. The relative decentring of the state challenges some key assumptions of constitutional thought. For example, sovereignty has historically been premised in the coming together of law, territory and authority in the nation state. But if the state now shares or negotiates power with a host of different actors, this account may no longer be adequate. Moreover, we now have to consider how far constitutional law itself has to be understood in terms of the interaction between local and global phenomena. To the extent that indigenous public law is being reshaped by constitutional imperatives which originate in other localities, or constitutional developments at the global level, we may have to abandon the presumption that constitutional law is inextricably linked to the nation state, and begin speaking in terms of constitutionalism beyond the state.

How does Scotland, with a devolved Parliament, but not a fully independent state, fit into this picture? One view is that the pressures which globalisation exerts upon nation states apply equally strongly at the sub-national level, perhaps more so as smaller units of government may have relatively weaker capacity to resist them. Accordingly, the constitutional position of Scotland vis-à-vis globalisation is simply an extension of the general challenge globalisation poses to the nation state. However, another view is that we should take into account how devolved government relates differently to globalisation, and the particular issues this raises. For example, some see the trend towards decentralisation – a feature of political life not just in the UK, but in a growing number of 'plurinational' democracies – itself as part of the reconfiguration of power outlined above. On this view, globalisation is more complementary than antagonistic to devolution, and may even result in a net gain of influence on the part of sub-state bodies.[14]

To put this discussion in context, three ways in which constitutional discourse has acquired a global dimension need to be considered: the relative homogenisation of constitutional theory and practice through the worldwide spread of charters of rights; the development of a discourse of supranational constitutionalism which focuses on the constitutional attributes of bodies like the EU or the WTO; and the emergence of what has been called 'the new constitutionalism', which argues that the disciplining effects of the global economy impose constitutional constraints on nation states. In the following three sections, each of these will be considered in turn. The general features of the phenomenon as discussed in the global constitutional literature are sketched first; the extent to which Scottish public law can be regarded as fitting into these global patterns is then outlined; and finally their impact upon the capacity of devolved Scotland to pursue her own policy agenda is considered.

---

14 See S Tierney, 'Reframing sovereignty? Sub-state national societies and contemporary challenges to the nation-state' (2005) 54 ICLQ 161.

THE GLOBALISATION OF CONSTITUTIONAL RIGHTS

One of the most remarkable legal phenomena of our time is the exponential growth in states adopting a charter of rights. Judicial review under a bill of rights originated in the US, and there was an initial period of constitutionalisation following the Second World War as fundamental rights featured prominently in the new constitutions of the defeated powers and states achieving independence from colonial rule.[15] However, the major period of constitution-making has been the past quarter century or so with constitutional rights now entrenched in southern Africa, through Central and Eastern Europe, in Australasia, South America and parts of the Middle East and Asia.[16] The principal catalyst for this process was the wave of democratisation which followed major events such as the transition from military rule in the Latin world, the fall of the Berlin Wall and the end of apartheid. As previously authoritarian states began to adopt new institutional arrangements, they largely drew on western liberal democracy.[17]

Bruce Ackerman calls these developments 'the rise of world constitutionalism'.[18] This does not mean there is a single global constitution. However, it suggests that a state's constitutional development is no longer solely tied to domestic factors, and that the differences between national constitutions are becoming less pronounced. Three indicia of constitutional globalisation are highlighted. First, there is considerable evidence of convergence in terms of institutional design as one model increasingly predominates, namely the constitution as higher law, under which judges scrutinise governmental acts for their compatibility with a core set of rights, including freedom of expression and religion, and basic procedural guarantees. Second, there is greater judicial fluency in comparative constitutional sources,[19] with cases from one jurisdiction forming the basis of decisions in another.[20] Third, in deciding these cases, courts around the world are said to be evolving common techniques of constitutional reasoning.[21] According to David Beatty, the worldwide adoption of bills of rights means that where governments limit individual freedom, they can only do so if this can be justified in accordance with the higher law of the constitution.[22]

Devolution and the globalisation of constitutional rights

The UK has not been immune to constitutional reform, and the period of New Labour rule since 1997 has seen considerable innovation. There is a strong tendency to focus on the internal implications of these developments, for example, whether

---

15 See H Klug, *Constituting Democracy: Law, Globalism and South Africa's Political Reconstruction* (2000), pp 62–66.
16 R Hirschl, 'The political origins of judicial empowerment through constitutionalization: lessons from four constitutional revolutions' (2000) 25 Law & Soc Inqy 91 at 92, fn 1.
17 Santos, *New Legal Common Sense*, above n 4, p 315.
18 B Ackerman, 'The rise of world constitutionalism' (1997) 83 VaLRev 771.
19 C McCrudden, 'A common law of human rights? Transnational judicial conversations on constitutional rights' (2000) 20 OJLS 499 at 506–510.
20 See, eg, U Werner, 'The convergence of abortion regulation in Germany and the United States: a critique of Glendon's Rights Talk thesis' (1996) 18 LoyLAIntl & CompLJ 571; L Leigh, in I Loveland (ed), *Importing the First Amendment: Freedom of Speech and Expression in Britain, Europe and the USA* (1998), p 51.
21 See D Beatty, *The Ultimate Rule of Law* (2004).
22 See D M Beatty, *Constitutional Law in Theory and Practice* (1995), ch 5.

devolution signals the break-up of Britain. However, it is argued here that it is also important to consider how far recent Scottish constitutional developments, in particular the domestic operation of the European Convention on Human Rights (ECHR), can be situated within global processes, and that to do so helps us better to understand the nature and impact of these reforms.

The key here is to see the worldwide spread of constitutional charters of rights as part of a broader project to export the rule of law which emerged in the 1990s. These 'rule of law' programmes are a high-profile example of Santos's globalised localism, as western governments and agencies (spending over a billion dollars in the process) emphasised the link between adopting western-style legal reforms and the promotion of good governance in transitional democracies.[23] A charter of fundamental rights was generally the flagship reform, but this also involved putting in place a basic legal infrastructure guaranteeing contracts and private property, together with root-and-branch restructuring of the judicial system.[24] There are clear parallels between this global discourse on rights and recent domestic constitutional debates. It has been argued that we have shifted away from the traditional political constitution, which was premised on ministers' accountability to Parliament, to a legal one, where courts and judges have a primary role in disputes over the use of public power.[25] According to Martin Loughlin, such a transformation envisages a new understanding of the rule of law as a juridical principle of limited government at the foundation of the constitutional order (as opposed to providing moral, but ultimately unenforceable, guidance on how government should act).[26]

There is much in the legislation giving domestic effect to Convention rights which would seem to align the UK with an emerging global rule of law consensus. The explicit rationale given for enacting the Human Rights Act 1998 (HRA) was to strengthen legal controls on governmental action;[27] similarly, the Scotland Act 1998 seemed to envisage a more prominent constitutional role for Scottish courts. One of the principal limits on the new Scottish Parliament is that it cannot pass legislation which is not Convention compliant,[28] and, unlike its Westminster equivalent, if it does so, such legislation can be struck down in the courts. The Scotland Act also places legal limits on Scottish Ministers performing acts which are incompatible with the Convention.[29] However, the fact that a constitutional document protects rights does not necessarily mean that courts will actively enforce them.[30] It is important to bear in mind in this regard that Scotland had further to

23 As the World Bank put it in 1994, '[t]he legal framework in a country is as vital to economic development as it is for political and social development.' Quoted by P McAuslan, in J Faundez (ed), *Good Government and Law: Legal and Institutional Reform in Developing Countries* (1997), p 25.
24 See World Bank, *World Development Report 1996 – From Plan to Market* (1996).
25 A Tomkins, *Public Law* (2003), pp 18–19.
26 See M Loughlin in G W Anderson (ed), *Rights and Democracy: Essays in UK-Canadian Constitutionalism* (1999), p 203.
27 See *Rights Brought Home: The Human Rights Bill* (Cm 3782, 1997), paras 1.4 and 2.2.
28 Scotland Act 1998, s 29.
29 Scotland Act 1998, s 57. See further, Chapter 10 in this volume.
30 Eg, while the 1789 French Declaration of the Rights of Man and the 1791 US Bill of Rights are now seen as seminal constitutional texts, it was not until the late and early twentieth century respectively that their provisions came to be systematically applied in legal proceedings: see A Stone, *The Birth of Judicial Politics in France* (1992) and D Kairys in D Kairys (ed), *The Politics of Law: A Progressive Critique* (1982), p 141. Such a phenomenon does not just arise with respect to historical tracts: see, eg, the Canadian Bill of Rights of 1960 (see The Constitutional Law Group, *Canadian Constitutional Law* (3rd edn, 2003), pp 677–681).

travel towards legal constitutionalism than the rest of the UK. While in the 1980s and 1990s (some) English courts and judges were holding that primary legislation had to be interpreted in light of fundamental common law rights,[31] there was little suggestion in Scotland that legal rights limited Parliament's sovereign will.[32] It was not inconceivable, therefore, that Scottish judges would retain the mindset of the political constitution, and adopt a deferential approach to the elected branches when interpreting the new constitutional legislation.

It now seems clear, though, that the legal constitution does not remain a theoretical option, and there is considerable evidence of the localisation of global trends in devolved Scotland. Some of the principal features of this jurisprudence are, first, the courts have shown that Convention rights do not set a purely perfunctory test, and have applied a relatively rigorous form of human rights review. Thus, in a number of high-profile cases the Scottish Executive failed the test of Convention compatibility, for example in challenges to the appointment of temporary sheriffs,[33] or to conditions in prison.[34] In these and other rights cases, the courts have shown they will not be easily deflected from a full human rights analysis, and where technical defences have been raised, they have been construed narrowly. For example, in *Napier*, it was argued that any breach of Article 3 occasioned by slopping-out was an administrative act or omission of the prison governor, and so did not engage section 57(2) of the Scotland Act. Lord Bonomy rejected this, finding that this was a policy matter within the responsibility of the Scottish Ministers.[35]

Second, and relatedly, changes of attitude towards the sovereignty of the Westminster Parliament can be discerned. The fact that many of the acts of public authorities are performed under statutory authority will not by itself induce deference by the courts and save them from human rights review.[36] Rather, they will only be exempted in very precise circumstances: for example, section 6(2) HRA only applies to acts which are actually required by primary legislation.[37] Moreover, the courts have on occasion used their new interpretative powers expansively, which to the extent that this rewrites Parliament's intention, can be seen to intrude on the once-exclusive domain of the sovereign legislature.[38]

---

31 M Hunt, *Using Human Rights Law in English Courts* (1997), ch 5.
32 *Moore v Secretary of State for Scotland* 1985 SLT 38 at 41. See also *Kaur v Lord Advocate* 1981 SLT 322. It was not until 1996 that a Scottish court, sitting in Edinburgh, applied the presumption that where legislation was ambiguous, the courts should give effect to the meaning which conformed with the European Convention on Human Rights: see *T, Petitioner* 1997 SLT 724 at 734C.
33 *Starrs v Ruxton* 2000 JC 208.
34 *Napier v Scottish Ministers* 2004 SLT 555.
35 *Napier v Scottish Ministers* at 585A.
36 Eg, in *Starrs v Ruxton*, although the Sheriff Courts (Scotland) Act 1971, s 11(4) provided that a temporary sheriff's appointment 'subsist[s] until recalled by the Secretary of State,' Lord Cullen simply declared (at 230F): 'I hold that the terms of s 11(4) are incompatible with Art 6(1) of the Convention.'
37 Thus, in *Starrs v Ruxton*, the Court of Criminal Appeal held that s 6(2) did not apply, despite the argument that it was in the public interest for a procurator fiscal to proceed with a prosecution even before a potentially suspect tribunal.
38 In *Brown v Stott* 2000 SLT 379, the Court of Criminal Appeal 'read in' words to s 172(2) of the Road Traffic Act 1988 such that although police officers could require suspects to give them information, this would not be admissible evidence in any ensuing prosecution. While the court was exercising its powers under the Human Rights Act 1998, s 6(2)(b) to read primary legislation in a manner compatible with Convention rights, as this effectively negated the purpose of the

Third, one of the consequences of human rights adjudication is that the style of public law argument is changing. This is not surprising as the courts are increasingly referred to, and indeed are under a statutory duty to consider,[39] comparative sources. In some cases, reference to comparative jurisprudence has directly affected the outcome of the decision, changing the previous position in Scots law in the process.[40] Perhaps more significantly, however, Scottish judges and lawyers are becoming more familiar with the judgments and modes of reasoning employed in more established traditions of legal constitutionalism.[41]

According to Beatty, underpinning constitutional jurisprudence throughout the world are the principles of rationality and proportionality. Although they do not empower courts to substitute their policy views in cases before them, they do require them to engage in a cost–benefit analysis weighing the importance of the governmental objective at stake against the severity of the restriction of individual freedom. The idea that laws and governmental action should be no more burdensome than necessary can be seen to explain some of the decisions discussed above. In *Starrs v Ruxton*, the appeal court effectively considered whether the objective of avoiding delay in the administration of justice outweighed the individual's right to a hearing before an independent and impartial tribunal under Article 6 ECHR. In *Napier*, the main factor in Lord Bonomy's decision that conditions in Barlinnie Prison amounted to inhuman or degrading treatment contrary to Article 3 ECHR was the disproportionate impact of the slopping-out regime on the health of the prisoner.[42]

It could be objected that the case for legal constitutionalism is overstated, that there are only a few cases where Executive Acts have been found to be invalid, and none (to date of writing) where legislation has been struck down on human rights (or other) grounds. But the real test of the advance of the legal constitution is how we frame and discuss questions of public policy. For example, in *Brown v Stott*,[43] the Judicial Committee, overturning the Court of Criminal Appeal, held that the Road Traffic Act 1988 legitimately required a drunk driver to incriminate herself, notwithstanding Article 6 ECHR. While this appears to defer to Parliament's views on road safety, it should be emphasised that Parliament is not free to make any judgment, but only one that does not disproportionately affect the right to a fair trial. While the courts eventually found that the line had been drawn correctly here, the validity of future policy choices will turn on whether their impact on Convention rights is judged to be appropriate. Thus, Scottish public authorities are increasingly operating within a culture of legal justification in so far as their actions impinge upon human rights.

---

provision in question, it can be seen to change the meaning of the 1988 Act quite considerably in relation to Parliament's original intentions. Although this decision was substantively reversed by the Judicial Committee of the Privy Council, the technique of reading in (or down) remains a potentially powerful means of shifting the balance of interpretative power in favour of the courts.

39 Human Rights Act 1998, s 2, in respect of decisions of the European Court of Human Rights.
40 See, eg, *McNab v HM Advocate* 2000 SLT 99.
41 See J Murdoch in E Örücü (ed), *Judicial Comparativism in Human Rights Cases* (2003), p 85.
42 See *Napier v Scottish Ministers* at 582C–584C.
43 2000 SLT 379.

Impact

The comparative constitutional literature divides on the impact of becoming part of this form of constitutional globalisation. For some, it should be seen in positive terms, ensuring that power is not exercised in an arbitrary or capricious manner.[44] Others, though, see it as a tool for preserving the status quo. Ran Hirschl claims that constitutionalisation was a deliberate response of various élites (whether white South Africans or Ashkenazi Israelis) to shifting political majorities which now threatened their positions. He argues that the turn to courts and bills of rights enabled them to preserve their existing powers by legal means which could no longer be guaranteed by electoral processes.[45]

These arguments are generally rehearsed with regard to nation states, but what is their relevance in the devolution context? In terms of opportunity, some saw joining the rights revolution as a way of giving concrete form to Scotland's greater attachment to social democratic values. The Scottish Constitutional Convention, for example, spoke of protecting rights in a way that improved upon 'prevailing international law and convention'.[46] Certainly, much of the field of social and economic rights is within the competence of the Scottish Parliament, and there would seem to be no bar to its passing a Scottish Human Rights Act going beyond the civil and political rights which represent the global common denominator. The substantive impact of globalisation on Scottish social democracy will be discussed in more detail later, but for the moment it can be noted that there has been little formal movement in this regard either in terms of legislation or doctrine. Remembering that globalisation consists of greater interconnectedness, Scotland is not so far providing an alternative constitutional model which may be localised elsewhere.

One particular argument in the critical literature should be highlighted, namely that bills of rights protect established interests in plurinational states by constraining nationalist politics.[47] This works on a general plane, by promoting unity among national citizens who share the same rights, and also in terms of more specific provisions limiting innovation at the sub-national level. While the former is somewhat intangible, it is noteworthy both that *Bringing Rights Home* (the White Paper which preceded enactment of the HRA) stressed the British origins of the ECHR, and that *Scotland's Parliament* (the devolution White Paper) found it unnecessary to mention the Scottish dimension of Convention rights at all.[48] As regards specific constraints, the Scotland Act contains some strong provisions designed to prevent the dissolution of the UK, for example, reserving decisions over the future of the Union between Scotland and England to the Westminster Parliament.[49] It should also be noted that the basic democratic right to elect a government operates differently in Scotland, and the plurality of votes which would return large Labour or Conservative majorities at Westminster, would never be sufficient to elect a Scottish National Party (SNP) administration at Holyrood.

---

44 Beatty, *The Ultimate Rule of Law*, above n 21.
45 R Hirschl, *Towards Juristocracy: The Origins and Consequences of the New Constitutionalism* (2004).
46 Scottish Constitutional Convention, *Scotland's Parliament. Scotland's Right* (1995), p 20.
47 See Hirschl, *Towards Juristocracy*, above n 45, p 75.
48 It seems ironic that such a major part of the devolution scheme would be introduced by an 'and applies to Scotland' paragraph in the HRA White Paper.
49 Scotland Act 1998, Sch 5, para 1(b).

This broader question, to which this discussion relates, of whether, post-devolution, Scottish courts will prevent the elected branches from pursuing certain political options, such as placing limits on the use of private property or holding a referendum on independence, has yet to be tested. However, putting this question in global context leads to three observations. First, comparative experience suggests it does not require headline striking down of laws to inhibit governments, and that the prospect of legal challenge is important when considering whether to adopt a particular policy.[50] The Scottish Executive now routinely evaluates the potential impact of Convention rights when introducing legislation.[51] Second, where the Scottish courts have sustained rights claims, this has been where due process has not been followed (as in *Starrs v Ruxton*), or where the individual's private sphere has not been respected (as in *Napier*). This can be seen, in line with the content of the European Convention on Human Rights, to embody the values of negative liberty,[52] which, in emphasising the right to be left alone, are potentially antagonistic to more interventionist approaches by government, particularly in economic policy. Third, and relatedly, this is largely in line with the attitudes of courts elsewhere: thus, if Scottish courts had to decide the vires of redistributive legislation, they would be referred to plenty of comparative jurisprudence which has been favourable to existing distributions of economic power.[53]

SUPRANATIONAL CONSTITUTIONALISM

A second approach that addresses the constitutional relevance of globalisation comes under the rubric of supranational constitutionalism. If the previous approach emphasises how one specific model of constitutionalism is being reproduced from state to state, this school of thought focuses more on how developments at the global level should be conceived in constitutional terms. In particular, it is argued that supranational bodies, such as the WTO and the EU, which perform important regulatory functions vis-à-vis the global economy, should be seen as sites of constitutionalism. Supranational constitutionalism thus represents a potentially more radical reconceptualisation of the subject, arguing that it is necessary to break the traditional link between constitutions and the nation state.[54]

The starting-point for supranational constitutionalism is that in the contemporary era, 'the performance of law and politics is no longer configured around or constrained by the territorial structures of the nation state'.[55] Neil Walker draws a distinction between the state on the one hand, and the polity on the other, which is

---

50 See P J Monahan and M Finkelstein, 'The Charter of Rights and public policy in Canada' (1992) 30 *Osgoode Hall LJ* 501 at 516–522.
51 Steps were also taken to pre-empt potential Convention challenges: see Convention Rights (Compliance) (Scotland) Act 2001.
52 A number of commentators have argued that the Human Rights Act thus represents a partial account of human rights, and that the emphasis on negative rights should be balanced by giving equal weight to the European Social Charter, which guarantees rights such as the right to work and a fair remuneration, whose protection may require more positive action on the part of the state: see K D Ewing in Anderson (ed), *Rights and Democracy*, above n 26, pp 78–83.
53 See G W Anderson, *Constitutional Rights after Globalization* (2005), ch 7.
54 See D Cass, *The Constitutionalization of the World Trade Organization: Legitimacy, Democracy and Community in the International Trading System* (2005), ch 2.
55 D Chalmers, 'Post-nationalism and the quest for constitutional substitutes' (2000) 27 JLS 178.

'the setting for the practice of politics'.[56] Whereas for much of modern history, the polity was regarded as being contained within the state's borders, the present era has seen the emergence of supranational bodies 'which overlap and rival states in terms of legal and political authority'.[57] According to Walker, constitutions are intrinsic to polities, and so if we regard, say, the EU as a polity, constitutional law can no longer solely be a characteristic of nation states. In other words, questions concerning the establishment of political power, the conditions of its exercise and the means of ensuring its accountability, which have been the mainstay of national constitutional law, also now have to be addressed at the global and supranational level.

However, it does not follow that state-based constitutional forms and concepts can now simply be applied at the supranational level. Rather, some of our core constitutional language will have to be 'translated' in order to be comprehensible in this new environment.[58] For example, are conceptions of citizenship which imagine a unitary relationship between rulers and the ruled still appropriate in the context of multiple layers of governance? In this section, the position of devolved Scotland vis-à-vis bodies such as the WTO and EU is considered in order to address two questions: in what ways does the supranational dimension affect our understanding of constitutionalism; and what impact does this have on some key issues concerning the governance of Scotland?

Changing conceptions of sovereignty

To talk of the EU or the WTO as constitutional entities does not mean that each possesses a fully worked-out constitutional order as with nation states. Rather, it is better to view their constitutionalisation as a process.[59] In this regard, Walker posits three sets of criteria which can assist in assessing how far these supranational bodies have progressed down the constitutional road. The first set he calls 'constitutive criteria' which address the extent to which these bodies should be regarded, and regard themselves, as providing the setting for the conduct of law and politics. One of the key elements here is a 'claim to foundational legal authority',[60] which foregrounds how far sovereignty has to be rethought in light of the ongoing reconfiguration of power.[61]

As traditionally understood, sovereignty expressed the idea of the state's absolute legal supremacy over its exclusive territory. This is under challenge in two important ways. First, supranational bodies claim authority on a functional basis (for example, the WTO exercises regulatory powers over world trade), and do not aspire to exercise the comprehensive territorial jurisdiction associated with states. Second, we are often now dealing with competing claims to sovereignty between supranational bodies and nation states (and sometimes between supranational bodies). Moreover, while each claim may provide its own answer to where sovereignty lies – for example, to questions of whether the supremacy of EU law in Member States derives from the supranational or national legal order – any conflicts

56 N Walker, in G de Burca and J Scott (eds), *The EU and the WTO: Legal and Constitutional Issues* (2001), p 35.
57 Walker, above n 56, p 36.
58 Walker, above n 56, p 36.
59 Walker, above n 56, p 35.
60 N Walker, 'The idea of constitutional pluralism' (2002) 65 MLR 317 at 342.
61 See N Walker in N Walker (ed), *Sovereignty in Transition* (2003), ch 1; N MacCormick, *Questioning Sovereignty* (1999).

this produces may be irresolvable.[62] Accordingly, Walker argues it may be best to abandon the search for some single ultimate authority, and instead accept that we live in an era of 'multiple and overlapping' claims to sovereignty.[63]

Some claims, though, are more persuasive than others. For instance, it is now commonplace to speak of the EU as a constitutional order,[64] reflecting how EU legal doctrines of supremacy and direct effect are now routinely accepted in the Member States. By contrast, there are no similar juridical doctrines pertaining to the WTO, although some argue, for example in so far as its normative framework for the global economy is internalised by states, that it is acquiring some attributes of sovereignty.[65] The relevance of these developments to Scotland might appear ancillary to their general impact on the UK. To the extent that the rise of supranational bodies results, as various commentators accept, in a relative diminution of national sovereignty, this also constrains those powers exercised at an internal devolved level. Thus, the successful assertion of EU sovereignty claims over agriculture and fisheries necessarily limits how the Scottish Executive can exercise the competence assigned to it in these fields by the Scotland Act.

However, while devolved Scotland would seem bound up with the UK's net loss of authority, in other ways it can be seen to benefit from a more fluid understanding of sovereignty. While in formal terms, the lack of statehood seems to close off avenues for making claims to sovereignty – for example, only nation states negotiate international treaties with supranational bodies – at a less formal level, there are now various mechanisms which enable distinctive Scottish claims to be made and heard. The concordat system in the UK enables Scotland to present her own interests vis-à-vis other levels of government, and so can seek to influence the UK position on matters within the competence of supranational bodies. As detailed elsewhere in this volume, the EU also provides for representation from regional bodies in European policy formation.[66] This of course does not mean that the Scottish voice will always prevail, or that Scotland is exercising full legal sovereignty; but it does suggest that we should situate post-devolution Scotland within a more plural account of sovereignty, in which it enjoys more political capacity (on which, Martin Loughlin reminds us, sovereignty finally depends)[67] than in the years before 1999.

Supranational constitutionalism in practice

Claims to sovereignty, while necessary, are not sufficient to establish the existence of supranational constitutionalism. Rather, Walker suggests we also have to turn our mind to a second set of criteria – 'governance criteria' – which considers the extent to which functions of governance are now carried out at the supranational level. The idea that there are now developed practices of constitutionalism beyond the state further challenges some of our basic ideas of public law. In particular, it supplants the traditional UK view of unitary political authority, with a more

---

62 See *Brunner v The European Union Treaty* [1994] 1 CMLR 57.
63 Walker, 'The idea of constitutional pluralism', above n 60, p 346.
64 See, eg, S Douglas-Scott, *Constitutional Law in the European Union* (2002).
65 See Cass, above n 54, ch 6.
66 See Chapter 3 of this volume.
67 See M Loughlin, *Sword and Scales: An Examination of the Relationship Between Law and Politics* (2000), p 137.

complex model in which questions concerning the exercise of political power are considered in terms of the relations between different (state, supra-state, and sub-state) sites of constitutional authority. Some writers have described this state of affairs as 'multilevel government (or governance)'.[68] This section now considers how far these governance criteria can be made out with regard to, and their impact upon, devolved Scotland.

The first element to discuss is the scope of supranational competence. According to Walker, claims to polityhood must be based either on supranational entities performing a critical mass of regulatory functions, or, if more sectorally limited, that their activities touch on a broad range of public policy issues. Put this way, it is clear that supranational bodies have extensive jurisdictional scope which is highly relevant to the contemporary governance of Scotland. Thus, while the Scotland Act provides for an internal division of competences within the UK, the practical implications of this will be meaningless unless we also take into account how this is shaped by the UK's relations with, at a minimum, the EU, the ECHR system and the WTO.

The general trend here is for supranational decisions to reach more and more areas of devolved competence. The expansion of the EU's field of operations from the economic to include, for example, social and environmental policy is well documented, and has intensified in some key areas. For example, in health care, one of the major devolved functions, the EU has emerged as an important new actor in setting the terms of policy debates. Later protocols have extended the rights protected under the ECHR from core procedural and political rights to include, for example, the right to private property. The WTO is also developing its range of activities in ways that potentially impact upon devolved competences. For example, the General Agreement on Trade and Services (GATS) seeks to extend free trade principles to services such as health and education.

For much that is within their responsibility, the devolved institutions have to turn their minds to the operation of supranational norms. The importance of doing so is reinforced by two further characteristics of governance which have been translated to the supranational level. All three entities mentioned have adjudicative bodies which claim interpretive autonomy over the scope of their jurisdiction, and whose decisions bind the UK internationally, and, to varying degrees, are directly applicable in Scottish courts. Moreover, each entity has, to varying degrees, some residual institutional capacity for ensuring the effectiveness of its decisions (for example, enforcement proceedings under Article 226 of the Treaty establishing the European Community). Thus, being conversant with supranational forms of government is not an optional extra, but integral to understanding contemporary public law issues in Scotland.

From one perspective, as with sovereignty, the impact of these developments on Scotland would again appear to be secondary to that on the UK generally. Looking at recent controversies where supranational norms have informed discussions of Scottish public policy – for example, the awarding of Executive contracts (EU and WTO provisions on public procurement), or attempts to protect the Scottish fishing industry (EU Common Fisheries Policy) or reform conditions in prison (ECHR Articles 3 and 8) – these are norms which apply throughout the UK. However, there are some ways in which the different position of devolved Scotland in relation to multilevel governance can be highlighted.

68 See T L Ilgen (ed), *Reconfigured Sovereignty: Multi-Layered Governance in the Global Age* (2003).

One issue which arises relates to the fact that while foreign affairs and EC matters are reserved, and so Scottish governmental institutions cannot act to create international obligations, in many non-reserved matters they can act in a way which engages, and potentially violates, those obligations which have been entered into by the UK. Moreover, any sanctions for such violations would be visited directly on the UK (although this would not preclude, for example, internal arrangements for recovering fines). As a consequence, the Scotland Act makes it clear that the devolved institutions are in a lower place in the hierarchy of multilevel governance than their UK equivalents. The Scottish Parliament is expressly barred from legislating in a manner which is incompatible with Community law, and if it acts inconsistently with the UK's international obligations (including WTO provisions), the Secretary of State has power to set this aside.[69] There are also some indications that the devolved institutions may be interacting differently with supranational, as opposed to national, bodies, and not always to their benefit. For example, Scott Greer notes that while the immediate period following devolution led to considerable divergence in health care policy in the UK, the recent entry of the EU in this field has produced homogenising pressures which restrict their freedom to innovate.[70]

The exercise of governance may prove hollow if this does not build new political relationships, and in that regard Walker suggests a third measurement of supranational constitutional phenomena under the heading of 'societal criteria'.[71] These focus on how far the processes described above have fostered new ideas of political community and participation above the nation state. He suggests that notions of supranational citizenship are most pronounced with regard to the EU – which, for example, confers a plethora of economic and, increasingly, political rights – and that while it has some way to go in the quality of its democratic representation, recent debates over the EU Constitutional Treaty may have contributed to the idea that there is a European *demos* with a direct interest in the EU's future governance.[72]

These shifting patterns of political identity can be seen to resonate in changes in the conduct of Scottish politics. In symbolic terms, this was perhaps most powerfully demonstrated when hundreds of thousands of people took to the streets of Edinburgh seeking to influence the G8 leaders' policies on Africa during their Gleneagles summit in July 2005. In part, this reflects the pragmatic sense that citizens' interests can now be prosecuted in a multiplicity of settings. For example, while the Scottish Executive holds regular discussions with other UK bodies through the concordats, it also seeks a voice on the international stage through its offices in Brussels and Washington. Campaigners are also sensitive to a more interconnected form of politics, as witnessed in the lobbying of the Scottish Executive to try to influence the UK's negotiating position in GATS.[73]

The greater cultivation of political relations at the supranational level is also in part related to the changing structural position of the nation state. For example,

69 Scotland Act 1998, ss 29 and 35.
70 See S L Greer, 'The territorial bases of health policymaking in the UK after devolution' (2005) 15 *Regional and Federal Studies* 501 at 513.
71 Walker, 'The idea of constitutional pluralism', above n 60, p 350.
72 See N Walker, 'The legacy of Europe's constitutional moment' (2004) 11 *Constellations* 368 at 384.
73 See A Dodds, 'The politicisation of trade in health and education services: black and white divisions over a "grey area"' (2004) 46 *Scottish Affairs* 56.

in light of the UK's relative loss of sovereignty, the SNP's political strategy has shifted from emphasising secession from the UK to advocating independence in Europe. The calculation here is that Scotland will have more influence and receive more benefits from interacting directly with supranational bodies than mediating its claims through the UK. Scotland is not, at time of writing, an independent state, but some writers argue that while what are described as 'sub-state national societies' are equally subject to globalisation, their more flexible approach to questions of sovereignty may mean that they are better placed to resist, and fashion innovative responses to, such pressures.[74] This returns us to the impact of globalisation on Scottish constitutional autonomy, and the question whether, in interacting with global forces, the devolved institutions have been able to pursue a distinctive approach which reflects Scottish interests and values. To consider this more fully, there follows a more substantive discussion of the politics of globalisation.

NEW CONSTITUTIONALISM

The new constitutionalism, according to Stephen Gill, is a "'global economic governance" project' designed to '"lock-in" the power gains of capital on a world scale'.[75] The context for this project is the rise of neoliberal economic policies since the 1980s which, Gill argues, seek to discipline national governments so that they do not interfere with the free market. New constitutionalism supports this by placing barriers in the way of redistributive policies through legal and political measures which are difficult to reverse. This school of thought, which has its roots in political science and international relations, provides two important points of contrast with the first two approaches. First, the starting-point for the new constitutionalism is not jurisprudential or institutional developments, but the global economy. It argues that political power is found not only in public institutional settings, and so in addition seeks to highlight the constitutional significance of the economic sphere. For example, multinational corporations are seen as important political actors whose actions and decisions have a direct impact on the lives of millions. Consequently, questions about the location of sovereignty, and the exercise and accountability of power, necessarily require us to focus on the relations between them, states and supranational bodies.

Second, the new constitutionalism advances a broader understanding of constitutionalism than is traditionally accepted within the legal academy (at least in the UK). What is constitutional about the new constitutionalism is not established principally by an analytical assessment of whether traditional constitutional functions are discharged within the global economy. Rather, it lies in the argument that the global economy places limits on the policies that governments can pursue. As a result, only policies which adhere to neoliberalism are deemed constitutionally legitimate.[76] This is done partly by direct means: supranational legal forms have a key role here, whether through the WTO

---

74 See Tierney, 'Reframing sovereignty?', above n 14, pp 172–173.
75 S Gill, 'The Constitution of Global Capitalism' (2000), *http://www.theglobalsite.ac.uk*, pp 11 and 6.
76 See H W Arthurs in T J Courchene (ed), *Room to Manoeuvre? Globalization and Policy Convergence* (1999), p 27.

imposing sanctions on states deviating from the global economic consensus, or bilateral treaties requiring domestic constitutional reform to qualify for inward investment.[77] It is also in part achieved by indirect means: for example, the international bond markets emerge as important constitutional actors to the extent that their credit ratings (which affect states' ability to borrow money) constrain public expenditure. The success of the new constitutionalism is said to lie not in the regular application of external constraints, but in the fact that this is often unnecessary, as states accept neoliberal values as 'normative bedrock' and conform their behaviour accordingly.

The new constitutionalism raises the political implications of constitutional globalisation more directly, and casts some of the previous discussion in a new light. In particular, it argues that the spread of constitutional rights and the rise of supranational governance in relation to the global economy show that the former also embody a narrow political agenda. For example, it has been pointed out that the forces behind rule of law projects are also those driving the liberalisation of trade,[78] leading some to speak of the emergence of a 'trade-related, market-friendly' paradigm of human rights.[79] Others suggest that bodies like the EU and WTO should be seen as vehicles for neoliberalism to the extent that they foster free trade and protect the rights of capital.[80] In response, some argue that rights, even within the WTO system, can be used to advance non-market values such as the protection of employment standards,[81] and in Europe, some see the EU, and particularly its social model, as a counterweight to neoliberalism and a potential alternative model of globalisation.[82]

These issues feed into a larger debate about the nature and extent of neoliberalism, and whether it is inevitable or irreversible, which it is beyond the scope of this chapter to address adequately, let alone resolve.[83] However, the broad question of whether there are structural limits to the sorts of policies national governments can pursue is highly relevant to the discussion about Scottish constitutional autonomy. If the new constitutionalism thesis holds up, Scotland may have less constitutional room to manoeuvre than the terms of the devolution legislation might indicate. For example, while the Scottish Parliament may have the formal authority to raise income tax by three pence in the pound (say to increase funding of education), it may in practice be constitutionally prohibited from ever exercising this power. James Tully argues that devolved levels of government, given their relative weakness, may be in an especially precarious position in relation to global economic forces, and may become 'trapped in a "race to the bottom"' as social protections are traded against the perceived need to remain competitive in the global economy.[84]

---

77 Gill, 'Constitution of Global Capitalism', above n 75, p 12. See also D Schneiderman, 'Investment rules and the new constitutionalism' (2000) 25 Law & Soc Inqy 757.

78 Santos, *New Legal Common Sense*, above n 4, ch 6.

79 U Baxi, *The Future of Human Rights* (2002), p 144.

80 See S Gill, *Power and Resistance in the New World Order* (2003), p 133.

81 R Howse and M Mutua, 'Protecting human rights in a global economy: challenges for the World Trade Organization' (2000): *http://www.ichrdd.ca/english/commdoc/publications/globalisation/wtoRightsGlob.html*.

82 J Habermas, 'So, Why does Europe need a Constitution?' (2001): *http://www.iue.it/RSCAS/Research/Institutions/Reform.shtml*.

83 See D Harvey, *A Brief History of Neoliberalism* (2005).

84 See J Tully, 'The unfreedom of the Moderns in comparison to their ideals of constitutional democracy' (2002) 62 MLR 204 at 211–213.

Against this, it is said that the smaller the unit of government, the less it can afford to incur the high social costs of, for example, mass unemployment, and so they are necessarily more flexible in their economic strategies.[85]

New constitutionalism and Scottish public policy

Debates about the scope for innovation in Scottish public policy following devolution can be seen to address some of these questions. There has been considerable interest since 1999 (albeit often in a UK context) as to whether the Scottish Parliament and Executive have been able to carve out distinctive approaches in a number of key policy areas.[86] In some controversial cases, Scotland has pursued different options from the rest of the UK – for example, the abolition of up-front tuition fees for students attending Scottish higher education institutions, or the provision of free personal care for the elderly. This raises the prospect that pre-devolution talk of a 'new politics', better able to respond to the needs and wishes of the Scottish people, may be realisable in practice. To explore some of the issues this provokes, two trends which it is argued are at the heart of the new constitutionalism are considered: the extension of market-based ideas and practices, and the narrowing of the range of political debate.

Scotland and the market: PFI and health reform

Gill sees one of the key elements of the new constitutionalism as the increasing marketisation of society. In practice, this was originally marked by the greater privatisation of formerly publicly-owned services like telecommunications and energy. However, he contends that processes of commodification now extend to more areas of social life, such as human reproduction (for example, surrogacy contracts) or security (for example, where private firms act as prison guards or 'police' gated communities). As a result, it is argued that politics are subordinated to economics, with more decisions being made on grounds such as efficiency and effectiveness, rather than broader political considerations of the general welfare.

Two high-profile ways in which these arguments have played out with regard to devolved Scotland can be highlighted. The first is the controversial Public Finance Initiative (PFI). Initially introduced on a UK-wide basis by John Major's Conservative government in the 1990s, and continued by the Scottish Executive, the idea was that private firms would tender for the construction of (for example) schools and hospitals at their own expense and risk, which, once built, would then be leased back to the public sector, often over a thirty-year period. Those opposing PFI argue that in the long run, it will cost more than if these projects had been met by public borrowing in the first instance. From one perspective, the turn to PFI can be seen as the policy preference of the Conservative, Labour and (at least in Scotland), the Liberal Democrat parties since the 1990s. However, the new constitutionalism asks us to consider how these policy preferences are shaped, and in particular, whether, when measured against the global trend towards neoliberalism, they can be seen to be the product of indigenous processes.

Both supporters and critics would agree that the very nature of PFI is designed to involve the private sector in new areas of policy delivery (for example, constructing

---

85 See P Katzenstein, *Small States in World Markets: Industrial Policy in Europe* (1985), ch 2.
86 See M Keating, *The Government of Scotland: Public Policy Making after Devolution* (2005), ch 1.

physical infrastructure such as the Skye bridge), but some critics go further and argue that the need to make contracts profitable to developers results in market-based decisions (for example, to reduce the number of beds in hospitals) which would otherwise not be taken.[87] Reversing the many PFI projects which have now been commissioned would prove very difficult in practice, given the enormous costs of buying out the private firms' contractual obligations.[88] It may also be the case that future administrations would find it difficult not to continue with PFI: Allyson Pollock argues that when New Labour came to power, it reasoned that GATS was likely to increase private sector access to WTO members' public services, and that pushing on with public-private partnerships would give the UK a competitive advantage.[89]

PFI may be a powerful indication of how certain policy options appear to be closed off to the Scottish Executive, but we should be careful not to generalise from one example. If we turn to health care, this may provide some counter-evidence that devolved Scotland has been less prone to market influences than other parts of the UK. In England, health policy has been characterised in terms of consumerism and competition, whether by grading the performance of hospitals (with the best designated as foundation hospitals), or freeing GPs, organised in primary care trusts, to contract with whomever they please in providing their services. Scotland has pursued a different approach, which, it is argued, places greater emphasis on 'professional leadership, consensus, uniformity and integration'.[90] Thus, for example, the Scottish Executive abolished the NHS trusts operating in Scotland. For some, this divergence can be seen to affirm a distinctive political culture in Scotland, more committed to public services.[91]

Others, though, suggest the scope for innovative health policy in Scotland may be reduced when considered in light of external pressures. We have already canvassed the argument that the entry of the EU into health care produces homogenising effects which constrain the extent to which Scotland can adopt a separate approach.[92] Others point to the potential effect of GATS: if, as some critics fear, public services such as health are deemed 'commercial' and so not exempt from competition, this could significantly open up the delivery of health care in Scotland to market forces.[93] It has also been argued that some of the headline acts discussed above may in fact indicate the limits of pursuing social democratic policies even within the UK's multilayered governance. Thus, when the UK government refused to provide the anticipated funds to cover free personal care,[94] raising Scottish taxes was not considered, leaving the Executive either to reduce services or make other

87 See Comment, *Scottish Left Review*, Issue 33 Mar/Apr 2006, p 2.
88 The Scottish Executive Financial Partnerships Unit estimates that £3.2 billion has been assigned to current projects, with £2.8 billion committed to future deals: *http://www.scotland.gov.uk/Topics/Government/Finance/18232/12308#anchor2*.
89 A M Pollock, *NHS plc: The Privatisation of Our Health Care* (2004), pp 53–54.
90 Keating, *Government of Scotland*, above n 86, p 176.
91 See C Spry, in G Hassan and C Warhurst (eds), *Anatomy of the New Scotland: Power, Influence and Change* (2002), p 113.
92 See Greer, 'Territorial bases of health policymaking', above n 70.
93 See A M Pollock and D Price, 'The public health implications of World Trade Negotiations on the General Agreement on Trade in Services and Public Services' (2003) 362 *The Lancet* 1072; and A Pollock, 'Will the NHS in Scotland be privatised?' (Centre for International Public Health Policy, University of Edinburgh): *http://www.wtcrf.ed.ac.uk/education/Talks/Allyson%20Pollock%20%2026%20Jan%202006.pdf*.
94 See I Macwhirter, in *Anatomy of a New Scotland*, above n 91, p 32.

charges, 'shift[ing] the burden of responsibility ... from society to the individual',[95] contrary to the Scottish Parliament's original intention.

New constitutionalism and the quality of Scottish democracy

One of the consequences of the new constitutionalism is said to be a narrowing of political discourse, as consensus is reached over the necessity of the global economy and a reduced role for the state.[96] On this account, the focus of politics (at least party politics) is how best to manage the market, rather than debating alternative forms of societal organisation.[97] Tully argues it is not surprising that globalisation has led to a 'decline in democratic deliberation':

> 'Political powers are abjured to the market or passed to global regulatory regimes by small groups of unelected and unaccountable negotiators in private meetings whose self-consciousness has been shaped by careers in ministries or large corporations, not in practices of citizenship.'[98]

As a result, people feel increasingly distanced from the events which shape their lives, and participation suffers. Whether one agrees with this analysis depends largely on how one measures the quality of democracy in the global age, which cannot be addressed directly in this chapter. However, some of these issues frame current discussion of the state of devolved politics.

One concern with devolution, shared by political parties, is the declining interest in Scottish parliamentary elections, with neither 1999 nor 2003 matching the turnout or enthusiasm of the 1997 referendum. In terms of the range of Scottish political debate, Michael Keating argues that while the Scottish Executive, particularly in economic policy, initially deviated little from the London lead of New Labour, with its emphasis on the market, there are now more differences, with social inclusion featuring more prominently in Scottish policy discussions.[99] Others though have lamented the lack of real choice between the mainstream Scottish parties,[100] and it seems likely that in the 2007 Scottish parliamentary elections, the platform of the principal opposition party will include a commitment to reducing corporate taxation and lowering the burdens on business. Moreover, the previously unthinkable idea of the Scottish Conservative Party maintaining a minority Labour administration in office has been floated in certain quarters.[101] Whether any political coalescence which has occurred would necessarily prevent a differently inclined Holyrood administration from pursuing more redistributive policies in the future (and what mechanisms might prevent this) remains to be seen. However, the fact that such a question can be posed might lead those of a new constitutionalist disposition to suggest that this is evidence of the (relative) entrenchment of market values, bringing Scotland into line with global patterns whereby alternative visions of society seem effectively beyond the reach of democratic politics.

---

95 A M Pollock, 'Social policy and devolution' (2001) BMJ 311.
96 See Arthurs in *Room to Manoeuvre*, above n 76.
97 See J Jenson and B de Sousa Santos, in Jenson and de Sousa Santos (eds), *Globalizing Institutions: Case Studies in Social Regulation and Innovation* (2000), p 12.
98 Tully, 'Unfreedom', above n 84, p 213.
99 Keating, *Government of Scotland*, above n 86, p 193.
100 J McAllion, 'What future Scottish democracy?' (2005) 29 *Scottish Left Review* 4.
101 See Editorial, 'Strangest bedfellows' *The Herald*, 5 June 2006.

CONCLUSION

To return to the opening discussion, it should now be clear that what happens elsewhere is often highly relevant to Scottish public law. Adapting Santos, we can say that devolved Scotland must now be seen in relation both to globalised constitutionalism, as fundamental rights, following the worldwide trend, assume a more prominent role in the Scottish legal system; and constitutionalised globalism, as supranational forms of political authority assume the constitutional attributes once regarded as exclusive to the state, and restructure local constitutional practices accordingly. Seeing constitutional globalisation in terms of the greater inter-connectedness between different constitutional levels and phenomena underscores that the global dimension is not an exotic realm of study, only relevant once we consider the domestic constitutional position. Rather, what this chapter has sought to demonstrate is that when we consider many of the key issues in Scottish public law, this necessarily engages with globalisation, and changes some of our basic conceptions of constitutionalism as a result. Thus, globalisation is not something happening 'out there',[102] but goes all the way through the governance of contemporary Scotland, and indeed recasts what we consider the domestic constitutional position to be.

This has some important practical implications for Scottish public law which has become a more complex endeavour than would have been the case even fifteen years ago, requiring a more flexible approach, a broader knowledge-base and a greater fluency in different constitutional traditions. Where students would once have learned about a single set of institutions within a supposedly unitary constitution, they now have to negotiate their way between three, sometimes four, different levels of authority to answer the basic constitutional questions about who can exercise power and under what conditions. Where practitioners working for Scottish public authorities would once, for example, have regarded the latter's commercial activities as raising (not particularly specialised) issues of Scots contract law, they now have to consider not only how this might be compatible with the Scotland Act, but also the UK's EU obligations (while also bearing in mind that the EU itself is a member of the WTO).

Perhaps the greatest significance of situating Scotland in the context of globalisation is to emphasise the high political stakes involved here. This focuses attention on the links between the various forms of constitutional globalisation and broader global processes. Does this, as one commentator suggests, lead to a more singular constitutional vision, which sees 'liberal rights [as] the common constitutional heritage of humankind'?[103] Moreover, are these rights more or less supportive of the prevailing form of economic globalisation? Or should devolved Scotland be seen as one part of a situation of 'constitutional pluralism',[104] with the potential to articulate its own distinctive constitutional values to other constitutional orders? However we answer these questions, it is evident that debates about the democratic implications of globalisation are also debates about the future quality of Scottish democracy (social or otherwise).

---

102 D Schneiderman in V C Jackson and M Tushnet (eds), *Defining the Field of Comparative Constitutional Law* (2002), p 239.
103 Schneiderman, above n 102, p 239.
104 See Walker, 'The idea of constitutional pluralism', above n 60.

PART II:
THE GOVERNANCE OF SCOTLAND

Chapter 5

Devolution and Democracy

Heather Lardy

REPRESENTATIVE DEMOCRACY AND PARTICIPATORY DEMOCRACY

This chapter considers how devolution is shaping the practice of democracy within Scotland. The new constitutional arrangements prescribe a representative democracy, but with several features which distinguish it from the form of representation practised in the pre-devolution system. An additional and prominent feature is the emphasis on the incorporation of elements of a more participatory style of democracy. The discussion which follows considers both aspects of the new regime: the changed structures of representation and the opportunities for participation in devolved Scotland. This introduction outlines the key features of both representative and participatory democracy and explains the relevance of each of those models of democracy to the features of devolved governance discussed in this chapter.

Representative democracy

In a representative democracy the dominant (or in some cases the exclusive) mode of participation by citizens in democratic life is voting in elections to select those by whom they will be represented. The core features of representative democracy are thus: regular, free and fair elections; extensive suffrage (right to vote); procedures for effective representation; stable political parties; and governance by democratically accountable electoral elites (whether individuals, political parties or coalitions of such individuals and groups, or their subsets). Representative democracy is often associated with the values of the political philosophy of liberalism, which commonly prevails in those states committed to representative government. Those values place a strong emphasis on ideas about the liberty of the individual, the rule of law, constitutionalism and human rights. Representative democracy is in this sense part of a political philosophy and not merely a mechanism for conducting elections.[1]

Those aspects of devolved democracy which relate especially to the core features of representative democracy concern the electoral system for the Scottish Parliament: its voting system and related electoral laws, and the roles of its representatives. Also relevant is the status of the right to vote in Scottish Parliament elections, and the place of election law generally within the constitutional law of devolved Scotland. Local governance reflects further changes to the practice of

---

1 Prominent examples of writers in the liberal tradition are J Rawls, *A Theory of Justice* (1971) and *Political Liberalism* (1993); R Dworkin, *Taking Rights Seriously* (1977) and *A Matter of Principle* (1985). On representative democracy see B Manin, *The Principles of Representative Government* (1997); D Judge, *Representation: Theory and Practice in Britain* (1998).

representative democracy following devolution: the implementation of a new voting system will produce different structures and patterns of representation.

The familiarity of representative democracy and its undoubted effectiveness as a means of managing the practice of some form of self-rule by large and diverse populations often combine to disguise its flaws. A major problem is the level of disconnection evident in the response of many potential voters in such democracies to election campaigns: low rates of voter turnout are a common aspect of modern representative regimes.[2] The causes of low turnout are difficult to identify precisely, but seem to range from lack of interest in politics generally to disaffection with the particular policies or attitudes advanced by candidates and parties. Levels of education about and awareness of electoral politics may also play a role, as may social attitudes and personal beliefs. A person who believes that her vote never counts or that her social group rarely benefits from the outcomes of electoral contests is less likely to vote than an elector who regards voting as a civic duty the exercise of which yields potentially significant social and personal benefits.

A related criticism of representative democracy is the dependence of the system on electoral regimes which require the reduction of the complex range of policy issues and choices facing the democracy to a list of points in an election campaign manifesto. In addition, representative democracy – and the dominance of electoral politics which accompanies it – limits opportunities for less polarised debate. It reduces the role of the average citizen to that of periodic voter in a ballot of headline policy agendas, in a competition in which power is traded between political elites. To the extent that non-voting may be a consequence of dissatisfaction with the general nature of democratic politics in a representative democracy, and with the emphasis which that politics places on polarised electoral competition, only fundamental changes to the manner in which citizens engage in such politics is likely to counter this trend. Such changes are advocated by those who propose a more participatory model of politics.

Participatory democracy

Participatory democracy is a collective term for a set of ideas, theories and practices which reflect upon the perceived defects of representative democracy. The latter is sometimes depicted by its critics as an arrangement whereby electors' preferences – formed without any necessary prior engagement in private reflection or public deliberation – are simply aggregated periodically by the application of voting systems in order to define the memberships of parliaments and the occupiers of governmental office. There is, on this view, no meaningful engagement by the voter with the democratic process. Participatory democrats seek to change this by widening the range of ways in which citizens engage in the political process, and by deepening the value which this fuller sort of participation generates both for the individual and for the democracy as a whole. Many advocates of participatory democracy work within a philosophical tradition which is sometimes labelled republicanism or communitarianism. This school of thought challenges defects which it perceives in the philosophy of liberalism, the system of thought which

2 In the 2001 general election for the Westminster Parliament the percentage of registered electors turning out to vote was 59.1 per cent, the lowest recorded turnout since 1918. See J Curtice, 'Turnout: electors stay home – again' (2005) 58 *Parl Affairs* 776.

underpins the theory of modern representative democracy. Republicanism seeks to moderate the emphasis which liberalism places on the individual in society, and emphasises instead the importance of interaction between the citizen and the community (or 'republic'). The theories advocate ways in which citizens may become engaged in this way, rather than living as disconnected individuals in the private world prescribed by liberalism.[3] The debate between defenders of representative democracy and proponents of participatory democracy is best viewed in this context, as part of a wider dialogue about what sort of political philosophy should prevail.

Citizen participation in (non-electoral) democratic decision-making may take many forms, such as taking part in consultation processes; communicating effectively with institutions (political parties, executive, legislatures and committees) and with elected representatives; and dialogue between civic groups (for example, interest groups and community organisations) and political institutions. Participation may also take place for a range of purposes: to air grievances; to establish connections which may be used to promote future dialogue; to contribute to the legislative agenda by commenting on proposed laws or suggesting new ones. Beyond such public or political goals, participation is argued by its proponents to have further and personal advantages for those taking part. It promotes self-development, a sense of active citizenship and ongoing connection with the democratic process. Voters are no longer passive recipients of ballot papers but active and engaged partners in the political process. Democracy becomes something which more closely approximates to rule by the people, rather than rule by the people's periodically elected representatives.

Considerable emphasis has been placed on the idea of participation by the architects of devolution, and it continues to be stressed by those charged with animating its institutions. The following discussion considers the potential contribution to participatory democracy which devolution may make, with particular reference to the Scottish Parliament. The discussion assesses the Parliament's founding principles, built environment and accessibility to the public. It reviews also the role of its committees, and the procedures for petitioning, consultation and enquiry. The Executive's role in fostering participation is also considered, as too is the potential contribution of e-democracy to strengthened participation. As the system of devolution remains predicated principally upon the ideas and practices of representative democracy, the discussion first reviews those features of devolved governance which lend distinctiveness to its particular system of representative democracy. The chapter closes with a brief consideration of non-devolved democracy – those aspects of Scottish governance which continue to be conducted at the United Kingdom level – and its relation to devolved democracy.

DEVOLUTION AND REPRESENTATIVE DEMOCRACY

The pattern of representation has changed significantly within Scotland since devolution. The resulting scheme is, to borrow the title of a report by the Select

---

3 See, eg, J Dryzek, *Deliberative Democracy and Beyond* (2000); R Goodin, *Reflective Democracy* (2003); P Hirst, *Associative Democracy* (1994); P Pettit, *Republicanism* (1997); I M Young, *Inclusion and Democracy* (2000).

Committee on Scottish Affairs, a multi-layer democracy.[4] The use of a system of proportional representation for the Scottish Parliament has produced very noticeable electoral effects. Both the 1999 and 2003 elections have produced Parliaments in which, as expected, no single political party has won an overall majority. Seats have been shared, as was the intention of the electoral system's designers, with a concern for a degree of proportionality between votes cast and seats won which is not evident in elections to the Westminster Parliament. Coalition government by the Scottish Labour and Liberal Democrat parties has operated as a result, and has become a distinguishing feature of Scottish governance, if not an immutable characteristic: debates continue about the possible shape of future Executives and the forms in which support (short of full coalition) might be given to the majority party in subsequent sessions. Proportional representation and the attendant coalition building have also had the result of awarding the status of official opposition to the Scottish National Party during the first two sessions of the Parliament, thereby enhancing the institutional standing of a party once resigned to the status of bit-part player on the Westminster stage.

The Scottish Parliament voting system

The voting system for the Scottish Parliament has been designed to have distinct characteristics from the Westminster system of FPTP (first past the post). A core feature of the devolution plan was a commitment to address the lack of proportionality in the FPTP system between votes cast for and seats won by a political party. The resulting system is a mixed one, combining the election of seventy-three constituency MSPs by FPTP with the election of a further fifty-six regional or list members using the so-called additional member system (AMS).[5] AMS employs the eight Scottish regions formerly used for elections to the European Parliament.[6] The total of 129 MSPs was a figure which the Scotland Act 1998 stipulated would be reduced in proportion to a corresponding reduction of Scottish representation at Westminster consequent upon devolution. Following opposition from the Scottish Parliament, which argued that its functioning would be impaired if its membership were to decrease, the UK government conceded that all 129 members would be retained. Legislation to that effect has now been passed.[7]

In 2005 the number of Westminster Parliament seats in Scotland was reduced from seventy-two to fifty-nine as a result of a review by the Boundary Commission for Scotland. In consequence, the boundary lines for Scotland's MPs are now different from those for constituency MSPs. Both of those sets of lines differ from those used to elect regional MSPs, and all of those boundaries are distinct from the wards used in local elections. The Arbuthnott Commission on Boundary Differences and Voting Systems was charged with considering the difficulties

4 Scottish Affairs Committee, *The Operation of Multi-Layer Democracy* (2nd report, 1997–1998, HC 460).
5 The Scottish Parliament is tied to fixed terms of four years, commencing with the first election on 6 May 1999: Scotland Act 1998, s 2. The Scotland Act also makes provision in s 3 for extraordinary general elections to be held outside the normal fixed term cycle in certain circumstances.
6 European Parliamentary Constituencies (Scotland) Order 1996 (SI 1996/1926).
7 Scottish Parliament (Constituencies) Act 2004. See Scotland Office, *The Size of the Scottish Parliament: A Consultation* (Dec 2001).

thrown up by this lack of coterminous boundaries. The Commission concluded that coterminous boundaries are desirable, but not essential. Lack of coterminous boundaries is not, in the Commission's view, a factor discouraging voters. The Commission took the view also that the boundaries for Scottish Parliament constituencies should respect local authority areas rather than Westminster constituencies. Scottish Parliament regions should be revised to reflect natural local communities and identities and should be built on local authority areas.[8] The emphasis which the Arbuthnott Report places on local authority areas as the basis of other boundaries is welcome. If it is followed, units of representation within the devolved democracy would be fashioned around the boundaries of the level of electoral system closest, in theory at least, to the people. Commentators had urged the Commission to recommend the adoption of the single transferable vote (STV), the system to be employed at local government elections in Scotland.[9] The Commission rejected this. Reporting in January 2006, it concluded that different electoral systems are appropriate for different institutions. It further recommended that more consideration be given to the issue later if the modifications to the existing system proposed in its report do not prove effective.[10] Those changes include the recommendation that the voting system be described as MMS – multi-member system – and not as AMS – the additional member system.[11] This is to discourage the perception that there is any difference in status, whether formally or in practice, between the constituency and the regional members. The Commission recommended also that the voting system not be portrayed as a modification of FPTP: all official documents should refer to the constituency vote and the regional vote and 'every effort [is] to be made to ensure equality of treatment and esteem of both parts of the system'.[12] In addition, the Electoral Commission should clarify the purpose of the regional vote (to address voter confusion about this) and revise the ballot paper to make clear the significance of the regional vote as a determinant of the share of seats in Parliament.

Another feature of the electoral system which has attracted criticism concerns the use of so-called 'closed' lists from which the electors select their regional or 'list' MSPs by voting for a list of candidates put forward by a political party, with no option to favour particular candidates on that list. The Select Committee on Scottish Affairs has recommended the use of open lists, and this has been endorsed recently by the Arbuthnott Commission.[13] This would permit voters to cast their ballot for a named party candidate, or for a party, expressing no preference for a candidate.[14] This system would arguably reduce the perception that the first loyalty of regional members is to their party, which currently controls their place on the list, rather than to the electorate.[15]

8 Commission on Boundary Differences and Voting Systems, *Putting Citizens First: Voting, Boundaries and Representation* (2006) (hereafter Arbuthnott Report), para 3.28.
9 See J Bradbury and J Mitchell, 'Devolution: between governance and territorial politics' (2005) 58 *Parl Affairs* 287 at 290–291.
10 Arbuthnott Report, above n 8, paras 2.11–2.13. The Commission did however recommend that STV should be introduced for European Parliament elections in Scotland by 2009: para 2.13.
11 The Commission considered and rejected the idea of a single vote multi-member system in which the elector's constituency vote would be presumed to be her choice for the list party also.
12 Arbuthnott Report, above n 8, para 4.48.
13 See Scottish Affairs Committee, above n 4; Arbuthnott Report, above n 8, paras 4.62–4.69.
14 Arbuthnott Report, above n 8, para 4.66.
15 Arbuthnott Report, above n 8, para 4.67.

The representatives: profile, roles and mandates

The composition of the Scottish Parliament is distinctive. There is a significantly higher number of women in the Parliament than in the House of Commons.[16] This increase is probably attributable in large part to the willingness of the political parties to engage in affirmative action aimed at placing women candidates in a proportion of winnable seats, and in prominent positions on their party lists.[17] There are also more members from minor parties and a number of independents.[18] This is attributable to the mixed electoral system, with its element of proportional representation. Citizen awareness of their representatives is, however, often limited. The Arbuthnott Commission has recommended that after every election, information should be supplied to every household detailing their representatives and their responsibilities, and there should be a publicly accessible national resource providing advice on how to contact elected representatives and public bodies.[19]

The Scottish Parliament Procedures Committee has identified the three main roles of MSPs as being (1) to pass laws; (2) to keep a check on the Scottish Executive; and (3) to act as a forum for national debate and for expressing the opinions of the Scottish people.[20] The principal distinction from the Westminster Parliament in terms of representation within the Scottish Parliament relates to the presence of two types of member: the constituency and the regional (or 'list') MSPs. After some initial uncertainty about the respective roles of the two types of MSP, clarification emerged in the form of principles proposed by a working group and incorporated into the Members' Code of Conduct, which states that all MSPs have equal formal and legal status.[21]

The orientation of constituency and regional MSPs towards constituency work or issues with a more regional or national focus is not determined principally by the basis of their election. Regional MSPs do engage in constituency work, a fact which has generated tension with some sitting constituency MSPs, who sometimes regard the intervention of the regional member as an attempt to build support within the constituency for a future electoral contest.[22] The Arbuthnott Commission has proposed changes to the roles and relations between regional and constituency MSPs, recommending that Scottish Parliament regions should be redrawn into more 'relevant and serviceable' areas and that the code of conduct for MSPs should be revised to provide a clear and positive role for both constituency and regional members to enhance representation for constituents and improve scrutiny of local and national services.[23] All MSPs

---

16 In the 2003–07 Parliament there are fifty women MSPs, constituting approximately 36 per cent of the total membership.
17 See A McHarg, 'Quotas for women! The Sex Discrimination (Election Candidates) Act 2002' (2006) 33 JLS 141.
18 In the 2003–07 Parliament there are five independent MSPs; seven representing the Green Party; six representing the Scottish Socialist Party and one representing the Senior Citizens' Unity Party.
19 Arbuthnott Report, above n 8, paras 5.39–5.42.
20 Scottish Parliament Procedures Committee, *The Founding Principles of the Scottish Parliament* (3rd report session 1, 2003, SP Paper 818).
21 Code of Conduct for Members of the Scottish Parliament (2nd edn, 2003), Section 9.2.3, Annexe 5.
22 T C Lundberg, 'Second class representatives? Mixed-member PR in Britain' (2006) 59 *Parl Affairs* 60.
23 Arbuthnott Report, above n 8, para 2.14

should be entitled to do constituency work, and all to deal with wider area issues, with a presumption that constituency MSPs will primarily do the former and regional MSPs the latter. These recommendations are welcome, and it is to be hoped that they will help to tackle the need to promote acceptance of the valuable functions which regional MSPs perform within the scheme of representation created by devolution. These functions pertain to the direct representation of constituents, responding to the concerns of Scottish electors, and also to the indirect promotion of better representation by MSPs: this happens through the introduction of an element of competition into the provision of representation. Voters dissatisfied with the response of a constituency MSP can approach the regional member for aid. And longer term, the presence of the regional member – who will often be a potential challenger for the constituency at a subsequent election – provides an incentive to the constituency MSP to provide a high level of representation to electors.[24]

Election law as a reserved matter

The franchise at local government elections – from which the right to vote in Scottish Parliament elections is derived – is named as a specific reservation in Schedule 5 to the Scotland Act 1998.[25] The Scottish Parliament is therefore unable to amend its own election law. It cannot decide to implement a reformed vision of the right to vote, such as, for example, reducing the voting age to sixteen or (more controversially) granting the right to vote to 'expatriate' Scots living elsewhere in the United Kingdom. Does this restriction matter? Arguably yes, because a parliament which cannot stipulate the boundaries of its electorate has no opportunity to redefine 'the people' by whom it is chosen (subject to the relevant human rights constraints). The Scottish Parliament must wait upon Westminster to act.

The rights to vote and to stand as a candidate in Scottish Parliament elections

Because the right to vote in Scottish parliamentary elections is governed by the franchise in local government elections it extends to peers and to European Union citizens resident in Scotland.[26] Otherwise, the voter qualifications are as for Westminster elections: Commonwealth citizenship (excluding persons who require, but have not obtained, leave to remain in the United Kingdom) or Irish citizenship; being eighteen or over on the day of the poll; and not being subject to any legal incapacity to vote (such as being a convicted prisoner).[27] All electors must be registered to vote, which requires residence in a constituency, or 'notional' residence on the part of homeless persons and others entitled to make

24 See Lundberg, above n 22, pp 72–75.
25 All other aspects of local election law are devolved.
26 Local Government Elections (Changes to the Franchise and Qualifications of Members) Regulations 1995 (SI 1995/1948).
27 Representation of the People Act 1983, ss 1–4 (as amended by Representation of the People Act 2000). On prisoners see *Hirst v United Kingdom (No 2)* App No 74025/01, 6 Oct 2005 in which a Grand Chamber of the European Court of Human Rights ruled that the blanket ban on prisoner voting employed by the UK (and adopted for Scottish Parliament elections) constituted a disproportionate interference with their rights under Article 3 of Protocol 1 of the Convention.

a 'declaration of local connection' in place of supplying an orthodox residential address.[28]

The rules governing candidature are similar to those governing Westminster elections, with modifications appropriate to the nature of the devolved system. Citizens of the European Union resident in Scotland are eligible, as are peers.[29] Certain of the exclusions listed in the House of Commons Disqualification Act 1975 apply.[30] The law currently permits candidates to stand simultaneously in constituency elections and in regional contests. There has been some debate about the desirability of these dual candidacies, since it provides an almost guaranteed seat to those unsuccessful constituency candidates favoured with a secure place on the party's list.[31] This matter was considered by the Arbuthnott Commission, which concluded that restricting dual candidacies would be undemocratic: its report found no survey evidence to suggest that dual candidacy is an issue for voters or a disincentive to their participation in the political process.[32] Further, banning it may breed tensions between constituency and regional candidates of a political party, the fortunes of the former being diminished by a strong performance by the latter. Smaller political parties would likely withhold candidates from constituency contests, fielding them instead in regional contests in which their chances are greater. This would arguably diminish 'the quality of constituency contests and unduly favour incumbent candidates'.[33]

The rights to vote and to stand for election contained in Article 3 of Protocol 1 of the European Convention on Human Rights,[34] and guaranteed by the Human Rights Act 1998, provide substantial protection to citizens seeking to challenge restrictive election laws. Their relevance to the scheme of devolved democracy lies in their potential application to any UK laws purporting to inhibit the electoral participation of Scottish voters in the institutions of devolved governance.[35]

Local government and representation

The arrangements for local government are a devolved matter. This includes the electoral system, and systems of local authority finance. The Local Governance (Scotland) Act 2004 has introduced a new voting system for local elections: the single transferable vote (STV). This reform was initiated in response to commitments made by the Scottish Labour party to its partners in coalition, the Scottish Liberal Democrats, and following the recommendations of the McIntosh

28 Representation of the People Act 1983, s 7A, added by Representation of the People Act 2000, s 6.
29 Scotland Act 1998, s 16.
30 Thus judges, civil servants, members of the armed forces and police, and members of non-Commonwealth legislatures are excluded. See also the disqualification of office holders specified in the Scottish Parliament (Disqualification) Order 2003 (SI 2003/409).
31 Such concerns have led to a proposed ban: see the Scottish Parliament (Candidates) Bill 2006, introduced by Lord Foulkes. See too *Better Governance for Wales* (Cm 6582, 2005) and the Government of Wales Act 2006, s 7, implementing a corresponding prohibition for Welsh Assembly candidates.
32 Arbuthnott Report, above n 8, paras 4.55 ff.
33 Arbuthnott Report, above n 8, paras 4.57–4.58.
34 'The High Contracting Parties undertake to hold free elections at reasonable intervals by secret ballot, under conditions which will ensure the free expression of the opinion of the people in the choice of the legislature'. This provision applies only to bodies which have legislative functions, such as the Scottish Parliament and not, therefore, to local government.
35 See, eg, *Hirst v United Kingdom (No 2)*, above n 27; H Davis, 'Constitutional reform in the United Kingdom and the right to free and fair elections' (1999) 4 EHRLR 411.

Report.[36] It has long been a goal of the Liberal Democrats to secure proportional representation for local government in Scotland. This new voting system will take effect for the first time at the local elections in May 2007.

Aside from its intrinsic merits as an electoral system, about which there is continuing debate, the introduction of STV for local elections is undoubtedly a noteworthy feature of the operation of devolved democracy. This reform is an instance of devolution generating potentially very significant reforms to democratic practice. The devolved institutions are passing on some of their own characteristics to governance at the local level: local representation will be made more proportional; and councils rendered more susceptible to coalition building. As commented during the debates on the Bill, the reform 'is about widening access and encouraging more people to consider standing, because they will be able to see that they have more chance of being elected'.[37]

Better representation or more representatives?

In the devolved regime, each Scottish citizen has a much expanded range of representatives. Each voter is now represented by eight MSPs (one constituency and seven regional members) and by one MP, as well as by local councillors and members of the European Parliament. Does this increase in the number of representatives mean that Scots are now better represented? Certainly, the voter can seek advice from a wider range of representatives on a particular problem, and perhaps hope to gain more guidance and support than was previously available. Voters may, however, be uncertain which representative to approach regarding a particular issue, and be deterred by this from approaching any: information and education is certainly needed (as the Arbuthnott Report recommends) to make voters aware of the respective roles of the various representatives.[38] Quality of representation requires more than merely an increase in the quantity of representatives. It requires also that the role of each representative is clearly defined, and clearly communicated to voters. It requires also that representatives are accessible, responsive and committed both to constituency duties and to their parliamentary roles.

Better representation depends on the performance of the Parliament as a whole as a forum in which the interests of Scottish citizens are identified, advocated and assessed. If the Parliament is providing a more fully considered and articulated account of those interests than was previously offered at Westminster, it may be possible to conclude that better representation is being offered. Certainly, the Parliament – and devolution generally – is allowing the Scottish polity to advance its concerns on matters on which it was not previously possible to differentiate a Scottish view, still less to legislate for it. The provision of free personal care for the elderly and the prohibition of smoking in enclosed public places represent prominent social policies, hallmarked as matters of particular concern to Scottish electors and resulting, arguably, in the more effective representation of Scottish views than was possible pre-devolution.[39]

36 *Report of the Commission on Local Government and the Scottish Parliament* (1999).
37 Tavish Scott MSP, then Deputy Minister for Finance and Public Services, speaking in the Stage 1 debate on the Bill: SPOR, 24 March 2004, col 6990.
38 Arbuthnott Report, above n 8, paras 5.37–5.42.
39 Community Care and Health (Scotland) Act 2002; Smoking, Health and Social Care (Scotland) Act 2005.

DEVOLUTION AND PARTICIPATORY DEMOCRACY

The institutional design of the Scottish Parliament is tailored to accommodate the need to encourage participation in political life by Scottish citizens. There are several features in particular which aim to contribute to a sense of interaction and engagement by individuals with the Parliament. The model of the Parliament is very different from that of Westminster, and designedly so. Citizens are welcomed to take part in, and to be part of, the life of the Parliament. Participation is written into the foundations of institution. The Parliament is reaching out to the citizenry; the extent to which this relationship is genuinely reciprocal is less clear.

Founding principles of the Parliament and participation

The Parliament's founding principles were originally set out by the Constitutional Steering Group (CSG), the body charged by the United Kingdom government with devising rules for the operation of the Parliament.[40] It has been noted that 'the CSG principles could easily have become a relatively meaningless set of pious aspirations, gathering dust on the devolution shelf'.[41] Instead, they have become an integral part of the fabric of the devolved democracy. Those principles are (1) power sharing; (2) accountability; (3) access and participation; and (4) equal opportunities. The Executive has adopted the principles also, as part of the Ministerial Code,[42] and they are mirrored in the Partnership Agreement regulating the coalition.[43] The principles express the following ideas about participation: a participatory system is one which requires that legislators and governors be prepared to share power with the citizenry, recognising that governance is a process in which we all take part if not daily then at least regularly and frequently. Participating only by voting in elections every few years is no substitute, reflecting a transient and rather shallow sharing of authority. Equal opportunities are also central to a participatory regime: participation must be open to all on equal terms. There must be no exclusion based upon discriminatory principles. The principle of accountability, a core practice of representative democracy, is also linked to the development of a participatory democracy: it demands that representatives answer to electors; and electors may exercise an initiative to call their representatives to account as a participatory practice in its own right.

The fact that founding principles have been given formal textual expression in the documents detailing the operation of the devolution framework is a constitutional novelty within the United Kingdom system of government. They do not, however, represent entirely novel ideas and indeed, it may be suggested that the principles were patterned on United Kingdom practice. Ideas and practices of accountability have, for example, long been an integral part of the Westminster system of government.[44]

On the other hand, the principle of access and participation is more innovative. It stipulates that 'The Scottish Parliament should be accessible, open, responsive and

---

40 Report of the Consultative Steering Group on the Scottish Parliament, *Shaping Scotland's Parliament* (1998).
41 B Winetrobe in J Jowell and D Oliver (eds), *The Changing Constitution* (5th edn, 2004), pp 175–176.
42 Available at *http://www.scotland.gov.uk/About/Ministers/14944/684*.
43 *A Partnership for a Better Scotland*, available at *http://www.Scotland.gov.uk/library5/government/pfbs.pdf*. On the status of the Principles, see Procedures Committee, above n 20.
44 See further, Chapter 7 in this volume.

develop procedures which make possible a participative approach to the development, consideration and scrutiny of policy and legislation.'[45] It is essential to the task of promoting citizen participation that the Parliament be seen by those it serves as an accessible place, both in its physical form and in its institutional aspects.

The Parliament building

The physical incarnation of the Parliament – the both beleaguered and feted building at Holyrood – has its own contribution to make to the development of accessibility and openness, and hence participation, within the new democracy. 'Parliamentary buildings are of particular metaphorical importance, as theatres in which countries act out their political lives.'[46] On this view, one clearly taken by its architects, the Scottish Parliament building is a powerful symbol of the distinctiveness of devolved governance. Critics of the building disagree, challenging variously its cost, location and design.

The building is purpose-built, which strengthens its status as a symbol of a new democracy rather than merely an adaptation of existing forms. The architecture is unmistakably modern; striking but less intimidating than the grand scale and gothic flourishes of the Palace of Westminster. The chamber is similarly distinctive, with its circular form and relatively large public gallery, both features suggesting inclusion and access. This is intended to be a place of debate and exchange between representatives in the welcome presence of citizens, rather than a forum for battles between polarised adversaries spectated upon by strangers. The reflections of Scots on Scottish democracy are inscribed in a tangible, accessible form on the exterior Canongate Wall of the Parliament. The building conveys a sense of being a place where shared aspiration and endeavour might counter the new Parliament's lack of history and tradition.

Although still young, the Scottish Parliament building is making its own contribution to the creation of an inclusive sense of Scottish citizenship. Citizens are encouraged to join in by, in the first instance, coming in to the place where the Parliament is held. Viewing the proceedings from the public gallery of the chamber or a committee room remains a rather passive means of interacting with the work of the Parliament, but it is nonetheless a form of participation which allows the visitors to hear representatives speak directly rather than through mediated reports. This may promote a sense of more direct connection to, and perhaps even a desire to take a more active part in, the political process. Even if it does not, simply watching parliamentarians at work is to witness their conduct in formal circumstances in which their duty of accountability is underlined by the presence of informal auditors.

Public access to the Parliament

All meetings of the Parliament, and most of those of its committees and subcommittees, take place in public.[47] Public access to the Parliament is protected

---

45 *Scotland's Parliament* (1999)
46 J Hastings and H Thomas, 'Accessing the nation: disability, political inclusion and the built form' (2005) 42 *Urban Studies* 527 at 532.
47 Standing Orders, rule 15.1. The exclusions regarding committees are set out in rule 12.3.5.

by the Standing Orders of the Parliament, which state that visitors are to be admitted to the public gallery of the chamber at all times.[48] The place of meeting is generally Holyrood, but the Standing Orders permit the meeting of the Parliament at any other place in Scotland.[49] Prior to the completion of the Holyrood building, and when the Parliament was required to vacate its temporary premises in the Church of Scotland General Assembly building, it did relocate to other Scottish cities.[50] It has not done so since and would no doubt be criticised on cost grounds should it do so. However, for citizens living at some distance from the capital and unwilling or unable to travel to visit the Parliament, mobile meetings might prove a useful means of facilitating access to and stimulating interest in the life and work of the Parliament. They would certainly raise the profile of the Parliament in the city or region, and spark political debate, even if predominantly about the Parliament's effectiveness and its cost. It may be argued that such visits would be of interest only to the political elite and to those citizens already converted to the Parliament's cause. While there may be some truth in this, the presence of the Parliament in a person's home town might generate or renew interest in the life and work of the institution in a way in which a trip to Edinburgh to see it in action might not. It would perhaps also promote a sense of ownership, of all Scots having the freedom to receive the Parliament into their (or a neighbouring) community rather than only a right to visit its static base.

Petitioning the Parliament

The public petitions system is perhaps one of the most striking developments in the new Scottish system of parliamentary democracy.[51] It enables individuals or groups to petition the Parliament directly on issues of concern.[52] There is no need for the petitioner to acquire a list of signatures of support, although some choose to do so.[53] The CSG took the view that 'it is an important principle that the Scottish people should be able to petition the Parliament directly'. Petitioning was viewed by the CSG not as a matter of rights, but as an aspect of the principle of power sharing, thus reinforcing the vision of an inclusive and non-confrontational politics in which citizens speak to their Parliament rather than battling to assert their rights against it. Petitions are, quite correctly, perceived as vehicles for promoting a political goal, rather than as a complaint mechanism for consumers of democratic services.[54]

Petitions are considered by the Public Petitions Committee, one of the mandatory committees of the Parliament. The Committee may take such action as it considers

---

48 Standing Orders, rule 15.2.
49 Standing Orders, rule 2.7.
50 The Parliament met in Glasgow in 2000 and in Aberdeen in 2002.
51 This is not a complete innovation, as there was a public petition system in the pre-Union Scottish Parliament. Petition systems are also common in the new democracies of central and eastern Europe: see D Arter, 'The Scottish Committees and the goal of a "New Politics": a verdict on the first four years of the Parliament' (2004) 12 *Journal of Contemporary European Studies* 71 at 75–76.
52 Standing Orders, rule 15.4.
53 The CSG felt that a signature threshold would discriminate against individuals living in remote areas and that it would in practice be difficult to verify the signatures: *Shaping Scotland's Parliament*, above n 40, Section 3.5, para 16.
54 See Arter, above n 51, p 76: 'The CSG viewed the right to petition not from a legalistic perspective of "basic rights" but as an important manifestation of the power-sharing principle.'

appropriate, including referring the petition to the Scottish Ministers, or to any other committee of the Parliament, or recommending that legislation be initiated.[55] The Committee has been called 'more symbolic than effective'.[56] While this may be a fair comment, it need not be a criticism. The Committee should be assessed at least as much on the basis of the processes of participation which it has the potential to open up to the public, as on its success in converting petitions into policies or laws. Viewed in terms of the opportunities for dialogue and exchange which it offers, the petitions procedure has been relatively successful. Petitioning has proved popular with the public, the Committee considering over a hundred petitions annually.[57] However, the opportunities for participation which the petition process offers are, like many other aspects of the new democracy, rather too contingent upon the motivation of the already politically engaged and aware electors. Little express encouragement is available to the disconnected and disengaged citizen who may view voting as a largely redundant exercise and is in that case unlikely to regard petitioning as a satisfactory remedy for the defects of electoral democracy. Even among the active electorate, there are surely many voters who respond rather passively to the choices offered by the ballot paper and who may need more than a user-friendly website to encourage them to become active communicants with their Parliament on issues of concern.

Parliamentary committees and participation

Theories of participatory democracy emphasise the enhancement of participation by individuals and groups of citizens within the political process in order to offset the dominance of the other – institutional – actors, principally parliaments, governments and their members. However, the emphasis upon citizens as participants does not diminish the role which institutional actors may perform in producing a more participative democracy. This may happen through institutional design or reform aimed at fostering citizen participation directly, or indirectly, by mediating between the dominant actors and individuals. The committees of the Scottish Parliament fit into this latter category: they are designed to be, just as their Westminster counterparts have evolved to become, effective participants in the democratic dialogue between citizens, government and Parliament. Committee proceedings, like that of the Parliament itself, are open to the public.[58] Committees also have a peripatetic aspect, sitting around Scotland to hear views, thus generating openness and accessibility to a wider number of people.[59] Convenerships of the committees are not in the gift of the governing parties. Committees employ the participative practices of consultation and inquiry (discussed separately below).

---

55 Standing Orders, rule 6.2. The Committee has not yet used this power to introduce a Bill in response to a petition.
56 J Mitchell in A Trench (ed), *Has Devolution Made a Difference? The State of the Nations 2004* (2004), p 39.
57 Annual reports of the Public Petitions Committee, available at *http://www.scottish.parliament.uk/business/committees/petitions/reports.htm*.
58 Except on certain occasions: see Standing Orders, rules 15.1 and 12.3.5.
59 The first committee to meet outside Edinburgh was the Enterprise and Lifelong Learning Committee in Oct 1999. More recently, the Public Petitions Committee sat in Dunfermline on 30 Jan 2006, following previous meetings in Dundee, Inverness and Ayr.

It is notable that the committees enjoy a right of legislative initiative, enabling them to counter, albeit to a very limited extent, Executive dominance of the law-making agenda.[60] It is expected that committees will engage with the citizenry in consultation about the design and content of their legislative initiatives.[61]

Consultation and inquiry

These two practices offer opportunities for citizen participation in the work of the Parliament. Each committee of the Parliament is empowered to conduct inquiries into such matters within its remit as it may consider appropriate or as the Scottish Parliament or another committee may require.[62] Such inquiries may be into legislative proposals (the committee's own or Executive plans). Alternatively, a committee may inquire into non-legislative matters, such as an issue of current affairs, or into a subject referred to it by the Public Petitions Committee. As part of such an inquiry, a committee may consult the public on the issues raised by the exercise.[63] This has become an established part of parliamentary practice, but the opportunity for participation which it offers remains restricted to those with the facilities and awareness to access the consultation details. By far the simplest way to do this is electronically, but this remains a medium which may exclude many potentially interested persons.

It is a distinctive feature of the legislative process that a Member's Bill must be preceded by a public consultation on the policy objectives of the Bill.[64] This consultation must last for at least twelve weeks.[65] The MSP may alternatively supply a written statement of reasons why, in her opinion, a case for the proposed Bill has already been made out with reference to specified published material, thereby making consultation unnecessary.[66] In such a case, a committee reviews this statement, and may decide that it is not satisfied that consultation is unnecessary.[67] The final proposal for the Bill must be accompanied by a summary of the consultation responses.[68] At Stage 1 of the Bill's legislative process (when the broad policy objectives of the Bill are put to the Parliament), the lead committee may recommend that it be voted down because the consultation on the draft does not demonstrate a reasonable case for the policy objectives or that

---

60 On this power see Arter, above n 51. The legislative agenda is still heavily dominated by the Executive. During its first session, the Scottish Parliament passed sixty-two Acts, of which fifty originated in the Executive and only three were initiated by committees (Protection from Abuse (Scotland) Act 2001, initiated by the Justice 1 Committee; Scottish Parliamentary Standards Commissioner Act 2002, by the Standards Committee; and Commissioner for Children and Young People (Scotland) Act 2003, by the Education, Culture and Sport Committee. In its second session, the Parliament has passed the Interests of Members of the Scottish Parliament Act 2006, initiated by the Standards and Public Appointments Committee.

61 Arter, above n 51, p 75.

62 Standing Orders, rule 6.2.2.

63 Current and past consultations can be viewed at *http://www.scottish.parliament.uk/vli/consultations/index.htm*.

64 Standing Orders, rule 9.14.3.

65 Standing Orders, rule 9.14.3(a).

66 Standing Orders, rule 9.14.3(b).

67 Standing Orders, rule 9.14.6.

68 Standing Orders, rule 9.14.9.

the proposal does not demonstrate that legislation is necessary to achieve those objectives.[69]

A further opportunity for participation by individuals and interested groups is in the work of the Parliament's many Cross-Party Groups, bodies concerned with a range of issues from cycling to human rights. Such groups must be parliamentary in character (that is, each must comprise at least five MSPs, at least one representing each party or group in the Parliament, in addition to any non-parliamentary members) and have a purpose which is of genuine public interest.[70] It is for the Standards Committee to determine this when a group applies for recognition. The meetings of such groups are held in public, and members of the public may speak (but not vote). Although participation in such a group (or attendance at its meetings) does not constitute taking part in a formal consultation, it does offer those involved the opportunity to engage directly with parliamentarians, and to take part in an enterprise with close links with the Parliament itself.

The Scottish Executive and citizen participation

Although most emphasis has been placed by politicians and commentators upon the ways in which the citizen may take part in the life and work of the Parliament, participation in the activities of the Executive is also an important, if less developed, theme within the devolution arrangements. The nature of the role of an executive obviously precludes some of the forms of participation which it is open to parliamentarians to offer. Few would suggest, for example, that the meetings of the Scottish Ministers be open to public scrutiny. There are, however, other ways in which the Executive seeks to encourage the public to engage with their governors. These methods are, however, rather weak and minimal when compared with the opportunities for participation offered by the Parliament. Taking part in government is still largely confined to a few peripheral aspects of executive activity, which have the capacity to generate only a rather superficial sense of connectedness between the citizen and the Executive.

The Executive regards consultation as an integral part of its working methods: 'Scottish Executive consultation exercises aim to provide opportunities for all those who wish to express their opinions on a proposed area of work to do so in ways which will inform and enhance that work.'[71] The Executive presents a consultation paper on the topic in question, and invites responses either to specific questions or on general themes. The Executive has so far demonstrated great zeal as regards this project, with approximately 700 archived consultations listed on its website alongside numerous current and forthcoming exercises. This apparent appetite for the views of the electorate is commendable, even if the consequences for policy-making of such consultation are not easy to determine.

As to the legislative process, consultation on Executive Bills may take place, but is not required. If it does happen, the nature and outcome of the consultation must be summarised in the Policy Memorandum accompanying the Bill.[72]

---

69 Standing Orders, rule 9.14.18.
70 Standards Committee, *Report on Regulation of Cross-Party Groups* (2nd Report, 1999, SP Paper 34).
71 *http://www.scotland.gov.uk/Consultations/About.*
72 Standing Orders, rule 9.3.3.

E-democracy and participation

The notion of electronic (e-)democracy is a prominent one within the political landscape of the twenty-first century.[73] The benefits it offers are stated to be of two types: the use of information communication technologies (ICT) to promote the efficient running of parliaments and other democratic institutions;[74] and the facilitation of participation by citizens in democratic life. E-democracy has been a prominent part of the Scottish Parliament's agenda since its inception.[75] Electors can watch the proceedings of the Parliament live on the web; petition the Parliament by email; or track the progress of a Bill on its web pages. The Executive is similarly enthusiastic about the prospect of digital democracy, being committed to the provision of all government services online. When it comes to polling day, however, voting so far remains a paper exercise, both as regards the casting and counting of votes.[76]

However well developed and funded e-democracy facilities are, the difficulty remains that they are arguably of most use to those groups in society which are already most likely to be politically aware and engaged. A related point is that access to the internet is not universally enjoyed within Scotland. Not all homes have internet access;[77] not all Scots have the ICT skills to engage with the Executive, the Parliament or its committees in this way. Not all those who do have access to the internet (at home or elsewhere) have the political education, awareness or desire to use it to reach out to their elected representatives or otherwise to take part in the democratic process. Promoting ICT skills and facilities and educating about the e-democracy opportunities that it offers is a prominent and now undoubtedly permanent part of the political agenda. There is a risk, however, that as this rises up the agenda, the relative emphasis on the development of other (non-electronic) avenues of connectedness to the electorate may be diminished. The latter strategy might reach more of those whose financial means or lack of confidence in their technological skills excludes them from the e-democracy regime. We ought also to remember that for all its promise of improved accessibility, e-democracy offers a form of participation in which electors relate to disembodied institutions or individuals. While this may suit some, others may consider it an impoverished way of taking part. It has also been commented that the use of ICT by political parties generally has served to give them greater control over the electorate, rather than to build structures

---

73 J Morison and D R Newman, 'On-line citizenship: consultation and participation in New Labour's Britain and beyond' (2001) 15 *International Review of Law Computers and Technology* 171; C F Smith and P Gray, 'The Scottish Parliament: [Re-]shaping parliamentary democracy in the information age' (1999) 52 *Parl Affairs* 429 at 429: 'the potential of ICTs to enable and support new democratic arrangements has, for the first time, become a visible stream in Scottish political discourse'. For a critical appraisal see V Sobchack, 'Democratic franchise and the electronic frontier' (2005) 27 *Futures* 725.

74 Smith and Gray, above n 73, p 436.

75 See *Scotland's Parliament, Scotland's Right* (1995), the final report of the Scottish Constitutional Convention; this is also reflected in the work of the CSG.

76 The Arbuthnott Commission has recommended that electronic vote counting be instituted by 2011: see above n 8, para 4.64.

77 Estimates of the extent of the so-called 'digital divide' vary: Smith and Gray, above n 73, p 435, suggested that only 10 per cent of homes are connected. The Executive's report on its policy on *Digital Inclusion: Connecting Scotland's People* (2001), which is currently being reviewed, claimed that 25 per cent of homes are online. It is likely that the proportion of homes which are online has increased significantly since these estimates were produced.

of mass participation.[78] It is perhaps not terribly surprising, although nonetheless worrying, that ICT tends to promote a perception of citizens as customers of political parties and clients of government, rather than as democratic actors.

Local governance and participation

Although often perhaps demoted in popular perception to the rank of a rather inconsequential aspect of democratic life, local governance has as much (and on occasion more) relevance to our daily lives than national government. Its concerns are often those we notice most vividly and immediately. Despite this, rates of participation in local government elections are generally lower than at parliamentary elections. At the 1999 local elections 59.58 per cent voted, and 49.6 per cent in 2003. Various possibilities exist to try to tackle this problem. One involves the use of so-called 'pilot schemes', designed to facilitate electoral participation at the local level by employing alternative methods of voting.[79] The pilots conducted so far have included the use of such techniques as all-postal ballots and mobile voting booths. As the conduct of local elections is a devolved matter, responsibility for instituting and managing such pilots now lies with the Executive. The techniques piloted ought to be monitored carefully to ensure that any increase in participation is not outweighed by the potential disadvantages of the method of voting being tested. If posting a ballot is more convenient – and can be safeguarded from the risks of fraud – the use of all-postal ballots may seem like a desirable reform. However, if all votes are cast by post rather than in a traditional polling station, this may encourage electors to view voting as a facet of private life rather than as a civic act. This in turn may discourage political debate and exchange by electors. Similar arguments may be made against other sorts of so-called 'remote voting' involving technologies such as text messaging and electronic voting. If taking part in elections comes to have the same value to citizens as acts such as paying a bill online or arranging to meet a friend by text, we risk losing some of the special character of democratic participation. It is important that we do not render the act of voting indistinct from the ways in which we take part in private, social and commercial life.

The Scottish Local Government (Elections) Act 2002 provided for the combining of local authority elections and Scottish Parliament elections. The rationale for this was to increase turnout at the polls for the former, by capturing voters who had turned out to vote for MSPs. The evidence that this has succeeded is far from clear.[80] The Arbuthnott Commission reviewed this practice and concluded that, on balance, local and Scottish Parliament elections should be decoupled.[81] This is not only to reduce the risk of voter confusion when presented with two different voting systems on the same day, but to counter the relegation of local election issues, which have tended to become eclipsed in media coverage and public debate by the higher profile Scottish Parliament elections. If the elections are decoupled – and the reasons for the recommendation do seem strong – there is a risk that cutting local

---

78 Smith and Gray, above n 73, p 439.
79 These were instituted by the Representation of the People Act 2000.
80 See the discussion of turnout at the 2003 elections in the Electoral Commission report, *Scottish Elections 2003, Official Report on the Scottish Parliament and Local Government Elections, 1 May 2003.*
81 Arbuthnott Report, above n 8, para 4.92.

elections loose from the Scottish parliamentary election timetable, and presenting voters with a poll based on a new and unfamiliar voting system may result in even higher rates of abstention.

A participatory democracy?

There is no doubt that devolution has brought changes to the ways in which Scottish citizens may participate in democratic life. It has also, by definition, offered more electoral opportunities. It does not necessarily follow, however, that the resulting democracy is genuinely more participatory in nature than its predecessor. It is certainly clear that the idea of enhancing electoral participation by facilitating other ways of taking part has formed a prominent part both in the design and in the practice of the Parliament. This does not seem, however, to have resulted in radical reform to the patterns of participation evident in the pre-devolution democracy.

The quest of the architects and actors of devolution to create a more genuinely participatory democracy has been qualified from the outset by the dominance of ideas of representative democracy within the United Kingdom political system, and the centrality of the practice of voting to that system. The aim has been to modify representative democracy, not to replace it. However participative the lives of citizens become, the central method of taking part in democratic life in Scotland is intended to remain voting. That does not mean that electoral democracy has remained unchanged by devolution. There are now more opportunities to participate in elections and a variety of different electoral systems to govern the outcomes. It is as yet unclear whether these changes have caused, or are likely to trigger, a change in the patterns or rates of electoral participation by Scottish electors. The devolution strategy of widening access and participation aims not only to offer alternatives to electoral participation, but also to boost voter turnout by reaching and engaging with electors who have previously chosen to abstain. These attempts are not so far proving particularly successful. The numbers of voters turning out to choose MSPs is relatively low. The turnout for the 1999 election was 59 per cent (significantly lower than the 71.3 per cent attained in the 1997 UK general election).[82] In 2003 turnout had fallen to 49.4 per cent.[83] Of special concern are the high rates of non-voting within economically disadvantaged and socially deprived groups.[84] The Arbuthnott Commission noted accordingly that it was 'concerned that differential turnout among social groups is likely to have negative consequences for democracy and the quality of the representation they receive'.[85] How, then, can participation in the Parliament's elections be promoted?

A simple and potentially effective means of trying to revivify electoral participation would be to establish a national holiday on polling day. The devolved institutions would arguably have the power to do this.[86] This may seem

---

82 See SPICe Research Paper 99/1: *Scottish Parliament Election Results*, 6 May 1999.
83 See SPICe Research Paper 03/25: *Election 2003*. See also D Denver and G Hands, 'Exploring variations of turnout: constituencies and wards in the Scottish Parliament elections of 1999 and 2003' (2004) 6 *British J of Pol and Int Rels* 527.
84 Arbuthnott Report, above n 8, para 6.6
85 Arbuthnott Report, above n 8, para 6.6.
86 Time is reserved, but not public holidays; however, there is the possibility that such a holiday, if regarded as being established exclusively for electoral purposes, might be regarded as part of the administration of parliamentary elections, and thus reserved to Westminster.

like a rather superficial suggestion, but it is based on the same ideas as those which underpin philosophies of participatory democracy.[87] It might encourage participation at the polls by removing the arguments of inconvenience or pressure of time. It would provide an opportunity for reflection prior to voting. And it would celebrate the occasion of the election as a shared public event, fostering a sense (even if minimal) of citizens taking part in a collective venture. Objections about cost would undoubtedly arise, but could be answered in terms of the projected benefit to the democracy of marking the special status of election days in this way.

A further source of suggestions for approaching this issue is the report of the Arbuthnott Commission. The report as a whole, as its title (*Putting Citizens First*) suggests, demonstrates an admirable concern with the position of the citizen as democratic participant. The review of constituency boundaries and voting systems, which might easily have been dominated by considerations of geography, statistics and electoral arithmetic, is rendered eminently more successful by its emphasis on the place of the citizen-participant within this matrix. The Commission has recommended that much greater stress be placed on educating school pupils about how citizens take part in democracy. There should also be a publicly accessible national resource providing advice about how to contact elected representatives and public bodies. These, combined with the main recommendations of the report regarding voting systems and boundaries, lead the Commission to the ultimately optimistic conclusion that '[t]here is a considerable potential for positive and radical renewal of participation'.[88]

The relationship between voting and taking part in the other forms of participation offered by devolution is an interesting and complex one. One might speculate that many, if not most, of those individuals taking advantage of the new non-electoral methods of participation are also active voters. It takes a certain minimum level of political commitment and awareness to engage in the ways offered by the Scottish Parliament, and this is found more commonly (although not exclusively) in those who are already active voters. Of course, not all non-voters are politically disengaged or unaware: some have made a conscious – perhaps even conscientious – decision to abstain from voting and to remain otherwise connected to political life. They may disdain the politics of electoral competition but enjoy the chance to take part in democratic life by petitioning the Parliament, for example. Those non-voters who are more fundamentally disengaged, however, are unlikely to exploit the opportunities for non-electoral participation which devolution has brought. Those parts of Scottish society which are trapped in a cycle of perpetual non-voting are unlikely to be aided into a more active citizenship by the range of non-electoral participations currently on offer. It must be ensured that non-electoral participation does not become the prerogative of the already politically literate and engaged, and that it reaches the needs of the under-enfranchised, those who possess an equal right to vote in law but an unequal propensity, for whatever reason, to exercise it in practice.

---

87 And has been advanced for elections in the United States by J S Fishkin and B Ackerman in *Deliberation Day* (2005). The purpose of the holiday they advocate would be to encourage voters to discuss – deliberate – the relevant electoral issues.

88 Arbuthnott Report, above n 8, para 6.9.

NON-DEVOLVED DEMOCRACY

Non-devolved democracy refers to all those aspects of Scottish democratic life which continue to be conducted principally at the United Kingdom level. Scottish MPs properly continue to enjoy full rights to participate in debate and to vote on those issues in the Commons. More controversially, they enjoy such rights regarding Commons debates and votes on matters of English home affairs which correspond to matters devolved to the Scottish institutions. This enables them to vote on proposed measures concerning, for example, health, education or hunting with hounds in England and Wales. This clearly represents a disequilibrium in the democratic system: English MPs could not vote on the smoking ban in Scotland enacted by the Scottish Parliament in the Smoking, Health and Social Care (Scotland) Act 2005, but Scottish MPs may join in the making – or thwarting – of a corresponding law for England. This ought to be a matter of concern to all democrats. The problem is one of a series of questions which have arisen concerning the governance of England in the post-devolution era, now characterised in an expanding literature as 'the English question': how should the constituent nations of the United Kingdom be represented in the Westminster Parliament, given that not all of those nations have devolved government and those that do enjoy differing degrees of devolution? Should there be a separate English Parliament? Or perhaps a reconstituted version of the Westminster Parliament sitting when appropriate as an exclusively English parliament to pass England-only laws (by restricting membership of legislative committees to English MPs, for example)? If Scottish MPs are to be denied rights to participate or to vote on devolved matters, how ought that reform to be implemented? Is the intervention of law required or would self-regulation by Parliament or even self-restraint by the Scottish MPs themselves be sufficient?

Space does not permit a full analysis of the extensive range of issues which the 'English question' raises.[89] From the perspective of non-devolved Scottish democracy, the English question compels a timely reassessment of our traditional understanding of the conduct of Scottish representation at Westminster. Scottish MPs represent Scottish citizens in a Parliament which serves the United Kingdom. Devolution has narrowed the role of the Scottish MP, requiring her to represent her electors on reserved matters only. The Scottish MP can no longer represent her electors directly on the whole range of home affairs matters which have been devolved. The relationship between participation in the devolved and non-devolved democracies is also complex. Which level of democracy – devolved or non-devolved – will Scottish citizens come to regard as the principal locus of their participative efforts? If the answer is devolved democracy – as seems feasible given the expanded opportunities for participation which it offers – what impact might this have on their perceptions of, and willingness to take part in, non-devolved democracy? It is too early in the devolution experiment to speculate usefully about these issues. Studies of voter turnout and attitude may over time suggest some answers. The relationship between the devolved and non-devolved democracies – as regards both representation and participation – is clearly likely to remain both interesting and dynamic.

89 See R Hazell, *The English Question* (2006).

CONCLUSION

Democracy in devolved Scotland may be described as predominantly representative and only partly participatory in character. The manner in which citizens take part has been given fuller and more consistent consideration during the process of setting up devolution and since the devolution reforms were instituted. The opportunities for participation remain, however, rather limited and citizens need to become acclimatised to the idea of doing some governing directly. 'Our democracy is still one in which we send others away to do it – in other words, democracy is done for us, not by us.'[90] Participating in a democracy is a responsibility. It demands commitment, time, effort and optimism. It is a civic duty with the potential to enrich – and even perhaps to completely reshape – our representative democracy. By taking a more active part, the citizen may also discover a sort of freedom and fulfilment which is absent when her role is restricted to receiving governance from others. It is to be hoped that participation will become a more dominant and well-developed theme in the devolved democracy in coming decades. So far, the promises of a more active citizenship which it offers remain largely unfulfilled.

---

90 Arbuthnott Report, above n 8, para 6.10.

Chapter 6

One Legal System, Two Legislatures: Scottish Law-Making After Devolution

Alan Page

INTRODUCTION

Devolution has meant that Scotland has gone from not having its own dedicated legislature, despite having its own legal system, to having two legislatures – the Scottish Parliament with law-making powers which extend across many aspects of Scottish life, including health, education, housing, land-use planning, agriculture, the environment and the general areas of civil and criminal law;[1] and the Westminster Parliament, which as a sovereign Parliament retains the power to legislate across the whole range of reserved and devolved matters, but which the UK government has said will not normally legislate on devolved matters except with the consent of the Scottish Parliament.[2]

This chapter examines the separate Scottish and United Kingdom dimensions of post-devolution Scottish law-making. The major theme of the chapter is the extent to which the Scottish Parliament is different from Westminster. For the proponents of devolution it was crucial that the Scottish Parliament should not simply be the 'Scottish Westminster'. The other theme is the continuing importance of the Westminster contribution to the Scottish statute book, in the devolved as well as the reserved areas, and hence the importance of the effective parliamentary scrutiny of Scottish provisions in Westminster Bills, at Holyrood as well as Westminster.

THE SCOTTISH DIMENSION

One hundred Acts and counting

Law-making has emerged as one of the defining activities of the Scottish Parliament. In the six years since devolution the Parliament has passed almost one hundred Acts, on subjects ranging from the abolition of feudal tenure to housing and homelessness and from freedom of information to family law, and in so doing confounded the expectations of those who thought that law-making would not feature prominently among the new Parliament's activities. The Consultative

---

1 Introducing the Executive's first legislative programme, the First Minister stressed the range and scope of the Parliament's law-making powers. The Parliament, he said, 'is in charge of a wide sweep of domestic policy, which will touch on the lives of every man, woman and child in the land. This is fundamental, radical change. This is, in every sense, a Parliament' (SPOR, 16 June 1999, col 403).

2 The principal reserved areas include the constitution, tax, social security, employment and trade, all other areas being devolved. For the UK Government's commitment not to legislate on devolved matters except with the consent of the Scottish Parliament, see below, n 101 and accompanying text.

Steering Group, which was set up to recommend the procedures the Parliament might adopt, did not envisage that the Parliament would have to pass significant numbers of Acts each year.[3] There were even some who questioned the need for much legislation in the new Scotland:

> 'So passionate were some of the expectations of devolution that some respectable voices argued that little or no devolved legislation would be needed. A nation that had voted decisively in favour of devolution would require precious little legislative governance.'[4]

Had it been suggested at the outset that in its first session (1999–2003) the Parliament would pass no fewer than sixty-two Bills the likelihood is that the suggestion would have been dismissed as absurd.

Nor has there been any confirmation of suggestions by the former Presiding Officer and others that once the 'backlog' arising from years of Westminster neglect had been cleared the demand for legislation would then drop.[5] Far from decreasing, the supply of legislative proposals appears to have increased to fill the increased time available in which to pass them. In its second session the Parliament has so far passed forty-one Bills with a further seventeen in progress. According to First Scottish Parliamentary Counsel, the demands for legislation from within and outside the devolved government of Scotland exceed its capacity to prepare it and the capacity of the Parliament to pass it, and 'appear to be endless'.[6]

Politicians, not surprisingly, have been quick to contrast the number of Acts passed by the Scottish Parliament with the number of Scottish Acts Westminster might have been expected to pass in the absence of devolution. In the ten years preceding devolution Westminster enacted between four and five Scottish Acts a year (forty-eight Acts between 1990 and 1999), which suggests that the volume of Scottish legislation nearly trebled over the first session of the new Parliament. These figures may exaggerate the extent of the increase. The headline figure of Acts passed by the Westminster Parliament takes no account of Scottish provisions in United Kingdom or Great Britain Bills, while some of the Acts passed by the Scottish Parliament have been very short indeed. Of the sixty-two Acts passed in the first session, more than a third (twenty-three) had fewer than ten sections.[7] Even so, it is undeniable that there has been 'a great increase in the volume of specifically Scottish legislative activity'.[8]

This 'palpable surge' in legislative activity for Scotland has been accompanied by 'a much reduced tendency for Scottish legislation to be borrowed from

---

3 *Shaping Scotland's Parliament, Report of the Consultative Steering Group on the Scottish Parliament* (1998), Section 3.5, para 2.

4 J McCluskie, 'New approaches to UK legislative drafting: the view from Scotland' (2004) 25 *Statute Law Review*, 136 at 138–139.

5 'I think in the fullness of time that backlog will have been cleared and I hope that we will have a little longer at each stage of the legislation than we have now': House of Lords Select Committee on the Constitution, *Devolution: Inter-Institutional Relations in the United Kingdom, Evidence Complete to 10 July 2002*, HL 147 (2001–02), Question 754. See also Procedures Committee, *The Founding Principles of the Scottish Parliament* (3rd Report, 2003), para 332.

6 McCluskie, above n 4, p 139.

7 While devolution has not meant the complete disappearance of 'compound' legislation, ie the practice of legislating on a number of disparate topics in a single Bill, there is less of it than in the past. More generally, the shortness of Acts of the Scottish Parliament is a function of the resources available to prepare them: McCluskie, above n 4, p 137.

8 T Mullen, 'Scottish Parliament legislation 1999–2002' (2003) 9 *European Public Law* 184.

England'.[9] Not only is there a lot more Scottish legislation but there is 'a great reduction in the parallelism with England and Wales that used to be a feature of many Scottish statutes'.[10] It has become customary to emphasise the constraints in the devolution settlement, but what is striking about the devolved Scottish statute book is how few Acts of the Scottish Parliament involve the adaptation of UK or GB-wide policy to take account of differences in Scots law or administration, the traditional form of Scottish legislation. There are instances, but they are concentrated in the first two years of the Parliament.[11] In their place we have seen a considerable increase in the amount of 'home grown' or 'self-generated' legislation. The results may not be eye-catching, as is frequently complained, but devolution has opened up greater scope for the adoption of distinctive policies – for Scottish solutions to Scottish problems – than is sometimes recognised or acknowledged.

This increase in self-generated legislation has not necessarily been at the expense of participation in wider UK developments. The Scottish Ministers have not been able to resist the temptation to help themselves to what the UK government has been doing by way of legislation, but they have been doing so by way of Sewel, or legislative consent, motions, rather than by promoting their own legislation, which underlines the continuing importance of Westminster legislation in the devolved areas.[12] Where the legislative task is simply one of adaptation, the preference would seem to be for it to be left to Westminster, 'who are within limits content to accept what we give them',[13] rather than for it to be undertaken by the Scottish Parliament itself.

Bounded competence

As already noted, the Scottish Parliament was not meant to be simply the 'Scottish Westminster', a 'legislative sausage machine' churning out laws on the Westminster model.[14] It was meant to be 'different'. One respect in which the Parliament clearly is different is that its powers are limited in a way in which, as a matter of strict constitutional theory at least, those of Westminster are not. The limits on the Parliament's legislative competence have a broad 'constitutionalist' as well as a narrower 'division of powers' significance.[15] They are about the protection

---

9 McCluskie, above n 4, p 138. For a more equivocal view, see M Keating, L Stevenson, P Cairney and K Taylor, 'Does devolution make a difference? Legislative output and policy divergence in Scotland' (2003) 9 *Journal of Legislative Studies* 110. On the basis of his analysis of the Scottish Parliament's legislative output over the first three years Mullen concludes that there has been 'significant if not radical policy divergence between Scotland and the rest of the United Kingdom': above n 8, p 185.

10 McCluskie, above n 4, p 138.

11 Census (Amendment) (Scotland) Act 2000, Regulation of Investigatory Powers (Scotland) Act 2000, Transport (Scotland) Act 2001, International Criminal Court (Scotland) Act 2001, Fur Farming (Prohibition) (Scotland) Act 2002 and Freedom of Information (Scotland) Act 2002, plus possibly National Parks (Scotland) Act 2000 and Regulation of Care (Scotland) Act 2000.

12 Below pp 126–129.

13 Interview with Scottish Executive.

14 SPOR, 5 Sept 2001, col 2211, David McLetchie MSP.

15 For Lord Reed the distinction is between restrictions which have 'the character of demarcation lines between the Scottish Parliament and the UK Parliament' and restrictions laying down 'more fundamental principles of a constitutional character': in J Beatson, C Forsyth and I Hare (eds), *Constitutional Reform in the United Kingdom: Principles and Practice* (1998), pp 21–22.

of fundamental rights and freedoms as well as about ensuring that the Scottish Parliament observes the division of competences between Edinburgh and London, and between London and Brussels. The Parliament thus has no power to legislate contrary to Convention rights as well as no power to legislate in relation to reserved matters or contrary to Community law.[16] It also has no power to legislate other than for or in relation to Scotland; in breach of various entrenched enactments, including the Human Rights Act 1998 (HRA), the key provisions of the European Communities Act 1972 which give effect to Community law in the UK, and much of the Scotland Act itself; or to remove the Lord Advocate as head of the system of criminal prosecution and investigation of deaths.[17]

Some of those limits mirror or are the equivalent of the 'limits' on the Westminster Parliament that flow from European Union membership and the 'incorporation' of the European Convention on Human Rights (ECHR). In contrast to the Westminster Parliament, however, the Scottish Parliament is subject to a strong rather than a weak form of judicial review.[18] Should it fail to observe the limits on its competence it is doing something it has no power to do and the courts have the power to strike down its legislation as ultra vires. Under the European Communities Act and the Human Rights Act, by contrast, there is no question of the courts striking down Acts of the Westminster Parliament as invalid; instead they are enjoined, in the case of a conflict with Community law, to deny effect to an Act of Parliament that cannot be read compatibly with 'enforceable Community rights'[19] or, in the case of a conflict with 'Convention rights', given the power to issue a declaration of incompatibility,[20] it being left to the government in both cases to take or to propose such remedial action as it considers appropriate.

At the outset judicial concern was expressed that the 'inescapable fact' that the Scottish Parliament is not a sovereign parliament had not been appreciated by the electorate,[21] but the limits themselves have not so far proved seriously controversial. No sooner had the Parliament's first Bill been enacted, the Mental Health (Public Safety and Appeals) (Scotland) Act 1999, than a challenge was mounted to its competence on human rights grounds.[22] Since then, however, there have been only two other challenges, both involving the Protection of Wild Mammals (Scotland) Act 2002, which is probably the most controversial piece of legislation the Parliament has passed to date.[23] Like the first challenge, both challenges were based on human rights as opposed to 'parish boundary' or 'pure' devolution grounds, making judicial review under the Scotland Act little different in practice from judicial review under the Human Rights Act. Had the decision not been taken to incorporate the ECHR for the UK as a whole the Scottish courts would have found themselves in a more exposed and arguably more difficult position, but for the moment at least it is the

---

16 Scotland Act 1998 s 29(2)(b) and (d).
17 Scotland Act 1998, s 29(2)(a), (c), and (e).
18 See the discussion of legislative review in Chapter 10 below.
19 European Communities Act 1972, s 2(4).
20 Human Rights Act 1998, s 4.
21 Lord Hope, 'Opinion: devolution and human rights' (1998) 4 EHRLR 373.
22 *A v Scottish Ministers* 2002 SC (PC) 63. The Judicial Committee of the Privy Council held that there was no conflict between s 1 of the Act and the right to liberty guaranteed by Art 5 ECHR.
23 *Adams v Scottish Ministers* 2004 SC 665; *Whaley v Lord Advocate* 2004 SC 78. At the time of writing a challenge is also threatened to the ban on smoking in public places.

Human Rights Act jurisprudence that is providing the doctrinal framework within which cases are being decided. Both challenges were also unsuccessful, suggesting that the fears of 'un gouvernement de juges' which were expressed at the time of devolution may have been a little premature.[24]

The absence of successful challenge does not mean, however, that the limits themselves are not treated with the utmost seriousness – by the Scottish Executive, which is the principal initiator of legislation, by the Parliament, and by the UK government, which has an interest in ensuring that the Parliament (and the Scottish Executive) remain within the boundaries of devolved competence (see further below).

'Power-sharing'

The Scottish Parliament was not just meant to be different in the sense of being a Parliament of limited competence, part of 'that wider family of parliaments', as the Lord President noted in *Whaley v Lord Watson of Invergowrie*, which though modelled in some respects on Westminster 'owe their existence and powers to statute and are in various ways subject to the law and to the courts which act to uphold the law'.[25] It was also meant to be different in the sense of not replicating what were commonly regarded as the worst features of the Westminster system. For the Scottish Constitutional Convention the hope was that the coming of a Scottish Parliament would usher in a way of politics that was 'radically different from the rituals of Westminster: more participative, more creative, less needlessly confrontational'.[26]

One respect in which the Parliament would be different would be that it would be elected by a form of proportional representation, which it was rightly assumed would lead to a break with the Westminster tradition of single-party government. But what being 'not like Westminster'[27] might mean for the exercise of the Parliament's legislative function was not widely discussed before devolution. For the Consultative Steering Group, the 'key' principles, later elevated to 'founding' principles, were 'power-sharing' and 'access and participation'.[28] The former was seen as requiring opportunities for members and committees as well as the Executive to legislate; it also meant enabling outside groups and individuals to participate in the making of legislation through an effective consultative process. The latter was likewise seen as requiring 'genuine' consultation.[29]

It is by no means clear, however, that this is radically different or even substantially different from Westminster. Private Members' legislation has been a feature of Westminster law-making for so long that it is difficult to conceive the circumstances in which a government might once more lay claim to a monopoly of the legislative initiative, and the importance of pre-legislative consultation with affected interests is widely acknowledged even if the reality may not always match up to the ideal.

---

24 A O'Neill, 'The Scotland Act and the government of judges' 1999 SLT (News) 61.
25 2000 SC 340 at 349.
26 *Scotland's Parliament, Scotland's Right* (1995), p 9.
27 The phrase is Winetrobe's: see B Winetrobe, *Realising the Vision: A Parliament with a Purpose* (2001), p 12.
28 *Shaping Scotland's Parliament*, above n 3, Section 2, paras 17–18, and Section 3.5. There were two other founding principles: 'accountability' and 'equal opportunities'.
29 See the discussion of participatory democracy in Chapter 5 above.

A clearer insight into what 'radically different' might mean is suggested by King's distinction between 'power-sharing' and 'power-hoarding' constitutional archetypes.[30] Power-sharing constitutions are characterised by the fragmentation of political power, bargaining, negotiation and deal-making, and a culture which stresses the values of accommodation and consensus over exclusion and conflict. Power-hoarding constitutions, on the other hand, are characterised by the concentration of political power in the hands of the government, the relative absence of competing centres of autonomous political power, and a political culture that legitimises and reinforces the hoarding of political power; its guiding normative principle is 'winner takes all'.[31] The labels are not meant to imply that one archetype is preferable to the other; both have their strengths and weaknesses. The potential strengths of power-sharing are a deliberative approach to policy-making, consensus and lasting solutions, while its potential weaknesses are delay, compromise and confusion. The potential strengths and weaknesses of power-hoarding are the obverse of those of power-sharing: coherence, speed and decisiveness of action against over-hasty, ill-considered and divisive decision-making. It comes as no surprise to learn that King's chosen example of a power-hoarding constitution is the United Kingdom. The Scottish Constitutional Convention might therefore be understood to have rejected the traditional 'winner take all' approach to the exercise of political power in favour of genuine power-sharing or a consensus-seeking one.

There is an obvious correlation between the concepts of power-sharing and power-hoarding and more traditional ideas of parliamentary and executive law-making. Under the UK constitution the law-making power belongs to Parliament, to the Queen in Parliament strictly speaking, but the conventional wisdom is that legislation is more an executive than a parliamentary function,[32] which wisdom would seem to fit rather well with the idea of the constitution as a power-hoarding constitution. A feature of power-hoarding constitutions is that parliaments are essentially weak institutions.[33] Pursuing the idea of a Scottish Parliament that is different, one might look therefore for a parliament that plays a more significant role in the legislative process than has traditionally been the case at Westminster. Such indeed seems to have been the goal of some commentators at the time of devolution. Crick and Millar thus looked forward to a system in which the Executive 'need not and should not have such total domination over the legislative process as has evolved at Westminster'.[34]

As the Parliament approaches the end of its second session, however, evidence of the Executive playing a less dominant role than at Westminster is decidedly thin. As at Westminster, most successful Bills are initiated by the Scottish Executive, the devolved government of Scotland. Fifty of the sixty-two Bills passed during the Parliament's first session (1999–2003) were Executive Bills, while thirty-five of the forty-one Bills passed so far during the second session have been Executive Bills (with ten of the further seventeen Bills in progress also being Executive Bills). Nor should this occasion surprise when one recalls both that the devolved system of government is modelled on the Westminster system, with an 'Executive' drawn

---

30 A King, *Does the United Kingdom Still Have a Constitution?* (2001), pp 7–9.
31 King, above n 30, p 10.
32 D Miers and A Page, *Legislation* (2nd edn, 1990), pp 4–7.
33 King, above n 30, p 9.
34 B Crick and D Millar, *To Make the Parliament of Scotland a Model for Democracy* (1995), p 5.

from the Parliament and dependent on its retention of the support of a majority in the Parliament for its continuation in office, and also the importance of legislation to the Executive in enabling it to spend money and to clothe its policies with the force of law (the tax-varying power is exercisable by resolution).[35] Without the power to legislate the Executive would not be able in any meaningful sense of the term to govern.[36] For the Consultative Steering Group it was essential that the arrangements for the programming of parliamentary business recognise 'the need for the Executive to govern, including enacting primary and secondary legislation and obtaining approval of its expenditure proposals'.[37]

The predominance of Executive legislation attracted criticism in evidence to a major inquiry conducted by the Parliament's Procedures Committee into the application of the founding principles in the first session. The Committee was quick to defend the 'substantial volume of Executive inspired law' as not necessarily at odds with the principle of power-sharing.[38] The bulk of legislation, it accepted, would continue to be initiated by the Executive, but it did envisage the proportion of non-Executive Bills increasing, and thought it vital that this process be encouraged by the allocation of sufficient resources, including the allocation of committee and plenary time:

'[W]e do not believe that the small number of Committee Bills passed to date is a cause for concern, but we do think that it would be reasonable to expect the number of Committee Bills and Members' Bills to rise in future years'.[39]

This expectation has not been met. Instead of an increase what has been seen is a decrease in the number of successful Bills attributable to backbench MSP or committee initiative. Of the twelve non-Executive Bills passed during the first session, eight were Members' Bills, three were Committee Bills, and there was one Private Bill. The equivalent figures for the second session so far are seven non-Executive Bills, of which only one is a Member's Bill, one is a Committee Bill and the remaining five are Private Bills. Of the seven non-Executive Bills in progress, four are Members' Bills and three are Private Bills.[40] These figures may exaggerate the extent of the decline – two of the Members' Bills in the first session were to all intents and purposes Executive Bills[41] – but the decline in the number of Members' Bills follows changes to the Members' Bill procedure which were introduced in 2004 with a view to averting the major difficulties it was anticipated the Parliament would face in accommodating rival demands for Executive and non-Executive legislation. The effect of these reforms, which included raising the threshold for introducing Members' Bills and the introduction of a requirement of cross-party support, the latter in line with the Procedures Committee's view that the main

---

35 Scotland Act 1998, s 73.
36 Miers and Page, above n 32, p 6.
37 *Shaping Scotland's Parliament*, above n 3, Section 2, para 6.
38 Procedures Committee, *Founding Principles*, above n 5, para 49.
39 Procedures Committee, *Founding Principles*, above n 5, paras 713–714.
40 In the twenty years preceding devolution there were one or two successful private Members' Scottish Bills a year at Westminster (thirty-four between 1979 and 1999). Since devolution there has been one Scottish Act at Westminster promoted by a private Member: Sunday Working (Scotland) Act 2003.
41 Leasehold Casualties, which the Executive would themselves have introduced as part of the land tenure reform package (also including Abolition of Feudal Tenure, Title Conditions, and Tenements), and Mortgage Rights, a classic 'hand-out' bill.

purpose of the Members' Bill procedure is to provide a channel for legislative ideas with 'broad general appeal', has been to make it more difficult for members to legislate, while at the same time underscoring the Executive's pre-eminence in initiating legislation.[42]

We might have cause to alter the picture of Executive dominance revealed by the origins of Bills if Bills were subsequently being amended against the wishes of the Executive – if what was being presented to the Parliament was merely a first attempt, which the Parliament through its committees was then free to remake in the light of its own consultations and ultimately its own assessment of where the public interest lay. The evidence, however, is not of an Executive that struggles to 'get' its legislation. As at Westminster, the vast majority of successful amendments come from the Executive (5,690 out of a total of 6,105 in the first session) or Executive backbenchers (191 out of 6,105), with only a handful coming from opposition members (224 out of 6,105). Shephard and Cairney purport to find evidence of increased 'parliamentary' – meaning opposition and backbench members' – influence in their analysis of amendments to Executive Bills in the first session, particularly in terms of the level of success of substantive amendments to Executive Bills, but the number of such amendments is extremely small.[43] In this respect as in others the evidence is of a legislative process that is not significantly different from that at Westminster.[44]

None of which, of course, means that the Executive is not committed to 'power-sharing', in the limited sense of the term employed by the Consultative Steering Group. It acknowledges the 'virtue' of non-Executive legislation and it is fully committed to consultation on Executive Bills.[45] But its basic belief, which is a power-hoarding rather than power-sharing one, is that possession of a parliamentary majority brings with it the right to have its wishes translated into law. As the former Minister for Parliament said in evidence to the Parliament's Procedures Committee, in terms little different from those that might have been used by a government at Westminster:

---

42 *A New Procedure for Members' Bill* (6th Report, 2004). As well as a higher threshold and a requirement of cross-party support, the Committee recommended that there should be a minimum of twelve weeks' consultation on proposals for Bills, a limit on the number of proposals or Bills that members may promote at any time, and that the Executive should be able to pre-empt members' legislation where it or the UK government is planning similar legislation. See more fully, A Page in R Hazell and R Rawlings (eds), *Devolution, Law Making and the Constitution* (2005), pp 15–16.

43 M Shephard and P Cairney, 'The impact of the Scottish Parliament in amending Executive legislation' (2005) 53 *Pol Studs* 303. As well as showing that most successful amendments come from the Executive, Shephard and Cairney's figures show that only a handful of successful amendments are of a substantive as opposed to a clarificatory or consequential nature (250 out of 6,105 or 4.01 per cent). Most of these come from the Executive (219 out of 250), but of that 219 it is claimed 62 were non-Executive inspired. The very small number of substantive amendments tends to confirm, however, that because there are fewer opportunities to get Bills right after they have been introduced there is a much greater emphasis on getting them in a form fit for enactment before they are introduced than is always the case at Westminster: see Page in *Devolution, Law Making and the Constitution*, above n 42, pp 20–21.

44 One respect in which it is different is that defeats on the Westminster model are almost unknown, which may be a reflection of a greater degree of political consensus in Scotland than in the rest of the UK, but which contributes to the widespread perception of the Parliament as 'boring'.

45 *The Founding Principles of the Scottish Parliament: Scottish Executive Response to the Report of the Procedures Committee of the Scottish Parliament* (Aug 2003).

'[T]he Executive's first and foremost duty is to deliver the programme for government on which it was elected. That has involved, and will continue to involve, an ambitious and substantial legislative programme.'[46]

What might force a change in Executive belief and with it a shift to a more genuinely power-sharing approach (for example, through over-sized coalitions, or an increased role for committees in the policy-making process) is the discovery that the coalition's majority is unworkable, but despite a smaller overall majority in the second session there is little to suggest that that is the case – the recent debacle over the Licensing Bill, when the ruling coalition broke down over whether off-licence opening hours should be determined centrally by the Parliament or by local licensing boards, being a notable exception.[47] In the meantime, legislation in the Scottish Parliament, it would seem, is as much a function of government as at Westminster.[48]

More effective scrutiny

Not being like Westminster might also be understood as meaning that legislation should be subject to more effective parliamentary scrutiny, the lack of effective scrutiny being one of the persistent criticisms of the Westminster legislative process.[49] For the Constitutional Convention it was important that, as a single-chamber legislature, the Parliament's procedures 'provide for the rigorous scrutiny of proposed legislation'.[50]

Pre-legislative scrutiny

In terms of pre-legislative scrutiny, there is the same emphasis on consultation and publication of Bills in draft as at Westminster. The Executive has put in place a 'coherent strategy' for consultation on Executive Bills,[51] which is generally well regarded despite its voluntary nature.[52] Commendable though its approach to pre-legislative consultation is regarded as being,[53] the Executive has some way to go before it is consistently hitting the target it originally set itself of two rounds of consultation on each Bill.[54] A similar picture emerges in relation to consultation on

46 Procedures Committee, *Founding Principles*, above n 5, para 52. The Committee did not challenge its right to do so: para 336.
47 For the debacle, see SPOR, 16 Nov 2005, cols 20675–20768.
48 Before the recent changes in Members' Bill procedure, the narrowness of the coalition's majority meant that the Executive was not necessarily in a position to 'kill' a Member's Bill with quite the same facility as at Westminster. It might therefore be forced to cede ground in a way which has no Westminster parallel. Tommy Sheridan's Abolition of Poinding and Warrant Sales Act 2001, which led to the Debt Arrangement and Attachment (Scotland) Act 2002, is the best example. The same pattern was repeated with his unsuccessful School Meals (Scotland) Bill, which provided the 'inspiration' for the Education (School Meals) (Scotland) Act 2003.
49 See most recently the report from the House of Lords Select Committee on the Constitution, *Parliament and the Legislative Process* (2003–04) HL 173 and earlier the report of the Hansard Society Commission on the Legislative Process, *Making the Law* (1992).
50 *Scotland's Parliament, Scotland's Right*, above n 26, p 24.
51 Procedures Committee, *Founding Principles*, above n 5, para 580.
52 See now *Scottish Executive: Consultation Good Practice Guidance* (June 2004).
53 Procedures Committee, *Founding Principles*, above n 5, para 952.
54 The policy memoranda which accompany Bills should show the extent of the consultation, but the distinction between an extended but single consultation process and separate rounds of consultation is seldom clear-cut.

draft Bills. The Executive's original intention apparently was that all Bills would be published for consultation, as part of the proposed second round of consultation, but publication in draft has been the exception rather than the rule. In the first session only a quarter (thirteen out of fifty) of Executive Bills were published for consultation.

Under the Consultative Steering Group's proposals, consultation would be undertaken by the Executive itself, with the process being overseen by the relevant subject committee of the Parliament. Committees themselves would not engage in consultation, although they might do so if they considered the Executive consultation inadequate.[55] They would also be involved in deciding who should be consulted and kept informed of progress.[56] There is little sense, however, of committee oversight of or involvement in the process. The impression is that committees prefer to wait and conduct their own consultation after the legislation has been introduced, which has led to complaints from the Executive that they are being 'standoffish' and a 'bit precious', and from affected interests of consultation overload.[57] Following its most recent consideration of the question, the Procedures Committee declined to make any general recommendations on the extent to which committees should engage in pre-legislative scrutiny, insisting that it must be for committees to decide how best to subject legislative proposals to scrutiny; committees should be free to embark on pre-legislative scrutiny 'where they wish to and have time – but neither should it be expected as a normal part of the legislative process'.[58] The Committee took the same laissez-faire approach to the question of the publication of Bills in draft, arguing it was for the Executive to decide where publication in draft could make a useful contribution to consultation and policy development.[59] There is of course no certainty that a power-hoarding Executive would welcome attempts by committees to become involved at an earlier stage in the legislative process, other than by making their views known as part of the consultation process, but the lack of committee involvement at the pre-legislative stage is suggestive of a legislative process that is, as has been indicated, little changed.

Legislative scrutiny

The legislative process itself, the basic elements of which are prescribed in the Scotland Act, is a conventional three-stage process with the three stages roughly corresponding to the second reading, committee and report/third reading stages at Westminster: a stage at which members can debate and vote on the general principles of the Bill; a stage at which they can consider and vote on its details; and a stage at which the Bill can be passed or rejected.[60] There is also provision for a reconsideration stage should a Bill be subject to a law officer's reference or a

---

55 *Shaping Scotland's Parliament*, above n 3, Section 3.5, para 5. It is clear from the reference in para 6 to committees concentrating on proposals which have already been the subject of participative involvement of interested parties that the Consultative Steering Group did not envisage committees duplicating Executive consultation.

56 *Shaping Scotland's Parliament*, above n 3, Section 3.5, para 6.

57 Procedures Committee, *Founding Principles*, above n 5, para 977.

58 *Timescales and Stages of Bills* (7th Report, 2004), para 107. Its predecessor in the first session acknowledged some inconsistency in committees' approach to pre-legislative consultation and suggested that the Convenors' Group consider establishing minimum periods and consistent standards for pre-legislative consultation: *Founding Principles*, above, n 5, para 346.

59 *Timescales and Stages of Bills*, above n 58, para 111.

60 Scotland Act 1998, s 36(1).

secretary of state's order under sections 33 or 35 of the Scotland Act after it has been passed.

Apart from the fact that the Scottish Parliament is unicameral, so that each stage is gone through only once, the Holyrood process differs from that at Westminster in two principal respects. First, before the stage one debate and vote on the principle of the Bill, which takes place in plenary session, a Bill is referred to one of the Parliament's subject committees which considers and reports on the principle of the Bill to inform the debate and vote in plenary session. The stage one inquiry is regarded as 'crucial to the effectiveness of the Parliament's whole legislative process' in that, as well as taking place in public, it allows affected interests, including those who may not have been consulted, direct access to the legislature and with it an opportunity to 'contribute to the formulation of a considered view both of the policy intention and of how it has been given detailed expression in legislation'.[61] The second principal difference is that the subject committees, which examine Bills before the stage one debate and again at stage two, combine the roles of select and standing committees at Westminster, the idea being to enable members 'to develop an expertise in particular areas and to bring an informed view to the consideration of legislation and scrutiny of the Executive'.[62]

There is little evidence, however, of the expected gains in terms of effectiveness of scrutiny being realised. The Scottish Parliament, it is said:

'does not yet have quite the same degree of legislative curiosity as at Westminster.... [It] tends to concentrate in its debates, even in Committee, on the policy and political dimensions of the Bills which it is scrutinising and tends to leave to one side questions about, for example, the particular application to particular cases of the provisions of its Bills'.[63]

The implication is that the Parliament might yet develop that 'curiosity'. Other observers have been less sanguine. For Lord Hope:

'The committee system, which was designed to provide an opportunity for careful, informed study of all the relevant detail, is not working as it should. Responsibility for both initial scrutiny of a Bill at Stage 1 and detailed scrutiny at Stage 2 rests with the same committee. At both stages this process tends to become the focus for political debate and point-scoring. Elected committee members lack the independence of mind and the opportunity for detachment and genuine self-criticism that is essential to effective scrutiny.'[64]

Concern about the effectiveness of parliamentary scrutiny was reflected in calls towards the end of the first session for some form of second chamber or 'revision' stage to compensate for the shortcomings of parliamentary scrutiny.[65] In the Parliament's defence the argument was that the parliamentary stages had been too rushed to allow for effective scrutiny. The Procedures Committee, in its examination of the application of the founding principles in the first session, found 'clear evidence that the committee system in the Scottish Parliament is under severe pressure of work, and that the quality of output is threatened by the

---

61 *Timescales and Stages of Bills*, above n 58, para 112.
62 *Shaping Scotland's Parliament*, above n 3, Section 2, para 13.
63 McCluskie, 'New approaches', above n 4, p 41.
64 'What a second chamber can do for legislative scrutiny' (2004) 25 *Statute Law Review* 8.
65 As to which, see Hope, 'Second chamber', above n 64, pp 12–14.

deadlines to which committees are working'.[66] If the devolution settlement was to operate as the Parliament intended when it adopted the founding principles, it continued, the Executive had to ensure, 'in seeking the time it needs to progress its electoral commitments, that committees are not so burdened that the quality of legislation, or other tasks that are central to committee work, is put at risk'.[67] In its reply to the Procedures Committee, the Executive conceded there had been pressures to complete Bill stages for public Bills 'more quickly than may have been ideal in some cases', before affirming its willingness 'to discuss timetabling issues with the parliamentary authorities having regard to the concerns raised and the need to ensure the timely passage of legislation'. Privately, it suggested that if the Parliament wanted to spend more time on legislation the answer might be for it to work harder; increased scrutiny, in other words, should not be at the expense of the Executive's legislative agenda.[68]

In the event the issue was not pressed to a conclusion. The Procedures Committee returned to the question of the speed of the process in the second session with a series of recommendations which

> 'should enable the quality and robustness of the Parliament's legislative output to be enhanced without threatening the legitimate expectation on the part of the Executive (and others) that they will be able to deliver legislative solutions within a reasonable timescale'.[69]

As the experience of Westminster demonstrates, however, effective scrutiny is not just a matter of procedures. It also depends crucially on those doing the scrutiny and the spirit with which they are imbued. Whether the reforms will lead to more effective scrutiny remains to be seen. But the fact that the Executive should have chosen not to force the issue is indicative of a Parliament in which Westminster assumptions about the exercise of legislative power do not automatically hold sway.

Post-legislative scrutiny

The question of post-legislative scrutiny – the review of legislation once it has been brought into force – has attracted attention in the Scottish Parliament as it has at Westminster.[70] In its report on the application of the founding principles in the first session the Procedures Committee argued that the Parliament was responsible for 'assessing the effect of legislation, whether it has achieved its stated purposes, whether it has had unanticipated consequences, and whether further legislation might be required'.[71] Noting that this 'key responsibility' had yet to become part of their routine work,[72] it recommended that subject committees should routinely

---

66 Procedures Committee, *Founding Principles*, above n 5, para 1016.
67 Procedures Committee, *Founding Principles*, above n 5, para 1018.
68 Comments by the First Minister to this effect were reported in *The Scotsman*, 26 June 2003. So far, however, there has been no sign of such a policy being pursued. The greater emphasis on getting Bills in a form fit for enactment before they are introduced as a result of the relative lack of opportunities for amendment may also serve to deprive the parliamentary stages of much of their interest from the standpoint of the Executive: instead of providing an additional opportunity to get a measure right, as at Westminster, they are simply reduced to a hurdle to be overcome: see Page, *Law Making and the Constitution*, above n 42, pp 20–21.
69 *Timescales and Stages of Bills*, above n 58, para 170.
70 See Law Commission, *Post-Legislative Scrutiny: A Consultation Paper* (No 178, 2006).
71 Procedures Committee, *Founding Principles*, above n 5, para 372.
72 Procedures Committee, *Founding Principles*, above n 5, para 1016.

consider whether to subject legislation which they have passed to post-legislative scrutiny, and that the Parliament's rules should be amended to require committees to give formal consideration to the need for post-legislative scrutiny and to report annually on all such work undertaken.[73] Although this recommendation was not implemented, examples of committees undertaking post-legislative scrutiny are not unknown.[74]

Scrutiny of legislative competence

The vulnerability of Acts of the Scottish Parliament to judicial review means that the exercise of the Parliament's legislative powers is dominated by questions of legislative competence to a much greater extent than is the case at Westminster. As Angiolini explains, the effect of the 'overarching constitutional framework' within which the Scottish Parliament and the Scottish Executive operate is:

> 'to raise the profile of law much higher than at Westminster. I do not say that Ministers at Westminster are careless about the law. The combination of European law and human rights law and the reserved matters in Sch 5 makes the legal issue – the issue of competence – much more of an immediate concern to the Scottish Ministers and administrators than is the case south of the Border'.[75]

As the Executive's chief legal adviser, it falls to the Lord Advocate to clear Executive Bills for introduction. An Executive Bill must be accompanied by a ministerial statement certifying that it is within the legislative competence of the Parliament,[76] and a minister cannot make a statement on legislative competence without the law officers' clearance. The Lord Advocate's involvement begins before the detailed preparation of a Bill has begun. The Scottish Executive has been much less willing than its UK counterpart to leave the preparation of individual measures to departments subject only to the threat that they will lose 'their' Bills if they are not ready on time. The machinery of control is provided by a committee known colloquially as the Lord Advocate's Star Chamber, which was first set up towards the end of 2002, and to which individual measures are referred once basic heads of policy have been agreed. The starting-point for the Lord Advocate's involvement is the question of legislative competence, but this has gradually broadened into a more general concern with the proper management of the legislative programme, that is, with ensuring that Bills are ready on time and that they are of an appropriate quality. Referral thus provides an opportunity to work out what is required to translate the policy into law, as well as early notice of any questions of competence that may arise.

A statement on legislative competence by itself is singularly uninformative: all that it states is that in the minister's view the provisions of the Bill in question 'would be within the legislative competence of the Scottish Parliament'. The lack of information has attracted criticism:

> 'It is not good enough that ministers assert in a one-line submission to the Scottish Parliament that a bill is compatible with ECHR. It should be incumbent on the

---

73   Procedures Committee, *Founding Principles*, above n 5, paras 381–382.
74   See eg Local Government and Transport Committee, *Inquiry into Issues Arising from the Transport (Scotland) Act 2001* (4th Report, 2005).
75   'Legislation, litigation and prosecution: the role of a Scottish law officer' 2003 JR 223.
76   Scotland Act 1998, s 31(1) and rule 9.3.3(a).

executive to produce a full statement with a rigorous analysis, explaining the ECHR implications of its legislative proposals.'[77]

This is not something the Executive has volunteered, but neither has there been any attempt, possibly because the machinery is lacking, to scrutinise the basis of statements in the manner of the Human Rights Committee at Westminster.[78] The evidentiary basis for the statement itself is not an especially onerous one. All that is required is that the minister be more satisfied than not, rather than satisfied beyond all reasonable doubt, that the Bill is within the legislative competence of the Scottish Parliament. (The same 'more likely than not' standard applies to section 19 HRA statements.)

A Bill must also be accompanied by a statement from the Presiding Officer stating whether or not in his view the provisions of the Bill are within legislative competence.[79] In order to obtain this statement a copy of the draft Bill, together with a note of the Executive's view on legislative competence, is sent to the Parliament's Legal Adviser three weeks before the date set for its formal introduction. During this three-week period the Parliament's Legal Adviser prepares advice to the Presiding Officer on legislative competence. According to the former Presiding Officer, if the Parliament's lawyers 'find things they are worried about, they talk directly to the Executive lawyers – a very good and healthy dialogue goes on and the Bills are often amended'.[80] On one occasion a Bill was sent back by the Presiding Officer after being scrutinised by the Parliament's lawyers and the explanatory memorandum amended to include a commitment to make subordinate legislation to address an omission in the Bill.[81]

A statement indicating that in the Presiding Officer's view a Bill (or specified parts of it) is outwith competence does not prevent the Bill from being introduced.[82] The Presiding Officer has said, however, that a Bill whose principal purpose (or one of whose principal purposes) is to make a provision 'manifestly outside' the legislative competence of the Parliament should not be introduced.[83]

Where non-Executive Bills show signs of making progress, the question of competence is gone into by the Legal Secretariat to the Lord Advocate and issues raised with the Bill's sponsors in the knowledge that where the Lord Advocate remains dissatisfied he may refer the question of whether it is within the legislative competence of the Scottish Parliament to the Judicial Committee of the Privy Council. Where the lead committee which considers a Member's Bill at stage one of the legislative process is of the opinion, having regard to the Presiding Officer's statement, that the Bill is clearly outwith the legislative competence of the Parliament, and that it is unlikely to be possible to amend it to bring it within legislative competence, it may recommend to the Parliament that the general principles of the Bill be not agreed to.[84]

77 Lord James Douglas Hamilton MSP, *The Scotsman,* 1 Dec 2001.
78 On the Human Rights Committee, see D Feldman, 'The impact of human rights on the UK legislative process' (2004) 25 *Statute Law Review* 91.
79 Scotland Act 1998, s 31(2).
80 *Devolution: Inter-Institutional Relations in the United Kingdom,* above n 5, Question 776.
81 *Devolution,* above n 80.
82 The Scottish Parliament, *Guidance on Public Bills* (2nd edn, 2001), para 2.14.
83 Recommendations on the content of Bills, reprinted in Annex A to the *Guidance on Public Bills,* above n 82.
84 R 9.14.18(b).

The importance attached to questions of competence within the Scottish Executive is undoubtedly increased by the fact that Bills are also scrutinised by the UK government to ensure that the Scottish Parliament and the Scottish Executive remain within the bounds of the devolution settlement. The Office of the Solicitor to the Advocate General within the Scotland Office examines Bills before they are first introduced, as well as formally when they have completed their parliamentary stages, with a view to ensuring that the UK government has 'early warning of issues of competence of Bills of the Scottish Parliament or actings of the Scottish Executive, and can engage in constructive dialogue with the Scottish Executive to address them'.[85] Where differences of opinion have arisen in the course of this process, we are told by the then Advocate General that these have been 'resolved amicably', with the possibility of a reference to the Judicial Committee of the Privy Council (JCPC) serving, in her words, as 'an incentive to the Scottish Executive to focus on keeping within the boundaries of devolved competence'.[86] Faced with the threat of a six-month delay to a Bill, and the consequent disruption to its legislative programme that a referral to the JCPC would entail, it would seem that the Scottish Executive has preferred to remove offending sections or redraft the legislation rather than invite the UK government to test its arguments in court.

That is not to say that a government of a different political complexion from the government at Westminster would be equally amenable to the same threat. A devolved administration that was keen to push the boundaries to devolved competence might well welcome the scope to 'constitutionalise' a dispute that a reference would afford. It might therefore invite the UK government to do its worst, in the knowledge that were it to succeed before the Judicial Committee the UK government would then have no choice but to back off or to amend the devolution settlement (or legislate in the devolved areas) without the Scottish Parliament's consent, which might well provoke a political crisis.

Subordinate law-making

The Parliament has no monopoly of law-making in Scotland. As in the rest of the UK, a significant amount of legislation is made by ministers in the exercise of delegated law-making powers. Ministers' delegated law-making powers are not confined to devolved matters. It was always anticipated that they should be given power to make subordinate legislation in relation to reserved matters, that is matters in respect of which primary legislation remains a matter for Westminster. The principal mechanism for conferring such functions on the Scottish Ministers is an executive devolution order made under section 63 of the Scotland Act, but as an alternative to an executive devolution order functions may be 'transferred', that is conferred directly on the Scottish Ministers, by Act of the Westminster Parliament. Devolution has seen a marked increase in the volume of 'Scottish' subordinate legislation (from 453 Scottish statutory instruments in 2000, the first full year after devolution, to 660 in 2005).[87]

The Parliament's arrangements for the scrutiny of subordinate law-making, and for the scrutiny of proposals for delegated law-making powers, are modelled on

85   HC Deb, vol 378, col 1126 W (25 Jan 2002).
86   L Clark, 'Three years on: the role of the Advocate General for Scotland' 2002 SLT (News) 143.
87   Not included in these figures are Scotland-only instruments made by UK/GB departments.

those at Westminster, with the Parliament's Subordinate Legislation Committee combining the technical scrutiny functions of the Joint Standing Committee on Statutory Instruments and the House of Lords Delegated Powers and Regulatory Reform Committee, the principal difference being that instruments are referred to subject committees for scrutiny on their merits, which should in theory at least yield more opportunities for the scrutiny of instruments and their underlying policy intentions than the 'palpably unsatisfactory' system at Westminster.[88] The Statutory Instruments Act 1946, which governs the 'laying' before Parliament and publication of statutory instruments, was also applied with modifications to Scottish statutory instruments.[89]

Whether the potential for greater scrutiny is being fully realised is open to question.[90] As at Westminster the sheer volume of subordinate legislation brings with it its own pressures. The more fundamental difficulty, however, is that the procedures to which instruments are subject, being a matter for the Executive – or else the UK government – when the legislation is being framed, are not necessarily conclusive of their importance. Some affirmative instruments are unimportant (the 'trivial affirmative') while some negative instruments are of major importance. There is no certainty therefore that instruments receive scrutiny in proportion to their merits.

The Parliament's procedures, on the other hand, are its own affair, and the Subordinate Legislation Committee has embarked on an inquiry into the existing arrangements with a view to instructing a Bill that will replace the Statutory Instruments Act 1946 in its application to Scottish statutory instruments. The Committee began by looking at the 'regulatory framework', that is the framework governing the making of subordinate legislation, an unfortunate choice of phrase because of the risk, which to some extent materialised, of confusing subordinate legislation with regulation, and in particular the imposition of burdens on business. The Committee's purpose might have been more aptly defined as being to examine the extent to which subordinate law-making in the devolved Scotland conforms to 'best practice' in subordinate law-making rather than best practice in regulation.[91]

In the second phase of its inquiry, the Committee turned its attention to the parliamentary scrutiny of subordinate law-making. Faced with clear evidence of a system that is not 'fit for purpose for a new Parliament', the Committee has recommended the replacement of the existing multiplicity of procedures with a new simplified procedure under which Scottish statutory instruments, with certain exceptions, would be laid in draft before the Parliament, which would be able to disapprove an instrument within forty days.[92] Under the new procedure the

88 House of Commons Select Committee on Procedure, *Delegated Legislation* (HC 152, 1995–96), para 1, a conclusion endorsed by its successor in 2000: *Delegated Legislation* (HC 48, 1999–2000), para 53.
89 Scotland Act 1998 (Transitory and Transitional Provisions) (Statutory Instruments) Order 1999 (SI 1999/1096).
90 For an initial, largely favourable, assessment, see C Himsworth, 'Subordinate legislation in the Scottish Parliament' (2002) 6 EdinLR 356.
91 Subordinate Legislation Committee, *Inquiry into the Regulatory Framework in Scotland* (31st Report, 2005). Compare in this respect the recent report from the House of Lords Merits of Statutory Instruments Committee, *The Management of Secondary Legislation* (HL 149, 2005–06), which argued in effect that 'better regulation' should be treated as encompassing the effective planning and management of the preparation, laying and scrutiny of secondary legislation.
92 Subordinate Legislation Committee, *Inquiry into the Regulatory Framework in Scotland* (Draft Report, SP 564).

Executive would be relieved of the need to obtain approval of instruments subject to the affirmative resolution procedure – it would be enough that they had not been disapproved. The Committee has recommended, however, that the Parliament be given advance notice of the Executive's programme of subordinate legislation, which would allow lead committees to concentrate their efforts on those instruments thought to merit the closest scrutiny. The Parliament itself would not be given the power to amend instruments, but the Executive would be able to amend a draft within the forty-day period in response to criticisms made by the Subordinate Legislation Committee, which reports a far higher percentage of instruments than the Joint Standing Committee on Statutory Instruments at Westminster (between 20 per cent and 30 per cent as opposed to about 5 per cent at Westminster). Legislation to implement the Committee's recommendations, which have been published for consultation, is not now expected until the Parliament's next session.

THE UNITED KINGDOM DIMENSION

Devolution has not altered the power of Westminster to legislate for Scotland. The Scotland Act affirms that the conferral of law-making powers on the Scottish Parliament 'does not affect the power of the Parliament of the United Kingdom to make laws for Scotland'.[93] Although devolution naturally invites concentration on the Holyrood dimension of Scottish law-making, the Westminster dimension remains important, more so than was anticipated at the time of devolution. At the time of devolution it was widely assumed that Westminster would more or less cease to legislate in the devolved areas. In his statement on the Executive's first legislative programme, the First Minister spoke of there being 'exceptional and limited circumstances in which it is sensible and proper that the Westminster Parliament legislates in devolved areas of responsibility.... [But] day in day out, it is here that the law of the land will be shaped and laid down'.[94] 'The usual rule', the Deputy Minister for Justice later announced, 'will be that legislation in devolved areas will be enacted by this Parliament. From time to time, however, it may make sense for a UK Act to include provisions about such matters.'[95] Westminster legislation in the devolved areas, however, has proved to be a far more common occurrence than was anticipated at the time of devolution. Since devolution there have been nearly seventy 'Sewel' or 'legislative consent' motions signifying the consent of the Scottish Parliament to Westminster legislation in the devolved areas.[96]

The reasons are not difficult to find. With hindsight it seems clear that claims about the frequency of Westminster legislation in the devolved areas underestimated the strength of the pull towards uniformity in the devolution settlement. One source of that pull is electoral expectations. In evidence to the Royal Commission on the Constitution, the late John Mackintosh argued that devolved governments in Scotland and Wales could not afford to face their electors and fall markedly behind the position being set in England. It was in this way that the position in Britain

93 Scotland Act 1998, s 28(7).
94 SPOR, 16 June 1999, col 403.
95 SPOR, 23 June 1999, col 697.
96 As well as Westminster legislation for devolved purposes, the Scottish Parliament's consent is sought for Westminster legislation altering the powers of the Scottish Ministers and Westminster legislation altering the legislative competence of the Scottish Parliament.

had determined the practice in Northern Ireland over a large area of decisions, which under the Government of Ireland Act were clearly allocated to Stormont.[97] The conclusion Mackintosh drew from this was that Westminster could afford to be relatively generous in the extent of the powers devolved, in the knowledge that pressure for uniformity would prevent significant deviation from the UK norm. What Mackintosh did not anticipate was that a devolved government might meet voters' expectations by the simple expedient of relying on Westminster.

A second source is the need 'to keep to an acceptable level any adverse cross-border consequences of policy differences',[98] including preventing firms or individuals from exploiting differences between the two jurisdictions. Reliance on UK bodies for the purposes of administration also seems to bring with it its own pressure for uniformity. In the case of the Regulation of Investigatory Powers Act 2000, for example, the argument was that UK bodies such as the intelligence and security services should be subject to the same law throughout the UK rather than being subject to the burden of operating according to different codes. Another source is the need to give effect to international – including EU – obligations. The devolution White Paper identified international obligations that touch on devolved as well as reserved matters as one area where it might be more convenient for legislation to be passed by Westminster.[99]

'Labour in power' in London and (in coalition) in Edinburgh is obviously also a factor in the frequency of legislative consent motions. The Scottish Ministers may see no reason why the law should not be the same, especially when they are members of the same political party as the government at Westminster. In the debate on the motion on the Anti-terrorism, Crime and Security Bill, the Deputy Minister for Justice made clear that the Executive's starting-point was that the law should be the same unless there were good reasons for adopting a different approach:

'Because we do not see the need for a distinctive approach on the other measures, we have sought to proceed with them by way of a Sewel motion. In the circumstances, the advantages of a rapid UK-wide approach take precedence.'[100]

But even if uniformity or consistency of approach is considered desirable there is nothing to prevent the Scottish Executive from promoting its own legislation. As a general rule, however, it has preferred to 'piggyback' on Westminster legislation. Again, there are a number of reasons for this. It may be faced with a stark choice between postponing 'worthwhile' reforms, or forgoing them altogether, and 'putting aside' or sacrificing its own legislative priorities to make room for separate Scottish legislation. It avoids any disruption to its own legislative programme. It affords access to Westminster's much greater policy-making capacity, while at the same time avoiding the need to disentangle the devolved from the reserved aspects of a proposal – on which the Parliament could not legislate. It also avoids the risk of legal challenge to the competence of Scottish legislation in politically controversial areas, through the doctrine of parliamentary sovereignty.

97 Royal Commission on the Constitution (Cmnd 5460, 1973), Written Evidence, vol 9 (1972), p 128.
98 *Report of the Royal Commission on the Constitution* (Cmnd 5460, 1973), para 826.
99 *Scotland's Parliament* (Cm 3685, 1997), para 4.4.
100 SPOR, 15 Nov 2001, col 3871.

Politically convenient or attractive though it may be, reliance on Westminster's concurrent legislative competence carries with it the obvious risk of abuse, of the Scottish Parliament being denied the opportunity to consider the details of legislation that is properly its concern. Much Westminster legislation in the devolved areas, it is reasonable to claim, makes only minor changes to the law. But some of it, for example on gender recognition and same-sex registered partnerships, has been on precisely the sorts of subjects on which the Scottish Parliament might have been expected to legislate after devolution. It is difficult to avoid the conclusion that one reason it was not asked to is because of the controversy that surrounded the repeal of section 2A of the Local Government Act 1986, which banned the promotion of homosexuality in schools. Sex and politics, it seems, do not mix well in the Scottish Parliament.

As an unexpected, and politically controversial, phenomenon the Scottish Parliament has been slow to adapt its procedures to Westminster legislation in the devolved areas. The expectation from the outset was that Westminster 'would not normally legislate with regard to devolved matters in Scotland without the consent of the Scottish Parliament'.[101] The procedures for obtaining the Scottish Parliament's consent, however, provided little assurance that Westminster was legislating in the devolved areas only where it was 'sensible and proper' to do so. Moreover, there were few real constraints on UK ministers or their Scottish counterparts once approval was given. The challenge for the Parliament was to treat Westminster legislation in the devolved areas with the same seriousness as it treats the other forms of legislation for which it is responsible.

Suggestions that the Parliament's Procedures Committee should be asked to review the procedures for obtaining the Parliament's consent to Westminster legislation in the devolved areas were initially slow to be acted on but, following a comprehensive review by the Committee, the Parliament has now put its procedures on a formal basis.[102] By embedding the main elements of scrutiny within the Parliament's formal procedures, the Committee sought to ensure that the Parliament had the information it needed at a sufficiently early stage to enable it to carry out the task of scrutiny effectively. It also sought, at a political level,

> 'to secure a degree of consensus about the general need for procedures of this sort and a shared understanding of how and when they should be used, and at the same time lay to rest some of the persistent misunderstandings that have arisen'.[103]

'We believe that it is in no-one's interests', the Committee argued, 'for a significant aspect of the Parliament's business, and its principal interface with the Westminster Parliament, to be so dogged by controversy and misunderstanding.'[104]

---

101 In the House of Lords on 21 July 1998 Lord Sewel said: 'we would expect a convention to be established that Westminster would not normally legislate with regard to devolved matters in Scotland without the consent of the Scottish Parliament' (HL Deb, vol 592, col 791, 21 July 1998). What became known as the Sewel convention is restated in the Memorandum of Understanding with the devolved administrations, which states that 'the UK government will proceed in accordance with the convention that the UK Parliament would not normally legislate with regard to devolved matters except with the agreement of the devolved legislature' (Cm 5240, 2001, para 13).

102 Procedures Committee, *The Sewel Convention* (7th Report, 2005).

103 *The Sewel Convention*, above n 102, paras 5-6

104 *The Sewel Convention*, above n 102, para 4.

But if the Scottish Parliament has been slow to respond to the continuing importance of Westminster legislation in the devolved areas the Westminster Parliament has been even slower. Before devolution Scottish legislative needs had been partially met by the introduction of distinctive Scottish procedures at Westminster, with a government's ability to make use of these procedures depending on its electoral position in Scotland.[105] Where these procedures were not being used, however, and a government's lack of a majority of seats in Scotland would mean that they could not be used, there was no guarantee of the sufficiency of consideration of Scottish provisions in Westminster legislation. What the continuing reliance on Westminster legislation in the devolved areas has underlined is the lack of effective parliamentary scrutiny of Scottish provisions in Westminster Bills – whether in the reserved or devolved areas.[106] The danger is that, against the background of devolution, the Scottish element of Westminster legislation will receive even less scrutiny than in the past: an unfortunate outcome for a process that was meant to reduce the democratic deficit in relation to Scottish legislation.[107] 'This "back to the future" approach', Winetrobe argues, 'might be accepted as just one more constitutional anomaly were it not operating on such a significant scale'.[108] Following suggestions by the Secretary of State for Scotland, the Scottish Affairs Select Committee is now examining the handling of Sewel Bills at Westminster. Whether its deliberations will result in any material improvement remains to be seen. The Scottish Parliament's Procedures Committee was less than optimistic: 'The reality is that the UK Parliament's consent to specific provisions in one of its Bills, important though it may be to us, is likely to remain a relatively insignificant factor from a Westminster perspective.'[109]

CONCLUSION

Devolution has seen an explosion in purely Scottish law-making – legislation that is made in Scotland by Scottish politicians – and with it what one politician has described as the 'most far-reaching and rapid updating of Scots law for three centuries'.[110] As the legislature of the devolved Scotland, however, the Scottish Parliament is less different than some of the proponents of devolution had hoped. It is different in that it is a Parliament of bounded competence, although so too arguably is Westminster, no matter how much it may assume otherwise, but not so different when it comes to the extent to which it is executive dominated or the effectiveness or otherwise of parliamentary scrutiny. It is not a carbon copy of Westminster – proportional representation and the fact of coalition government alone are perhaps enough to ensure that it is not – but neither is it radically different.

---

105 C Himsworth, 'The Scottish Grand Committee as an instrument of government' (1996) 1 EdinLR 79. Since devolution these procedures have largely fallen into disuse. There have been only two Scotland-only Acts since devolution – Sunday Working (Scotland) Act 2003 and Scottish Parliament (Constituencies) Act 2004.
106 House of Lords Select Committee on the Constitution, *Devolution: Its Effect on the Practice of Legislation at Westminster* (HL 192, 2003–04), Appendix 1, paras 52–53.
107 A Page and A Batey, 'Scotland's other parliament: Westminster legislation about devolved matters in Scotland since devolution' [2002] PL 502.
108 In *Devolution, Law Making and the Constitution*, above n 42, p 56.
109 *The Sewel Convention*, above n 102, para 139.
110 W Alexander in W Alexander (ed), *Donald Dewar: Scotland's First First Minister* (2005), p 210.

At the same time Westminster remains important – more so than was anticipated at the time of devolution. The Scottish Ministers have not had to look elsewhere for inspiration in framing their legislative priorities but at the same time they have not been able to resist the temptation to help themselves to what UK government is doing by way of legislation. The continuing importance of Westminster legislation in the devolved areas highlights the importance of the effective scrutiny of Scottish provisions in Westminster Bills – at Holyrood as well as Westminster. The context may have changed but the challenge of ensuring the effective parliamentary scrutiny of legislation remains.

Chapter 7

Public Accountability in Scotland

Barry K Winetrobe

INTRODUCTION

This chapter examines the constitutional concept of accountability in Scottish public law. The theory and practice of accountability in the UK is outlined, and then tested against the situation in post-devolution Scotland, primarily in relation to devolved aspects of government, but also briefly in relation to those matters still reserved to the UK level. Improved accountability was one of the intended benefits of devolution. Part of the impetus for devolution stemmed from a perceived accountability deficit in the previous arrangements for the governance of Scotland. However, in so far as devolution has transformed the UK from a primarily unitary system of governance into a more multi-layered and asymmetrical system, this has also provided the opportunity for experimentation within each of these national and sub-national units, including in forms of accountability. To what extent, then, has devolution transformed the accountability of Scottish government? Is devolved governance a better, more accountable version of UK government? And what impact has it had on the scrutiny and accountability of that part of Scottish government which remains in the hands of Whitehall and Westminster?

Bearing in mind that devolution is still too young to allow more than tentative conclusions to be drawn, this chapter will not attempt a comprehensive survey of all that can fall within the elastic term of 'accountability', much of which is covered elsewhere in this volume. This chapter concentrates on what is, or is potentially, different in Scotland. It looks at political, rather than legal, financial or other means of accountability. It should be noted that these various forms of accountability can overlap. In particular, as devolution is itself essentially a creature of statute, legal accountability, especially through judicial review, is always a relevant factor. There may also be greater scope in this new governance than at present in the UK for the criminal law, as in the ethical regulation of MSPs,[1] where, in one case dealt with by the Parliament, the procurator fiscal was initially involved.[2]

ACCOUNTABILITY: UK THEORY AND PRACTICE

The concept of accountability is deeply embedded in British constitutional theory and practice, so much so that its meaning has become blurred; it has

---

1 Scotland Act 1998, s 39, and the Interests of Members of the Scottish Parliament Act 2006.
2 *Complaint against Kenneth Macintosh MSP*, Standards and Public Appointments Committee (4th Report, 2005), SP Paper 374, 9 June 2005.

become a 'chameleon-like term',[3] a 'hurrah word'.[4] Nevertheless, the core idea of accountable government can be simply stated as one where the governors are responsible to the governed. Hence it underpins the elements of constitutionality, legality, democratic control and limited government inherent in the UK's form of governance. Accountability is a way of describing governance relationships and control, where it reverses the apparent hierarchy of the governors' day-to-day control over the governed into a relationship where the governed are intended to be in a constitutionally dominant position over the governors. This may involve merely the rendering of an account by government actors to the governed of their stewardship of activities and decisions within their remit (*explanatory* accountability or 'accounting'). Or, more substantially, it may require acceptance of any errors or failings in those activities or decisions, and of the duty to ensure their correction and/or to accept any resulting blame or sanctions (*amendatory* accountability or 'being held to account').

When examining accountability relationships, several components have to be distinguished. We need to know: *who* is accountable *to whom, for what,* and *how*? The traditional British model answers these questions by saying that ministers are responsible to Parliament, for policy and its implementation, primarily through mechanisms such as questions, debates and committee scrutiny. In the British constitution, this fundamental expectation of public constitutional accountability as being primarily parliamentary accountability is embodied in the twin constitutional conventions of collective and individual ministerial responsibility.[5] These doctrines seek to define the accountability relationships between the Parliament and the Executive, and within the latter, between ministers, and between ministers and their officials, especially as they both relate to the Parliament. The doctrines developed in the eighteenth and nineteenth centuries when executive power was shifting from the sovereign personally to political ministers acting in the sovereign's name; the role and scope of the state was very much less than it is today, and it was possible for ministers to have some personal knowledge of, and direct control over, the implementation of policy in their departments; and civil servants were becoming less the 'placemen' of powerful social and political actors, and more professional, permanent officials appointed on objective criteria.

According to Marshall, the doctrine of collective responsibility has three strands to it: the *confidence* rule, which requires that the government as a whole must resign if it no longer has majority support in the House of Commons; the *unanimity* rule, which means that individual ministers must publicly support government policy or resign if they cannot do so; and the *confidentiality* rule, which prevents discussions between ministers from being made public.[6] Initially developed as a bulwark against monarchical power, the contemporary significance of collective responsibility is as a means of preserving executive unity and solidarity, so that government speaks with one voice to Parliament and the people.[7] It also enables full and frank discussion within government, prior to policy being presented

---

3 R Mulgan, 'Accountability: an ever-expanding concept?' (2000) 78 *Pub Admin* 555.
4 M Bovens in E Ferlie et al (eds), *Oxford Handbook of Public Management* (2004), p 182.
5 See G Marshall, *Ministerial Responsibility* (1989).
6 Marshall, above n 5, pp 2–4.
7 See generally *The Collective Responsibility of Ministers: an Outline of the Issues* (HC Research Paper 04/82, Nov 2004).

and defended by all ministers.[8] From the perspective of accountability, collective responsibility helps to answer the 'who' question (as well as the 'for what' and 'to whom' questions), as it ensures that the same accounting for government policy will be given whoever within government provides it. The doctrine is in tune with the British equation of united government with strong and effective government. However, for those seeking to hold government to account, it may appear less helpful, in terms of making informed assessments and evaluations of how and why policy was developed; what alternatives were considered; why particular decisions were taken or not taken; whether implementation of policy has matched intended aims and objectives, and so on.

Individual responsibility also addresses the 'who' and 'for what', as well as the 'to whom', questions, as it requires 'political' ministers, rather than 'non-political' officials to be accountable to Parliament and the public for what happens within that minister's area of responsibility.[9] Having thereby established the essential constitutional chain of accountability, the more pressing questions tend to focus on the substance or content of the convention, especially in the complex arena of public administration.[10] For what is a minister accountable, both in the senses of rendering an account, and of being held to account? When is it appropriate for either or both aspects of accountability to come into play, and to what extent does that expose officials to more direct accountability in either or both these senses, especially before Parliament? Because government is not a world of technical administration, but the practical world of politics and personalities, these constitutional issues of accountability can become the arena for partisanship, where the immediate focus is more on blame and sanctions, especially resignation or dismissal (where support from party leaders and colleagues may be decisive),[11] rather than a disinterested investigation of some aspect of policy and administration, with a view to learning lessons.

Ministerial accountability to Parliament is a relationship under continual strain and tension, where the government inevitably has the upper hand. Parliaments – so far as they are autonomous – constantly seek ways of holding to account a government so preferentially positioned. Effective accountability requires a parliament to have robust mechanisms of holding the governors to account. At the same time, a parliament has several other roles, primarily that of legislator, and is essentially a political rather than a technocratic institution, where the priorities of its actors will not be defined solely in terms of accountability functions. In the Westminster model of representative democracy, parliaments hold ministers to account on behalf of the people; these ministers sit within, and as part of, these parliaments, and members need to balance their party and governmental/opposition allegiances with their representative obligations to their constituents and the wider public. This makes the web of accountability potentially complex, especially where there may be little clear distinction between accounter and accountee, and where

8 All this now has to take account of freedom of information legislation, though such schemes tend to exempt, to some degree, such internal discussions and advice between ministers and/or officials.
9 See generally *Individual Ministerial Responsibility: Issues and Examples* (HC Research Paper 04/31, April 2004).
10 In practice, the ultimate sanction, of loss of office, tends to result from personal or private misconduct, rather than from 'official' failings.
11 N Baldwin and N Forman in N Baldwin (ed), *Parliament in the 21st Century* (2005), p 280.

the parliament's members can themselves be accountable to the public for how they hold the government to account.

In the latter decades of the twentieth century, there were reforms at Westminster designed to enhance its accountability mechanisms, especially through the creation of the modern select committee system from 1979, and the adoption of explicit resolutions in both Houses in March 1997 designed to set out the basic principles of parliamentary accountability.[12] In addition, there have been developments in accountability mechanisms which have little or no direct connection with parliaments, such as ombudsmen, auditors and inspectors, and which, unlike parliaments, are exclusively or primarily mechanisms of accountability.[13]

At the same time there were, and continue to be, fundamental changes in the structure, organisation and operation of UK public administration, including those inspired by 'new public management' thinking, with many public sector functions being delivered, not directly by central departments headed by ministers, but by bodies with varying degrees of independence from central departments. These included 'next steps' executive agencies operating at 'arm's length' from Whitehall departments but without separate legal personality; non-departmental public bodies (NDPBs or 'quangos') outside the departmental structure, and the delivery of functions by private bodies, sometimes under contract to the public sector. Though some of these forms of structure were not new (public boards were common in the nineteenth century, and twentieth century nationalisations brought similar accountability problems, especially after 1945),[14] the scale since the 1980s has been more extensive, and has rendered substantially redundant the traditional notion of a minister accountable to Parliament for the activities directly within his/her remit.

As an aim of these administrative reforms was to loosen direct political 'interference' and oversight, to allow agencies to operate more efficiently and innovatively, it was inevitable that these changes would have a major impact on traditional accountability practice. Relationships between ministers and these bodies tended to become akin to private sector 'managerial accountability', where governments set strategic goals, provide some or all of the necessary resources, and hold those given the task of carrying out these activities to account for their efficient, effective and economic operation. Ministers could claim that their accountability for these activities should depend on the extent of their actual or appropriate involvement, and that, while accountable, in an explanatory sense, for all activities, they are 'responsible' in the amendatory sense (especially in terms of blame or sanctions) only for those aspects in which they are actually or should be involved.

While governments since the 1980s continued to insist that the traditional model remained essentially intact (partly because it justified their own 'control' over these supposedly freer bodies), parliaments had constantly to play 'catch up' in tracking and holding to account this more fragmented public sector, not just in their mechanisms but also in deciding for what ministers can be held accountable.[15]

12 HC Deb, vol 292, cols 1046–1047 (19 March 1997); HL Deb vol 579, col 1057 (20 March 1997). See D Woodhouse, 'Ministerial responsibility: something old, something new?' [1997] PL 262; *The Osmotherly Rules*, HC Standard Note SN/PC/2671, Aug 2005.
13 Mulgan, 'Accountability', above n 3, p 565.
14 See T Prosser, *Nationalised Industries and Public Control* (1986).
15 For a study of the accountability of agencies, see P Giddings, *Parliamentary Accountability* (1995).

All this has led to what appears like a constant reformulation of the principles and practice of constitutional accountability, and of individual ministerial responsibility in particular, primarily carried on in 'negotiations' between the UK government and the select committees, especially the Public Administration Committee (and its predecessors) and the Liaison Committee (composed of the committee chairs).[16] Westminster has resisted governmental reformulations which distinguish between 'policy' and 'operational' matters, especially if it means that ministers are to be regarded as 'responsible' only for the former, thereby potentially leaving large accountability gaps, or that ministers evade justified blame or sanctions, including loss of office. However, there has been a greater focus (especially since the Scott Report into the Arms for Iraq affair)[17] on explanatory aspects, especially in parliaments, in particular, having access to all information necessary to carry out their scrutiny functions in an informed and effective manner.

Notwithstanding this fragmentation of the public sector, and the rise of notions of more direct accountability between government and people, which may wholly or in part be said to 'bypass' parliaments and parliamentarians, both governments and parliaments have publicly adhered to the parliamentary accountability model. The cultural insularity of the UK Parliament, and its dominance by the executive, has tended to reinforce this model, not necessarily in appropriate or effective ways, to the exclusion of the essential democratic limb of the model which is that all this accountability is undertaken on behalf of the people. In theory, Parliament is the prism through which the government discharges its accountability to the people, but in practice the accountability relationship between Parliament and government has become a virtually closed one, almost excluding the very accountability to the people for which it is supposed to operate as the medium. Accountability is, in essence, the accountability of ministers to Parliament.

RETHINKING ACCOUNTABILITY FOR DEVOLVED SCOTLAND

To what extent do the theory and practice of accountability differ in today's Scotland? Prior to devolution, accountability was applied uniformly across the UK, subject to the different ways that each country within the UK was governed, with the Scottish system the most distinctive outside England. By 1997, 'administrative devolution'[18] had developed into a sophisticated governance system, operating largely through a territorial department, the Scottish Office, with its own ministerial team under the Secretary of State for Scotland, as well as the functional departments and ministers which governed the UK and England, with particular procedures and practices within the Westminster Parliament to handle Scottish business. Nevertheless, Scottish Office ministers were chosen from the majority party at Westminster and bound by collective responsibility, which limited the scope for distinctive Scottish policy initiatives. It was also widely perceived that the

---

16 M Flinders, 'The enduring centrality of individual ministerial responsibility within the British constitution' (2000) 6 *Journal of Legislative Studies* 73; D Woodhouse, 'The reconstruction of constitutional accountability' [2002] PL 73; M Flinders, 'Shifting the balance? Parliament, the Executive and the British constitution' (2002) 50 *Pol Studs* 23.

17 HC 115, 1995–96; A Tomkins, *The Constitution After Scott* (1998).

18 See J Mitchell, *Governing Scotland* (2004).

arrangements for handling Scottish business (especially legislation) at Westminster were marginalised and inadequate.

Devolution provided not just further decentralisation within the UK, but also an opportunity for rethinking many aspects of our governance arrangements. This arose for two main reasons. First, devolution had to be established through Westminster legislation, requiring relationships that were previously embodied in unwritten conventions to be expressed in statutory form. Secondly, innovative constitutional thinking was encouraged by, and explicit in, the way that the devolution policy, which was eventually implemented once Labour gained power in 1997, developed in the 1980s and 1990s. This was by an extra-governmental process (as the Conservative government was opposed to devolution) involving many opposition parties and other groups and bodies in wider Scottish civil society, which were determined to promote not just devolution, but, within it, a better form of governance.

Conventional wisdom has it that there was a relatively linear progression from the referendum result in 1979 to the establishment of devolution two decades later. Key steps in this evolution included the *Claim of Right* in 1988; the Scottish Constitutional Convention (SCC) 1989-1995; the cross-party constitutional reform agenda which triumphed at the 1997 election; and finally the Consultative Steering Group (CSG),[19] the July 1997 White Paper[20] and the Scotland Act 1998. For supporters of devolution, process was just as important as substance, ushering in the era of 'new politics', a form of governance that would be both different from, and better than, that practised at Westminster and Whitehall, underpinned by the central, pro-active role of the people. It would be some sort of uniquely Scottish synthesis of traditional representative democracy and a more direct or participatory democracy born out of supposed Scottish constitutional notions of the 'sovereignty of the people'. Though this view missed out much of the wider political contexts of the time,[21] it shaped the context for the constitutional rethinking that included a redefinition of accountability.

This rethinking developed from early 'sovereignty of the people' rhetoric, rejecting as 'non-Scottish' notions of unlimited parliamentary sovereignty, through attempts to reconcile both strands of thinking, and finally to a recognition that any practical devolution scheme would be firmly based on traditional UK constitutional principles, albeit with a dash of 'direct democracy'. What emerged was a blend of the old and the new, within which 'accountability' was not just the removal of the perceived democratic deficit in existing Scottish governance (especially the imposition of policies, such as the poll tax, by a UK government with little or no elected representation in Scotland) but one of the 'principles' underpinning this better government of Scotland.

The 1997 White Paper skilfully proposed a form of decentralisation within the existing UK constitutional framework, and as part of the Labour Government's wider constitutional reform package, dressed up with just enough of the 'new politics' rhetoric to claim continuity with what had gone before. Devolution would

---

19 This was established in late 1997, and reported in January 1999: *Shaping Scotland's Parliament*, (1999).

20 *Scotland's Parliament* (Cm 3658, 1997).

21 K Wright, *The People Say Yes* (1997); A Brown, 'Designing the Scottish Parliament' (2000) 53 *Parl Affairs* 542; J Mitchell, 'The creation of the Scottish Parliament: journey without end' (1999) 52 *Parl Affairs* 649; P Grice, 'The creation of a devolved parliament' (2001) 7 *Journal of Legislative Studies* 1.

'strengthen democratic control and make government more accountable to the people of Scotland'; 'connect and involve people with the decisions that matter to them'; and 'bring a sense of ownership to political debate'.[22] Its specific key proposals – such as the nature of the devolved government, and its relationship with the Parliament ('The Scottish Executive, which will be accountable to the Scottish Parliament, will exercise executive responsibility in relation to devolved matters. The relationship between the Scottish Executive and the Scottish Parliament will be similar to the relationship between the UK Government and the UK Parliament');[23] ministerial control over quangos, and the additional member system of elections – reaffirmed existing doctrines of constitutional accountability, through ministerial accountability to parliament, and a 'representative' relationship between the people and the organs of government.

This approach was consolidated in the CSG Report in January 1999, *Shaping Scotland's Parliament*.[24] Its centrepiece was a set of four key principles, designed to deliver the Parliament envisaged by the SCC and the Scotland Act, and 'to provide an open, accessible and, above all, participative Parliament'.[25] These principles were: sharing the power; accountability; access and participation; and equal opportunities. As far as accountability was concerned, the Report stated that 'the Scottish Executive should be accountable to the Scottish Parliament and the Parliament and Executive should be accountable to the people of Scotland'. The Report devoted a whole chapter to 'accountability', in the belief that much of the Parliament's work would consist of Executive scrutiny.[26] As well as considering means of financial and EU scrutiny, it divided accountability mechanisms into ones by which the Executive would be held to account by the full Parliament, by committees and by individual MSPs.

When they came into being in 1999, both the Parliament and the Executive signed up to the CSG approach. In one of the first parliamentary debates, Henry McLeish (then an Executive cabinet minister) declared that 'the Executive will be much more accountable to the Parliament in Scotland than the government is to the Parliament in Westminster',[27] and the Executive explicitly incorporated the CSG principles in its *Scottish Ministerial Code*, published in August 1999.[28] However, the important question concerns what impact this desire for improved accountability has actually had in practice. Has the 'new politics' talk remained simply aspirational rhetoric, devoid of any substantive meaning or relevance to day-to-day devolved governance? Or has it become embedded in the operational culture and ethos, as well as the practice of the devolved institutions, especially the Parliament?

DEVOLVED ACCOUNTABILITY IN PRACTICE

In order to discover which path has been taken since 1999, it is necessary to examine some key aspects of accountability as it has operated in practice in devolved

22 *Scotland's Parliament*, foreword by the Scottish Secretary, Donald Dewar. See also para 1.1.
23 *Scotland's Parliament*, para 2.6.
24 This Group was set up and administratively supported by the Scottish Office, and chaired by the devolution minister, Henry McLeish.
25 CSG Report, para 2.4.
26 CSG Report, Section 3.4, and also paras 2.23–2.27.
27 SPOR, 9 June 1999, col 367.
28 Para 3.1.

Scotland, noting where Scottish theory and practice have applied or diverged from traditional UK notions of accountability. In other words, in devolved Scotland who is accountable to whom, for what and how? The section considers, first, the essential principles on which accountability is based, concerning the 'who', 'to whom' and 'for what' questions. It then considers various other aspects of accountability practice, largely focusing on the 'how' question.

Ministerial responsibility

It was to be expected that collective responsibility would be applied by a devolved Scottish government. In fact, it should be more important than at Westminster because, as the electoral system makes single-party majority government a rarity, collective responsibility is the key mechanism in holding a coalition government together, by not just keeping united ministers within, but also across, the governing parties. Accordingly, the Scottish version of the doctrine has been termed *collective coalition responsibility*.[29] This doctrine underpins the Executive's internal guidance, such as the *Scottish Ministerial Code* (in other respects a 'tartanised' version of the *Ministerial Code*)[30] and the *Guide to Collective Decision Making*, which reproduce detailed guidance on the meaning and application of collective responsibility, as between ministers (including ministers of the two coalition parties), but also between ministers and their officials. The *Guide*, which has no UK parallel, is implicitly focused on collective responsibility as it applies in a coalition situation, and derived from the initial partnership agreement between the two governing parties, Labour and Liberal Democrat. The latter, according to the *Guide*'s preface, written by the permanent secretary, 'makes it clear that, in order to work together effectively to deliver their programme, "the partnership parties will need goodwill, mutual trust and agreed procedures which foster collective decision-making and responsibility"'. The *Guide* also contains, for example, guidance on the respective roles of the First Minister (the Labour party leader) and the Deputy First Minister (the Liberal Democrat leader).[31]

The clearest example so far of the operation of collective responsibility in practice was the resignation of Tavish Scott, deputy Minister for Parliament, in March 2001 over fisheries policy. Despite supporting the Executive in a crucial division (which the Executive lost), he subsequently resigned, not, as may perhaps have been expected, as a consequence of any perceived failure on his part, as party business manager, to prevent a significant Liberal Democrat rebellion, but on his own initiative because of his disagreement with Executive policy. This provided the opportunity for the Parliament's first ex-ministerial resignation speech, when, during the re-run fisheries debate a week later, he said:[32]

'I resigned last Friday because I sought to convince ministerial colleagues of those arguments for more short-term aid, but I failed. I was not able to change colleagues'

29 B Winetrobe, 'Collective responsibility in devolved Scotland' [2003] PL 24.
30 M Shephard in J Fleming and I Holland (eds), *Motivating Ministers to Morality* (2001).
31 The post of Deputy First Minister is entirely non-statutory, and was presumably created to provide a suitably senior status for the leader of the 'junior' coalition partner. Thus far, that person has also held a substantive ministerial portfolio.
32 SPOR, 15 March 2001, cols 600–601. See also the exchange of letters with his party leader, the Deputy First Minister, Jim Wallace, reproduced in a Liberal Democrat press release of 9 March 2001.

minds last week.... As I was not able to support government policy on fisheries, I had no alternative but to resign. Let me be clear: when one is a minister, one supports the government. If one cannot support the government, one resigns.'

Another example, which involved both ministers and ministerial parliamentary aides,[33] occurred over Glasgow hospital reorganisation in 2002.[34] Several local Labour MSPs openly opposed the Executive-supported policy, and attended local protest meetings, including a meeting with the Health Minister, justifying their actions by emphasising their dual roles in the government and as constituency MSPs. Though some took their opposition to the extent of not positively supporting the Executive in every relevant vote, none was dismissed or required to resign,[35] with the Executive publicly claiming, notwithstanding its own guidance, that collective responsibility had been properly applied.

A further example of apparent disagreement on Executive policy, over the fire dispute in late 2002, by the Education Minister, Cathy Jamieson, again did not lead to resignation or dismissal. However, her dissent was more implied than explicit, when she failed to endorse comments by the First Minister describing the strike as 'unacceptable'. Nevertheless, this came at a time when the junior Justice Minister, Richard Simpson, (whose department handled the fire service) had to resign when he was reported as describing the striking fire-fighters as 'fascist bastards', an example of individual ministerial responsibility in action.

By contrast, as at Westminster, the confidentiality aspect of collective responsibility appears to apply even beyond ministerial office. When, as a new member of the European and External Relations Committee in 2005, the former Deputy First Minister, Jim Wallace, was asked for the usual declaration of interests, he 'stated that he considered himself bound by ministerial collective responsibility on matters in which he had been directly involved'.[36]

Prior to the Simpson episode, the main test of individual responsibility came with the Scottish Qualifications Authority (SQA) school examinations affair in 2000, when many students received wrong, incomplete or late results. In addition to criticism of SQA (an executive NDPB) itself, there was scrutiny of the role of the Education Minister, Sam Galbraith (although responsibility for the SQA was, at the relevant time, split between the Education and Enterprise and Lifelong Learning departments and ministers). The affair was the subject, inter alia, of two parliamentary committee inquiries, and a plenary no confidence debate. Though the minister survived the immediate crisis (he was reshuffled in October 2000 to the Environment portfolio, and eventually left the government and the Parliament in 2001), the scrutiny highlighted issues of the extent of ministerial oversight and control of arm's length bodies, mainly argued in terms of existing UK practice as it was understood.[37] Woodhouse saw this case as an example of how UK constitutional accountability has developed in recent times.[38] However, Himsworth has suggested that her analysis 'appears to take little account of the possibility of

33 The equivalent of a parliamentary private secretary. The *Scottish Ministerial Code* applies collective responsibility to them.
34 See further, Winetrobe, 'Collective responsibility', above n 29.
35 One MPA resigned immediately on his own initiative.
36 Minutes of 13th Meeting, 2005, 13 Sept 2005, item 1.
37 E Clarence, 'Ministerial responsibility and the Scottish Qualifications Agency' (2002) 80 *Pub Admin* 791.
38 Woodhouse, 'Constitutional accountability', above n 16, pp 82–83.

different constitutional relationships', though he does not elaborate beyond a warning that 'one should be cautious in a convention-dependent field such as this to assume that the principle of ministerial responsibility ... will, in fact, turn out to develop in precisely the same way in Scotland'.[39]

The ultimate form of accountability mechanism for a minister or a government is a confidence motion. At Westminster, the consequences are a matter of constitutional convention rather than law, although, as in 1924 and 1979, they can lead to the fall of a government or an immediate general election.[40] The Scotland Act 1998 made this a statutory mechanism, ensuring that the passing of a no confidence motion in the Scottish Executive by the Parliament leads to the resignation of the whole government, including junior ministers and the law officers.[41] The Parliament's standing orders (SOs) both set out the procedures for these motions,[42] and allow for similar motions in respect of an individual minister.[43] Though the latter, being governed by SOs rather than statutory, if passed by the Parliament, do not legally require any consequences such as resignation, it is likely that the force of British conventional practice would lead to the resignation or dismissal of the criticised minister. So far, there have been two instances of a confidence motion, both against individual ministers, and both unsuccessful,[44] and one further *de facto* motion of no confidence against a minister, also unsuccessful.[45]

A related form of 'confidence accountability', which has no Westminster parallel, is the requirement for parliamentary endorsement of ministerial appointments. The Parliament nominates one of its members to the sovereign to be First Minister,[46] and has to agree to the First Minister's ministerial appointments (subject to the sovereign's approval).[47] SOs specify the method of parliamentary involvement in such appointments,[48] which is limited to the filling of vacancies to the appropriate ministerial tier (Scottish Minister, law officer or junior minister), and so give the Parliament no formal say in the allocation or re-allocation of ministerial portfolios when reshuffles occur where there is no vacancy to be filled.[49] In practice, for an Executive with a majority, such parliamentary endorsement is virtually guaranteed.

These few examples cannot be the basis of any firm conclusion as to how ministerial responsibility operates in devolved Scotland. What they do suggest is that the intention of the Scottish Executive (and, presumably, of the UK

---

39 C Himsworth in P Craig and A Tomkins, *The Executive and Public Law* (2006), p 207 and fn 78.
40 J Seaton and B K Winetrobe, 'Confidence motions in the UK Parliament' (1994) 62 *The Table* 34.
41 Scotland Act, ss 45(2), 47(3)(c), 48(2) and 49(4)(c).
42 If such a motion is supported by at least twenty-five members it must be included in a proposed business programme.
43 Rule 8.12.
44 Sam Galbraith, over the SQA affair in 2000, SPOR, 13 Dec 2000, cols 841–864; Sarah Boyack, over tendering of trunk roads management contracts, SPOR, 15 Feb 2001, cols 1279–1305.
45 Malcolm Chisholm, over hospital reorganisation and closures, SPOR, 30 Sept 2004, cols 10747–10801. This expression of no confidence was contained in a more extensive motion, moved by the Conservatives in their own debating time, and was responded to by the criticised minister, not by the First Minister.
46 Scotland Act 1998, s 46.
47 Scotland Act 1998, ss 47–49.
48 Rules 4.1, 4.3, 4.6 and 4.7.
49 For internal guidance, largely to accommodate coalition government, on how such decisions are made, see the *Scottish Ministerial Code*, paras 4.1–4.3.

government also) that the UK model would operate, subject to any particular circumstances (such as the existence of coalition government, as discussed above), has been borne out in practice thus far. This is not surprising, given the pressures of managing inter-party, as well as intra-party, dissent in the Executive, and the limitations imposed by the Scotland Act on the structure of the Executive, and its relationship with the Parliament. Himsworth's suggestion of some divergence over time may yet come about, but that will depend, as do so many of the topics discussed in this section, on factors such as the willingness of the Executive and the Parliament to continue with familiar structures of the devolved administration (departments, agencies, NDPBs and the like) and of the appropriate accountability mechanisms applied to them.

Questions, debates and statements

Parliamentary debates, questions (written and oral) and ministerial statements are important accountability devices in Holyrood, as at Westminster, and generally speaking, operate in similar ways, though with some procedural innovations. For example, the Parliament has tried ways of enabling statements to be the trigger not just for an immediate question-and-answer session, but also for more substantive debates. It also holds general debates (similar to Commons 'debates on the adjournment') without motions or decisions, to encourage non-partisan discussion of appropriate issues. The daily members' business debate at the close of business is longer (forty-five minutes) and a more genuine and meaningful debate, in terms of the numbers of participants, than the equivalent Commons adjournment debate.

However there have been criticisms that some plenary debates, especially Executive ones, avoid controversial or topical issues. This puts even more onus on non-Executive debates to be of a partisan or critical nature. Many of these difficulties arise from standing orders which do not, unlike Commons SO number 14(1), explicitly provide that all plenary time not otherwise allocated 'belongs' to the government, although that seems to be the situation in practice,[50] especially in the Executive's view. How ministerial policy announcements should be made to the Parliament is as much a problem at Holyrood as at Westminster. There has been a more open acceptance (though not endorsement) of the 'inspired' or 'planted' question, even to the extent of these being noted in the *Business Bulletin* by its own symbol. As with committees, there are pressures on plenary time (1.5 days per sitting week), much of which is taken up by specified business, such as question times, and by legislative business.

The Parliament's arrangements for parliamentary questions (PQs) are also generally similar to the Westminster model, even to the extent of the early creation of a dedicated First Minister's Question Time. This was not included in the initial SOs, but swiftly added, because it was thought to be a clear gap in Executive accountability.

The scale of written PQs has proved problematic for the Executive. It tried to dispense with them during recesses, as at Westminster, but, though current rules now provide for longer lead times for answers during long recesses, the Parliament

---

50 This is ameliorated somewhat by the ability of others, such as individual members, committees or the Bureau to lodge motions on business, procedural or substantive matters, which can be taken if included in a business programme.

successfully resisted this. This can be contrasted with the Commons, where the government has rejected such moves because it has

> 'always taken the view that the House should retain the principle of tabling questions during periods when the House is sitting and ministers are in attendance to respond to parliamentary scrutiny. Ministers remain accountable for the work of their department, and members can and do correspond with them during recesses'.[51]

Despite some analysis of the proper role of PQs,[52] Holyrood does not generally focus on the quality and relevance of parliamentary *answers* as a way of scrutinising the effectiveness of PQs as an accountability mechanism. This can be contrasted, for example, with the regular audit of PQs which the Commons Public Administration Committee conducts.[53]

Parliamentary committees

The committee system was designed to be the main mechanism for public engagement and power-sharing, as well as being a core instrument for holding government to account. Unlike at the House of Commons, committees at Holyrood are 'all-purpose' bodies dealing with policy, legislative and budgetary scrutiny, and petitions. Holyrood committees also operate much more transparently than those at Westminster. Whereas Westminster committees are essentially private bodies, only meeting in public for evidence-taking, the Parliament's committees are generally required to operate in public, with most meeting papers published online in advance.

Information is essential to a parliamentary committee's scrutiny role, and its ability to hold government to account. Committees have detailed mechanisms for commissioning research, and for operating through reporters (based on continental 'rapporteur' systems). However, Commons select committees are improving in these areas, with the creation of a dedicated Scrutiny Unit, and, since 2002, operating with a set of defined, published 'core tasks', which provides a foundation for enhanced accountability, both of the government to Parliament and of the committees to the public.[54] Holyrood committees publish individual, but extremely brief, annual reports, and the Procedures Committee recently rejected a proposal from the Conveners' Group (roughly equivalent to the Commons' Liaison Committee) to remove the SO requirement for the committees to produce them. It suggested that the Group might review its guidance on producing them, to enable committees to make them 'more relevant and interesting', and also sent it information on the House of Commons system of 'core tasks' for select committees, as a possible model.[55]

---

51 Written Answer by Leader of the House, HC Deb, vol 437, col 882W (18 Oct 2005).
52 The Procedures Committee in 2000 emphasised that the duality of PQs, having 'both an information gathering aspect and a political aspect', contributes to accountability: 1st Report, 2000, SP Paper 169, Aug 2000, para 44.
53 See, eg, the 7th such report by the Committee, *Ministerial Accountability and Parliamentary Questions* (5th Report, 2004–05), HC 449, March 2005.
54 See HC Standard Note SN/PC/3161, Aug 2004.
55 Letter to Conveners Group, 27 April 2006, Paper PR/S2/06/8/8, reproduced in Procedures Committee papers for its 9 May 2006 meeting.

Like Commons select committees, Holyrood committees tend to be periodically restructured to reflect changes in ministerial or departmental portfolios. However, the Executive practice (carried over from the pre-devolution Scottish Office) of not matching ministerial and departmental portfolios, compounds the difficulties parliamentary committees generally have in the UK in 'keeping up' with government organisational arrangements.

Much of the Holyrood committee system's innovativeness is in the area of 'openness and participation' (process issues) rather than in 'accountability' (outcome issues), although, in principle, a more transparent, inclusive and participative process should itself be regarded as a necessary, if not sufficient, condition for effective scrutiny.[56] The multi-purpose remits of the Parliament's committees make them busy, and also limit their autonomy, as so much of their business is determined externally. These problems are compounded by regular turnover in membership, which dilutes the specialisation the unitary system was designed to encourage. They also all have Executive majorities, because the Parliament interprets the statutory requirement to 'have regard' to party balance[57] as replicating that plenary balance. The 2003 Procedures Committee *Founding Principles* report rejected the idea that Executive majorities inhibit the committees' accountability role, or that they are especially inappropriate for mandatory committees, such as Procedures and Standards and Public Appointments.[58]

Parliament's information-gathering powers

To exercise its accountability role effectively, a parliament has to be able to require government to provide it with the information it needs. This has been difficult at Westminster, whenever its notionally unlimited power to call for 'persons, papers and records' clashes with the government's unwillingness to allow ministers and officials to appear or answer questions as fully as Parliament would wish. The government's approach is set out in its guidance (the 'Osmotherly Rules'), which operates in practice despite not being formally endorsed or approved by Parliament.[59]

As the devolved Parliament's information-gathering powers derive directly from provisions in the Scotland Act, it should be more able to enforce its will in similar circumstances.[60] Executive ministers and officials have to obey a valid demand for the appearance of witnesses or production of documents. In practice, no such demand has yet been made, as the Parliament has operated by invitation.[61] However, the Executive believes that matters should operate under 'Osmotherly' conditions, and, when problems arose in late 2000 over committee inquiries into

---

56 M Sandford and L Maer, *Scrutiny Under Devolution: Committees in Scotland, Wales and Northern Ireland* (2003); D Arter, *The Scottish Parliament: a Scandinavian-Style Assembly?* (2004).

57 Scotland Act 1998, Sch 3, para 6(2).

58 Procedures Committee Principles Report, vol 1, paras 659–664. By contrast, the House of Commons Standards and Privileges Committee has an equal number of Government and Opposition members.

59 *Departmental Evidence and Response to Select Committees*, July 2005; *Erskine May's Parliamentary Practice* (23rd edn, 2004), p 761.

60 Scotland Act 1998, ss 23–26, which, by standing orders, have been applied to the Parliament's committees: s 23(8) and rule 12.4.1.

61 There was an unsuccessful attempt to force the Parliament to use its statutory powers to order the BBC to disclose material desired by the (non-statutory) Fraser Inquiry into the Holyrood Building Project: SPOR, 31 March 2004, cols 7227–7256.

the SQA affair, it took the opportunity to persuade the Parliament to accept this regime. At a day's notice, and without any prior scrutiny, it lodged a motion[62] which imports restrictive 'Westminster' principles to the Parliament, by applying a public interest test of confidentiality of governmental policy discussions between ministers and officials into the exercise of the unqualified statutory powers.[63]

This was compounded by the issuing, weeks later, of Executive guidance which was little more than a 'tartanised' version of the Osmotherly Rules.[64] The Executive believed that the Parliament's resolution had endorsed its view of its parliamentary accountability, and this had discharged earlier promises from the Presiding Officer and the First Minister that no 'MacOsmotherly Rules' would be promulgated without prior parliamentary approval.[65]

Thus, the Parliament had in less than two years virtually agreed a self-denying ordinance on the exercise of its statutory powers, in favour of the 'Osmotherly' approach, which, unlike the House of Commons, it had even explicitly endorsed. This irony was compounded further by there being virtually no formal parliamentary scrutiny of the content or operation of this guidance, nor any substantive demand for its reform, despite some, albeit limited, Westminster parliamentary involvement in the revision of the UK 'Rules' in July 2005.[66]

At the time of writing, the Shirley McKie/Scottish Criminal Record Office fingerprinting affair may test the committees' powers to obtain adequate information from the Executive, as ministers have resisted calls for some form of public inquiry, preferring a parliamentary inquiry. The Justice 1 Committee has begun such an inquiry, but early indications are that the Executive is unwilling to release some information even to the Parliament on the grounds of legal confidentiality.[67]

Parliamentary scrutiny of constitutional and governance matters

A major deficiency in the Parliament's committee system is its scrutiny of the 'core executive'. This includes the organisation, structure and operation of the Scottish administration; its public bodies; 'modernising/efficient government' initiatives; ministerial-official relationships; inter-governmental, external and parliamentary relations; freedom of information; public appointments, and so on. As with Whitehall, the devolved Scottish administration is more than the Executive ministers and its nine central departments. As at April 2006, it comprised nineteen executive agencies, thirty-one executive NDPBs, forty-four advisory NDBPs, thirty-eight tribunals, twenty-three health bodies, one public corporation and two nationalised industries, as well as temporary bodies such as task forces.[68]

62 Entitled *Executive Accountability to Parliament*. This resolution may have derived from the March 1997 Westminster accountability resolutions, noted earlier.
63 SPOR, 1 Nov 2000, cols 1197–1240. See the general note to s 23 in the Explanatory Notes to the Scotland Act (2004).
64 *Scottish Executive and Responses to Committees of the Scottish Parliament* (2001).
65 Permanent Secretary's foreword; SPOR, 25 Nov 1999, cols 994–995 and 1001.
66 See the memorandum (containing a draft revised version) and evidence of the Leader of the House to the Liaison Committee, 19 Oct 2004, HC 1180, 2003–04.
67 Scotland Act 1998, s 23(9) enables people to refuse to produce information they would be entitled to refuse to produce in proceedings in a court in Scotland. See the Justice Minister's written answers on 20 March 2006 and 13 April 2006, S2W-23155 and S2W-24584 respectively.
68 Statistics derived from lists on the Scottish Executive website, April 2006: *http:// www.scotland.gov.uk/Home*.

While some of these issues are examined by committees[69] – the Finance Committee has been a consistent scrutineer of the Executive's various 'modernising government' initiatives, and relocation policies – and some committee remits have been extended from time to time to accommodate them,[70] there is no single, dedicated committee that examines them comprehensively, as is done at the House of Commons by its Public Administration Select Committee. The Procedures Committee has considered proposals for such a single committee from time to time, but without any resulting reforms.

A dedicated committee is no guarantee that such core issues would be scrutinised effectively by the Parliament. Scrutiny by different committees may ensure a more diverse range of views. Nevertheless, the absence of a dedicated committee has ensured fragmented, inconsistent and incomplete scrutiny of the 'core executive' and devolved governance as a whole. As Westminster has long experienced,[71] the constantly changing structure of the public sector, especially the development of bodies at 'arm's length' (such as 'next steps' executive agencies, and quangos/NDPBs), itself makes effective scrutiny problematic.[72] Parliaments have to play 'catch-up' in devising appropriate scrutiny mechanisms to cope with these changes,[73] and where such issues are a 'secondary' or more recent part of a committee's remit, they may take second place to matters within a committee's 'core' or original remit.[74]

The Procedures Committee, in its *Founding Principles* report, suggested that it would be consistent with those principles if the Parliament became 'an active partner' in these developments.[75] It also recognised the inadequacy of current scrutiny of quangos and similar bodies, and urged the Parliament to develop 'a high-profile, well-resourced and systematic approach to scrutinising such bodies. Without such an approach, accountability and power-sharing are unlikely to prove adequate'.[76] This received short shrift from the Executive, which advocated existing notions of ministerial accountability; in its response to the Committee's report, it stated that 'it could not support any proposals which cut across these lines of accountability', and that it was 'of course important to recognise that, under the terms of the Scotland Act 1998, the Scottish administration and the Parliament are distinct statutory bodies with separate management structures'. Ministers even questioned the need for any proposed change in the Procedures Committee's remit

---

69 Eg, the Finance Committee's remit is taken to include public service reform issues, and the Procedures Committee examines procedural aspects of Parliament-Executive relations.

70 The European Committee now includes 'external relations' in its remit since March 2003; 'public appointments' was added to the Standards Committee's remit in March 2005, and some Executive 'public service' functions have been added to the Local Government Committee's remit since 2000.

71 See *The Regulatory State: Ensuring its Accountability*, House of Lords Constitution Committee (6th Report, 2003–04), HL 68, May 2004; M Flinders, in P Giddings (ed), *The Future of Parliament* (2005).

72 See R Parry, 'Delivery structures and policy development in post-devolution Scotland' (2002) 1 *Social Policy and Society* 315; I Kirkpatrick and R Pyper, in T Butcher and A Massey, *Modernising Civil Services* (2003); R Parry, 'The civil service response to modernisation in the devolved administrations' (2005) 21 *Financial Accountability and Management* 57.

73 Eg, on executive agencies, see Giddings, *Parliamentary Accountability*, above n 15.

74 This has been the case with the Local Government Committee in recent years.

75 *The Founding Principles of the Scottish Parliament*, Procedures Committee (3rd Report, 2003), SP Paper 818, March 2003, para 566 (Procedures Committee Founding Principles Report).

76 *Founding Principles*, para 557.

to cover constitutional or governance issues, believing that they should be dealt with on a case-by-case basis.[77]

The fallout from the Fraser Inquiry into the Holyrood Parliament Building Project, which reported in September 2004, demonstrated how limited is the pressure for significant 'core executive' scrutiny. When the Executive suggested that lessons would be learned, many in the Parliament and media thought this meant some radical review of the devolved civil service. The permanent secretary did request an external (by a civil service commissioner) examination of whether any disciplinary action was justified in respect of any action by Executive officials. This resulted in a report, finding no misconduct by officials, but making various recommendations on project management and similar processes.[78] Amid cries of whitewash and demands for more radical reform (such as a fully devolved civil service), the affair soon faded away, in the absence of any real parliamentary focus or appetite for pursuing these matters further.

This parliamentary accountability gap may hide a further gap at governmental level over civil service issues. There is little public indication of the extent to which the Executive itself contributes to the UK government's development of its policies and practices towards civil service and related machinery of government issues. These are not just technical matters of structure or personnel management; they reflect formulations of the core principles that underpin public accountability of government. For example, there is, at the time of writing, a draft (UK) Civil Service Bill, following many years of discussion within and between Westminster and Whitehall, and itself the subject of widespread and lengthy consultation. More recently, the UK government has been consulting on a new draft of the Civil Service Code (last amended in 1999 to take account of devolution), but, from the available evidence, the Executive has not been an active participant in this exercise, on the basis that it is a reserved matter. According to the Executive, once the UK code is finalised and an Executive version issued (reflecting not differences in substance, but in terminology), 'arrangements will be made to notify the Scottish Parliament'. In the meantime, Executive staff were being encouraged to respond to the UK consultation exercise.[79]

This rather passive approach contrasted with the assertions of the then Public Service Minister, Andy Kerr, responding to the Fraser Inquiry debate in 2004, that there is 'flexibility within the Scottish Executive to act differently, without referring elsewhere for approval' and vehemently rejected claims that 'we cannot make any changes without being told what to do by Whitehall':[80]

> 'Our civil servants are accountable to us as Scottish Ministers and we in turn are accountable to the Scottish Parliament. We have the power and the flexibility to introduce change if we think that it is needed. In short, Scottish civil servants may refer to London, but they do not defer to London.'

Another problematic aspect of Executive–Parliamentary relations has been the extent to which MSPs could directly approach, and seek assistance from, Executive officials: a practice which would test traditional UK constitutional arrangements

---

77 Scottish Executive Response, Responses to Recommendations 67–70, Aug 2003.
78 Scottish Executive Press Notice, 25 Nov 2004.
79 Information from the Executive, March 2006.
80 SPOR, 22 Sept 2004, col 10415.

at central government level, but seems natural to those with a local government background. As the European Committee's convener, Hugh Henry, put it during the committee's second meeting, in August 1999:

> 'I still find it hard to get my mind round the concept of the split of the Executive as servants of the Scottish Ministers rather than of the whole Parliament. For me, that raises the issue of accountability.... I hope that we have not just mirrored the Westminster model and that ... we will start, over the next few years, to examine how civil servants are responsible and accountable to the whole Parliament, rather than to a particular minister.'[81]

The Executive reinforces the traditional model in its internal guidance and in agreed protocols relating to MSPs, committees[82] and SPICe (the Parliament's research and information service). Its guidance on contacts with MSPs reminds its officials:[83]

> 'to bear in mind their constitutional position.... It would be a clear breach of the [Civil Service] Code were civil servants simultaneously to assist opposition parties ... in the formulation or development of their policies.... in any direct or indirect contacts with MSPs who are not Scottish Ministers civil servants must avoid either suggesting or commenting on policy options or engaging in debate about the merits of the Executive's policies.'

Some in the Parliament have tried to press for a more direct relationship, but when it was raised very early on, during the debate establishing the committees in June 1999, the deputy Minister for Parliament, Iain Smith, following the consistent view of UK governments,[84] said that 'we must recognise that, under existing terms, civil servants are not directly answerable to this Parliament, as they remain responsible to the ministers and to the Executive'.[85]

Other than some discussion in the Procedures Committee in May 2000[86] and in its *Founding Principles* inquiry 2001–03, the Parliament has not been willing or able to pursue these questions in any systematic way. This leaves a crucial gap at the heart of the Parliament's mechanisms for holding the Executive to account.

Commissioners

One Scottish innovation is the extent of the creation of a set of statutory 'constitutional commissioners', nominated by the Parliament and appointed by the monarch, rather than being appointed by the Executive.[87] The idea has its genesis in Westminster's 'officers of Parliament', where it applies to the Parliamentary Commissioner for Administration (PCA) and the Comptroller

---

81 European Committee, Meeting 2, 1999, 18 Aug 1999, col 48.
82 *Protocol Between Committee Clerks and the Scottish Executive* (1999).
83 *Guidance on Contacts with Members of the Scottish Parliament* (Aug 2003), paras 2–3.
84 Eg, in its November 1996 response to a Commons committee report on ministerial accountability and responsibility, the government defended 'the fundamental principle that civil servants are servants of the Crown, and not servants of the House': Public Service Committee, 1st special report, HC 67, 1996–97, para 10.
85 SPOR, 8 June 1999, col 277.
86 Procedures Committee, Meeting 7, 2000, 23 May 2000.
87 The Scottish Parliamentary Standards Commissioner is appointed directly within the Parliament.

and Auditor General, and is more developed in several Commonwealth countries.[88] Compared with Westminster, the devolved Scottish system is more widespread (six posts, with more perhaps to come)[89] and far more Parliament-centred in operation. Like auditors, inspectors and ombudsmen elsewhere, they provide a form of 'horizontal' or 'diagonal' accountability mechanism for public institutions, especially the Executive, the Parliament and other devolved public authorities.[90] For example, the Information Commissioner ensures that the Executive and other public bodies make their information available to the public; the Commissioner for Public Appointments oversees the integrity of ministerial appointments to public bodies, and the Public Services Ombudsman investigates complaints of maladministration against the Executive and other public bodies.

This development has been encouraged by the idea that it provides independence from the Executive, seen as a necessary characteristic for officials holding such sensitive constitutional oversight posts. However, this comes at the cost of dependence on the Parliament, which appoints, supports and resources them, and also brings with it a complex, and still developing, web of accountability. The Finance Committee has been especially keen that the commissioners' independence should not mean that they are entirely unaccountable to the Parliament. Its convener, Des McNulty, has said that the commissioners' 'proper independence' and 'arm's-length relationship with the Parliament ... should not be at the expense of proper approval and financial accountability. There can be no blank cheques for anybody in modern Scotland'.[91] The Committee has, at the time of writing, launched an inquiry into the commissioners' 'accountability and governance'.

As with judges and others with adjudicatory/investigatory functions, there is a trade-off between independence and accountability. This is not a zero-sum exercise, as there has to be an appropriate balance between the autonomy necessary for the commissioners to do their jobs effectively, and control by, or their accountability to, the Parliament, so that it can itself account for its spending on these officials. A parliament may be tempted to exercise its power of dismissal and financing powers when a commissioner's activities impinge directly on it, such as with the Standards or Information Commissioners, or when a commissioner takes public stances on controversial public policy matters, as has the Children's Commissioner over asylum and immigration policies affecting children.

It is too early to assess either the commissioners' role in holding government to account, or their own accountability to the Parliament and public. Though appointed by or through the Parliament, they, unlike the UK PCA, were not explicitly created as a parliamentary mechanism, intended to support parliamentary accountability. There is no MSP filter for any of the commissioners; they deal directly with the public. The benefits of independence from ministerial control may

---

88 O Gay and B Winetrobe, *Officers of Parliament: Transforming the Role* (2003); O Gay, in Giddings, *The Future of Parliament*, above n 71.

89 Standards Commissioner; Auditor General for Scotland; Scottish Public Services Ombudsman; Scottish Information Commissioner; Commissioner for Children and Young People; and Commissioner for Public Appointments in Scotland. At the time of writing, there is an Executive Bill to create a Scottish Commissioner for Human Rights, and a Member's Bill to establish a Commissioner for Older People.

90 Bovens in Ferlie, *Oxford Handbook*, above n 4.

91 SPOR, 21 Dec 2005, col 21985.

mean that this system will enhance devolved governance. On the other hand, more direct parliamentary 'interference' in commissioners' activities, in the name of the Parliament's own obligations of financial and wider accountability, may replicate problems that are common in the accountability of governmental public bodies.

ACCOUNTABILITY FOR NON-DEVOLVED MATTERS

We need to recall that devolution is not the whole story of Scottish governance.[92] Much, perhaps most, of it is still carried out at the UK level, notwithstanding the huge focus of the Scottish media and 'civic society' on devolved governance rather than on Westminster and Whitehall. There are still UK ministers, including a Secretary of State for Scotland, and a territorial department, the Scotland Office (since 2003, part of the Department for Constitutional Affairs). Westminster, though with fewer Scottish MPs since 2005, retains some distinctiveness in its Scottish business. And, through a network of intergovernmental relations constructed since 1999, the Scottish Executive plays a role in non-devolved policy and administration, in partnership with the UK government.

To what extent can the two Parliaments hold the two Executives to account for non-devolved matters affecting Scotland, and how is that accountability role shared between these various institutions? These are significant questions, which can only be explored briefly in the context of this chapter. Notwithstanding the drafting of the Scotland Act, there is no clear, fixed boundary between devolved and non-devolved matters. As well as the scope for conflicting interpretations of provisions defining, for example, reserved matters in Schedule 5, there are areas where functions or powers may be shared between the two executives,[93] or granted to the Scottish Executive without corresponding legislative competence being granted to the Scottish Parliament ('executive devolution').[94] Core reserved issues such as finance and the civil service also impact directly on devolved governance, and there are other areas where both administrations' activities may overlap.[95]

Some of the layers of accountability of pre-1999 'administrative devolution' (such as through the multi-functional Scottish Office and its secretary of state, and the range of specialised parliamentary procedures for handling Scottish business), have remained, albeit in modified or truncated form, to deal with non-devolved matters. In addition the advent of devolution has brought forth new forms of relationship, through concordats, conventions and the like, so that the two parliaments and two executives do not, as far as possible, tread on each other's toes, and, within the paramount sovereignty of the UK institutions, respect each other's practical areas of competence.[96] Nevertheless, the accountability arrangements for non-devolved Scottish matters are, in practice, arguably as bad as, if not worse than, they were prior to devolution, especially in relation to legislative scrutiny. Other than 'high' constitutional issues encapsulated by the

92 Also omitted from this chapter are the important tiers of Europe and of local government.
93 Eg, under Scotland Act 1998, s 56.
94 Scotland Act 1998, s 63.
95 As in the UK government's foreign policy and the Executive's 'external relations' strategies.
96 For an excellent overview, see *Devolution: Inter-Institutional Relationships in the United Kingdom*, HL Constitution Committee (2nd Report, 2002–03), HL 28, Jan 2003. See also A Trench (ed), *Devolution and Power in the United Kingdom* (forthcoming).

shorthand of the 'West Lothian Question' or the 'English Question',[97] though, accountability for the governance of non-devolved matters affecting Scotland is not much examined these days.[98]

With some exceptions, ministers from one jurisdiction have rarely appeared before the committees of the other Parliament, something which hinders effective accountability across the two jurisdictions. For example, when asked to appear before a Holyrood committee examining the (UK) Constitutional Reform Bill, the Lord Chancellor declined:

> 'I do not think it would be appropriate for me to accept your invitation on this occasion. I believe you readily appreciate that my accountability is to the Westminster Parliament and that it is rightly a matter for Scottish Ministers to account to the Scottish Parliament for the devolved matters within the Bill.'[99]

This highlights the need for the two parliaments to give further consideration as to how they allocate between them their accountability roles for Scottish governance.

CONCLUSION: ENHANCED ACCOUNTABILITY?

Devolution, by 'adding democracy to administrative devolution'[100] through the creation of a Parliament, was intended to remove a perceived 'democratic deficit'. As such, it could be expected that one of its aims, and one of its measures of success, would be the enhanced accountability of the governors of Scotland to its people. However, many key players in establishing devolution knew that any devolution scheme would be created by, and operate within, existing UK constitutional law and practice, which included Scotland's already distinctive governance system. For Scottish devolution, therefore, the default model was not simply the UK, but the already existing 'Scotland-in-the-UK' system, with its own department and ministers for many areas of policy. As such, devolution was a matter of adding a Scottish Parliament to the existing system of Scottish administrative devolution. It is no surprise that both the UK and Scottish governments expected devolved governance to resemble and reflect the existing UK model. Indeed, in so far as devolution had removed the previous democratic deficit, what it would resemble would not be the previous Scottish version of UK governance, which had catered for Scottish distinctiveness, but something much more akin to the default UK position.

The most intensive internal parliamentary examination of devolved accountability was the Procedures Committee's inquiry into the operation of the CSG principles, which, after two years, produced a massive report in March 2003.[101]

---

97 See R Hazell, *The English Question* (2006).
98 But see the Constitution Unit's series of monitoring reports, summarised in chapters in the Unit's annual 'State of the Nations' compilations. See, eg, G Lodge, M Russell and O Gay, in A Trench (ed), *Has Devolution Made a Difference?* (2004).
99 Reproduced in Paper J2/S2/04/19/7 of the Justice 2 Committee's 12 May 2004 meeting; Devolution Guidance Note 12, *Attendance of UK Ministers and Officials at Committees of the Devolved Legislatures*.
100 J Mitchell, 'Citizenship in a multi-tiered polity', paper presented to APSA Annual Conference, Washington, USA, Sept 2005, p 15.
101 Procedures Committee, *Founding Principles*. For a critique, see Himsworth in *The Executive and Public Law*, above n 39, p 209.

The Committee's analysis recognised the influence of traditional UK notions of parliamentary accountability, and contrasted the 'relatively fresh' notion of parliamentary power-sharing with accountability, which it described as 'a profoundly traditional function of parliaments'. It defined accountability in terms both of accountability of the Executive to the Parliament collectively, and 'the means by which the Members of the Parliament generally are held to account by the electorate, mainly by voting periodically in a general election'.[102] It concluded that 'the Parliament is performing effectively in its duty to scrutinise the Executive', though it

'also found significant gaps in Executive accountability to the Parliament, in budget scrutiny; scrutiny of the civil service, and, especially, of the Executive's "arm's length" agencies; and aspects of the legislative process and parliamentary questions'.[103]

The Executive is comfortable with these largely familiar lines of accountability. True, it has adjusted to a relationship with its Parliament, which is in some ways unfamiliar in London, especially in business management, and the scale of parliamentary scrutiny – by committees, PQs, debates etc – is certainly much greater than in the days of Scottish Office accountability to Westminster. However, the mechanisms of parliamentary accountability are generally not that much different from those at Westminster.

The Executive has succeeded in convincing the Parliament that, however refined they may be, the basic UK accountability principles still operate in devolved Scotland. The pressures of the legal, statutory, financial and practical infrastructure of devolved and UK governance ensure that outcome, as does the generally high level of intra-party and inter-party cohesion within the coalition parties in government and in the Parliament. Some areas are dealt with by negotiation and compromise, as with the scale and handling of PQs. In others, the Executive has persuaded the Parliament to accept its way of thinking, as in the November 2000 accountability resolution. Attempts to make binding parliamentary resolutions (especially those which are the result of an Executive defeat) which 'instruct' the Executive on some aspect of public policy, have been resisted by the Executive, which claims that it will take account of the will of the Parliament when making its decisions.[104]

In the absence of a dedicated scrutiny committee, the 'core Executive' is held to account by the Parliament mainly through familiar mechanisms (questions, debates, statements and so forth) which tend to place a premium on party political (or, more accurately, 'government versus opposition') considerations; through various committees, each operating individually according to its own agendas, and through the persistent efforts of some backbenchers.[105] Notwithstanding Robin Cook's dictum that good scrutiny makes for good government, there are obvious advantages for an executive in fragmented and inadequate parliamentary scrutiny. However good the Holyrood scrutiny system may be in holding the devolved

102 Paras 286–287.
103 Para 1008.
104 Eg, see the agreed resolution on 22 Sept 2005 on 'dawn raids' for the removal of failed asylum seekers: SPOR, cols 19370–19395, and First Minister's Questions, 24 Nov 2005, cols 21126–21134.
105 S Deacon in K MacAskill, *Agenda For a New Scotland: Visions of Scotland 2020* (2005).

government to account in specific policy areas such as health or education, there is a clear accountability gap in the scrutiny of devolved governance itself, which needs to be filled.

In other respects, though, there may be a risk of too much accountability, not just in terms of Executive complaints of excessive workload due to PQs, or that devolution has brought government much 'closer to home', but because MSPs will be keen to justify their existence by scrutinising all aspects of the devolved administration's activities, even arm's-length bodies.[106]

The overall verdict must be that the traditional accountability model is alive and well in Scotland, albeit with refinements and variations. While, prior to devolution, differences of practice took account of the distinctiveness of Scottish governance within the UK model, now such differences are more a result of internal pressures within the new devolved environment itself, or as a result of external pressures from the media in the devolution hothouse of a small country. Because it is so constitutionally grounded in the UK model, accountability practices in devolved Scotland have not in fact moved very far in the direction of direct accountability, if at all, despite early suggestions that this might be the case.

Chris Himsworth has reminded us that discussions of governance and accountability assume that the Scottish Executive is a 'government' much like, albeit in its own way, the UK government. Yet, he argues, if it is a government, it is 'a much more restrained and domesticated constitutional animal', where many typical governmental powers and functions, such as defence, foreign relations, taxation and social welfare, are wholly or partly outwith its competence, and so it may be that such assumptions of similarity between the administrations in London and Edinburgh are 'simply misplaced'.[107]

This is an intriguing view which may provide a helpful perspective when assessing the operation of accountability since 1999. Perhaps the accountability gaps which have arisen have done so because of failed attempts to apply inappropriate UK-style mechanisms to the devolved governance system in Scotland. It may be that 'new politics' approaches, often being little more than familiar UK reforms dressed up in new language, have not taken hold for similar reasons. As Bradley and Ewing note, 'the principle of accountable government is ultimately more important than ministerial responsibility. If there appears to be any conflict between the two, the former principle ought to prevail'.[108]

What is needed is a fresh look at what devolved governance is really like, and to what accountability mechanisms and 'standards' it should be subject. This reminds us that accountability is, or should be, a product of the governmental system to which it applies, and that, as has been seen at Westminster, its effectiveness is, largely, a factor of its appropriateness to that system as it evolves. This means that any innovations or variations in post-devolution accountability in Scotland could stem from either (or both) changes in accountability arrangements as applied to substantially familiar governmental structures, or to changes in these structures themselves. As suggested here, the Executive thus far has been content to operate and apply a familiar UK model, and the Parliament has been largely unwilling

---

106 M Denton and M Flinders, 'Democracy, devolution and delegated governance in Scotland' (2006) 16 *Regional and Federal Studies* 63.

107 Himsworth in *The Executive and Public Law*, above n 39, pp 215–216.

108 A Bradley and K Ewing, *Constitutional and Administrative Law* (13th edn, 2003), p 116.

or unable to impose major institutional changes on the Executive or in its own accountability mechanisms. But even where both the Parliament and the Executive are willing to change the 'terms of accountability engagement', there remains the issue of how much of this terrain may also be effectively circumscribed by UK legislation (such as the 'reserved' nature of the civil service under the Scotland Act), convention and practice. The experience of the last seven years suggests that such an investigation by the Parliament remains necessary.

Chapter 8

Local Government in Scotland

Chris Himsworth*

INTRODUCTION

A theme which runs through the whole of this book is the impact on the public
law of Scotland of the devolution of powers under the Scotland Act 1998 to the
Scottish Parliament and the Scottish Executive. In this chapter that theme also
dominates. Although this would not have been the terminology used at its creation
by King David in the twelfth century, local government has, throughout its history,
been the most prominent manifestation of Scotland's 'multi-level governance'. The
constitutional position of Scottish local authorities has been defined by reference to
the relationships they have maintained with the legislature from which they have
derived their powers and the government ministers and departments with which
they have maintained a form of 'partnership' in the representation of local interests
and in the provision of public services at the local level. From the Union of 1707,
that legislature was the Westminster Parliament and, from the creation of the
Scottish Office in 1885 and the post of Secretary of State for Scotland in 1925, they
were the institutions of the UK government to which Scottish local government
related. It was in that central-local relationship that the condition of Scottish local
government was, in ways to be discussed later in this chapter, principally defined.
Although the relationship varied over time, there were many tensions and, from a
local government point of view, it was often a relationship in which the dominant
power of central government gave it an inappropriately high degree of control over
the local authorities.[1]

Devolution in 1999, however, brought a new situation in which, for the most part,
the Scottish Parliament has replaced the UK Parliament as the principal legislature
in respect of local government matters and the Scottish Executive has assumed the
role formerly played by the Secretary of State for Scotland. This might be viewed
as a merely formal change. A 'central government' based primarily in Edinburgh
but with responsibilities to London was replaced by a 'central government' entirely
based in Edinburgh and accountable to an Edinburgh-based Parliament. But the
question raised at the time of devolution[2] was whether greater changes might be

---

*   I am most grateful to Mr Anil Gupta of COSLA for his comments on a draft of this chapter.
    Remaining errors of fact or interpretation are my own responsibility.

1   Recent texts on local government law have included C M G Himsworth, *Local Government Law
in Scotland* (1995); J McFadden, *Local Government Law in Scotland: an Introduction* (2004). See
also C M G Himsworth and C M O'Neill, *Scotland's Constitution: Law and Practice* (2003), ch 7
and *Stair Memorial Encyclopaedia*, 'Local Government' (Reissue, 1999) and 'Constitutional Law'
(Reissue, 2002), paras 438–467. Earlier accounts include J Bennett Miller, *Administrative and
Local Government Law in Scotland* (1961).

2   See the White Paper *Scotland's Parliament* (Cm 3658, 1997), ch 6 and C M G Himsworth, 'New
devolution: new dangers for local government?' (1998) 24 *Scottish Affairs* 6.

produced. In particular, the new Scottish Executive might be tempted to use the powers available to it through legislation in the Scottish Parliament to expand its own role in the overall governance of Scotland, at the expense of the powers of local government. The resulting squeeze on local government might radically affect the relationship between the two levels.

The principal aim of this chapter is to offer provisional thoughts on this issue – 'provisional' because the period since devolution is too short a time in which to make final judgments. There are, however, straws in the wind. Before reaching the substance of that discussion it is necessary to put in place some other building blocks of the argument. The next section considers the structure of local government in Scotland, the internal constitution of local authorities, their powers and responsibilities, and the ways in which these are financed. The following section considers the claims which can be made on behalf of local government to a form of autonomy and protection from undue central intervention. The next two sections consider the central pressures on local government and the state of central-local relations, both before and after 1999. The final section contains provisional conclusions.

STRUCTURE, FUNCTIONS AND FINANCING OF LOCAL GOVERNMENT

Structure

The present structure of local government in Scotland dates back to 1996 when the thirty-two councils created by the Local Government etc (Scotland) Act 1994 were established in what was the third major reorganisation of local authorities of the twentieth century. The foundations of modern local government had been laid in the late nineteenth century with the creation of the county councils to provide services, especially in the rural areas, to complement those already provided by the burghs. Reform in 1930 under the Local Government (Scotland) Act 1929[3] brought a much-needed consolidation and rationalisation of functions in a new system. The old parish councils were abolished but replaced by district councils (with few real powers) producing, outside the four cities of Aberdeen, Dundee, Edinburgh and Glasgow, a pattern of 'two-tier' local government in which responsibilities were shared between the thirty-three county councils, on the one hand, and, on the other, the 'large burghs', 'small burghs', and districts which lay within their territories. In the four cities, their councils as 'single-tier' authorities exercised all local functions. By the 1960s, however, the time had come for further reform. The existing responsibilities for school education, roads, public health, and housing had greatly expanded and had been joined by new responsibilities for town and country planning, social work and others. In addition, the existing pattern of authorities with its five different types and different distributions of responsibilities had produced a system which was unduly complex, insufficiently accountable to the people it served, and poorly adapted to the changing demography of Scotland. This, at least, was the view of the (Wheatley) Royal Commission on Local Government in Scotland which was appointed in 1966 and reported in 1969.[4] Local

---

3 The later Local Government (Scotland) Act 1947 was a reforming and consolidating measure but it did not alter the general structure of local government.
4 Cmnd 4150.

government needed both greater democracy and greater strength and effectiveness. The 430 existing authorities needed to be replaced by a much smaller number, with responsibilities reallocated according to the requirements of efficiency of the different services, in terms of the size of both population and territory. What these recommendations produced, after some adjustment, was the Local Government (Scotland) Act 1973 which established, for mainland Scotland, a two-tier system with effect from 1975. There were nine regional councils with responsibility for the large-scale functions of education, social work, strategic planning, roads and transport, and the police and fire services. In addition, there were fifty-six district councils (including the four former city councils) with responsibility for local planning,[5] housing and environmental health. Under this scheme, single-tier local government migrated from the cities to the islands where three islands councils (Orkney, Shetland and the Western Isles) became all-purpose authorities, subject, however, to amalgamation arrangements (with the Highland Region) in relation to police and fire services.

As well as the local authorities properly so called, the 1973 Act provided for the creation of what were called 'community councils'.[6] These were not to be another tier of councils with executive powers but would instead represent the views of local communities and, as required, be the custodians of local traditional ceremonies. Community councils were not directly established by the Act but would come into existence, under schemes formulated by district councils, on the initiative of local people. A consequence was that the pattern of community councils actually set up was, and has remained, rather uneven.

Whilst the arguments of functional efficiency had persuaded the Wheatley Royal Commission of the need for a two-tier structure of local government across much of Scotland, this did not protect that structure from criticism on other grounds. Any two-tier system can be criticised for the potential confusion, especially in the minds of the general population, that may be created by the division of responsibilities between the tiers. More importantly, the bigger regions (in particular, Strathclyde region with about half of Scotland's population) came to be criticised for their bureaucratic remoteness and their capacity for political opposition to the Conservative governments of the 1980s and 1990s. This led to a process of consultation[7] which fell far short of the depth of inquiry reflected in the Wheatley Report and which produced the Local Government etc (Scotland) Act 1994. This established the thirty-two all-purpose authorities which lack the political clout of the former regions and arguably, because of the small size of many of them – eleven authorities have a population of less than 100,000 – they are ill equipped for efficient service delivery. On the other hand, although this was not at all in the minds of the Conservative government which created it, the new system was probably better suited than its predecessor for the launch of Scottish devolved government in 1999. An additional tier of local government in the overall multi-level architecture might have created early complications.

Within the structure of modern local government, there have been two principal defining characteristics: one is democratic elections and the other, subject to

5   Except in the Highland, Borders and Dumfries and Galloway regions where planning powers
    were allocated to the regions.
6   Part IV.
7   Culminating in a White Paper *Shaping the Future – The New Councils* (Cm 2267, 1993).

recent adaptations, has been the reliance upon 'government by committee'.[8] As to elections, the emergence of the local franchise has broadly tracked developments at the national level, save that, as with elections to the Scottish Parliament but unlike Westminster elections, the local electorate includes members of the House of Lords and also resident nationals of European Union states. Those entitled to stand for election to local councils must be, with effect from 2007, at least eighteen years of age;[9] and must have a local connection.[10] Until the council elections to be held across Scotland in 2007, the system of elections has been based on first-past-the-post contests in the wards into which council areas were divided. The 1994 Act provided for three-yearly elections. More recently, however, the Scottish Local Government (Elections) Act 2002 has put local authorities on the same four-year cycle as the Scottish Parliament itself, with the next elections to be held in May 2007. More importantly, a second post-devolution development has produced the Local Governance (Scotland) Act 2004 which abolishes first-past-the-post elections and introduces elections based on the single transferable vote (STV). The Act provides for the division of each local government area into new electoral wards to each of which either three or four councillors will be elected.

Internal organisation

Thus, it is the thirty-two councils to be elected (from 2007) in this way that are established under the 1994 Act, and it is on these councils that are conferred the statutory responsibilities which flow from that Act and from other legislation to be discussed below. As a practical matter, however, it would be impossible for the councillors (numbering over fifty in the larger authorities) to meet as a council and make all the decisions required of them by that legislation. By one means or another much of the decision-making has to be conferred on others and one radical response adopted recently by some English authorities under Part II of the Local Government Act 2000 has been the creation of a directly elected mayor[11] to whom most of the powers of the authority are delegated. The 2000 Act does not extend to Scotland and there is not the option here for directly elected mayors (or provosts) on this model. Instead, councils may have a provost (or lord provost or convener) elected from amongst their own membership to chair the council and to carry out ceremonial functions on their behalf. But as to the organisation of decision-making on behalf of the authority, the traditional option open to Scottish councils has been to retain certain key issues for determination by the council itself[12] but then to take advantage of powers available under the Local Government Acts[13] to delegate the bulk of their decision-making either to committees (or sub-committees) of the council or to senior officials. Local authorities have a general power to engage staff to enable them to discharge the

---

8 K C Wheare, *Government by Committee* (1955).
9 Local Governance (Scotland) Act 2004, s 8 (reducing the age from 21).
10 Defined by the Local Government (Scotland) Act 1973 (henceforth '1973 Act'), s 29.
11 Other possibilities are the 'leader and cabinet executive' and 'mayor and council manager' models.
12 Some are *required* to be determined at this level, eg the annual determination of the level of council tax.
13 Most notably s 56 of the 1973 Act.

council's functions, whether in an advisory or decision-making role. *Certain* officials (for instance, an officer responsible for financial affairs) are statutorily required.

Before the reorganisation of 1975, the typical practice of large authorities was to delegate virtually all their responsibilities to a large number of committees defined by function. Later the number of committees was reduced and the decision-making committees were joined by a co-ordinating committee of senior councillors usually known as a policy and resources committee. More recently, some councils have gone a stage further by raising the status of that committee into a central executive committee, with other council committees then taking on a monitoring and scrutinising role.[14] Some councillors are 'executive members' with responsibility for specific functions, whilst others, on this model, become 'back-benchers' with the duty to hold the executive to account.

Important to the understanding of all these models of internal organisation of local government is that authorities have, for many years, been administered on party political lines. Nearly 80 per cent of councillors are elected on a political basis and control of a council's decision-making, whether at the level of the full council or executive committee or, where retained, functional committees, is organised along political lines, whether subject overall to the control of a single party or of a coalition of parties.

In addition to the powers of internal delegation offered by section 56 of the Local Government (Scotland) Act 1973, the section also enables authorities to arrange for the discharge of their functions either by another authority or in combination with another authority or authorities, by the use of joint committees or boards. Since 1975, there has been an important use of joint working imposed by central government to produce the merged police and fire services in the Northern (Highlands and Islands) and Lothian and Borders areas.

Transparency and standards

An important characteristic of local government has been its relatively high degree of exposure, in comparison with central government, to public scrutiny. Under rules dating principally from 1960[15] and 1985,[16] there has been a requirement of public access, subject only to specified exceptions, to the meetings (including committees and sub-committees) and also to the agendas, minutes and other papers of local authorities. That provision has been expanded in scope by the inclusion of local authorities within the ambit of the Freedom of Information (Scotland) Act 2002, under which, again with specified exceptions, individuals may request information held by public bodies.

Another significant enhancement of provision has been in the area of ethical standards in local government. Once again, there has been long-standing regulation. Anti-corruption Acts[17] have sought to curb bribery and there has also been provision for the declaration of interests by councillors and officials

---

14 The *Report of the Leadership Advisory Panel* (2001) (the MacNish Report) referred to some six or eight councils being organised in this way.
15 Public Bodies (Admission to Meetings) Act 1960.
16 Local Government (Access to Information) Act 1985.
17 Prevention of Corruption Acts 1906 and 1916 and Public Bodies Corrupt Practices Act 1889.

and for a code of conduct.[18] Such provision has, however, been strengthened by the Ethical Standards in Public Life etc (Scotland) Act 2000 which introduced a new statutory code of conduct and established the Standards Commission for Scotland whose task it is to ensure that the code is upheld and to investigate alleged breaches.

Local authority functions

Turning to the actual powers of local authorities, the UK tradition has been for these to be enumerated (often with a high degree of specificity) in statutes relevant to a particular functional sector. Thus, an authority's education powers are currently contained in the Education (Scotland) Act 1980 (as amended and as supplemented, for example, by the Standards in Scotland's Schools etc Act 2000). An authority's planning powers are contained in the Town and Country Planning (Scotland) Act 1997 (as amended)[19] and so on. Much of this legislation continues to be contained in pre-devolution Westminster statutes, but increasingly supplemented or replaced by Holyrood Acts. Only a relatively small number of local authorities' powers are set out in the Local Government Acts[20] themselves although their important general powers to make byelaws for their areas are, for instance, contained in the Local Government (Scotland) Act 1973.[21]

There is a general assumption which underpins local authority statutory powers which is that authorities must remain strictly within the limits of the powers actually conferred. This derives simply from the application to them of the normal principles of ultra vires which courts apply to public authorities in general when their activities are judicially reviewed. These are principles, however, which, in the recent history of local government, have been thought to operate very restrictively against local authorities and in such a way as to curb local enthusiasm and initiatives.[22] Unlike central government (including now the Scottish Executive) which may invoke the prerogative and other common law powers of the Crown, local authorities have no such access to common law sources of legal power. On the other hand, some *statutory* recognition has been given to the need for some flexibility in the extent of their powers. Under section 69 of the Local Government (Scotland) Act 1973 a local authority has 'the power to do anything ... which is calculated to facilitate, or is conducive or incidental to, the discharge of any of [its] functions'.[23] Whilst conferring a degree of statutory flexibility, section 69 does not confer the power to go beyond the powers otherwise laid down. In particular, it does not confer a 'general competence' to do things thought by an authority to be

---

18 1973 Act, s 38 and Pt I of the Local Government and Housing Act 1989 consequential upon the (Widdicombe) *Report on the Conduct of Local Authority Business* (Cmnd 9797, 1986).

19 Shortly to be substantially further amended by the current Planning etc (Scotland) Bill.

20 The practice of the Westminster Parliament was to make general provision for Scottish local government in measures called 'Local Government (Scotland) Acts' (the Local Government etc (Scotland) Act 1994 was a minor deviation) as supplemented by provisions in (GB) Local Government Acts. Since devolution, the practice of the Scottish Parliament has varied to include the Local Government *in* Scotland Act 2003 and the Local *Governance* (Scotland) Act 2004.

21 Section 201 and see Civic Government (Scotland) Act 1982, s 112 (power to make management rules).

22 See the (English) (Maud) *Report on Management of Local Government* (1967), para 283.

23 But see *McColl v Strathclyde Regional Council* 1983 SC 225.

in the interests of its area. A limited power of this sort was, however, contained in section 83 of the 1973 Act.

More recently, the section 83 power has been repealed and replaced by a new power, which is in broader terms, contained in section 20 of the Local Government in Scotland Act 2003. This enables a local authority 'to do anything which it considers likely to promote or improve the well-being of (a) its area and persons within that area; or (b) either of those'. The power to advance well-being is further defined[24] to include the power to incur expenditure, give financial assistance to any person, enter into arrangements or agreements, co-operate with, or facilitate or co-ordinate the activities of any person or exercise functions on behalf of a person, or provide staff, goods, materials, facilities, services or property. As with the former section 83 power, the new power may be exercised in relation to the whole or only a part of an authority's area and in relation to all or only some of the people in the areas. It may also be used to affect persons or places outwith an authority's area if this is likely to improve well-being within it.[25] The use of the power is subject to the need to have regard to guidance provided by the Scottish Ministers.[26] There are also a number of specific restrictions on the use of the power, including a prohibition on doing something forbidden by another enactment[27] or to impose charges for the delivery of services such as schools, libraries and fire-fighting.[28] A second new function introduced by the 2003 Act has been the duty of all local authorities to undertake 'community planning' in their areas.[29] This relates to the planning and provision of public services and involves consultation with public and community bodies and thereafter the obligation to (a) invite and (b) take suitable action to encourage those bodies 'to participate appropriately in community planning'. There is provision for local authorities to co-operate in the performance of this duty and a reciprocal duty to participate in community planning is imposed not only on local authorities but also on a list of other public bodies including health boards, chief constables, Scottish Enterprise and Highlands and Islands Enterprise.[30] The Scottish Ministers themselves must also promote and encourage the use of community planning[31] and may issue guidance on community planning.[32]

Finally, in this section on the powers of local authorities, another constitutionally significant source of powers has lain in the opportunity for an authority to seek new powers directly from Parliament with specific application to the authority and its area. Until 1999, the relevant Parliament was, of course, the Westminster Parliament and the normal procedure adopted was that involving, in the first place, a 'provisional order' made by the Secretary of State and subsequently confirmed by Parliament under the Private Legislation (Procedure) (Scotland) Act 1936.[33]

24 Local Government in Scotland Act 2003 (henceforth '2003 Act'), s 20(2), subject to extension by order by the Scottish Ministers under s 20(5), (6).
25 2003 Act, s 20(4).
26 2003 Act, s 21. Guidance was issued in 2004.
27 Not a simple matter to scour the statute book for possible restrictions!
28 2003 Act, s 22.
29 2003 Act, s 15.
30 2003 Act, s 16(1). The list may be modified by the Scottish Ministers: s 16(3)–(7).
31 2003 Act, s 16(8).
32 2003 Act, s 18. Guidance was issued in 2004.
33 Although some local Acts, eg the Orkney Act 1974 and the Zetland Act 1974, were passed under Parliament's private bill procedures.

That procedure and its predecessors had been used to extend the powers of individual authorities (especially the cities) to enable them to perform functions not authorised under public general Acts of Parliament. Since 1999, the Scottish Parliament has had a private legislation procedure[34] and a new procedure has recently been adopted.[35] Private legislation has been important in the authorisation of railway and tram construction but local authorities themselves have not so far taken advantage of the procedure. It may be that the general power to advance well-being will be a useful alternative to the need to obtain special additional powers by private legislation.

Finance

Essential to the carrying out of the statutory functions of local authorities are sufficient financial resources. From one source or another, local authorities must have available to them the capital funding to build roads, bridges, schools and the other buildings essential for the discharge of their responsibilities. Equally, on a recurrent basis, local authorities must have the funding necessary to pay the salaries of the teachers, social workers, planners, administrators, technicians and all the other staff required for the delivery of their services, as well as for all the related building maintenance, vehicles and other equipment.[36] The distinction between the ways in which capital investment, on the one hand, and recurrent expenditure on the other is funded is one which has been maintained, albeit in different ways, throughout modern local government practice. In this section recurrent expenditure is dealt with first.

The period from the beginning of the twentieth century to date has demonstrated three principal features of the funding of recurrent expenditure. The first is that, with the exception of a very small proportion raised by local authorities in fees and charges for the delivery of their services,[37] the main sources of income have been taxes imposed and raised locally by the authorities and grants from central government. The second feature has been that the twentieth century saw a radical change in the balance of that funding. In the early 1900s, about 90 per cent of local authority revenue was raised locally. By the end of the century, some 80 per cent of local revenue came in the form of grants from central government and only 20 per cent from local taxes. Thirdly, throughout this period, with the single exception of the ill-fated experiment of the community charge or 'poll tax' during 1989 to 1993, the local tax has taken the form of a property tax, that is, a tax imposed on the owner or occupier of property, with the amount payable, therefore, varying according to the valuation placed on the property concerned. In the period to 1989, the tax was the 'rate' which was imposed on both domestic (residential) and non-domestic (business) property by reference to its (notional) annual rental value. Since 1993 the non-domestic rate has been retained but with the level of the tax determined not by the local authorities but by central government,[38] and the income redistributed to the authorities (see below).

34 See Himsworth and O'Neill, *Scotland's Constitution*, above n 1, pp 333–336.
35 Standing Orders, Ch 9A and Procedures Committee (4th Report, 2005) SP Paper 334.
36 And the interest payments to service the debts resulting from capital investments.
37 Eg fees for applications for licences, consents for building or planning control or charges for the use of facilities.
38 For 2006–07, see Non-Domestic Rate (Scotland) Order 2006 (SSI 2006/92).

Whilst, therefore, the non-domestic rate has become a centrally-determined tax, the *local* tax since the implementation of the Local Government Finance Act 1992 in 1993 has been the council tax. This is a charge levied annually by all local authorities on houses in their area. The amount payable depends on three principal factors: the value of the property, the number of residents and the rate of tax prescribed by the local authority. Rather than attributing an individual valuation to each property in the area, the local assessor (whose office operates independently of the local authority) allocates properties to one of eight valuation 'bands', established according to capital values of 1991. Individual property valuations are then subject to modifications in respect of discounts and allowable benefits.

With the valuation of the property determined, the level of tax to be levied is fixed by the local authority at the end of its annual budgeting process and it is the fact that it is the council itself (and, by law, a decision of the full council rather than a committee or official on its behalf)[39] which decides the level of tax that gives the tax its local character. It is, on the face of it, the opportunity for the council to take into account the cost of the services it intends to provide in the following year, together with the amount of grant expected to be received from the Scottish Executive, and to fix the level of tax accordingly. In practice, it is, however, a quite substantially constrained exercise, for three main reasons. First, councils determine levels of tax in an environment in which room for manoeuvre is limited. With most of their resources devoted to the salaries of employees engaged in tasks it would be very difficult significantly to reduce, tax levels are not very flexible. Equally, councils make their decisions against the backdrop of publicly-announced assumed levels of expenditure, central grant and hence council tax made by the Executive. Expectations are created that levels of council tax will not be significantly higher than predicted. Secondly, the fact that councils currently derive some 80 per cent of their income from Executive grants reduces their capacity to use the council tax to increase overall expenditure and service provision. Thirdly, the determination of tax levels takes place in the shadow of statutory powers available to the Scottish Ministers to 'cap' the level of tax fixed by a council if they are satisfied that the estimated expenses of the authority are excessive.[40] In recent years, these powers have not been invoked and, most recently, their use has probably been ruled out in respect of local expenditure in 2006–07[41] but their very existence casts a shadow over locally autonomous decision-making.

Turning to the Scottish Executive's contribution towards the revenue expenditure of local authorities, the principal formal provision for this is made in an annual Local Government Finance (Scotland) Order.[42] In respect of each authority, this sets two figures. One is the amount of non-domestic rate income (see above), allocated to the authority not on the basis of the amount actually raised locally but according to a population-based formula.[43] The second is the amount of 'revenue support grant'. The calculation of this element is more complex but details are published in circulars issued by the Scottish Executive. In essence, the calculation involves the determination for each authority of its 'total estimated expenditure'

39 1973 Act, s 56(6).
40 Local Government Finance Act 1992, s 94 and Sch 7.
41 *The Scotsman*, 11 Nov 2005. At that point, capping seemed to have been definitely excluded but later press reports appeared to suggest that it was again on the agenda.
42 For 2006–07, see SSI 2006/29.
43 Local Government Finance Act 1992, s 108 and Sch 12.

(based principally on estimated costs of service provision plus the cost of servicing loans) from which are deducted amounts to be transferred to the authority as non-domestic rate income and certain 'specific' grants allocated to the authority in respect of particular services (especially the police service). A further deduction is incorporated which takes account of an authority's own capacity to contribute to its expenditure from council tax income. The resulting amount of revenue support grant is, therefore, a figure which is deemed to have taken account both of the council's estimated needs and the funding resources otherwise available. The intended effect is that the Executive makes a substantial overall grant contribution, incorporating a measure of 'equalisation' of resources across the wealthier and poorer authorities but producing a situation in which all councils may set the same level of council tax to achieve the same level of service provision. The criteria on which each year's local government finance order is made are the subject of intensive (and sometimes acrimonious) consultation between the Executive and the Convention of Scottish Local Authorities.

In addition to their recurrent or revenue expenditure, local authorities must also provide for their capital expenditure in respect of the acquisition or enhancement of their buildings and other assets. Until the implementation of the Local Government in Scotland Act 2003, this was expenditure met almost exclusively by borrowing and subject to limits set by the Scottish Ministers.[44] The 2003 Act has now introduced a more flexible regime according to which capital expenditure may also be met from revenue income as well as capital grants from the Executive[45] and then by borrowing (some of which is financially supported by the Executive) and also from receipts from asset disposals. One way in which local authorities can expand services involving capital expenditure is by attracting private funding under Private Finance Initiative schemes.

All the spending arrangements of local authorities are conducted against the background of two forms of regulatory control. Recently created under section 1 of the Local Government in Scotland Act 2003 has been the duty of local authorities to make arrangements which secure 'best value',[46] a term defined as 'continuous improvement in the performance of the authority's functions'. An authority is obliged to maintain 'an appropriate balance' among the quality of its performance, the cost to the authority, and the cost to other persons of any service; and it must have regard to efficiency, effectiveness, economy and the need to meet equal opportunity requirements. It must also discharge its duties to secure best value in a way which contributes to the achievement of sustainable development. In addition, local authorities must have regard to any guidance on the performance of these duties provided by the Scottish Ministers.[47] Substantial guidance has been published.[48]

This 'best value' obligation is related to a form of regulation of longer standing. One of the functions of the Controller of Audit and the Accounts Commission to which he reports is to take account of this obligation and monitor performance of it.[49] Replacing earlier arrangements for the external audit of the accounts of local

---

44 1973 Act, s 94.
45 2003 Act, s 37.
46 Effectively replacing earlier requirements of compulsory competitive tendering for local authority contracts.
47 2003 Act, s 2.
48 Scottish Executive, 2004.
49 2003 Act, ss 6, 55–56. These provisions replaced earlier obligations to monitor on grounds of economy, efficiency and effectiveness.

authorities, the Local Government (Scotland) Act 1973 gave the Controller and Commission powers to test the compliance of local authorities with accounting rules and the law – powers which have since been steadily expanded into the much broader areas of best value and community planning.

LOCAL GOVERNMENT'S CLAIM TO AUTONOMY

The primary purpose of local government is the provision of public services at the local level. It is clearly of the highest importance that, in a country which values its schools, its social work services, the quality of its local roads and so on, these services be provided effectively and efficiently. It is not inevitable, however, that they are provided by locally elected councils. Questions may be asked about whether they should be provided by public authorities at all. In England, responsibility for domestic water supply and the provision of sewerage services has been removed from local authorities and transferred instead to private water companies. In Scotland, the same services were removed from local authorities, but not into private hands. Instead they were, in 1996, placed with three regional water authorities, before they were merged in 2002 into a single agency, Scottish Water. Other services are provided by public agencies, such as the Scottish Environment Protection Agency. The National Health Service in Scotland is provided by a pattern of fifteen health boards, on which local councillors are represented, and health trusts. All these services are, of course, provided locally, with local offices and often involving the participation of locally-appointed representatives in a process sometimes described as 'field administration'. What these arrangements lack is the characteristic which identifies local government, properly so called, which is the democratically-based legitimacy which derives from direct local elections. It is this which distinguishes the constitutional position of local authorities. It is what ensures that they are not merely outposts of central government or quangos subject to the discipline of central appointment and policy direction but enjoy, or ought to enjoy, the autonomy that separate election justifies. Local government is *government* rather than mere administration.

The claim of local government, or local *self-government*, to autonomy and the necessary elements of that claim are well expressed in the European Charter of Local Self-Government, a Council of Europe treaty originally promulgated in 1985 and to which the UK became a party, under the new Labour government, in 1997.[50] The preamble to the Charter speaks of local authorities as 'one of the main foundations of any democratic regime' and states that local self-government 'entails the existence of local authorities endowed with democratically constituted decision-making bodies and possessing a wide degree of autonomy with regard to their responsibilities'. Local authorities should 'regulate and manage a substantial share of public affairs'.[51] The rights of local elected representatives should be assured.[52] Any administrative supervision of local authorities should normally be aimed only at 'ensuring compliance with the law and with constitutional principles'.[53] Local authorities should have financial resources which are 'adequate' and of which they

50 The Charter was ratified on 24 April 1998.
51 Art 3.1.
52 Art 7.4.
53 Art 8.2.

may dispose freely.[54] Part at least of these resources should derive from local taxes and charges of which local authorities have the power to determine the rate.[55] Their finances should be 'diversified and buoyant' and there should be financial equalisation procedures designed to compensate financially weaker authorities.[56]

Despite these bold statements of principle, there are weaknesses in the Charter regime. The Charter's language may be thought to be unduly general and vague. What, for instance, are 'adequate' resources? Similarly, the Charter's guarantees are frequently expressly stated to be subject to national statutory or constitutional provision. And the Charter's terms, unlike those of the Council of Europe's Convention on Human Rights with its own distinguished court at Strasbourg, are not directly enforceable in any international court or tribunal. Instead, however, the implementation of the Charter's provisions is monitored, on behalf of the Committee of Ministers, by the Congress of Local and Regional Authorities of Europe. What the European Charter standards reaffirm is a commitment to a principle of subsidiarity which extends beyond its application at the nation-state level right through to the level of local self-government. It asserts the need for democratic, powerful and effective local government: qualities that were reaffirmed in Scotland in the Wheatley Report of 1969. The underlying assumption is that these qualities of strength are the necessary pre-conditions of a healthy 'partnership' relationship between local and central government.

CENTRAL–LOCAL RELATIONS PRIOR TO DEVOLUTION

The language of 'partnership' can, however, be deceptive. At least in a British context, it will never be likely to be an equal partnership between central and local government. The legislative power available to central governments and their ability to use the parliamentary majorities which they command to change the rules of the game, coupled with their greater financial and other resources, will always tend to give them the upper hand. There are centralising forces at work which tend to undermine local strength and it was because of these tendencies across Europe that the adoption of the Charter became important.

It is not merely, however, some crude lust for power that has prompted central government intervention in the work of local authorities. There have been a number of other factors. The European Charter requires that powers given to local authorities 'shall normally be full and exclusive'[57] but the truth is that the boundaries between matters of exclusively local concern and those justifying central involvement are not absolute. Local transportation issues merge with national issues, requiring a measure of central government intervention in the interests of co-ordination. Whilst most development planning and development control decisions may have a local focus, some others (for instance, in respect of major power plants) have national consequences and again justify ministerial powers under the planning Acts. A rather different justification for central powers, at least from a central government perspective, is that some leading aspects of policy to which a government may have a strong political commitment are nevertheless

54 Art 9.1–9.2.
55 Art 9.3.
56 Art 9.4–9.5.
57 Art 4.4.

almost entirely in local authority hands when it comes to delivery. School education is a good example where it is almost unthinkable that central governments could adopt an entirely 'hands-off' approach. Historically, apart from setting the general framework in legislation, governments have sought to intervene through school inspection (whether by inspectors responsible directly to ministers or to more autonomous agencies) the determination of the ground rules for the curriculum or public examinations, or, as more recently in England, through the establishment of schools (city academies) which are semi-detached from local authority control.

Another major concern of central governments is with the financing of local government. This derives, in part, from their wider responsibility for overall levels of public expenditure which has led to controls over local authority borrowing or capital spending; controls over levels of annual grants to local authorities; controls over the levels of other centrally-determined sources such as, in recent years, the business rate; and, perhaps most controversially, the reserve power to 'cap' levels of income otherwise determined locally, nowadays the council tax. Another financial concern of central governments has been with the political impact of local decisions on taxation and spending, an impact which may be felt as much centrally as locally. If there are 'central' worries in Scotland or England at present about the future of the council tax, they result not from the merits and demerits of the tax objectively assessed as a fair and efficient source of local revenues but from the possible adverse political fallout from a property revaluation and its effects on taxpayer burdens. The driving force behind the much-despised and short-lived community charge (or poll tax) experiment of 1989–93 was, in part, ideological commitment, but also a fear of the national political consequences of the revaluation of properties for domestic rating purposes which would otherwise have been necessary. A similar political concern has driven the Scottish Executive's recently-stated commitment to reduce the level of Scottish non-domestic rates and achieve a level playing field across Scotland and England.[58]

The other general central concern with local funding has been to ensure, through adjustments in the levels of government grants, a measure of 'equalisation' between the inherently richer and poorer authorities. Central government is called on to ensure fairness across the board. And this national responsibility has wider consequences. Subsidiarity requires the allocation of decision-making power to the local authorities. This necessarily and desirably carries with it the opportunity for different policies to be adopted locally and for different spending priorities to be implemented according to local choice. But central governments have never been able to free themselves entirely from responsibility for differences of provision, especially those that amount to a fundamental failure to deliver. In more recent times there has also been a growing central concern for effectiveness and efficiency in local government, reflected in the enhancement of the powers of external auditors to ensure the delivery of 'best value'.

Although the controls exercisable by ministers over local authorities may have been dominated by those directed towards the control over total (and, in some cases, more specific) levels of spending and, more recently, by efficiency controls, ministerial controls have always ranged much more broadly. Statutory texts are capable of either overstating or sometimes understating the working significance of specific controls which has varied greatly over time but few modern statutory

---

schemes confer powers on local authorities without also conferring powers on ministers to make regulations determining, in large measure, how the powers are to be exercised. Similarly, ministers commonly include a power for them to issue 'guidance' on how local authority functions are to be discharged, coupled with the duty of local authorities to 'have regard' to any guidance issued. It has been seen that the Scottish Ministers have issued such guidance in relation to the power to advance well-being and the duties to secure best value and to engage in community planning. Sanctions in the form of 'enforcement directions' may thereafter be imposed in the event that a local authority fails to discharge its functions accordingly.[59] Another device available to ministers is that of requiring that local authority plans are approved by ministers. The need for approval of structure plans under the town and country planning legislation is a good example.[60] Another example, also drawn from the planning regime, is the opportunity for individuals to appeal against local authority decisions to ministers[61] and yet another device is that of the power of inspection. Local authority schools are subject to inspection by HM Inspectorate of Education and there are also powers of inspection in relation to the police and fire services as well as social work services.[62] Many of these powers of control have a routine aspect. They are part of the general culture of local authority decision-making and its supervision. Underpinning other powers of control, however, is the 'default' power to intervene in the case of a serious failure of a local authority to discharge its functions. Rarely used but of continuing symbolic importance is the power of the Scottish Ministers under section 211 of the Local Government (Scotland) Act 1973 to make an order, enforceable in the Court of Session, requiring action, following a local inquiry, in circumstances where an authority has failed to discharge a statutory duty.

As a footnote to this brief survey of central–local relations, there should be added a word about the role of the local authorities' representative association, the Convention of Scottish Local Authorities (COSLA). On the 'central' side of the relationship, the pre-devolution entity was, of course, the Secretary of State for Scotland, assisted by junior ministers and the civil servants of the Scottish Office. On the 'local' side were the local authorities and it is true that relationships were struck in the direct interaction between the Scottish Office and the members and officials of individual authorities. It is also the case, however, that across most of its activities, local government has interacted collectively with central government through COSLA. At some points, this is statutorily endorsed in legal requirements that ministers must consult with bodies representative of local government (COSLA is not identified by name but that is what is meant) before proceeding to take certain decisions. The most important example is the requirement of consultation prior to the making of the annual local government finance order[63] and this always involves a very intense engagement in an area at the heart of the overall

59 2003 Act, ss 23–27.
60 Town and Country Planning (Scotland) Act 1997, s 10. See also the requirement for approval of integrated waste management plans (Environmental Protection Act 1990, ss 44ZA–ZD inserted by s 34 of the Local Government in Scotland Act 2003).
61 Town and Country Planning (Scotland) Act 1997, s 47. See also the power under s 46 to 'call in' planning applications for decision by the Scottish Ministers or by a reporter on their behalf.
62 And see now the Joint Inspection of Children's Services and Inspection of Social Work Services (Scotland) Act 2006.
63 Local Government Finance Act 1992, Sch 12, para 2(2).

relationship between the parties. In addition, however, and on a non-statutory basis, COSLA is engaged in constant dialogue with central government on other matters of common concern.

Although some of the illustrations have been updated to take account of developments in the post-1999 era, the analysis of central–local relations in this section has been primarily concerned with the pre-devolution constitutional arrangements. It is obviously important to have this in place before turning to consideration of the effects of devolution. Above all, it is necessary to avoid any impression of a pre-devolution 'golden age' of local autonomy. It is, on the contrary, better to see the pressures on local government in the closing years of the twentieth century as simply the most recent chapter of a story of fraught relations between central and local government – in Scotland, as in England and Wales – in which financial controls had dominated and which had begun at least as far back as the ministerial judgment in 1974 that 'the party was over' for local government.[64] It is not surprising that, whilst restating many of its strengths, the review undertaken in 1998 by the Congress of Local and Regional Authorities of Europe was critical of many (especially financial) aspects of British local government.[65]

IMPACT OF DEVOLUTION[66]

The Scotland Act 1998 made no provision directly affecting the structure or functions of local authorities in Scotland. It was not, for instance, the occasion for a further reorganisation of the system established in 1996. For the most part, of course, the Act focused instead on the creation of the Scottish Parliament and the Scottish Executive and, broadly speaking, it can be said that, because local government is not a reserved matter under Schedule 5 to the Act, it falls within the legislative competence of the Scottish Parliament and within the devolved competence of the Scottish Executive. We have already seen that local government has been an area of vigorous legislative activity by the Parliament and the powers formerly exercised by the Secretary of State for Scotland (those, for instance, for the financing of local authorities) have, since 1999, been exercisable by the Scottish Ministers.

Although it has not used its powers in this way, it would clearly be within the competence of the Parliament fundamentally to reorganise the structure of local government and, because nearly all the functions of local authorities are also within its legislative competence, the Parliament can modify these functions by adding new ones or taking others away. A very small number of local authority functions are, however, not within the Parliament's competence, for instance, consumer protection and weights and measures.[67] At other points, local government is an area where the Parliament's competence has been deliberately expanded. The Parliament cannot generally legislate in the field of taxation but it *is* competent to make laws on 'local taxes to fund local authority expenditure'.[68] The Parliament can

---

64 Anthony Crosland MP, signalling the end of an era of growth in local government expenditure.
65 See Congress Report 1998 CG(5) and Recommendation (49) 1998.
66 For an early study, see M Bennett, J Fairley and M McAteer, *Devolution in Scotland: The Impact on Local Government* (2002).
67 Scotland Act 1998, Sch 5, Pt II, Section C7, 9. For this reason a local authority is defined by the Act as a 'Scottish public authority with mixed functions'.
68 Scotland Act 1998, Sch 5, Pt II, Section A1.

also amend the system of local elections, although not the franchise[69] and, as we have seen, the STV electoral system has been applied to local government by the Local Governance (Scotland) Act 2004.

Within this framework provided by the Scotland Act, the Scottish Parliament and Executive stepped into the shoes of their UK counterparts. In formal terms, they inherited the pre-devolution relationships with Scottish local government. However, it was anticipated in the devolution White Paper, *Scotland's Parliament*,[70] that the powers available to the Parliament might be used in such a way as to affect adversely the quality of local government and the UK government went to some trouble to caution against this. It pointed out that the UK had just become a signatory to the European Charter of Local Self-Government and declared that the Scottish people would be served best by the Scottish Parliament and Executive working closely with strong, democratically-elected local government. This was a relationship which was crucial to the good governance of Scotland and the effective provision of services to its people.

To encourage progress along these lines, the UK government set up a Commission on Local Government and the Scottish Parliament under the chairmanship of Neil McIntosh. It had a remit to consider (a) how to build the most effective relations between local government and the Scottish Parliament and Scottish Executive, and (b) how councils could best make themselves responsible and democratically accountable to the communities they served. The Commission carried out a substantial consultation exercise and reported in June 1999[71] to recommend that central and local government should commit themselves to joint agreements setting out working relationships. Rather like the concordats now agreed between the Scottish and UK ministers there should be a 'covenant' between the Scottish Parliament and the thirty-two local councils, supported by a standing joint conference to consider matters of mutual concern. There should be a separate formal agreement between local government and the Scottish Ministers. In addition, the Commission recommended a new statutory power of general competence for local authorities; a review of local government finance; the reform of election arrangements and the electoral system; the review by councils of the way in which they conduct their business, including the formalisation of political leaderships as council executives; and the strengthening of community councils.

Some of these recommendations have been carried forward, as described above. A Partnership Framework between the Scottish Executive and the Convention of Scottish Local Authorities was agreed in May 2001. This was a document based on 'parity of esteem and the principles of subsidiarity underlying the European Charter of Local Self-Government' and which committed the Executive to consultation, the exchange of information and meetings on matters of local government concern. In the Scottish Parliament, the first substantive policy debate was on local government[72] and the Parliament's Local Government Committee devoted some time in the 1999–2003 session to the discussion of a covenant between the Parliament and local government. A draft was prepared which provided, as with the Partnership Framework, for consultation in a relationship which was to be 'effective

---

69 Sch 5, Pt II, Section B3.
70 Cm 3658 (1997), ch 6.
71 *Report of the Commission on Local Government and the Scottish Parliament* (June 1999).
72 SPOR, 2 July 1999, col 878.

and meaningful'. A Standing Joint Conference would be established to undertake periodic reviews of the relationship and of the working of the covenant. However, the covenant was not concluded in the work of the first session of the Parliament because of a number of unresolved difficulties. While the Local Government Committee thought it possible that its successor in the second session might wish to pursue the matter further, it also thought that events had demonstrated that the Parliament was not, in practice, likely to 'absorb' local government powers. Perhaps more fundamentally, following legal advice, it referred to the retention of the Parliament's powers to legislate on local government matters 'irrespective of the views of local government representatives, or others. Any covenant could not alter this fundamental legislative position'. The Committee was questioning the case for a covenant purporting to bind the Parliament – which may be reasonable in itself but it did mean the loss of the other standing arrangements for collaboration as well. On the other hand, the Local Government Committee, in the face of Executive reluctance to set up a general inquiry into local government finance at that time, conducted its own inquiry, making recommendations that the balance between central and local funding of local government should be put in a 50:50 basis rather than 80:20; that properties should be revalued regularly for council tax purposes; that the non-domestic rate should be returned to local control; and that a further inquiry should be held into the feasibility of introducing a local income tax.[73] The coalition document of May 2003 committed the Executive to establishing an independent review of local government finance[74] and the Local Government Finance Review Committee, chaired by Sir Peter Burt, was duly established on 16 June 2004, with an expectation that it would report by mid-2006. The remit of the Committee is to review the different forms of local taxation, including a reformed council tax, against criteria set by the Scottish Executive (such as fairness, stability, buoyancy and accountability) and to identify the pros and cons of change. By March 2006 the Committee had completed its public deliberations and was proceeding to prepare its report.

CONCLUSIONS

At the beginning of this chapter, the point was made that it is still too early to draw anything other than very provisional conclusions about the impact of devolution on Scottish local government. This is especially true if the 'impact of devolution' is understood in the limited sense of the direct consequences of the insertion of a new tier of government – the devolved institutions consisting of the Scottish Parliament and the Scottish Executive – between local government and the UK Parliament and government. Some changes since 1999 may certainly be directly attributable to that constitutional innovation. On the other hand, local government was already undergoing a degree of transformation prior to 1999 and it would have been surprising if, even without devolution, some change had not occurred, although no doubt with the range of possibilities affected to a degree by the different party political conditions at Westminster. And some of the changes which *have* occurred as a result of post-devolution legislation by the Holyrood Parliament may

73 SP Paper 551, Session 1 (2002).
74 *A Partnership for a Better Scotland*, p 46.

be attributable not to the new constitutional architecture as such but to reforms which were achieved because of the political configuration in coalition government at Holyrood. The prime example here is the forthcoming introduction in 2007 of proportional representation by STV under the Local Governance (Scotland) Act 2004. Thus, among a range of variables which have impacted on Scottish local government, it is difficult to isolate those specifically attributable to the broader constitutional change, less still to assess the *degree* of influence they have had in a fluid situation.

Among other trends have been what one leading commentator described as one of the 'juridification' of local government.[75] Partly as a result of legislative intervention and partly as a result of greater activism on the part of the courts themselves, the direction of local government was increasingly being determined not by the political judgments of elected members but by judgments of courts, mainly in the process of judicial review. This was at a time when, in particular, the decisions of the English Court of Appeal and the House of Lords in *Bromley London Borough Council v Greater London Council*[76] had demonstrated a particularly virulent intrusion into local authority decision-making.

The increasing significance of judicial review in relation not only to local authorities but also to all other institutions of government has been a continuing phenomenon. Although the number of cases directly affecting local government may have been relatively small, the scope for additional judicial regulation introduced by the Human Rights Act 1998 and its consequences for local authority decision-making have added to the potential effects of 'juridification'. As noted earlier, the grant to local authorities of a measure of 'general competence' in the form of the power to 'advance well-being' seems unlikely in practice to unshackle local authorities from the discipline of judicial control. The judge continues to be over their shoulder.[77]

But the coming of the Human Rights Act may also be seen as a part of a wider package of strengthening regulation of local government. Since 1975, local authorities have been subject to investigation on grounds of 'injustice in consequence of maladministration', a function entrusted, since 2002, to the Scottish Public Services Ombudsman[78] in a change which, despite its 'one-stop shop' attractions, may have left that form of review less sensitive to the political accountability of local government, for example by virtue of the ombudsman's obligation to report, even on local investigations, to the Parliament to which local authorities owe no duty of accountability. Local government audit is of even longer standing but the expansion of the remit of the Controller of Audit and the Accounts Commission into the monitoring of 'best value' is an important extension of external regulation. The imposition of the 'best value' duty on local authorities does, in itself, have the capacity to reduce discretionary and political decision-making, although it is also true that proposals for managerial economies introduced on only an advisory basis have a less intrusive impact. In related ways, the strengthening of the 'standards' regime in local government, especially by the creation of the Standards

75 M Loughlin, *Legality and Locality* (1996), ch 7.
76 [1983] 1 AC 768.
77 *The Judge over your Shoulder* is the title of a pamphlet (mainly for use by central departments) about their vulnerability to judicial review published by the Treasury Solicitor's Department (3rd edn, 2000).
78 See Chapter 14 below.

Commission and the (inevitable) inclusion of local authorities under the umbrella of the freedom of information rules have contributed to the further regulation of local authorities. Whilst no one could, in principle, be heard to speak out against the incorporation into local government of the values of human rights, the rule of law, financial probity, and good administration and transparency, the collective impact of these externally-regulated standards leaves reduced scope for political freedom in decision-making and political accountability. In combination with the generally reduced number and size of local authorities introduced from 1996 and the probable effect of the introduction of STV and the broadening of multi-party governance, there has been a draining of the political power of local authorities, a trend which has been reinforced by the creation above them of the devolved institutions. It is, as yet, unclear what the current review of local government finance will bring but it seems unlikely to produce buoyant new sources of revenue for authorities. If the UK does shortly enter a period of economic downturn, there may be a squeeze most acutely felt by local authorities as the Scottish Executive comes under pressure to reallocate reduced resources.[79]

In these circumstances, it may be that, despite their new role of 'community planning', local authorities will lose their political distinctiveness and become merely a part of a new pattern of local administration (made up of a variety of bodies both public and private) which is malleable at the hand of the devolved institutions. In some respects, this may generate a closer working relationship between local government and the Scottish Executive but, as one commentator has observed, '[t]here is the rub. Access, interdependence, and structures for partnership do not necessarily have much to do with the protection of local government autonomy'.[80] Local authorities may instead expect to be deployed in ways which suit the wider purposes of an overall (central) vision of policy-making. The new planning legislation foreseen in the Executive's White Paper, *Modernising the Planning System* (2005), will increase central intervention in the planning process. Intervention in school education has already been seen in the shape of new powers for the Scottish Ministers under the School Education (Ministerial Powers and Independent Schools) (Scotland) Act 2004. Housing is ceasing to be the local authority service it once was, with substantial transfers of stock to housing associations. Another warning came in the form of the proposed 'Single Correctional Agency' (a body which would have merged (local) social work and (central) prison service responsibilities) a project later abandoned by the Executive as a result of concerted lobbying from local government. The creation of a new strategic transport agency as Transport Scotland and of new regional transport partnerships under the Transport (Scotland) Act 2005 are, however, examples of strategic intervention which have progressed. The police and fire services[81] have for many years been vulnerable to suggestions that they be converted to operate at a 'national' level but the recent emphasis on the need for a strategic response to terrorism and other larger-scale threats to security will make the police case, in particular, even more compelling.

Taken together, these developments present a stark warning to Scottish local government. They combine a programme of specific powers of Executive

79 A phenomenon already arguably present in the uneven distribution of the burden of 'efficiency savings'. See SP (Finance Committee) OR, 20 Sept 2005.
80 C Jeffery, 'Devolution and local government' (2006) 36 *Publius* 57.
81 See now the powers to constitute joint fire and rescue boards under the Fire (Scotland) Act 2005.

intervention with a series of new strategic initiatives to remove local authorities from the centre stage of local governance. Meanwhile, the focus is also turning towards the structure of local government itself.[82] It seems almost inevitable that local authorities will face one of two major reforms, both involving strong Executive-driven intervention. One would be an extension of 'community planning' to produce widespread mandatory co-operation between local authorities in relation to those functions requiring large areas and substantial resources. The other would go further to produce a new reorganisation of local government, with mergers of existing authorities to bring about a big reduction in numbers. The evolving logic of the devolution settlement will, it seems, produce a system of local governance much more closely integrated with, but also much more directly subordinated to, the new institutions in Edinburgh. As in the past, changes will doubtless occur in the name of 'partnership'!

The questions may still be asked: What difference does devolution itself make to the role of local government? Are there not as many similar changes occurring south of the border? And the answer is that, although there *are* clear parallels between the trends in England and Scotland, there will be a much stronger tendency over time to view the Scottish Executive as an upper (regional) tier of government capable of absorbing, whether directly or by quangos on its behalf, functions previously treated as part of local government proper. The late Professor John Mackintosh's evidence to the Wheatley Commission in the 1960s[83] should be remembered. His pre-devolution proposal, roundly rejected as too 'constitutional' by the Commission at that time, was for a two-tier system of local government in which the upper tier would simply have been an all-Scotland local authority. That was then. But now, with devolution delivered, his vision may yet be achieved by another route!

82 See First Minister Jack McConnell, SPOR, 9 Feb 2006, col 23253.
83 Cmnd 4150, paras 683–686.

Chapter 9

The Scottish Judiciary

Scott Crichton Styles

INTRODUCTION

Strictly speaking, the Scottish judiciary encompasses all who sit in a judicial role in Scotland from justices of the peace and sheriffs up to the House of Lords, but the focus of this chapter will largely be on the Court of Session and High Court of Justiciary, with some reference to the district court, the sheriff court, the House of Lords and the Privy Council. Scotland is a small jurisdiction of just over five million inhabitants, with a correspondingly small judiciary. The size of the Court of Session increased steadily over the twentieth century from its historic number of fifteen[1] to the present day thirty-two judges, but this is still a small court; indeed the English Court of Appeal is larger than the whole Court of Session. There are 140 permanent sheriffs who serve in Scotland's forty-nine sheriff courts, which are combined in groupings of various sizes to comprise six sheriffdoms, each presided over by a sheriff principal. There are also eighty part-time sheriffs.

The Scottish judiciary stands at the very heart of the Scots body politic. It is the most important organ of central government to have survived in unbroken continuity since the earliest days of the early modern Scottish state.[2] The office of sheriff existed in Scotland at least as far back as the twelfth century, and it is well recognised that the 'foundation' of the College of Justice by James V in 1532 merely put on a statutory footing the authority of an already extant court.[3] Since the sixteenth century the Court of Session has survived the travails of Reformation and the Union of the Crowns, and after a hiatus during the Cromwellian period, it was revived as part of the Restoration settlement in Scotland. Crucially the court and the existence of Scots law as a separate body of legal knowledge not only survived the Union of Parliaments but even had its continued existence guaranteed by the Act of Union.[4] The existence of Scots law as a distinct jurisdiction in a unitary state led to the odd position that the Scottish courts became the guardians of what was left of the Scots body politic as well as of the actual content of Scots law.

Throughout the nineteenth century and up until the end of the twentieth century the Court of Session conducted its judicial business under remarkably little public scrutiny or even interest: the Faculty of Advocates, surely Scotland's

1 The College of Justice Act 1532 provided for a total of fifteen judges.
2 Act of Union 1707, Art XIX. The Act also preserved the then existing local government institutions, the royal burghs: Art XXI.
3 R K Hannay, *The College of Justice* (1933); A A M Duncan, in *An Introduction to Scottish Legal History* (Stair Society, vol 20, 1958); M Godfrey, 'The assumption of jurisdiction: Parliament, the King's Council and the College of Justice in sixteenth-century Scotland' (2001) *The Journal of Legal History* 21.
4 Act of Union 1707, Arts XVIII and XIX.

most successful ever 'trades guild', maintained its position as monopoly pleader before the Court of Session and monopoly supplier of candidates for the Session bench; and the actual content of development of the doctrines of Scots law aroused little interest outside bench, bar, academic lawyers and the more scholarly solicitors. Three main reasons can perhaps be given for this public disinterest in Scots law generally and in the Scots bench in particular. First, it is a fact that in most places and at most times the content of any given legal system is largely seen as a series of 'technical rules' of interest to no-one but the lawyers and their clients. Most law, most of the time, and therefore most judicial business is of little interest to the wider public. The one major exception to this is of course the perennial interest in crime. Secondly, in so far as the Scots public was aware of Scots law at all being different from English law this was seen as a 'good thing'; the existence of a separate Court of Session was seen as a source of pride and of remuneration for a section of the Scots bourgeoisie. Thirdly, the doctrine of the supremacy of Parliament, developed out of the Restoration settlement and achieving its full flowering in the influential writings of A V Dicey,[5] largely removed the operation of the courts, north and south of the border, from areas of political controversy. When the doctrine of parliamentary sovereignty was combined with the increasingly democratic composition of Parliament then the effect was that almost all legal questions which were controversial in a political or policy sense were dealt with by Parliament and not by the courts. Generally the pre-devolution Scottish courts proved very reluctant to depart from the Diceyan orthodoxy of parliamentary supremacy.[6] Indeed the classic case, both north and south of the border, is a Scots one: *Edinburgh and Dalkeith Railway Company v Wauchope*.[7] The one exception to this was *MacCormick v Lord Advocate*[8] in which Lord President Cooper hinted at a distinctive Scottish attitude to parliamentary sovereignty, indicating that, in some unexplained way, the principle of unlimited parliamentary sovereignty did not apply in Scotland.[9] The meaning of this was unclear and would have been unlikely to survive an appeal to the House of Lords in the 1950s had one been held.

Guarnieri and Pederzoli have created[10] a useful typology by which to classify the nature of the judicial role against the two variables of 'judicial creativity' and 'judicial autonomy'. Using this analysis, they distinguish four types of judicial role – 'executor', 'delegate', 'guardian' and 'political' – which are mapped as follows:[11]

		Political Autonomy	
		Low	High
Judicial Creativity	**Low**	executor	guardian
	High	delegate	political

5 *Introduction to the Study of the Law of the Constitution* (1885).
6 See, eg, *Gibson v Lord Advocate* 1975 SC 136; *Sillars v Smith* 1982 SLT 539; *Pringle, Petitioner* 1991 SLT 330; *Murray v Rogers* 1992 SLT 221; and *Fraser v MacCorquodale* 1992 SLT 229.
7 1842 Bell's App Cas 252 at 279, where Lord Campbell famously stated: 'All that a court of justice can look to is the parliamentary roll.'
8 1953 SC 396.
9 Eg, Lord Cooper states at 412: 'I have not found in the Union legislation any provision that the Parliament of Great Britain should be "absolutely sovereign" in the sense that Parliament should be free to alter the Treaty at will'. See further, Chapter 2 in this volume.
10 C Guarnieri and P Pederzoli, *The Power of Judges* (2002), pp 68–76.
11 Above n 10, p 70.

According to this typology, a judge who is an executor is merely 'a faithful and passive executor of the legislative will' with no room for judicial creativity.[12] If a judge is a delegate, 'judicial creativity may or must be exercised in a manner that is subordinate to the political branches',[13] a view Guarnieri and Pederzoli consider is particularly prevalent in common law countries, especially England. A judge who exercises a guardian role 'may or must oppose the prevailing attitudes of representative institutions in order to fulfil the judge's role of guaranteeing citizens' rights',[14] a role especially prevalent where judges have power of judicial review. Finally, judges have a political role where they are seen as 'relatively independent not only from the political branches but also from the legal system' and where they 'act as true policy-makers developing rules "based on judgments on social benefit"'.[15] Reference will be made to this typology from time to time in the remainder of this chapter.

Although the 1970s and 1980s saw the increasing use of judicial review in the UK, it is the constitutional changes introduced by the Blair government which have threatened to push the courts into more political areas of decision-making, moving the judges from a delegate role to a more dynamic one. As Tomkins remarks: '[o]ne striking feature of the reforms witnessed in Britain since 1997 has been the growth in authority of the judiciary',[16] and this is part of a more general phenomenon in western states of what has been referred to as the 'judicialisation of politics'[17] or, to put the matter the other way round, the politicisation of judging.

The constitutional revolution wrought by the Blair government at the end of the 1990s preserved the position of the Court of Session, but the combined effects of the two main pieces of constitutional legislation – the Scotland Act 1998 and the Human Rights Act 1998 – were in some ways contradictory in regard to the overall position of the Court of Session within the Scots constitution. The establishment of an independent Scottish Executive and Parliament arguably diminished the relative importance of the Court of Session within Scotland. No longer could it claim to be the sole guardian of some mystic flame of Scots law. On the other hand, devolution can be seen as increasing the powers of the judiciary because the decisions of the Executive, and even the very Acts of the Scottish Parliament, are now subject to the possibility of being struck down by the courts. The combined effect of the Human Rights and Scotland Acts has been to turn the Court of Session into a *de facto* constitutional court, with much greater power to strike down Scottish legislation, at least *de jure*, than the corresponding power which it and the English higher courts have in respect of legislation enacted by the Westminster Parliament, as such Acts can only at most be declared 'incompatible' with the European Convention on Human Rights (ECHR). However, although now enjoying the powers of a constitutional court,[18] the Court of Session is clearly not a supreme court because it is at present subject to the authority of the House

---

12 Above n 10, p 69.
13 Above n 10, p 71.
14 Above n 10, p 71.
15 Above n 10, p 74.
16 In P P Craig and A Tomkins (eds), *The Executive and Public Law* (2006), p 26.
17 T Vallinder, in C N Tate (ed), *The Global Expansion of Judicial Power* (1995), p 13.
18 S Tierney has written eloquently about the 'constitutionalisation' of the Scottish judiciary; see 'Constitutionalising the role of the judge: Scotland and the New Order' (2001) 5 EdinLR 49.

of Lords and the Judicial Committee of the Privy Council, and will be subject to the newly constituted UK Supreme Court when that body finally comes into operation, replacing the Lords and the Privy Council. The actual details of how the Court of Session has exercised these powers are dealt with elsewhere in this volume,[19] and this chapter will focus on the nature of the court itself, its impartiality, independence, composition and accountability.

THE JUDICIAL META-VALUES

For a judiciary to discharge its functions credibly the judges must be appointed and hold office in a way that satisfies the criteria of independence, impartiality, accountability and competence. These criteria are so central to the judicial role that they may be understood as *judicial meta-values*. Independence and impartiality are *essential* meta-values in that, without them, no matter what the expertise of the individual judges, the judicial system as a whole will lack legitimacy. Competence is a substantive quality present (or absent) in each individual judge which the judicial selectors hopefully discern in the right candidates. As such it is closely related to, and will be discussed in the context of, the judicial appointments system itself, which is in turn part of the accountability of the judiciary. Accountability has only recently come to the foreground of desirable judicial qualities and, although highly desirable, it is certainly not currently regarded as an essential meta-value. Thus, although Article 6 ECHR provides for a trial before an 'independent and impartial tribunal', it makes no mention of accountability, nor indeed of competence.

Impartiality and independence – distinct but linked

The concepts of independence and impartiality are closely linked, even yoked, in much discussion of the judicial meta-values, above all in the wording of Article 6 ECHR. In *Findlay v United Kingdom*, the European Court of Human Rights said:

> 'The Court recalls that in order to establish whether a tribunal can be considered as "independent", regard must be had inter alia to the manner of appointment of its members and their term of office, the existence of guarantees against outside pressures and the question whether the body presents an appearance of independence.
>
> 'As to the question of "impartiality", there are two aspects to this requirement. First, the tribunal must be subjectively free from personal prejudice or bias. Secondly, it must also be impartial from an objective viewpoint, that is, it must offer sufficient guarantees to exclude any legitimate doubt in this respect.
>
> 'The concepts of independence and objective impartiality are closely linked.'[20]

Nevertheless, although 'closely linked', the two concepts are distinct. Judicial independence is primarily institutional and systemic. It concerns the relationship between the judiciary collectively and the state; that is, the principle that the judiciary as a whole must also be independent of the executive and the legislature. Institutionally, independence is secured primarily by the security of tenure of office enjoyed by judges. Impartiality is partially institutional but also partially personal,

19 See Chapters 10 and 16.
20 (1997) 24 EHRR 221, para 73.

and concerns the relationship between a sitting judge or judges and the parties before the court in the instant case. Institutionally, impartiality is secured by the immunity from suit enjoyed by judges, by legal and conventional rules which prevent judges engaging in overtly political activities and, above all, by rules requiring judges to act neutrally when deciding cases. Personally, it is the ability of a judge to decide a case with an open mind, as free as possible from conscious bias, and certainly free from pressures or inducements from either the state or the parties to the action. The concepts of independence and impartiality are in an asymmetrical relationship to each other, in that a judiciary which is not independent of the state will always carry the suspicion of being a partial judiciary, at least in cases involving the state. By contrast, however, independence is no guarantee of impartiality towards the litigants. When independence and impartiality are combined there are the conditions which make possible the rule of law.

This chapter will consider first the arrangements for the selection of judges in the light of the concepts of competence and accountability, and then proceed to discuss the values of impartiality and independence.

JUDICIAL COMPETENCE AND ACCOUNTABILITY

As noted above, accountability has only recently become a focus of concern in considering the nature of the judicial office and in practice it is arguably the weakest and least important of the meta-principles. Logically, accountability encompasses both the procedures for the appointment and for the dismissal of judges. Thus we may distinguish between accountability in the appointment processes, and accountability for actions whilst in office, which latter topic will be discussed below in the context of judicial independence. Unfortunately, the very scope and meaning of the term 'accountability' itself have recently become a matter of dispute. Le Sueur contrasts the original meaning of accountability as being 'understood mainly as a command-and-control relationship' with the contemporary usage whereby 'the terminology of "accountability" is now used far more broadly, to include, for example, public dialogue without the presence of any relationship of subordination or the possibility of sanction'.[21] Bogdanor makes a similar distinction but in a more vivid way when he distinguishes between 'sacrificial' accountability, where dismissal is possible, and 'explanatory' accountability, where it is not.[22] This broader use of the term 'accountability' is misleading in that it may imply that radical change is occurring where in fact none is. Accordingly, for the most part, the present author will restrict accountability to its narrower sense, and refer to explanatory accountability as scrutiny.

Accountability in appointment

The notion of judicial accountability is at its most obvious and least problematic when considering the selection and appointment of judges. The basic principle is that, as judges will have power over the citizen, then the citizen should have some

21 A Le Sueur, 'Developing mechanisms for judicial accountability in the UK' (2004) 24 LS 73 at 74.
22 V Bogdanor, 'Parliament and the judiciary: the problem of accountability', 2006 Sunningdale Accountability Lecture available at *http://www.iiasiisa.be/iias/aisun/sunningdale_2006.pdf.*

say in the selection of the judiciary. Accountability in appointment is not in fact a characteristic to be required of the judiciary themselves but rather it is one relevant to the appointing body, which in Scotland is now the Scottish Executive. Three interconnected issues must be considered: the criteria for selecting judges; the judicial selection mechanism; and the representativeness of the judiciary.

Eligibility and criteria for judicial appointment

Eligibility for judicial appointment has long been governed by statute but, until recently, no formal criteria for appointment existed. Traditionally, the way 'merit' (that is, competence, knowledge and technical expertise in the law) has been ascertained in common law jurisdictions[23] is by only appointing judges who have had a significant amount of experience as legal practitioners. Indeed, for nearly three centuries eligibility for appointment to the Court of Session was restricted to Scottish advocates of at least five years' standing,[24] but in 1990 it was widened to include sheriffs principal and sheriffs who have held office for at least five years and solicitor-advocates who have had rights of audience before both the Court of Session and the High Court of Justiciary for at least five years.[25] Eligibility for appointment as sheriff principal or sheriff is restricted to those persons who have been legally qualified, as either an advocate or a solicitor, for at least ten years.[26] For appointment to the Court of Session bench, the statutory five years' call to the Bar was always understood very much as a minimum requirement. In practice candidates needed to be Queen's Counsel of several years' standing, and this would still appear to be the case for appointments direct from the Bar. Although merit was presumably a factor in at least some appointments it was never actually provided for or defined by statute.[27] However, in Scotland the Judicial Appointments Board has now issued a document entitled *Criteria for Judicial Appointment* and 'a high level of legal knowledge and experience' is the very first quality mentioned. As a principle, no-one could be against merit as a criterion of judicial appointment but its application is not unproblematic (see further below). Furthermore, there is the question of whether factors other than 'pure merit' should be considered, in particular whether the bench should seek to embody the diversity of the society over which it presides in the composition of its members (to be discussed further below).

Judicial selection mechanism

Prior to devolution, judicial appointments were made by the Queen acting on the advice of the Secretary of State for Scotland, but the real decisions were taken by the Lord Advocate.[28] The traditional system was one that was entirely opaque and maximised the unaccountable discretion of the Lord Advocate. Politics as an explicit

---

23 Civil law jurisdictions tend to have a career judiciary: see Guarnieri and Pederzoli, above n 10, ch 1.
24 Treaty of Union 1707, Art XIX. This Article also provided that Writers to the Signet of at least ten years' standing were eligible for appointment, provided that they satisfied a test by the Faculty of Advocates but no Writer has ever been appointed to the Court of Session under these provisions.
25 Law Reform (Miscellaneous Provisions) (Scotland) Act 1990, s 35 and Sch 4, paras 1–3.
26 Sheriff Courts (Scotland) Act 1971, s 5.
27 The Constitutional Reform Act 2005 seems to be the first piece of legislation to specifically provide for merit as part of the criteria for English judicial appointments; s 63(2) states that 'Selection must be solely on merit.'
28 For appointment as Lord President or Lord Justice-Clerk the formal recommendation to the Queen came from the Prime Minister.

feature of judicial appointments lingered far longer in Scotland than England.[29] As late as the early 1970s a significant factor in the selection of an advocate for the Session Bench was his political connections[30] and, most anomalously of all, the Lord Advocate (a member of the government) would appoint himself to the bench when the opportunity arose. From the 1970s onwards, there was increasing disquiet about the explicitly political nature of judicial appointments[31] and a major milestone was reached when Lord Wylie, Lord Advocate from 1970–74, announced that advocate-deputes would no longer be appointed on a party basis, that appointments to the bench would be made on merit and that he would not appoint himself to the bench. However, complaints about political bias or simple cronyism did not disappear altogether and subsequent Lords Advocate continued to appoint themselves to the bench.

The Scotland Act 1998 transferred to the First Minister the responsibility for making recommendations to the monarch for the appointment of a Lord of Session. The First Minister has an obligation to consult the Lord President before making the recommendation,[32] but at first the *de facto* position of the Lord Advocate as judge-maker was unaltered. However, the combined effects of devolution and the incorporation of the ECHR, together with a more general sense of the increasing importance of transparency and accountability in the public sphere, meant that there was a wide consensus for replacing the Lord Advocate's patronage with a more modern system of judicial selection. Eventually, this resulted in the Scottish Executive delegating the power of judicial appointments to the Judicial Appointments Board for Scotland (JAB), which began its work in June 2002.[33] The JAB was created by executive fiat but the present Scottish Executive plan to eventually place it on a statutory footing.[34] Although the creation of the Board marked the first real attempt at institutionalising the idea of accountability into the system for appointing Scottish judges, the JAB can nevertheless be criticised both on its composition and procedures and also on the criteria by which it makes its decisions.

The JAB is a quango appointed by, and responsible to, the Scottish Executive consisting of ten members, including the chairman. There is an even balance of legal and lay members. The five legal members represent the various constituencies of the legal system: a senior solicitor, a senior advocate, a Lord of Session, a sheriff

29 Up until 1912 appointments to the High Court of Justice and the Court of Appeal were made on a political basis, and those to the Lords were on a similar basis into the 1920s. See further R Stevens, *The English Judges: their Role in the Changing Constitution* (2002).

30 Of the twenty-nine Lords of Session appointed between 1919 and 1945, eleven were law officers, four were MPs or parliamentary candidates and three who had been Dean of the Faculty of Advocates were also law officers. Between 1945 and 1969, of twenty-four appointments ten were law officers, three MPs or parliamentary candidates and one had been a dean as well as law officer; see S C Styles, 'The Scottish judiciary 1919–1986' 1988 JR 41 at 47.

31 As the standard textbook at the time on the Scottish legal system commented 'there is too little chance of promotion to the Bench for the advocate who is politically inactive, unless he should attain the office of Dean or Vice Dean': D M Walker, *The Scottish Legal System* (5th edn, 1981), p 310.

32 Scotland Act 1998, s 95(4). For appointment as Lord President or Lord Justice-Clerk the formal recommendation continues to be from the Prime Minister.

33 In the summer of 2000, a public consultation exercise was carried out by the Scottish Executive: *Judicial Appointments: An Inclusive Approach*. Responses to the consultation paper demonstrated substantial support for the creation of an independent Judicial Appointments Board and, in March 2001, the Justice Minister, Jim Wallace, announced the setting up of such a Board.

34 The Executive announced its intention to place the JAB on a statutory basis in February 2006: *Strengthening Judicial Independence in a Modern Scotland*, para 6.4.

principal and a sheriff. The criteria set out by the JAB establish two main grounds for appointing judges: legal competence and personal qualities. The current system recognises the non-expertise of lay members by explicitly excluding them from judging candidates' *professional* competence,[35] allowing them a role only in assessing their *personal* qualities. However, the lay members also serve a useful function in ensuring good practice, preventing any overt cronyism and, hopefully, properly representing the views of non-lawyers. Unfortunately, the lay members of the JAB, as presently constituted, cannot really be said to represent the wider Scottish citizenry in any meaningful sense, as they are a typical quango coterie of establishment insiders.[36] Thus, although the JAB was intended to create a more accountable and transparent system, it may be doubted if it has achieved these ends.

As a quango the JAB is both undemocratic and unaccountable. At the moment actual judicial appointments are still made by the First Minister, with the JAB only making recommendations, but in reality the First Minister's decision is now a mere formality. The tensions involved here have been clearly expressed by the chair of the JAB, Sir Neil McIntosh:

> "'I think it's right that in essence the appointment should rest with the First Minister who is democratically accountable. So the actual process of being a recommending rather than an appointing board is I think the right one.'
>
> 'And if a recommendation were not accepted for political reasons?'
>
> "'I think we would all have to consider our position. I mean that would simply be undermining the whole reason for our existence.... I should stress that every recommendation we've made to date has been accepted and there has been absolutely no political interference. We're a fiercely independent group of people so from that point of view I don't think our independence would in any way be challenged by still being a recommending rather than an appointing body.'"[37]

In this model it would appear that the First Minister is accountable to the JAB rather than the other way round! Moreover, how can the First Minister provide democratic accountability if he has no discretion to refuse a recommendation? Accountability presupposes discretion; where an office-holder has no discretion then he or she cannot rationally be held accountable for any actions which run in their name. The schema envisaged by the Scotland Act is that responsibility rests with the First Minister who is accountable to the Scottish Parliament and to the Scottish people. However the existence of the JAB effectively thwarts the clear meaning of the Scotland Act by allowing the First Minister to disclaim any responsibility for an appointment, but at the same time there is no meaningful mechanism for making the JAB itself accountable, because it can always 'hide behind' the First Minister. Ironically, therefore, the existence of the JAB actually diminishes accountability.[38]

---

35 Scottish Executive, *Strengthening Judicial Independence*, above n 34, para 6.23.

36 The five lay members appointed in 2002 consisted of three men and two women, of whom all but one had been knighted or received an OBE or MBE. The professional background of the members was respectively that of a local government chief executive, a human resources professional from the Royal Mail, a businessman, a legal academic and a university principal.

37 P Nicholson, 'Opening up the Bench: Interview with Sir Neil McIntosh, Chairman of the Judicial Appointments Board for Scotland' (2003) 48/12 JLSS 44.

38 Exactly the same arguments apply in respect of the Judicial Appointments Commission, which will recommend Scottish candidates for appointment to the House of Lords/Supreme Court, created by the Constitutional Reform Act 2005.

Whilst the legal position is clear (the JAB merely *advises* the First Minister, who remains free to accept or reject its advice), the manner in which the First Minister exercises his/her powers should be clarified so that s/he can be held accountable for the decisions which s/he makes in appointing judges. A more radical change to increase accountability in appointment would be to place responsibility for judicial appointments in the hands of those who are themselves directly accountable to the citizenry, namely the MSPs. This could be done in either a minimalist or maximalist way. A minimalist option would be to have the four main Scottish political parties represented by an MSP sitting on the JAB, such members to act entirely independently, creating a legitimacy which is lacking in quango appointees. The maximalist option would be to make judicial appointments a task for a committee of the Scottish Parliament, in addition to or in replacement of the JAB. Legal expertise on appointments could be provided by consultation with the Lord President and by the law officers who could either advise or perhaps sit on this committee. This committee might even hold confirmation hearings in the style of the US Senate for Supreme Court appointments.

Nor, as an institution, is the JAB much more transparent than the old system of appointments by the Lord Advocate. It operates in secret and gives no reasons for its decisions, the only major differences being that the criteria are public, the posts are advertised, and individuals must submit an application, whereas under the old system the Lord Advocate simply informed individuals that he was willing to appoint them and asked if they would accept. However, although the criteria for appointment are public, they are so broad that the JAB effectively makes appointments with the same lack of transparency and unfettered discretion as the appointments made by the Lord Advocate. The only guidance laid down by the Scottish Executive merely stresses that appointments must be made on merit, though with the subsidiary aim of making the judiciary as representative as possible.[39]

Sceptics, on the other hand, may question whether the form of judicial selection matters at all. Bell has pointed out[40] in his survey of judicial appointment methods in Europe:

> '[A] salutary lesson is provided by the latest *Eurobarometer* findings (July 2003). Table 1.1c on trust in relation to non-political national institutions shows absolutely no correlation between satisfaction with the legal system and the way judges are appointed. Those with independent agencies can register 80% confidence (Denmark) or 66% (Sweden), but equally 43% in Spain (and a majority dissatisfied). Independent councils of the judiciary are found in France (43% satisfaction, but 51% dissatisfaction), Italy (44%) and Portugal (46%), but they fare no better than the UK (47%). What matters to the population is not how people are appointed, but whether they are effective in delivering justice.'

So it would appear that the method of appointment matters much less than the quality of the appointees and the way they act, at least as regards the general public.

---

39 The remit of the Judicial Appointments Board for Scotland is: to provide the First Minister with a list of candidates recommended for appointment to the offices of judge of the Court of Session, sheriff principal, sheriff and part-time sheriff; to make such recommendations on merit, but in addition to consider ways of recruiting a judiciary which is as representative as possible of the communities which it serves; and to undertake the recruitment and assessment process in an efficient and effective way.

40 J Bell, 'Judicial appointments: some European experiences', p 6, available at *http:// www.law.cam.ac.uk/staff/view_staff.php?profile=jsb48*.

But this begs the question of whether the composition of the bench is presently much affected by the selection mechanism, again raising the question of the representativeness of the bench.

The representativeness of the judiciary

The judiciary in Scotland, and likewise in England and Wales, have been marked by a striking homogeneity in the composition of their memberships, which was, until recently, uniformly white, male and middle class.[41] Until comparatively recently this homogeneity aroused little comment or interest, but since the 1960s there has been an increasing stress on issues of equality and diversity throughout society, with an increasing emphasis placed on equality of opportunity and the outlawing of discrimination on grounds of race, gender and so on. Quite rightly, these principles raised concerns about the nature of the judicial selection process, but, for many, the issue of a representative bench is about more than ensuring equal opportunities for individual candidates for judicial office; it is also about the nature and exercise of judicial power itself. There are two reasons for this. First, as judges act in an increasingly political role, exercising discretion in inherently contested political and moral areas, then the issue of the views of the individual judges concerned becomes more important. Secondly, some critics, especially those on the radical left, have argued that judges' homogeneous social background gives them a common set of preconceptions and attitudes which inevitably, if often unconsciously, make them biased in favour of certain social and political values.[42] Some go further still, and argue that judges' views are so strongly affected by their unconscious attitudes as to make an impartial trial impossible. However, such an approach seems to be based on a conflation of the notion of preconception with bias, an issue discussed further below.

Nevertheless, to a greater or lesser extent, judicial attitudes do matter and some would argue that that is why the composition of the bench matters: a more diverse bench is needed to reflect the diversity of modern Scottish society. Equally there are those who reject this approach and argue that the very notion of 'representativeness' is highly problematic in this context: 'I do not understand the call for a court to be representative. We are never told what sort of representation is contemplated or how it is to be achieved.'[43] Perhaps, as Kentridge argues, a more useful notion than 'representativeness' is that of 'diversity' on the grounds that diverse life experiences bring new perspectives to the bench, a point well made by Lady Justice Hale:

> '[A] a generally more diverse bench, with a wider range of backgrounds, experiences and perspectives on life, might well be expected to bring some collective change in empathy and understanding for the diverse backgrounds, experience and perspectives of those whose cases come before them.'[44]

The difficulty is that the term 'representative' has at least two different meanings. In the first sense it implies a *delegate*, someone who, by his method of appointment

---

41 See I D Willock, 'Scottish judges scrutinised' 1969 JR 193; C M Campbell, 'Judicial selection and judicial impartiality' 1973 JR 255; Styles, above n 30.
42 See generally J A G Griffith, *The Politics of the Judiciary* (5th edn, 1997)
43 Sir Sydney Kentridge, 'The highest court: selecting the judges' (2003) 62 CLJ 55 at 60.
44 Lady Justice Hale, 'Equality and the judiciary: why should we want more women judges?' [2001] PL 489 at 501.

(typically election) is an advocate for a given set of views or group(s) of people. The second meaning of representative is as an *exemplar* of a group of people, and it is this latter sense which Kentridge tries to express by using the term diversity. Unless the selection of judges is made democratic in some way, by direct or indirect election, it is not clear that judges can ever be representative in the delegate sense. Such a development is highly unlikely in the foreseeable future, since judicial selection by election could be viewed as compromising the independence and impartiality of the judiciary. Nevertheless, many would hold that as the role of the judiciary, post-devolution, moves to a more political one, disquiet over the ability of a disproportionately white, male judiciary to represent the wider views of society will become more acute:

> 'Until relatively recently there was general agreement that the roles of the two branches of government [executive and judiciary] were absolutely distinct, and that a clear divide could be drawn between the formation and implementation of policy by elected representatives and its interpretation by independent judges who reached their decisions with reference solely to the law.... However, as the power of senior judges has grown, it has become more difficult to sustain this bright line between the functions of judges and politicians. The emergence of the judiciary as the third branch of government, checking and scrutinising the executive, has narrowed the gap between the functions of the senior judiciary and elected politicians. Judges are not politicians in wigs but they are increasingly required to reach decisions in relation to politically controversial issues which cannot be resolved without reference to policy questions. As the differentiation between law and politics blurs, the efficiency argument against the use of methods such as quotas to bring about greater diversity become less compelling and the benefits to be gained from a more diverse judiciary in terms of democratic legitimacy and public confidence grow.'[45]

The one concrete move that there has been towards a more diverse Scottish bench has been the appointment of women judges. Even prior to devolution and the resultant changes in the mechanism for appointing judges the problem of the lack of women judges was recognised. Hence in 1996 the first woman, Hazel Aronson, was appointed to the Court of Session bench, under the judicial style of Lady Cosgrove, and by 2005 four out of the thirty-two judges of the Court of Session were women. Of the 140 sheriffs twenty-four are now female, one from an ethnic minority background. Notwithstanding the Scottish Executive's guidance that the JAB should aim for a more representative judiciary, it is not at all clear that the existence of the Board has made any real difference on this issue. Rather, it is likely that more women are being appointed because that is now part of the general agenda of society.

However, even if it is accepted in principle that a more diverse judiciary is desirable, the question still arises as to what sort of diversity is desirable. At the moment the type of diversity to be encouraged seems to be of the visible sort, namely gender, ethnicity and race, but important as these are there are other equally significant aspects of diversity in society, such as religion, politics and, above all, class. By definition, for as long as judges are selected from the ranks of silks, and perhaps also senior solicitors, the bench will be composed entirely of individuals who in the course of their working lives have enjoyed a six-figure income and standard

45 K Malleson, 'Rethinking the merit principle in judicial selection' (2006) 33 JLS 126 at 133–134.

of living far beyond that of most citizens.[46] Such high earnings will inevitably give judges, whether male or female, a rather different perspective on life from that of the average citizen. Moreover, given that entry barriers to the legal profession increasingly favour the well-off and privately educated this is not a situation which is likely to change and if anything is getting worse.[47] As Ewing observes:

> 'There are in fact two interconnected problems standing in the way of a representative bench; one is the method by which people are recruited and the other is the pool of people who are eligible to be recruited. Reform of the former is important, but it will make little significant difference without a corresponding reform of the latter.'[48]

Combined with the changing nature of the judicial role, noted above, this insight suggests that the only real way to make a difference to the composition of the bench is to break away from the presumption that success in legal practice, particularly as a silk, is the best way of assessing the competence or merits of candidates. As Ewing iconoclastically observes:

> 'It is by no means clear why participation in a private labour market should be a qualification for [judicial] appointment at all, or indeed how a minimalist reform will secure a more representative bench.... Access would remain confined (except for the token academic) to successful practitioners, that is to say, to people who spend their lives in the service of wealthy clients, imbued with the values and enriched with the money of wealthy clients.'[49]

In other words, if we really wished to see a fundamental widening in the diversity of the bench we would need to radically expand the pool of potential candidates. At a minimum eligibility for appointment could be extended to all who are legally qualified including all solicitors, and arguably even legal academics, combined with a new definition of 'merit' which made it clear that a successful court practice is not to be the only, or even the main, criterion for judging merit. But arguably even that expanded 'pool' would not be properly representative of the community: to do that one would need to make all citizens eligible. If the pool were opened up to all citizens it would be much easier to recruit judges from ethnic minorities and other unrepresented groups because the systemic barriers which hinder such individuals from making a career as a lawyer would be rendered irrelevant. However, given the need for legal competence, such a change is highly unlikely, with the result that the diversity of the bench, except perhaps in gender terms, is unlikely to increase significantly in the future, and the Scottish Bench will continue to be composed predominantly of wealthy former advocates and solicitors whose life experiences are far removed from those of the mass of the population over whom they preside.

---

46 In England the Judicial Sub-Committee of the Review Body on Senior Salaries investigated the pre-appointment earnings of High Court judges and found that the median pre-appointment earnings at 2004 rates was £430,565, and that of Circuit judges was £181,212. See *Major Review of the Judicial Salary Structure – Consultation Document* (June 2005).

47 According to the *Sutton Trust Briefing Note: The Educational Backgrounds of the UK's Top Solicitors, Barristers And Judges* (June 2005) in 2004, over two thirds of the barristers at the top English chambers had attended independent schools, as had three quarters of the judges, and over half the partners at the leading law firms.

48 K D Ewing, 'A theory of democratic adjudication: towards a representative, accountable and independent judiciary' (2000–2001) 38 *Alta L Rev* 708 at 719.

49 Above n 48, p 720.

JUDICIAL IMPARTIALITY

Once judges have been appointed, the primary judicial meta-value is that they should act impartially. Judges' immunity from suit (but not criminal liability) in respect of acts undertaken in their judicial capacity is a longstanding protection for judicial impartiality. Without it, it has been said that '[n]o man but a beggar or a fool would be a judge'.[50] The immunity also protects judicial independence because it prevents the state raising actions against judges because of their judicial decisions.[51] This immunity, whilst widely seen as essential to judicial impartiality and independence, is not unproblematic either in application or effect, but lack of space precludes a discussion of these issues here. Similarly, lack of space precludes discussion of the restrictions on judges' political activities (also a matter of some uncertainty and controversy) except in so far as is relevant to their ability to decide cases impartially.

As noted above, impartiality is an *essential* meta-value required of every judge, for without it no decision by a judge can have credibility: 'impartiality and the appearance of it are the supreme judicial virtues'.[52] The reason for this is that the very concept of judging a case *fairly* (whether in a court of law or even in the most informal extra-legal circumstances) presupposes *neutrality* on the part of the judge. The judge must hear both sides and then make his decision, but if he has decided the outcome even before he has heard the case then, as well as being unfair, the question arises why the disadvantaged party should submit his case to judgment in the first place. As Lord Hope stated in *R v Bow Street Metropolitan Stipendiary Magistrate and others, ex parte Pinochet Ugarte (No 2)*:[53]

> 'One of the cornerstones of our legal system is the impartiality of the tribunals by which justice is administered. In civil litigation the guiding principle is that no one may be a judge in his own cause; *nemo debet esse judex in propria causa*. It is a principle which is applied much more widely than a literal interpretation of the words might suggest.'

Impartiality does not, however, mean that a judge comes to a case without any preconceptions. Such a state is simply impossible, as Judge Jerome Frank observed:

> 'If ... "bias" and "partiality" be defined to mean the total absence of preconceptions ... then no-one has ever had a fair trial and no-one ever will. The human mind ... is no blank piece of paper.... Interest, points of view, preferences, are the essence of living.'[54]

It is therefore necessary to distinguish the preconceptions or general attitudes of a judge from bias.

The Scots and English courts have developed a distinction between *actual* bias and *apparent* bias and that distinction has been paralleled by the European Court

---

50 Stair, *Institutions*, iv.i.5, approved in *Haggart's Trustees v Lord President* (1824) 2 Shaws Rep 125 at 134. See also *McCreadie v Thomson* 1907 SC 1176.
51 'The judge's right to refuse to answer to the executive or legislative branches of government or their appointees as to how and why the judge arrived at a particular judicial conclusion is essential to the personal independence of the judge, one of the two main aspects of judicial independence': *Knowles' Trial* (1692) 12 How St Tr 1179, per McLachlin J.
52 Lord Devlin, *The Judge* (1979), p 4.
53 [1999] 1 All ER 577 at 592.
54 *In re Linahan* 138 F2d 650 at 651–652 (2d Cir, 1943)

of Human Rights.[55] Actual bias is, at least according to the reported cases, almost unknown in the modern legal systems of the UK. It has been defined as a situation where a judge 'has a personal interest which is not negligible in the outcome, or is a friend or relation of a party or a witness, or is disabled by personal experience from bringing an objective judgment to bear on the case in question'.[56] But is actual bias really so rare? Anecdotal reports from those who work in the courts would suggest not, and arguably its apparent rarity is due to the deference of counsel and judicial courtesy, which results in courts being extremely reluctant to ascribe actual bias to a fellow judge. For example, in *Jones v National Coal Board*,[57] where the trial judge had persistently interrupted the hearing and made his views on the case very clear, although the Court of Appeal ordered a re-trial for lack of fairness, it did not actually state the judge was biased. Similarly, in *Bradford v McLeod*,[58] a sheriff, in a conversation which took place at a social function during the miners' strike in 1984, remarked that he 'would not grant legal aid to miners' in the presence of a solicitor representing the National Union of Mineworkers. The sheriff subsequently refused to recuse himself in cases involving criminal actions against striking miners and the case went to the Court of Criminal Appeal where it was held that the sheriff should have recused himself on the grounds of *apparent* bias, but Lord Ross went out of his way to stress he found no actual bias.[59] However to the present author this seems a straightforward example of *actual* bias: the judge had declared publicly his prejudice against granting miners legal aid. Nevertheless, it is because impartiality is concerned with the *possibility* of bias by the judge that *apparent* bias is as significant as actual bias, for if judges were allowed to hear cases in which they are apparently biased confidence in the entire judicial system would be undermined.[60] As Lord Devlin wrote:

> 'The social service which a judge renders to the community is the removal of a sense of injustice. To perform this service the essential quality which he needs is impartiality, and next after that the appearance of impartiality. I put impartiality before the appearance of it simply because without the reality the appearance would not endure. In truth, with the context of service to the community the appearance is the more important of the two.'[61]

In a similar vein Lord Nolan stated: 'I would only add that in any case where the impartiality of a judge is in question the appearance of the matter is just as important as the reality.'[62]

The current test for apparent judicial bias is 'whether the fair-minded and informed observer, having considered the facts, would conclude that there was a real possibility that the tribunal was biased'.[63] Given that the courts are extremely

---

55 See *Piersack v Belgium* (1983) 5 EHRR 169 where the distinction is made in terms of objective and subjective bias.

56 *Davidson v Scottish Ministers (No 2)* 2005 1 SC (HL) 7 at para 6 per Lord Bingham of Cornhill.

57 [1957] 2 QB 55.

58 1986 SLT 244

59 1986 SLT 244 at 247 per Lord Justice-Clerk Ross.

60 *R v Sussex Justices, ex parte McCarthy* [1924] 1 KB 256 at 259 per Lord Hewart CJ: 'Justice should not only be done, but should manifestly and undoubtedly be seen to be done.'

61 Lord Devlin, *The Judge*, p 3.

62 *R v Bow Street Metropolitan Stipendiary Magistrates and others, ex parte Pinochet Ugarte (No 2)* [2000] 1 AC 119 at 139.

63 *Porter v Magill* [2002] 1 All ER 465 at 494 per Lord Hope.

reluctant to make findings of actual bias, the important distinction in practice is between apparent bias which automatically debars a judge and that which does not. Traditionally,[64] the automatic disqualification rule was thought to apply only in cases where the judge had a pecuniary or proprietary interest in the outcome of the litigation. However, it was widened to include non-financial interests by a broader understanding of the *nemo judex* principle in *Pinochet (No 2)*,[65] where it was held unacceptable for Lord Hoffmann to sit in an appeal related to the former Head of State of Chile whilst he was also a director of a charity closely allied to Amnesty International, Amnesty being an intervener in the case:

> '[A]lthough the cases have all dealt with automatic disqualification on the grounds of pecuniary interest, there is no good reason in principle for so limiting automatic disqualification. The rationale of the whole rule is that a man cannot be a judge in his own cause. In civil litigation the matters in issue will normally have an economic impact; therefore a judge is automatically disqualified if he stands to make a financial gain as a consequence of his own decision of the case. But if, as in the present case, the matter at issue does not relate to money or economic advantage but is concerned with the promotion of the cause, the rationale disqualifying a judge applies just as much if the judge's decision will lead to the promotion of a cause in which the judge is involved together with one of the parties.'[66]

There have been two post-devolution Scottish cases in the wake of *Pinochet (No 2)* where the partiality of a judge has been successfully raised: *Hoekstra v HM Advocate (No 3)*[67] and *Davidson v Scottish Ministers (No 2)*.[68] These cases are important because they focus on previously expressed views of the judges in question. In *Hoekstra*, it was successfully argued that the fact that Lord McCluskey had written an article in a national newspaper which was highly critical of the ECHR was enough to render him apparently biased in an appeal in which Convention rights were being relied upon, and a rehearing of the case before a different panel of judges was ordered. Interestingly, it was not the content of his criticisms which the court considered led to his presumed bias, but the *context* and *tone* in which he expressed his concerns.[69] But such a distinction seems to smack of a patronising 'not in front of the servants and children' attitude. Why should views stated in serious tones in a scholarly journal not constitute bias, but views expressed forcefully in a newspaper do so? In fact, even scholarly criticism, if too forcefully expressed, can lead to a presumption of bias, as happened in *Locabail (UK) Ltd v Bayfield Properties Ltd*,[70] where the judge, who was a tort expert, was deemed biased because he had written articles which were too pro-claimant. This problem returned to haunt the judiciary in *Davidson*, which was concerned

64 *Dimes v Grand Junction Canal* (1852) 3 HLC 759, especially at 793 per Lord Campbell.
65 [2000] 1 AC 119.
66 At 135 per Lord Browne-Wilkinson.
67 2000 JC 391.
68 2005 1 SC (HL) 7.
69 'We stress that, in reaching this conclusion, we attach particular importance to the tone of the language and the impression which the author deliberately gives that his hostility to the operation of the Convention as part of our domestic law is both long-standing and deep-seated. The position would have been very different if all that Lord McCluskey had done was to publish, say, an article in a legal journal drawing attention, in moderate language, to what he perceived to be the drawbacks of incorporating the Convention into our law': 2000 JC 391 at para 23 per Lord Justice-General Rodger.
70 [2000] QB 451.

with whether the fact that Lord Hardie had made statements while he was Lord Advocate about the effect of a statute had rendered him apparently biased in a case which turned on the interpretation of that statute. The House of Lords held that such comments did indeed raise an appearance of bias but stressed that this was not based purely on a separation of powers argument. Rather it depended on what the judge had done in Parliament in his legislative capacity, and the court went out of its way to stress that former Lords Advocate were not per se 'ineligible to be judges or to hear a very wide range of cases'.[71] The combined effect of these cases is to give at least putative grounds to challenge a judge's impartiality if he has written on the matter in question or dealt with it previously, especially in some other extra-judicial capacity. In this context, it is interesting also to reflect on the composition of the bench in *Kearney v HM Advocate*,[72] one of several cases (discussed further below) on the question of whether the use of temporary judges was compatible with Article 6 ECHR. In that case the leading judgment is given by Lord Hope, but as he himself admits in the judgment: 'I have to confess that I bear much of the responsibility for the way the system [of temporary judges] was introduced and for the way in which, before the coming into force of the Scotland Act, it was operated.'[73] It is therefore surprising that Lord Hope did not feel obliged to recuse himself on grounds of prior involvement with the case, as surely this was a clear case where apparent bias might arise.

In fact, in the immediate post-devolution era the Court of Session took such a strong line on the importance of impartiality in the context of planning decisions that it was in danger of ignoring the need for democratic accountability. However, its initial decision in *County Properties Ltd v Scottish Ministers*[74] was overturned by the Inner House[75] following the decision of the House of Lords in *R v Secretary of State for the Environment, Transport and the Regions, ex parte Alconbury Developments Ltd.*[76] The Inner House held that although neither the Scottish Ministers nor a planning reporter appointed by them constituted an independent and impartial tribunal for the purposes of Article 6 ECHR, there was no breach of Article 6 because the process for determining such planning questions viewed as a whole (including the right of appeal to the Court of Session) satisfied Article 6. Subsequently, one 'Robbie the Pict' unsuccessfully challenged the impartiality of Scottish judges on the grounds of membership of certain secret societies, drawing attention in particular to judicial membership of the Freemasons and the Speculative Society.[77] Robbie's challenges were perhaps not taken entirely seriously by either the courts or the media. But in a small jurisdiction such as Scotland, where the higher judiciary has been drawn almost exclusively from a very narrow group of individuals (namely, the Faculty of Advocates), problems of partiality are likely to arise with even greater frequency than they would in a larger country, given the interconnected nature of the governmental, business and judicial elites. Robbie might also have usefully raised the possible effects of membership of the New Club and Muirfield Golf Club!

71 2005 SC (HL) 7 per Lord Bingham at para 20.
72 *Kearney v HM Advocate* [2006] UKPC D1.
73 *Kearney* at para 29.
74 2000 SLT 965.
75 2001 SLT 1125.
76 [2001] 2 WLR 1389.
77 See *Robbie the Pict, Petitioner (No 2)* 2003 JC 78. The Speculative Society is a dining club composed of male Edinburgh University undergraduates and graduates.

JUDICIAL INDEPENDENCE

The final issue to be considered is what happens if judges fail to meet our expectations of impartiality, or otherwise turn out to lack the necessary competence for the job. If, as discussed above, effective accountability for judicial appointments has proved difficult to secure in practice, the notion of accountability in office is even more problematic because in many ways it is diametrically opposed to the principle of independence, especially with regard to the dismissal of judges. Nevertheless, as with judicial appointments, there have been recent changes in this area in response to concerns about lack of accountability. The Commonwealth's Latimer House Guidelines on securing judicial independence, drawn up in 1998, divide accountability in office[78] into headings of 'discipline' and 'public criticism'. These are understood as qualifications of the fundamental principle of judicial security of tenure and parallel Bogdanor's distinction between 'sacrificial' and 'explanatory' accountability.

Sacrificial accountability

Security of tenure and judicial discipline

The near absolute security of tenure enjoyed by Scottish judges is an essential precondition of their institutional independence from the state. As stated earlier 'sacrificial accountability' effectively means the possibility of dismissal but, by definition, the easier it is to dismiss a judge then the less independent is the judge. In effect, independence and sacrificial accountability are incompatible values in the operation of a judiciary. In the UK, at least since the 'Glorious Revolution',[79] the emphasis has been on securing the independence of the judiciary rather than on making the judges accountable. Judicial independence post-1689 was ensured by granting tenure of office *ad vitam aut culpam*. The Act of Settlement made the mechanism for judges' removal from office in England and Wales the extremely onerous one of a motion passed by both Houses of Parliament, a mechanism used only once.[80] The effect of this was that judges could act free of fear or favour of the executive or legislature, and the removal of a judge became solely a matter of discipline on fault grounds. Prior to the enactment of the Scotland Act no statutory provision existed for the removal from office of a judge of the Court of Session. The procedure laid down by the Act of Settlement had not been applied to Scotland, although it had been suggested that it would have been prudent for the Crown to seek the support of both Houses before dismissing a judge.[81] The Scotland Act filled this gap in the law[82] and included provisions for the removal of judges of the Court of Session analogous to the statutory scheme which already existed for

---

78 The Guidelines do not refer to accountability 'in office' but merely to 'accountability', but that is because they deal with appointment under a separate heading.

79 The Claim of Right of 1689 provided that 'changing the nature of the judges' gifts *ad vitam aut culpam* into commissions *durante beneplacito* [is] contrary to law'.

80 In 1830 an Irish judge, Sir Jonah Barrington, misappropriated £700 paid into the Admiralty Court of Ireland and was subsequently dismissed after an address was presented to the Crown by Parliament.

81 See A W Bradley and K D Ewing, *Constitutional and Administrative Law* (11th edn, 1993), p 378.

82 Scotland Act 1998, s 95(6)–(11) and Scotland Act 1998 (Transitory and Transitional Provisions) (Removal of Judges) Order 1999 (SI 1999/1017).

the removal from office of sheriffs under the Sheriff Courts (Scotland) Act 1971 section 12.[83] Now, where serious concerns exist about a Court of Session judge, a tribunal, chaired by a member of the Judicial Committee of the Privy Council, may be constituted to investigate that person's fitness for office. If the tribunal reports that the person in question is unfit for office, the First Minister may make a motion to the Scottish Parliament for the judge's removal from office, and if the Scottish Parliament passes this resolution, by not less than two thirds of the total membership of the Parliament, the First Minister can make a recommendation to the Queen that the judge in question be removed from office. At the time of writing it is likely that these transitional provisions will be replaced by primary legislation of the Scottish Parliament.[84]

According to the existing, and proposed, statutory arrangements a judge may only be dismissed by reason of inability, neglect of duty, or misbehaviour. The first of these three criteria is the straightforward one of physical or mental incapacity; the other two are examples of *culpa*, fault, as envisaged by the Claim of Right. All of these criteria are quite extreme and unlikely to arise often in practice and so the sacrificial accountability they provide is of a very narrow kind. There is the further difficulty that there is no real mechanism for disciplining judges for unacceptable behaviour that is not so severe as to merit dismissal. In England this problem has recently been addressed by creating[85] the post of Judicial Appointments and Conduct Ombudsman, independent of government and judiciary, who will hear complaints about the judiciary. Whilst the need for reform in this area has been recognised in Scotland,[86] this particular option seems likely to be rejected and instead the Executive has proposed that the power to discipline judges should rest with the Lord President.[87] Arguably, accountability would be better served by a more independent complaints process, such as the creation of a Judicial Ombudsman, as in England or, better still, a Judicial Performance Committee such as is found in the majority of American states.[88]

Temporary sheriffs and judges and independence and impartiality

Security of tenure has traditionally been understood as meaning appointment for life or, since the 1960s, at least until a fixed retirement age. However, the practice has developed of appointing judges and sheriffs for temporary periods, often as a prelude to permanent appointment, one rationale for which can be understood as allowing the competence of potential judges to be tested prior to their acquiring full security of tenure. Following the incorporation of the ECHR, though, the compatibility of temporary judicial office with the Article 6 guarantees of independence and impartiality was tested in three key cases: *Starrs v Ruxton*,[89]

---

83 Two sheriffs have been removed under this procedure: in 1977 Peter Thomson for promoting a referendum on Scottish home rule; and in 1992 Ewen Stewart was removed as unfit to hold judicial office: see *Stewart v Secretary of State for Scotland* 1998 SC (HL) 81. A third sheriff, Hugh Neilson, was in September 2004 made the subject of an investigation into fitness for office conducted, on behalf of Scottish Ministers, by the Lord President and Lord Justice-Clerk but he resigned before the investigation could be concluded.

84 Scottish Executive, *Strengthening Judicial Independence*, above n 34, para 7.1.

85 Constitutional Reform Act 2005, s 62 and Sch 12.

86 Scottish Executive, *Strengthening Judicial Independence*, above n 34, ch 8, esp paras 8.3–8.4.

87 Scottish Executive, *Strengthening Judicial Independence*, above n 34, para 8.15.

88 See D Pannick, *Judges* (1987), pp 96–103 who supports the creation of such a commission.

89 2000 JC 208.

Clancy v Caird[90] and *Kearney v HM Advocate*.[91] In *Starrs v Ruxton*, the High Court of Justiciary held that temporary sheriffs[92] sitting on criminal business were not independent and impartial tribunals within the meaning of Article 6(1) given their lack of security of tenure (appointments were made for one year only and were subject to recall within that period) and the restrictions applied by the Lord Advocate in determining who was eligible for reappointment. This case highlighted the close interconnection between the concepts of independence and impartiality: a lack of substantive independence was held to create a risk of *apparent* bias, even although it was accepted there had been no actual bias. In contrast to *Starrs*, the Inner House in *Clancy v Caird* held that the employment of temporary judges in the Court of Session was on terms which provided sufficient guarantees against any reasonable perception of lack of independence and impartiality because the case did not involve the Crown and because the employment of temporary judges was a matter for the Lord President not the Lord Advocate. *Clancy* was a civil case and so the issue of temporary judges sitting in criminal cases eventually had to be dealt with by the Privy Council in *Kearney v HM Advocate*. In *Kearney* it was stressed by the Privy Council that:

> 'It is not … in doubt that a person exercising judicial functions should not be placed in a position where his freedom to discharge those functions without fear or favour, affection or ill-will, might be or appear to be jeopardised by his relationship with the executive.'[93]

However, the position of temporary judges in criminal cases was distinguished from that of the former temporary sheriffs as none of the factors identified in relation to temporary sheriffs applied. A temporary judge presiding over a criminal trial therefore has no relationship with the Lord Advocate which could undermine his independence. Perhaps surprisingly, *Clancy* and *Kearney* both held that a time-limited appointment does not, of itself, breach Article 6, provided there is security of tenure during office. This acceptance that judicial office may be held for relatively short periods of time is, ironically, a major weakening of the judicial tenure provisions provided for by the Claim of Right and the common law and this opens up one radical possibility for making judges more accountable: making appointments to the bench for fixed but renewable terms, say five or six years. This would then allow for the possibility that a judge who has been found wanting could merely not have his term of office renewed. In practice, however, this is extremely unlikely to be adopted as it is too bold a break with the Scots and English tradition of judges holding office till death or retirement, and it would probably also significantly decrease the attractiveness of judicial office to senior lawyers.

Explanatory accountability

The Scottish judiciary is subject to several forms of explanatory accountability.

---

90 2000 SC 441.
91 [2006] UKPC D1.
92 The power to create temporary sheriffs was conferred on the Secretary of State for Scotland by the Sheriff Courts (Scotland) Act 1971, s 11(2).
93 *Kearney v HM Advocate* per Lord Bingham of Cornhill at para 4.

Legal scrutiny

Judges must hear cases in public and are generally expected to justify their decisions by giving reasons, that is, their legal opinion. This obligation does set some real limits to judicial action in that the very act of public explanation will tend to inhibit purely arbitrary or unjustifiable decisions. The judicial hierarchy of course binds a judge and it follows that the decisions of lower judges are subject to some sort of review. Evidently this does not apply to judges who sit at the apex of the judicial hierarchy. In Scotland the appeal courts are in an asymmetrical position in that the Court of Criminal Appeal is the Supreme Criminal Court but the Court of Session is subject to appeals to the House of Lords. In any case it is only the decision which can be reviewed; the position of the judge is not affected no matter how often his decisions are reversed by a superior court, although there is perhaps some reputational harm suffered by a judge if this happens too frequently.

Scrutiny by civil society

Scrutiny by civil society includes criticism by politicians (in and outwith Parliament), the media and in legal and scholarly journals. There is no doubt that political scrutiny of the judges is increasing as criticism of the judiciary by politicians, including government ministers, has become increasingly common in recent years.[94] As regards criticism in Parliament judges, individually and collectively, have traditionally been insulated from such attacks by parliamentary procedure but there is a growing trend among politicians to attack the judiciary outside Parliament in the media. This kind of scrutiny is important but does not provide accountability, because there are no consequences for the judges concerned other than the possibility of reputational harm. Bogdanor suggests one possible new form of political scrutiny by proposing that, after they have been appointed, judges could be cross-examined on their judicial philosophy by parliamentary committees.[95] Another type of accountability that could usefully be introduced has been proposed by Ewing,[96] namely a register of interests analogous to that which exists for MPs. Such a register would, provided that the information which had to be disclosed was sufficiently wide, be a positive step towards an accountable judiciary (in that failure to disclose could mean a loss of office) and would enhance the procedure by which judicial impartiality is maintained.

Perhaps the most important informal form of scrutiny to which judges are subject is criticism in the media. Such criticism can range from the tabloid rants of the popular press to scholarly criticisms in the academic and legal press. Although such scrutiny has the advantage of being external to the judicial system it has the disadvantage that questions may well be asked about the credibility or locus of these critics. As Ewing remarks:

> 'Admittedly, there is the possibility of public criticism in the press, the existence of which is extremely important, or indeed criticism in the law reviews as the ultimate and most penetrating form of censure. But the former speak for the proprietors (and have no democratic legitimacy), while no one reads the self-appointed critics in the latter and fewer still (rightly) take them seriously.'[97]

94 See, eg, R Verkaik, 'Judges "have become whipping boys to hide ministerial failings"' *The Independent*, 5 July 2006.
95 'Parliament and the judiciary', above n 22, p 6.
96 'A theory of democratic adjudication', above n 48, p 722.
97 'A theory of democratic adjudication', above n 48, p 724.

In recent years there has been an increasing tendency for judges themselves to express their views in print, especially in the more scholarly press, and this is an important form of, self-imposed, explanatory accountability. But, in the light of *Hoekstra (No 3)* and *Davidson (No 2)* such views will have to be carefully expressed in future if they are to avoid raising a possibility of apparent bias.

CONCLUSION

The last ten years has seen more changes in the position, role and power of the Court of Session than the previous 100 years, a transformation that may well see the senior judiciary moving, in Guarnieri and Pederzoli's typology, from a 'delegate' role to a 'guardian' role or even a 'political' one. So far the political effects of devolution have been diluted by the fact that the same party, Labour, is in power in both London and Edinburgh; the party has fulfilled the role of co-ordinating policy and avoiding clashes between the two Parliaments. But this situation will not last indefinitely and it is almost inevitable that situations may arise where conflict is much more likely, say a Scottish National Party-led coalition in Edinburgh and a Conservative government in London. In that situation there may well be many issues about the respective competences of the two Parliaments and governments, some of which will inevitably be litigated and those decisions, whatever they are, will almost certainly be seen in a political light. Taking together the possible effects of devolution, human rights legislation and other extensions of the judicial role, when the judges start to act in an increasingly political way it is likely that the complex issues of judicial accountability, independence and impartiality discussed in this chapter will come to the political fore, and that there will be increased demands for accountability and increased questioning of their impartiality.

As regards the latter, whilst the independence of the judiciary per se is unlikely to be challenged, their impartiality may be subject to more challenge on legal grounds and to more insistent questioning by politicians and the media. Following *Davidson (No 2)* it may be difficult for certain devolution cases to be heard by judges who are former law officers. Likewise the effect of *Hoekstra (No 3)* and *Locabail* may even be to prevent judges who have written on constitutional matters from sitting in devolution cases, for suspicion of apparent bias. As regards the former, current arrangements may not satisfy future demands for increased accountability, and it may become necessary to clarify the nature and extent of judicial accountability and how it can be reconciled with independence. Greater scrutiny is the price the judiciary will pay for their increased powers and increasingly political role in a devolved Scotland.

PART III:
CONTROLLING PUBLIC POWER IN SCOTLAND

Chapter 10

Parliamentary Sovereignty and the Judicial Review of Legislation

Aidan O'Neill QC

INTRODUCTION

It is sometimes suggested that one cannot properly talk of 'United Kingdom constitutional law' because of the underlying differences between English and Scots law on such fundamental issues as the rights and liabilities of the Crown[1] and the nature and extent of parliamentary sovereignty.[2] Arguably, too, Scots law historically contained less recognition and protection than did English law for what would now be regarded as the fundamental rights and freedoms of the individual.[3] But the reality is that there is simply insufficient material in the Scottish case law to allow one to reconstruct a complete and coherent theory of the relationship between government and individual in Scotland which consistently differed (and differs) in its essential aspects from the position as applied in England from time to time.

The UK constitution is, in any event, a dynamic and evolving affair. There is no one foundational written document, nor any Founding Fathers (or Mothers) whose views are thought to carry particular significance. Even if the constitutional position in Scotland pre-1707 as regards the relationship between individuals, the courts and the state did indeed differ from that of England, Article XVIII(2) of the Treaty of Union provided that 'the laws concerning public right, policy and civil government may be made the same throughout the whole United Kingdom'. And the judges in Scotland have typically relied upon this provision to support the claim that 'the constitution of Scotland has been the same as that of England since 1707 [and] there is a presumption that the same constitutional principles apply in both countries'.[4] The result has been that the courts in Scotland have tended simply to follow established English lines of authority on constitutional issues such as

---

1 See Chapter 13 in this volume.

2 See *MacCormick v Lord Advocate* 1953 SC 39 at 41 per Lord President Cooper. See further Chapter 2 in this volume.

3 In *Mackintosh v Lord Advocate* (1876) 2 App Cas 41 (HL(Sc)) at 59–60 Hemming QC cites a paper by J F Macqueen QC, read at the Manchester Congress of Social Science on 8 Oct 1866, to the following effect:

   'The blessings of the English Constitution, however, were not extended to Scotland [at the Union in 1707]. The Scotch consequently have no Magna Charta, no Bill of Rights, no Habeas Corpus.... Personal freedom depends on the temper of the existing government, or rather on the discretion – peradventure the caprice – of the Lord Advocate. When that high functionary incarcerated a gentleman supposed to entertain dangerous political opinions, the Lord Advocate justified himself in the House of Commons by the proud boast that he represented the Scottish Privy Council, and that his powers were unlimited. Under the sway of a benignant sovereign Caledonian grievances have practically disappeared. But the grave question remains whether it is consistent with the dignity of an intellectual people that their political rights should depend on the clemency of the government.'

4 *Macgregor v Lord Advocate* 1921 SC 847 at 848 per Lord Anderson.

the liability of government departments in negligence,[5] the application of general statutory provisions to the Crown,[6] the susceptibility of government departments to coercive orders from the courts,[7] or the possibility of, and the conditions for, finding the Executive to be in contempt of court.[8] Admittedly, the doctrinal traffic is not always one way. On the issue of whether the courts could overrule the Executive's claim to be able to withhold documentation relevant to court proceedings on the grounds of public interest immunity the House of Lords relied upon Scottish authority[9] to overrule the earlier English rule[10] that it was not open to the courts to look behind any such claim by the Executive.[11] But the tendency remains one of seeking harmonisation throughout the UK, rather than a desire to preserve constitutional differences between Scotland and England.

Older UK constitutional paradigm

From the Union of Parliaments of 1707 through to the entry of the UK into the European Communities in 1973 the UK constitution could be characterised as one which sought to instantiate (more or less) the following as fundamental constitutional principles: the sovereignty of Parliament and the separation of powers. The interaction of these two principles resulted in the following propositions of basic constitutional law for the UK: (1) it is for (the Westminster) Parliament to make the laws; (2) it is for ministers of the Crown to govern within the limits of the law set down by Parliament; (3) it is for judges to interpret (but not question) that law and enforce its limits;[12] and (4) international legal obligations entered into by the Crown have no effect within the domestic forum unless and until expressly incorporated into national law by Parliament.[13] On the accepted constitutional theory of the sovereignty of Parliament what would be regarded as anomalous or exceptions to the constitutional rule would be any substantial law-making outside the bounds of Parliament, whether by the Crown exercising executive powers, or by the judges applying statutory law in ways never intended by Parliament or by the judges embarking on major changes in the existing common law.

Paradigm shift in the UK constitution?

On the face of it the Scotland Act 1998 (SA) has expressly departed from the tendency toward constitutional harmonisation by introducing within the UK a wholly new constitutional model which is based on judicial rather than parliamentary primacy. It is certainly crucial to any proper understanding of the

---

5   *Macgregor* at 853 per Lord Salvesen.
6   *Lord Advocate v Dumbarton District Council* 1990 SC (HL) 1.
7   *Davidson v Scottish Ministers (No 1)* 2006 SC (HL) 41.
8   *Beggs v Scottish Ministers* 2005 SC 342.
9   *Glasgow Corporation v Central Land Board* 1956 SC (HL) 1.
10 Set out in *Duncan v Cammell Laird & Co Ltd* [1942] AC 624.
11 *Conway v Rimmer* [1968] AC 910 at 938, 950 per Lord Reid.
12 See *R v Secretary of State for the Home Department, ex parte Fire Brigades Union* [1995] 2 AC 513 at 567–568 per Lord Mustill (dissenting).
13 See *R v Lyons* [2003] 1 AC 976 per Lord Hoffmann at paras 27–28. The rules of customary international law may be incorporated into the domestic legal system without express incorporation: see *Lord Advocate's Reference (No 1 of 2000) re nuclear weapons* 2001 JC 143 (HCJ) and *R v Jones* [2006] 2 WLR 772.

role of the judiciary in relation to the Scottish Parliament that it be recognised that that Parliament has not been accorded the status in law of a sovereign body. Thus, notwithstanding that they require specific royal assent as a condition of their validity, Acts of the Scottish Parliament (ASPs) are defined in the Human Rights Act 1998 (HRA) as 'subordinate legislation' (s 21).[14] And SA section 29(1) provides that 'an Act of the Scottish Parliament is not law so far as any provision is outside the legislative competence of the Parliament'. The powers of the Scottish Parliament and Executive are delimited and circumscribed by the provisions of the statute which set them up. What has been created in the Scottish Parliament is a democratic legislature whose Acts are subject to control by the judiciary, both in terms of pre-legislative judicial review by the Judicial Committee of the Privy Council *and* post-enactment judicial review by all courts in the UK hierarchy. Possible conflict between the Westminster Parliament and the Holyrood Parliament on claims that the new body is exceeding its limited powers is thus made into a juridical rather than a nakedly political matter.

But the tendency – the internal dynamic – within the constitution toward doctrinal harmonisation remains. In that light, it is submitted that the introduction of the principle of judicial supremacy in the context of devolution will have effects and resonance even within the non-devolved aspects of the UK constitution. In addition to the granting of legislative and administrative devolution to Scotland, Wales and Northern Ireland, other significant changes in the constitution include the UK's entry into the European Union, the incorporation into domestic law of substantive provisions of the European Convention on Human Rights, and the institutional reform of the House of Lords, both as a legislative body (in removing the attendance and voting rights of (all but ninety-two of) the hereditary peers)[15] and as a judicial body (in removing the Lords of Appeal in Ordinary and setting up a distinct UK Supreme Court).[16] It is suggested that the cumulative result of these legislative changes has been to make the older constitutional paradigm – based on the principle of unfettered sovereignty of the Westminster Parliament – increasingly untenable as an accurate description of the manner in which legislative, judicial and executive power in fact operates in the UK as a whole.

It is suggested in this chapter that we are in the throes of a constitutional paradigm shift, of a legal revolution which has been initiated (perhaps unwittingly) by the Westminster Parliament but which is now being (perhaps more consciously) effected and furthered by the judges particularly of the House of Lords (and Privy Council) who have increasingly shown themselves, in the words of Lord Nicholls,

14 Though in *Adams v Advocate General* 2003 SC 171, the Lord Ordinary, Lord Nimmo Smith, observed, *obiter*, at 201:

'[D]espite the reference in the Human Rights Act to Acts of the Scottish Parliament being subordinate legislation, such Acts have in my opinion far more in common with public general statutes of the United Kingdom Parliament than with subordinate legislation as it is more commonly understood. Indeed, the definition of subordinate legislation in the Scotland Act makes this distinction clear. The Parliament is a democratically-elected representative body. It has under sec 28(1) a general law-making power, except in relation to reserved matters and the other matters specified in sec 29(2). In consequence of this, it can not only pass its own Acts, it can amend or repeal, in their application to Scotland, pre-devolution acts of the United Kingdom Parliament. An Act of the Scottish Parliament, once passed, requires Royal Assent to become law. It is of a character which has far more in common with a public general statute than with subordinate legislation, though it might be preferable to regard it as being *sui generis*.'

15 House of Lords Act 1999.
16 Constitutional Reform Act 2005.

as being 'prepared to depart from a strict and narrow interpretation of the judiciary's adjudicative role'.[17] If this apparent constitutional change is being carried forward by the actions of the judges – in what under the older constitutional paradigm might have been characterised as a *trahison des juges* – this is a revolution without revolt since the change being wrought is not in the formal structures of the law, but in our understanding of the existing legal and constitutional structures. Lord Hope has stated that 'the principle of parliamentary sovereignty itself which ... has been created by the common law is built upon the *assumption* that [the Westminster] Parliament represents the people whom it exists to serve'.[18] Lord Justice Laws has also noted that 'the doctrine of [Westminster] parliamentary sovereignty cannot be vouched by Parliamentary legislation; a higher law confers it and must of necessity limit it'.[19] What has been created by the courts as a common law principle may, presumably, be altered by the courts exercising their jurisdiction to develop the common law. And Lord Nicholls observes:

> 'In common law countries much of the basic law is still the common law. The common law is judge-made law. For centuries judges have been charged with the responsibility of keeping this law abreast of current social conditions and expectations. That is still the position. Continuing but limited development of the common law in this fashion is an integral part of the constitutional function of the judiciary.... In all cases development of the common law, as a response to changed conditions, does not come like a bolt out of a clear sky. *Invariably the clouds gather first, often from different quarters, indicating with increasing obviousness what is coming*'[20] (emphasis added).

In this context, the particular issue which this chapter explores is the extent to which the judges may claim and seek to exercise a power of judicial review over primary legislation and the implications that the existence of such a power has for constitutional analysis. Ultimately the thesis put forward is that there is a momentum in favour of a shift in the central descriptive motif which characterises the UK constitution. There is a move from the primacy of the legislature to one in which the judges have the last word on matters of constitutionality. The constitutional revolution in the UK is clearly not yet completed,[21] but the changes in the judicial role within the polity which have been expressly mandated by the devolution statutes indicate the direction in which we are headed.

GATHERING CLOUDS: COMMONWEALTH
CONSTITUTIONALISM AND THE PRIVY COUNCIL

Although the Judicial Committee of the Privy Council has been accorded a role as a UK domestic court by the devolution statutes (the Scotland Act 1998 (SA), the Northern Ireland Act 1998 (NIA) and the Government of Wales Act 1998 (GWA)), the vast bulk of the work of the Privy Council remains that of deciding upon Commonwealth cases. The Board considers on average around sixty overseas

---

17 *In re Spectrum Plus Ltd (in liquidation)* [2005] 2 AC 280 per Lord Nicholls at para 16.
18 *R (on the application of Jackson) v Attorney-General* [2006] 1 AC 262 per Lord Hope at para 126.
19 Sir John Laws, 'Law and democracy' [1995] PL 72 at 87.
20 *In re Spectrum Plus Ltd (in liquidation)* per Lord Nicholls at para 16.
21 See *International Transport Roth GmbH v Home Office* [2003] QB 728 (CA) per Laws LJ at para 71.

appeals each year compared to only two or so devolution issue cases decided annually. The 'new Commonwealth' constitutions which were drafted by the Foreign and Commonwealth Office (FCO) in the years following the 1939–45 War gave the Privy Council a role not simply as a final court of appeal on the Westminster model but as the supreme/constitutional court for the various Commonwealth nations, entrusted with the task of ensuring that the authorities of the newly independent states stayed within the bounds of the constitution. In this latter role the Privy Council gradually began to develop new techniques of legal reasoning which sought to establish a rationale and justification for post-enactment judicial involvement in the legislative decisions of the democratic legislature. The FCO 'standard constitutions' for the former colonial territories also commonly contained provisions authorising the courts to construe ordinary laws of the territory in a manner which ensured their constitutionality (and fundamental rights compatibility). The Commonwealth courts were enjoined to read statutes which appeared on their face to be incompatible with the constitution 'with such modifications, adaptations, qualifications and exceptions as may be necessary to bring them into conformity with the constitution'.[22] Thus, as the highest court in Commonwealth cases the Privy Council has not regarded itself as being constrained to *apply* the language of the statute in question but instead, in order to avoid striking down a provision as void because unconstitutional, sees itself as constitutionally authorised to effect modifications or amendments to the statutory language in order to bring the provision into conformity with the constitution.[23] This might be thought to be the judiciary exercising a quasi-legislative power rather than a purely interpretative one.[24] Perhaps conscious of this, the Privy Council has stated that the constitutionality of a parliamentary enactment is presumed unless it is shown to be unconstitutional, and that the burden on a party seeking to prove invalidity is a heavy one.[25]

This 'new Commonwealth' case law of the Privy Council of the period since the end of the 1939–45 War is also of particular interest in the development of its fundamental rights jurisprudence. When it was signed and ratified by the UK in 1950, the European Convention on Human Rights (ECHR) also applied to its then dependent territories, the vast majority of which subsequently went on to become independent nations within the Commonwealth. As part of the process of decolonisation, the FCO included in the constitutional instruments which set up the former colonies as independent nations, and which were expressed to be the supreme law of the new state, entrenched fundamental rights provisions modelled on the terms of the ECHR.[26] Thus in this 'new Commonwealth' case law the Privy Council has from the early 1980s been referred to,[27] and from the early

---

22 See, eg, *R v Hughes* [2002] 2 AC 259.
23 See, eg, *Rojas v Berllaque (Attorney-General for Gibraltar intervening)* [2004] 1 WLR 201 per Lord Nicholls at para 24.
24 See *Ghaidan v Godin-Mendoza* [2004] 2 AC 557 per Lord Millet at para 64 and per Lord Rodger of Earlsferry at para 120.
25 See *Mootoo v Attorney-General of Trinidad and Tobago* [1979] 1 WLR 1334 at 1338–1339 and *Grant v Jamaica* [2006] 2 WLR 835 at para 15.
26 See, generally, A W B Simpson, *Human Rights and the End of Empire* (2001).
27 The first reported references by counsel before the JCPC to ECtHR jurisprudence are to be found in *Ong Ah Chuan v Public Prosecutor* [1981] AC 648 (on appeal from the Court of Criminal Appeal of Singapore). *Riley v Attorney-General of Jamaica* [1983] 1 AC 719 appears to mark the first occasion on which judges expressly referred to this jurisprudence (Lord Scarman and Lord Brightman (dissenting) at 734).

1990s regularly come to rely upon, relevant decisions of the European Court of Human Rights (ECtHR).[28] One of the techniques developed by the Privy Council has been to treat the matter of the interpretation and application of constitutional fundamental rights provisions terms in a generous and purposive manner: as Lord Wilberforce stated in *Minister of Home Affairs v Fisher*, 'avoiding what has been called "the austerity of tabulated legalism"', suitable to give to individuals the full measure of the fundamental rights and freedoms referred to'.[29] In the same case, Lord Wilberforce also emphasised that the proper understanding and application of a constitutional instrument called for 'principles of interpretation of its own, suitable to its character ... without necessary acceptance of all the presumptions that are relevant to legislation of private law'.[30]

Spill-over into Human Rights Act case law

In its Commonwealth case law (as influenced by the ECtHR), the Privy Council increasingly saw its role to be that of upholding and protecting the fundamental rights of the individual even against the duly sanctioned decisions of the majority, as expressed by their representatives within the various Commonwealth nations' Parliaments. This growing familiarity with the case law and jurisprudential techniques of the Strasbourg institutions has been instrumental in developing the conditions for a judicial human rights culture in the UK following the coming into force of the fundamental rights provisions of the devolution statutes and the HRA. The evidence for this is to be found in the spill-over of concepts derived from the Privy Council's constitutional Commonwealth jurisprudence into purely domestic UK case law which occurred almost as soon as the UK courts were vested with a fundamental rights jurisdiction by the devolution statutes and the HRA.

Thus in *R v Director of Public Prosecutions, ex parte Kebilene*, a case decided by the House of Lords after the enactment but before the coming into force of the HRA, Lord Hope explicitly referred to and relied upon this Commonwealth case law in the following terms:

> 'In *Attorney-General of Hong Kong v Lee Kwong-kut* [1993] AC 951, 966 Lord Woolf referred to the general approach to the interpretations of constitutions and bills of rights indicated in previous decisions of the Board, which he said were equally applicable to the Hong Kong Bill of Rights Ordinance 1991. He mentioned Lord Wilberforce's observation in *Minister of Home Affairs v Fisher* [1980] AC 319, 328 that instruments of this nature call for a generous interpretation suitable to give to individuals the full measure of the fundamental rights and freedoms referred to, and Lord Diplock's comment in *Attorney-General of The Gambia v Momodou Jobe* [1984] AC 689, 700 that a generous and purposive construction is to be given to that part of a constitution which protects and entrenches fundamental rights and freedoms to which all persons in the state are to be entitled. *The same approach will now have to be applied in this country when issues are raised under the Human Rights Act of 1998 about the compatibility of domestic legislation and of acts of public authorities with the fundamental rights and freedoms which are enshrined in the Convention*'[31] (emphasis added).

28 *Attorney-General of Hong Kong v Lee Kwong-kut* [1993] AC 951 marks the first Privy Council decision when a *majority* of the Board refers to and relies upon ECtHR jurisprudence.
29 [1980] AC 319 at 328.
30 At 329.
31 [2000] 2 AC 326 at 375.

Similarly, in *R v Lambert*, Lord Hope cited two Privy Council Commonwealth decisions[32] in which the Board was prepared to read in or interpolate markedly different formulations from the actual words contained in the relevant legislative provisions in order to bring them into conformity with the fundamental rights guaranteed by the constitution. He stated that these two decisions provided good examples 'of the use of an interpretative obligation of the kind that has now been written into our domestic law by section 3(1) of the 1998 Act'.[33]

Spill-over into devolution case law

Significantly, in passing the devolution statutes, the UK Parliament decided that the Privy Council should become a UK court *superior to* the House of Lords.[34] This might be interpreted as providing statutory backing to the importation of the Privy Council's Commonwealth jurisprudence into the domestic UK sphere. This seems at least to have been the intention of the government, as was made clear by Lord Sewel, in the course of its promoting the Scotland Bill through the House of Lords, when he stated as follows:

> 'The Government believe that it is important that the decisions of the Judicial Committee of the Privy Council are binding in all legal proceedings other than proceedings before the JCPC itself. Amendment No 292EA would mean that they were not binding upon this House, and we do not accept that position.
>
> 'Devolution issues will seldom be decided by this House. In normal circumstances, under Schedule 6 of the Bill any devolution issue which arises in judicial proceedings in this House will be referred to the Judicial Committee unless this House considers it more appropriate that it should determine the issue itself. *We think it is appropriate that this House should not be able to depart from the earlier decisions made by the JCPC. We believe that the JCPC is ideally placed to resolve disputes about vires. It has a vast experience of dealing with constitutional issues from the Commonwealth, making the provision that the JCPC's decisions of the highest status will ensure that clear decisions with a clear status are produced and that devolution issues are treated consistently.* That is the advantage behind the line that we are advocating'[35] (emphasis added).

Consistently with this, the scheme of the devolution statutes, and in particular the Scotland Act, may best be understood as introducing, within the domestic sphere, a model for constitutionalism which has been tried and tested in the new Commonwealth states under the supervision of the Judicial Committee of the Privy Council over the last fifty years. And, as has been seen, this is a constitutional model based on *judicial primacy* rather than on the *legislature's sovereignty*. Thus the quasi-legislative power given to the court under the model constitutions for Commonwealth states to construe local statutes 'with such modifications as may be necessary to bring them into conformity with the Constitution' is now echoed in SA section 101(2) which instructs the UK courts to read a provision of devolved legislation which might otherwise appear to be ultra vires (because outwith devolved competence) 'as narrowly as is required for it to be within competence, if such a

---

32 *Vasquez v The Queen* [1994] 1 WLR 1304 and *Yearwood v The Queen* [2001] UKPC 31 on appeal from Belize and Grenada.
33 *R v Lambert* [2002] 2 AC 545 at para 85.
34 See SA s 103(1); NIA s 82(1); and GWA Sch 8, para 32(b).
35 HL Deb, vol 593, col 619 (8 Oct 1998).

reading is possible'.[36] And the UK courts have, under the devolution statutes, been given the express power to remove or limit the retrospective effect of their decisions that any devolved legislation passed by the devolved legislatures or made by the devolved executives is in fact ultra vires and hence a nullity.[37] Further, the UK courts are also authorised to suspend the effect of any such decision for any period and on any conditions to allow the defect identified in relation to the devolved legislation to be corrected.[38] In deciding whether to make any such order of suspension or limitation of retrospectivity the courts are to have regard, inter alia, 'to the extent to which persons who are not parties to the proceedings would otherwise be adversely affected'.[39] It is particularly noteworthy, from the point of view of constitutional spill-overs and paradigm shifts, that in framing these provisions of the devolution statutes account was taken by the UK drafters of the similar provision in Article 172(1) of the South African Constitution, a constitution which relies upon judicial primacy over the legislature in the protection of fundamental rights.[40]

In a classic instance of constitutional 'spill-over' of the specifics of the devolutionary settlement into the UK's general constitutional law, *In re Spectrum Plus Ltd*,[41] a seven-judge House of Lords bench relied upon the fact that the UK courts had been given the express power under the devolution statutes to remove or limit the retrospective effect of their decisions regarding the vires of devolved legislation to hold the courts now had a general inherent power at common law to vary the retrospectivity of their decisions. The earlier observations of Lord Goff of Chieveley to the effect that 'a system of prospective overruling, … although it has occasionally been adopted elsewhere (with, I understand, somewhat controversial results) has no place in our legal system',[42] were held no longer accurately to reflect the actual constitutional position post-devolution. It could no longer be said to be contrary to the proper role accorded to judges under the UK constitution that they should claim and exercise this power in appropriate cases, even where not specifically empowered to do so by the legislature.

NEW CONSTITUTIONALISM AND THE SCOTLAND ACT

SA section 29 provides that an Act of the Scottish Parliament will be 'not law' so far as any provision of it contravenes the various limits on the legislative competence of the Scottish Parliament which are laid down under the Scotland Act. Thus the Scottish Parliament may not pass an ASP which contains provisions which 'relate to' matters specified in SA Schedule 5 as being reserved to the Westminster Parliament (see SA s 29(2)(b) and (3)). What is meant by 'relate to' is further expanded

---

36 The parallel provision in Northern Ireland is NIA s 83(1) which requires the courts when considering potentially ultra vires legislation passed by the Northern Ireland Assembly or made by a Northern Ireland authority to construe it 'in a way which makes it within that competence or, as the case may be, does not make it invalid'.

37 See SA s 102(2)(a); NIA s 81(2)(a); and GWA s 110(2)(a). For an example of the court in Scotland considering the possible use of its SA s 102 powers see *Shelagh McCall v Scottish Ministers* [2005] CSOH 163 per Lord Carloway at para 18.

38 See SA s 102(2)(b); NIA s 81(2)(b); and GWA s 110(2)(b).

39 See SA s 102(3); NIA s 81(3); and GWA s 110(3).

40 See *Minister for Home Affairs v Fourrie* [2005] ZACC 7 for an example of the exercise of this power.

41 [2005] 2 AC 280.

42 *Kleinwort Benson Ltd v Lincoln County Council* [1999] 2 AC 349 at 379.

in SA Schedule 4, paragraph 3 as meaning, in effect, substantive modification or amendment rather than simple restatement of the reserved enactments in question. The Scottish Parliament is, however, empowered to pass what might be termed 'harmonisation measures' – namely provisions which make incidental and proportionate modifications of Scots private law (defined in SA s 126(4)) or Scots criminal law (defined in SA s 126(5)) as these apply to reserved matters, provided that the purpose of these amendments is to ensure consistency in the application of law as between reserved and non-reserved matters (see SA s 29(2)(b) and (4)). But certain statutes of the Westminster Parliament (specified in SA Sch 4, para 1) are given specific protection against any amendment by the Scottish Parliament (see SA s 29(2)(c)). Further, the Scottish Parliament has no power to remove the Lord Advocate from his position as head of the systems of criminal prosecution and of the investigation of deaths in Scotland (see SA s 29(2)(e)), and its laws are prohibited from having any 'extra-territorial effect' in the sense of purporting to form part of the law of a country or territory other than Scotland, or seeking to confer or remove functions exercisable outside Scotland (see SA s 29(2)(a)). The Scottish Parliament may also not enact provisions which are incompatible with Community law (see SA s 29(d)) and, in this at least, is in much the same position as the Westminster Parliament. By virtue of UK courts' acceptance and application of the (Community law) doctrine of the primacy of Community law over all and any provisions of national law[43] the courts will not enforce any national law, no matter its provenance, in so far as it is incompatible with Community law.[44] But it is the Scotland Act's prohibition on legislation which is incompatible with Convention rights being made by either the Scottish Parliament (s 29(2)(d)) or by the Scottish Executive (s 57(2)) which has had the most impact to date on the relationship between the courts and the devolved legislature.

Protection of fundamental rights under the Scotland Act

Although there has been a certain degree of co-ordination between the devolution statutes and the HRA in terms of fundamental rights protection, there are some significant differences among the four statutes in relation to how these rights are to be protected. The phrase 'Convention rights' has been given the same meaning in the four statutes;[45] and the same 'victim status' is required for individual *private* parties for them to be able to complain of violation of their Convention rights by public authorities and seek an appropriate remedy from the courts.[46] But unlike the HRA, the three devolution statutes *all* give a role to the various law officers (the Attorney-General, the Attorney-General for Northern Ireland, the Advocate General for Scotland and the Lord Advocate) to raise 'policing' proceedings concerning the Convention compatibility of acts of the devolved administrations and legislatures. These are matters which the law officers would *not* be able to raise under the HRA because they would not be 'victims'[47] and hence would have no

---

43 See Case 6/64 *Costa v ENEL* [1964] ECR 585 and Case 106/77 *Amministrazione delle Finanze dello Stato v Simmenthal (No 2)* [1978] ECR 629.
44 See *R v Secretary of State for the Home Department, ex parte Factortame Ltd (No 2)* [1991] 1 AC 603 at 658–659 per Lord Bridge of Harwich.
45 See HRA s 1(1); SA s 126; NIA s 98; and GWA s 107(5).
46 See HRA s 7(1) and (7); SA s 100(1); NIA s 71(1); and GWA s 107(2).
47 See SA s 100(2); NIA s 71(2); and GWA s 107(3).

title and no right to raise any complaints as regards breach of Convention rights under the HRA. On this matter the devolution statutes go further than the HRA in defining the range of persons who may take the devolved institutions to court on Convention rights issues, that is, individual victims plus the law officers.[48] But the Scotland Act departs from the schema for the protection of fundamental rights laid down both in the HRA, and in the other two devolution statutes, on one significant issue. It provides that, with the exception of the Lord Advocate when prosecuting any offence or in his capacity as head of the systems of criminal prosecution and investigation of deaths in Scotland, the Scottish Ministers *cannot* pray in aid the provisions of HRA section 6(2) (which allow for the possibility of the Westminster Parliament providing for a *lawful* breach of Convention rights by public authorities).[49] As Lord Hope has observed:

'The purpose of ... paragraphs [(a) and (b) of HRA section 6(2)] is to prevent section 6(1) being used to undermine another of the [Human Rights] Act's basic principles. This is that in the final analysis, if primary legislation cannot be interpreted in a way that is compatible with them, parliamentary sovereignty takes precedence over the Convention rights.'[50]

The Scottish Ministers by contrast – and unlike any other public body or devolved authority[51] – are bound absolutely as a matter of vires by the requirements of the Convention. No provision is made for the possibility of any 'lawful' breach of Convention rights by the Scottish devolved authorities relying upon, or seeking to enforce, Convention incompatible provisions of Westminster legislation. Thus, because the Scottish Ministers and Parliament have no HRA section 6(2) defence open to them, a declarator by a court (whether under HRA s 4 or at common law) that a provision of Westminster legislation is incompatible with the requirements of the Convention will have the effect of rendering ultra vires any act or omission of the Scottish Ministers or Parliament which relies upon the Westminster provision in question.

This decision not to afford the Scottish devolved institutions the possibility of an HRA section 6(2) defence is one with radical constitutional implications for the whole of the UK that have perhaps not yet been fully realised. For the decision means that, in relation to the assessment of the lawfulness of acts of the Scottish Ministers, Westminster statutes are placed in a position which is normatively subordinate to the requirements of the Convention. Because the Scottish Ministers have no HRA section 6(2) defence, Convention rights have the same effect against the Scottish Ministers as do directly effective provisions of Community law: both render their acts ultra vires. Thus any Convention incompatible provision of a Westminster statute effectively falls to be 'disapplied' as regards the Scottish

---

48 But see, now, the Equality Act 2006, s 30(3) which gives the new Commissioner for Equality and Human Rights statutory title to raise actions before the courts in Scotland, England and Wales in any proceedings relevant to its functions (including human rights issues in 'reserved matters') notwithstanding its lack of 'victim status'. Northern Ireland is already being served by the Northern Ireland Human Rights Commission which under NIA s 69(5)(b) is able to 'bring proceedings involving law and practice relating to the protection of human rights', a category which includes, but is greater than, Convention rights.

49 See SA s 57(2), (3).

50 *R (Hooper) v Secretary of State for Work and Pensions* [2005] 1 WLR 1681 at 1700 per Lord Hope of Craighead.

51 See NIA s 71(3)(a) and (4)(a) and GWA s 107(4)(a).

Ministers, just as any Community law incompatible provision of a Westminster statute is to be disapplied as regards acts or emanations of the UK state.[52] The Scotland Act provisions have thus unequivocally placed the ultimate responsibility for ensuring compliance with the Convention rights by the devolved authorities in Scotland with the judges, rather than with the democratically-elected Parliaments or the publicly-accountable Executive. Thus had there been no successful appeal to the Privy Council against the decision of the Scottish criminal appeal court in *Brown v Stott*[53] then the prosecuting authorities in Scotland would simply have been unable, by reason of Convention incompatibility, to lead and rely in court on evidence of an admission (regarding the identity of the driver of a car) which the accused was compelled to make to the police under the Road Traffic Act 1988, section 172(2)(a).[54] And, similarly, the result of the decision of the court of criminal appeal in *HM Advocate v McIntosh*[55] (which was also overturned on appeal to the Privy Council)[56] was that the Scottish authorities would not have been able to rely upon the provisions of the Proceeds of Crime (Scotland) Act 1995, section 3(2), relating to the recovery of the proceeds of drug trafficking.

Consistently with this approach mandating judicial primacy within the Scottish constitution, SA section 100(4)(a) allows Convention rights challenges to be brought in relation to 'making any legislation'. This is again to be contrasted with the intent and effect of the HRA which seeks to remove the possibility of Convention rights-based challenges to the legislature's making of (or failure to make) primary or secondary legislation: thus, HRA section 6(3) prohibits any Convention-based challenge to the exercise of parliamentary functions. Further, SA section 100(4)(b) allows *any* act or failure to act by a member of the Scottish Executive to be subject to Convention rights challenge. It is accordingly broader in scope than the HRA which, by section 6(6), limits the scope of failures reviewable on Convention grounds by excluding failures to '(a) introduce in, or lay before, Parliament a proposal for legislation; or (b) make any primary legislation or remedial order'. The intent of the SA, by contrast, is clearly to allow for, among other omissions, failures by the Scottish Ministers to make positive legislative provisions required by the Convention rights, to be reviewable on Convention grounds under that Act. Finally, SA section 100(3) permits the courts to make orders for payment of damages by way of just satisfaction in respect of Convention rights challenges brought under the Scotland Act by individuals otherwise qualifying as 'victims'.[57]

Judicial review of legislation under the Scotland Act

Notwithstanding the fact that the Scotland Act has granted the courts an explicit power of judicial review of legislation there has been, to date, only a handful of challenges under SA, whether to primary legislation emanating from the Scottish Parliament (ASPs) or to secondary legislation made by the Scottish Ministers (SSIs). In *Adams v Advocate General*, Lord Nimmo Smith held at first instance that

---

52 See *Factortame (No 2)* [1991] 1 AC 603.
53 2000 JC 328.
54 *Brown v Stott* 2001 SC (PC) 43.
55 2001 JC 78.
56 2001 SC (PC) 89.
57 See *R v HM Advocate* 2003 SC (PC) 21 per Lord Hope at para 39 and Lord Rodger of Earlsferry at para 17.

the SA provided a comprehensive framework for the operation of the legislative procedures of the Scottish Parliament itself as well as the Parliament's relationship to the courts such that traditional common law grounds of judicial review were excluded and any challenge to the validity of ASPs has to be made within the four corners of the constituting statute.[58] But no challenge to any ASP or SSI to date has been made on any ground other than alleged Convention incompatibility and no court challenge to the validity of devolved legislation has been brought by any of the UK's law officers otherwise empowered under the Act to raise such actions. Instead the challenges to date have all been brought by individuals claiming to be victims of a breach of their Convention rights. And in no case to date has the court yet exercised its powers to strike down as unconstitutional any such devolved legislation.

Medical treatability and detention in secure hospitals

In *A v Scottish Ministers* there was an unsuccessful challenge to the Convention compatibility of the emergency legislation which had been passed by the Scottish Parliament with retrospective effect and targeted and specific intent to close a perceived loophole in the law whereby persons who had been sentenced after trial to be detained indefinitely in a secure hospital were able to secure their release on the grounds that they were not now held to be suffering from any treatable mental illness.[59] Medical opinion had shifted since these individuals had been sentenced such that their condition – psychopathic disorder manifested by abnormally aggressive or seriously irresponsible conduct – was not now regarded as being capable of receiving treatment likely to alleviate or prevent a deterioration in their condition.[60] The Privy Council held that the Scottish Parliament's legislation was justified by considerations of continued safety of the general public as well as the staff and inmates of ordinary prisons, all of which could properly be used to justify the continued detention of restricted patients in hospital, whether or not their mental disorder was treatable.[61]

Hunting with dogs

There have been a number of challenges to the Convention compatibility of the Scottish Parliament's attempt to outlaw hunting of wild mammals with dogs. In *Whaley v Lord Watson of Invergowrie* a pre-emptive attempt was made by an individual, whose livelihood would be affected by the ban, to prevent the presentation before the Parliament of a Member's Bill which dealt with the issue. The basis for the interdict was the allegation that the promoter of the Bill had breached the Parliament's rules relating to members' interests in that the drafting of the Bill had effectively been paid for by an outside interest, an animal welfare lobbying group. The challenge was rejected by the Inner House on the somewhat

---

58 2003 SC 171 at 200E–I per Lord Nimmo Smith.

59 See *Ruddle v Secretary of State for Scotland*, 2 Aug 1999, Sheriff J Douglas Allan (unreported) ordering the release of a patient suffering from a psychopathic disorder where the treatability test was not satisfied.

60 *Reid v Secretary of State for Scotland* 1999 SC (HL) 17 at 39 per Lord Clyde.

61 *A v Scottish Ministers* 2002 SC (PC) 63. See too *Hutchison Reid v United Kingdom*, 20 Feb 2003 (ECtHR), [2003] RJD 3319.

narrow technical grounds that the individuals concerned had no title and interest to complain of any breaches of the Parliament's Standing Orders. The Parliament's susceptibility to judicial review was, however, robustly affirmed by the court in the following terms:

'[T]he [Scottish] Parliament [i]s a body which – however important its role – has been created by statute and derives its powers from statute. As such, it is a body which, like any other statutory body, must work within the scope of those powers. If it does not do so, then in an appropriate case the court may be asked to intervene and will require to do so, in a manner permitted by the legislation. In principle, therefore, the Parliament like any other body set up by law is subject to the law and to the courts which exist to uphold that law. . . .

'[I]n many democracies throughout the Commonwealth, for example, even where the parliaments have been modelled in some respects on Westminster, they owe their existence and powers to statute and are in various ways subject to the law and to the courts which uphold the law. The Scottish Parliament has simply joined that wider family of parliaments. Indeed, I find it almost paradoxical that counsel for a member of a body which exists to create laws and to impose them on others should contend that a legally enforceable framework is somehow less than appropriate for that body itself. . . .

'While *all* United Kingdom courts which may have occasion to deal with proceedings involving the Scottish Parliament can, of course, be expected to accord all due respect to the Parliament *as to any other litigant*, they must equally be aware that they are *not* dealing with a Parliament which is sovereign: on the contrary, it is subject to the laws and hence to the courts. For that reason, I see no basis upon which this court can properly adopt a "self-denying ordinance"[62] which would consist in exercising some kind of discretion to refuse to enforce the law against the Parliament or its members. To do so would be to fail to uphold the rights of other parties under the law.'[63]

The Bill was duly presented to the Parliament and passed by it as the Protection of Wild Mammals (Scotland) Act 2002. The Act was then subject to a post-enactment Convention compatibility challenge by those whose livelihoods would be affected by the hunting ban. This challenge was unsuccessful both in the Outer House[64] and the Inner House.[65] The petitioners chose, however, not to exercise their right of appeal to the House of Lords.

Fixed fees legal aid in summary prosecutions

In *Buchanan v McLean*[66] a collateral challenge was brought as to the compatibility with the Convention right to a fair trial of the new criminal legal aid regulations introduced in Scotland with effect from 1 April 1999 by the Criminal Legal Aid (Fixed Payments) (Scotland) Regulations 1999.[67] It was argued on behalf of the accused that these new criminal legal aid regulations breached the Convention principle of equality of arms, by substituting a fixed fee scale, the adequacy of

62 See the opinion of Lord Woolf MR in *R v Parliamentary Commissioner for Standards, ex parte Al Fayed* [1998] 1 WLR 669 at 670.
63 2000 SC 340 (IH) at 348H, 349D–E, 350B–C.
64 See *Adams v Advocate General* 2003 SC 171.
65 See *Adams v Scottish Ministers* 2004 SC 665 and *Friend v Lord Advocate* 2006 SC 121.
66 2002 SC (PC) 1.
67 SI 1999/491.

which cannot be challenged in any particular case, for the previous 'time and line' basis for reimbursing solicitors in respect of their investigation, preparation and conduct of the defence in summary criminal trials. It was submitted that any decision of the prosecuting authorities (whose funds are not similarly limited in any particular case) to initiate proceedings where the defence funds are so arbitrarily limited would potentially constitute action by the Lord Advocate incompatible with the accused's Convention rights under Article 6(3)(b) 'to have adequate time and facilities for the preparation of his defence', under Article 6(3)(c) 'to defend himself in person or through legal assistance of his own choosing or, if he has not sufficient means to pay for legal assistance, to be given it free when the interests of justice so require', and under Article 6(3)(d) 'to examine or have examined witnesses against him and to obtain the attendance and examination of witnesses on his behalf under the same conditions as witnesses against him'. The Lord Advocate, and those acting under his authority, are statutorily bound to respect all of these rights when bringing prosecutions. In the event, the Privy Council dismissed the challenge in the particular case on the basis that it was clear that a solicitor had been willing to take up and argue the case, notwithstanding the limits placed on his remuneration. The Board noted, however, that if it could be shown that no legal representation was available to an individual because of the legal aid limits, this might constitute a breach of his Convention rights. Lord Clyde exhorted the Scottish Ministers in his judgment to amend the regulations by introducing an element of flexibility whereby fixed fees could be increased at the discretion of the Legal Aid Board in appropriate circumstances. This hint was duly taken up by the Scottish Ministers.[68]

Individual punishment and public protection in mandatory life sentences

A sentence of life imprisonment is the penalty which judges have been required by law to impose on all adults found guilty of murder since the abolition of the death penalty in the UK in 1965. In practice, however, except in the tiny minority of cases, life does not mean life. The mandatory life sentence has, instead, generally been treated as a *maximum* possible period of detention. Once they have been deemed to have served a sufficient period of imprisonment by way of punishment for their crime, convicted murderers become eligible for parole allowing them to be released on licence from prison so long as they are deemed no longer to represent a danger to the public. The question then arises how, why and by whom is the period necessary to serve as punishment for the crime to be determined. Over time, the ECtHR's jurisprudence has established that this decision is a matter for judges alone and cannot be left by contracting states for determination by ministers, who may be subject to populist and political pressures in particular cases in making these sentencing decisions. The Convention Rights (Compliance) (Scotland) Act 2001 was passed by the Scottish Parliament, inter alia, to introduce a regime which would respect the Convention rights of persons convicted of murder in Scotland by removing all ministerial discretion on the matter of the date of release from prison of those serving a mandatory life sentence. The problem that arose in *Flynn and others v HM Advocate*[69] was that the introduction of this new system for those

---

68 Criminal Legal Aid (Fixed Payments) (Scotland) Amendment Regulations 2002 (SSI 2002/247).
69 2004 SC (PC) 1.

already serving mandatory life sentences meant that the High Court of Justiciary was required to determine for the first time the length of time to be served by way of punishment for the crime for which they had been convicted. In a number of cases this resulted in life prisoners becoming ineligible for consideration for parole where they had previously been eligible because the court determined that a longer term should be served by way of punishment than the minister had assumed under the previous system, resulting in situations which were perceived by the affected prisoners as retrospective lengthening of their terms of imprisonment. In rejecting a challenge to the Convention compatibility of the 2001 Act the Privy Council held that the legislation had in fact been misunderstood by the High Court and that a properly Convention compatible reading should have taken into account and given appropriate weight to the parole board hearing dates previously notified to the individuals to ensure that new procedures did not operate in any significant way to the disadvantage of the prisoners concerned.

Retrospective application of new criminal legal aid fees regime

In *McCall v Scottish Ministers*[70] the petitioner sought judicial review of the manner of introduction of the Criminal Legal Aid (Scotland) (Fees) Amendment Regulations 2005[71] which set the rates for counsel's fees in the criminal courts. The Scottish Legal Aid Board purported to apply the new regulations to all fees where the proceedings were concluded on or after 4 April 2005 which meant that, where a case concluded after that date, *all* the work done by counsel prior to the commencement date would be paid on the basis of the new Schedule albeit that it came into force after that work had been done. In some cases, the work in question would have been completed months before the Schedule came into force, resulting in the counsel affected receiving considerably less under the new Schedule than they would have done under the old scheme, even though they had undertaken the work on the basis of the applicability of that earlier scheme. Lord Carloway in the Outer House held that the fees for work carried out prior to the coming into force of the new Schedule constituted 'possessions' for the purposes of Article 1, Protocol 1 – the Convention right to respect for property – and that the manner of the retrospective implementation of the new Schedule could not be justified as a proportionate or fair interference with the petitioner's acquired property rights in accrued fees due for work already done. In the light of this decision the Scottish Ministers amended the legislation in question before any order was made invalidating it.[72]

PRECEDENTS FOR JUDICIAL PRIMACY IN UNITED KINGDOM CONSTITUTION

The fact that the Scotland Act has followed the constitutional model which provides for judicial rather than legislative primacy should not be regarded as utterly radical and alien to our domestic constitutional traditions for a number of reasons.

---

70 2006 SC 266.
71 SSI 2005/113.
72 Criminal Legal Aid (Scotland) (Fees) Amendment (No 3) Regulations 2005 (SSI 2005/656).

Constitutional statutes in the UK

There is a growing judicial acceptance that certain Acts of Parliament are to be regarded as 'constitutional statutes', which status carries with it certain consequences for the interpretation and application of their terms.[73] Thus in a House of Lords decision on the proper interpretation of the NIA – and, in particular, on the question whether or not candidates had been validly elected by the Northern Ireland Assembly to the offices of First Minister and Deputy First Minister – Lord Bingham observed that the Act was 'in effect a constitution' and as such deserving of a generous and purposive interpretation 'bearing in mind the values which the constitutional provisions are intended to embody'. And Lord Hoffmann stated that 'the principles laid down by the Belfast Agreement ... form part of the admissible background for the construction of the Act just as much as the Revolution, the Convention and the Federalist Papers are the background to construing the Constitution of the United States'.[74] Similarly, in *R v HM Advocate* Lord Rodger of Earlsferry picked up the language of constitutionalism, noting that:

> 'the Scotland Act is a major constitutional measure which altered the government of the United Kingdom' and that 'in enacting a constitutional settlement of immense social and political significance for the whole of the United Kingdom, [the Westminster] Parliament has itself balanced the competing interests of the government of the United Kingdom, of the Scottish Executive, of society and of the individuals affected'.[75]

Recovery of the pre-1707 Scottish constitutional tradition

Although the point is not without difficulty, there has long been academic and judicial discussion which states that the claim that a Parliament has untrammelled legislative sovereignty to do as it wills (even to act contrary to fundamental rights) is not a constitutional provision which has ever formed part of Scots law. Thus in *MacCormick v Lord Advocate* Lord President Cooper observed that '[t]he principle of the unlimited sovereignty of Parliament is a distinctively English principle which has no counterpart in Scottish constitutional law' and that '[t]he Lord Advocate conceded this point by admitting that the Parliament of Great Britain "could not" repeal or alter ... "fundamental and essential" conditions' of the Treaty of Union.[76]

European Community law

The effect of the already noted acceptance in UK domestic law of the principle of primacy of Community law over national law[77] has been such that it is no longer legally, politically or constitutionally proper to talk of unlimited parliamentary sovereignty at Westminster. The courts are given a role under Community law

---

73 *Thoburn v Sunderland Council* [2003] QB 151 at 186–187 per Laws LJ.
74 *Robinson v Secretary of State for Northern Ireland* [2002] UKHL 32 at paras 11 and 33. See, to like effect, *In re Northern Ireland Human Rights Commission* [2002] UKHL 25 per Lord Slynn of Hadley at para 12.
75 *R v HM Advocate* 2003 SC (PC) 21 per Lord Rodger of Earlsferry at paras 16 and 50.
76 1953 SC 396 at 407–408. See further Chapter 2 in this volume.
77 See *R v Secretary of State for the Home Department, ex parte Factortame Ltd (No 2)* [1991] 1 AC 603.

to correct the 'mistakes' of the national legislature by the principle of 'conforming interpretation'[78] whereby the courts might 'write in' words into statutory provisions which have been omitted by the legislature in order to ensure conformity with the requirements of Community law.[79] The fact that UK courts can, by virtue of Community law, now effectively treat provisions of an Act of Parliament as 'invalid' and disapply them in the particular case by granting (interim and final) injunction/interdict against their application[80] and can award (*Francovich*)[81] damages to individuals affected by the application of offending provisions of the national statute[82] shows that the constitutional position following the UK's entry into the EU is perhaps somewhat more complex than a simple Diceyan analysis which might have applied heretofore. A shift begins to take place whereby the central constitutional model is increasingly seen as one of judicial primacy rather than parliamentary supremacy and it is this new model which comes to be regarded as the explanatory norm.

Influence of the Human Rights Act

The new constitutional model for the relationship between courts, legislature and executive provided for in European Community law has been used by the House of Lords to sanction an extremely expansive approach to the duty of Convention compatible interpretation of legislation imposed by HRA section 3. The strength of this interpretative duty – and the dominant influence of the Community law model in the judges' understanding of it – is seen in the House of Lords' decision *Ghaidan v Godin-Mendoza*[83] where their Lordships held that HRA section 3 gave the court powers that were at least as strong as their duty and powers to rewrite national legislation to comply with the requirements of Community law. Thus, by a 4:1 decision (Lord Millett dissenting), the House of Lords found that a surviving member of a same-sex couple who was residing in a privately-rented house immediately before the death of his partner, the original tenant, was to be regarded for the purposes of the Rent Act 1977, Schedule 1, paragraphs 2 and 3 as 'the surviving spouse of the original tenant', so as to be entitled to become the statutory tenant of the property in the same way that a person who was living with the original tenant 'as his or her wife or husband' would have been treated. This decision differs little in its substantive effect from the decision of the South African Constitutional Court in *Minister for Home Affairs v Fourie*[84] which held that the statutory and common law exclusions of same-sex couples from the possibility of marrying was unconstitutional, notwithstanding that the South African constitution is one explicitly based on the model of judicial primacy.

---

78 See Case C-106/89 *Marleasing SA v La Comercial Internacional de Alimentación SA* [1990] ECR I-4135 at 4159.

79 See, eg, *Pickstone v Freemans plc* [1989] AC 66 and *Litster v Forth Dry Dock & Engineering Co Ltd* [1990] 1 AC 546, recently discussed in *Customs & Excise v IDT Card Services Ireland Ltd* [2006] EWCA Civ 29.

80 *Factortame (No 2)* [1991] 1 AC 603.

81 See Joined Cases C-6, 9/90 *Francovich and Bonifaci v Italy* [1991] ECR I-5357; and Joined Cases C-46/93 and C-48/93 *Brasserie du Pecheur SA v Federal Republic of Germany*; *R v Secretary of State for Transport, ex parte Factortame Ltd (No 4)* [1996] ECR I-1029, para 58.

82 *R v Secretary of State for the Home Department, ex parte Factortame Ltd (No 5)* [2000] 1 AC 524.

83 [2004] 2 AC 557. See in particular Lord Steyn at 574–576, and Lord Rodger of Earlsferry at 599–602.

84 [2005] ZACC 7.

The only limitation on the HRA section 3 interpretative obligation, according to the House of Lords decision in *Ghaidan*, is that in reading words into the legislation or in deleting offending words, the courts have to be satisfied that such emendation could not be said to go 'against the grain' by overriding some cardinal feature of the legislation in question, or otherwise raise generally policy issues that a court cannot properly seek to resolve by a process of judicial rewriting.[85] Thus, although the HRA is said to embody a constitutional model which remains faithful to the idea of parliamentary sovereignty, this is perhaps difficult to reconcile with the breadth of discretion which HRA section 3 is said to give to the courts to construe unambiguous legislation in a Convention compatible manner. HRA section 3 allows, indeed requires, the court to give an interpretation to a legislative provision which may be entirely contrary to the expressed will of Parliament at the time of passing the provision in question, if this is necessary to ensure Convention compatibility. The very strength of this 'interpretative' obligation might indicate that there is in fact little distinction between the two constitutional models, of legislative as opposed to judicial primacy, when it comes to the protection of fundamental rights.

Judges as guardians *against* Westminster Parliament of constitutional rights

More generally, the classic Diceyan analysis of an untrammelled or wholly unlimited Westminster parliamentary sovereignty has come under increasingly close scrutiny by the judges, even in non-Community law and non-Convention rights cases.[86] Lord Hoffmann noted in one pre-HRA case:

> 'In the absence of express language or necessary implication to the contrary, the courts ... presume that even the most general words were intended to be subject to the basic rights of the individual. In this way the courts of the United Kingdom, though acknowledging the sovereignty of Parliament, apply principles of constitutionality little different from those which exist in countries where the power of the legislature is expressly limited by a constitutional document.'[87]

And in *A v Secretary of State for the Home Department* – the challenge to the regime of the special detention, without charge or prospects of a trial, of foreign nationals said by the Executive to be suspected of having connections with terrorism – Lord Bingham, giving the leading speech (which was expressly concurred in by six of his brethren on the bench), unequivocally proclaimed the legitimacy of the judges' role in reviewing the lawfulness of the Executive's approach to this issue (albeit that the Executive's stance had been expressly sanctioned by Parliament) noting that 'the function of independent judges charged to interpret and apply the law is universally recognised as a cardinal feature of the modern democratic state, a cornerstone of the rule of law itself'.[88]

In *Jackson v Attorney-General*, the matter before the court looked very like (and in reality was) a direct challenge to the validity of an Act of Parliament, the

---

85 See *R v Holding* [2006] 1 WLR 1040 (CA) at 1050–1051, paras 47–48.

86 See *Watkins v Home Office* [2006] 2 WLR 807 at 827–828, para 61 per Lord Rodger of Earlsferry.

87 *R v Secretary of State for the Home Department, ex parte Simms* [2000] 2 AC 115 at 131 per Lord Hoffmann.

88 [2006] 2 AC 68 per Lord Bingham at para 42.

Hunting Act 2004, which made the hunting of wild animals with dogs unlawful. But rather than simply throw the matter out of court as clearly and obviously an 'unconstitutional' attempt to impugn the sovereignty of the Westminster Parliament, the Appellate Committee convened itself as a court of nine judges and recharacterised the issue as a justiciable one: namely what was the true interpretation of the Parliament Act 1911? Lord Steyn took the opportunity to state that the classic Diceyan account of the absolute sovereignty of Parliament was 'out of place in the modern United Kingdom'. And while he accepted that 'the supremacy of Parliament is still the general principle of our constitution' he did not regard it as 'unthinkable' that circumstances might arise – he cited as examples an attempt to abolish judicial review or the ordinary role of the courts – as a result of which the judges might expressly modify this principle to hold that 'even a sovereign Parliament acting at the behest of a complaisant House of Commons might not lawfully interfere with such constitutional fundamentals'.[89]

Similarly, in *In re Spectrum Plus Ltd (in liquidation)*, Lord Hope gave, in his summary of the current UK constitutional position, pole position to the judicial power to uphold, against all comers, the rule of law and the protection of fundamental rights, when he noted that the House of Lords as a judicial body

> 'must respect any limits on its jurisdiction that have may been imposed by Parliament, *so long as* these are compatible with our treaty obligations under Community law and with the rights that are defined by section 1(1) HRA as the "Convention rights". A statutory limitation which was found to be incompatible would have to be read down under the doctrine of direct effect or under section 3(1) of the 1998 Act to remove the incompatibility'.[90]

JUDICIAL DEFERENCE TO THE LEGISLATURE

The direct judicial review of primary and secondary devolved legislation in such constitutional challenges raises interesting questions regarding the proper relationship of the courts to the democratically-elected legislature. Since the limits of the new devolved legislative bodies and administrations are set out in statute, the task of ensuring that the devolved institutions stay within the limits of the powers granted to them is one for the courts. As already noted the devolution statutes have created democratic institutions whose acts are, however, subject to control by the judiciary.

Lord Rodger's robust remarks in *Whaley v Lord Watson*, equating the Scottish Parliament with any other statutory institution to be treated by the courts as 'any other litigant', must now be seen in context. They may perhaps be read now as no more than an assertion that the internal workings and privileges of the Scottish Parliament are not to be regarded as immune from judicial scrutiny. However, once that Parliament has duly acted in a legislative capacity, the court recognises the legitimacy that inheres to the substance of the resulting statute, by virtue of its being produced by a democratically-mandated assembly. This does not mean that the terms of the statute are immune from substantive judicial review, rather that the doctrine of proportionality should be applied in a careful and nuanced

---

89 *Jackson* [2006] 1 AC 262, para 102.
90 *In re Spectrum Plus Ltd* [2005] 2 AC 280, para 69.

way, with the court not rushing in to substitute its assessment of policy matters for that of the legislature. This certainly seems to have been the approach taken by both the Inner House of the Court of Session and the Privy Council in *A v Scottish Ministers* in deciding to uphold the validity of the Scottish Parliament's legislation. A deferential approach to the will of the Westminster Parliament as expressed in legislation also seems to characterise the few Convention rights-based challenges to the interpretation and application of Westminster legislation which have been brought to date before the Privy Council exercising its devolution jurisdiction.[91]

Clearly, a balance has to be struck. The courts have to recognise the importance of the democratic mandate given to both the Westminster and the Edinburgh Parliaments. They have to recognise too that the rights conferred under the Convention have to be interpreted and applied in their social context: they are fundamental rights but not, in all circumstances, absolute ones in the sense of overruling all considerations of the public interest. As Lord Hope noted in *Kebilene*:

> 'Difficult choices may have to be made by the executive or the legislature between the rights of the individual and the needs of society. In some circumstances it will be appropriate for the courts to recognise that there is an area of judgment within which the judiciary will defer, on democratic grounds, to the considered opinion of the elected body or person whose act or decision is said to be incompatible with the Convention.'[92]

Still, while Parliaments articulate the public interest, in the final analysis it is the courts which must ensure due respect for individuals' (and minorities') rights. It is, therefore, vital for the proper functioning of the constitution that the public have faith in the impartiality of their judiciary. But the issues concerning what standard of review the courts ought to adopt would be rather different in the context of non-fundamental rights challenges. Where the conflict is between two sets of democratically-elected institutions, the notion of judicial deference may be of itself insufficient; the court might be deferring to different institutions each with their own democratic legitimacy and mandate. In these circumstances, the court might be required to make a more substantive assessment of the relative constitutional importance of the Scottish and Westminster Parliaments. In this regard it should be borne in mind that the Scotland Act does not dissolve the 1707 Union: SA section 37 specifically provides that the English Union with Scotland Act 1706 and the Scottish Union with England Act 1707 continue to have effect, subject to the new Act. And SA section 1(1), which states that 'there shall be a Scottish Parliament', does not restore the old Estates of Scotland but rather establishes the new Scottish Parliament as a subordinate legislative body ultimately remaining (like parish councils in England) subject to the control of the Parliament of the United Kingdom at Westminster. The power of the Westminster Parliament to make laws for Scotland is unaffected by the Scotland Act (see s 28(7)). It is clear, however, that the acquisition of broad powers of legislative judicial review creates a challenging new role for the judges. It raises large questions which have yet to be faced: for example as to the interrelationship between the principle of judicial respect for the democratic will of the Scottish people (as expressed by the Scottish Parliament)

---

91 *Brown v Stott* 2001 SC (PC) 43 and *McIntosh, Petitioner* 2001 SC (PC) 89.
92 [2000] 2 AC 326 at 381.

and the enforcement by the judges of the limits laid down on that legislature in accordance with the democratic will of the peoples of the UK (as expressed by the Westminster Parliament and government in the provisions of the Scotland Act).

CONCLUSION

Under the Diceyan theory of absolute parliamentary sovereignty, there was no possibility of judicial review of legislation duly passed or confirmed by the Westminster Parliament. As Ungoed-Thomas J in *Cheney v Conn* observed, in dismissing a claim by a taxpayer that taxes were being levied from him unlawfully because a substantial part of the tax so raised was allocated to the construction of nuclear weapons and so contravened the Geneva Conventions Act 1957:

> 'What the statute itself [*in casu*, the Finance Act 1965] enacts cannot be unlawful, because what the statute says and provides is itself the law, and the highest form of law that is known in this country. It is the law which prevails over every other form of law, and it is not for the court to say that a parliamentary enactment, the highest law of this country, is illegal.'[93]

It is apparent from the more recent cases cited above that while a certain lip-service continues to be paid to the older constitutional paradigm of parliamentary sovereignty, the reality is that the judges no longer consider it to be an absolute, or perhaps even the primary, principle of the UK constitution. Instead it is clear that the judges now consider that there are justiciable limitations on the freedom of the Westminster Parliament to legislate and that it is the proper constitutional role of the judges to ensure that those limitations are observed by the legislature and enforced by the courts. Under the older paradigm the judges could aspire to nothing more than ascertaining the intention of Parliament in framing laws in particular terms and, having established that intention, to interpret and apply the laws consonantly with it. But the new role which the judges seem to be fashioning for themselves is that of guardians of the values underpinning the constitution and, in particular, the fundamental rights of the individual against excesses of the state and the tyranny of the majority.

Judges in the UK do in fact now exercise powers of direct judicial review of legislation and hold that the UK Parliament has acted unlawfully in cases when provisions of national legislation are found to contravene provisions of Community law intended to confer rights upon individuals. And a power of direct judicial review of legislation is also conferred under the Scotland Act which requires judges to strike down ASPs which exceed the limits of the power of that legislature as set down in its constituting statute, the Scotland Act, and to disapply – at least vis-à-vis the Scottish devolved institutions – any Convention-incompatible provisions of primary Westminster legislation. Finally a power of indirect judicial review of Westminster legislation is also now operated by the judges, both by virtue of the strong interpretative obligation in favour of Convention compatibility imposed by HRA section 3, as well as by the requirements of Community law compatible interpretation exemplified in the judgment of the European Court of Justice in *Marleasing*.[94]

---

93 [1968] 1 WLR 242 at 247.
94 [1990] ECR I-4135 at 4159.

Notwithstanding the terms of the English Bill of Rights of 1688 and the Scottish Claim of Right of 1689 (which have been understood as asserting parliamentary sovereignty as a constitutional fundamental) it would appear that the judges, under their new guise as the ultimate guardians of the constitution, are becoming increasingly emboldened to claim the general right to exercise, in appropriate circumstances, a power of suspending of laws, or the execution of laws passed by Parliament, where those laws threaten to breach basic constitutional norms, and in particular fundamental rights. A constitutional historian might indeed seek to argue that all this shows is that the seventeenth-century civil war which raged in these islands is not yet over.[95] Instead a third force, not Parliamentarian nor Royalist but judicial, is now gaining the upper hand to effect what may properly be called a constitutional revolution since it may be thought simply to seek to restore the primacy of the (judge-made) common law over the presumption of statute law and so vindicate the claims of Coke CJ in 1610 when he stated that the judges could lawfully:

> 'controul acts of Parliament, and sometimes adjudge them to be utterly void: for when an Act of Parliament is against common right and reason, or repugnant, or impossible to be performed, the common law will controul it and adjudge such Act to be void'.[96]

If that is indeed once again going to become a basic principle of the UK constitution, the new task for our constitutionalists and our judges is to develop principles of legitimacy which can justify the extent of any priority of the individual's fundamental rights over the claims of the legislature and the executive to protect the general public interest in a democracy as well as principles for determining the legitimate relationships among the Scottish, UK and European legislatures and executives governing the land. Legal practice will require a substantive moral and political theory. There is much work to be done. The revolution is not yet completed: *la lotta continua*.

---

95 See, eg, *M v Home Office* [1994] 1 AC 377 at 395 per Lord Templeman.
96 *Dr Bonham's case* (1610) 77 Eng Rep 646 at 652.

Chapter 11

Border Disputes: the Scope and Purposes of Judicial Review

Aileen McHarg

INTRODUCTION

Commenting on *Anisminic Ltd v Foreign Compensation Commission*,[1] Sir William Wade famously described judicial review as a 'constitutional fundamental'.[2] Yet it is not entirely identical north and south of the border. Whilst the Court of Session has repeatedly confirmed that the grounds of review are essentially the same,[3] the threshold issues which determine the practical effects of judicial review – standing,[4] remedies, procedure and the scope of review – differ substantially. Regarding scope (the subject of this chapter) the Inner House in *West v Secretary of State for Scotland*[5] explicitly declined to follow the English approach, citing both historical and principled justifications.

Given the differences, particularly procedural, between the Scottish and English legal systems, some disparities in relation to these threshold issues are only to be expected. However, although questions of scope and procedure or remedies cannot be entirely divorced, the former raises much more fundamental issues concerning the appropriate reach of judicial review principles. Moreover, as with any legal concept, attitudes towards such boundary questions are intimately connected with views about the purpose(s) that the relevant law is considered to serve. Thus, in England, the question of how to justify the extension of judicial review to non-statutory powers exercised by public and also powerful private bodies was the trigger for an intense debate about its constitutional foundations.[6] Accordingly, if the scope of review rests upon a different basis in Scotland compared to England, the possibility arises that it also performs different constitutional functions in the two jurisdictions. Prima facie, this would require both explanation and justification.

There are, nevertheless, broad similarities in the scope of review in Scotland and England. Although in both jurisdictions the majority of cases involve public bodies, in neither does the scope of review depend upon a simple distinction between public and private *institutions* (see figure 1). Rather, both treat some decisions by public bodies as falling outwith the scope of review – typically those

---

1 [1969] 2 AC 147.
2 See now H W R Wade and C F Forsyth, *Administrative Law* (9th edn, 2004), pp 720–721. See also The Rt Hon Lord Clyde and D J Edwards, *Judicial Review* (2000), para 8.03.
3 See, eg, *West v Secretary of State for Scotland* 1992 SC 385. There is, however, an important difference regarding the extent of review for error of law: see further below.
4 See Chapter 12.
5 1992 SC 385.
6 D Oliver, 'Is the ultra vires rule the basis of judicial review' [1987] PL 543; and see generally C F Forsyth (ed), *Judicial Review and the Constitution* (2000).

involving employment, contractual or commercial functions, which, prima facie, are governed by ordinary, private law rules. Conversely, both sometimes permit judicial review of private bodies – typically ones involved in delivering public services or performing regulatory or disciplinary functions. This general approach is attributable to the absence of any systematic public/private distinction in either Scots or English law, resulting in a preference for subjecting governmental actors, where possible, to the same legal rules and remedies as private actors,[7] as well as in a haphazard institutional distribution of government functions, with distinctions being further blurred in recent decades by privatisation and contractualisation policies.

Figure 1

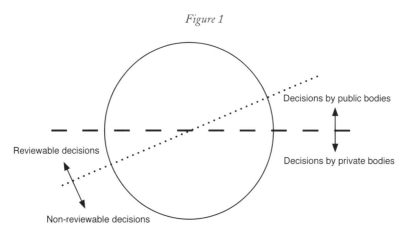

Where Scots and English law differ is in the tests they employ for determining the boundaries of review. In England, this depends upon the presence of a sufficient 'public element', since judicial review is regarded as a public law remedy.[8] In Scotland, by contrast, the public/private distinction has been rejected and the touchstone of reviewability is instead whether the decision-maker is exercising a jurisdiction, or the presence of a 'tripartite relationship'.[9] At the margins, consequently, the Scots and English courts may reach different conclusions about the reviewability of very similar decisions. However, neither test has proved straightforward to apply, and both have provoked theoretical controversy.

   This chapter thus has two, related, aims. One is to examine the nature of the tests for reviewability adopted in Scotland and England, the reasons for divergence, and the extent to which they differ in practice: in particular, whether the Scottish approach truly avoids a public/private distinction. Secondly, it considers the relationship between the scope and purposes of judicial review, and, in light of theoretical debates about the public/private distinction and the constitutional foundations of review, analyses why both the Scottish and English tests have proved problematic, and whether continued divergence can be justified.

---

7 Classically stated by A V Dicey, *The Law of the Constitution* (10th edn, 1959), who regarded it as
   a necessary feature of the rule of law.
8 *O'Reilly v Mackman* [1983] 2 AC 237; *R v Panel on Takeovers and Mergers, ex parte Datafin plc*
   [1987] QB 815.
9 *West v Secretary of State for Scotland* 1992 SC 385.

APPLICATION FOR JUDICIAL REVIEW AND SCOPE OF SUPERVISORY JURISDICTION IN SCOTS LAW: CONFUSION AND CLARIFICATION

Contemporary debates in both Scotland and England about the scope of judicial review stem from the introduction in each jurisdiction of a special procedure by which to invoke the supervisory jurisdiction of the Court of Session and the High Court respectively. Previously, there had been no distinction in Scotland in the procedure or remedies used for judicial review compared with ordinary actions, whereas in England, although special, so-called 'prerogative', orders did exist, judicial review could also be sought via the ordinary remedies of declaration or injunction. In neither country, consequently, had the boundaries of review been precisely defined. The introduction of specific review procedures, however, made it necessary to determine when those procedures *had* to be used, and also when they *could* be used.

The starting-point for this development was a joint recommendation from the Scottish and English Law Commissions in 1969 that there should be a broad inquiry into administrative law, conducted on a UK-wide basis. This was, however, rejected, each Commission being asked instead to review existing remedies with a view to evolving simpler and more effective procedures. In 1971, the Scottish Law Commission reported that, although Scots law did not suffer the same procedural difficulties as English administrative law,[10] there might nevertheless be advantages in introducing a flexible petition for review of official acts and omissions.[11] No further action was taken but, meanwhile, the English Law Commission recommended the creation of a single procedure for obtaining all the available remedies in public law cases.[12] The Application for Judicial Review (AJR) was implemented in 1977 as Order 53 of the Rules of the Supreme Court,[13] later confirmed by section 31 of the Supreme Court Act 1981 and now contained in Part 54 of the Civil Procedure Rules (renamed the Claim for Judicial Review (CJR)).[14]

The case for a Scottish AJR was revived in 1983, in *Brown v Hamilton District Council*,[15] a homelessness case which had taken four years to resolve. Giving judgment in the House of Lords, Lord Fraser said that: 'it is for consideration whether there might not be advantages in developing special procedure in Scotland for dealing with questions in the public law area'.[16] In response, the Lord President therefore set up a working party chaired by Lord Dunpark:

'to devise ... a simple form of procedure, capable of being operated with reasonable expedition, for bringing before the court ... complaints by aggrieved persons (1) against acts or decisions of inferior courts, tribunals, public bodies, authorities or officers ... alleging that the acts or decisions are ultra vires'.[17]

---

10 See *Report on Remedies in Administrative Law* (Law Com No 73, Cmnd 6407, 1976).
11 *Remedies in Administrative Law* (Scot Law Com No 14, 1971), paras 4.3, 13.5.
12 Above n 10.
13 Rules of the Supreme Court (Amendment No 3) 1977 (SI 1977/1955).
14 Civil Procedure (Amendment No 4) Rules 2000 (SI 2000/2092).
15 1983 SC (HL) 1.
16 At 50. See also *Stevenson v Midlothian District Council (No 2)* 1983 SC (HL) 50 at 60.
17 *Report to Rt Hon Lord Emslie, Lord President of the Court of Session by the Working Party on Procedure for Judicial Review of Administrative Action* (1984), para 1.

Following the working party's recommendations, the AJR was introduced in 1985 by Rule of Court 260B,[18] now contained in Chapter 58 of the Consolidated Rules of Court.[19]

This background clearly shows that both sets of procedural reforms had common objectives and that, in Scotland as well as England, the assumption was that the AJR would apply to official or public acts and decisions. However, rule 260B was not so limited, stating merely that: '[a]n application to the supervisory jurisdiction of the court which immediately before the coming into operation of this rule would have been made by way of summons or petition, shall be made by way of an application for judicial review'. Unlike the English prerogative orders, judicial review in Scotland had never been explicitly confined to public powers or duties. Moreover, although the two procedures had certain common features – an emphasis on speed and flexibility, discretionary remedies and the use of nominated judges – there were also some important differences. Whereas the English Law Commission sought to balance advantages to applicants – removal of technical restrictions on the availability of the various remedies – with protections for public bodies against excessive or unmeritorious challenges – a three-month time-limit and the requirement to seek leave (permission) from the court to proceed – the Dunpark working party made no such recommendations. Accordingly, there was confusion about whether the scope of the Scottish procedure should be the same as in England or determined on some other basis.

Several early cases did follow the English approach,[20] the most important being *Tehrani v Argyll and Clyde Health Board*,[21] in which the Inner House (Second Division) held that a petition for review of the summary dismissal of a consultant surgeon was incompetent because it did not involve a sufficient element of public law. Moreover, Lord Wylie stated that he saw no good reason for differences between Scots and English law to develop in this field and that it would be regrettable if they did.[22] The appropriateness of this approach was, however, doubted in other cases,[23] and in an influential article by Lord Clyde.[24] The supervisory jurisdiction in Scots law was, he argued, a broadly-based remedy, historically based in equity. The different role of the court in judicial review compared with ordinary actions was not related to the public or private nature of the rights or duties under consideration, nor of the parties involved but instead, because it was a supervisory rather than an original jurisdiction, concerned merely with the legality and not the merits of decisions. Thus it was neither historically accurate nor desirable in principle to restrain the free exercise of an equitable jurisdiction by importing a public/private distinction. He repeated this view in *Watt v Strathclyde Regional Council*,[25] in which the First Division held that the council's refusal to amend teachers' contracts

18 Act of Sederunt (Rules of Court Amendment No 2) (Judicial Review) 1985 (SI 1985/500).
19 Act of Sederunt (Rules of the Court of Session) 1994 (SI 1994/1443).
20 *Connor v Strathclyde Regional Council* 1986 SLT 530; *Safeway Food Stores Ltd v Scottish Provident Institution* 1989 SLT 131; *Bank of Scotland v IMRO* 1989 SC 107.
21 1989 SC 342.
22 At 372–373.
23 Eg *Criper v University of Edinburgh* 1991 SLT 129; *Jackson v Secretary of State for Scotland* 1992 SC 175.
24 In W Finnie, C M G Himsworth and N C Walker (eds), *Edinburgh Essays in Public Law* (1991). See also A W Bradley, 'Applications for judicial review – the Scottish model' [1987] PL 313; Anon, 'Arbitration and judicial review' 1990 SLT (News) 113.
25 1992 SLT 324.

to implement a statutory review committee's recommendation was amenable to review. Outer House judges were thus faced with conflicting authority and a third Inner House decision, *West*, was required to provide clarification.

West involved a prison officer who was refused a discretionary reimbursement of removal expenses on being transferred between prisons, which he argued was unreasonable and in breach of his legitimate expectations. The petition was easily dismissed as involving merely an ordinary contractual dispute which was not therefore amenable to judicial review. However, the court also sought to resolve the uncertainty over the relevance of the public/private distinction in Scots law and to give guidance on the scope of the supervisory jurisdiction for the future.

Giving judgment for the court, Lord President Hope traced the development of the supervisory jurisdiction, identifying a consistent line of authority since the early nineteenth century to the effect that, where an excess or abuse of power or jurisdiction conferred upon a decision-maker is alleged, the Court of Session has inherent power to correct it. He placed particular emphasis on *Forbes v Underwood*,[26] which held that the Court of Session alone had power to compel an arbiter to proceed. This case was significant because it showed that the principle upon which the supervisory jurisdiction is exercised is not affected by distinctions between public bodies and those exercising jurisdictions under private contracts. This was confirmed by later cases such as *McDonald v Burns*,[27] concerning expulsion of nuns from a convent, and *St Johnstone Football Club v Scottish Football Association*.[28] According to Lord Hope, the essential feature in all these cases was the existence of a 'tripartite relationship': between a person or body to whom a jurisdiction, power or authority has been delegated or entrusted, whether by statute, agreement or any other instrument, and the person or persons in respect of or for whose benefit that jurisdiction, power or authority is to be exercised (no such tripartite relationship being present in *West* itself).

Turning to *Brown v Hamilton District Council*, Lord Hope argued that in referring to the desirability of a new procedure for 'public law' cases, Lord Fraser was not trying to define the scope of the supervisory jurisdiction; rather his use of this terminology was explained by the fact that the House of Lords had that same day delivered judgment in two English cases defining the CJR as an exclusive procedure for public law cases.[29] In any case, rule 260B could not have introduced such a restriction: it was a procedural change only, made by Act of Sederunt, which could not therefore alter the substantive law as to the nature or scope of the supervisory jurisdiction. To describe judicial review as a public law remedy, dependent upon the existence of a public law element, was thus to introduce concepts which had played no part in the development of the jurisdiction in Scotland. However, the statements to this effect in *Tehrani* were, Lord Hope considered, merely obiter since counsel for the petitioner had conceded that he had to prove the existence of a public law element (and the case was correctly decided on its facts). Nevertheless, he disagreed with Lord Wylie about the desirability of following English authority: the introduction of the public/private distinction into English law had been motivated by entirely different concerns

---

26 (1886) 13 R 465.
27 1940 SC 376.
28 1965 SLT 171.
29 *O'Reilly v Mackman* [1983] 2 AC 237; *Cocks v Thanet District Council* [1983] 2 AC 286.

from those applicable in Scotland, and had continued to cause difficulty and uncertainty. Accordingly, the competency of review petitions in Scotland was not confined to cases accepted as amenable to review in England.

SCOPE OF SUPERVISORY JURISDICTION: SCOTS AND ENGLISH LAW COMPARED

The rejection in *West* of the public/private distinction was widely welcomed in Scotland,[30] and also attracted interest from some English writers critical of its use in their own jurisdiction.[31] However, other commentators have been more sceptical about both the correctness of the reasoning in *West* and the appropriateness of the alternative test it propounded.[32] A number of questions therefore arise. Was the Inner House right to reject the characterisation of judicial review as a public law remedy? To what extent does the Scottish approach really differ from the English in practice? Does it avoid the problems encountered in England? And does it really avoid invoking a public/private distinction?

It is important to realise that there are two aspects to the scope of review which are not always clearly distinguished. The first is a purely procedural issue: if one wishes to invoke judicial review principles in respect of a particular decision, when is it necessary to raise an AJR/CJR as opposed to an ordinary action? The second aspect is substantive: in respect of what decisions may the grounds of review be competently invoked?

The procedural issue

It is the procedural aspect of the public/private distinction which has attracted the greatest criticism in England. The difficulties stem from the historical existence, already noted, of two procedural routes by which to seek judicial review. Although the CJR allowed all remedies to be invoked in a single procedure, the Law Commission did not intend this to be exclusive; claimants would still be able to bring ordinary proceedings for declarations or injunctions.[33] Nevertheless, since this would allow applicants to evade the protections for public authorities, particularly the time-limit, built into the CJR, the House of Lords declared in *O'Reilly v Mackman*[34] that it would normally be an abuse of process to permit someone seeking to establish that a public authority had infringed their public law

---

30 See, eg, W J Wolffe, 'The scope of judicial review in Scots law' [1992] PL 625; W Finnie, 'Triangles as touchstones of review' 1993 SLT (News) 51 at 51; 'Administrative Law', in *Stair Memorial Encyclopaedia*, vol 1 (Reissue, 1999), para 115; Clyde and Edwards, *Judicial Review*, paras 8.27–8.30.

31 See, eg, J Alder, 'Hunting the chimera – the end of *O'Reilly v Mackman*' (1993) 13 *Legal Studies* 183 at 203; D Oliver, *Common Values and the Public-Private Divide* (1999), p 287; Wade and Forsyth, *Administrative Law*, p 646; I Cram and J Bell, 'Towards a better public law?' (1996) 74 *Pub Admin* 239 at 245.

32 See, eg, Finnie, above n 30; C M G Himsworth, in B Hadfield (ed), *Judicial Review: a Thematic Approach* (1995), p 291; C M G Himsworth, in M Supperstone et al (eds), *Judicial Review* (3rd edn, 2005), para 21.3.24; V M Smith, 'Contract or tripartite arrangement – *Rooney v Chief Constable, Strathclyde Police*' 1998 JR 193 at 196; A O'Neill, *Judicial Review in Scotland: a Practitioner's Guide* (1999), paras 1.40–1.41.

33 *Remedies in Administrative Law*, above n 10, para 34.

34 [1983] 2 AC 237; *R v Panel on Takeovers and Mergers, ex parte Datafin plc* [1987] QB 815.

entitlements to proceed via ordinary action. This general rule (known as procedural exclusivity) was, however, subject to two exceptions: first, where the parties agreed to the alternative procedure; second, and more significantly, where the public law challenge arose as a collateral issue in an action based on private rights, for example, where a negligence action involved impugning the validity of a planning decision,[35] or where a defence to proceedings for eviction from local authority accommodation involved challenging the validity of a rent increase.[36]

The application of this 'collateral challenge' exception proved highly problematic, in determining both what constituted a 'private right' and when the public law issue was merely 'collateral' to the private law challenge. Moreover, since a case wrongly begun by ordinary action could not be transferred into the CJR, this meant that otherwise meritorious claims could fail on what was coming to be seen as merely a technicality. Against this background, the House of Lords in *Roy v Kensington and Chelsea and Westminster Family Practitioner Committee*[37] endorsed a broad view of the collateral challenge exception, namely that the CJR was only mandatory when *no* private rights were at stake.[38] However, whilst this reduced the practical significance of procedural exclusivity, allowing more cases to proceed via ordinary action, it did not remove objections to the existence of the rule in principle. For one thing, there is no logical connection between its underlying rationale (the need to protect public bodies against unmeritorious or late challenges) and the basis of the collateral challenge exception. Thus, it seems merely to suggest that challenges founded on private rights are more important than those based solely on judicial review principles.[39] Secondly, whereas cases based on common law grounds of action, in contract, tort or property law, have been readily allowed to proceed by ordinary procedure irrespective of the importance of the judicial review challenge in establishing the claim, the tendency has been to insist that actions based on statutory rights, which crystallise only after a discretionary decision in the claimant's favour by a public body, continue to be brought via the CJR.[40] In other words, certain types of private rights also seem to be regarded as more important than others.

Given these problems, it is unsurprising that the Scottish courts would wish to avoid a procedural public/private distinction, and it is clear that, in practice, the introduction of the AJR in Scotland has not caused the same degree of difficulty.[41] As the Dunpark working party intended,[42] *West* confirmed that it was an exclusive procedure for *all* applications to the supervisory jurisdiction. Moreover, since there is no specific time-limit there is not the same incentive for applicants to evade the AJR, nor for respondents to resist ordinary actions. Nevertheless, tactical considerations may still influence choice of procedure. For instance, an ordinary action brought in the sheriff court may be cheaper than an AJR, and where the

---

35 Eg *Davy v Spelthorne Borough Council* [1984] AC 262.
36 Eg *Wandsworth London Borough Council v Winder* [1985] AC 461.
37 [1992] 1 AC 624.
38 Subsequent cases went even further; eg, *Mercury Communications Ltd v Director-General of Telecommunications* [1996] 1 All ER 575 held that ordinary actions should be allowed to proceed *unless* they amounted to an abuse of process – reversing the presumption in *O'Reilly*.
39 P Cane, *Administrative Law* (4th edn, 2004), pp 118, 123.
40 *British Steel plc v Customs & Excise Commissioners* [1997] 2 All ER 366.
41 T Mullen et al, *Judicial Review in Scotland* (1996), ch 4; *Stair Memorial Encyclopaedia*, above n 30, para 116.
42 Above n 17, para 8.

respondent body is domiciled in England, a delict or contract action may be available in Scotland, but judicial review is not.[43]

Moreover, the exclusive nature of the supervisory jurisdiction in Scotland does not in fact prevent judicial review issues being raised outwith the AJR. According to Clyde and Edwards:

> 'Where the substance of the action is a private right or the issue is raised as a properly pleaded defence, the exclusivity of judicial review is not a ground for insisting that questions as to the legality of a decision-maker's decision can only be raised in judicial review. The exclusivity of the judicial review procedure relates to the power of the court and to the effect of the remedy which can be obtained.'[44]

The essential issue appears to be whether the action truly involves attacking the validity of a decision (reduction only being available via judicial review)[45] or is rather an action, such as an action for damages, which presupposes the invalidity of the decision but does not require it to be reduced. This can be a difficult distinction to draw,[46] and may be problematic in that a case might impugn the validity of a decision whilst technically leaving it intact, a consideration which may incline the court to find that judicial review is required.[47] However, the important point is that the question whether an action truly invokes the supervisory jurisdiction seems to require a judgment very similar to the pre-*Roy* position in England about the significance of the judicial review issue to the proceedings before the court. In fact, according to Edwards:

> '[T]here *is* an important conceptual distinction between acts, such as delictual acts, which give rise directly to a right to damages or other civil remedies, and acts, such as administrative acts, which must first be deprived of legal effect before such a right can arise.... *If nothing else, [the English] public law/private law distinction assists in focusing this basic point*'[48] (emphasis added).

Thus, whilst Scots law may avoid the language of the public/private distinction, the procedural issues at stake in Scotland and England appear to be very similar, and indeed arise in any jurisdiction with a separate judicial review procedure.[49] The real difference therefore lies in the *content* of the two procedures. It is the restrictiveness of the English procedure, and judicial ambivalence about its justifiability,[50] which is the main reason for the greater practical difficulties it has produced. As the gulf between judicial review and ordinary procedures has narrowed with the reform of the Civil Procedure Rules – defendants may now apply to have ordinary actions stopped if there has been unreasonable delay or they have no real chance of success, whereas the permission stage of the CJR is no longer conducted ex parte – so too

---

43 Civil Jurisdiction and Judgments Act 1982. See *Bank of Scotland v IMRO* 1989 SC 107; *Fotheringham & Son v British Limousin Cattle Society Ltd* 2004 SLT 485.

44 Clyde and Edwards, *Judicial Review*, para 8.16.

45 *McDonald v Secretary of State for Scotland (No 2)* 1996 SC 113.

46 See, eg, *McDonald*, above n 45; *Sleigh v City of Edinburgh District Council* 1987 SC 70; *Hands v Kyle & Carrick District Council* 1988 SC 233; *Shetland Line (1984) Ltd v Secretary of State for Scotland* 1996 SLT 653; *Vaughan Engineering Ltd v Hinkins & Frewin Ltd* 2003 SLT 428; *Fotheringham & Son*, above n 43.

47 See *Vaughan Engineering Ltd*, para 35.

48 D J Edwards in D Curtin and D O'Keeffe (eds), *Constitutional Adjudication in European Community and National Law* (1992), p 294.

49 Cram and Bell, above n 31, pp 245–246.

50 P P Craig, *Administrative Law* (5th edn, 2003), p 804.

have the practical problems caused by procedural exclusivity diminished.[51] Although it has occasionally been argued that the Scottish procedure is not restrictive *enough*, providing insufficient certainty for public bodies,[52] the inevitable price would be increased litigation over the scope of the AJR.

The substantive issue

Whilst the procedural dimension of the scope of judicial review is purely contingent, dependent upon the existence of a separate AJR/CJR procedure, the substantive dimension is unavoidable, irrespective of the procedure by which review is sought, akin to the need to determine which relationships are properly described as contracts, or when a duty of care in negligence is owed. Moreover, although both jurisdictions take a symmetrical approach to the procedural and substantive scope of review, this is not essential. In other words, in England, because the CJR is regarded as a public law procedure, a public element is also required before the substantive principles of judicial review can be invoked. However, it would be possible to restrict the CJR to public law cases whilst allowing judicial review principles to be applied in other cases, their scope being determined on some other basis.[53] Similarly, in Scotland, because the AJR is *not* limited to public law cases, the grounds of review are assumed not to be so restricted either. Again, though, there would be no contradiction in classifying judicial review as a public law remedy, albeit applicable to certain decisions taken by private bodies, just as the Scottish courts accept that contract is a private law remedy, even when public bodies are parties to particular contracts.

Rejection of public/private distinction: historical argument

In fact, it is questionable whether *West's* denial of the relevance of a public/private distinction to the scope of review in Scotland is historically accurate. In *Forbes v Underwood*, for example, the position of arbiters was explicitly compared to that of judges and other public officers.[54] Similarly, the leading House of Lords authority – *Moss's Empires v Assessor for Glasgow* – states that '[i]t is within the jurisdiction of the Court of Session to keep *inferior judicatories* and *administrative bodies* right'.[55] Indeed, Himsworth argues that the older cases focus almost exclusively on bodies having a 'public' character, in the sense that they judge, they administer or they regulate.[56] Exceptions such as *McDonald v Burns* or *St Johnstone Football Club* are, he claims, too narrowly argued (and the former too peculiar factually) to support a general proposition that purely private bodies are reviewable.[57]

---

51 *Clark v University of Lincoln and Humberside* [2000] 1 WLR 1988; see Craig, *Administrative Law*, pp 828–829.
52 Eg N Collar, 'Mora and judicial review' 1989 SLT (News) 309 at 310–311. Mora, taciturnity and acquiescence can be pled in cases of unreasonable delay – *Hanlon v Traffic Commissioner* 1988 SLT 802 – but it is a plea on the merits not an absolute bar to proceedings. Otherwise, the standard prescription periods apply.
53 In fact, Oliver argues that this is the true position in England: ie, there is no substantive public/private divide, it being of procedural and remedial relevance only. See, eg, D Oliver in *Judicial Review and the Constitution*, above n 6, p 323.
54 (1886) 13 R 465 at 467–469 per Lord President Inglis.
55 1917 SC (HL) 1 at 11 per Lord Shaw (emphasis added); see also at 6 per Lord Kinnear.
56 'Public employment, the supervisory jurisdiction and points *West*' 1992 SLT (News) 257 at 261. See also A McGrade, *The Supervisory Jurisdiction of the Court of Session and the Impact of West v Secretary of State for Scotland* (unpublished LLM dissertation, University of Glasgow, 1997).
57 *Thematic Approach*, above n 32, pp 296–297.

Further, contrary to Lord Hope's assertion of a historically consistent line of authority, others have painted a more confused picture of the development of the supervisory jurisdiction.[58] Indeed, according to the Law Commission, since Scots law was deficient in both literature and case law it was difficult to present a coherent account of the law.[59] Even the terminology used has not been consistent. The term 'supervisory jurisdiction' is relatively recent, the older cases such as *Forbes* referring to the Court of Session's 'supereminent jurisdiction', a broader term which includes, for example, petitions to the nobile officium.[60] Himsworth concludes that 'the historical emergence of the "supervisory jurisdiction" of 1985 is not merely a story of changing nomenclature but also one of contested concepts at the core of the Court of Session's own powers'.[61]

Paradoxically, the historical case supporting a public/private distinction in England is equally contestable, the term 'public function' having been used no earlier than 1967.[62] Although the prerogative orders were restricted to public bodies and public duties, judicial review via declaration and injunction was widely applied in both public and private contexts without any general distinction being drawn.[63] Indeed, the ultra vires principle was originally developed to control joint stock railway companies created by private Acts of Parliament before being extended to governmental institutions.[64] It is the difficulty of reconciling these earlier cases with modern authority which causes some English writers to question whether the scope of judicial review does or should rest upon a public/private distinction.

In fact, contrary to the claims of some Scottish writers,[65] the development of judicial review in both jurisdictions appears to have been broadly similar in functional terms, if not in the precise procedures and remedies employed. Thus, the courts in both countries gradually assumed supervisory functions over administrative bodies previously exercised by the Privy Councils (the Scots having been abolished in 1708, and the English greatly diminished in powers after the Glorious Revolution), supplementing their existing jurisdiction to control inferior courts.[66] Moreover, these similarities are hardly surprising, since judicial review has developed in the context of a unitary state with largely common government institutions and a single final civil appeal court. Nevertheless, even if there were compelling historical evidence regarding the (ir)relevance of the public/private distinction, it is doubtful whether it should be determinative of the modern scope of review. As Drewry points out, 'the early development of legal remedies belongs to the prehistory of a very modern area of jurisprudence'.[67] Judicial review has been dramatically transformed and expanded since the 1960s, propelled by specific concerns about the control of contemporary governmental power and by a changing

---

58 See J D B Mitchell, 'The scope of judicial review' [1959] PL 197.
59 *Remedies in Administrative Law*, above n 11, para 4.4; see also para 5.5.
60 Himsworth, above n 56, pp 259–260.
61 Above n 56, p 260.
62 In *R v Criminal Injuries Compensation Board, ex parte Lain* [1967] 2 QB 864.
63 See, eg, Oliver, above n 6; Alder, above n 31.
64 Sedley LJ in Forsyth, *Judicial Review and the Constitution*, pp 296–298. However, companies were not initially regarded as purely private organisations: see M Stokes in W Twining (ed), *Legal Theory and Common Law* (1986), p 162.
65 See Clyde, above n 24, p 290; Clyde and Edwards, *Judicial Review*, para 2.02.
66 See Clyde and Edwards, *Judicial Review*, ch 2; McGrade, above n 56, ch 2; Wade and Forsyth, *Administrative Law*, pp 13–14.
67 In Supperstone et al, *Judicial Review*, para 2.1.4. See also S Bailey in Forsyth, *Judicial Review and the Constitution*, p 421.

understanding of the constitutional role of the courts. Hence, Drewry argues, earlier judicial activity was mostly directed at problems very different from those before the courts today.[68]

Rejection of public/private distinction: argument from principle

If defining the scope of review is thus a more creative process than was acknowledged in *West*,[69] the question remains whether Lord Hope was right to regard the adoption of a public/private distinction as being undesirable *in principle*.

As he correctly noted, the English courts have not found the distinction easy to apply, and there is also a powerful theoretical critique which argues that it is simply too indeterminate to supply a satisfactory legal test.[70] Rather than the world being neatly divided into public and private spheres, the former pursuing public purposes and the latter private purposes, the real picture, it is suggested, is one of institutional hybridity and interpenetration, and of shifting boundaries between public and private functions, with the passage of time, political perspective and the purpose for which classification is made. In this context, formal tests for identifying decisions which are sufficiently public to be subject to judicial review – based on institutional form or the legal source of powers – tend to produce anomalous results,[71] while functional tests, which look to the nature of the activity being undertaken rather than the decision-maker's identity or the source of their power, are inherently vague because there is little agreement on how functions should be classified and the same activities are often undertaken simultaneously by public and private bodies.[72]

Thus, although the Court of Appeal in *Datafin*[73] officially rejected a source-based approach in favour of a functional one, in practice the English case law oscillates between the two, sometimes with conflicting results. For example, *R v National Coal Board, ex parte National Union of Mineworkers*,[74] decided in the wake of the divisive 1984–85 miners' strike, held that a colliery closure decision by the publicly-owned coal board was an executive, business or management decision equivalent to one taken by a privately-owned company, and hence not amenable to judicial review. However, in *R v British Coal Corporation, ex parte Vardy*,[75] involving a decision to close ten collieries which had provoked considerable public sympathy for the affected miners, *NUM* was not followed on the basis that a statutory consultation procedure, by which Parliament had intended to restrict British Coal's freedom to dismiss employees, had not been complied with.

The persistence of a formalistic approach is particularly noticeable in relation to bodies whose powers derive solely from contract, the most criticised aspect of

---

68 In Supperstone et al, *Judicial Review*, above n 67, para 2.2.3.
69 Himsworth, above n 56, p 259.
70 For discussion see, eg, P Cane in J Eekelaar and J Bell (eds), *Oxford Essays in Jurisprudence* (3rd Series, 1987), pp 64–71.
71 Eg, if statutory bodies are subject to review this would technically include companies, the establishment and powers of which are governed by the Companies Act 1995.
72 Eg, both government and private institutions provide health and education services, act as employers and enter into commercial relationships for the supply of goods and services. On the distinction between formal and functional tests see generally C Harlow, '"Public" and "private" law: definition without distinction' (1980) 43 MLR 241 at 253–258.
73 [1987] QB 815.
74 [1986] ICR 791.
75 [1993] ICR 720.

the English jurisprudence.[76] These are treated as inherently private, and therefore excluded from judicial review, no matter what functions they perform,[77] nor whether claimants have truly consented to their powers.[78] In general, though, the courts apply what Cane terms a 'contextually functional', rather than 'purely functional' approach,[79] looking for evidence of government involvement, in the case of private associations, or specific statutory regulation or other distinguishing features, in the case of government contracts, as indicators that public functions are being performed. In other words, judges attempt to ground their decisions about the nature of particular functions in something more concrete than their personal instincts about publicness and privateness. Nevertheless, disagreements are still possible about what contextual factors are relevant in particular cases,[80] and, inevitably with any shift towards a more formal approach, slight variations in the contextual characteristics of particular cases can produce different and seemingly anomalous results.[81]

Again, therefore, it is understandable that the Scottish courts might want to avoid basing the scope of judicial review on a public/private distinction, provided, however, that a more suitable alternative is available.

The West test in practice

The Scottish approach does appear to be superior in one respect, namely in accepting that contractually-based decisions are not automatically excluded from judicial review. This recognises that contracts can sometimes create decision-making powers that are not adequately controlled by the initial agreement:

> '[I]f the ... governing authorities of the body go altogether beyond the sphere of the constitution of the association – if they deal with a member in the way that they are not authorised by their constitution to deal with him – *if they attempt to exercise over him a power or authority which he by becoming a member did not give them* ... he will not be precluded from seeking redress'[82] (emphasis added).

Thus, private associations may be reviewable in Scotland, even if they are not part of any governmental regulatory scheme and, although there is no Scottish authority, judicial review of contracted-out public services would not be precluded merely because the functions were governed by contract. Nevertheless, the jurisdictional test established in *West* suffers from two major flaws which seriously compromise its ability to justify, and resolve disputes about, the scope of the supervisory jurisdiction.

---

76 See, eg, D Pannick, 'Who is subject to judicial review and in respect of what?' [1992] PL 1; J Black, 'Constitutionalising self-regulation' (1996) 59 MLR 24 at 41–42; Wade and Forsyth, *Administrative Law*, pp 638, 644; S A de Smith, Lord Woolf and J Jowell, *Principles of Judicial Review* (1999), pp 64, 70.

77 See, eg, *R v Insurance Ombudsman Bureau, ex parte Aegon Life* [1994] COD 426 (non-statutory ombudsman not reviewable); *R v Servite Houses, ex parte Goldsmith* [2001] LGR 55 (provider of contracted-out local authority housing services not reviewable).

78 See, eg, *R v Jockey Club, ex parte Aga Khan* [1993] 1 WLR 909 (Jockey Club not reviewable, although exercised monopoly control over horse racing).

79 *Administrative Law*, p 39.

80 Eg contrast the decisions of Bingham and Hoffmann LJJ in *Aga Khan*, regarding whether actual or merely potential government involvement was required.

81 Eg, compare *Poplar Housing Association Ltd v Donoghue* [2002] QB 48 with *R (Heather) v Leonard Cheshire Foundation* [2002] 2 All ER 936.

82 *McMillan v The Free Church* (1859) 22 D 290 at 314. See also *Blair v Lochaber District Council* 1995 SLT 407 at 409; *Crocket v Tantallon Golf Club* 2005 SCLR 657, para 31.

The first set of problems arises from Lord Hope's claim that reviewable jurisdictions are characterised by the presence of tripartite relationships. This is at
once a highly formalistic criterion and practically indeterminate. The difficulty is
that tripartite relationships can be identified in many situations – such as private
trustees,[83] sporting referees[84] and company boards[85] – which are not usually
regarded as being routinely subject to review. Judgments are therefore required
about which tripartite relationships count, and this has given rise to conflicting
decisions. For instance, for Lord Hope, *St Johnstone Football Club* clearly involved
a tripartite relationship, since the Scottish Football Association's council had been
entrusted by its articles of association with a limited decision-making jurisdiction.[86]
However, in *Fraser v Professional Golfers' Association*, Lord Eassie held that a mere
delegation to employees, officers or agents was not sufficient to create a tripartite
relationship, since incorporated and unincorporated associations have no choice
but to act through intermediaries.[87] Similarly, in *Fotheringham & Son v British
Limousin Cattle Society Ltd*,[88] the court did not consider that official recognition of
a self-regulatory organisation (SRO) for the purposes of compliance with an EC
directive, which conferred binding legal effect on the Society's pedigree certificates,
was sufficient to create a tripartite relationship. But this is difficult to reconcile with
Bank of Scotland v IMRO[89] (decided before *West*, but not since doubted), which held
that a financial services SRO was reviewable precisely because it was woven into a
statutory regulatory regime.

In fact, there are particular challenges in fitting statutory powers into the
tripartite model.[90] Although it has sometimes been accepted that Parliament may
constitute the third party to the relationship,[91] this creates two problems. First,
many relationships are regulated by statute (such as parent and child, employer
and employee) but again fall outwith the scope of review, so additional criteria are
needed to distinguish statutory obligations which create reviewable jurisdictions
from those which do not.[92] Secondly, it is unclear at what level of generality
statutory regulation becomes relevant. For instance, *Hardie v City of Edinburgh
Council*[93] held that a teacher's removal from a list of supply teachers was reviewable
although there was no statutory duty to maintain such a list, since the court
considered that the council's general obligation to secure the provision of education
created the necessary tripartite relationship. However, in *West* itself the general
statutory obligations on the prison service were not regarded as relevant. Given
these difficulties, other cases have suggested that it is not always necessary to prove
the existence of a tripartite relationship,[94] or that the test applies only to contractual

---

83 Wolffe, above n 30, p 631.
84 Himsworth, above n 56, p 261.
85 Wolffe, above n 30, pp 632–633.
86 See also *Irvine v Royal Burgess Golfing Society of Edinburgh* 2004 SCLR 386; *Crocket v Tantallon
    Golf Club*.
87 1999 SCLR 1032 at 1037.
88 2004 SLT 485.
89 1989 SC 107.
90 See Finnie, above n 30, pp 53–54.
91 See, eg *Boyle v Castlemilk East Housing Co-operative Ltd* 1998 SLT 56.
92 Cf Finnie, above n 30, p 54; Himsworth, in Supperstone, *Judicial Review*, para 21.3.23.
93 2000 SLT 130.
94 Eg, *Naik v University of Stirling* 1994 SLT 449 at 451–452; *Joobeen v University of Stirling* 1995
    SLT 120 at 122; *McIntosh v Aberdeenshire Council* 1998 SCLR 435 at 442. See also Clyde and
    Edwards, *Judicial Review*, para 8.33.

powers,[95] again raising questions about what alternative tests might be relevant. Others still have abandoned the tripartite analysis altogether in favour of explicitly functional criteria, such as whether the decision is 'administrative' or 'judicial',[96] or alternatively 'commercial' in character,[97] or simply invoking the true nature of the issues involved.[98] As Himsworth notes, '[i]f that is not the readmission of a "public law" test, it is not at all clear what it is'.[99]

However, even if additional criteria can be found to identify the existence of a jurisdiction, there are more fundamental problems in linking the scope of review to the concept of jurisdiction. For one thing, it does not account for the review either of prerogative powers or decisions by central government bodies deriving from their capacity as legal persons.[100] Neither set of powers is delegated by an identifiable third party, but rather arises by operation of law, and in the case of common law powers, these are not unique to public bodies. Since such decisions do appear to be reviewable in Scotland,[101] this must rest upon some other conceptual basis, such as the nature of the functions being performed, the decision-maker's identity or their reasons for acting. In addition, although there is conceptual unity between the concept of jurisdiction and some grounds of review, this is not true for all of them.[102] The grounds raised in *West*, for example – breach of legitimate expectations and unreasonableness – could have been established irrespective of any jurisdictional limits on the Prison Service's powers. This point is not merely academic, because some cases appear to conflate questions about the *relevancy* of particular jurisdictional grounds with the *competency* of the petition itself, effectively excluding the possibility of review on non-jurisdictional grounds. For instance, in *Stannifer Developments Ltd v Glasgow Development Agency*,[103] a contractual tendering process was allegedly conducted unfairly, but the court held that because there were no express statutory constraints on the bidding process, it did not constitute the exercise of a jurisdiction.[104] Similarly, in *JDP Investments Ltd v Strathclyde Regional Council*,[105] concerning the sale of council property allegedly in breach of the Crichel Down guidelines,[106] Lord Hamilton held that the application of the guidelines could arguably amount to the exercise of a jurisdiction, but he could not decide this issue without first determining what part, if any, they had played in the making of the relevant decision. Whether a decision is potentially reviewable should, however, be determinable independently of whether there are any *grounds* for review in a particular case.

The scope of review in Scotland is thus every bit as vague and contradictory as it is in England. According to Clyde and Edwards, this lack of precision is only

95   Eg, *Blair v Lochaber District Council* 1995 SLT 407 at 409. See also O'Neill, *Judicial Review*, para 1.37.
96   *Blair* at 409–410.
97   *Stannifer Developments Ltd v Glasgow Development Agency* 1998 SCLR 870.
98   *Joobeen v University of Stirling* 1995 SLT 120 at 122.
99   'Further *West*? More geometry of judicial review' 1995 SLT (News) 127 at 131.
100 Wolffe, above n 30, p 632; Finnie, above n 30, p 54.
101 For prerogative powers, see *McDonald v Secretary of State for Scotland* 1996 SLT 16; for other non-statutory powers see, eg, *Al Fayed v Lord Advocate* 2004 SC 568.
102 Wolffe, above n 30, p 631.
103 1998 SCLR 870.
104 See also *Fraser v Professional Golfers' Association* 1999 SCLR 1032.
105 1996 SCLR 243.
106 Governing the resale of compulsorily purchased property.

to be expected in an equitable and supervisory jurisdiction.[107] However, whilst some uncertainty at the margins is probably inevitable, it is unsatisfactory in both practical and theoretical terms if the conceptual underpinnings of at least the central instances of judicial review cannot be stated confidently. Without a clear idea of what judicial review is *for*, far from being the principled enterprise claimed by Lord Hope, it risks becoming a sea of single instances in which judges' responses are shaped by the perceived merits of the cases before them. Accordingly, in order to resolve this issue, as well as to understand why it has proved so problematic in both countries, it is necessary to examine more closely the nature of the public/private distinction and the constitutional foundations of judicial review.

PUBLIC/PRIVATE DISTINCTION AND PURPOSES OF JUDICIAL REVIEW

Nature of public/private distinction and functions of judicial review

The Scottish courts' experience suggests that, in determining the scope of judicial review, it is hard to avoid employing some sort of public/private distinction, notwithstanding the apparently vague and controversial nature of the judgments this involves. Indeed, it may be argued that, in contrasting jurisdictions with purely contractual relationships, the *West* test *itself* implicitly invokes such distinctions. Whereas in a bilateral relationship, the petitioner can (at least in theory) sufficiently protect her interests vis-à-vis the decision-maker either by negotiation or the threat of taking her business elsewhere, this is not possible in a tripartite relationship, because the decision-maker must act in accordance with the terms of her jurisdiction, over which the petitioner exercises no direct control (see figure 2). Hence this involves two sets of distinctions, between authority-based and consensual relationships, and between constrained and unconstrained decision-

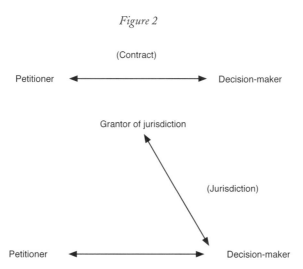

Figure 2

making powers (acting in pursuit of someone else's purposes versus acting on one's own account), which are stereotypically associated with government and private actors respectively.

However, these are not the only characteristics associated with publicness and privateness. In fact, one reason why public/private classifications are so contentious and contradictory is because the distinction involves not one, but a series of dualisms which overlap, but do not entirely converge (see figure 3). The same decisions may thus be classified as *both* public and private, depending upon which characteristics are emphasised, and this also helps to explain apparent similarities in the functions and values of public and private law. For example, Oliver points out that many private law relationships resemble to some extent that between government and citizen, such as fiduciary relationships or employment relationships, and are therefore subject to similar 'duties of considerate decision-making' to those imposed via judicial review.[108] She admits, however, that these duties are not necessarily identical and that the governmental or non-governmental nature of the decision or the decision-maker sometimes makes a difference.[109]

Figure 3

Public	Private	Judicial Review
Authority	Consent	} Protective function
Other's purposes	Own purposes	
Collective action	Individual action	} Directive function
General interests	Specific interests	

For present purposes, the important point is that recognising the multi-faceted nature of the public/private distinction helps to clarify the true difference between the approaches to defining the scope of review in Scotland and England. It is not that one jurisdiction rejects while the other accepts the relevance of the distinction; rather each emphasises *different aspects* of publicness and privateness. Thus, while *West* stressed the importance of non-consensual relationships and decision-making constraints, the English courts are interested primarily in identifying decisions made on behalf of the public collectively, and which affect the public interest.[110] Moreover, this difference matters because each pair of characteristics entails a different function for judicial review. The stress on formal characteristics of publicness in Scotland suggests a *protective* function for the courts: policing jurisdictional boundaries to ensure that decision-makers do not exceed the powers delegated to them and thereby abuse their authority over those subject to their jurisdiction. However, the English courts' stress on the more substantive aspects of publicness suggests a *directive* function for judicial review: setting 'standards of good administration' to ensure that power exercised in the public's name or which affects public interests is directed towards appropriate ends.

The distinction between the protective and directive functions of review should not be overstated. The former also seeks to direct powers towards proper ends, in terms of complying with the spirit as well as the letter of jurisdictional constraints.

---

108   See *Common Values* above n 31, chs 6–9.
109   *Common Values* above n 31, pp 250–255.
110   Cf de Smith et al, *Principles of Judicial Review*, above n 76, p 65.

Similarly, the standards of good administration are primarily concerned with protecting individuals against potential abuses of power. However, individual protection is balanced by concern for the needs of the community at large and, whilst the standards of good administration include compliance with specific jurisdictional limits, these are by no means exhaustive. In other words, a directive rather than protective function for judicial review suggests a more ambitious role for the courts: actively shaping the legitimate exercise of public power, rather than merely enforcing conditions set elsewhere. Thus, as already noted, Scottish writers emphasise the equitable role of the supervisory jurisdiction – a matter of ensuring that no wrong goes without a remedy[111] – and hence the residual nature of judicial review.[112] More generally, the courts continue to stress the importance of the legality/merits distinction: that it is not for them to interfere in decisions which are within the scope of the decision-maker's jurisdiction.[113] Unlike the English courts, they therefore still adhere to the problematic distinction between intra vires and ultra vires errors of law,[114] and they have played little part in developing the modern grounds of review, largely reacting to innovations south of the border.[115] By contrast, English judges have become increasingly confident in asserting the fundamental constitutional values embodied in the grounds of review and the importance of the courts in ensuring respect for those values.[116]

In many cases, this functional divergence makes little or no difference to the practice of judicial review in each jurisdiction. In the paradigm case, where the various characteristics of publicness converge – where a minister or local authority administers a statutory scheme in the public interest which impacts adversely on an individual's interests – the outcome will be the same whether review is conceived as primarily protective or directive. However, at the margins of review, where the component parts of the public/private distinction begin to disaggregate, the differences become more apparent. Thus, as noted above, the Scottish courts struggle to accommodate the non-jurisdictional aspects of judicial review, where its directive functions are most prominent, whilst the English courts appear to have lost sight of the protective functions performed in earlier cases in respect of private associations.

Nevertheless, in each jurisdiction the neglected aspects of the public/private distinction continue to exert a pull. Tensions arise, first, because the distinctions being relied upon by the courts are not self-executing. There are, for instance, many gradations between wholly consensual and wholly coercive relationships, and how a particular decision is classified will depend partly upon judgments about the petitioner's need for protection and the suitability of applying judicial review norms.[117] For example, in *Fotheringham & Son*, one reason why the court refused

---

111 Clyde and Edwards, *Judicial Review*, paras 2.08, 3.01, 4.03.
112 For Clyde and Edwards, the absence of an alternative remedy is one of the principal limits on the scope of judicial review (see para 8.46).
113 See, eg, *Crocket v Tantallon Golf Club* 2005 SCLR 657, para 31.
114 *Watt v Lord Advocate* 1979 SC 120; *O'Neill v Scottish Joint Negotiating Committee for Teaching Staff* 1987 SC 90; *Codona v Showmen's Guild of Great Britain* 2002 SLT 299. In England, all errors of law are reviewable: *R v Hull University Visitor, ex parte Page* [1991] 4 All ER 747.
115 Himsworth in Hadfield, *Thematic Approach*, p 305; O'Neill, *Judicial Review*, para 1.05.
116 See, eg, S Sedley, 'The sound of silence: constitutional law without a constitution' (1994) 110 LQR 270; J Laws, 'Law and democracy' [1995] PL 72; and compare *Leech v Secretary of State for Scotland* 1992 SC 89 with *R v Secretary of State for the Home Department, ex parte Leech (No 2)* [1994] QB 198.
117 Cf Cane, *Administrative Law*, pp 42–43, who notes similarly that there is no objective test of how integrated into a statutory scheme a function must be in order to qualify as public.

to find that the society was exercising a jurisdiction was because it had no *de jure* monopoly over the issue of pedigree certificates for the breed of cattle in question; there was no legal restraint on the formation of another breeders' association which could seek official recognition itself. Since the petitioners were alleging a breach of the Competition Act 1998, the court may have felt that the matter was more appropriately dealt with according to market principles, rather than judicial review. Conversely, the absence of monopoly has not been significant in cases regarding the reviewability of golf clubs,[118] perhaps recognising that membership decisions in this context involve an element of status, not purely commercial considerations. It is, however, one thing to insist that private clubs comply with their own rules, and to accord some procedural protection to ensure that those rules are applied fairly; it is quite another to require them to comply with the same standards of rationality and substantive fairness expected of government bodies.

Further complicating these judgments is the fact that the different pairs of public characteristics emphasised by the Scottish and English courts do not in practice arise in neat and mutually exclusive packages. Rather, they are found in multiple combinations and, when it is unclear whether a particular decision is reviewable or not, the presence or absence of other public characteristics may be sufficient to tip the balance. For example, prerogative powers undeniably involve the exercise of authority, but are subject only to very attenuated jurisdictional constraints.[119] Nevertheless, since they are exclusively governmental powers and there is a clear public interest in their proper use, it is not surprising that the Scottish courts should wish to ensure that they are reviewable to the same extent as in England. In a case such as *Fraser*, on the other hand, where a trainee golf professional sought to reduce an examiner's decision to fail him, simply because he was subject to the Professional Golfers' Association's *de facto* authority was not enough to make the decision reviewable in the absence of specific constraints on the examiner's powers, there being no strong public interest in or governmental flavour to its actions either. In England, similarly, the protective function of judicial review sometimes exerts an influence. Admittedly, this usually acts as a limiting factor on the scope of review, seen most clearly in relation to public contracts. Although when exercising contractual functions the government is still acting on behalf of the public, and should arguably therefore comply with the same standards of good administration as apply to its other functions,[120] the courts generally take the view that public employees and other contractors are sufficiently protected by private law, unless some specific public interest factor[121] or jurisdictional constraint[122] sets a particular case apart. Sometimes, however, the fact that a private body exercises *de facto*[123] or *de jure*[124] coercive powers may incline the court to find that it is performing a public function, even if there is no, or only limited, government involvement in its activities.

---

118 *Irvine v Royal Burgess Golfing Society of Edinburgh* 2004 SCLR 386; *Crocket v Tantallon Golf Club* 2005 SCLR 657.

119 Ie, the scope of particular prerogatives is fixed at common law, but this does not necessarily prevent them from being used in new ways: see, eg, *R v Secretary of State for the Home Department, ex parte Northumbria Police Authority* [1989] QB 26.

120 See, eg, S Arrowsmith, 'Judicial review and the contractual powers of public authorities' (1990) 106 LQR 277.

121 Eg *CCSU v Minister for the Civil Service* [1985] AC 374.

122 Eg *R v British Coal Corporation, ex parte Vardy* [1993] ICR 720.

123 See, eg *R v Panel on Takeovers and Mergers, ex parte Datafin* [1987] QB 815 at 845 per Lloyd LJ.

124 Eg, *R (A) v Partnerships in Care Ltd* [2002] 1 WLR 2610.

Constitutional foundations of judicial review

One might conclude from this analysis that a more satisfactory approach to the scope of review in both Scotland and England would be to acknowledge the multidimensionality of the public/private distinction and the dual functions of judicial review. It should first be considered, however, whether there is any deeper constitutional significance in, or justification for, the divergence between the Scottish and English approaches.

The jurisdictional test applied in Scotland echoes the traditional understanding of the constitutional foundations of judicial review, based on the ultra vires principle. This is usually regarded as being grounded in respect for parliamentary sovereignty and it supplies the rationale for the legality/merits distinction: the courts' function is to enforce Parliament's authority by ensuring that agencies do not exceed the powers granted to them; but judges too must respect Parliament's will by not arrogating to themselves decisions which have been assigned elsewhere.[125] However, Scots law demonstrates that this reasoning can equally be applied to non-statutory jurisdictions, which suggests that the true constitutional justification for the ultra vires principle is the separation of powers. In other words, the courts' role is to interpret and uphold legal limits on decision-making powers (by whomsoever imposed), but not themselves to impose such limits; parliamentary sovereignty merely supplying the most compelling justification for this judicial formalism.

By contrast, the 'functional turn'[126] in English administrative law is associated with the rise of an alternative constitutional justification for judicial review. This approach sees judicial review principles as independent creations of the common law, grounded in the rule of law. This theory, it is argued, more accurately explains the modern practice of judicial review, since control of prerogative and common law powers has nothing to do with policing legislative (or other) grants of power. Nor can the application of non-jurisdictional grounds of review, or even the proper extent of jurisdictional control, realistically be attributed to legislative (or other) intent.[127]

Contemporary defenders of the ultra vires principle concede much of this case.[128] They accept that it does not justify review of non-statutory (or non-jurisdictional) powers and they admit that the idea that *specific* parliamentary intent can be found for each ground of review (that is, the idea that when a body is held to have acted ultra vires for, say, breach of natural justice the court is merely upholding Parliament's intention that it should comply with the principles of natural justice) is a fiction. In reality, these grounds have been created by judges and their specific content is justified by other constitutional principles. Nevertheless, it is important, they claim, to retain the 'fig leaf' of assuming that Parliament, in general terms, intends statutory powers to be exercised in accordance with judicial review principles in order to ensure that the courts remain within their proper constitutional bounds and pay proper deference to Parliament's role in setting the terms on which public power should be exercised.

---

125 See Craig, *Administrative Law*, pp 5–7.
126 Cane, *Administrative Law*, p 10.
127 See, in particular, essays by D Oliver, P P Craig and Laws LJ in Forsyth, *Judicial Review and the Constitution*.
128 See essays by C F Forsyth and by M Elliott in Forsyth, *Judicial Review and the Constitution*; and C F Forsyth and M Elliott, 'The legitimacy of judicial review' [2003] PL 286.

In fact, they argue, not only does the common law approach jeopardise the legality/merits distinction, by allowing judges to assess the substantive justifiability of executive decisions,[129] but at its strongest, it may bring the courts into direct conflict with Parliament. This is most obvious in relation to ouster clauses: unless it is presumed that the grounds of review are part of the ultra vires principle, to deny that a decision taken in breach of a non-jurisdictional ground is protected by an ouster clause amounts to a blatant refusal to give effect to Parliament's intent. However, the dangers of judicial supremacism can also be seen in relation to the scope of review in the context of SROs and contracting-out. Part of the reason for preferring these mechanisms to statutory regulation or direct public service provision is precisely because private bodies are not subject to the same constraints as public ones. If, taking a functional approach, the courts nevertheless declare that SROs and private contractors are performing public functions and so still subject to judicial review, this denies political actors the freedom to choose how best to pursue particular policy objectives.[130]

Adherents of the common law school reject the charge of judicial supremacism, arguing that Parliament can always exclude judicial review, or alter specific grounds, provided it makes its intention sufficiently clear. The debate between the two camps has thus largely become confined to a narrow, technical dispute about whether the common law can supplement legislative intent or whether the latter is all-encompassing. The real significance of the debate, however, lies in the differing attitudes it reveals toward the role of judges in controlling public power – between those who welcome and those who remain suspicious of (overt) judicial activism – the fundamental fault line dividing administrative law scholars. Nevertheless, the debate does not expressly address the appropriateness of the various judicial review principles or their application in particular contexts.[131] In particular, though the ultra vires approach reminds the courts to be cautious in applying the grounds of review, it does not actually guarantee judicial restraint since any level of judicial intervention can be formally reconciled with legislative intent.[132] In other words, it is only by acknowledging that judicial review is a creative process that its limits can properly be addressed.[133]

CONCLUSION: SCOPE AND PURPOSES OF JUDICIAL REVIEW RECONSIDERED

The constitutional foundations debate reinforces the conclusion that neither a wholly protective nor a wholly directive function for judicial review is satisfactory. Whilst judges inevitably play an active role in determining the limits of lawful decision-making, this needs to be tempered by awareness of the legitimate role of

---

129 This is best illustrated by the doctrine of substantive legitimate expectations: see *R v North and East Devon Health Authority, ex parte Coughlan* [2001] QB 213.

130 See, eg, *R (Heather) v Leonard Cheshire Foundation* [2001] EWHC Admin 429, para 48(iii), per Stanley Burnton J; but cf contra P P Craig, 'Contracting-out, the Human Rights Act and the scope of judicial review' (2002) 118 LQR 551.

131 A Halpin, 'The theoretical controversy concerning judicial review' (2001) 64 MLR 500 at 508; T R S Allan, 'The constitutional foundations of judicial review: conceptual conundrum or interpretative inquiry?' (2002) 61 CLJ 87 at 101.

132 N Bamforth in Forsyth, *Judicial Review and the Constitution*, p 114; N W Barber, 'The academic mythologians' (2001) 21 OJLS 369 at 379.

133 Barber, above n 132, p 379.

other actors in setting conditions for the exercise of power and of the need for those conditions to be policed. Clearly, there is room for different views about where the balance between these two functions should be struck. However, there is no evidence that the divergence in approaches to the scope of review in Scotland and England is based on a considered difference of opinion about the proper constitutional role of the courts. Nor, indeed, does there seem to be much justification for fundamental divergence on this issue, given the ongoing similarities in the structure and content of executive power north and south of the border.[134]

Accordingly, the Scottish courts' continued adherence to the concept of jurisdiction as the basis of judicial review looks simply like conservatism, while their acceptance of English authority on the grounds of review though rejecting that on scope is plain incoherent, since both are influenced by prevailing attitudes to the role and foundations of judicial review. It is, of course, commendable that they have not lost sight of the protective function of judicial review, and, from this perspective, the scope of review need not be identical in Scotland and England given that there may be differences in the alternative remedies available.[135] However, the directive function of judicial review must also be acknowledged: to see it merely as an expression of the equitable principle that no wrong should go without a remedy is to seriously misrepresent its contemporary significance in shaping the exercise of governmental power.

It has been argued in this chapter that using a public/private distinction to determine the scope of review would, provided its multifaceted nature is acknowledged, be better able than the *West* test to accommodate these dual functions. It has also been argued that this would not actually be such a radical departure from current practice as it might appear. Moreover, the Scottish courts already have to make such distinctions when determining the scope of the duty to comply with Convention rights in section 6 of the Human Rights Act 1998 (HRA).

The boundary questions arising under the HRA are not identical to those in judicial review. The Act draws a distinction between 'core' public authorities, which must comply with Convention rights in all their actions, and 'hybrid' public authorities, defined as 'any person some of whose functions are functions of a public nature',[136] which are bound in respect of their public functions, but not if the nature of a particular act is private (see figure 4).[137] It thus relies on both institutional criteria, when identifying core public authorities, and functional criteria, in relation to hybrid ones.[138] In addition, section 6 must be interpreted in the light of the Strasbourg jurisprudence concerning when state responsibility is engaged under the Convention itself and, as a UK statute, it should also be interpreted uniformly throughout the country. The most important difference, however, is that the obligations imposed by section 6, unlike judicial review, are non-reciprocal: that is, an actor cannot simultaneously be a public authority which must respect the rights of others and itself a bearer of rights so as to satisfy the victim test in

---

134 Although Himsworth notes that, if significant differences in the political accountability of Scottish compared with UK ministers were to emerge this might justify a difference in their legal accountability: Supperstone et al, *Judicial Review*, para 21.1.4.

135 Eg, arbitrators have never been reviewable in England because a specific statutory framework provides similar controls: Arbitration Act 1950.

136 HRA s 6(3)(b).

137 HRA s 6(5).

138 See *Aston Cantlow and Wilmcote with Billesley Parochial Church Council v Wallbank* [2004] 1 AC 546, para 41, per Lord Hope.

HRA section 7.[139] The significance of this point for the present discussion is that it indicates that the HRA performs a directive rather than a protective function: it 'points to an ethical bottom line for public authorities'.[140] Hence, the mere fact that a body exercises a jurisdiction should not be sufficient to indicate that it also performs public functions. Rather, whether it can be said to be acting on the public's behalf and/or whether its decisions engage the public interest should be the more important considerations,[141] although the exercise of non-consensual and/or constrained powers may be relevant in making those judgments.

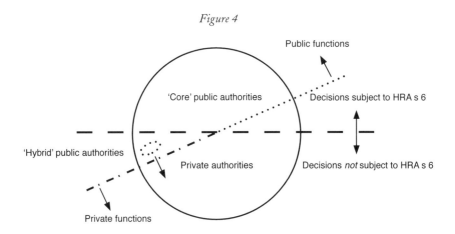

Figure 4

Thus, decisions about the scope of section 6 and the scope of judicial review need not be identical. Nevertheless, the fact that human rights and traditional judicial review challenges will often be raised together may in time – there has as yet been no significant Scottish authority on section 6[142] – encourage the Scottish courts to employ the language of the public/private distinction in judicial review cases, and also to pay greater attention to their directive role in setting conditions for the legitimate exercise of public power. Admittedly, reliance on the public/ private distinction would require complex and sometimes contentious contextual judgments about the reviewability of particular decisions, although it is unlikely to produce the procedural problems experienced in England. However, the difficulties encountered in applying the *West* test suggest that formalistic criteria offer false promise of greater certainty. The public/private distinction would at least more accurately reflect the conceptual underpinnings of contemporary judicial review practice, and it might also enable the Scottish courts to develop a truly distinctive take on the legal control of power in the modern state.

139 At least for core public authorities. Hybrid authorities can apparently be victims in relation to private acts (*Aston Cantlow*), but the position is unclear in respect of their public functions. See H Davis, 'Public authorities as "victims" under the Human Rights Act' (2005) 64 CLJ 315; H Quane, 'The Strasbourg jurisprudence and the meaning of a "public authority" under the Human Rights Act' [2006] PL 106.
140 Jack Straw MP, quoted in Joint Committee on Human Rights, *The Meaning of Public Authority Under the Human Rights Act* (7th Report 2003-04, HL 39, HC 382), para 48.
141 Cf JCHR, above n 140, para 140.
142 But see *Grampian University Hospitals NHS Trust v Frame* 2004 SCCR 173, which held that an NHS Trust was a governmental organisation and hence not a victim within HRA s 7.

Chapter 12

Standing to Seek Judicial Review

Tom Mullen

INTRODUCTION

The grounds of judicial review of administrative action are near identical in Scots law and English law,[1] but different approaches have been taken to the ancillary questions of remedies, procedure and standing to sue. Such ancillary rules are important as they affect the ability of litigants to obtain judicial review. Taking remedies first, there are important differences in the way that these have developed in the two jurisdictions. English law developed special remedies for challenging administrative action originally referred to as prerogative writs, and later as prerogative orders, including certiorari, mandamus and prohibition. However, ordinary private law remedies such as injunction and declaration could also be used in certain cases.[2]

The law of remedies in England and Wales was highly complex and issues of the scope of remedies sometimes became intertwined with the grounds of judicial review. Litigants often faced a difficult task in deciding which remedies to seek. The procedures applied to prerogative orders were different from those applying to declaration and injunction, the standing requirements varied according to the remedy sought, and sometimes difficult questions arose as to the scope of the remedies. This somewhat unsatisfactory state of affairs has been improved considerably by reform of remedies and procedure, although some new difficulties have been created in the process.[3]

Scots law never developed any remedies which were specific to public law. General remedies ordinarily available in civil litigation are equally applicable to judicial review cases. Thus, the remedy of reduction which in the context of private law may be used to set aside, for example, a contract procured by misrepresentation, may also be used to invalidate an unlawful administrative decision. It is, therefore, functionally equivalent to the English quashing order (formerly certiorari).[4] Similarly, there were no special procedures for challenging administrative decisions, and actions invoking the supervisory jurisdiction would normally be begun by summons or petition. Standing to sue did not generally appear to vary according to the remedy sought but was considered in relation to the substantive rights in dispute. As a consequence, litigants before the Scottish courts were rarely

---

1 See, eg, *Brown v Hamilton District Council* 1983 SC (HL) 1.
2 For a useful general account of the English law of remedies, see P P Craig, *Administrative Law* (5th edn, 2003), pt 3.
3 See Craig, *Administrative Law*, ch 23.
4 New terminology for the prerogative orders was introduced in 2000. Certiorari became a quashing order, mandamus a mandatory order and prohibition a prohibitory order: see Civil Procedure Rules, rule 54.2.

faced with the difficulties sometimes faced by litigants in England and Wales in relation to remedies and procedure.

However, by the late 1970s the supervisory jurisdiction of the Court of Session was virtually moribund with at most a handful of cases being brought each year.[5] No doubt this was due in part to the limited awareness on the part of the litigants and legal advisers of the relevant legal principles, but it was also likely to be due in part to the delay and expense associated with ordinary civil litigation in the Court of Session. Two applications for judicial review of decisions on the rights of homeless persons focused attention on these difficulties.[6] In both cases, Lord Fraser of Tullybelton suggested that there might be advantages in developing special procedures for cases raising questions of public law analogous to those which had been developed in England. This led to the setting-up of a committee chaired by Lord Dunpark which recommended the adoption of a simple form of procedure for judicial review.[7] The proposals were implemented (albeit with significant departures from the committee's recommendations) with effect from 30 April 1985 by adding a new rule of court, rule 260B. Following consolidation of the Rules, the procedure is now contained in Chapter 58 of the Rules of Court.

The procedure is relatively simple and straightforward and gives the judges significant discretion. Although inspired by the example of the English judicial review procedure, there are a number of departures from the English model which operates under Part 8 (as modified by Part 54) of the Civil Procedure Rules.[8] First, it was made clear that the new judicial review procedure was the only competent procedure for cases invoking the supervisory jurisdiction, a point on which the English procedure was silent and which provoked a great deal of litigation.[9] Second, there is no time-limit – the English procedure requires an application to be brought within three months – although an applicant may be treated as personally barred from suing for undue delay in seeking judicial review.[10] Third, there is no presumption, as there is in England and Wales, that judicial review is unsuitable for resolving disputes of fact. So, examination and cross-examination of witnesses will be permitted where that is necessary to resolve disputes of fact.[11] Fourth, and perhaps most significant, there is no requirement in Scotland to apply to the court for permission to seek judicial review.

Research has suggested that the introduction of the special procedure did substantially speed up the process of judicial review.[12] It is also clear that there has been a dramatic and sustained increase in the number of petitions for judicial review lodged, as compared to the period before its introduction. Sixty-six petitions were lodged in 1988, 117 in 1992 and since then the number has never dropped below 100 and in several years has exceeded 150.[13] The three largest categories in

---

5 A Page in M Adler and A Millar (eds), *Socio-Legal Research in the Scottish Courts*, vol 2 (1991).
6 *Brown v Hamilton District Council* 1983 SC (HL) 1; *Stevenson v Midlothian District Council* 1983 SLT 433.
7 *Report to Rt Hon Lord Emslie, Lord President of the Court of Session by the Working Party on Procedure for Judicial Review of Administrative Action* (1984).
8 These procedures replaced Order 53.
9 Beginning with *O'Reilly v Mackman* [1983] 2 AC 237. See Craig, *Administrative Law*, ch 23.
10 *Hanlon v Traffic Commissioners* 1988 SLT 802.
11 *Walker v Strathclyde Regional Council (No 2)* 1987 SLT 81.
12 T Mullen, K Pick and T Prosser, *Judicial Review in Scotland* (1996).
13 Mullen et al, above n 12 and successive *Civil Judicial Statistics*. Civil Judicial Statistics Scotland 2002, available at *http://www.Scotland.gov.uk/library5/justice/cjs02-02.asp#t210*.

the period covered by the research (1988–93) were immigration control, housing (especially homelessness) and licensing (especially liquor licensing) accounting for 60 per cent of all cases in 1988–93.[14] Subsequent civil judicial statistics suggest that immigration control has remained the largest category although it is clear that the composition of that category has changed and it has in recent years been dominated by asylum cases. Housing has generally continued to be the second largest category, albeit not as prominent as in 1988–93, and the proportion of the case load made up by licensing cases has fluctuated.

The specialised procedure for judicial review has been a largely successful innovation. The process has been considerably speeded up and as a consequence, legal costs have been reduced, consciousness of judicial review as a means of challenging administrative decisions has been raised, and the procedural reforms have not, as in England and Wales, created any new obstacles for litigants to surmount.[15] There remain concerns about access to justice both in terms of the availability of legal aid for funding cases and of the availability of knowledge and expertise. However, the special procedure for judicial review does not cause or contribute to these problems.

There are, therefore, grounds for concluding that the procedures and remedies available provide a reasonably effective means of bringing challenges to the legality of administrative action before the courts, at least relative to other procedures in the ordinary courts. There is room for argument about the effectiveness of judicial review in comparison to other means of challenge such as appeals to specialist tribunals and complaints to ombudsmen but that is an issue beyond the scope of this chapter.

The position with regard to the remaining ancillary issue – that of standing to sue (*locus standi*) – is less satisfactory. Here, a comparison between Scots law and the common law jurisdictions shows Scots law in a poorer light, largely because of the excessively narrow approach it continues to take to this issue, compared to the more liberal approach now adopted in England and elsewhere. The issue of standing is concerned with who is the appropriate person to bring a case before the courts. It does not follow from the fact that an administrative decision or action is arguably illegal, that anyone and everyone is entitled to take legal action to have the question of its legality decided. The traditional Scots law terminology for dealing with the issue of standing is that of title and interest to sue.

It is important to distinguish standing in this narrow sense from two other issues which may be raised using the language of title and interest to sue. The first is that of 'ripeness' for review (whether the question raised is clearly focused, and neither hypothetical nor premature). The second is that of justiciability: whether an issue is suitable for resolution by the courts at all.[16] This chapter is concerned with standing in the narrow sense of the term, and the questions of whether there is a real issue to decide and of justiciability will be considered only in so far as they have a bearing on standing in that sense.

---

14 Mullen et al, above n 12, pp 17–22.
15 Mullen et al, above n 12, ch 8.
16 See, eg, *MacCormick v Lord Advocate* 1953 SC 396 in which Lord Cooper suggested that the question whether an alteration of a particular aspect of Scots private law was 'for the evident utility' of the subjects within Scotland was not a justiciable issue, being essentially a political question.

The requirement of having title and interest to sue applies in civil proceedings generally, but in disputes between private parties questions of title and interest rarely arise as issues distinct from the merits. The person or range of persons who may sue is generally clear from the nature of the right which is being asserted or denied. It is, therefore, rare to find an action being raised or defended by someone who is arguably the wrong person. Questions of standing arise more frequently in the context of administrative law where the link between unlawful administrative action and the range of persons who may complain of it is sometimes less clear.

Legislation sometimes settles the question of who may challenge a particular act or decision, most obviously when rights of appeal are created, and in these cases judicial review may be excluded by the principle of exhaustion of remedies whereby a litigant is expected to use any statutory remedies that are available rather than seeking judicial review,[17] but Parliament frequently legislates without directly addressing the question of who may sue for acts and decisions which are unlawful in terms of that legislation, leaving the courts to decide who is to be permitted to sue.

In analysing and evaluating rules of standing it is important to make a distinction between, on the one hand, cases in which the litigant has a specific personal interest in the outcome of the litigation and, on the other, cases in which the litigant is seeking to assert the interests of other identifiable individuals or the public interest ('representative standing'). It is important to have standing rules which are appropriate for both sorts of litigants. Cane[18] has made a useful distinction between three different types of representative standing: 'associational standing', 'public interest standing' and 'surrogate standing'. Associational standing refers to the situation in which a body or group, which may or may not be incorporated, raises an action on behalf of identifiable persons who are its members or whom it otherwise claims to represent, for example, a trade union suing on behalf of a particular group of workers over some aspect of their employment conditions. Public interest standing refers to the situation in which an individual or group seeks to represent the interests of the whole public or a section of it rather than identified or identifiable individuals. Surrogate standing refers to the situation in which one person is the nominal pursuer/petitioner but represents the interests of another who may be regarded as the real applicant.

This chapter will first explain the Scots law of standing to seek judicial review (with reference to the distinctions just made) and then evaluate it. Cane's third category, surrogate standing, will not be discussed separately as there are few, if any, Scottish administrative law cases falling into this category.

TITLE AND INTEREST TO SUE: GENERAL

The classic exposition of the law of standing is contained in the speech of Lord Dunedin in *D & J Nicol v Dundee Harbour Trustees*,[19] a case in which harbour trustees were authorised by statute to operate ferry services on the River Tay. The House of Lords held that this activity was ultra vires as the use of the ships for pleasure cruises could not be regarded as reasonably incidental to the purpose

---

17 The principle is not absolute: see 'Administrative Law' in *Stair Memorial Encyclopaedia*, vol 1 (Reissue, 2000), para 118.
18 P Cane, 'Standing up for the public' [1995] PL 276.
19 1915 SC (HL) 7.

specifically authorised in the statute, namely running a ferry service. In defending the action, the harbour trustees had argued that the pursuers had no title to sue. In considering this plea, Lord Dunedin began by emphasising that title and interest are distinct and separate requirements and both must be established in order to permit a litigant to sue. He went on to say:

> 'By the law of Scotland a litigant, and in particular a pursuer, must always qualify title and interest. Though the phrase "title to sue" has been a heading under which cases have been collected from at least the time of Morison's Dictionary and Brown's Synopsis I am not aware that anyone of authority has risked a definition of what constitutes title and interest to sue. I am not disposed to do so, but I think it may fairly be said that for a person to have such a title he must be a party (using the word in its widest sense) to some legal relation, which gives him some right which the person against whom he raises the action either infringes or denies.'[20]

He then gives a number of examples including a suit brought by the owner of property to vindicate his ownership of it, a suit brought by one party to a contract to compel the other party to perform it, and a suit brought by a beneficiary against a trustee. The third example extended to cases in which persons were not technically trustees but did owe a fiduciary duty to others. In such cases the latter could sue the former for breach of the fiduciary duty such as wrong-dealing with the property. *Nicol* was an example of this third category. The pursuers had title to sue in their capacity as harbour ratepayers. Importantly, they did *not* have title to sue in their capacity as rival traders (all being operators of pleasure cruise boats in the area). Such a capacity gave them interest, but not title to sue.

Although Lord Dunedin disclaimed any intention to lay down a definition, this dictum has been highly influential and frequently referred to in later cases. As expressed by Lord Dunedin, the relationship between the party suing and the party being sued is essentially one of legal form. The examples he gives are all well-established relationships giving rise to rights and duties in private law. Even though the relationship between the parties in *Nicol* was created by statute it was viewed as a traditional private law relationship.

The best known dicta relating to interest to sue are those of Lord Ardwall in *Swanson v Manson*[21] who said[22] that the law courts, 'are not instituted for the purpose of deciding academic questions of law, but for settling disputes where any of the lieges has a real interest to have a question determined which involves his pecuniary rights or his status' and that, 'no person is entitled to subject another to the trouble and expense of litigation unless he has some real interest to enforce or protect'.

Taking the dicta in *D & J Nicol* and *Swanson v Manson* together it can be observed that early in the twentieth century the Court of Session was prepared to grant or withhold standing on the assumption that the function of the courts is to resolve disputes (a) which involve the rights of individuals, and (b) where the outcome will materially affect the interests of one of the parties to the case. When applied in the context of administrative law, this may be called the private rights model of judicial review.

---

20 1915 SC (HL) at 12.
21 1907 SC 426.
22 At 429.

To summarise, title and interest to sue are preliminary questions which should, in principle, be distinguished from the merits of the case and they are distinct requirements. A potential litigant must have both in order to be permitted to sue. A person may have title but no interest, or have an interest but no title to sue. This may be contrasted with the position in England where the test for standing to seek judicial review is that 'the applicant has a sufficient interest in the matter to which the application relates',[23] no distinction being made between title and interest.

Having explained the general approach of the Court of Session to title and interest we can now consider its application in different contexts, considering first cases in which litigants seek to vindicate personal interests and then cases of representative standing.

PERSONAL INTEREST

The law in Scotland has developed to a stage where a person who has a particular personal interest in a matter (using the word interest in a non-technical sense) will normally be accepted as having standing to seek judicial review. A decision directly addressed to a person, such as a decision to revoke a licence, will invariably confer title and interest to sue. Even when the decision is not directly addressed to a person, where there is a real personal interest, title and interest will generally be recognised. Several such cases have concerned commercial interests. For example, meat importers, dealers and fleshers had title and interest to challenge the validity of a byelaw restricting the holding of meat auctions at a public market,[24] an ice-cream seller had title and interest to challenge conditions imposed in licences for the sale of ice cream[25] and an airline was permitted to challenge air traffic distribution rules which directed them to a particular airport which was less convenient for the airline and many of its customers.[26] Other cases have concerned professional interests, for example, where schoolteachers had title and interest to seek a declarator that a statutory consultative council intended to be representative of all teachers was not properly constituted.[27] In many of these cases, in order to arrive at a conclusion on the issue of title and interest, the court examined the statutory scheme in some detail but in others the conclusion that title and interest existed appeared to follow simply from the fact that the person was adversely affected by the decision. For example, in *Rossi v Edinburgh Magistrates*, Lord Robertson commented, 'his title is his trade'.[28]

However, the courts have not been entirely consistent, and there are examples of a stricter approach being taken from time to time. In *D & J Nicol* it was held that a trader had no title to protect his business from unlawful competition by a public authority. This was an example of interest without title. This did not prevent D & J Nicol suing as they had title to sue as harbour ratepayers, but where there is only

---

23 Supreme Court Act 1981, s 31(3).
24 *Scott v Glasgow Corporation* (1899) 1 F (HL) 51.
25 *Rossi v Edinburgh Magistrates* (1904) 7 F (HL) 85.
26 *Air 2000 Ltd v Secretary of State for Transport* 1989 SLT 698; *Air 2000 Ltd v Secretary of State for Transport (No 2)* 1990 SLT 335.
27 *Cannon v Secretary of State for Scotland* 1964 SLT 91.
28 (1904) 7 F (HL) at 90.

the relationship of trade competitor it is assumed, on the authority of *Nicol*, that there is no title to sue.[29]

Trade competitors were also excluded in the more recent case of *PTOA Ltd v Renfrew District Council*.[30] Although Lord Dawson's judgment does not expressly categorise the petitioners as trade competitors, he did base his decision on the general dicta of Lord Dunedin quoted above. An association of taxi drivers sought judicial review of a decision to grant taxi licences to taxi drivers from outside the area of the licensing authority. Lord Dawson held that the association would have had a legal interest to sue as the livelihood of its members could well have been affected but that it had no title to sue as there was no legal relationship of the appropriate type between them and the licensing authority.

This decision may be contrasted with the decision in *City Cabs (Edinburgh) Ltd v City of Edinburgh District Council*[31] in which a taxi operators' association successfully challenged a decision of a licensing authority to increase the number of licences available in their area. On the face of it this case is very similar to the Renfrew case. The petitioners were of the same type, the statutory scheme of regulation was the same, both were challenges to a policy decision by the licensing authority and both actions were raised to protect commercial interests. However, the question of title and interest was not argued in the Edinburgh case.

Simpson v Edinburgh Corporation[32] provides a good example of a restrictive approach being taken in cases concerning non-commercial interests. The University of Edinburgh obtained planning permission to demolish two sides of a square in order to allow the construction of modern buildings. The pursuer, who owned a dwellinghouse in the square, attempted to challenge the decision to grant planning permission as ultra vires on the ground that it was contrary to the city's development plan. The pursuer averred that the square in its existing form was one of character, architectural interest and strong historical associations, and that the proposed developments would destroy the character of the square and adversely affect the amenity of his house. Lord Guest held that the pursuer had no title to sue as the legislation concerned regulated the development of land, and was primarily concerned to protect the interests of the public, and was not intended to confer a right of action on interested neighbours. However, if similar facts arose today, the court's answer might well be different given the developments which have taken place in planning legislation and practice which have extended third-party rights in the planning process, and the possibility of referring to more recent decisions of the English courts which have given a more expansive definition to the phrase 'person aggrieved' (the test used in legislation in both jurisdictions to determine who is entitled to challenge planning decisions in court).[33]

So, although a person with a genuine interest in the outcome of litigation will normally be treated as having title and interest to sue, there are examples of a more restrictive approach, and in particular it has been assumed in some cases (if not in all cases) that a trading interest is not by itself sufficient to give title to

---

29 *Clyde Steam Packet Co v Glasgow and South-Western Railway Co* (1897) 4 SLT 327; *Stair Memorial Encyclopaedia*, above n 17, para 125.
30 1997 SLT 112.
31 1988 SLT 184.
32 1960 SC 313.
33 It has also been argued that relevant authority was not cited in *Simpson*: see *Stair Memorial Encyclopaedia*, above n 17, para 118.

sue. There is some evidence to suggest that the law on title and interest is not a major problem in practice. Research by Page[34] and by Mullen, Pick and Prosser[35] which reviewed unreported as well as reported cases suggested that in recent years title and interest have not often been an obstacle to litigants with points of standing rarely being raised and, if raised, frequently not pressed. However, it is arguable that the generally relaxed approach merely highlights the injustice to those litigants who are denied access to judicial review on the grounds that they lack standing.

REPRESENTATIVE STANDING

Associational standing

As indicated above 'associational standing' refers to the situation in which an organisation sues on behalf of its members or other identifiable individuals whom it claims to represent. There have been several examples of this in the Scottish cases. In *Association of Optical Practitioners Ltd v Secretary of State for Scotland*[36] the association's title and interest to challenge a decision fixing opticians' fees on behalf of its members was not challenged. In *Educational Institute of Scotland v Robert Gordon University*[37] a teaching union attempted to challenge on behalf of its members new conditions of service being imposed by a university on its teaching staff. On the issue of standing, Lord Milligan said:

> 'Where, as here, a trade union is able to allege that among its members are persons who are likely to be adversely affected by an ultra vires decision of the respondents and that it is unrealistic for such members individually, both on timetabling and prospects of acceptance grounds, to challenge the decision individually, it seems to me that the trade union has not only an interest to challenge the decision but also title to do so.'

The approach taken here is essentially pragmatic: the members (who are assumed to have title and interest to sue) might find it difficult to sue themselves, hence it is reasonable to allow the union to sue on their behalf. Lord Milligan also observed that there was a strong case for recognising title to sue where the decision complained of had not yet affected some of the members of the organisation.

Lord Milligan's opinion in the *Robert Gordon* case followed comments by Lord Clyde in the *Scottish Old People's Welfare Council* case that he could 'see no reason in principle ... why, simply because a group of members of the public combine to sue where each could do so as an individual, the mere fact of their combining together into an association should deprive them of a title'.[38]

It is, therefore, clear that the Scottish courts are, in principle, receptive to claims of associational standing (although the term itself has not been used in any reported case). The most obvious limitation of representative standing appears to be that it is essentially derivative: the members of the association must themselves have title and interest to sue. It is also worth noting that an unincorporated association

34 Above n 5, p 58.
35 Above n 12, pp 52–54.
36 Court of Session, 10 Dec 1985 (unreported).
37 Court of Session, *The Times*, 11 July 1996.
38 *Scottish Old People's Welfare Council, Petitioners* 1987 SLT 179 at 185.

having no separate legal persona must in general sue through office-bearers or other authorised representatives.[39]

Public interest standing

As indicated above, 'public interest standing' refers to the situation in which an individual or group seeks to represent the general public or a section of it. It can be distinguished from 'associational standing' by the fact that there is no membership link, and it is the whole public rather than a specific group which is being represented.

Before discussing cases in which litigants have attempted to assert public interest standing it is useful to dispose of one potentially confusing issue, that of the *actio populuaris*. There is a specified class of rights in Scots law known as public rights. Any person who is within the class of person entitled to enjoy the right has title and interest to enforce it in the courts.[40] The class of public rights that may be enforced in this way includes the right to use the foreshore, public rights of way, public rights to use land for recreation, or as a bleaching green, public rights of pasturage, public rights of navigation and the right to use a public market. The type of action used to vindicate such a right is referred to as an *actio popularis*, and the court's decision on the issues disputed in such cases will be treated as *res judicata* against all other members of the public preventing the same issues being raised in any future litigation. The doctrine of public rights is of little practical value in the context of the supervisory jurisdiction. The doctrine only applies to a limited range of specific rights including those described above. The rights arise at common law and are public in the sense that they are enjoyed by all members of the relevant public in common. They are not specifically rights against government or the broader range of bodies subject to the supervisory jurisdiction, and any interference with such a right is just as likely to come from a private party as from a public body. The *actio popularis* will, therefore, not generally be available to persons and groups seeking to challenge on behalf of the public the unlawful exercise of statutory powers by public bodies.[41]

The most expansive approach to public interest standing to date in a Scottish case was arguably that taken by Lord Ross in *Wilson v Independent Broadcasting Authority*.[42] The case arose from the devolution referendum of 1979. The IBA allocated party political broadcasts for the period leading up to the referendum so that each of the four Scottish parliamentary political parties had one broadcast. The effect of this would be that three of the four programmes broadcast would be in favour of a 'Yes' vote. Lord Ross granted an interim interdict to prevent the broadcasts going ahead on the basis that the respondents were prima facie in breach of their duty under section 2(2)(b) of the Independent Broadcasting Act 1973 to ensure a proper balance was maintained in the programmes broadcast. Broadcasts before a referendum at which the electorate was being invited to answer a question 'Yes' or 'No' could not be treated as if they were ordinary party political broadcasts.

---

39 *Renton Football Club v McDowall* (1891) 18 R 670.
40 *Stair Memorial Encyclopaedia*, above n 17, para 123.
41 Examples of where an action may arise from the improper exercise of statutory powers or failure to perform statutory duties include cases of obstruction of, or interference with, public rights of passage: *Stair Memorial Encyclopaedia*, above n 17, para 123.
42 1979 SC 351.

The petitioners described themselves as chairman and vice-chairman of the 'Labour Vote No Committee' a group opposed to the official Labour party policy of campaigning for a 'Yes' vote. Lord Ross implicitly distinguished title from interest. Having said that he regarded it as significant that Parliament had imposed duties on the respondents but not provided specific remedies for breach, he went on to say:

> 'In Scotland, I see no reason in principle why an individual should not sue in order to prevent a breach by a public body of a duty owed by that public body to the public. It may well be that the Lord Advocate could be a petitioner if the interests of the public as a whole were affected ... but I see no reason why an individual should not sue provided always that the individual can qualify an interest.'[43]

Sufficient interest arose from the fact that the petitioners were entitled to vote in the referendum, and that they belonged to an organisation campaigning for a 'No' vote.

It is not clear whether Lord Ross intended to make a firm distinction between title and interest and, therefore, whether the first sentence in the quotation should be read as referring to title to sue only but that does seem to have been the intention. The point was addressed again in *Scottish Old People's Welfare Council, Petitioners* (the 'Age Concern' case).[44] The petitioners sought to challenge the legality of a circular issued by the Chief Adjudication Officer concerning the making of cold weather payments under social security legislation. The substantive argument made by the petitioners was that certain instructions in the circular which restricted the circumstances in which cold weather heating payments could be made were erroneous in law and ultra vires. The petitioners were a voluntary association, better known as Age Concern Scotland, whose objects included the promotion of the interests of old people in Scotland.

Lord Clyde considered that the association had title to sue on the basis that the duties imposed by the legislation were owed to the public:[45]

> 'The purpose of legislation is to make state benefit available to any member of the public who may qualify for it and it is not unreasonable to see the duty of the proper administration of the legislation as a duty owed to the public. On that basis it can be concluded that any member of the public has at least a title to sue and the only remaining question would be whether he had an interest to do so.'

As indicated above, the association's title rested on the fact that its members each had title to sue and that their combining to litigate should not make a difference. Ultimately, however, the petitioners lacked the necessary standing because they lacked a sufficient interest.[46]

> 'It is not said that the association or any of its members have claimed the benefit in question or are attempting to do so. Indeed while some of them members may be in a position to claim it is certainly not evident that all the members are potential claimants. The petitioners are not suing as a body of potential claimants but as a body working to protect and advance the interests of the aged. Their purpose in the present

---

43 1979 SC at 356–357.
44 1987 SLT 179.
45 1987 SLT at 185.
46 1987 SLT at 187.

context is not to claim benefit for themselves or their members but to secure that
benefit is available in all cases where they believe it is deserved.'

Taken in isolation these remarks might seem to be a straightforward rejection of the
notion of pure public interest, as opposed to associational, standing, but Lord Clyde
went on to stress that the implementation of the circular lay wholly in the future,
that no claims had yet been submitted following the circular, and that it was not yet
clear how far, if at all, the advice contained in the circular would be followed. So the
question of who was an appropriate person to sue was arguably bound up with the
question whether the substantive issues raised by the petition were too hypothetical
and remote.

Nonetheless, the Age Concern case clearly suggested that pressure groups and
individuals would find it difficult to establish standing to seek judicial review in
Scotland in cases where neither the individual nor a member of the group had a
personal interest greater than that of any other person in the outcome.

Any lingering doubts that Scots law was not particularly receptive to the idea
of public interest standing were dispelled by the Mike Tyson case, *Rape Crisis
Centre v Secretary of State for the Home Department*.[47] Mike Tyson, a former World
Heavyweight Boxing champion who had a conviction for rape in the United
States, applied for leave to enter the UK to take part in a boxing match. Amidst
great public controversy, the Home Secretary decided to grant entry clearance in
accordance with rule 320(18) of the Immigration Rules[48] having previously met
representatives of the boxer. That rule stated that a person who had a conviction
for a serious offence would not normally be admitted to the UK unless there were
strong compassionate reasons. Clearly, the proviso did not apply, but the Secretary
of State exercised the residual discretion which he possessed under the Immigration
Rules to admit Tyson. The petitioners challenged the decision on procedural rather
than substantive grounds, arguing that the Secretary of State ought to have called
for representations from interested members of the public. Lord Clarke held that
there was no procedural impropriety. More importantly for present purposes, he
also held that the petitioners had no title to sue. He thought that had there been
title, the petitioners would have had interest, so the petitioners' inability to bring
the case was based on title alone. Lord Clarke quoted Lord Dunedin's dictum from
D & J Nicol and then said that: '[i]t is a fallacy to suppose that because of the public
interest in ministers acting lawfully and fairly that public interest *by itself* confers on
every member of public a right to challenge a minister's act or decision'.[49]

The person or body seeking to challenge the decision must show that, having
regard to the scope and purpose of the legislation, or measures under which the act
is performed, or the decision is made, he or they have such a right conferred upon
them by law, either expressly or impliedly. The scope and function of the legislation
and the Immigration Rules did not provide a legal nexus between the petitioners
and the Secretary of State when he was exercising his discretion under them.

Lord Clarke also quoted the expansive dicta of Lords Ross and Clyde from the
Wilson and Age Concern cases, and indicated that he did not regard these cases as
contradicting the test for title to sue that he had formulated. It appears, therefore,
that for him the distinction between these cases and the case before him was to

47 2002 SLT 389.
48 HC 395, 1994–95.
49 2002 SLT 389 at 394.

be found in the scope and purpose of the legislation. Whereas it was possible to interpret the broadcasting legislation and the supplementary benefits legislation as creating duties owed to the general public, it was not possible to interpret the immigration legislation in this way.

Public interest standing in England

A much more liberal approach has been taken to public interest standing in England where both pressure groups and public bodies have been permitted to seek judicial review to protect the public interest. Standing in judicial review cases in England has a general statutory basis in section 31(3) of the Supreme Court Act 1981 which states that the court shall not grant leave to make an application for judicial review unless it considers that the applicant 'has a sufficient interest in the matter to which the application relates'. This general test replaced the separate tests previously employed in relation to different remedies.

The decision of the House of Lords in *IRC v National Federation of Self-Employed and Small Businesses Ltd*[50] gave a clear signal that the test of 'sufficient interest' was to be liberally interpreted. The Federation wished to challenge a tax amnesty that the Inland Revenue had negotiated with certain trade unions. Although the House of Lords did not recognise the Federation as having sufficient interest, Lord Diplock in the course of his speech made these comments:

> 'It would in my view be a grave lacuna in our system of public law if a pressure group, like the federation, or even a single public-spirited taxpayer, were prevented by outdated technical rules of *locus standi* from bringing the matter to the attention of the court to vindicate the rule of law and get the unlawful conduct stopped.'

That is precisely the approach that the English courts subsequently took. Both public-spirited individuals and pressure groups were permitted to seek judicial review of alleged illegalities in which the applicants had no specific personal interest. As regards individuals, in *R v Felixstowe Justices, ex parte Leigh*[51] a journalist was given standing to challenge a decision of local justices that they should have anonymity in reports of proceedings, and in *R v Secretary of State for Foreign and Commonwealth Affairs, ex parte Rees-Mogg*[52] a member of the House of Lords was given standing to challenge the government's decision to ratify the Maastricht Treaty establishing the European Union.

As for pressure groups, in *R v Inspectorate of Pollution, ex parte Greenpeace (No 2)*[53] Greenpeace was given standing to challenge the decision to permit the development of a new thermal oxide reprocessing plant at Sellafield on the basis that it was an entirely responsible and respected body with a genuine concern for the environment, and that it had 2,500 supporters in the Cumbria region.[54]

50 [1982] AC 617.
51 [1987] QB 582.
52 [1994] QB 552.
53 [1994] 4 All ER 329.
54 The fact that it had 400,000 supporters in the UK as a whole carried less weight. The case also indicates that the categories of associational and representative standing may overlap. However, this does not seem to be a case of pure associational standing as the court's decision to grant standing was not based solely on the fact that Greenpeace claimed to represent the interests of its members, but also on the seriousness and complexity of the issues, the organisation's expertise and the fact that otherwise there might be no effective way of getting the matter into court.

The high watermark of pressure group standing was achieved in *R v Secretary of State for Foreign and Commonwealth Affairs, ex parte World Development Movement Ltd*[55] in which a decision of the Foreign Secretary to grant aid to the Malaysian Government under section 1(1) of the Overseas Development and Cooperation Act 1980 to help finance the construction of the Pergau dam was successfully challenged on the ground that aid was not given for the purpose of 'promoting development' as required by the Act. The pressure group had neither members who were directly affected by the action nor indeed any members in Malaysia, so the case was as pure an example of 'citizen standing' as one would expect to find. The factors that were important in granting standing were, according to Rose LJ, the importance of vindicating the rule of law, the importance of the issue raised, the likely absence of any other responsible challenger, the nature of the breach of duty against which relief was sought and the prominent role of the applicants in giving advice, guidance and assistance with regard to development aid.

The most prominent exception to the trend of liberalising standing is *R v Secretary of State for the Environment, ex parte Rose Theatre Trust*.[56] An historic theatre was discovered in central London when a site was being developed. A trust company set up to preserve the theatre sought judicial review to challenge the Secretary of State's refusal to list the site as an ancient monument under section 1 of the Ancient Monuments and Archaeological Areas Act 1979. Mr Justice Schiemann held that a decision not to list an ancient monument was one of those governmental decisions in respect of which the ordinary citizen does not have sufficient interest to seek judicial review, and that merely by combining together a group of persons could not acquire any greater interest than they possessed as individuals. However, this seems to be an isolated example of a stricter approach in the light of subsequent decisions such as those in the Greenpeace and Pergau dam cases.

Another strand of the more liberal approach to standing taken in England is evident in relation to the ability of statutory bodies to litigate on behalf of the public. In *R v Secretary of State for Employment, ex parte Equal Opportunities Commission and Day*[57] the House of Lords granted declarations that the statutory limitations on the employment rights of workers which distinguished between part-time and full-time workers were unlawful because they indirectly discriminated against women contrary to EC anti-discrimination law. The EOC had sufficient interest to bring proceedings. Lord Keith commented:

> '[i]n my opinion it would be a very retrograde step now to hold that the EOC has no *locus standi* to agitate in judicial review proceedings questions related to sex discrimination which are of public importance and affect a large section of the population'.[58]

A more liberal approach to standing has also been taken in the United States[59] and in several Commonwealth jurisdictions in recent decades conferring on public-spirited individuals and pressure groups the right to litigate on matters of

---

55 [1995] 1 All ER 611.
56 [1990] 1 QB 594.
57 [1995] 1 AC 1.
58 [1995] 1 AC at 26.
59 See, eg, *Association of Data Processing Services v Camp* 397 US 150 (1970); *Flast v Cohen* 392 US 83 (1968) and *United States v SCRAP* 412 US 669 (1973).

public concern. So, the distinctiveness of the Scots law of standing with regard to representative standing lies not only in the distinction which it continues to maintain between title to sue and interest to sue (which applies equally to cases of personal interest), but also in a generally stricter approach to recognising standing where individuals and groups are seeking to vindicate the public interest.

HUMAN RIGHTS AND DEVOLUTION

Before evaluating the Scots position it is appropriate to consider the special rules of standing that have been introduced for certain constitutional issues arising under the Human Rights Act 1998 and the Scotland Act 1998. The Human Rights Act allows the rights protected by the European Convention for the Protection of Human Rights and Fundamental Freedoms ('Convention rights') to be used in legal argument in a variety of ways. Where a person's Convention rights have been violated by a public authority it will normally be possible to obtain a remedy from the UK courts. Section 7(1)(b) of the Human Rights Act states that a person who claims that a public authority has acted incompatibly with a Convention right may rely on the Convention right concerned in any legal proceedings. This permits human rights-based arguments to be raised in the course of a statutory appeal or in defence to any legal action raised by a public authority, and in many cases these will be the appropriate procedures for vindicating human rights claims. Section 7(1)(a) permits a person to bring proceedings against the authority in question in the appropriate court or tribunal. Therefore, where other remedies are not available, a person may challenge an alleged violation of Convention rights by way of a petition for judicial review. However, there is an important limitation in section 7. In either case the person must be a 'victim' of the unlawful act, and a person is a victim only if he would be regarded as a victim for the purposes of Article 34 of the Convention if proceedings were brought in the European Court of Human Rights. The ECtHR has interpreted this provision in such a way as to limit its use as a vehicle for either associational or public interest standing,[60] and UK courts are obliged to have regard to the Strasbourg case law (although they are not bound by it) by virtue of section 2 of the Human Rights Act. Standing under the Human Rights Act (which does not vary as between Scotland and the rest of the UK) may, therefore, be regarded as a continuation of the private rights model of standing.

The Scotland Act imposes on the Scottish Parliament and the Scottish Executive vires limitations which include but go far beyond Convention rights. It also makes provision for standing both in respect of human rights and challenges to vires generally. Section 100 was intended to align standing requirements for Convention rights challenges under the Scotland Act and the Human Rights Act and, therefore, repeats the victim test from Article 34.[61] Schedule 6 defines a range of questions relating to the vires of legislation and actions of the Scottish Executive as 'devolution issues' and states that proceedings for the determination of a devolution issue may be raised by the Lord Advocate, the Advocate General for Scotland, the Attorney-General or the Attorney-General for Northern Ireland

---

60 See J Miles in N Bamforth and P Leyland (eds), *Public Law in a Multi-layered Constitution* (2003).

61 An exception is made by subsection (2) for the law officers throughout the UK who may raise proceedings even where they are not victims.

depending on the jurisdiction in which the action is to be raised. This provision allows the law officers to raise an action for the express purpose of resolving an issue relating to vires. No provision is made for the standing rights of any other persons which means that the ability of these others to challenge decisions and actions of public authorities by way of judicial review in terms of the Scotland Act depends on the general rules of standing already outlined.

The enactment of human rights legislation has also led to changes in the rules of intervention. Prior to the Human Rights Act and the Scotland Act the Scottish courts had not developed a practice of permitting intervention in the public interest as had the courts in England and Wales.[62] However, following the Human Rights Act, the rules of court were amended to permit persons to seek leave to intervene in judicial review proceedings to address a matter of public interest raised by the proceedings.[63] So, individuals and pressure groups that lack standing to petition for judicial review may be able to intervene in proceedings raised by others.

PURPOSE OF STANDING RULES

In order to evaluate the existing Scottish rules the purpose(s) which is/are served by the restrictions on standing must first be considered, and the question of the purposes of standing cannot be separated from the more general question of the purposes of administrative law. The traditional answer to the question – exemplified in the dicta quoted above from *D & J Nicol* and *Swanson v Manson* – of what standing rules are for is that the purpose of the courts and legal process is to enable persons to assert and protect their legal rights. Therefore, the law should allow only those whose legal rights have been infringed to litigate. This is the private rights model of standing. Secondly, the courts should only be used when there is something at stake, that is, that the person raising the legal action stands to gain or lose by it. Importantly, this view of the function of the courts has not been restricted to disputes between private parties, but has been extended to cases involving public authorities, hence the rejection of claims on grounds of lack of title alone in *PTOA Ltd v Renfrew District Council* and in the Tyson case without adequate consideration of whether the circumstances of the former are comparable to those of the latter.

However, if we examine the purpose of litigation in the context of administrative law, the unsuitability of applying without qualification concepts derived from private law litigation becomes clear. What then is/are the purposes of administrative law? The orthodox view for most of the twentieth century was that the primary function of judicial review was to ensure the public bodies kept within the limits of the powers granted to them by Parliament.[64] The private rights model of judicial review described above is broadly compatible with this ultra vires model of judicial review since keeping public bodies within the limits of their powers ought to ensure that they do not interfere with individual rights, but it does not exhaust the possibilities of the ultra vires model. If public bodies have legal duties which are not owed to

---

62 For discussion of the relaxation of the rules on intervention, see C Harlow, 'Public law and popular justice' (2002) 65 MLR 1 and Miles, above n 60.

63 Act of Sederunt (Rules of Court of Session) (Amendment No 5) Public Interest Intervention in Judicial Review 2000 (SSI 2000/317).

64 See, eg, dicta of Lord Shaw in *Moss's Empires v Assessor for Glasgow* 1917 SC (HL) 1 at 11.

specific persons, or powers which may be exceeded without invading individual rights then the private rights model will not ensure that all unlawful public action is open to challenge. First, illegality which particularly affects specific individuals may go unchallenged because the individual's very real interest is not characterised as an enforceable legal right (as in *PTOA Ltd v Renfrew District Council*). Second, illegality which affects the public generally may go unchallenged because many statutory duties are owed to, and the exercise of many powers affects, either the public as a whole, or large sections of it, so there may well be no-one who has a greater interest than members of the public generally. If it is indeed the principal aim of administrative law to ensure that public bodies observe the limits of their powers, that suggests that any citizen should be able to assert the public interest in court without being required to show a personal special interest if the alternative is that in that context unlawful administrative action will go unchallenged for want of a specifically interested pursuer.

In England, at least in theory, these gaps could have been filled by the Attorney-General who was empowered to bring proceedings in the public interest, but in Scotland the Lord Advocate has not adopted a practice of bringing civil actions in the public interest.[65] In any event, there are serious difficulties with the notion of relying on a government minister to take legal action against a government department even if he might be expected to take action against other public bodies, and neither the Attorney-General nor the Lord Advocate has made a practice of litigating against central government. Even on the orthodox view of the purpose of administrative law – keeping public bodies within the limits of their powers – there is, therefore, a rationale for public interest standing.

Accordingly, the approach of the Scottish courts to standing is at odds with the orthodox view of the function of administrative law, a view which has been accepted by the courts themselves in cases such as *Moss's Empires* and *West v Secretary of State for Scotland*.[66] It is also increasingly out of step with by now well-established developments (which have been accepted by the Scottish courts) in the substantive grounds of judicial review. It has for some time been accepted that a person whose legitimate expectations have been defeated may seek judicial review. Legitimate expectations, by definition, are neither common law nor statutory rights. So, here the law has accepted that *interests* rather than rights are a legitimate basis for judicial review.

The orthodox view is not the only possible view of the functions of administrative law. More recently, alternative conceptions have emerged including that the purpose of administrative law is to establish standards of good administration[67] and to require administrators to follow them, or that it should function as a surrogate political process.[68] These conceptions both provide more far-reaching rationales for public interest standing. The former might suggest that standing be accorded to citizens whenever that is likely to contribute to improving standards of administration. The latter necessitates liberal rules of standing as advocates of this view suggest that the legal process can make up for deficiencies in the political

---

65 See Rt Hon Lord Clyde and D Edwards, *Judicial Review* (2000), para 10.31. The precise extent of the Lord Advocate's powers to litigate to assert the public interest are not entirely clear.

66 1992 SC 385.

67 See comments of Lord Donaldson MR in *R v Lancashire County Council, ex parte Huddleston* [1986] 2 All ER 941 and Chapter 11 above.

68 R Stewart, 'The reformation of American administrative law' (1975) 88 Harv LR 1669.

process, providing legal accountability where political accountability is lacking. The legal process can hardly do that if access to it is impeded by restrictive rules of standing.

As the argument above indicates, it is not necessary to posit alternative views of the functions of judicial review to support arguments for widening standing beyond traditional limits as the case for widening standing can easily be accommodated within the traditional view, but it is certainly worth noting that all three conceptions of the functions of judicial review converge on the need for relatively liberal standing rules. One alternative conception of the functions of administrative law which might support a *restrictive* approach to standing is that advanced by Allan in which judicial review is principally concerned with the protection of individual rights. Allan has argued[69] that cases such as the Pergau dam case and the Fire Brigades Union[70] case are not appropriate exercises of judicial review because no individual rights were at stake. However, this approach seems to give too little weight to the value of ensuring that government acts in accordance with law, and it is not clear that there are alternative and *effective* means of securing respect for legality in such cases.

Enough has been said to indicate that liberalisation of the rules of standing may be supported from a variety of perspectives on the purpose of judicial review. It would be preferable for Scots law to fall into line with the rest of the UK and apply a test of 'sufficient interest' in order to determine access to judicial review. Such a test would have two strands along the lines of a proposal made by the Law Commission in 1994 which in fact reflects the current approach of the English courts.[71] A person who is adversely affected by an administrative act or decision would automatically be entitled to sue, whilst for cases in which no-one had a personal stake the test would be whether it is in the public interest for the petition to be made. There is nothing worth keeping in what are currently distinctive Scottish aspects of the law of standing. The truth is that the most distinctive aspect – the separation of title and interest – serves no useful function. First, the requirement to show title is not necessary for the purpose of distinguishing between the frivolous litigant and those with a serious interest in the outcome of litigation: the requirement of interest is perfectly capable of performing that function on its own. Second, as we have seen, the requirement to show title may exclude those who have a substantial personal interest in challenging illegal acts, such as trade competitors. Third, it adds confusion because litigants are not able to predict when lack of title will be successfully argued against them. And finally, the separation of title from interest causes particular confusion in the context of public interest standing because public interest petitioners are told in some cases that they have title but lack interest, but in others they have interest but lack title, with the reasons for the difference not being clear.

Thus far, the Scottish courts have shown themselves reluctant to develop the law in this area. However, this may be partly a function of the fact that nearly all of the cases in the last two decades have been Outer House decisions, so the Inner House has not had a recent opportunity to address the issues.[72] However, a relatively low

---

69 *Constitutional Justice* (2001), pp 172–173.
70 *R v Secretary of State for the Home Department, ex parte Fire Brigades Union* [1995] AC 513.
71 Law Commission, *Administrative Law: Judicial Review and Statutory Appeals* (Law Com no 226, 1994), para 5.22.
72 *Adams v Scottish Ministers* 2004 SC 665 concerned the somewhat restrictive 'victim' test in Scotland Act, s 100(1).

number of appeals reaching the Inner House has been a consistent feature of judicial review in Scotland since the introduction of judicial review procedure in 1985, so perhaps the time has come for the Scottish Parliament to legislate on the subject.

It is appropriate to consider possible objections to the proposal that Scots law should adopt a 'sufficient interest' test for standing. It is hard to see what the objection would be in the context of cases in which the litigant has a specific personal interest. In principle, a person materially affected by unlawful administrative action ought to be able to seek judicial review. In practice, a standing point is rarely pressed in such cases and no adverse consequences seem to follow. There is perhaps more room for argument if it is assumed that adoption of a sufficient interest test will result in a broadening of standing to allow public-spirited citizens to assert the public interest. There are a number of objections to the notion that individuals and pressure groups should be permitted to litigate to advance the general public interest where no persons are specially affected, which may be summarised as follows:[73]

1. Relaxing rules of standing to permit a citizen action will result in a flood of unnecessary litigation brought by cranks and busybodies.
2. Strict rules of standing are necessary to conserve scarce judicial resources which should be used for real rather than hypothetical disputes.
3. An undue burden will be placed on the Executive by the need to defend litigation.
4. There is a risk of cases being inadequately presented by parties with no real interest in the outcome.
5. Relaxing standing will result in cases being brought before the courts in abstract or hypothetical form which may force the courts to make unwise decisions.

The first objection has long been considered a weak one by academic writers.[74] There is little empirical evidence to suggest that there are large numbers of persons prepared to litigate for frivolous reasons and there are strong disincentives to engaging in *any* litigation, most obviously the high cost of going to court, which includes the possibility of having to pay the other side's legal costs in the event of failure. If it is felt that there is a need for additional protection against frivolous litigation then the rules on costs can be adjusted.

If it is accepted that the adjusted numbers of additional judicial review cases which will result from relaxed rules of standing are likely to be small that helps to dispose of the second objection: the need to conserve scarce judicial resources. The evidence from England is that, despite the evident relaxation in standing which has occurred there, the vast majority of cases continue to be brought by individuals (and corporations) with a personal stake in the outcome.[75]

As to the third objection, it may be said that all litigation against government imposes a burden on it with possible adverse consequences of additional cost to the taxpayer and diversion of officials from their primary tasks of carrying out their functions. Where the pursuer is specifically affected by the decision challenged, and the claim is upheld by the courts then society considers this a price worth

73 See P Hogg, *Constitutional Law of Canada* (3rd edn, 1992), Section 6.2 and Craig, *Administrative Law*, pp 743–748.
74 K Scott, 'Standing in the Supreme Court – a functional analysis' (1973) 86 Harv LR 645.
75 L Bridges, G Meszaros and M Sunkin, *Judicial Review in Perspective* (1995), ch 3.

paying. If the primary purpose of administrative law is to ensure the legality of government action, then it is hard to see why the price would no longer be seen as worth paying merely because the action is brought by a pressure group or public-spirited citizen.

The objection must, therefore, be either that allowing the citizen action will lead to such a large increase in the number of claims as to affect the judgment as to whether the price is worth paying, or that interests which are widely shared are less worthy of protection than interests which are peculiar to specific individuals.

There is little evidence to support the first possibility. As indicated above, the cost of litigation provides a strong deterrent to engaging in groundless litigation and this is true for pressure groups as well as individuals. Nor is it obvious, as a matter of principle, why the fact that many people share an interest makes it less worthy of protection than individual interests. Also, from a constitutional perspective, it is difficult to make the argument that Parliament, in imposing duties owed to the general public, implicitly treats those as of lesser importance than individual rights.

The fourth objection is also groundless. There is simply no evidence to suggest that how effectively a case is presented depends upon the extent or nature of the person's interest in it. Indeed, it is curious that this objection should be raised at all given that court cases are usually argued by lawyers who (except under contingent fee arrangements) have no personal interest in the outcome. It also ignores the fact that pressure groups and public-spirited citizens generally do feel very strongly about the outcomes of the cases in which they are involved and that pressure groups may well have expertise in relation to the issues in dispute.

The fifth objection was that the courts may make unwise decisions on questions which are put before them in abstract or hypothetical form. The underlying assumption here, which also underlies the second objection, is that relaxing the rules on standing will increase the likelihood of the courts being asked to answer abstract or hypothetical questions which are unsuitable for judicial resolution. There is a short answer to this. As indicated in the introduction, it is necessary to distinguish between three distinct questions: who is the appropriate person to sue, whether the issue is 'ripe' for review (clearly focused, not hypothetical, not premature), and whether an issue is justiciable. If an issue has not yet properly crystallised the courts can reject the application for judicial review as premature. The fact that the action has been raised by a public interest or associational pursuer does not make it harder or easier to decide whether an application is premature.

Similarly, the nature or identity of the pursuer should not make it more difficult to identify, or to resolve, questions of justiciability. Contrast *MacCormick v Lord Advocate* with *Gibson v Lord Advocate*.[76] In both cases, the court was invited to declare that an Act of the UK Parliament was contrary to the Treaty of Union. In the former case, the pursuer objected to the use of the title Queen Elizabeth II by the current monarch on the grounds that she was the first Elizabeth to rule over the United Kingdom. In the latter case, the pursuer challenged the European Communities Act 1972, one consequence of which was that the EC common fisheries policy would apply to UK waters giving 'foreign' fishermen access to stocks previously reserved for UK fishermen. It was alleged that this was contrary to the Treaty of Union as an alteration in private law which was not 'for the evident utility

76 1975 SC 136.

of the subjects of Scotland'. In *MacCormick* it was held that whether an Act of Parliament was consistent with the Treaty of Union was not a justiciable question, a ruling which was followed in *Gibson*. Mr Gibson could argue that he had a personal stake in the outcome of the litigation in that he was a fisherman. MacCormick was clearly a public-interest pursuer. There is no indication that the nature of the pursuer's interest made any difference to the way the court dealt with the question of justiciability in either case. If there is a concern that the courts might engage with issues prematurely or decide questions that are not justiciable then that should be addressed directly by elaboration and careful application of criteria for rejecting claims on these grounds. It is neither necessary nor appropriate to address these potential problems indirectly by excluding the possibility of the public-interest pursuer.

There is no logical connection between the nature or the identity of the pursuer and the degree to which the issues in a case are abstract or hypothetical or justiciable. However, it is probably the case that the objection is pragmatic: that even though it is clear that broadening standing does not logically entail that the issues raised in cases will be abstract and hypothetical or non-justiciable, it is simply more likely in practice that citizen actions will raise these issues. This is so because of the nature of the legal provisions which are likely to be the subject of contention by public-interest pursuers. It is when legal duties are broad, highly discretionary and owed to the public as a whole that the 'need' for public-interest pursuers is felt. By their nature, pressure groups and public-spirited citizens will be making challenges in areas in which the exercise of powers and the performance of duties require the making of choices on matters of social and political controversy, so that there is in practice likely to be a greater risk of the courts being asked to address non-justiciable questions. It probably has to be admitted that this pragmatic judgment is correct, but excluding public-interest pursuers from the courts is a lazy way of dealing with it, and will screen out cases in which the issues are clearly justiciable. As indicated above, it is better for the courts to address the problem directly by considering carefully the justiciability of issues put before them.

The most powerful case against liberal rules of standing (and indeed of intervention) has been put forward by Harlow.[77] She draws attention to the fact that not only have rules of standing (in the strict sense) been relaxed, but also that a much more liberal approach to intervention has been taken in the English courts in recent years, with various non-governmental bodies and pressure groups such as the UN High Commissioner for Refugees, Liberty, Amnesty International and JUSTICE being permitted to intervene regularly. This, according to Harlow, has resulted in 'a shift away from the traditional bipolar and adversarial lawsuit familiar to common lawyers to something more fluid, less formal and possibly less individualistic in character'. It has two adverse consequences. One is that it risks undermining the traditional virtues of the legal process including certainty, finality and independence '[i]f we allow the campaigning style of politics to invade the legal process'. The second is that it risks undermining the system of representative democracy by encouraging the substitution of legal for political accountability.

It is important to note that Harlow's concerns do not relate to standing alone, but also to the liberalisation of intervention. It is the possibility of intervention rather than extended standing which more obviously threatens to undermine

---

77 Above n 62.

the 'traditional bipolar and adversarial lawsuit'. Clearly intervention requires to be subject to certain controls and safeguards, but space does not permit full argument on the issue of the proper scope of intervention. It would indeed be unfortunate if an expansion of standing were to lead to a substitution of legal for political accountability. Two points may be made about that. The first has been made already: it is important for the courts to elaborate and apply principles of justiciability. This will limit the extent to which they deal with issues which ought to be resolved in political fora. The second is that political and legal accountability are not necessarily mutually exclusive alternatives.

CONCLUSION

The Scottish legal system can pride itself on having developed simple and straightforward procedures and easily understood and applied remedies for dealing with unlawful administrative action. The same cannot be said for the law of standing to sue. There is no coherent rationale for the distinction between title to sue and interest to sue and this distinction contributes to the confusion and inconsistency in this area of the law which results in rules which are too restrictive both as regards the specially affected and the public-interest petitioner. There is no merit in retaining this particular distinctive feature of Scots law, and it would be preferable to substitute (by legislation if necessary) an approach broadly comparable to the approach being taken by the English courts.

Chapter 13

The Crown in Scots Law

Adam Tomkins

INTRODUCTION

In considering, as this book does, the extent to which Scots public law exists as a discrete subject within the legal systems of the UK, an examination of the Scots law of the Crown might be expected to be central. In justifying his book *An Outline of Constitutional Law*, first published in 1938 with the express aim of helping Scottish solicitors pass their examinations, W I R Fraser stated that almost 'no book deals with constitutional law from the point of view of the Scottish lawyer' and that, while 'there are several English textbooks, ... on some branches of the subject they are of little assistance to the student of Scots law'. Fraser cited as his only examples of this 'the history and present organisation of the law courts' and the 'important differences between Scottish and English procedure in actions against the Crown'.[1] Sixty-five years later, when Himsworth and O'Neill published their new textbook on *Scotland's Constitution*, next to no mention was made in it of the Crown, of Crown proceedings, or of the distinctive things that Scots law (it is claimed) has to say about these topics.[2]

The only relevant comment made in Himsworth and O'Neill's book is the following:

> 'One constitutional consequence of the elision of the functions of ministers and monarch ... and also of the vagaries of language and conceptual imprecision over time, has been the emergence of the concept of the "Crown". Sometimes a term used to refer simply to the person of the sovereign, sometimes to the sovereign as an institution of government and sometimes to the entire collectivity of sovereign and ministers ... the concept of the "Crown" has been useful in defining a distinct governmental entity for legal purposes.... However, confusion has arisen over the extent to which immunities from legal proceedings possessed by the sovereign personally extend also to ministers.'[3]

While the explanation of the term 'the Crown' contained in this passage is a useful one, it is striking that, having introduced the concept and having then stated that 'confusion' surrounds it, Himsworth and O'Neill proceed immediately to dismiss further consideration of the Crown as focusing on the 'dignified' rather than on the 'efficient' aspects of the contemporary constitutional order.[4] They say nothing about the nature, or the detail, of the 'confusion' that has arisen over the extent

---

1 W I R Fraser, *An Outline of Constitutional Law* (1938), preface to the first edition.
2 C M G Himsworth and C M O'Neill, *Scotland's Constitution: Law and Practice* (2003).
3 *Scotland's Constitution*, p 214.
4 *Scotland's Constitution*, p 215. The distinction between the 'dignified' and the 'efficient' elements of the constitution was famously first drawn by Bagehot: see W Bagehot, *The English Constitution* (1867) (ed P Smith, 2001), p 5.

of the Crown's legal immunities. Even if their implicit functionalist claim that public lawyers should concentrate on the efficient over the dignified is accepted, the question remains whether Himsworth and O'Neill are correct to assert that the Crown and the 'confusion' that surrounds it are no obstacle to the efficient working of today's constitution. The argument in this chapter will be that, even if attention is confined to the efficient at the expense of the dignified, the problems of the Crown should not be ignored.

Himsworth and O'Neill's brief explanation of the Crown as a concept in Scots law is nonetheless a convenient starting-point. Three points are made in it which are worth drawing out. The first is the 'elision' of the functions of ministers and monarch. Clearly, the term 'the Crown' derives directly from the fact that the United Kingdom is a monarchy. Its head of state is Her Majesty Queen Elizabeth II. Similarly, before the Union of 1707, both Scotland and England were monarchies. Historically, government (or at least central government) was exercised more or less directly by the monarch and his or her courtiers. Over the course of time, the exercise of government was transferred from courtiers (responsible primarily to the monarch) to ministers in Parliament (responsible primarily to Parliament). While ministers are *responsible* to Parliament, they continue to derive a number of their *powers* from the Crown (rather than from the parliamentary authorisation contained in statutes)[5] and, as will be seen, they continue to enjoy a number, albeit a limited number, of the legal *privileges and immunities* accorded to the Crown.

The second point to note is what Himsworth and O'Neill suggest about the 'vagaries of language' and the 'conceptual imprecision' that seem always to accompany legal analysis of the Crown. While 'the Crown' may sometimes refer to the monarchy, and while it may sometimes refer to the government, it is often used in a way in which neither monarchy nor government is an exact synonym for what 'the Crown' represents. One of the things that is frequently stated about public law in the UK is that, whether Scots law or English law is under consideration, there is no developed concept of 'the state' in UK constitutional law.[6] One of the reasons for the Crown's importance, as a legal term of art, is the work that it performs in the absence of a developed notion of the state. It is as a result of such 'vagaries of language' and 'conceptual imprecision' that the confusion over the extent of the Crown's immunities, to which Himsworth and O'Neill refer, arises.

The third point to highlight is the fact that the Crown is a label that can be used to mean different things in different contexts. Sometimes it refers to the 'person of the sovereign', sometimes to an institution of government, and sometimes to 'the entire collectivity of sovereign and ministers'. It is important to bear this in mind.

---

5 These powers, generally referred to as royal prerogative powers, include the power to make treaties, the power to conduct diplomatic relations with other states, the power to deploy British armed forces both within and beyond the borders of the UK, the powers to employ civil servants, appoint peers, grant honours, and to issue and revoke passports, among others. All of these powers are now exercised by ministers, rather than by the monarch. For discussion in the context of Scots law, see *Burmah Oil v Lord Advocate* [1965] AC 75. Some prerogative powers continue to be exercisable only by the monarch (and not by ministers): these include the power to appoint the Prime Minister, the power to dissolve Parliament, the power to dismiss the government and the power to grant the royal assent to legislation. On the contemporary exercise of the monarch's powers, see A Tomkins, *Public Law* (2003), pp 62–72

6 See M Loughlin, in M Sunkin and S Payne (eds), *The Nature of the Crown: A Legal and Political Analysis* (1999).

One of the reasons why 'the Crown' has no neat and tidy legal definition is because it is a term that may be used to refer to a number of legally and politically different entities.

CONTEMPORARY PRACTICAL SIGNIFICANCE

All of this may sound somewhat arcane. While the law of the Crown is decidedly both mysterious and technical, this is not to say that it is of no practical consequence. In order to appreciate why one should bother to unpick the various uncertainties of this area of public law, consider, for example, the following scenarios, all of which are drawn from real cases in Scots public law.[7] Suppose first that you are hit and injured by a car that is owned by the Ministry of Defence and is being driven, in the course of his professional duties, by a member of Her Majesty's Armed Forces. You sue in the Scottish courts for compensation. Next, suppose that you are a company, incorporated in Scotland, with property overseas. That property is deliberately destroyed in war by British Armed Forces to prevent it falling into enemy hands. You seek compensation in the Scottish courts. Thirdly, suppose that the Ministry of Defence instructs a firm of contractors to build a security fence around its property and that, in doing so, the contractors encroach onto the highway, requiring a lane temporarily to be closed. Suppose further that the local highway authority (that is, the local council) has not given permission – as it is required by statute to do – for the encroachment onto the highway, and it takes legal action in the Scottish courts.

Consider now the position of three prisoners, each detained in a Scottish jail. The first is of the view that he has been subjected to numerous illegal searches at the hands of prison officers, and he seeks in the Scottish courts an interdict ordering the searches to cease, along with damages in respect of the searches he has suffered in the past. The second considers that the overcrowded and unsanitary conditions under which he has been detained are so obnoxious that they constitute 'inhuman or degrading treatment' contrary to Article 3 of the European Convention on Human Rights (ECHR). He, too, sues in the Scottish courts for damages and for an order that he be moved to detention under conditions that satisfy the requirements of Article 3. The third considers that privileged correspondence between himself and his lawyers has been routinely opened and interfered with by the prison authorities and that this is contrary both to the ECHR and to statute. Like the other prisoners, he sues in the Scottish courts for an order requiring the prison authorities not to interfere with his privileged correspondence.

What these various scenarios have in common is that in each instance, even if the petitioners or pursuers have an otherwise sound legal argument, they will struggle to gain the remedies they seek for the common reason that they will, in some shape or form, come up against the Crown. The Queen herself, of course, would be the defender in none of the actions brought. The Lord Advocate, (before devolution) the Secretary of State for Scotland or, (since devolution) the Scottish Ministers, are the most probable candidates to play that role. A principal legal argument deployed by the defender in each case will be that there is no liability, or no jurisdiction in the court to grant an order or interdict, because the case somehow touches upon the legal privileges that surround the Crown.

---

7 The cases from which these scenarios are drawn are discussed later in this chapter.

It is these privileges that contemporary Scots law accords to the Crown that is the main subject-matter of this chapter. The argument proceeds in three sections. First the legal extent of the term 'the Crown' is considered. As the various scenarios above illustrate, one thing that Scots lawyers rarely mean by 'the Crown' is 'the King or Queen'. While the Crown is central to a legal analysis of all of the above scenarios, the monarch him- or herself has nothing to do with any of them. Secondly, something of the immunities and privileges of the Crown – the special legal rules pertaining to the Crown – are considered. Thirdly, the law that governs the liability of the legal proceedings that may be brought, and the remedies that may be obtained, against the Crown are considered in detail. This is an aspect of Scots public law that is, at the time of writing, rapidly evolving, with one major House of Lords decision having been handed down in December 2005[8] and another expected, alas shortly after this book goes to press, in early 2007.[9] More will be said about this below.

LEGAL EXTENT OF 'THE CROWN'

Illustrative of the difficulties of knowing what is and what is not to be included within the legal definition of the Crown is the case of *British Medical Association v Greater Glasgow Health Board*.[10] A dispute arose between certain consultant surgeons and the Greater Glasgow Health Board about the appointment of a director of the plastic and oral surgery unit at Canniesburn hospital. An agreed procedure existed whereby such disputes could be addressed and resolved. Notwithstanding this procedure, however, the health board advertised the position. The consultants presented a petition for suspension and interdict against the health board. The health board claimed that the petition was incompetent on the basis that it (the board) was entitled to immunity under the Crown Proceedings Act 1947, section 21. Section 21 is a provision central to a number of the concerns encountered in this chapter, and it is as well now to set it out in full. It provides as follows:

'(1) In any civil proceedings by or against the Crown the court shall, subject to the provisions of this Act, have power to make all such orders as it has power to make in proceedings between subjects, and otherwise to give such appropriate relief as the case may require:
Provided that:—
(a) where in any proceedings against the Crown any such relief is sought as might in proceedings between subjects be granted by way of injunction or specific performance, the court shall not grant an injunction or make an order for specific performance, but may in lieu thereof make an order declaratory of the rights of the parties; and
(b) in any proceedings against the Crown for the recovery of land or other property the court shall not make an order for the recovery of the land or the delivery of the property, but may in lieu thereof make an order declaring that the plaintiff is entitled as against the Crown to the land or property or to the possession thereof.
(2) The court shall not in any civil proceedings grant any injunction or make any order against an officer of the Crown if the effect of granting the injunction or

---

8 *Davidson v Scottish Ministers* 2006 SLT 110 (HL).
9 *Beggs v Scottish Ministers* 2005 SC 342 (IH), currently on appeal to the House of Lords.
10 1989 SC (HL) 65.

making the order would be to give any relief against the Crown which could not have been obtained in proceedings against the Crown.'

Notwithstanding the English terms in which the provision is drafted ('injunction' instead of 'interdict', and so on), section 21 is expressly stated to apply to Scotland.[11]

The argument in *British Medical Association v Greater Glasgow Health Board* was whether the health board could claim the immunity from interdict accorded to the Crown under section 21. The Lord Ordinary (Lord Prosser) ruled that it could not. He reasoned that a health board is not the Crown: 'it may be an agent of the Crown but in my opinion it cannot be regarded as itself an officer of the Crown in the sense envisaged by section 21(2)'.[12] The respondents reclaimed to the Inner House, which ruled that the Lord Ordinary was correct. In an important judgment the Lord Justice-Clerk (Ross) stated as follows:

'I accept that health boards are established by the Secretary of State who is required to set up hospital boards. I also accept that health boards are set up for the purpose of exercising certain of the Secretary of State's functions with respect to the administration of health services. I also accept that in terms of the statute [the National Health Service (Scotland) Act 1978] the Secretary of State has virtual control of health boards.... In my opinion, even though a health board falls to be regarded as providing services on behalf of the Crown, it does not follow that the health board falls to be accorded Crown status. The respondents contended that if a body was performing functions of the Crown and only functions of the Crown, then they were Crown bodies. In my opinion, however, that submission is fallacious. It is necessary to distinguish, as the Lord Ordinary did, between the nature of the functions performed on the one hand and the status of the person who performed them on the other hand. It is not every body which performs functions on behalf of the Crown which falls to be treated as the Crown. A body which is acting on behalf of the Crown may be entitled to claim Crown immunity so long as it is acting on the instructions and at the direction of the Crown, but that does not mean that such a body falls to be treated as being the Crown.'[13]

The Lord Justice-Clerk was prepared to hold that 'the Crown', for present purposes, included 'ministers of the Crown and members of the civil service acting under the direction of ministers', but he saw 'no justification' for further extending the Crown also to cover bodies such as health boards which exercise functions delegated to them by ministers.[14]

On appeal to the House of Lords their Lordships unanimously dismissed the appeal, Lord Jauncey giving the only reasoned speech. Lord Jauncey ruled that 'the critical question' was 'not whether health boards perform functions on behalf of the Crown ... nor whether health boards for the purposes of statutory immunity or other purposes fall to be treated as the Crown ... but whether the [consultants'] petition amounted to "proceedings against the Crown" for the purposes of section 21'.[15] In answering that question, Lord Jauncey embarked on a close examination of the legislative history and purpose of the Crown Proceedings Act. His Lordship

11 Crown Proceedings Act 1947, s 42.
12 1989 SC (HL) at 71.
13 1989 SC (HL) at 74, 76.
14 1989 SC (HL) at 77.
15 1989 SC (HL) at 93–94.

noted that 'if Parliament had intended that actions against regional hospital boards and hospital management committees should be treated as proceedings against the Crown, it would have been very simple to have so provided'. The absence of such an express provision from the Act suggested, according to Lord Jauncey, that health boards and the like should not be construed as being included within the definition of the Crown for these purposes. His Lordship concluded that:

> '[T]he general purpose of the Crown Proceedings Act 1947 was to make it easier rather than more difficult for a subject to sue the Crown. To hold that the Act had clothed with immunity from prohibitory proceedings a body which prior to its passing would have enjoyed no such immunity would be to run wholly counter to its spirit'.[16]

Lord Jauncey's opinion suggests that there may be as many as three different sorts of answers to the question, 'what is the Crown?', and that the answer may be substantively different in each case. Here, the pertinent question was whether the health board fell within the definition of the Crown for the purposes of *proceedings* against the Crown. That matter is to be kept separate, in Lord Jauncey's view, from the matter of whether a body performs *functions* on behalf of the Crown, and from the matter of whether a body may enjoy some form of statutory *immunity* accorded to the Crown. *British Medical Association v Greater Glasgow Health Board* is authority for the proposition that the definition of the Crown may be narrower in Scots law when the issue to be resolved concerns Crown proceedings than it might be if the issue concerned either the functions or the immunities of the Crown.

CROWN IMMUNITIES

One of the most important immunities that the law accords to the Crown is its immunity from statute. Certainly, this is the Crown's most lucrative legal immunity, as it is on this basis that the Crown is regarded as not being obliged to pay tax. The Crown is not bound by statute; taxation is a matter exclusively of statute; *ergo* the Crown is not bound to pay tax (or so the argument runs). Accordingly, the conventional wisdom is that such tax as the Crown does pay is voluntary. This is not the place to offer a detailed analysis of the legal reasoning that has led to this conclusion, controversial and, in some respects, flawed as it may be.[17] The starting-point of the analysis does, however, need to be considered: namely the rule that the Crown is not bound by statute. This immunity was examined in detail by the Court of Session and the House of Lords in *Lord Advocate v Strathclyde Regional Council* and *Lord Advocate v Dumbarton District Council*.[18] The dispute between the parties arose when the Ministry of Defence (MOD) wished to erect a secure perimeter fence around its controversial base at Faslane, where Britain's fleet of Trident nuclear submarines is based. The construction of the fence required the MOD's contractors to encroach upon and to close part of the highway running alongside the base. The councils were, respectively, the local highways and planning authorities. They had not given the statutory permissions that were normally required before such

16 1989 SC (HL) at 95.
17 See A Tomkins in *The Nature of the Crown*, above n 6.
18 The two cases were heard and decided together: see 1988 SLT 546 (IH) and [1990] 2 AC 580 (HL).

work may be carried out.[19] On this basis they took enforcement action against the contractors and the MOD, action in respect of which the Lord Advocate, acting on behalf of the Crown, sought judicial review. The Lord Advocate's argument was that the statutory provisions requiring the local authorities to authorise the work did not bind the Crown and that the MOD and the contractors were therefore entitled to proceed with the work without first having to secure authorisation from the highways and planning authorities.

The Lord Ordinary ruled that the Lord Advocate was correct but the Inner House (the Lord President (Lord Emslie), Lord Grieve and Lord Brand) unanimously held that the local authorities' reclaiming motions should be allowed. On appeal to the House of Lords their Lordships unanimously allowed the appeal and restored the order of the Lord Ordinary, Lord Keith giving the only reasoned speech. Thus the Crown won in the end, securing a ruling that, as will be seen, was remarkably beneficial to itself. The contrast between the approaches taken in the Inner House and in the House of Lords is striking.

Lord Emslie started from the proposition that the notion that the Crown enjoys a general immunity from statute is one that has been recognised in Scots law only since the 1707 Union with England, there being 'no trace of any such doctrine' as applied to the interpretation of Acts of the Scottish Parliament before the Union.[20] The Lord Ordinary had ruled that:

> '[T]here is no difference between the principle in its application to legislation for Scotland and its application to legislation for England.... I can find in the authorities ... no good reason for drawing any distinction between England and Scotland in regard to the principle.... While I would be naturally cautious about importing terminology from English cases I feel the less diffident in the present case since the doctrine with which I am dealing has no indigenous roots in Scotland'.[21]

Accordingly, the Lord Ordinary held that, in Scots law as in English law, the Crown was not bound by statute unless the statute stated otherwise either expressly or by necessary implication. 'Necessary implication', for this purpose, means that the statute would be meaningless or that its purpose would be impossible to achieve if the Crown were not bound by it. Lord Emslie criticised this approach, ruling that it led the Lord Ordinary to adopt a broad formulation of the Crown's legal position for which there was 'no Scots authority'.[22] In identifying what he considered to be the proper Scots formulation of the Crown's legal position, Lord Emslie considered the history and the purpose of its evolution as a rule. It emerged, he said, 'in an age when the Crown was virtually unfettered in the exercise of arbitrary power and when anything enacted in a statute would be likely to constitute a derogation of its position'. In this context, the rule was designed 'to protect the Crown against divestiture of any of its rights, privileges or interests'.[23] Taking this purpose into

---

19 The relevant legislation in force at the time was the Roads (Scotland) Act 1984 and the Town and Country Planning (Scotland) Act 1972. See now the Planning and Compulsory Purchase Act 2004, s 90, which amends the Town and Country Planning (Scotland) Act 1997, expressly providing that the 1997 Act and related legislation 'binds the Crown'.
20 1988 SLT 546 at 553, citing *Somerville v Lord Advocate* (1893) 1 SLT 172 per Lord Kyllachy. Lord Keith in the House of Lords accepted that this had been the legal position in Scotland prior to the Union: see [1990] 2 AC 580 at 588.
21 1988 SLT 546 at 550 per the Lord President.
22 1988 SLT at 553.
23 1988 SLT at 552, citing *Magistrates of Edinburgh v Lord Advocate* 1912 SC 1085.

the present day, ruled Lord Emslie, means that the rule is not to be construed as a *general* immunity from statute, as the Lord Ordinary had held, but as an immunity that applies only where necessary to protect the Crown's rights, privileges or interests. Such English cases as were cited to the Court of Session, in which the rule had been more broadly expressed, were, in Lord Emslie's view, not binding on the court for the reason that they were all 'divestiture' cases, whereas the present case was not. In the present case the Crown had no right, privilege or interest that the statutes in question were taking away.

Lords Grieve and Brand agreed with the Lord President, resulting in the Court of Session holding that the rule of statutory construction that the Crown was not bound by statute unless the statute in question stated otherwise either expressly or by necessary implication fell to be applied to a statute only when the provisions in question would bind the Crown to the prejudice of its rights, interests or privileges. This ruling, as has been seen, was overturned on appeal to the House of Lords, where their Lordships held that the approach of the Lord Ordinary had been the correct one. Lord Keith reasoned as follows:

> 'An Act of the United Kingdom Parliament may apply to the whole of the kingdom or only to particular parts of it. There would appear to be no rational grounds upon which a different approach to the construction of a statute might be adopted for the purpose of ascertaining whether or not the Crown is bound by it according to the jurisdiction where the matter is being considered. In the case of an Act in force over the whole of the United Kingdom the answer must be the same whether its application to the Crown in Scotland or in England or in Northern Ireland is in issue. It is not conceivable that Parliament could have a different intention as regards the application of the Act to the Crown in various parts of the Kingdom. Likewise, where Parliament is legislating for Scotland only it cannot, for that reason alone, be held to have a different intention from what it would have had if legislating for England only.'[24]

For this reason, in Lord Keith's view, it was appropriate to examine the English authorities on the point. As Lord Emslie had conceded, those authorities formulate the Crown's immunity in the general terms preferred by the Lord Ordinary. Unlike Lord Emslie, Lord Keith did not accept that the English authorities could be distinguished on the basis that they dealt exclusively with matters that may divest the Crown of its rights, privileges or interests. In Lord Keith's opinion, however, it was not only a matter of precedent: it was also a matter of logic. He ruled that 'a statute must, in the absence of some particular provision to the contrary, bind the Crown either generally or not at all. There is no logical room for the view that it binds the Crown when the Crown is acting without any right to do so but not when the Crown does have such rights.'[25]

The House of Lords has not always been as indifferent as it was in this case to the safeguarding of distinctively Scottish rules pertaining to the law of the Crown. An immunity that the Crown enjoys in both Scots and English law is that which is now known as 'public interest immunity' (PII), formerly known as 'Crown privilege'. The doctrine of PII enables the Crown to seek to prevent evidence coming into open court where the Crown asserts that it would be contrary to the

24 [1990] 2 AC 580 at 591.
25 [1990] 2 AC at 599. This case must now be read in the light of the reforms made by the Planning and Compulsory Purchase Act 2004 (see n 19 above). That Act does not affect the tenor of Lord Keith's ruling but does mean that it no longer applies in the specific context of planning law.

public interest for it to do so. Suppose, for example, that the evidence touches on national security, or on the commercial confidentiality of a sensitive government contract. If a minister takes the view that it would be contrary to the public interest for such evidence to be disclosed, he or she may sign a PII certificate to that effect. One of the leading authorities in the modern law of PII is the House of Lords case *Duncan v Cammell Laird and Co*, decided under English law.[26] One of the propositions for which *Duncan v Cammell Laird* was authority is that the courts have no jurisdiction to look behind a ministerial claim to PII. Once a minister has signed a PII certificate, the House of Lords ruled, the evidence to which the certificate relates may not be disclosed. In *Glasgow Corporation v Central Land Board* the House of Lords accepted that this rule did not apply in Scotland:[27]

'[T]he common law of Scotland differs from that of England in regard to the liability of the Crown to be sued and has developed independently in regard to the right of discovery or recovery of documents in possession of the Crown.... [D]esirable though it may be that in matters of constitutional importance the law of the two countries should not differ, ... it would be clearly improper for this House to treat the law of Scotland as finally determined by a decision upon an English appeal'.

The legal position in Scotland, their Lordships ruled, was that the courts were able to look behind a ministerial certificate. Whether the balance of the public interest lay with disclosure or not was, ultimately, a question for the court rather than for the minister, albeit that in addressing this matter the court would of course give due weight to the minister's view. Twelve years later the House of Lords brought English law into line with Scots law, overruling this particular aspect of *Duncan v Cammell Laird*.[28]

CROWN PROCEEDINGS, REMEDIES AND LIABILITY OF THE CROWN

'Historically the position of the private litigant vis-à-vis the Crown differed in Scotland and England. While actions founded in tort and delict could be brought against the Crown in neither country, other actions could be brought as of right in Scotland, whereas in England it was necessary to proceed by petition of right. Indeed, interdict was available against the Crown in Scotland although such a remedy was, I understand, inconceivable in England. It could be said that Scots law took a more robust view of the individual's rights against the Crown than did the law of England.'

So stated the Scottish law lord, Lord Jauncey, in *British Medical Association v Greater Glasgow Health Board*.[29] The recent history of the Scots law governing remedies against the Crown is a confused and unhappy one, with both the Scots courts,

---

26 [1942] AC 624. For discussion, see A Tomkins, *The Constitution after Scott: Government Unwrapped* (1998), ch 5.

27 1956 SC (HL) 1 at 9 per Viscount Simonds. Mitchell wrote that this was the first House of Lords case to contain clear statements that the rules governing the Crown need not be identical in both England and Scotland. See J D B Mitchell, 'The royal prerogative in modern Scots law' [1957] PL 304 at 305.

28 See *Conway v Rimmer* [1968] AC 910. In other respects *Duncan v Cammell Laird* continues to be authoritative: see Tomkins, above n 26.

29 1989 SC (HL) 65 at 94.

on the one hand, and the UK government and Parliament, on the other, having reformed and interpreted the law so as significantly to dilute the traditionally 'robust view' that Lord Jauncey attributed to Scots law. It may be, as will be seen below, that the House of Lords has recently solved the problem, but before coming to the purported solution it is necessary first to identify something more of the problem.

In 1928, J R Philip wrote that 'for a considerable time ... the Scottish courts have been absorbing English authority upon the law of the Crown as litigant'.[30] This process started, according to Philip, around 1840. This is not the place for an excursus into the nineteenth-century history of Scots law and the Crown.[31] Rather, analysis commences with the 1921 case of *Macgregor v Lord Advocate*.[32] Macgregor was knocked down and severely injured by a car that was driven, in the course of his duty, by a soldier. Had this happened in England, Macgregor would not (at the material time) have been able to sue the Crown for damages, although he may have been able to proceed by the more cumbersome procedure of petition of right, a procedure unknown in Scots law. Macgregor argued that Scots law was different in that, unlike in England, the Crown could be sued in respect of a wrong. The Lord Ordinary held that 'the constitution of Scotland has been the same as that of England since 1707' and dismissed Macgregor's claim. Macgregor reclaimed to the Inner House, but unsuccessfully. The Lord Justice-Clerk (Scott Dickson) ruled in the following terms:

'I have always understood, both from my reading and experience of Scots cases, that an action of damages for negligence such as the present – an action for reparation as it is properly called in Scotland – will not lie against the Crown for the reason that the Crown is not liable for the wrongous acts of its servants.'

Agreeing with the Lord Ordinary, the Lord Justice-Clerk held that 'the position of the Crown in such matters must be the same on both sides of the border' and that English decisions on the matter 'correctly express' the law of Scotland.[33]

This ruling was roundly criticised in the pages of the *Juridical Review*, H R Buchanan writing that:

'It is doubtful whether prior to the Union of 1707 the common law of Scotland accorded any prerogative or privilege to the Crown, at any rate within the field of private law. And the terms of the Act of Union should have sufficed to prevent innovation on the common law of Scotland in this respect, apart, of course, from specific statutory enactment.'[34]

The procedure under which legal proceedings could be taken against the Crown in Scots law was set out in statute. The Crown Suits (Scotland) Act 1857 – which remains in force today – provides in section 1 that

30 J R Philip, 'The Crown as litigant in Scotland' (1928) 40 JR 238 at 239.
31 On which, see, as well as Philip's article (above n 30), H R Buchanan, 'Some aspects of the royal prerogative' (1923) 25 JR 49; J D B Mitchell, 'The royal prerogative in modern Scots law' [1957] PL 304 and W J Wolffe, in W Finnie, C Himsworth and N Walker (eds), *Edinburgh Essays in Public Law* (1990), p 351.
32 1921 SC 847.
33 The result of the case was effectively overturned by the Crown Proceedings Act 1947, s 2.
34 Buchanan, above n 31, p 53. Philip, above n 30, is to similar effect. In *Davidson v Scottish Ministers* 2006 SLT 110 Lord Rodger described the ruling in *Macgregor* as 'unfortunate' (para 66).

'Every action, suit, or proceeding to be instituted in Scotland on behalf of or against Her Majesty, or in the interest of the Crown, or on behalf of or against any public department, may be lawfully raised in the name and at the instance of or directed against the appropriate Law Officer'.

That is to say, to sue the Crown in Scots law you proceed against the Lord Advocate (as Macgregor had done). The Court of Session ruled in *Macgregor* that the 1857 Act did not provide authority to the effect that the Crown could be sued in Scotland for damages. Rather, the legislation, according to the Lord Ordinary, must 'be controlled and modified by the constitutional principle' that the Crown cannot be sued in an action claiming damages for a wrong. The statute, in other words, is 'confined to those actions which may competently be raised'. The Crown Suits (Scotland) Act is, in this sense, procedural rather than substantive. It does not confer upon litigants in Scotland new causes of action, but merely sets out the procedure according to which competent actions are to be brought.

The English petition of right procedure was not abolished until 1947, when the Crown Proceedings Act was passed. This legislation, twenty-six years in the making,[35] was designed to put the Crown on more or less the same footing as any other litigant in contract and tort cases in English law. Like the Crown Suits (Scotland) Act 1857, it was largely procedural in nature. It is relevant for present purposes because certain provisions of the Act, including section 21, set out above, were stated to extend to Scotland, as well as to England and Wales. Section 21, it will be recalled, prohibits the making of injunctions against the Crown, albeit that courts may, in lieu thereof, make orders declaratory of the rights of the parties. In *McDonald v Secretary of State for Scotland* a prisoner raised an action in the sheriff court against the Secretary of State, averring that he had been subjected to many illegal searches and seeking interdict against the Secretary of State, or anyone on his behalf, from searching him without lawful authority, together with damages.[36] The Secretary of State argued that the action was incompetent, on the basis that section 21 prohibits the courts from issuing interdict against ministers of the Crown. On appeal from the sheriff court the Court of Session agreed with this argument.

In the course of his judgment the Lord Justice-Clerk (Ross) acknowledged that, on this interpretation, the Crown Proceedings Act 1947 had changed the law of Scotland and had done so in a way adverse to the interests of citizens engaged in legal proceedings against the Crown. The court accepted that, prior to the passing of the 1947 Act, courts in Scotland 'did on occasion pronounce interdict and interim interdict against the Crown'[37] and that, as the court construed the terms of section 21, that right had been taken away in 1947. Notwithstanding the fact that section 21 allows courts to make declaratory orders, the impossibility of obtaining interdict against the Crown has a significant impact on litigants, in that interim

---

35 See J M Jacob, 'The debates behind an Act: Crown proceedings reform 1920–1947' [1992] PL 452 and, at more length, *The Republican Crown: Lawyers and the Making of the State in Twentieth Century Britain* (1996).

36 1994 SC 234.

37 1994 SC at 238, citing *Russell v Magistrates of Hamilton* (1897) 25 R 350 and *Bell v Secretary of State for Scotland* 1933 SLT 519 as examples. In *Davidson v Scottish Ministers* Lord Marnoch in the Inner House commented that these cases, while 'often cited' in support of this proposition, on closer examination provide 'a somewhat shaky foundation' for it: see 2002 SC 205 at para 10 of his judgment. Nonetheless, the Inner House in *Davidson* accepted that it had become 'generally accepted' (Lord Weir at para 6 of his judgment) that Scottish courts had enjoyed the power to issue interdict against the Crown.

declaratory orders are not available. The real benefit to litigants in Scotland of being able to secure interdict against the Crown, prior to 1947, lay in their being able to secure interim interdict. As Fraser suggested in his *Outline of Constitutional Law*, 'from a purely practical point of view interdict procedure is especially valuable because it includes procedures for obtaining an immediate interim interdict, either to preserve the status quo pending the final decision of the court, or to prevent the commission of a threatened wrong'.[38] The conclusion, in the words of the Lord Justice-Clerk, was that 'one effect of the Crown Proceedings Act 1947 has been to deprive litigants in Scotland of a right which they previously had'.[39]

It should be noted that, shortly before *McDonald's* case was decided, the House of Lords had held in an English appeal that, notwithstanding the terms of section 21, English courts could grant injunctions against ministers of the Crown in judicial review proceedings. In *M v Home Office*[40] the House of Lords held, contrary to earlier authority,[41] that judicial review proceedings in England were not 'civil proceedings', and therefore did not fall within the prohibition contained in section 21. In *McDonald* the Court of Session declined to follow that line of reasoning and apply it to Scotland, holding that *M v Home Office* was an authority only in English law and that the present case, not being a petition for judicial review but an action commenced in the sheriff court, could not be understood as being anything other than 'civil proceedings'. As such, section 21 applied to it, and the court was for that reason barred from granting interdict against the Secretary of State.

The argument in *McDonald* was effectively rerun in *Davidson v Scottish Ministers*,[42] albeit that *Davidson*, unlike *McDonald*, originated as a petition for judicial review. Davidson, a prisoner in a Scottish jail, considered that the conditions under which he was detained were so overcrowded and insanitary that they violated his right under Article 3 of the ECHR not to be subjected to inhuman and degrading treatment. In judicial review proceedings he sought an order requiring the Scottish Ministers to have him transferred to conditions of detention compliant with Article 3. The Inner House was unreceptive to the argument that section 21 of the 1947 Act should be interpreted as not applying to petitions for judicial review in Scotland, holding that such petitions were 'civil proceedings' for the purposes of the section and that, as a result, interdict was unavailable where the proceedings concerned the Crown.[43] Lord Weir stated that, while he considered it 'desirable' that the law governing remedies against the Crown be the same in both Scotland and England, if the proper construction of section 21 'leads to a different result, then that divergence is one that will have to be faced'. 'It would be entirely improper,' he warned, 'to do violence to the proper construction of the provision in order to achieve uniformity.'[44] Lord Weir acknowledged that the result is unsatisfactory – both because of the difference between English and Scots law and because of the fact that litigants in Scotland were denied a right which, since

38 W I R Fraser, *An Outline of Constitutional Law* (2nd edn, 1948), p 165, cited by the Lord Justice-Clerk in *McDonald* 1994 SC 236 at 239.
39 1994 SC at 239.
40 [1994] 1 AC 377.
41 See *R v Secretary of State for Transport, ex parte Factortame* [1990] 2 AC 85.
42 2002 SC 205 (IH) and 2006 SLT 110 (HL).
43 The Crown Proceedings Act 1947, s 38(2), as amended by the Scotland Act 1998, provides that 'officer', in relation to the Crown, includes not only ministers of the Crown but also members of the Scottish Executive. This is discussed further, in relation to *Beggs*, below.
44 2002 SC 205 at para 10 of his judgment.

M v Home Office, their counterparts in England enjoyed – but insisted that 'the only cure for this state of affairs lies in the hands of Parliament'.[45]

On appeal, the House of Lords took a different view. Their Lordships unanimously held that, as Lord Nicholls expressed it, 'when applied in Scotland references to civil proceedings in section 21 are to be read as not including proceedings invoking the supervisory jurisdiction of the Court of Session in respect of acts or omissions of the Crown or its officers'.[46] The Scottish law lords hearing the appeal, Lords Hope and Rodger, each gave reasoned opinions in which they agreed with Lord Nicholls' holding.[47] The reasoning of the House of Lords was purposive. The purpose of the Crown Proceedings Act 1947 was, as has been seen, to make it *easier* to take effective legal action against the Crown. On this all are agreed, judges and commentators alike.[48] Section 21 of the Act is not, therefore, to be read as taking away a procedural right in respect of Scotland that had formerly existed and that it was intended to provide for litigants in England. Notwithstanding the fact that the section plainly states that interdict shall not be granted in civil proceedings against the Crown, and notwithstanding the fact that there is no separate category in Scots law (unlike in English law) of public law proceedings,[49] the House of Lords ruled that section 21 is not to be interpreted as meaning that interdict cannot be granted against the Crown on a petition for judicial review. Their Lordships ruled that it was not wrong of the Court of Session in *McDonald* to hold that, in the context of that case, section 21 prevented the court from being able to issue interdict, as that case, properly understood, was an action for assault, such action being 'a private law action of damages for a delict', as Lord Rodger put it.[50] That ruling, however, should not apply outwith the context of private law actions. As Lord Hope expressed it, 'judicial review proceedings where the supervisory jurisdiction of the Court of Session is being invoked against the Crown are public law proceedings',[51] meaning that they fall outside the scope of the expression 'civil proceedings' in section 21, and that the prohibition contained in that section on courts issuing interdict against the Crown does not apply in the context of petitions for judicial review.

As was mentioned above, the Crown Proceedings Act 1947 was more than a quarter-century in the making. It developed out of a government report that had been commissioned by the Lord Chancellor (Lord Birkenhead) in 1921. It is plain that neither the report nor the Act itself paid sufficient regard to the impact the legislation would have on Scots law. While, as has been seen, several provisions of the Act applied to Scotland as well as to England and Wales, it was with English law in mind that the Act, and the government reports on which it was based, were drafted. The likely problems that the Act would cause to Scots law were first pointed out as long ago as 1928. In an appraisal of the government report that would lead, eventually, to the 1947 Act, Philip wrote, with classic understatement, that 'the

45 At para 18 of his judgment.
46 *Davidson v Scottish Ministers* 2006 SLT 110, para 33.
47 At para 53 (Lord Hope) and para 88 (Lord Rodger). Lords Carswell and Mance also agreed.
48 See, eg, Sir William Wade, in *The Nature of the Crown*, above n 6.
49 Compare, eg, *O'Reilly v Mackman* [1983] 2 AC 237 (English law) with *West v Secretary of State for Scotland* 1992 SC 385 (Scots law).
50 *Davidson v Scottish Ministers* 2006 SLT 110, para 90.
51 At para 53. This contrasts with Lord Hope's insistence as Lord President in *West v Secretary of State for Scotland* that the scope of judicial review in Scots law should not be determined by reference to phrases such as 'public law'. See further, Chapter 11 in this volume.

advantage to English and Scots law would be mutual if, before the draft Crown Proceedings Bill becomes law in England, the position of the Crown as litigant in Scotland were examined with the thoroughness and precision which marks the English report'.[52] Philip's plea was ignored and, as we have seen, it took the courts fifty-eight years to solve the problems caused to Scots law by the wording of section 21. As Lord Sutherland noted in *McDonald v Secretary of State for Scotland*, 'this may be seen as one of the natural hazards of enacting legislation for the United Kingdom without having proper regard to the wholly different pre-existing law and procedures in England and Scotland'.[53]

Important as it undoubtedly is, *Davidson* will not long remain the last word on these issues. A few months before the House of Lords handed down its opinions in *Davidson* the First Division of the Inner House delivered its judgment in *Beggs v Scottish Ministers*.[54] This judgment, as was noted earlier, is currently on appeal to the House of Lords. Beggs, a prisoner in a Scottish prison, complained that his privileged correspondence with his solicitors and with the Scottish Prisons Complaints Commissioner had been opened by the prison authorities in breach of the relevant provisions of the Prison Rules. The Scottish Ministers gave an undertaking to the court that, in future, the Prison Rules would be complied with and that Beggs' privileged correspondence would not be interfered with. When his privileged correspondence continued to be interfered with Beggs returned to court, arguing that the Scottish Ministers should be found in contempt of court for breaching their earlier undertaking. Counsel for the Scottish Ministers argued that the Court of Session had no jurisdiction to find the Scottish Ministers in contempt of court, as section 21 of the Crown Proceedings Act 1947 prohibited the making of coercive orders against the Crown. The Court of Session held, however, that it was 'not satisfied that the proceedings ... represent proceedings against the Crown'.[55] The court reasoned that the Scottish Ministers are a creation of statute (see the Scotland Act 1998, section 44). As such, they are:

'circumscribed both by the limits of devolved competence and by reference to compatibility with Convention rights and Community law. The validity of acts of the [Scottish Ministers] may be determined by a court of law as a devolution issue. In this respect [they] may be compared with the Scottish Parliament, which is not sovereign but is subject to the laws and hence to the courts. In the present case we are concerned with the exercise by the [Scottish Ministers] of their statutory functions under the Prisons (Scotland) Act 1989. While the exercise of such statutory functions on behalf of Her Majesty is devolved to the Scottish Ministers, it is erroneous, in our view, to regard proceedings against them in respect of any of those functions as proceedings against the Crown itself'.[56]

A move is plainly being attempted here to divorce the new Scottish institutions (both the Executive and the Parliament) from the old, British (or perhaps even English) notions of royal prerogative and parliamentary sovereignty, which have acted to insulate government and Parliament in the UK from full judicial scrutiny and review. The Scottish Parliament is not a sovereign body, we are told, but is

52 Philip, above n 30, p 249.
53 1994 SC 234 at 247–248.
54 2005 SC 342.
55 At para 22. The judgment of the court was delivered by the Lord President (Cullen).
56 At para 24.

subject to the laws and to the courts in a way that is not (yet?) shared by the UK Parliament in Westminster. Likewise the Scottish Ministers are to be regarded as creatures of statute rather than as an emanation of the Crown.

Welcome as it may be to seek to move away from ancient and unhelpful notions of the Crown, there are three ways in which the court's analysis in *Beggs* may be questioned. First, it is generally unwise in constitutional law to analogise from the legislative branch to the executive. Just because Acts of the UK Parliament have traditionally been regarded, at least in English law,[57] as enjoying legal supremacy does not mean to say that the decisions of the UK government possess the same, or even a similar, constitutional status. On the contrary, it is elemental to an understanding of the British constitution that the doctrine of the rule of law, properly understood, pertains to the government and not to Parliament[58] and that, whereas decisions and actions of government ministers may be judicially reviewed, Acts of Parliament generally may not be. So too here, even though the Scottish Parliament is clearly not a sovereign legislature in the Diceyan sense, it does not follow from this fact that the Scottish Ministers should benefit any less from the legal immunities accorded to the Crown than the Secretary of State for Scotland did before devolution.

Secondly, the reasoning of the Inner House seems to go against an amendment made by the Scotland Act 1998 to section 38(2) of the Crown Proceedings Act 1947. That provision, as amended, provides that 'officer' in relation to the Crown includes, among others, 'a Minister of the Crown and a member of the Scottish Executive'. In explaining this amendment to the House of Lords as it was debating the Scotland Bill, the then Lord Advocate (Lord Hardie) explained that it was designed to 'make clear the status which we intend the Scottish administration [to] have: a part of the Crown separate and distinct from the United Kingdom government, in effect Her Majesty's government in Scotland in relation to devolved matters'.[59] In a subsequent debate the Lord Advocate reinforced his earlier comment by stating that 'Scottish Ministers will be part of the Crown and will be protected by the provisions of the Crown Proceedings Act 1947'.[60] The Inner House is, of course, free to interpret the provisions of legislation in a way which is different from the interpretation given by ministers in Parliament while the legislation was debated but, nonetheless, the ruling in *Beggs* does seem difficult to square with the express statement contained in section 38(2) that the Scottish Ministers are officers of the Crown.

A final problem with the Inner House's analysis is that it seems to have overlooked section 21(2) of the Crown Proceedings Act. This subsection governs the circumstances in which the courts may grant coercive orders against officers of the Crown (as opposed to their granting of such orders against the Crown itself, which is governed by section 21(1)). Section 21(2), it will be recalled, provides that the courts shall not grant an injunction (or interdict) against an officer of the Crown 'if the effect' of doing so 'would be to give any relief against the Crown which could not have been obtained in proceedings against the Crown'. In his opinion in *Davidson* Lord Rodger observed that the effect on its ruling of this subsection had

---

57 Scottish courts have sometimes expressed a different view: see, most famously, *MacCormick v Lord Advocate* 1953 SC 396.

58 See *Entick v Carrington* (1765) 19 St Tr 1029.

59 HL Deb, vol 593, col 650 (8 Oct 1998).

60 HL Deb, vol 593, col 2044 (28 Oct 1998).

been overlooked by the Inner House in *Beggs*, implying perhaps that it ought not to be overlooked when *Beggs* comes to be argued before their Lordships.[61]

CONCLUSION

Notwithstanding the problems identified with the reasoning of the Inner House in *Beggs*, what the court is attempting to achieve in that case is surely to be applauded. The court is seeking a welcome move away from notions of the Crown. The move is desirable for all the reasons explored in the preceding pages of this chapter. Put simply, the Crown gets in the way. The problem is not that it gets in the way of litigants, but that it gets in the way of the rule of law itself. Government ought to conduct itself in accordance with principles of accountability and political responsibility, but also – just like the rest of us – in accordance with the law. In particular, when the government breaches or is about to breach the law sufficiently interested or directly affected citizens ought to be able to commence legal proceedings remedying the breach or preventing the threatened breach. The reality is that, at times, this will require the courts to employ coercive powers against the government, just as they may have to against other parties. Neither the government nor those in the private sector always do what is politely requested of them. On occasion the coercive authority of the courts of law is required: *M v Home Office* is one notable example; *Beggs* is another. There is no justification for the government to be able to play the immunities and privileges of the Crown as a joker, or as a trump card, to avoid the ordinary force of the law.

On one level it is extraordinary that these matters still require to be dealt with even into the twenty-first century. After all, the comments made in the previous paragraph are hardly revolutionary. The only point being made is the really rather basic one that the government should act in accordance with the law and that the law ought not to grant special immunities or privileges to the government simply because its activities are carried out in the name of the Crown. On another level, however, that these matters do still have to be dealt with reveals something fundamental about the nature of the constitution and about the nature of our public law. It reveals that there continues to be inadequate separation between the executive and judicial 'branches' (to adopt the American expression) of the constitutional order. English law has never understood the British constitution to be based on the eighteenth-century notion of the separation of powers: that is to say, the notion of the separation of powers which seeks to divide the state into three branches – legislature, executive and judiciary – and to separate these three branches in terms of both their functions and their personnel. This is why English law has always struggled to uphold the rule of law in the face of the Crown.[62]

Scots law, at least before the Union of 1707, understood governmental relations differently. As Lord Jauncey recognised in the quotation cited above, the position of the private litigant (or the citizen) vis-à-vis the Crown was historically different in Scotland from the position in England in that, as he expressed it, 'Scots law took a more robust view of the individual's rights against the Crown than did

---

61 2006 SLT 110, para 61. See further on s 21(2), D J Edwards, 'Interdict and the Crown in Scotland' (1995) 111 LQR 34.
62 See Tomkins, *Public Law*, ch 2.

the law of England'.[63] This robustness was a legal reflection of the way the
Scots historically viewed their monarch. George Buchanan, Scotland's greatest
political theorist before the union with England, argued as early as 1579[64] that
kingship is 'essentially an elective office', and that 'what has been established
by the community may likewise be revoked'.[65] Kings, thought Buchanan, are
'instrumental' to the needs of their subjects: 'they are appointed not for themselves
but for the people'.[66] What is essential is that 'the ruler's authority is to be used for
the good of the community'.[67] If it is not so used, the community may – indeed,
should – seek to resist and replace their appointed ruler. Law, in this scheme,
far from offering immunities to kings, is 'intended above all to govern the ruler
himself, to counteract the universal tendency for the authority established for the
public weal to turn into arrogant despotism'.[68] Now, Buchanan was not the only
theorist of monarchy in early modern Scotland, and not all such theorists agreed
with him,[69] but his views are at least indicative of the fact that the Scots were well
ahead of the English in thinking that the relation of monarch to subject does not
have to be (and should not be) akin to that of master to slave. Half a century ago
J D B Mitchell warned that Buchanan's work must 'be regarded rather as political
tracts than as expositions of accepted legal theories'[70] but, as Lord Jauncey's
statement indicates, Buchanan's views were, at one time, widely reflected in Scots
public law. As W J Wolffe correctly claimed:

> 'Scots law was historically sceptical of Crown claims.... [I]t regarded the Crown as
> bound by general statutory words. It had no general preference in competition with
> other creditors. It was subject to interdict proceedings and probably to diligence. It
> could sue and be sued, in contract, and possibly in delict. The courts did not regard a
> ministerial claim of privilege in relation to disclosure of documents as conclusive.'[71]

And so on. As Wolffe also remarked, English law was in most of these situations
'diametrically opposite'.[72]

The argument here is not meant to suggest that, in the mists of time before
union with England, there existed a perfect and fully formed Scots public law of
the Crown that made no distinction between Crown and government on the one
hand and citizenry on the other. Such a view would be plainly preposterous, and
would be asking far more of sixteenth- and seventeenth-century law than it could
possibly have delivered. But the argument here is meant to suggest that, historically,
Scots law and English law approached the matter of the Crown from different and
contrasting starting-points, in which Scots law was, as Wolffe expressed it, largely
'sceptical of Crown claims' and in which English law assumed that 'the Crown

---

63 See above, text at n 29.
64 In his *De Iure Regni Apud Scotos*. See J H Burns, *The True Law of Kingship: Concepts of Monarchy in
    Early Modern Scotland* (1996), ch 6.
65 See Burns, above n 64, p 187. In this and the succeeding quotations I am using Burns' translation
    from Buchanan's Latin.
66 Burns, above n 64, p 198.
67 Burns, above n 64, p 198.
68 Burns, above n 64, p 200.
69 Perhaps his best-known critic was his erstwhile pupil, King James VI (later James I of England),
    advocate of the divine right of kings, among other matters. See, eg, his 'Trew Law of Free
    Monarchies' (1598), in J P Sommerville (ed), *King James VI and I: Political Writings* (1994).
70 Mitchell, above n 31, p 306.
71 Wolffe in *Edinburgh Essays in Public Law*, n 31 above, p 357 (Wolffe's footnotes omitted).
72 Wolffe in *Edinburgh Essays in Public Law*, p 357.

can do no wrong' and that 'the Crown cannot be sued in its own courts'. Through an unhealthy combination of poor legislative drafting of Westminster statute, a chronic shortage of Scottish case law, and the inability of Scots law to resist the force of English precedent, the twentieth century saw the gradual, faltering but incomplete merger of the two approaches, which (like the Union of 1707 itself, maybe) was perhaps as much as 80 per cent English takeover, leaving relatively little of the indigenous Scots law behind. That said, it was not all one-way traffic. The distinctive approach of Scots law has on occasion been preserved and, indeed, has sometimes even formed the basis of reform in English law: see, for example, the rule concerning the conclusivity of a PII certificate, discussed above.[73] This is very much the exception rather than the rule, however, as is indicated by the changes surveyed above to the rules of Scots law that the Crown may be sued in delict;[74] that the Crown is bound by statute unless that statute would divest the Crown of its rights, interests or privileges;[75] and that interdict and interim interdict are available in proceedings against the Crown.[76]

The recent change effected by the decision of the House of Lords in *Davidson* cannot be seen as an attempt to reverse this trend. There is no sense that what their Lordships were doing in that case was driven by an eagerness to reassert the distinctive identity of Scots public law. On the contrary, their Lordships' motivation was a desire to eliminate a difference between the laws of Scotland and England, a difference that had emerged as a result of the changes made to English law in *M v Home Office*.[77] Thus, the result in *Davidson* was inspired by a judicial desire that the law in Scotland and in England should be *the same*, and was not due to what Fraser described as the 'important differences between Scottish and English procedure in actions against the Crown'.[78] Moreover, the change made by their Lordships in *Davidson* was made at the expense of insisting on a strained interpretation of the Crown Proceedings Act – an interpretation, it will be recalled, which the Court of Session had rejected as untenable.[79] It was also made at the expense of introducing a distinction into Scots law – a distinction between civil proceedings and public law proceedings – which is quite alien to it. Both the terms of the statute and the traditions of Scots law have been unceremoniously pushed aside in order to make room for the desired result. *This*, it turns out, is the far from 'natural' hazard of enacting legislation for the UK 'without having proper regard' to the position in Scots law.[80] *Davidson* does nothing to diminish the impression that contemporary Scots law of the Crown is inchoate, largely unprincipled, and increasingly dependent, for both its content and its interpretation, on the law of England, manifestly deleterious to the interests of citizens (as litigants) as that particular source of law has traditionally been in this context.

Mitchell concluded his account of the Crown in Scots law with the plea that its 'genuine, deep-rooted' differences from English law be remembered and taken

---

73 See *Glasgow Corporation v Central Land Board* 1956 SC (HL) 1.
74 See *Macgregor v Lord Advocate* 1921 SC 847.
75 See *Lord Advocate v Strathclyde Regional Council*; *Lord Advocate v Dumbarton District Council* 1988 SLT 546 (IH); [1990] 2 AC 580 (HL).
76 See *McDonald v Secretary of State for Scotland* 1994 SC 234.
77 There is no evidence that the changes made to English law in *M v Home Office* were inspired by the position in Scots law.
78 Fraser, *An Outline of Constitutional Law*, preface to first edition.
79 See above, text and nn 44–45.
80 Cf Lord Sutherland, 1994 SC 234 at 247–248.

into account.[81] It may be that the judgment of the Inner House in *Beggs* will be permitted to give Scots law a new lease of life in this regard, suggesting as it does an account of the relationship between devolved government and the courts that is both bold and distinctive. Whether its new sprouting will be allowed to take hold and flourish in what has been a largely hostile climate, only time – and the House of Lords – will tell.

81 Mitchell, above n 31, p 320.

Chapter 14

The Scottish Public Services Ombudsman: Revolution or Evolution?[1]

Brian Thompson

INTRODUCTION

The establishment of a devolved Scottish Parliament in 1999 was not only a major change to Scotland's system of public law in its own right, but it has also been the catalyst for further important developments. One such change has been the creation of the Scottish Public Services Ombudsman (SPSO) by the Scottish Public Services Ombudsman Act 2002. By establishing a 'one-stop shop' for investigation of complaints of maladministration across the public sector in Scotland, the SPSO appears to be a major departure from the previous UK practice of having sector-specific ombudsmen, and, indeed, sector-specific redress mechanisms more generally. Moreover, the consultation exercises which preceded the establishment of the SPSO[2] operated on the premise that the foundations of the British public sector ombudsman model should be revisited. In fact, though, as will be argued in this chapter, the SPSO does not constitute a major departure from that model as its functions and operational practices had evolved by 2002. Indeed, the one-stop shop principle had already been recommended for adoption in England by the 2000 Collcutt Report.[3] Although that idea has not yet been implemented in England,[4] it has subsequently been adopted in Wales, by the Public Services Ombudsman (Wales) Act 2005.[5]

The primary aim of this chapter is to examine the structure, powers and operation of the SPSO and to evaluate its performance over its first few years. Before doing so, however, the chapter traces the development of the ombudsman concept in the UK, situating it within the context of the wider system for redress of grievances against public bodies, and of debates about the functions that ombudsmen should perform. The chapter ends by considering possible future development of the Scottish ombudsman, as part of a broader, integrated system of administrative justice.

EVOLUTION OF REDRESS MECHANISMS IN THE UK

It is almost forty years since the creation of the first British ombudsman, the Parliamentary Commissioner for Administration or Parliamentary Ombudsman[6]

1 I am very grateful for the assistance given by the Scottish Public Services Ombudsman, Professor Alice Brown, and Deputy Scottish Public Services Ombudsman, Mr Eric Drake. Any errors and omissions are mine and they should not be taken to share the views expressed.
2 Scottish Ministers, *Modernising The Complaints System* (2000, SE/2000/84); Scottish Ministers, *A Modern Complaints System* (2001, SE/2001/139).
3 P Collcutt and M Hourihan, *Review of the Public Sector Ombudsmen in England* (2000).
4 But see M Elliott, 'Asymmetric devolution and ombudsman reform in England' [2006] PL 84 for discussion of recent Cabinet Office proposals for closer co-operation amongst the English public sector ombudsmen.
5 See M Seneviratne, 'A new ombudsman for Wales' [2006] PL 6.
6 Parliamentary Commissioner Act 1967 (PCA).

(PO), which added a new component to the provision of redress for citizens aggrieved with providers of public services. The range of redress mechanisms in the 1960s included (a) the political, whereby an MP or local councillor took up a constituent's case, (b) the judicial, which included the somewhat rarely sought judicial review and the even rarer action for compensation, and (c) statutory appeal procedures, which included tribunals and inquiries. The Whyatt report,[7] which advocated the creation of a British ombudsman modelled on the ombudsmen in Sweden and Denmark and on the British parliamentary officer, the Comptroller and Auditor General, considered these mechanisms to be flawed. Both political and judicial redress mechanisms lacked power to obtain access to departmental files; litigation was expensive and judicial review at that time was rather restricted in its scope as well as procedurally cumbersome so that its utility was limited; and tribunals and inquiries were unsystematic in their availability. Thus the PO was given significant investigative powers,[8] its jurisdiction was broadly defined as being to investigate injustice caused by maladministration,[9] and it was free to access for the citizen, as well as being procedurally uncomplicated, once a complaint had been accepted. However, reflecting the fact that the office was intended to complement rather than replace existing redress mechanisms, cases could only be accepted for investigation where there was no alternative remedy, unless the PO felt that it was unreasonable for the complainant to use that alternative,[10] and the case had to be referred to the PO by an MP[11] (the so-called 'MP filter'). In addition, if a complaint was upheld the 'guilty' department was not obliged to remedy the injustice, although the PO could issue a further report where of the opinion that the injustice had not been or would not be remedied.[12] The PO reports to a parliamentary select committee, which provides a further means of putting pressure on agencies to comply with its findings.

Since 1967, the ombudsman concept has developed further and has also affected the general development of redress mechanisms in the public sector, particularly internal complaints procedures. To begin with, the ombudsman institution was extended[13] to the National Health Service (NHS) in 1972[14] (the Health Service Commissioners, hereafter referred to as HSO) and to local government in 1974–75[15] (the Commissions for Local Administration in England and Wales and the Commissioner for Local Administration in Scotland, hereafter referred to as LGO). Secondly, since none of the three public services ombudsmen was authorised to accept a complaint unless an attempt had previously been made by the

---

7 Justice, *The Citizen and the Administration: the Redress of Grievances* (1961).
8 PCA, s 8(1)–(2).
9 PCA, s 5(1).
10 PCA, s 5(2).
11 PCA, s 5(1).
12 PCA, s 10(3).
13 First to Northern Ireland and to its devolved parliament by Parliamentary Commissioner Act (Northern Ireland) 1969, now Ombudsman (Northern Ireland) Order 1996 (SI 1996/1298), and then to local government and the NHS, Commissioner for Complaints Act (Northern Ireland) 1969, now Commissioner for Complaints (Northern Ireland) Order 1996 (SI 1996/1297).
14 National Health Service (Scotland) Act 1972 and National Health Service Reorganisation Act 1973. Initially matters of clinical judgment were not included but after they were added to the remit by the Health Commissioners (Amendment) Act 1996, s 6, they became the largest single complaint in the workload.
15 Local Government Act 1974; Local Government (Scotland) Act 1975.

complained-against agency to respond to it, this was one factor behind a growing trend for public bodies to establish their own complaints-handling mechanisms. The first substantial study of agency redress systems by Birkinshaw in 1985[16] revealed a somewhat patchy picture, with some agencies having very good provision and others hardly any arrangements. Moreover, much of it was informal and, in general, arrangements were not well publicised. The Citizen's Charter initiative,[17] launched in 1991, included the provision of redress as part of its aim of improving public services. A Complaints Task Force was created which produced guidance and good practice on complaints-handling.[18] Alongside guidance published by the LGO[19] and by a review of the NHS,[20] a consensus has emerged as to what constitutes good practice in complaints-handling. This includes:

- good publicity about the complaints' system;
- defining a complaint and what the system can and cannot deal with;
- indicating what the likely redress might be;
- separation of complaints from disciplinary issues;
- support for complainants;
- setting and publication of time-limits for the various stages of the system;
- escalation of stages from immediate and informal action to more formal investigation;
- awareness of the complaints system by all staff in the public body, with training for those handling complaints, and responsibility for the system vested in senior staff; and
- evaluation of complaints in relation to both the lessons which might be learned from the matters complained about and complainants' experience of the complaints process.

It is, however, important to bear in mind that complaints cover a wide range. The current Cabinet Office definition is 'any expression of dissatisfaction that needs a response'.[21] Harlow and Rawlings suggest that in ascending order of seriousness there are grumbles/grievances, complaints and disputes.[22] At the minor end of this spectrum, for example, a complaint may amount to no more than a request for more information. Maladministration and injustice, which the ombudsmen are mandated to investigate, also embrace a broad range, from delay and discourtesy to a failure to apply relevant policies or to inform/advise people of relevant

---

16 P Birkinshaw, *Grievances, Remedies and the State* (1985).

17 *The Citizen's Charter: Raising the Standard* (Cm 1599, 1991), which was succeeded by *Service First: The New Charter Programme* (1998) and *Modernising Government* (Cm 4310, 1999).

18 See work done by the Citizen's Charter Complaints Task Force – *Effective Complaints Systems: Principles and Checklist* (1993) and *Putting Things Right* which also included a *Good Practice Guide* (1995).

19 Commission for Local Administration in England, *Devising a Complaints System* (1992). This had been preceded by Commission for Local Administration in England and Local Authority Associations, *Complaints Procedures: A Code of Practice for Local Government and Water Authorities* (1978) and the LGO's latest version's title reflects the fact that arrangements are not new but established: *Running a Complaints System* (2002).

20 A Wilson (Chairman), *Being Heard: The Report of a Review Committee on NHS Complaints Procedures* (1994).

21 Cabinet Office, *How to Deal With Complaints* (1998), p 8.

22 C Harlow and R Rawlings, *Law and Administration* (1997), p 401.

information or procedures.[23] Thus they can extend from the minor to the very serious, the latter including examples such as a flat being rendered uninhabitable and furnishings damaged by water due to poor supervision of repairs,[24] demands for recovery of substantial amounts of money after overpayment of tax credits[25] and adverse outcomes in medical treatment.[26]

A further important distinction arises from a study by the National Audit Office, which suggested that agencies channel expressions of dissatisfaction into two streams: complaints and appeals.[27] Complaints are regarded as being about administrative blame and are indicators of defective processes or poor handling of an individual's case. Appeals are expressions of dissatisfaction with a substantive decision and, as in social security for example, the decision may be appealed to a statutory independent tribunal. In effect the complaints stream deals with service and the appeals stream with rights.[28]

If one may say that the range of complaints is a dimension of width, there is also one relating to height in the sense that there is a complaints 'pyramid' or 'ladder' with different tiers. The first tier is the agency and the final one is the ombudsman. This idea developed following comments by the PO and its select committee on the redress proposals in the Citizen's Charter which discussed the need for an external review tier above the internal agency complaints process but made little reference to the public services ombudsmen.[29] As a consequence, in many (though by no means all) of the central governmental departments and agencies which generate the most complaints there are now what might be called intermediate complaints handlers, in that they have autonomy in dealing with complaints which come to them from the work of the agency, but they are not fully independent as they are appointed and funded by the departments in question. The Revenue Adjudicator was the first of this new type of complaints-handler and its remit was later expanded to deal with Customs and Excise.[30] Similarly, the Independent Case Examiner was created to deal with the large volume of complaints against the Child Support Agency.[31] In both of these arrangements the complainant must first have used the agency's own complaints procedure, but in pursuing further redress the PO could be approached directly. One particularly complex multi-tiered scheme was the UK-wide NHS complaints scheme, introduced in 1996, under which the complainant had to go through successively the first stage of local resolution and then independent review (or have been denied a review) before the HSO could accept a case.[32]

23 The Crossman catalogue is examples of maladministration given during the passage of the 1967 legislation 'bias, neglect, inattention, delay, incompetence, inaptitude, perversity, turpitude, arbitrariness and so on': HC Deb, vol 734, col 51 (18 Oct 1966).
24 Commissioner for Local Administration in Scotland, *Annual Report 1984*, para 27(7).
25 *Tax Credits: Getting Things Right* (HC 124, 2005–06).
26 Eg, problems in a GP deputising service meant that a patient died: case E.1927/98–99 in Health Service Commissioner, *Annual Report* 1999–2000 (HC 542, 1999–2000), para 2.3.
27 National Audit Office, *Citizen Redress: What Citizens Can Do if Things Go Wrong with Public Services* (HC 21, 2004–05), p 18.
28 B Thompson in M Harris and M Partington (eds), *Administrative Justice in the 21st Century* (1999), p 463.
29 Select Committee on the Parliamentary Commissioner for Administration, *The Implications of the Citizen's Charter for the Work of the Parliamentary Commissioner for Administration* (HC 158, 1991–92).
30 See P Morris, 'The revenue adjudicator – the first two years' [1996] PL 309.
31 M Seneviratne, *Ombudsmen: Public Services and Administrative Justice* (2002), pp 84–86.
32 See the new NHS arrangements in Scotland since April 2005: Scottish Executive, *Can I Help You? Learning from Comments, Concerns and Complaints* (2005), Part 3.

ROLE OF THE OMBUDSMAN

Within this complex system of redress, there are two distinct roles which an ombudsman might perform. Borrowing Harlow and Rawlings' metaphors, these can be described as 'fire-fighting' and 'fire-watching'.[33] According to the fire-fighting conception, the ombudsman's primary function is to resolve citizens' grievances, operating as a kind of administrative small claims court. By contrast, the fire-watching conception emphasises inspection and audit functions, so that rather than processing a higher volume of cases the ombudsman plays a more strategic role, giving investigations into particular cases a broader impact, particularly in dealing with systemic problems. Thus deficiencies can be identified, improvements made and recurrence of that type of maladministration prevented. To change the metaphor, the strategic investigation can have a 'ripple effect'. Heede uses the term 'control' to describe this function, defining it as 'the process through which administrative behaviour is investigated and hopefully influenced with the purpose of improvement', and she contrasts it with 'redress', her term for the fire-fighting role.[34]

While there is broad agreement about the nature of these roles, there has been considerable debate about the emphasis which each should be given. The Whyatt Report, and subsequent evaluations by Justice, have advocated the redress role,[35] whereas Harlow was one of the first to favour the strategic, improvement role.[36] The initial statutory framework was rather ambiguous as to which of these roles was intended, since the ombudsman was conceived, as noted above, against a background of perceived defects in *both* political and legal redress mechanisms. Thus, while the PO was a *parliamentary* institution, aimed at assisting MPs in their general function of holding the government to account, it was also intended to provide individual citizens with a more effective means of obtaining redress from government. This ambiguity is important because different conceptions of the ombudsman role carry rather different implications for the structure of the institution, its powers and operating practices.

Access

One of the most controversial issues has concerned whether complainants should have direct access to the PO. The abolition of the MP filter has been supported by Justice for many years, pointing out that, in comparison with ombudsmen in other countries, the PO deals with a much smaller number of cases, thus depriving some citizens of redress. Comparison with the LGO, where the equivalent 'councillor filter' was removed in 1989, tends to support this contention. Work on the so-called 'lost cases' in England and Scotland[37] demonstrated that complaints which had been made directly to the LGOs were not subsequently referred by a councillor and so the lack of direct access was an obstacle to redress. After 1989, the number of complaints received by the LGO increased substantially. On the other hand, supporters of the MP filter argue that the PO's investigative methods were not

---

33 *Law and Administration*, above n 22, ch 13.
34 K Heede, *European Ombudsman: Redress and Control at the Union Level* (2000), pp 94–95.
35 See Justice, above n 7, and *Our Fettered Ombudsman* (1977).
36 C Harlow, 'Ombudsmen in search of a role' (1978) 41 MLR 446.
37 J G Logie and P Q Watchman, *The Local Ombudsman* (1990), pp 37–59.

designed for a greater volume of complaints and that it is appropriate for MPs to help bring about resolution of the more straightforward cases, leaving the more complex or contested ones for the PO.[38]

This argument has apparently been won by those who urge the removal of the MP filter, with even a majority of MPs in a 2004 survey now in favour of direct access.[39] However, the government, despite having accepted the Collcutt Report's recommendation to this effect,[40] has not yet taken the opportunity to include it in legislation.[41]

Investigations

The proponents of the control or improvement model have criticised the ombudsmen's lack of power to begin investigations on their own initiative rather than waiting for complaints to be made. Hayes,[42] a Northern Ireland Ombudsman, has advocated not only own-initiative investigations but widening investigations beyond the terms of the original complaints. This proactive approach can maximise the strategic potential of the ombudsman, and own-initiative investigation is a power which the vast majority of ombudsmen in other countries enjoy. Despite support by the select committee for experimentation,[43] the Collcutt Report stated that 'the ombudsman function must remain grounded in addressing injustice caused to an individual and own-initiative investigation appears inconsistent with impartiality'.[44] The review also reported that the ombudsmen themselves were not seeking this power and they thought it would alter significantly their relations with bodies under their jurisdiction.[45]

Jurisdiction

Although the requirement to find *injustice* in consequence of maladministration, and the prohibition on questioning the merits of decisions taken without maladministration,[46] might suggest a redress role, maladministration has in fact been interpreted in a way which could promote the improvement of public services, in relation to the treatment of 'bad rules'. This was done at the instigation of the select committee at a very early stage in the PO's existence following the Sachsenhausen case in which the PO did not think he could criticise the merits of the 'Butler rules' which set out the criteria for the award of compensation to prisoners of war and which were known to be restrictive.[47] The select committee

---

38 See Harlow, 'Ombudsmen', above n 36.
39 See 'Summary Results of the Survey of Members of Parliament on the Work of the Ombudsman' on the website *http://www.ombudsman.org.uk/about_us/FOI/whats_available/documents/surveys/ mp_survey_04.html*.
40 HC Deb, vol 372, cols 464W–465W (20 July 2001).
41 In its consultation paper on a draft Regulatory Reform Order, the government stated that reforms could be implemented using this special type of delegated legislation, apart from removal of the MP filter for which it would not be 'an appropriate vehicle', Cabinet Office, *Reform of Public Sector Ombudsmen Services in England* (2005), para 31.
42 M Hayes in J Hayes and P O'Higgins, *Lessons From Northern Ireland* (1990), p 50.
43 B Thompson, 'Integrated ombudsmanry: joined–up to a point' (2001) 64 MLR 459 at 464.
44 Collcutt and Hourihan, above n 3, para 6.15.
45 Collcutt and Hourihan, above n 3, para 6.14.
46 PCA, s 12(3).
47 *Third Report from the Parliamentary Commissioner for Administration* (HC 54, 1967–68), para 66.

suggested that if the impact of a rule is found to give rise to concern then the PO may ask the department to review it. If that review found the rule to be faulty then the PO could legitimately inquire what had been done to redress the situation and if it was not changed what were the grounds for maintaining it? Thus it would be possible to find maladministration in the review of the rule.[48]

A second jurisdictional issue which has been controversial is the overlap between the ombudsman and other remedies. The ombudsmen's discretion to accept cases if it is unreasonable to insist on exhaustion of other remedies can be regarded as helpful to complainants, potentially giving them a choice of a remedy,[49] and so this might again emphasise the redress role. However, taking a more strategic view of the impact of redress mechanisms on public services, Bradley was concerned that it might lead to the creation of 'two hierarchies of conflicting norms',[50] thereby causing confusion for public bodies and citizens alike. One example of potential overlap arises from the extension of the HSO's jurisdiction in 1996 to include complaints arising from the exercise of clinical judgment, in respect of which redress might also be available via damages action in the courts. However, the use of the NHS complaints procedure for clinical issues is intended for complainants who are not seeking damages,[51] thus perhaps reflecting the distinction highlighted earlier between service-improvement via the ombudsman, and redress for rights violations via the courts.

Remedies

For proponents of the redress model, the fact that the ombudsmen may only make recommendations is a significant defect, since it means that someone who has been found to have a legitimate grievance might ultimately receive no remedy. In Northern Ireland there is a method which would allow a complainant whose complaint has been upheld by an ombudsman (the Commissioner for Complaints) to go to court and seek either an order or award of damages for the injustice caused by maladministration.[52] There was a period during which the LGOs were unhappy with their own enforcement powers, since all they could do if they were dissatisfied with a council's response was to issue a second report, which was also often ignored. Calls were therefore made to extend to the rest of the UK provisions for judicial enforcement similar to those in Northern Ireland.[53] Although the legislation was amended, it merely required councils to consider second reports and, if they

48 *Second Report from the Select Committee on the Parliamentary Commissioner for Administration* (HC 350, 1967–68), para 17.
49 Justice-All Souls, *Administrative Justice: Some Necessary Reforms* (1988), para 5.27.
50 A W Bradley, 'The role of the ombudsman in relation to the protection of citizens' rights' (1980) 39 *Cambridge LJ* 304 at 332.
51 The handling of a complaint under the NHS procedure is suspended if the complainant instigates, or notifies an intention to instigate, a legal action. See Scottish guidance, *Can I Help You?* above n 32, Part 4, para 14.3 and in England, *Guidance to Supplement Implementation of the National Health Service (Complaints) Regulations 2004* (2004), para 14.3.
52 Originally Commissioner for Complaints Act (Northern Ireland) 1969, s 7; see now Commissioner for Complaints (Northern Ireland) Order 1996 (SI 1996/1297), art 16. See, also, the new Welsh provision which allows the ombudsman to certify to the High Court that a listed authority has without lawful excuse wilfully ignored an investigation report which found injustice or hardship (Public Services Ombudsman (Wales) Act 2005, s 20).
53 (Chairman: D Widdicombe) *Report of the Committee on the Conduct of Local Authority Business* (Cmnd 9797, 1986), para 9.69, and Justice-All Souls, above n 49, pp 113–132.

were not intending to comply with the recommended remedy, provided for the publication of a notice in local newspapers giving the LGO's required action and the council's reasons for non-compliance.[54] The reasons given for not conferring enforcement powers were (a) that the actual number of cases where second reports were ignored was not large (around 6 per cent of initial investigation reports),[55] and (b) that it would adversely affect the relationship between LGOs and councils to the probable detriment of complainants.[56] Subsequently the incidence of second reports has decreased.

There has been no real difficulty over the acceptability of complaints upheld by the PO and HSO. The PO's power to issue a special report where injustice has not been or will not be remedied has been exercised only on four occasions, with the third and fourth occurring in 2005 and 2006.[57]

Outcomes

It can be seen that the legislation establishing the public sector ombudsman did not clearly promote either a fire-fighting role – the lack, at least initially, of direct access and of enforceable remedies – nor a fire-watching role – by denying own-initiative investigations. Subsequently, a better balancing of these roles has been attempted, with the LGO being the trailblazer. The initial investigative process implemented by the PO devoted a great deal of effort to determining whether a complaint was within jurisdiction and, if so, conducting a thorough investigation and producing a report. The LGO was the first ombudsman to interpret its statutory powers not to initiate or to discontinue an investigation so as to facilitate a local settlement of the case, rather than issuing a statutory investigation report.[58] The PO did not introduce a similar change to its working practices until April 2000, prompted by a desire to achieve resolution, but also to speed up the average time taken to dispose of cases and reduce a burgeoning backlog.[59] This increased emphasis on resolving rather than investigating complaints is clearly an improvement from the point of view of the ombudsmen's redress role. There is, however, a danger that the use of a local settlement might be used by an agency to 'buy off' a complainant and thereby avoid a deeper investigation. In Northern Ireland, the ombudsman has indicated that, if an investigation is stopped because of a settlement but it is nevertheless thought that there might be a systemic problem then the agency would be invited to conduct a review. If serious maladministration or a persistent failure to observe reasonable standards is disclosed then a full investigation would be mounted.[60]

---

54 Local Government and Housing Act 1989, s 26.
55 A Whetnall, *Report of the Financial Management and Policy Review of the Commission for Local Administration in England Stage II* (1996), p 157.
56 Seneviratne, *Ombudsmen*, above n 31, pp 219–220.
57 *'A Debt of Honour': the Ex Gratia Scheme for British Groups Interned by the Japanese During the Second World War* (HC 324, 2005–06) and *Trusting in the Pensions Promise: Government Bodies and the Security of Final Salary Occupational Pensions* (HC 984, 2005–06).
58 *Annual Report 1980*, paras 27–28; the Scottish LGO adopted a similar revision: *Annual Report 1983*, paras 10–11.
59 A draft Regulatory Reform Order has been proposed which would amend the ombudsmen's legislation to allow for the resolution of a complaint in addition to or instead of an investigation in *Reform of Public Sector Ombudsmen Services in England* (2005). For commentary see M Elliott, above n 4.
60 B Thompson, *Textbook on Constitutional and Administrative Law* (1993), pp 338–339.

The Collcutt Report, which very much favoured changing the emphasis from acceptance or rejection of the complaint to the action or resolution proposed by the ombudsman, also acknowledged the concern that ombudsmen might become a 'small claims court' and recognised that investigations must be retained for the identification and publicising of systemic problems.[61] Indeed, it was suggested that, in some cases, most likely in health, the investigation itself might constitute the resolution, and that investigations might also be required where (a) there has been a lack of co-operation from the bodies complained about, and (b) the public interest requires the uncovering of what happened.[62]

All of the ombudsmen have the power to issue special reports.[63] The PO's practice of producing them seems to have been restarted in the 1990s by Sir William Reid, although the LGO produced its first one only in 2003. Analysis suggests that some of these reports amount to a kind of audit, while others are more detailed versions of ordinary reports but have been issued as special reports to bring them to the attention of other potential complainants, to respond to public interest in the particular public service or to generate pressure on the agency to provide redress and make improvements.[64] One of the LGOs has said that it is using special reports to distil lessons from several complaints on a particular topic and so inform councils of wider lessons.[65] A variation on this is found in the English HSO's report on the reform of the NHS complaints procedure, where the aim was to point out the deficiencies in the interim arrangements so that the later version could be improved.[66]

Advisory functions

The LGO was empowered by legislation passed in 1989 to provide advice and guidance on good administrative practice.[67] As was noted earlier, one issue on which the LGO has provided guidance is complaints-handling. Other guidance derived from their experience includes principles of good administrative practice and specific guidance on remedies, repairs to council housing and disposal of land. As their caseload increased, so summary details about reports of investigations published in the annual report were hived off into an annual digest in which more details of selected investigation reports are published.

One initiative begun after 2000 by the LGO is the practice of writing a letter to the chief officer of a body which has had an investigation report in which the lessons to be drawn from the complaint are highlighted.[68] This has also been adopted by the PO after a trial with the Department of Work and Pensions,[69] by far the most frequently complained-against agency within the remit of the PO.

---

61 Above n 3, para 6.9.
62 Above n 3, para 6.10.
63 PCA, s 10(4); Local Government Act 1974, s 23 and Health Service Commissioner Act 1993, s 14(4)(b).
64 R Kirkham, 'Auditing by stealth? Special reports and the ombudsmen' [2005] PL 740 at 746.
65 J White, 'Special reports – a new way of getting the message across' *The Ombudsman*, Jan 2005, p 14.
66 *Making Things Better? A Report on Reform of the NHS Complaints Procedure in England* (HC 413, 2004–05).
67 Local Government (Scotland) Act 1975, s 21(4A) inserted by Local Government and Housing Act 1989, s 23.
68 Select Committee on the Office of the Deputy Prime Minister, *The Role and Effectiveness of Local Government Ombudsmen* (HC 458, 2004–05), QQ 126–130.
69 *Annual Report 2003–04* (HC 702, 2003–04), p 1.

It is suggested that while the legislative design for the ombudsmen in the UK, with its mix of filters on access, jurisdiction and recommended remedies, favours the improvement role, the reality is that all ombudsmen will take seriously the function of resolving complaints within their jurisdiction, and indeed giving helpful advice about complaints outside their remit. The audit-style investigation was simply too protracted for some cases and the backlog probably undermined the PO's perceived utility.[70] Accordingly, mixing investigations with action short of an investigation probably helped to manage the workload better and improve reputation.

SCOTTISH PUBLIC SERVICES OMBUDSMAN

When devolution took effect in 1999 there were four separate statutory ombudsmen dealing with complaints about public services in Scotland: the PO, who continued to deal with reserved services such as social security and tax; the HSO; the LGO; and a newly created Scottish Parliamentary Commissioner for Administration (SPCA), who took over responsibility for dealing with maladministration in devolved public services from the PO. In fact, the post was held by the same person who occupied the office of PO, but now complaints were referred by MSPs and reports were made to the Scottish Parliament.[71] This was, however, intended to be a transitional arrangement only, as section 91 of the Scotland Act 1998 required the Scottish Parliament to make provision for investigating complaints of maladministration in respect of any action taken by or on behalf of a member of the Scottish Executive or any other office-holder in the Scottish administration. Rather than simply confining reform to the limited requirements of section 91, the Scottish Executive took the opportunity to conduct a wide-ranging review of complaints mechanisms in Scotland, culminating, as already noted, in the establishment of a single public sector ombudsman, the SPSO.

Jurisdiction

The Executive's consultation exercise elicited universal approval for the proposal that the separate ombudsman jurisdictions should be merged to form a 'one-stop shop'. This would mean that there would be one organisation with a single 'face' to the public which should make complaining to it easier. The Collcutt Report in England had proposed a college of ombudsmen, but in Scotland it was decided to have a single ombudsman with a number of deputies.[72] This was thought to allow for greater flexibility in the allocation of resources, as the expertise of the staff in the separate ombudsmen offices could be retained but they would now have the opportunity to broaden their experience.[73]

The criteria proposed for the inclusion of ombudsmen in the 'one-stop shop' were that they:

---

70 G Drewry and C Harlow, 'A "cutting edge"? The Parliamentary Commissioner and MPs' (1990) 53 MLR 745.
71 Scotland Act 1998 (Transitory and Transitional Provisions) (Complaints of Maladministration) Order 1999 (SI 1999/1351).
72 Scottish Public Services Ombudsman Act 2002 (SPSOA), s 1.
73 SE/2000/84, para 2.7.

- operated in the public sector;
- were established by statute;
- dealt with matters falling within the legislative competence of the Scottish Parliament; and
- were entirely independent of the departments or authorities which they investigate.[74]

Other redress mechanisms were, however, included because for various reasons their subject matter would be appropriately located in the one-stop shop: the Housing Association Ombudsman for Scotland (HAOS), even though housing associations were not public bodies; complaints about mental health services, taken from the Mental Health Welfare Commission; and complaints against Scottish Enterprise and Highlands and Islands Enterprise. As to precisely which bodies are subject to investigation by the SPSO, the consultation document originally proposed that this should be defined in general terms as including all public bodies in Scotland. Nevertheless, the 2002 Act continues the practice of listing in a schedule those bodies which fall within jurisdiction,[75] as it was ultimately decided that this would be clearer.[76]

The SPSO's jurisdiction does, however, include four matters which were previously excluded from investigation. These are complaints against those who had stopped providing family health services following retirement; court administration; events leading up to the award of a contract or other commercial transaction; and the internal organisation and management of schools under local authority control.[77] Whilst the ban on the investigation of most contracts and commercial transactions remains, and this is one exclusion in the British public services ombudsman model which has generated substantial opposition,[78] preparatory matters were proposed to be investigable, including, for example, the tendering process, although as will be seen below the SPSO does not think the legislation[79] really reflects this intention. There was some concern that it might be difficult to draw a line between educational matters still beyond jurisdiction,[80] and internal management and organisation which are now investigable, but there was general support for this extension of jurisdiction.

There was also widespread approval from the consultation respondents for the Scottish Executive's view that it would not be helpful to define maladministration in the legislation.[81] It should be noted that these respondents were familiar with the ombudsmen and their work. In addition, during the consultation process, a survey was conducted of people who had complained to the Scottish ombudsmen, which revealed that the majority had been dissatisfied with the outcome of their complaint. It appeared that this was because they had unrealistic expectations based on a misunderstanding of the ombudsman's role and powers. This was to be countered by ensuring that better information was provided about the ombudsman.[82]

---

74 SE/2000/84, para 2.3.
75 SPSOA, Sch 2.
76 SE/2001/139, para 3.5.
77 SE/2000/84, paras 3.7–3.9, 3.62–3.63.
78 Seneviratne, *Ombudsmen*, above n 31, pp 106–109.
79 SPSOA, Sch 4, para 7.
80 SPSOA, Sch 4, para 10.
81 SE/2000/84, para 3.4; SE/2001/139, paras 3.8–3.10.
82 SE/2001/139, paras 3.09–10, and pp 55–56.

As the HSO could accept cases alleging service failure as well as those alleging maladministration, it was decided not only to retain this provision but also to extend it to the other listed bodies (with the exception of family health service providers and registered social landlords).[83] Service failure is defined as 'any failure in a service provided by an authority' and 'any failure of the authority to provide a service which it was a function of the authority to provide'.[84] The decision was taken to extend this concept beyond health because it was felt to be anomalous not to have it apply more widely.[85] It is, however, unlikely that this does in fact significantly extend the scope of maladministration. As far as registered social landlords are concerned, the HAOS had power to investigate any action which it considered to be in the public interest to do so, and this wider remit was retained in the legislation.[86]

Access

Complainants have direct access to the SPSO, although they can still be referred by their MSP or councillor. Complaints to the SPSO must still be made by the person aggrieved, although a representative authorised in writing may act on his/her behalf.[87] A representative might also be allowed to make a complaint where the person aggrieved has died or is unable to act.[88] Complaints should normally be in writing, which includes those submitted electronically; however, the SPSO has discretion to accept oral complaints.[89] In the consultation paper, it was proposed that oral complaints might be accepted where there were language or learning difficulties or there is exceptional urgency.[90]

It was decided not to confer upon the SPSO a power of own-initiative investigation because of concerns about encroaching on internal audit arrangements and a conflict with the SPSO's primary role of investigating individual complaints. There was, however, support for strengthening the links between the SPSO and other ombudsmen, commissioners and auditors in Scotland and the UK, in the hope that the sharing of information amongst these offices would minimise the risk of missing cases of maladministration.[91] In addition, an authority may request an investigation by the SPSO.[92] This is meant to cover a situation where there has been criticism of an authority's actions or procedures but no complaint to the ombudsman from a person aggrieved. The Scottish Executive took the view that an authority's request for an investigation should be a matter of last resort, as the authority would have to demonstrate that it had attempted to resolve the issue, and it must have been the subject of a public allegation that injustice or hardship had been caused to one or more members of the public. If the SPSO is not satisfied that both of these conditions have been met then the request will be refused.

83 SPSOA, s 5.
84 SPSOA, s 5(2).
85 SPOR, 5 March 2002, cols 2795–2798; SPOR, 21 March 2002, cols 10487–10489.
86 SPSOA, s 5(1)(e).
87 SPSOA, s 9(1).
88 SPSOA, s 9(3).
89 SPSOA, s 10(3).
90 SE/2001/139, paras 4.7–4.10.
91 SE/2001/139, paras 4.16–4.17. The SPSO is therefore required to disclose some information to specified public officials (SPSOA, s 20, Sch 5) and to consult with parliamentary, health, local government and housing ombudsmen in Great Britain if a matter could be investigated by them (s 21).
92 SE/2001/139, paras 4.18–4.19; SPSOA, s 5(5).

Powers

The SPSO must, in the course of considering a complaint or a request, consult the PO and any of the public services ombudsmen in England and Wales if the matter could involve an issue which that other ombudsman could investigate.[93] Consultation with other ombudsmen may cover the conduct of an investigation, and/or the form, content and publication of a report of an investigation.[94] If the SPSO considers it necessary, the person who made the complaint or request must be informed how to complain to that other ombudsman.[95]

The SPSO has inherited its predecessors' extensive powers of obtaining evidence, including the power to bring proceedings for contempt of court if there is obstruction in an investigation or, if a person acts or fails to act in an investigation which, if the investigation were a proceeding in the Court of Session, would constitute a contempt of court. Accompanying these powers is a correlative duty of confidentiality. Information given to the SPSO may only be required to be disclosed for the purposes of:

(1) the investigation and any report on it;
(2) any inquiry or proceedings for an offence under the Official Secrets Acts or perjury, relating to an investigation; or
(3) any proceedings for obstruction or contempt relating to an investi- gation.[96]

However, a member of the Scottish Executive or a minister of the Crown may issue a notice preventing disclosure of material if, in their opinion, to do so would be prejudicial to the safety of the state or otherwise contrary to the public interest. The confidentiality provisions do not apply to co-operation and consultation with other ombudsmen.[97] In health cases the SPSO has a power to disclose information if that would be in the interests of health and safety of patients.[98]

Process

The consultation paper proposed that the new legislation would not specify the investigation procedure as it would be better to allow flexibility and enable the SPSO to adapt according to experience or changes in circumstances.[99] During the consideration of the Bill, however, the SPCA, Sir Michael Buckley, was concerned about what he felt was an emphasis upon investigation which could be in conflict with the more informal methods which ombudsmen were now using.[100]

As noted above, Sir Michael had been reforming the operating methods of the PO, particularly since 1997, and he had carried these reforms over into his SPCA work. He wished to move away from the initial audit approach in which effort was devoted to screening, that is determining if a complaint was within jurisdiction.

93 SPSOA, s 21(1).
94 SPSOA, s 21(3).
95 SPSOA, s 21(2).
96 SPSOA, s 19(2).
97 SPSOA, s 21(5).
98 SPSOA, s 19(3).
99 SE/2001/139, paras 5.1–5.2.
100 Local Government Committee, *Stage 1 Consideration of the Scottish Public Sector Ombudsman Bill* (SP Paper 496, 2002), Annex C.

In the new procedure,[101] which amalgamated screening and investigation, the working assumption had changed from screening out complaints so as to retain those for thorough investigation, to one where, unless a case was clearly outside jurisdiction, it would be given to a caseworker to pursue inquiries and take action to bring the case to a soundly-based conclusion. This could range from ruling it out of jurisdiction, through taking action short of an investigation which would resolve it, to the completion of an investigation with a report. Where investigations were begun they could be discontinued because it turned out that they were outside jurisdiction, or because the department accepted there was a problem and had put it right or agreed to put right mistakes and provide redress.

As a result of Sir Michael's intervention, the legislation was amended to make it clear that the SPSO may take any such action in connection with a complaint as is considered helpful in deciding whether to initiate, continue or discontinue an investigation, including action taken with a view to resolving the complaint.[102]

Outcomes

The SPSO's reporting requirements are uniform across all the different public services. If an investigation is not to be conducted, the complainant or their authorised representative and the complained-about authority should receive reasons. If an investigation report is issued, this must be given to the parties, Scottish Ministers and the Scottish Parliament. Reports must also be advertised and made available to the public by the complained-against body, but the SPSO has discretion to direct otherwise if that is in the public interest or the interest of the complainant or other persons.[103]

If the SPSO thinks that injustice or hardship will not be remedied then a report may be laid before the Scottish Parliament.[104] In other words, like the other British ombudsmen, the SPSO's recommendations are not legally enforceable. The reason given for retaining this approach was there would be no need for follow-up action where there was no substantial difference between the SPSO's recommendations and the action taken/proposed by the authority. The Scottish Executive was 'confident that this arrangement will allow a reasonable degree of flexibility, while being sufficiently rigorous to encourage compliance with ombudsman recommendations'.[105]

Housekeeping

The arrangements for the appointment, tenure and dismissal of the SPSO and deputies are adapted to suit the devolution settlement.[106] Like the PO, appointment is by the Crown, but on the nomination of the Scottish Parliament, and dismissal is by a resolution passed by a two-thirds majority of MSPs. The SPSO or deputy could resign. The term of office is five years which may be renewed but normally only

101 *Scottish Parliamentary Commissioner for Administration Annual Report 1999–2000* (SP Paper 184, 2000), paras 2.2–2.4.
102 SPSOA, s 2(4), (5).
103 SE/2001/139, paras 7.1–7.3; SPSOA, s 15.
104 SE/2001/139, para 7.5; SPSOA, s 16.
105 SE/2001/139, para 7.5
106 SPSOA, s 1, Sch 1.

once. The pay, allowances and pensions of the SPSO and deputies are determined by the Parliamentary Corporation. Their approval is also required for staffing levels and the terms and conditions of employment and payment arrangements which the SPSO proposes. The SPSO must submit annual accounts to the Auditor General for Scotland for audit. The consultation document proposed that the new institution should be called the Scottish Public Sector Ombudsman. The title was changed to Scottish Public *Services* Ombudsman at the suggestion of the Local Government Committee in its Stage 1 report on the Bill, following evidence which suggested that the inclusion of housing meant that the term public sector was misleading.[107] There had been a desire to find a more gender neutral term, but ombudsman was preferred to ombud and other options.[108]

OPERATION AND EVALUATION OF THE SPSO

The SPSO has had its jurisdiction expanded to cover institutions of further and higher education from autumn 2005,[109] and in April 2005[110] its involvement in complaints about the NHS was accelerated due to the abolition of the independent review stage. Now, if a complainant is unhappy with the outcome of the initial local resolution stage, resort is direct to the SPSO. This change resulted from a review of the complaints procedure conducted throughout the UK.[111] It found serious flaws, not least with the independent review stage, which was perceived as not genuinely independent and defective in the time taken to obtain clinical assessors, as well as in the communication of reports and application of their recommendations. The Scottish Executive consultation on reform[112] proposed, amongst other things, a choice between (a) the retention of independent review to be conducted by a new health complaints agency, and (b) the abolition of independent review and consequently the earlier involvement of the SPSO. Some 70 per cent of respondents preferred the latter option.[113]

These two developments suggest a degree of satisfaction with the SPSO, but what criteria should be used in evaluating it? One possibility would be to use the SPSO's key principles:

(1) to be open, accountable and accessible in providing the service;
(2) to be independent, free and fair in responding to complaints, and
(3) to raise awareness of our service and promote good practice by Scottish public services.[114]

---

107 SP Paper 496 Session 1 (2001), paras 89–91.
108 SE/2001/139, paras 9.7–9.8.
109 Further and Higher Education (Scotland) Act 2005, s 27 which amends SPSOA, s 3 and Sch 2.
110 Directions to health boards, special health boards and the Agency on Complaints Procedures which are reproduced in a document with guidance, see Scottish Executive, *Can I Help You?* above n 32.
111 The York Health Economics Consortium and NFO System Three Social Research, *NHS Complaints Procedure: National Evaluation Report* (2001).
112 Scottish Executive, *Complaints Procedure: Patient Focus and Public Involvement* (2003).
113 Scottish Executive, *Revision of the NHS Complaints Procedure in Scotland: Response from the Scottish Executive* (2003), para 19. The new shorter procedure may reduce the barriers to complaining which a multi-tiered process may create.
114 *Scottish Public Services Ombudsman Annual Report 2002–2003*, p 3.

These principles are broadly neutral as between the view that ombudsmen should concentrate on fire-fighting and the opposing view that they would be better to concentrate on fire-watching and their realisation is desirable from both perspectives. The context in which the SPSO is to operate suggests that it is seen primarily as a fire-fighter although significant developments have taken place along both dimensions of the ombudsman role. The SPSO has been placed at the top of a complaints ladder which is reached by complainants who are dissatisfied with the outcome of their resort to the internal complaints system of the listed authority whose service had caused the grievance. The SPSO is independent and not created solely to help elected representatives redress their constituents' grievances. Moreover, the complaint-handling process has evolved from an audit-style investigation to one more focused on resolution and by action short of investigation. On the other hand, the concern with faster resolution is in partnership with a focus upon improving service by disseminating the lessons learnt from complaints, which previously had received a much lower priority.

The following evaluation of the SPSO will focus on the different elements of the complaints process (complaints-acquisition; complaints-handling; and complaints outcomes), and will briefly also examine mechanisms of accountability, in order to assess whether the institution satisfies its stated key principles, but taking into account both dimensions of the ombudsman role.

Complaint acquisition

The factors that affect the initial acquisition of complaints are: general awareness of the SPSO, barriers to access and jurisdictional limitations. These are relevant from a fire-fighting perspective because they limit opportunities for redress for specific complaints and from a fire-watching perspective because they deprive the ombudsman of signals that suggest that an area requires investigation or, in the case of jurisdictional limitations, insulate areas of administrative action from scrutiny.

Awareness

Improving public awareness of the office is important from both the fire-fighting and the fire-watching perspective. It is clear, however, that the fire-fighting role has been adjusted to the extent that the SPSO is not intended to be the first rung on the complaints-handling ladder. The listed authorities have their own complaints systems and the SPSO is required not to investigate complaints unless such internal procedures have been exhausted or it is not reasonable to expect the complainant to do so.[115]

If the view is now that it is better to encourage local and informal resolution of complaints, it remains important to ensure that complainants are aware that they can take matters further. Listed authorities are obliged to take reasonable steps to publicise the right to complain to the SPSO.[116] It is clear, however, that awareness is still an issue. Studies of the ombudsmen throughout Great Britain have shown that there is limited awareness of them and that this is lowest amongst those in lower socio-economic groups and the young.[117] A 2001 study in Scotland indicated that 43 per cent had heard of the ombudsman service but only 8 per cent considered that

115 SPSOA, s 7(9), (10).
116 SPSOA, s 22.
117 MORI, *Ombudsmen Awareness Survey* (2003), p 7.

they would use it to complain. This compared with an awareness by 93 per cent of the Citizens' Advice Bureaux and 62 per cent who would consider using their service.[118] A more recent (2003) study also found that the more Citizens' Advice Bureaux advisers know about ombudsmen, the more favourably disposed they are to them, and that they are more likely to refer cases to the ombudsmen than the proportion of the public likely to do so.[119] In the light of these findings, therefore, the strategy employed by the SPSO in its first three years of providing its own publicity material, but also working with and through the listed authorities and bodies like Citizens' Advice Scotland, makes sense. In addition, the SPSO has been involved with others in producing and promoting a booklet (also available online) entitled *Route Map: Your Guide to Complaining about Public Service in Scotland* and in the 2004–05 annual report[120] it was stated that in 2005–06 the SPSO would be considering how to deal with under-represented groups, in terms of identifying them and improving their awareness of SPSO functions.

Access

The question of direct access has been resolved but there may be other barriers which discourage those who are aware of the SPSO from making complaints. One possible barrier is the requirement to complain in writing. Although the SPSO has discretion to accept oral complaints if there are special circumstances, there are concerns that to allow this more generally might encourage vexatious and frivolous complaints and also might create conflicts of interest if ombudsmen staff assist the complainant in drafting the written complaint.[121] However, surveys show that the public prefer to use the telephone rather than write when submitting a complaint, with young, black and ethnic-minority groups less inclined to write.[122] In the 2003 study, 21 per cent stated that requiring writing would make it less likely that they would contact the ombudsmen.[123]

The SPSO's front-line staff who deal with telephone inquiries have been trained to operate as the first contact able to provide information and forward an inquirer to a colleague who investigates complaints. The SPSO, while distinguishing between inquiries and complaints received, has not reported on whether there is any 'slippage' between oral contacts which appear to constitute issues within jurisdiction and the subsequent making of a complaint. Nor has the SPSO reported on the exercise of the discretion to accept oral complaints. As was noted above, evidence from the LGO does suggest that complaints may be 'lost' if complainants are required to 'recomplain' by some other means. Moreover, other complaints schemes, such as the NHS complaints scheme in England and Scotland, do allow complaints to be made orally.[124]

118 *Scottish Public Services Ombudsman Annual Report 2002–03*, p 15.
119 MORI, above n 117, p 14.
120 At p 35.
121 Scottish Executive, *Scottish Public Sector Ombudsman Bill: Report of Consultation on the Proposals* (2001), para 21; SE/2001/139, para 4.8.
122 MORI, above n 117, p 7.
123 MORI, above n 117, p 13.
124 National Health Service (Complaints) Regulations 2004 (SI 2004/1768), reg 9(2). In Scotland the *Directions to Health Boards, Special Health Boards and the Agency on Complaint Procedures*, para 8, stipulates complaints are to be in writing but the guidance allows for acceptance of complaints in writing, by telephone and in person: Scottish Executive, *Can I Help You?*, above n 32, Part 3, para 49.

Citizens may also be deterred from complaining because they feel it will not do any good or might even make things worse. For example, patients may fear being removed from their GP's list if they make a complaint.[125] The SPSO's attitude to this problem is that such fears can be allayed by their work with listed authorities to help them create and operate good, well-publicised complaints systems. Certainly in relation to health service complaints there are particular issues such as a continuing patient–doctor relationship and ignorance of medical matters which make it more likely that complainants need not only information and advice about avenues of redress, but also help and support in making a complaint. The Deputy SPSO overseeing the health service work has noted that '[i]t is important that advice and support in making complaints is available for those who need it'.[126] Health boards are required to have arrangements for information, advice and support for patients and carers in relation to complaints and arrangements have been made with Citizens' Advice to provide such a service independent of the NHS.[127]

Jurisdiction

As has been seen, jurisdictional restrictions have historically been a major obstacle for complainants to the ombudsmen to overcome, and considerable resources have been devoted to determining whether or not complaints can be accepted. From the latter perspective, the SPSO's outreach strategy to work with advice agencies and listed authorities is probably cost effective, as these bodies are easily identifiable and more likely than the general public to understand the SPSO's jurisdiction. Nevertheless, significant jurisdictional barriers remain. As with the SPSO's predecessors, the data reported in the SPSO's first two annual reports (these data not reported in 2004–05) show that the major reason why complaints were not accepted or investigations discontinued continues to be the absence of clear evidence of maladministration or injustice in the complaint. In the 2004–05 annual report, the SPSO also stated that the legislation restricts the ability to take complaints about contractual matters and noted a discrepancy between the legislation on contractual matters and the Scottish Executive's guidance to the legislation, suggesting that amendments might be needed to bring the Act more into line with the Parliament's intentions.[128]

Complaint-handling

The main issues in relation to the handling of complaints are the process which is employed to consider them, and the outcomes of complaints.

Process

The distinction between fire-fighting and fire-watching is relevant to process. As indicated above, the fire-fighting conception tends to place a premium on resolving a high volume of complaints, whereas fire-watching tends to encourage a more thorough form of investigation. In merging the different predecessor ombudsmen the SPSO had to devise a new complaints process. This was implemented at the end

125 York Health Economics Consortium, above n 111, para 4.29.
126 *Scottish Public Services Ombudsman Annual Report 2004–05*, p 14.
127 Scottish Executive, *Can I Help You?* above n 32, Part 4, paras 1.1–1.3.
128 At p 10.

of 2003 and revisions were introduced in late 2005. The procedure for considering complaints adopted by the SPSO emphasises screening cases in rather than out and stresses the pre-investigation, determination/resolution of complaints.[129]

SPSO Complaints Process 2003–05

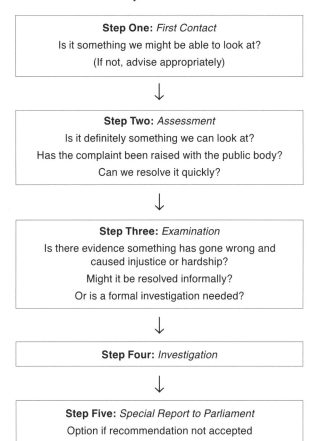

The revision has occurred at steps three and four. In part this is because it was felt that there was confusion for complainants between examination and investigation. Now if a complaint is going to be looked at further it is called investigation.[130] Under the revised procedure it is more likely that a complaint will be investigated providing that it is within jurisdiction and the listed authority has had an opportunity to respond to it. If the complaint is premature then the complainant will be advised of this and also of how to pursue the complaint with the listed authority. When the investigation has been concluded a draft report is sent to the listed authority and the complainant asked for their view on the evidence. If they make comments those will be considered and amendments may be made.[131] The draft report will indicate if the SPSO thinks maladministration and injustice have occurred and, if

129 *Scottish Public Services Ombudsman Annual Report 2003–04*, pp 14–15.
130 *Scottish Public Services Ombudsman Annual Report 2004–05*, p 6.

so, remedial action will be proposed. The SPSO seeks to ensure fairness by copying communications to both complainant and listed authority and giving reasons when cases are not accepted or investigations discontinued. An investigation report with findings will still be produced if the complaint has been resolved to the complainant's satisfaction. The report will record the remedy. The changes to the complaint-handling process are directed more at fire-watching than the fire-fighting role as a small number of cases had previously proceeded to investigation and it is only investigation reports which can be published. Now the wider dissemination of the lessons which may be learned from each upheld complaint is enhanced by producing a commentary on each batch of investigation reports.

Complaint outcomes

From a fire-fighting perspective it might be thought sufficient to ensure that complaints are appropriately resolved, meaning that appropriate decisions are made on whether to uphold complaints and that appropriate remedies are obtained (unless grievances are resolved informally). From a fire-watching perspective it is also important that any systemic problems are addressed and that investigations lead to promotion of good practice. The consideration of a complaint by the SPSO will result in one of four potential outcomes: (1) it is rejected or an investigation discontinued because it is outside jurisdiction; (2) a settlement is agreed; (3) an investigation is reported which upholds (or partially upholds) or does not uphold the complaint; (4) a special further report is laid where the SPSO is of the opinion that the injustice/hardship has not been or is unlikely to be remedied.

Resolution

While ombudsmen have developed their practices so that they now seek to achieve informal resolutions as quickly as they can, it has, as already noted, historically been the case that the great majority of complainants are dissatisfied with their experience of an ombudsman.[132] This is mainly because their complaints are outside jurisdiction, but even amongst those whose complaints are upheld there is dissatisfaction with the remedy achieved. Better information and advice for complainants may reduce the false hopes which complainants perceive about what the SPSO can do for them.

So far, the SPSO has not felt it necessary to lay any special reports and it therefore remains to be seen how effective they will prove to be where an upheld complaint has not been remedied. Some respondents to the consultation felt that the second report procedure had worked satisfactorily in the past in relation to the LGO, since both the ombudsman and the council could publicly express their views.[133] If, however, any MSP wanted to take up the complainant's case following a special report, it is not clear what parliamentary procedure might be used. In

---

131 *Scottish Public Services Ombudsman Annual Report 2003–04*, p 15.
132 See the summary on the Scottish survey in SE/2001/139, pp 55–56 and customer satisfaction surveys for the English LGO: MORI, *Complainants Survey 1999* and A Sansom, *The Local Government Ombudsman – Customer Satisfaction Study* (2005). In the 1995 study, 73 per cent were dissatisfied and of those whose complaint was upheld 48 per cemt were dissatisfied. The 2005 study used a different methodology and comments that the 1999 dissatisfaction figures did not differentiate between the content of the decision letter and the letter's clarity, wording or layout.
133 Scottish Executive, above n 121, para 91.

relation to the PO in such situations the House of Commons Select Committee on Public Administration, which oversees the PO, would pursue the case and take evidence from either the permanent secretary or a minister. But the PO context is different as the PO helps MPs to hold ministers and their departments to account, and the SPSO has no equivalent parliamentary committee to oversee its work. It is thus to be hoped that the lack of problems with enforcement of complaints upheld by the ombudsmen in Scotland continues.

Promoting good practice

The SPSO does make recommendations to prevent recurrence of deficiencies and these recommendations will be followed up to check that they have been implemented. The 2004–05 Annual Report stated the SPSO's intention to institute a practice of writing annual letters to chief executives which will 'provide a summary of the outcome of our investigations of complaints into their organisations together with an analysis of the trends and issues' and it will also identify 'the key lessons to be learned and make suggestions for changes to processes and procedures. Where possible we will supplement these letters with individual meetings with the ombudsman or one of the deputies'.[134] In addition, the change in complaints-handling process noted above, which will result in the publication of more investigation reports, is being implemented by publishing groups of reports and including a commentary upon them by the SPSO drawing out important points, and they are also published on the SPSO website.

One area in which the SPSO has sought to promote good practice is in relation to the internal complaints systems used by the listed authorities. The SPSO feels that the diversity of systems in use acts as a barrier to their effectiveness and so work is being undertaken to devise a common template.[135] The key precepts which the SPSO recommends are that complaints systems should be:[136]

Easy to access
Fair
Flexible
Ensure confidentiality
Clear and
Timely
Integrated with other systems to provide
Valuable feedback and
Engender trust from service users and staff

Although this template is commendable, it is not identical in all respects to the UK-wide criteria for the award of a Charter Mark developed by the Cabinet Office.[137] Devolution is, of course, intended to allow for local innovation, but this should not be at the expense of uniformity where appropriate. Accordingly, it would be desirable if the SPSO were to consult not only with their listed authorities but also the Cabinet Office and their counterparts in the rest of the UK when developing guidance as to good administrative practice.

134 *Scottish Public Services Ombudsman Annual Report 2004–05*, p 7.
135 *Scottish Public Services Ombudsman Annual Report 2004–05*, pp 8–9.
136 *Scottish Public Services Ombudsman Annual Report 2004–05*, p 31.
137 See *Charter Mark Standard* (2003), sub–criterion 4.3, pp 21–22.

Another proposal for promoting good practice which was made in the 2004–05 annual report was that the legislation should be amended to enable the listed authorities to make an apology without an admission of liability.[138] Experience so far has led the SPSO to believe that this would be appreciated by complainants, and it is a practice which has been adopted by several states in Australia. But, of course, if the apology is insincere then it may in fact have the opposite effect to what this proposal seeks to achieve, namely to escalate the complaint.

Accountability

The theme of the SPSO's 2004–05 annual report was accountability. It is a delicate task to marry independence with accountability. The legislation provides for the making of annual reports and accounts, plus reports of investigations, and the ultimate recourse for those dissatisfied with the SPSO, whether complainant or listed authority, would be judicial review.[139] The SPSO has, however, developed additional mechanisms for internal and external accountability.[140] These are: published service standards; procedures for the review of decisions; and internal audit and quality assurance procedures. There is a commitment to change following feedback and developments in good practice. An external advisory group has been established but its membership and terms of reference have not been published. The SPSO has also announced an intention to commission an external audit of its work.

FUTURE PROSPECTS

There is a possibility that future development of the ombudsmen and complaints-handling across the UK will take place within a wider framework of 'administrative justice'. This term was used in a White Paper proposing significant reform of tribunals[141] to include both the work of public bodies as well as all of the mechanisms for redress of grievances arising from that work. The White Paper recommended that redress mechanisms should be improved, with more advice and support for citizens to resolve grievances fairly, quickly, effectively and efficiently, using a wider range of methods, with the hope that problems could be resolved before they escalated. This concept of 'proportionate dispute resolution' would also contribute to 'getting things right first time'. The White Paper also proposed the creation of an Administrative Justice Council, building on the existing Council on Tribunals, the tasks of which would include keeping under review the performance of the administrative justice system as a whole, as well as its component parts (in particular ombudsmen, tribunals and the courts and their relationship with each other) to ensure that they are clear, complementary and flexible, suggesting research

---

138 *Scottish Public Services Ombudsman Annual Report 2004–05*, p 7.
139 Despite earlier indications to the contrary, the reviewability of both the LGO's and the PO's decisions was established in *R v Commissioner for Local Administration, ex parte Eastleigh Borough Council* [1988] 3 All ER 151 and *R v Parliamentary Commissioner for Administration, ex parte Dyer* [1994] 1 All ER 375, respectively. Both have been successfully reviewed on a couple of occasions.
140 *Scottish Public Services Ombudsman Annual Report 2004–05*, p 5.
141 *Transforming Public Services: Tribunals, Complaints and Redress* (Cm 6234, 2004).

priorities and advising government on legislative changes and improvements to the administrative justice system.

The expectation, following inter-governmental consultation, is that these reforms will extend to Scotland in respect of reserved matters. It is also to be hoped that the Scottish Executive in conjunction with the Scottish Parliament will embark upon a similar development for institutions within their jurisdiction. The Scottish Committee of the Council on Tribunals would be the appropriate starting-point, not least because the SPSO is an ex officio member and would be very well placed to contribute to the proposed tasks. The SPSO is already working in conjunction with other officials and is seeking to ensure that new policy and legislative initiatives take account of the office. In response to the consultation on a proposed Police Complaints Commissioner for Scotland in the Police, Public Order and Criminal Justice (Scotland) Bill, for example, the SPSO pointed to the 'one-stop shop' principle and indicated that in some countries the jurisdiction of the public services ombudsman includes police operations. The SPSO correctly noted that whether or not to establish a separate police ombudsman is a policy matter, but argued that if there is separation then the inter-relations of their jurisdictions must be looked at very carefully and that there could be scope for co-operation and sharing of services.[142] Similar points were made about overlapping jurisdictions, co-operation and sharing of services in responding to a consultation about the Scottish Human Rights Commissioner Bill.[143]

If there were to be greater integration of the ombudsmen and other redress mechanisms, this would blur the distinction, identified above, between complaints, dealing with service matters, and legal processes, concerned with rights, and hence might shift the ombudsmen in the direction of the 'citizen's rights defender' model which has been adopted in emerging democracies in Eastern Europe and South Africa.[144] As things stand, the British model of ombudsmanry has not moved very far from the original idea that their role was to assist elected representatives in resolving citizens' grievances and holding government to account. However, the SPSO is a step or two further away from this model than its predecessors and this raises the question of what its link ought to be with the Scottish Parliament. The PO values the connection with its select committee and, while the SPSO was not created as a *parliamentary* ombudsman, it might be useful if its links with the Parliament were more permanent than merely responding to committees' consultations. Association with a committee could enhance the SPSO's accountability and effectiveness both in securing service improvement and individual redress if listed bodies were to be unco-operative after complaints had been upheld. On the other hand, the SPSO's jurisdiction is not limited to bodies which are directly accountable to the Scottish Parliament. Historically, parliamentary accountability was resisted for the LGOs given sensitivity about maintaining the constitutional independence of local government, and such concerns are unlikely to have diminished in post-devolution Scotland.

---

142 Justice 2 Committee, *Second Report 2006 Stage 1 Report on the Police, Public Order and Criminal Justice (Scotland) Bill, vol 2 Evidence* (SP Paper 491, 2006).
143 Justice 1 Committee, *First Report 2006 (Session 2) Scottish Commissioner for Human Rights Bill, vol 2 Evidence* (SP Paper 508, 2006).
144 See R Gregory and P Giddings (eds), *Righting Wrongs: The Ombudsman in Six Continents* (2000).

CONCLUSIONS

The SPSO's three key aims are linked to both the redress and improvement roles, but it is arguable that it is the former which predominates. In practice, such has been the success in securing statutorily-sanctioned resolution of complaints that only a few have ended with an investigation report which could be placed in the public domain and be a resource for achieving improvement in administration. Steps have been taken so that more investigation reports are now published with a commentary which seeks to distil and disseminate the lessons. In order to gauge the success of the SPSO's endeavours to promote good practice in Scottish public services measures will have to be devised to ascertain if lessons from complaints have been learnt and applied. Such measures will have to be more sophisticated than regarding a decreasing number of complaints received at the top of the ladder by the SPSO as equalling fewer problems through better administration. A decrease might reflect lack of awareness by citizens or the fact that initial handling of the complaint discouraged them from going to the SPSO. A system which aims to improve administrative practice, whether or not it has an own-initiative investigation power, does need complaints. Accordingly awareness surveys should be carried out, as well as research into users' experience of the SPSO service. The SPSO's outreach work has, so far, been mainly concentrated upon agencies and advisers. A high-profile case might help raise awareness amongst citizens. There is, of course, a danger that the publicity generated by a 'row' over failure by a listed body to remedy an injustice sends the wrong message of weakness if the injustice is not eventually remedied. Consideration might also be given to creating a special project team focusing on a particular area and publishing a special report which leads to improvements in administration and a raised effective profile for the SPSO.

As devolution develops, policies and institutional design in administrative justice may be more tailored to Scottish circumstances rather than adding another institution for another role. In a small country like Scotland, with only around five million people, the integrated public services ombudsman model has significant advantages, and it might be that the police service could be added to it in the future. It would be a new departure for the British model of ombudsmanry to develop as a defender of human rights, as has happened in Eastern Europe. The Equality Act 2006 merges anti-discrimination with human rights and so co-operation between the SPSO and a Scottish human rights commissioner may well be more appropriate than further integration. Nevertheless, it is suggested that the Scottish Parliament and Executive should follow up the 'one-stop shop' principle by moving on to a more broadly-based conception of administrative justice and considering how the SPSO might be integrated with other mechanisms for redress and improvement. An Administrative Justice Council is needed and it ought to report to a specific committee of the Scottish Parliament.

Chapter 15

Tribunals in Scotland

Sarah Craig

INTRODUCTION

Tribunals are now a well-established part of the administrative landscape. The majority provide a means for challenging decisions by government officials. Others, such as the employment tribunals and the rent assessment committees, exist to resolve disputes between private parties. The tribunal system in the UK has developed somewhat haphazardly. A variety of considerations has prompted the creation of particular tribunals, and in general the reasons for creating tribunals have not differed as between Scotland and the rest of the UK. Whatever the reasons for establishing tribunals in particular cases, however, the preference for allocating decision-making functions to tribunals has often been based on the assumption that they are different from courts, and have certain advantages over courts as vehicles for dispensing justice. According to the Franks Committee, which reported in 1957, '[t]ribunals have certain characteristics which often give them advantages over courts. These are cheapness, accessibility, freedom from technicality, expedition and expert knowledge of their particular subject'.[1] Courts, by contrast, were considered to be slow, elaborate and costly, and judges were non-specialist. In tribunals, disputes could be disposed of quickly and cheaply, for the benefit of the public purse as well as for that of the claimant.[2]

However, it has generally been accepted since the Franks Report that tribunals (with few exceptions) are properly to be regarded as court substitutes. This does not mean simply that they are required to decide disputed questions of fact and law (and of the application of law to facts). It also means that in their structures and processes they are expected to observe values associated with adjudication. The Franks Committee insisted that tribunals be regarded as machinery for adjudication rather than as part of the administrative process, and that their proceedings should be characterised by openness, fairness and impartiality.[3]

Tribunals are certainly different from courts to some degree. They do not, in general, apply strict rules of evidence, their procedures tend to be less complicated than ordinary court procedures, and in some tribunals the parties are less likely to be represented than they are in the courts. Also the members of the tribunal routinely include non-lawyers. This means that the objectives of cheapness, speed and the application of expert knowledge are often achieved. However, the assumption that tribunals are an informal and accessible method of doing justice, which has, for example, been used to justify the absence of provision for legal aid in many

---

1 *Report of the Committee on Administrative Tribunals and Enquiries* (Cmnd 218, 1957), p 9.
2 H W R Wade and C F Forsyth, *Administrative Law* (9th edn, 2004), p 907.
3 Franks, above n 1, paras 23–25, 40.

tribunals, needs to be subject to careful scrutiny. Informality is relative. Tribunals, where no-one wears wigs and gowns and evidence is rarely given upon oath, may seem informal to the lawyer, but they may seem formal to the citizen in comparison with other life experiences. Moreover, tribunals are free from technicality only in terms of evidence and procedure. The substantive law which they are required to apply may well be exceedingly complex.

A number of studies[4] have demonstrated that ordinary users are placed at a further disadvantage because they are unfamiliar with the process. Where the user is in dispute with a government department, as is the case in social security and immigration appeals, they are usually appealing for the first time[5] and in these circumstances: '[i]t is illusory to imagine that the unrepresented claimant is in a position of parity with the public body'.[6] It may, therefore, be beyond the capacity of many people to represent themselves effectively at tribunals. Moreover, appellants may be misled by the informality of the tribunal procedure into thinking that the tribunal will reach decisions in an informal way too,[7] deciding cases according to substantive notions of justice or fairness rather than according to law. The leading study of the subject found that (contrary to official rhetoric) inquisitorial methods were rarely used and claimants rarely received the assistance they needed.[8] Many users found that the appeal process was more formal than they expected and that this prevented them from airing their grievances about what had happened to them.[9] Other studies have confirmed that people find it difficult to represent themselves and that, where they have chosen to do so, they find the process more complex and legalistic than they expected and regret their decision afterwards.[10] In the light of this research, and bearing in mind that the ordinary person is much more likely to encounter a tribunal than the mainstream court system, the extent to which the traditional attachment to informality should be maintained, and what consequences, if any, ought to flow from the desire to maintain informality is, arguably, the key question facing the tribunal system today.

This central issue arises regardless of where in the UK tribunals are situated or of the extent of their geographical jurisdiction. Nevertheless, the way in which it has been and can in future be addressed is affected by the fact that the UK is a state containing more than one legal system and by the increasingly multi-level nature of its governance arrangements. Thus, there is – and always has been – a Scottish dimension to the tribunal system. First, there are a number of specifically Scottish tribunals. Secondly, there are differences in the way certain UK-wide tribunals operate in Scotland as compared to the rest of the country. Thirdly, there are variations in the arrangements for oversight and accountability in different

---

4 For an overview, see M Adler and J Gulland, *Tribunal Users' Experiences, Perceptions and Expectations* (2003).
5 Adler and Gulland, above n 4, pp 22–23.
6 P P Craig, *Administrative Law* (5th edn, 2003), p 264.
7 H Genn, 'Tribunals and informal justice' (1993) 56 MLR 393.
8 H Genn and Y Genn, *The Effectiveness of Representation at Tribunals* (1989).
9 R Young in M Harris and M Partington (eds), *Administrative Justice in the 21st Century* (1999), p 290.
10 J Baldwin, N Wikely and R Young, *Judging Social Security* (1992), p 174; L Dickens, *Dismissed: A Study of Unfair Dismissal and the Industrial Tribunal System* (1985), p 88; Genn and Genn, above n 8, p 21; J Gregory, *Trial by Ordeal: A Study of People Who Lost Equal Pay and Sex Discrimination Cases in Industrial Tribunals During 1985 and 1986* (1989), p 23; R Sainsbury, *Survey and Report into the Working of Medical Appeal Tribunals* (1992), pp 52–53.

parts of the UK. The aim of this chapter is therefore to consider the implications of this Scottish dimension in addressing the problems associated with tribunals. In particular, it examines the implications for tribunals in Scotland of a review of tribunals recently carried out on behalf of the UK government (the Leggatt Review),[11] a subsequent White Paper on the future of grievance machinery in the public sector[12] and the resultant legal and administrative changes which underpin the establishment in April 2006 of the new Tribunals Service.[13]

TRIBUNALS IN SCOTLAND

The majority of tribunals have jurisdiction across the whole of Great Britain or the UK, including those dealing with employment, social security benefits, immigration control and taxation. What these four examples have in common is that UK legislation provides most of the substantive law, and this legislation applies in the same way throughout the UK. In many cases, therefore, where a separate tribunal has been created for Scotland this is simply because Scots law in the relevant area is significantly different. Examples include the Crofters Commission, the Lands Tribunal for Scotland, and the rent assessment committees. However, distinctive aspects of Scots private law may also apply in some UK-wide tribunals, most obviously in employment tribunals, where Scots law on employment contracts may be different from English law.[14] Indeed, the Scottish features of employment tribunals have, to a significant extent, survived their incorporation into the Tribunals Service.[15] In some cases, although there is a separate tribunal, the social policy objectives underlying the law are, broadly speaking, UK objectives. In others, the tribunal responds to a distinctively Scottish policy agenda, most obviously children's hearings, which are an integral part of the Scottish systems of juvenile justice and child protection.

Whether a new tribunal may be established for Scotland, or the arrangements for an existing Scottish tribunal modified now depends upon the terms of the devolution settlement. Certain policy matters are reserved to the UK Parliament by the Scotland Act 1998. Accordingly, the existence and operation of any tribunal in these areas is a matter for Westminster. The separate Scottish tribunals that existed in 1999, when legislative and executive power was devolved, all fall within devolved areas. The Scottish Parliament may, therefore, abolish or amalgamate any of them, transfer their jurisdiction to other bodies, or otherwise modify their operation. The Parliament also has power to create new tribunals and the Mental Health Tribunal for Scotland[16] and the additional support needs tribunals[17] for

---

11 *Tribunals for Users: One System, One Service* (March 2001).
12 Department for Constitutional Affairs, *Transforming Public Services: Complaints, Redress and Tribunals* (Cm 6243, 2004) (henceforth *Transforming Public Services*).
13 The Constitutional Reform Act 2005, Pt 4 changes the rules for judicial appointments, including the appointment of chairs of some UK tribunals. The Tribunals, Courts and Enforcement Bill (Cm 6885) was presented to Parliament as a draft Bill in session 2005–06. The draft Bill proposes reform of the 'second-tier' appellate tribunals and the establishment of the Administrative Justice and Tribunals Council to replace the Council on Tribunals.
14 *Clink v Speyside Distillery Co Ltd* 1995 SLT 1344.
15 See pp 309–310 below.
16 Established by the Mental Health (Care and Treatment) (Scotland) Act 2003.
17 Established by the Education (Additional Support for Learning) (Scotland) Act 2004.

Scotland are new tribunals which have been created since devolution. Thus the constitutional framework leaves to the Scottish Executive and Scottish Parliament substantial room for innovation in tribunal justice (including related issues such as legal aid) at least within devolved areas of policy. Conversely, those interacting with UK tribunals in Scotland, whether as appellants, respondents, members or otherwise, must accept the judgment of Westminster on how those tribunals should be structured and how they should operate. In the remainder of this chapter, the Scottish dimension of tribunals will be illustrated principally by reference to three tribunals, one specifically Scottish and two operating at UK level. At this stage, therefore, it is appropriate to outline their characteristics.

Children's hearings

Children's hearings were set up following the report of the Kilbrandon Committee in 1964.[18] Its basic philosophy is now expressed in section 16(1) of the Children (Scotland) Act 1995: '[w]here … a children's hearing decide … any matter with respect to a child the welfare of that child throughout his childhood shall be their paramount consideration'. What is unique about the Scottish system is that it deals with a child who has committed an offence in the same forum, and with the same range of disposals, as a child against whom an offence has been committed or who is otherwise in need of care or protection. In other words, the system is based on the principle that children who have committed offences need guidance, protection and control just as much as those against whom offences have been committed.

Because of their adversarial nature, the courts were considered an inappropriate place for deciding what should be done to promote the welfare of the children appearing before them.[19] A child may be referred to a children's hearing on a variety of grounds each of which in some way indicates that the child is in need of guidance or protection. A children's hearing is a tribunal of lay persons drawn from a panel appointed on behalf of the Scottish Executive by the Scottish Minister for Education and Young People. Responsibility for deciding to refer cases to a hearing rests with the Children's Reporter who also presents to the hearing the case that the child is in need of compulsory measures of supervision. However, it is the responsibility of the members of the hearing alone to decide whether compulsory measures of supervision are necessary and what measures, if any, to impose.[20] Children's hearings have a different relationship with the courts from that of other tribunals. Where the grounds for referral are disputed or there is a question as to whether the child or family has properly understood them the case is referred to the sheriff who decides whether the grounds for referral are established. This recognises that while the court, with its procedures for testing evidence, is the better forum for establishing facts, it is not the better forum for deciding what to do after the facts have been established.

Children's hearings are, therefore, an example of a tribunal which has had to incorporate legal representation into a process which values informality very highly. Representation has been introduced to children's hearings if the child is not otherwise able to present his or her case effectively or if secure accommodation is

---

18 *Report on Children and Young Persons, Scotland* (Cmnd 2306, 1964).
19 K McK Norrie, *Children's Hearings in Scotland* (2nd edn, 2005), p 2.
20 Children (Scotland) Act 1995, s 70.

being considered as an outcome[21] and the role of the representative is to act as the child's advocate, adviser and 'procedural watchdog', but not to adopt an adversarial approach.[22]

Employment tribunals

Employment tribunals exist to resolve disputes between workers and employers. They have a wide jurisdiction in employment matters, including claims of unfair dismissal and of unlawful discrimination. In contrast to many tribunals, which exist to settle disputes between government departments and individuals, the former only get involved in employment tribunals in their capacity as employers.

The procedure followed at employment tribunals is that the aggrieved worker initiates the case by submitting a claim within strict time-limits. The employer will then submit a response, after which the tribunal may issue directions as to how the case should proceed. If a fixed period for conciliation applies to the case, or if the parties wish to try and negotiate a settlement, the Advisory Conciliation and Arbitration Service (ACAS) will become involved. Case management discussions may take place, and if settlement cannot be achieved, the case will be heard by a legally qualified chair and two lay members.

Prior to the introduction of the Tribunals Service, employment tribunals in Scotland were linked to their sponsoring department, the Department for Trade and Industry. Despite this link to a British department, Scottish employment tribunals were, from their inception, separately constituted as regards rules of procedure, appeals, appointment of members and administration. There were also differences in tribunal practice. For example, in Scotland there was less reliance on written statements and greater reliance on oral evidence[23] and, unlike in England and Wales, witnesses were excluded from the hearing room until after they had given evidence.[24] Some of these differences still remain.[25]

Further differences still apply to appeal arrangements. In Scottish cases, appeals may be made from an employment tribunal on a point of law to the Employment Appeal Tribunal sitting in Edinburgh and thereafter further appeals on a point of law are made to the Inner House of the Court of Session, whereas appeals in English cases lie to the Court of Appeal. Final appeal is to the House of Lords. The substitution of the Inner House for the Court of Appeal in Scottish appeals is standard in UK tribunals.

Following their move to the Tribunals Service, employment tribunals in Scotland have preserved their independence in relation to judicial appointments. They have their own president and vice-president who, like the chairmen themselves, are appointed by the Lord President of the Court of Session,[26] and not by the Lord Chancellor. Although in future the Lord Chancellor and the Judicial

---

21 *S v Miller* 2001 SLT 531.
22 See Norrie, *Children's Hearings*, p 73.
23 Department for Trade and Industry, *Moving Forward: The Report of the Employment Tribunal System Taskforce* (2002), para 8.26.
24 Department for Trade and Industry, above n 23, para 8.6.
25 Discussed further at pp 315–317 below.
26 Employment Tribunals (Constitution and Rules of Procedure) Regulations 2004 (SI 2004/1861).

Appointments Commission will make many judicial appointments within the new Tribunals Service,[27] the government has undertaken to respect the separate arrangements prevailing in Scotland for such appointments.[28]

Asylum and Immigration Tribunal

The immigration appeals system was initially set up in 1969 to provide Commonwealth citizens (but not aliens) with appeals against some immigration decisions. Their aim was to provide 'a sense of protection against oppression and injustice, and … reassurance against fears of arbitrary action on the part of the Immigration Service'.[29] Their scope was extended by the Immigration Act 1971 and subsequent legislation. In Scotland, appeals against decisions on immigration and asylum matters made by the Home Office have been heard at the Glasgow hearing centre since the late 1990s. Until April 2005, the Glasgow hearing centre was part of the Immigration Appellate Authority which provided a two-tier appeals structure, with immigration adjudicators providing the first tier and the Immigration Appeal Tribunal providing the second. The Asylum and Immigration Tribunal (AIT) has now replaced the Immigration Appellate Authority's structure with a (largely) single-tier appeals process. Immigration and asylum appeals in Scotland are also subject to the supervision of the Court of Session, although this has been limited by statute.[30] However, unlike employment tribunals, immigration and asylum appeals in Scotland have always been part of a UK-wide service using the same rules and procedures. Such differences as there have been in Scotland relate primarily to practice and to provision of state funding for representation.

Tribunals in this area are different from most other tribunals in one important respect: their formality and complexity are openly acknowledged and this is recognised in the way the tribunals and their members have been described. A study into 'immigration courts' recognised that they were generally known by this name[31] and legally qualified members of the AIT are now known as immigration judges. The Lord Chancellor appoints immigration judges[32] and there are no separate arrangements for Scotland.

The AIT is part of the Tribunals Service, but in many respects it is treated as a 'special case'. For example, while the government plans to introduce a separate Appellate Tribunal (similar to the Employment Appeal Tribunal) to oversee the first-tier tribunals in the Tribunals Service, immigration and asylum appeals are not included in these plans. The White Paper explains this as follows:

'The Asylum and Immigration Tribunal has been created as a single-tier organisation in part to reduce the impact of the abuse of the present two-tier appeal system in asylum cases. It would be contrary to the underlying principles for the creation of the AIT if an appeal were to lie from it to another tribunal.'[33]

27 Constitutional Reform Act 2005, Pt 4 and Sch 14.
28 *Transforming Public Services*, above, n 12, para 6.49.
29 *Committee on Immigration Appeals*, chaired by Sir Roy Wilson (Cmnd 3387, 1967), cited by I A Macdonald and F Webber (eds), *Macdonald's Immigration Law and Practice* (6th edn, 2005), p 1160.
30 Nationality, Immigration and Asylum Act 2002, ss 103A et seq.
31 M Travers, *The British Immigration Courts* (1999).
32 Nationality, Immigration and Asylum Act 2002, s 81 and Sch 4 (as substituted by Asylum and Immigration (Treatment of Claimants etc) Act 2004, s 26).
33 *Transforming Public Services*, para 7.18.

Change has been a constant feature of asylum and immigration appeals in recent years, often in response to policy concerns.[34] So while the tensions that exist between the administrative target of quick disposal of cases and the interests of the appellant in receiving a fair hearing are present throughout the administrative justice system, these tensions play a particularly significant role in immigration and asylum appeals. In 2005, the United Nations High Commission for Refugees attributed the recent fall in asylum applications in European countries to the introduction of more restrictive asylum policies,[35] and the UK Parliamentary Joint Committee on Human Rights has said that aspects of the appeals system may fail to protect some appellants with well-founded claims.[36] The AIT makes decisions in this difficult setting.

The procedure at the AIT starts with a case management review hearing, where the immigration judge identifies the key issues under appeal and gives directions for the conduct of the full appeal hearing.[37] These directions normally require the appellant to produce written statements of all witnesses' evidence, a skeleton argument and a list of authorities. The full hearing takes place before one or more immigration judges, and the decision is usually issued later in writing, with reasons.

If the appeal is refused, a written application for reconsideration can be made to the tribunal within five working days, on the ground that the immigration judge has made a material error in law in reaching his decision. If refused, the application can be remade to the Court of Session, again within five working days, where it is considered without a hearing. A successful application for reconsideration will result in a rehearing before a different immigration judge (or judges) at the AIT. In limited situations, an onward appeal can be taken to the Inner House of the Court of Session.[38]

INFORMAL AND FAIR? – THREE POSSIBLE SOLUTIONS

As noted above, the key issue facing tribunals today is the proper role of informality in their decision-making. The current approach of attempting to provide a some-what less formal version of the methods and processes of the ordinary courts clearly has substantial weaknesses, notably the risk of making erroneous decisions arising from the inability of unrepresented appellants to present their cases adequately, and creation of expectations on the part of appellants that cannot be satisfied. However, it is important to recognise that traditional adjudication as practised in the ordinary courts may have certain virtues. This helps to explain why informality has in practice been so difficult to achieve in many tribunals.

There are two constraints which limit what tribunals may do in the name of informality. The first is the desire to ensure procedural fairness. The procedures of

---

34 The Immigration, Asylum and Nationality Act 2006 will introduce further significant changes to rights of appeal to the AIT which are not discussed here.
35 *Asylum Levels and Trends in Industrialised Countries* (2005).
36 See, eg, UK Parliamentary Joint Committee on Human Rights, Scrutiny of Bills, *Sixth Progress Report* (13th Report, 2003–04, HL 102/HC 640); *Asylum and Immigration (Treatment of Claimants Etc) Bill: New Clauses* (14th Report, 2003–04, HL 130/HC 828); *Scrutiny of Bills: Seventh Progress Report* (17th Report, 2003–04, HL 157/HC 999).
37 Asylum and Immigration Tribunal (Procedure) Rules 2005 (SI 2005/230), rule 45.
38 Nationality, Immigration and Asylum Act 2002, ss 103A et seq.

the ordinary courts may look formal but their aim is to ensure that each party has an equal opportunity to be heard. Hence tribunals generally attempt to reproduce the essentials of court process albeit with less complexity and formality. The second constraint is that, as noted above, the law which tribunals have to apply is often complex. Complex statutes and regulations govern the issues at stake and tribunals are legally bound to decide in accordance with them. They are not entitled to consider what is a 'just' or a 'fair' outcome if it would be incompatible with the relevant law.

Bearing these constraints in mind, the issue of informality might be approached in several ways. One approach is to rely on the higher courts' power to put right any problems which have arisen. A second approach is to acknowledge openly that appeals to tribunals are formal processes and reorganise tribunals accordingly. A third approach is to take the idea of informality seriously and to alter tribunals fundamentally to replace the current model with a genuinely informal process for dealing with citizens' grievances. These three approaches, which are discussed in detail below, are not necessarily mutually exclusive. It may be that different approaches might predominate in different tribunal contexts. For example, what might work in children's hearings might not work in employment disputes.

As already noted, the problem being addressed is not a peculiarly Scottish one, but there is evidence that tribunals in Scotland have sometimes dealt with the issues of formality in tribunals in different ways from their counterparts in England, and the continued existence of a separate legal system coupled with devolution of legislative and executive power means that different solutions may be sought in future.

Supervision by the higher courts

Intervention by the higher courts, whether by way of a statutory appeal or judicial review, is the traditional mechanism for correction of errors in first-instance decisions. Clearly, this is likely to address only one of the problems associated with informality: that of error in tribunal decisions. It is hard to see how intervention by the courts would assist in dealing with the problem of appellants' misperceptions of the tribunal process. There is, in the case of most tribunals in Scotland, a right of appeal to the Inner House of the Court of Session (often restricted to a point of law) and, where this has not been limited or excluded by statute,[39] there is also a common law right to seek judicial review on the ground that the conduct of an appeal does not comply with administrative law principles.[40] The right of appeal to the higher courts is the legacy of the Franks Committee, whose report led to the Tribunals and Inquiries Act 1958.[41] The Franks Report valued specialist tribunals and made no attempt to unify the tribunals themselves. Instead, it emphasised the importance of fair procedures and supervision by the higher courts through judicial review. For all tribunals in Scotland, including both UK-wide tribunals, which are administered by the Tribunals Service (on behalf of the Department for Constitutional Affairs), and specifically Scottish tribunals, which are the responsibility of the Scottish Executive, judicial supervision takes place within the Scottish legal system.

---

39 See, eg, the limited right to judicial review contained in the Nationality, Immigration and Asylum Act 2002, s 103A.
40 An application for judicial review would initially be heard in the Outer House.
41 Now replaced by the Tribunals and Inquiries Act 1992.

Although more restrictive time-limits, or other procedural constraints, may apply to statutory appeals, the scope of challenge in a statutory appeal on a point of law is broadly similar to that available when invoking the supervisory jurisdiction of the court in judicial review. Substantive grounds of challenge would include allegations that the tribunal's decision was tainted by an error of law, that findings of fact were manifestly contrary to the evidence, and that the tribunal had exercised its discretion (if any) unreasonably. In addition, the higher courts may set aside a tribunal's decisions if its procedures do not comply with principles of procedural fairness. Human rights legislation has added to the scope for challenge both on substantive and procedural grounds. Tribunals and indeed courts are obliged to respect the rights conferred by the European Convention on Human Rights (ECHR) in making their decisions by section 6 of the Human Rights Act 1998, although this is qualified by the obligation to give effect to primary legislation of the UK Parliament in certain circumstances even if that would infringe human rights.[42] For tribunals which fall within devolved competence, the limitations on legislative and executive competence imposed by the Scotland Act 1998 are also relevant here.[43]

Particular attention has been focused on the effect on the tribunal system of the incorporation of Article 6 ECHR into domestic law. Article 6(1) provides that:

'In the determination of his civil rights and obligations or of any criminal charge against him, everyone is entitled to a fair and public hearing within a reasonable time by an independent and impartial tribunal established by law: judgment shall be pronounced publicly.'[44]

Superficially, Article 6 appears to replicate the requirements of the common law doctrine of natural justice. However, following the incorporation of the ECHR, there were two reasons for considering that there might be advantages to litigants in relying on Article 6 to mount challenges on grounds of procedural fairness. One was the possibility that the requirements of Article 6 would prove to be more exacting than those of the common law doctrine. The other was that, whereas the application of natural justice to a decision can be excluded by statute, the role given to the Convention rights by the Scotland Act and the Human Rights Act, means that in practice human rights norms are much more difficult to exclude.[45] One possible consequence of the incorporation of human rights norms, therefore, was that it would lead to further judicialisation of the tribunal system.

A preliminary question which has caused some confusion is whether Article 6 applies to all tribunal proceedings or only to some. The European Court of Human Rights initially interpreted the phrase 'civil rights and obligations' in Article 6(1) rather narrowly as referring to rights and obligations in the field of private law and was unwilling to extend the term to include people's rights in relation to

42 Human Rights Act 1998, s 6(2).
43 See further Chapters 10 and 16 in this volume.
44 Public pronouncement of judgments is subject to restrictions on press and public involvement on the grounds of morality, public order or national security, and to restrictions for the protection of juveniles and private life.
45 On the other hand, breach of Art 6 by the primary decision-maker may in some circumstances be cured by appeal to or review by a body which does comply with Art 6 (see, eg, *Bryan v United Kingdom* (1996) 21 EHRR 342; *R (Alconbury Developments Ltd) v Secretary of State for the Environment, Transport and the Regions* [2001] 2 WLR 1389), whereas breaches of natural justice cannot be cured by judicial review.

administrative bodies, on the basis that this would interfere with the executive's right to implement policy through administrative acts. Over time, however, the Strasbourg Court's approach has changed in relation to some administrative acts, particularly where rights analogous to private rights have been infringed such as in the field of social security.[46] Nevertheless, the court has remained rigid in its refusal to extend Article 6(1) rights to immigration decisions, where it has not been considered appropriate to interfere with the discretion of the administrative body.[47] In the administrative justice field, the unsatisfactory consequence of this is that Article 6(1) has been found to apply to some administrative tribunals and not to others. However, a number of UK commentators now take the view that for domestic purposes we should act as if Article 6(1) applies to all tribunals. Sir William Leggatt's Review of Tribunals recommended drawing no distinction between tribunals to which Article 6(1) applies and those to which it does not,[48] and the government has accepted Leggatt's view that, in order to satisfy the Article 6 requirement of 'independence', tribunals should no longer be administered by the government department responsible for the relevant policy area. In England, the Court of Appeal has been prepared to treat asylum appeals as if the Article 6(1) procedural rights applied in substance, saying that: '[i]n this day and age, a right of access to a tribunal or other adjudicative mechanism established by the state is as important and fundamental as a right of access to the ordinary courts',[49] and the Court of Session has taken a similar approach.[50] Other decisions also suggest a reluctance to follow the Strasbourg Court's exclusion of certain 'public law rights'.[51] Accordingly, it appears that in practice tribunal determinations will in general be treated as covered by Article 6 within the UK.

Apart from the decision to separate tribunals from departments, thus far, the effects on tribunals of the incorporation of Article 6 into domestic law have been significant but not dramatic. The main concerns have related to independence and to provision of legal aid. Prompted by concerns about Article 6 challenges, the Lord Chancellor's Department decided to give greater security of tenure to part-time tribunal chairs by extending the standard period of appointment to five years.[52] Otherwise, it is not clear that the courts are applying stricter standards of procedural fairness because of Article 6. The courts have stressed that the common law test for bias is to the same effect as the Convention's requirement of an independent and impartial tribunal,[53] although it does appear as if the reformulation of the test for bias in *Porter v Magill*[54] was influenced by ECHR jurisprudence. Moreover,

46 *Ringeisen v Austria* (1971) A13, para 94; *Salerno v Italy* (1992) A245-D; *Salesi v Italy* (1993) 26 EHRR 187.
47 *Maaouia v France* (2001) 33 EHRR 42; *Mamatkulov v Turkey* (2003)14 BHRC 149. The court has found that Article 13 (the right to an effective remedy) applies where another Article has been violated, such as Article 3 (the prohibition on torture or inhuman and degrading treatment). See, eg, *Vilvarajah v UK* (1991) 14 EHRR 248; *Chahal v UK* (1996) 23 EHRR 413; *Jabari v Turkey* [2001] INLR 136.
48 *Tribunals for Users*, above n 11, para 2.17. See also Wade and Forsyth, *Administrative Law*, p 928.
49 *R v Secretary of State for the Home Department, ex parte Saleem (Asifa)* [2000] Imm AR 529.
50 *Koca v Secretary of State for the Home Department* [2005] CSIH 41.
51 See, eg, *Begum v Tower Hamlets London Borough Council* [2003] 2 AC 430.
52 See Lord Chancellor's Department Press Notices, 127/00, 12 April 2000 and 284/00, 27 July 2000.
53 *Lawal v Northern Spirit Ltd* [2004] 1 All ER 187; *Charanjit Singh v Secretary of State for the Home Department* 2004 SC 416.
54 [2002] 2 AC 357.

the courts have not used Article 6(1) to impose fixed 'court-like' procedures on all administrative decisions.[55] In general, the approach of the Scottish courts to questions of procedural fairness appears to be broadly comparable to that taken by the English courts.

Provision for legal aid has also been extended. The catalyst for this in Scotland was *S v Miller*[56] in which the fairness of proceedings at a children's hearing was challenged on various grounds. The Inner House decided that, although the provision of legal representation was not required in all cases, a child ought to be given free legal representation at a children's hearing where it was in the interests of justice to do so because representation was required for the child to present his or her case effectively. It was also held that existing arrangements for legal aid were not Convention-compliant. Following this case, regulations were enacted so that funded legal representation can be made available to a child (but not his or her parents) at a hearing. The hearing or a business meeting appoints the legal representative from a panel, which is usually made up of safeguarders and curators ad litem, and the local authority makes the arrangements for attendance and payment.[57] In addition, funding for representation at tribunal hearings under the Assistance by Way of Representation (ABWOR) scheme has been extended to immigration and asylum appeals, mental health, employment and VAT tribunals in Scotland.[58] The extension of ABWOR to employment tribunals in Scotland, when there is no equivalent provision in England and Wales, indicates that the devolution settlement allows for a variation of approach even in relation to UK tribunals.

To summarise, human rights legislation has extended the grounds on which the superior courts can supervise the quality of tribunal decision-making. However, the role of the courts cannot be seen as the answer to the problems associated with informality. Their function deals with only one of the concerns: the likelihood of erroneous decisions being made. Even as regards that, it is surely preferable to focus on how to ensure that tribunals get decisions right first time, rather than relying solely on mechanisms that correct errors after they occur.

'Court-like' processes – witness statements

The second approach identified above was to acknowledge that tribunal proceedings are formal processes, similar in essential respects to courts, and to allow tribunals to copy aspects of court procedure where that appears appropriate. Again, this might be done to improve the quality of decision-making because the procedures reduce the likelihood of error. It might also contribute to solving the problem of appellants' misperceptions precisely because it would make tribunals appear more like courts. This approach has obvious attractions in the more adversarial tribunals in which the respondent is committed to 'winning' the case. Employment tribunals and tribunals dealing with immigration control have always tended to operate in a much more adversarial fashion than other tribunals.[59] As noted above, in the latter case,

---

55 *Begum v Tower Hamlets LBC* [2003] 2 AC 430.
56 2001 SLT 531.
57 Nb, the local authority, and not the Scottish Legal Aid Board, is responsible for the arrangements: Children's Hearings (Legal Representation) (Scotland) Rules 2002 (SSI 2002/63).
58 Legal Aid (Scotland) Act 1986 and Advice and Assistance (Assistance by way of Representation) (Scotland) Regulations 2003 (SSI 2003/179).
59 Genn and Genn, above n 8.

they are even referred to as 'courts'. The argument that the unrepresented appellant will be able to present their own case effectively is particularly unconvincing in these contexts and an insistence on formal procedures may provide at least some protection for appellants. Perhaps because these tribunals identify more with the ordinary courts and share their ethos, there have, as noted above, been significant variations in Scottish practice even though these are UK tribunals.

For example, the fact that, in Scotland, employment and immigration tribunals have in the past placed less emphasis on written witness statements than the equivalent English and Welsh tribunals stems from the fact that the normal way to present witnesses' evidence in Scottish civil courts is still orally, not in written form. Affidavit evidence is relatively unusual and precognitions are privileged as between client and solicitor: they are not prepared with a view to being presented as evidence in court, and are not disclosed to the court. However, such Scottish differences may be vulnerable to changes to practice in UK tribunals inspired by reforms of the procedure of the ordinary courts in England and Wales. Following Lord Woolf's reports into access to justice, changes were made to the civil justice system in England and Wales[60] to encourage early settlement of cases, and these changes included requiring parties to disclose details of their claim at an early stage, and to make witness statements available to the court and the other parties. It has now become standard practice for such witness statements to stand as the evidence-in-chief of the relevant witness.[61]

However, it may actually be in the interests of appellants (whether represented or not) to have evidence heard orally. The practice of hearing witnesses rather than taking statements as read ensures, according to an employment practitioner in Scotland, that no unfair advantage is gained by having a well-crafted witness statement, and that evidence is tested by cross-examination. This in turn gives a greater impression of due process having been observed.[62]

These changes have been applied to employment and immigration tribunals as well as to the ordinary courts in England and Wales. Since 2001 it has been the practice to lodge witness statements in immigration and asylum appeals[63] and, more recently, in some employment tribunals in Scotland. However, some account has been taken of Scottish views. In 2002, the Employment Tribunals Taskforce remarked on the different Scottish approach to written statements as follows:

'We noted the increasing use of witness statements in England. Some felt strongly that they can be costly to representatives and time-consuming to prepare, may not necessarily be accurate and could be damaging to an unrepresented applicant if there is no opportunity for cross-examination. On the other hand, we were told by the judiciary that they can assist in reducing valuable hearing time. In England and Wales, we were told that the use of witness statements was found to be valuable and they are increasingly being taken as read. The use of such statements does not occur in Scotland where they are generally not encouraged and evidence is given in the traditional oral fashion.'[64]

---

60 *Interim Report on Access to Civil Justice* (June 1995).
61 *Access to Civil Justice: Final Report by Lord Woolf to the Lord Chancellor* (July 1996), para 53.
62 L Marr, 'The Scottish and English Employment Tribunal Practice and Procedure – the Best of Both Worlds?' (available at *http://www.legal500.com*).
63 Immigration Appellate Authority, *Chief Adjudicator's Practice Direction of 27 July 2001*.
64 Department of Trade and Industry, above n 23, para 8.26.

Common rules of procedure for employment tribunals were introduced throughout the UK in October 2004.[65] The Employment Tribunals Task Force correctly predicted that these might address this difference in procedure between Scotland and England and rule 10(2) now allows a chairman to order that witness statements be prepared and exchanged. However, this practice is not as widespread as in immigration and asylum appeals, where it is standard practice to require that such statements be produced.[66] The discernible emphasis on oral evidence, rather than on witness statements, at employment tribunals in Scotland has therefore been maintained.

Scottish differences have been recognised in other aspects of employment tribunals. The common procedure rules acknowledge Scottish practice and allow the tribunal chair to exclude witnesses from the hearing room.[67] It remains to be seen whether Scottish practices will continue to be permitted to diverge in this UK tribunal, or whether the influence which the English and Welsh civil justice system, through the Department for Constitutional Affairs, has on the Tribunals Service will change practice in Scotland.

The tension between pressures for more formality and pressures to retain informality has also been felt in the children's hearings. However, apart from the introduction of paid legal representation for children, there has been little change to the practice of the children's hearings.[68]

UK-wide reforms – removing 'court-like' processes

The third way of dealing with the complexity in tribunals is more radical. It is to challenge the idea that a court-like forum is appropriate at all. This approach lies behind the UK government's reform programme, outlined in a recent White Paper.[69] This has been partially implemented through the introduction of the Tribunals Service and the enactment of the Constitutional Reform Act 2005, and further legislation is planned.[70] The programme promises radical reform of the way that tribunals approach their work, and will affect UK-wide tribunals in Scotland. These reforms need to be understood in the context of the Leggatt Review, from which they grew. This marked a significant departure from previous approaches to the organisation of the tribunal system. Its emphasis was on unification, rather than specialisation, and on sharing skills and resources to the mutual benefit of different parts of the tribunal system and the users of the system:

> 'It should never be forgotten that tribunals exist for users, and not the other way round. No matter how good tribunals may be, they do not fulfil their function unless they are accessible by the people who want to use them, and unless the users receive the help they need to prepare and present their cases.'[71]

Leggatt clearly reaffirmed the traditional view of tribunals as informal, accessible fora for dispute resolution that has prevailed since Franks. For example, he described

---

65 Employment Tribunals (Constitution and Rules of Procedure) Regulations 2004.
66 Asylum and Immigration Tribunal (Procedure) Rules 2005 (SI 2005/230), rule 45.
67 Employment Tribunals (Constitution and Rules of Procedure) Regulations 2004, rule 27.
68 A Scottish Executive consultation, *Getting it Right for Every Child* (2005), resulted in proposals for action which have not yet been implemented.
69 *Transforming Public Services*, above n 12.
70 See n 13, above.
71 *Tribunals for Users*, Overview, para 6.

representation as 'work[ing] against the objective of making tribunals directly and easily accessible to the full range of potential users',[72] and the measures in his review were designed to ensure that legal representation would only be required in a residual category of complex cases. Leggatt also rejected the argument that, because employment tribunals increasingly resembled courts, they should become courts, stating that this would be 'a retrograde step'.[73]

The specific changes proposed by Leggatt included unifying procedural rules, sharing tribunal premises and administrative systems and exploring less formal processes, including alternative methods of dispute resolution. The idea of sharing (appropriately qualified) judicial staff across different tribunals was also mooted.

The 2004 White Paper, *Transforming Public Services: Complaints Redress and Tribunals*, accepted Leggatt's key recommendation of a unified Tribunals Service and this was set up as an agency within the Department for Constitutional Affairs in April 2006. In the 2004–05 session, Bills[74] were presented to the UK Parliament which were intended to bring about further reforms to tribunals and, while only limited reforms (to the procedures for appointing some tribunal chairs)[75] made it to the statute book at that time, the government's intention is that the other key reforms – including a simplified two-tier tribunals structure (consisting of a tribunal tier and appellate tier) and a new Administrative Justice and Tribunals Council to replace the existing Council on Tribunals – will still take place.[76] Taken as a whole, these reforms have a more ambitious agenda than Leggatt. The task of the new Tribunals Service is to improve the whole end-to-end system of administrative justice, and not just tribunals. It emphasises resolution of disputes prior to hearings, encourages the reconsideration of decisions if more evidence becomes available and makes dispute resolution, and not the administration of appeals, its objective:

'We need to go further and to re-engineer processes radically so that just solutions can be found without formal hearings at all.... The organisation will inherit existing jurisdictions and procedural rules but its overarching mission will be dispute resolution and we expect it, in conjunction with departments, users and representatives, to develop new ways of operating.'[77]

The current reforms therefore respond to the perception that tribunals are not user-friendly by changing the way that tribunals deal with cases. The new proposals discourage traditional oral hearings involving examination and cross-examination of witnesses. It is assumed that, as with the ombudsmen, sound decisions which respect the rights of parties should be achievable without formal hearings. Where oral hearings do take place, tribunals will also be expected to change the way that they work by ensuring that hearings are not daunting or legalistic, and by providing comprehensive and comprehensible information about the process. Procedures that prompt active reconsideration of decisions before a hearing will be encouraged and the existing use of virtual hearings, using telephone and video conferencing, is to be expanded.[78]

72 *Tribunals for Users*, para 4.21.
73 *Tribunals for Users*, para 3.22.
74 Courts and Tribunals Bill and Constitutional Reform Bill.
75 Constitutional Reform Act 2005, Pt 4.
76 See draft Tribunals, Courts and Enforcement Bill, n 13 above.
77 *Transforming Public Services*, para 6.20.
78 *Transforming Public Services*, para 6.20.

This departure from oral hearings is not entirely consistent with the Leggatt Review, which acknowledged that oral hearings were often more 'user-friendly' than written processes and were helpful in ensuring that justice was seen to be done.[79] It recommended that the use of alternative methods of dispute resolution (ADR) should be explored where it was appropriate to do so, either because the nature of the case made it suitable for ADR, or because there was scope for negotiation, for example where a stark 'win' or 'lose' result was not appropriate. Leggatt cited employment and land disputes as appropriate for ADR since the parties might wish to have a continuing relationship once the subject-matter of the dispute had been dealt with.[80] However, the Tribunals Service proposals take Leggatt's recommendations on ADR further, recommending that they be introduced generally and not just for certain subject-matters. The Service has the aim of 'moving out of courts and tribunals disputes that could be resolved elsewhere through better use of education, information, advice and proportionate dispute resolution'.[81]

The aims of the Tribunals Service also go further than those of the Leggatt Review as regards representation. The Leggatt Review, whilst taking the view that the vast majority of appellants should be enabled to understand and put their cases properly themselves,[82] was careful to emphasise that not all appellants would be able to do so, and noted that funded representation was available for certain tribunals (such as immigration and mental health). Leggatt recommended that the criteria for funding representation should be complexity or difficulty for the appellant rather than the type of tribunal – thus making it possible for funded representation to be extended to a wider range of tribunals. However, these caveats are not emphasised in the White Paper, which presents even more strongly than Leggatt the view that, in general, appellants should be able to represent themselves. According to the White Paper: '[t]he case for representation and advocacy is based on assumptions about the nature of the tribunal process. As the process changes, so does the need for support'.[83] This suggests that a reduction, rather than an increase, in current levels of representation is expected.

These proposals indeed suggest radical change to a tribunal system no longer seen in isolation from other aspects of dispute resolution, and a genuine attempt to replace court-like procedures with something different. But there must be doubts about whether this ambitious vision can be realised in a way that does not disadvantage appellants. The generalised way in which the proposed reforms are presented leaves a number of questions unanswered. It may well be the case that reform along these lines will make tribunals more user-friendly, or provide user-friendly alternatives, but it is not clear that it will remove all the causes of appellants' misunderstanding of, and dissatisfaction with, the current tribunal system. To give an example, those appealing administrative decisions may get the chance in the new user-friendly system to tell their story in their own way, but will they be any more likely to realise that decisions must be made according to law rather than to open-ended criteria of fairness and justice? More importantly, whilst the reformed process might reduce the need for the advocacy skills which the current system requires by ensuring informality of process, it does nothing to address the problem

79 *Tribunals for Users*, para 8.16.
80 *Tribunals for Users*, paras 8.17 et seq.
81 *Transforming Public Services*, para 1.13.
82 *Tribunals for Users*, para 4.21.
83 *Transforming Public Services*, para 10.15.

of legal complexity. Indeed both Leggatt and the White Paper can be accused of underestimating the range of tribunals in which complex legal issues arise. So, it may still be true in many disputes that appellants will not be able to present cases effectively themselves. In addition, the reforms will not address the factors which encourage adversarialism in certain tribunals such as employment tribunals and those concerned with immigration control. These limitations on the possibility of achieving much less formal processes are to some extent acknowledged, for example, in the separate treatment given to employment and immigration tribunals in the White Paper, but arguably the pressures that encourage adversarialism have not been sufficiently acknowledged.

Both the Leggatt Review and the subsequent reforms relate only to tribunals which operate across the UK or in relation to England and Wales. They will, therefore, have important effects on the Scottish justice system but will not apply to those tribunals for which responsibility has been devolved. The Scottish Executive kept a watching brief on the Leggatt Review and the White Paper but, disappointingly, has not yet produced proposals of its own relating to devolved tribunals. So, it is not clear whether there will be divergent approaches to tribunal justice operating within Scotland in the near future. The implications of these developments for Scotland are discussed below.

THE FUTURE FOR TRIBUNALS IN SCOTLAND

At the beginning of this chapter three dimensions of difference for tribunals in Scotland were suggested. These were: the existence of specifically Scottish tribunals; differences in the way certain UK tribunals operate in Scotland; and different arrangements for oversight and accountability. Separate Scottish tribunals are likely to continue to exist as the reasons for their creation remain valid. However, although there have long been separate tribunal structures, the approach to tribunal justice has been broadly the same as in the rest of the UK, and has been that set out by the Franks Committee. Given that the Scottish Executive has not yet bought into the current reform programme it is possible that a divergence of methods between Scottish tribunals and the UK tribunals will be seen in future. It would be desirable for the Executive to engage more with the reform process and to take a view on whether the White Paper proposals are desirable in principle, and the extent to which they can or ought to be applied to Scottish tribunals. The reform programme also raises the question of whether the distinctly Scottish elements within UK tribunals will remain. The formal structure of devolution places no obstacle to elimination of Scottish differences, but it would be in the spirit of devolution for the case for Scottish differences within UK tribunals to be assessed on their merits in each case rather than for it to be assumed without argument that arrangements must be uniform.

As the Tribunals Service develops, it will remain to be seen how Scottish interests engage with the Service and the extent to which existing Scottish practice will be maintained. There have been signs that it may be possible to adjust the UK-wide reforms for Scotland: for example, as mentioned above, the employment tribunals service review attempted to apply best practice from different traditions while also focusing on reforming the process so that it was 'fit for purpose'.[84] However, it must

---

84 Department for Trade and Industry, above n 23, p 11.

be acknowledged that the thrust of the reform programme is to make tribunals *less* like courts, whereas Scottish differences (such as the practice of excluding witnesses from the hearing before they have given evidence in employment tribunals) have sometimes been inspired by the desire to replicate formal aspects of court procedure. There may, therefore, be pressure to eliminate Scottish differences.

These comments are not made on the assumption that elimination of Scottish differences would necessarily be a bad thing. Aspects of the reform programmes may well be beneficial, such as early reconsideration of decisions and proportionate dispute resolution in appropriate cases. In addition, oral hearings and representation should not be treated as a panacea and UK-wide tribunals in Scotland might benefit from reforms which promote alternatives to traditional oral hearings. What is important is that each proposal be evaluated on its merits to ensure that it is genuinely for the benefit of tribunal users.

One area in which differences in the way UK tribunals operate in Scotland is likely to remain is in public funding for representation. This is because responsibility for legal aid is devolved. As noted above, the scope of the ABWOR scheme has been expanded to cover more tribunals. The availability of legal aid has been of particular concern in the area of asylum and immigration. One of the concerns that the Council on Tribunals expressed about the new appeals system was the effect which legal aid arrangements in England and Wales are having on the availability of advice, assistance and representation.[85] Some of the restrictions on legal aid which prevail in England and Wales do not, therefore, apply in Scotland, where legal representation before the asylum and immigration tribunal and (in complex cases) before the employment tribunal is funded by the ABWOR[86] scheme. However, the Community Legal Service system of awarding franchises is so different from the case-by-case system operating in Scotland that it is difficult to draw direct comparisons, and both systems can be difficult to access.[87] The operation of two such different schemes in Scotland and England can lead to anomalies, for example where English solicitors appear at an asylum and immigration tribunal hearing in Scotland. They may have difficulty getting paid for their work under the Community Legal Service scheme for England and Wales, and may not be aware that they should arrange with Scottish solicitors for them to appear using the Scottish ABWOR scheme. This can be a barrier for people living in Scotland who may be detained under the Immigration Acts in English detention centres, but whose legal representatives are in Scotland, or for people living in England who are detained in Scotland, but who have English solicitors.

Oversight and accountability

Apart from the change which has seen UK tribunals move into the Tribunals Service in order to improve their independence, the proposed reforms will also change the supervision and oversight of tribunals in two other respects. The first is the proposal, mentioned above, to introduce an appellate tribunal which will replace and therefore

---

85   Council on Tribunals, *Annual Report 2004–2005* (HC 472, SE/2005/173, 2005), ch 5, para 15.
86   Legal Aid (Scotland) Act 1986 and Advice and Assistance (Assistance by Way of Representation) (Scotland) Regulations 2003 (SSI 2003/179).
87   In 2004–05 ABWOR was used in only 140 employment tribunal cases: Scottish Legal Aid Board, *Annual Report 2004-2005* (2005), Appendix 3, Table 3.4.

have the same status as the Court of Session.[88] While the implications of this reform for the Scottish legal system deserve scrutiny, the implications for Scotland of the second change, to the Council on Tribunals, are already causing concern.

The Council on Tribunals is currently the principal oversight body for the tribunals system. Its functions are to review and report on the constitution and working of tribunals and other matters referred to it.[89] The Council has a Scottish Committee which oversees the procedures both of UK-wide tribunals operating in Scotland, and of the separate Scottish tribunals. The White Paper proposes the formation of a new Administrative Justice Council out of the existing Council on Tribunals. The changes in the short term will not be dramatic, but in the longer term it is intended that the Council will evolve into an advisory body for the whole administrative justice sector, and its remit will reflect the new emphasis on improving administrative decisions before they reach tribunals.[90] In addition to its current duties, the Council's expanded remit will include keeping under review the performance of the administrative justice system as a whole, drawing attention to matters of particular importance or concern; reviewing the relationships between ombudsmen, tribunals and the courts; identifying priorities for, and encouraging the conduct of, research; and providing advice and making recommendations to government on changes to legislation, practice and procedure which will improve the workings of the administrative justice system.[91]

The failure of the Scottish Ministers to respond to the Leggatt Review or to the White Paper has caused particular anxiety in relation to the arrangements for oversight in Scotland. It is difficult to see how the Scottish Committee of the Council on Tribunals will fulfil its role in the light of the change in role of its parent organisation. One example is training. It is envisaged that the Judicial Studies Board and the Council on Tribunals will work together to provide the training resources which the proposed radical changes to UK-wide tribunals will demand. In Scotland, training has hitherto depended on the initiative of individual tribunals and the role which the Judicial Studies Board will play here is less clear, particularly since the Board has no remit to train Scottish judges in the civil courts. Aware of the importance of training[92] and of the enhanced role which the UK Council on Tribunals has been promised, the Scottish Committee wants to remain attached to the UK body[93] and issued annual reports in 2004 and 2005 which expressed concerns that devolved tribunals might be left behind if they were not able to benefit from the training and sharing of expertise which the Tribunals Service will provide to UK-wide tribunals.[94]

CONCLUSION

The future is, therefore, uncertain. There is a vision for the future of tribunals at UK level. It is not clear whether the Scottish Executive has any vision for the future

---

88 *Transforming Public Services*, para 7.28. See reference to Courts and Tribunals Bill, above n 13.
89 Tribunals and Inquiries Act 1992, s 1. The Council also has functions in relation to inquiries.
90 *Transforming Public Services*, para 11.13.
91 *Transforming Public Services*, para 11.13.
92 At present the Scottish Committee maintains a register of training resources.
93 Scottish Committee of Council on Tribunals, *Annual Report 2003-2004* (SE 2004/203), foreword.
94 Scottish Committee of Council on Tribunals, *Annual Report 2004-2005* (SE/2005/188), para 20.

of tribunals in Scotland. It is clear that UK tribunals operating in Scotland will be subject to significant change, but not clear which of their distinctively Scottish aspects will survive. At present, there are signs that the devolved tribunals will continue to develop in the traditional, piecemeal manner, and indeed new tribunals are still emerging, such as the additional support needs tribunal and mental health tribunals.[95] Potentially, Scotland could have the best of both worlds, learning from the beneficial aspects of the reformed UK-wide service, and applying them to devolved tribunals, while retaining the positive attributes of the latter. These benefits will only come about if sufficient commitment and resources are devoted to the development of all tribunals in Scotland.

---

95 C Turner, 'Seen to be fair?' (2005) 50/11 JLSS 24; M Ross, 'MHTs take another look' (2006) 51/3 JLSS 20; D Hanlon and K McGill, 'Safeguards before the MHTs' (2006) 51/4 JLSS 28.

Chapter 16

Protecting Human Rights in the Scottish Legal System

Jim Murdoch

INTRODUCTION

If devolution is the most visible part of the constitutional reform package introduced by the 1997 Labour Government, 'incorporation' of the European Convention on Human Rights (ECHR) by the Human Rights Act 1998 (HRA) and the Scotland Act 1998 (SA) may prove to be its most controversial. Previously virtually ignored in domestic legal proceedings (particularly in Scotland), the Convention was finally welcomed as a legitimate source of legal authority. However, within six or so years of this conferment of formal standing in the legal system, the same government was voicing executive frustration with judicial determinations concerning politically-sensitive matters such as the detention of terrorists and the deportation and extradition of non-nationals from the UK. Human rights legislation had become a site of constitutional struggle in which the rule of law was being pitted against executive attempts to deal with perceived threats to community safety.

This chapter seeks to outline the status of the ECHR and its jurisprudence in the Scottish legal system, to consider the extent to which the domestic courts have given effect to Convention rights since 1999, and to assess the degree of success the Convention has had in redrawing or realigning domestic law and practice. This focus upon the Scottish dimension will mean excluding from consideration some of the more high-profile controversies that have emerged to date. The leading Scottish cases have not generated the same coverage in the UK media as some of the cases brought in the English courts (notably those arising from the application of anti-terrorism legislation) and Scotland – small and relatively homogenous – can never hope to generate the number of human rights cases that will arise south of the border. However, there is no reason, in principle, why human rights challenges to UK legislation should not arise in Scotland (for example, where terrorist suspects are detained in Scotland) and some cases arising from specifically Scots law, such as challenges to the position of temporary sheriffs and to the practice of 'slopping-out' in Scottish prisons, have had important consequences for Scottish government going far beyond their effect on the rights of the individuals making those challenges. It is important, therefore, to analyse the differences that exist in the protection of human rights in Scots law. This chapter will first explain how the Scottish approach to the protection of human rights differed before incorporation of the ECHR, then explain the effect of the human rights legislation, before going on to discuss the experience of operation of that legislation thus far, concluding with an analysis of attempts to ensure that human rights values are fully embedded in government and society.

THE STARTING-POINT: THE ECHR AND SCOTS LAW BEFORE 1999

Until comparatively recently, the interests that we now refer to as human rights were discussed and taught in the language of 'civil liberties'. Scots law relating to civil liberties differed to a significant degree from that applying in the rest of the UK because, in many cases, rules of law impinging on those liberties had not been harmonised at UK level, most obviously in the areas of substantive criminal law and criminal process. Nevertheless, the protection of civil liberties displayed the same general features as in the rest of the UK and the underlying constitutional framework was the same. The topic of civil liberties in university law programmes tended to be marginalised and presented as an adjunct to courses on constitutional law. The latter typically began with an exploration of Dicey's exposition of the rule of law which stressed the inherent superiority of judicially-created protection of individual rights over codified statements of rights, which were alleged often to amount to mere rhetoric. The content of the civil liberties topic usually consisted of a handful of judicial decisions largely concerning the application of the criminal law in cases involving public assembly[1] and expression,[2] and on the workings of the system of criminal procedure,[3] including protection against ill-treatment during detention through rules excluding unfairly obtained evidence.[4] However, the oft-quoted aphorism that human rights in Scotland (as in Britain as a whole) were essentially residual – that is, everything was permitted except that which was prohibited – failed to recognise the role that Parliament had played in providing positive entitlements, often necessitated by judicial conservatism as exemplified by timid and excessively deferential decision-making by the courts.[5] For example, statutory provisions provided a high level of procedural safeguards for accused persons by strictly limiting the maximum length of pre-trial detention.[6] Religious tolerance in a country where schisms were frequent had been promoted by a statutory separation between Church and State,[7] and Parliament also responded to demands for separate state-supported denominational schooling by Irish Roman Catholic parents who found that the brand of Christianity on offer in the public school system had a distinctly Presbyterian flavour.[8] More recently, and most obviously, human rights have been advanced by race relations and other equalities legislation.

But the legal foundations for human rights rested less upon firm rock than upon shifting sands. Although the legislature had intervened to promote rights on occasion, it could not be assumed that the legislature and executive would

---

1 Eg, *Deakin v Milne* (1882) 10 R (J) 22; *Aldred v Langmuir* 1932 JC 22.
2 Eg, *Galletly v Laird* 1953 SLT 67; *Watt v Annan* 1978 SLT 198.
3 Eg, *Bell v Black and Morrison* (1865) 5 Irv 57.
4 As in *Chalmers v HM Advocate* 1954 JC 66.
5 See, eg, the English case of *Malone v Metropolitan Police Commissioner* [1979] Ch 344, in which phone-tapping by the police was held to be lawful because it was not specifically prohibited. The European Court of Human Rights subsequently found the absence of legal regulation of phone-tapping in the UK to be a violation of Art 8 ECHR (*Malone v United Kingdom* (1984) 7 EHRR 14) and Parliament responded by passing the Interception of Communications Act 1985.
6 Ie, through the '140 day rule', which still forms part of Scots law: see Criminal Procedure (Scotland) Act 1995, s 65 (as amended).
7 Church of Scotland Act 1921, s 1; see further, F Lyall, *Of Presbyters and Kings: Church and State in the Law of Scotland* (1980).
8 See, eg, J Murdoch, 'Religion, education and the law' (1989) 34 JLSS 258.

always respect fundamental rights. Moreover, although international and regional developments in human rights protection meant that executive and legislative action could in theory be measured against external standards, these developments largely passed by the Scottish legal system (and thereby, public administration in general). In particular, although the UK ratified the ECHR in 1953 and accepted the right of individual petition in 1966, these developments had no direct legal consequences at the domestic level as Strasbourg jurisprudence had no ready route into the deliberations of the Scottish courts. This did not mean that the ECHR had no impact upon the Scottish legal system. The right of individual petition allowed those whose rights were not protected by Scots law to use the Strasbourg machinery to pursue their grievances. There was a steady, but certainly not spectacular, use of the right of individual petition, and although there were certain successes there were far more failures.[9]

Strasbourg cases emanating from Scotland, of course, often but not invariably have a distinctively Scottish dimension. Where Scots law and practice were effectively replicated elsewhere in the UK (for example, some of the prisoners' cases emanating from Scottish prisons[10] and corporal punishment (albeit administered by the tawse rather than cane))[11] the geographical source of the challenge was of little obvious importance. On the other hand, a number of cases determined in Strasbourg have concerned specifically Scottish practices, and have led the UK government to make significant modifications to distinctly Scottish legal provisions or administrative rules. This was particularly so in the area of criminal proceedings.[12] For example, cases such as *Granger v United Kingdom*,[13] *Boner v United Kingdom* and *Maxwell v United Kingdom*[14] led to the end of the automatic right of appeal against conviction or sentence and to the introduction of the requirement that leave to appeal be obtained,[15] while in *McMichael v United Kingdom*, a crucial aspect of the operation of the children's hearing system was condemned.[16]

The reluctance of the Scottish courts to give any weight to the Convention was in contrast to the position in England and Wales where there was some obvious movement on the part of the judges, particularly in the 1980s and early 1990s, to begin to try to shape a new legal awareness. Whether this resulted from the general renaissance in administrative law, prompted in part by recognition of the limits of reliance upon the legislature to restrain a dominant executive, or was merely a natural consequence of the longstanding use of international obligations

9 For a survey, see R Reed and J Murdoch, *A Guide to Human Rights Law in Scotland* (2001), paras 1.10–1.16.
10 See eg, *Boyle and Rice v United Kingdom* (1988) Series A no 131; *McCallum v United Kingdom* (1990) Series A no 183; and *Campbell v United Kingdom* (1992) Series A no 233-A.
11 *Campbell and Cosans v United Kingdom* (1982) Series A no 48.
12 But cf comments of Lord Hope in *Anderson v HM Advocate* 1996 JC 29 at 34 suggesting that Scots criminal law was in general Convention-compliant: Article 6 reflects 'principles which ... have, for a long time, been established as part of the law of this country'.
13 (1990) Series A no 174.
14 (1994) Series A no 300-B; and (1994) Series A no 300-C.
15 These cases illustrate that a successful challenge before the Strasbourg Court may result in what appears to be a reduction of the rights of persons in domestic law. The prior system of the automatic right of appeal, when combined with a restriction on legal aid to appeals which appeared to have merit, meant that many appellants appeared unrepresented whereas the Crown was always represented. Imposing a requirement of leave to appeal meant that the UK was able to ensure that appellants would, in general be represented, and Art 6 complied with.
16 (1995) Series A no 307-B.

in interpreting statutory ambiguities, by the end of the Thatcher administration the use of the Convention as an informal source of law was well recognised in England and Wales and in Northern Ireland, just as it was in other legal systems which had yet to 'transform' the Convention into domestic law. In Scotland, however, Convention arguments were not available either as an aid to statutory interpretation or as a source of public policy with which to develop the common law, in direct contrast to the situation in other jurisdictions (such as England and Wales, Northern Ireland, the Republic of Ireland,[17] and even the Nordic countries).[18] The only context in which the Convention was given any weight – but only to a limited extent and only in respect of particular judges who appeared more open to such submissions – was in judicial review proceedings, and then only in respect of certain areas (particularly immigration controls).[19]

In 1992, in a lecture on the importance of European influences on Scots law, Lord Hope warned of the risk of 'isolation by unfamiliarity' not only with EU law but also with ECHR jurisprudence. At the heart of the problem was a self-imposed obstacle: judicial reluctance to hear arguments based upon European law meant that counsel were unlikely 'to spend days researching into a topic on which the judge [was] likely to cut them short [and as] a result, judges were not having relevant European jurisprudence cited to them, and thus European law was not finding its way into their judgments'.[20] But this was a self-imposed catch-22, for the more courts were asked to consider Convention arguments, the more reluctant they seemed to do so. This situation resulted from the decisions in *Kaur v Lord Advocate*[21] and *Moore v Secretary of State for Scotland*,[22] the twin watchdogs at the doors of the Scottish legal system which effectively prevented entry of the ECHR into domestic law in the absence of a statute 'transforming' the treaty into domestic law. *Kaur* and *Moore* effectively (but not necessarily technically, for it was always open to the House of Lords to have taken a different line)[23] prevented the use of Convention arguments. In both of these cases, attempts to rely on Convention rights were bound to fail because the pleadings rested upon rather speculative constitutional and legal arguments. In particular, *Kaur* is hardly more than a reaffirmation that international law and domestic law are two distinct spheres and that legislative approval is required to transform international obligations entered into by the Executive into domestic law. However, it also provided the opportunity for the Outer House to reject as a matter of constitutional propriety the growing English case law which was encouraging at this early stage the use of the Convention as an aid to statutory interpretation. This decision was given more decisive weight four years later by the Inner House in *Moore v Secretary of State for Scotland* in disposing of party-litigant submissions. The result was that for the next two decades, there was only sporadic use made of Convention arguments in

---

17 See, eg, M Hunt, *Using Human Rights Law in English Courts* (1997); and essays by P Gardner and C Wickremasinghe and by B Dickson in B Dickson (ed), *Human Rights and the European Convention* (1997).
18 See M Scheinin (ed), *International Human Rights Norms in the Nordic and Baltic Countries* (1996).
19 See further J Murdoch in Dickson (ed), *Human Rights*, above n 17.
20 *From Maastricht to the Saltmarket*, Society of Solicitors in the Supreme Courts of Scotland, Biennial Lecture 1992, pp 16–17.
21 1981 SLT 322.
22 1985 SLT 38.
23 But see *Lord Advocate v Scotsman Newspapers* 1989 SC (HL) 122 at 167 per Lord Templeman.

Scotland. The rich seam of Convention jurisprudence was left largely unmined, a situation only in part in practice altered by the relaxation in judicial attitudes marked in 1996 in *T, Petitioner*[24] in which – in observations strictly obiter – Lord Hope sought to cast *Kaur* and *Moore* aside as hopelessly outdated and inappropriate. This judgment did not tackle the constitutional doubts expressed in *Kaur* that use of the Convention without legislative approval was inappropriate and seemed to limit use of the Convention to cases of statutory interpretation, but did prompt some greater, albeit limited, use of the Convention in legal argument.[25] However, the impact of *T, Petitioner* was short-lived, for parliamentary mandates for the application of Convention jurisprudence appeared within a short period of time.

CONSTITUTIONAL REFORM

It is worth recalling that there was (and still is) a party-political dimension to the issue of incorporation of the ECHR. As late as the mid-1990s, many in the Labour Party still considered that the most appropriate way ahead for the effective protection of human rights in Britain was not through the 'incorporation' of the European Convention on Human Rights but through specific legislative reforms spelling out in some detail the scope and content of individual rights. The judiciary were not to be trusted. For the Conservative Party, the matter was more straightforward: it was the notion of 'human rights' that was not to be trusted, particularly if this came with a European flavour. Only the Liberal Democrats advocated incorporation, albeit from a perspective far removed from likely political power. However, the New Labour leadership was converted to the cause of incorporation and the 1997 election manifesto included a commitment to translate the ECHR into domestic law. The plans were subsequently outlined in the White Paper, *Rights Brought Home: The Human Rights Bill*[26] which led to the enactment of the HRA.

How these proposals related to the devolution proposals was clearly an issue as the actions of devolved institutions might result in the UK being in violation of its international obligations under the ECHR. The White Paper on devolution to Scotland[27] made clear that the principal means of restraining the Scottish Parliament and Scottish Executive from violating Convention rights would be the device of judicial determination of challenges to the exercise of devolved legislative and executive powers rather than executive veto exercised from London.[28]

The former option was the more obvious in political terms, but when taken along with the proposals in the Human Rights Bill to increase the scope of judicial review powers and to authorise the courts to issue declarations of incompatibility, critics were concerned that not only would there be a significant enhancement of judicial authority but also that this could be seen as parliamentary abrogation of

---

24 1997 SLT 724. See A Brown, 'The European Convention on Human Rights in Scottish courts' 1996 SLT (News) 267.
25 See, eg, *McLeod v HM Advocate* 1998 SCCR 77; *Ucak v HM Advocate* 1998 SCCR 517; and *Ward v Scotrail Railways Ltd* 1999 SC 255.
26 Cm 3782, 1997.
27 *Scotland's Parliament* (Cm 3658, 1997).
28 But note the power of the Secretary of State to intervene in certain cases prior to royal assent: SA, s 35.

the task of protecting human rights, a responsibility considered more properly that of the legislature.[29] A second crucial question concerned the issue of whether one set of statutory provisions or two would be needed to confer this mandate upon the judiciary. It might have been possible for the HRA itself to have included the necessary provisions, but practical considerations probably ruled this out even although many claims of human rights violations could raise issues under both HRA and SA. Thus, both HRA and SA are relevant to the protection of human rights in Scotland. Under SA, the observation and implementation of obligations under the ECHR are not reserved matters.[30] Accordingly, ensuring compliance with human rights norms is primarily the responsibility of the Scottish Parliament and Scottish Executive within the framework of controls established by the two statutes.

The provisions of the two statutes became effective in stages. Since May 1999 (when executive power was devolved), it has been possible to bring challenges to executive action based upon the human rights provisions of SA in the Scottish courts, and since 1 July 1999 (when legislative power was devolved to the Scottish Parliament) it has similarly been possible to test provisions of Acts of the Scottish Parliament. The HRA entered into force on 2 October 2000, and from that date it became possible to make claims of human rights violations under both Acts.

In both cases, such claims involve 'Convention rights', that is, the rights and fundamental freedoms set out in Articles 2 to 12 and 14 of the Convention, Articles 1 to 3 of Protocol 1, and Article 1 of Protocol 13, all as read with Articles 16 to 18 of the Convention and subject to any designated derogation or reservation of the Act.[31] The definition of Convention rights is amplified by HRA, section 2 which provides that a court or tribunal determining a question which has arisen in connection with a Convention right must take into account any judgment, decision or declaration or advisory opinion of the European Court of Human Rights, any decision on admissibility or report on the merits given by the (former) European Commission of Human Rights, or any decision of the Committee of Ministers (that is, before the entry into force of Protocol No 11), so far as relevant to the proceedings.[32] Thus, the UK courts are obliged to have regard to the Strasbourg case law in deciding whether Convention rights have been violated, but are not strictly bound to follow decisions of the Strasbourg institutions.

Both HRA and SA seek to give effect to Convention rights in four broad ways: through rules of statutory interpretation, through methods for the resolution of incompatibility between statutes and Convention rights, through the imposition of express limitations upon powers of public bodies, and through the institution of proactive checks in an attempt to reduce the likelihood of parliaments legislating in a manner incompatible with the Convention. The brief comparison of both sets of statutory provisions which follows will show how the manner of 'incorporation' of the Convention rights varies as between devolved and non-devolved matters.

---

29 See, eg, essays by M Tushnet and by K Ewing, in C Gearty and A Tomkins (eds), *Understanding Human Rights* (1996).
30 SA, Sch 5, para 7(2).
31 HRA, s 1(1) and (2), amended by the Human Rights Act 1998 (Amendment) Order 2004 (SI 2004/1574); ('designated derogation' is defined by s 14, and 'designated reservation' by s 15 to mean the UK's reservation to Art 2 of Protocol 1 to the ECHR): SA, s 126(1).
32 HRA, s 2.

Logically, the discussion of proactive checks should come first, but these are more easily understood once the limitations on the competence of the Scottish Parliament and Executive have been explained.

Interpretation of primary and subordinate legislation

Section 3 of HRA states that primary and subordinate legislation is to be read and given effect in a way that is compatible with the Convention rights, so far as it is possible to do so. This applies to legislation whenever enacted.[33] But this provision does not affect the validity, continuing operation or enforcement of any incompatible primary legislation, or of any incompatible subordinate legislation if (disregarding the possibility of revocation) primary legislation prevents removal of the incompatibility.[34] Thus the HRA does not impliedly repeal previous legislation enacted by the Westminster Parliament which is incompatible with the Convention, or prevent the enactment of subsequent legislation incompatible with the Convention. The task of a court is to determine whether a provision can be read in a manner which prevents the need for a declaration of incompatibility (see below).[35]

The requirement in HRA, section 3 to read legislation 'so far as it is possible to do so' in a Convention-compatible way, applies to Acts of the Scottish Parliament which are defined as subordinate legislation for the purposes of HRA.[36] In addition, SA, section 101(2) provides that an Act of the Scottish Parliament is 'to be read as narrowly as is required for it to be within competence, if such a reading is possible'.[37] Despite the different wording and emphasis, the intention and effect of both provisions appear to be the same: to enable the courts to give effect to rather than to invalidate legislation[38] and to require courts as far as they can to read into legislative provisions relevant Convention principles and values. In practice, though, as far as HRA, section 3 is concerned, there have been variations in the way in which the provision has been applied, between narrower views which restrict the possible scope for interpretation of statutes and broader approaches which expand the scope of interpretation.[39]

Resolution of statutory incompatibility

If primary legislation cannot be read in a manner compatible with the Convention, the HRA enables specified courts[40] to make a declaration that the statutory provision

---

33 HRA, s 3(2)(a).
34 HRA, s 3(2)(b) and (c).
35 See further *R (Wardle) v Crown Court at Leeds* [2002] 1 AC 754, per Lord Hope of Craighead at para 79, and Lord Clyde at para 155; *R v A (No 2)* [2001] 1 AC 45, per Lord Steyn at para 45; *R v Lambert* [2002] 2 AC 545, especially per Lord Hope of Craighead at paras 78–94; and *Gunn v Newman* 2001 SC 525.
36 HRA, s 21(1).
37 See, eg, *Flynn and others v HM Advocate* 2004 SC (PC) 1, discussed in Chapter 10 of this volume.
38 See HC Deb, vol 583, col 536 (18 Nov 1997) (regarding HRA) and HL Deb, vol 593, col 1953 (28 Oct 1998) (regarding SA).
39 See, eg, *R v A (No 2)* [2002] 1 AC 45; *R (Anderson) v Secretary of State for the Home Department* [2003] 1 AC 837; and *Ghaidan v Godin-Mendoza* [2004] 2 AC 557. For discussion in a Scottish case, see *Advocate-General for Scotland v MacDonald* 2001 SLT 819, 2003 SLT 1158 (HL).
40 HRA, s 4(5). In proceedings arising in the Scottish courts, this means the House of Lords, the Judicial Committee of the Privy Council, the High Court of Justiciary sitting otherwise than as a trial court, and the Court of Session.

is incompatible with a Convention right. Such a declaration can also be made where a provision of subordinate legislation is incompatible and where primary legislation prevents removal of the incompatibility.[41] The legislation is worded in such a way as to confer a power rather than a duty. However, a declaration of incompatibility does not affect the validity, continuing operation or enforcement of the provision in respect of which it is given, and is not binding on the parties to the proceedings in which it is made.[42] So, the courts may not under HRA invalidate primary legislation of the UK Parliament. Rather, it is envisaged that the government (or where appropriate Scottish Executive)[43] will use its powers to take remedial action (by order) to remove the incompatibility.[44] In contrast, the provisions of SA dealing with Acts of the Scottish Parliament go further. An Act of the Scottish Parliament is not law so far as any provision of the Act is outside the legislative competence of the Parliament,[45] including where provisions are incompatible with Convention rights.[46] The courts may thus strike down an offending provision. The powers of the courts are also wider than those under HRA. If a court or tribunal decides that any provision of an Act of the Scottish Parliament is not within its competence, or that subordinate legislation is ultra vires, the court or tribunal has the power to make an order removing or limiting any retrospective effect of the decision, or suspending the effect of the decision for any period and, on any conditions, in order to allow the defect to be corrected.[47] Again, this power appears to envisage that the Scottish Executive will bring forward proposals to remove incompatibility.

Limitations on powers of public bodies: duty to act compatibly with Convention rights

At first glance, there are more similarities between the two statutes in this area. HRA, section 6 makes it unlawful in general for a public authority to act[48] in a way which is incompatible with a Convention right unless, as the result of one or more provisions of primary legislation, the authority could not have acted differently.[49] Similarly, SA, section 57(2) provides that a member of the Scottish Executive has no power to make any subordinate legislation, or to do any other act, so far as the legislation or act is incompatible with any of the Convention rights or with Community law. The differences lie in the limitation inherent in these sections.

41 HRA, s 4(1)–(4).
42 HRA, s 4(6).
43 Cf Reed and Murdoch, *Human Rights*, para 1.87, fn 1: 'It seems that powers under the Human Rights Act 1998, s 10 can also be exercised by a Scottish Minister in relation to matters falling within devolved competence: see the complex provisions of the Scotland Act 1998, s 53 and Sch 4, paras 1, 12 and 13. Similar powers are conferred in any event on the Scottish Ministers by the Convention Rights (Compliance) (Scotland) Act 2001.'
44 HRA, s 10. Section 10 allows for the amendment of primary and subordinate legislation both in response to a declaration of incompatibility, and in response to an adverse finding of the Strasbourg Court against the UK.
45 SA, s 29(1).
46 SA, s 126(1).
47 SA, s 102.
48 An 'act' includes a failure to act, but not a failure to introduce in, or lay before, Parliament a proposal for legislation; or make any primary legislation or remedial order: HRA, s 6(6).
49 HRA, s 6(2). This exception appears to cover the situation where the public authority is not required by primary legislation to act as it has done, but where it was acting so as to implement the legislation and all possible ways of implementing the legislation would involve a breach of Convention rights: see *Millar v Dickson* 2001 SCCR 741.

HRA section 6 provides a general statutory defence to a public authority that primary legislation required it to act as it did. However, there is no such general defence under the SA. There is a limitation on the scope of section 57(2), but it applies only to the Lord Advocate and only to certain of his functions.[50] It is also worth noting that, for the purposes of section 57(2), the term 'act' is interpreted broadly to include the implementation of an executive or administrative decision.[51]

The scope of section 6 is extended by section 6(3)(a) which provides that the term 'public authority' includes a court or tribunal. Thus, the courts are also under a duty to act in a manner which is compatible with Convention rights. This means that in addition to the duty of compatible interpretation of legislation, the courts have a duty to apply and develop the common law consistently with the Convention rights, which may apply both in cases involving other public authorities and in disputes between private parties.[52]

Although the courts are clearly included, one of the key problems in applying HRA, section 6 has nonetheless been the meaning to be given to the term 'public authority'. A 'public authority' also includes 'any person certain of whose functions are functions of a public nature',[53] but in relation to a particular act, a person is not a public authority by virtue only of being a person certain of whose functions are functions of a public nature if the nature of the act is private.[54] Here, the legislative intention is to distinguish between 'obvious' public authorities (such as central and local government and the police), all of whose acts are unlawful if incompatible with the Convention, and entities which are public authorities only by virtue of HRA, and whose acts are unlawful by reason of being incompatible with the Convention only if not of a private nature. This aspect of the statute has proved troublesome to the courts, however, for the distinctions between public and private authorities and public and private functions are not always obvious, and courts have struggled with this provision from the outset.[55] The outcome has been a rather restricted approach and concern that there are 'real gaps and inadequacies in human rights protection'.[56]

Legislative process

As indicated above, both statutes include proactive measures designed to reduce the likelihood of questions of incompatibility arising in respect of legislation. The HRA

---

50 SA, s 57(3) which covers the Lord Advocate's functions in respect of prosecution and the investigation of deaths. See also Chapter 10 in this volume.
51 *HM Advocate v Burns* 2000 SCCR 884; cf *HM Advocate v Campbell* 1999 SCCR 980 (no 'act' of the public prosecutor before disputed evidence is sought to be led).
52 For examples, see *Venables v News Group Newspapers Ltd* [2001] Fam 430, per Dame Elizabeth Butler-Sloss, paras 24–27 and *Karl Construction Ltd v Palisade Properties plc* 2002 SLT 312.
53 HRA, s 6(3)(b).
54 HRA, s 6(5). See further Rt Hon Lord Clyde and D Edwards, *Judicial Review* (2000), para 6.47.
55 Compare and contrast, eg, *Poplar Housing and Regeneration Community Association Ltd v Donoghue* [2002] QB 48, with *R (Heather) v Leonard Cheshire Foundation* [2002] 2 All ER 936. See further D Oliver, 'The frontiers of the state: public authorities and public functions under the Human Rights Act' [2000] PL 476 and M Carss-Frisk, 'Public authorities: the developing function' [2002] EHRLR 92; C Donnelly, '*Leonard Cheshire* again and beyond: private contractors, contract and section 6(3)(b) of the Human Rights Act' [2005] PL 785; and Joint Committee on Human Rights, *The Meaning of Public Authority under the Human Rights Act* (7th Report, 2003–04, HL39/HC 382).
56 Joint Committee on Human Rights, *The Work of the Committee in the 2001–05 Parliament* (19th Report, Session 2004–05, HL112/HC 552), para 148.

requires a minister of the Crown in charge of a Bill in either House of Parliament to make a statement (in writing and to be published in such manner as the minister making it considers appropriate) before the second reading of the Bill, either to the effect that in his view the provisions of the Bill are compatible with the Convention rights ('a statement of compatibility') or to the effect that, although he is unable to make a statement of compatibility, the government nevertheless wishes the House to proceed with the Bill.[57] A statement made to the Westminster Parliament probably does not give rise to a justiciable issue by virtue of parliamentary privilege under the Bill of Rights 1689.

The SA provides, in contrast, not one but multiple devices seeking to minimise the possibility that the Scottish Parliament legislates outwith its competence. First, a member of the Scottish Executive in charge of a Bill must state that in his view the provisions of the Bill would be within the Parliament's competence.[58] Second, the Presiding Officer of the Parliament must state, on or before introduction of the Bill, whether in his opinion the provisions would be within competence.[59] Third, any of the law officers may refer a Bill to the Judicial Committee of the Privy Council for determination of whether it is within competence.[60] Fourthly, the Secretary of State may make an order prohibiting submission of a Bill for royal assent on grounds which include incompatibility with international obligations.[61] A Bill may not be presented for royal assent where the Judicial Committee has decided it is not within competence, or if a referral has not been determined or the time within which a referral may be made has not elapsed, or if the Secretary of State has made an order.

However, these provisions which aim to prevent the Scottish Parliament from legislating incompatibly with Convention rights do not in themselves influence the determination by the courts of a legal challenge to the competence of a provision of an Act of the Scottish Parliament, and decisions by the minister in charge of a Bill and by the Presiding Officer that a Bill is within the vires of the Scottish Parliament are 'no more than statements of opinion which do not bind the judiciary'; in any event, the fact that a law officer has decided not to refer a Bill to the Judicial Committee is not of consequence in determining a subsequent challenge to the compatibility of a Bill in legal proceedings.[62] Where a pre-royal assent reference has been made by a law officer, however, the Judicial Committee's decision will be binding on lower courts but will not prevent the Judicial Committee itself from reconsidering an appeal or reference made on a devolution issue.[63]

Other differences between the statutes

There are further differences between the two statutes in relation to rights of action and matters of procedure and remedies for which each makes separate provision. Both the HRA and the SA restrict the right to raise an action claiming

57 HRA, s 19. An analogous practice has been adopted in respect of statutory instruments: HL Deb, vol 608, col 76WA (10 Jan 2000).
58 SA, s 31(1).
59 SA, s 31(2).
60 SA, s 33. See also ss 34, 36.
61 SA, s 35.
62 *A v Scottish Ministers* 2002 SC (PC) 63 at 66 per Lord Hope of Craighead. Under the HRA, the position on justiciability is likely to be similar, but this has not yet been determined.
63 SA, s 103(1).

a violation of Convention rights or otherwise relying on the Convention rights in legal proceedings to those who are victims within the meaning of Article 34 of the ECHR.[64] Any claim that an Act of the Scottish Parliament or an action of a member of the Scottish Executive is ultra vires on human rights grounds amounts to a devolution issue in terms of SA, Schedule 6 and thus requires certain procedures to be followed, including intimation to the Lord Advocate and Advocate General and the possibility (or duty in the case of tribunals from which there is no appeal) of referral to the appropriate higher court. In contrast, the HRA provides no special procedures for dealing with claims arising under it. Perhaps more significantly, the House of Lords is the court of last resort for issues raised under the HRA in matters other than Scottish criminal cases, but in contrast, the Judicial Committee of the Privy Council is normally the court of last resort for devolution issues.

The availability of relief is not unrestricted. HRA, section 7 provides that a person who claims that a public authority has acted (or proposes to act) in a manner incompatible with Convention rights may bring proceedings against the authority under the Act in the appropriate court or tribunal, or rely on the Convention right or rights concerned in any legal proceedings.[65] The appropriate court or tribunal is any civil court or tribunal which has jurisdiction to grant the remedy sought.[66] Unlike the situation under SA, proceedings must be brought timeously under HRA, as there is a requirement that proceedings must be brought within the period of one year beginning with the date on which the act complained of took place or such longer period as the court or tribunal considers equitable having regard to all the circumstances (subject to any rule imposing a stricter time-limit in relation to the procedure in question).[67] As to remedies, under HRA a court or tribunal may grant such relief or remedy, or make such order, within its powers as it considers just and appropriate in relation to any act (or proposed act) of a public authority which the court finds is (or would be) unlawful under the statute,[68] but damages may be awarded only by a court which has power to award damages, or to order the payment of compensation in civil proceedings.[69] Damages may not be awarded under either statute unless that would be necessary to afford just satisfaction and in determining whether to award damages and the amount of the award the court must take account of the principles applied by the European Court of Human Rights.[70]

EXPERIENCE TO DATE: 'GIVING EFFECT' TO CONVENTION RIGHTS

It is thus clear that neither HRA nor SA amounts to full incorporation of the ECHR into domestic law, but rather each requires domestic courts to take

64 HRA, s 7(1), (7); SA, s 100(1).
65 'Legal proceedings' include proceedings brought by or at the instigation of a public authority, and an appeal against the decision of a court or tribunal: HRA, s 7(6).
66 Human Rights Act 1998 (Jurisdiction) (Scotland) Rules 2000 (SSI 2000/301), rule 3. SA, s 100 is to the same effect as HRA, s 7 but does not authorise the making of rules regarding the appropriate court.
67 HRA, s 7(5).
68 HRA, s 8(1).
69 HRA, s 8(2).
70 HRA, s 8(3), (4); SA, s 100(3).

Convention jurisprudence into account in determining certain legal issues. This in turn implies that domestic lawyers cannot merely rely upon Strasbourg jurisprudence, but must also consider the way in which and the extent to which the two statutes protect Convention rights, and, given that the Strasbourg case law is persuasive rather than binding, how Convention rights have been interpreted at a local level. Further, since decisions of domestic courts may on occasion fail to meet minimum Strasbourg requirements, consideration of whether a further challenge via the Convention machinery is appropriate may be called for.

The legal profession and use of human rights arguments in the courts

The effectiveness of both statutes depends upon the ability and willingness of the legal profession to identify and to employ human rights arguments. For supporters of human rights legislation, the preparedness of the legal profession was potentially an issue. As already noted, legal education hardly gave prominence to the subject, while *Kaur* and *Moore* may have dampened any enthusiasm for the best part of two decades. However, before the legislation came into force, a welter of seminars was organised by and for the professional bodies and for the judiciary in order to help acclimatise the legal system. At the same time, internal 'audits' attempted to pinpoint actual and potential shortcomings in public sector agencies. This proactive work was of some significance, and was most marked in the presentation of legislative proposals by the new Scottish Executive that ultimately resulted in the Bail, Judicial Appointments etc (Scotland) Act 2000 and the Convention Rights (Compliance) (Scotland) Act 2001. An alternative perspective was provided by opponents of human rights legislation such as Lord McCluskey who argued, using an oft-quoted aphorism borrowed from Canada, that the Convention would prove to be 'a field-day for crackpots, a pain in the neck for judges and a gold mine for lawyers'.[71]

Experience, however, has been very different. It was perhaps inevitable that the initial enthusiasm for raising Convention-based challenges would be followed by a cooling-off of interest. Research carried out for the Scottish Executive into the use made of Convention rights arguments in the Scottish courts (but not tribunals) confirmed what many had predicted: there had indeed been an initial surge in the use of human rights arguments followed by a reduction and thereafter a settling-down in their use. This was particularly so in criminal cases: over a thousand human rights issues were raised in the first nineteen months (that is, until the end of 2000), but this number soon dropped and stabilised at around 175 to 200 per annum. Placed in the context of the total number of prosecutions in Scotland, these cases represented only a very small fraction (a little over 0.25 per cent) of the total criminal case load.[72] More interestingly, there were a number of 'hot spots' in Scotland where human rights cases were clustered, rather than being randomly distributed across Scotland. As far as civil cases were concerned, it was more difficult to ascertain the number of cases in which human rights arguments had been raised (criminal cases were recorded by the Crown Office as a matter of course), but the research seemed to indicate (albeit tentatively) that human

---

71 *Scotland on Sunday*, 6 Feb 2000.
72 See P Greenhill et al, *The Use of Human Rights Legislation in the Scottish Courts* (2004), pp 11–12. See also T Mullen et al, 'Human rights in the Scottish courts' (2005) 32 JLS 148.

rights points were being raised more often in the Court of Session than in the sheriff court. It was not surprising that judicial review proceedings were the most significant category of Court of Session cases given the purpose and content of the Convention; nor was it unexpected that summary applications should be the most prevalent form of procedure in which human rights arguments arose in the sheriff court given the scope of the subject-matters which fall under this procedure (which include appeals against local authority decisions affecting individuals' interests, such as assumption of parental rights).[73]

The research also confirmed the predictions that, in criminal cases, the bulk of challenges would be under the Article 6 guarantee of a fair hearing, and within this category, would involve the requirement of 'trial within a reasonable time'. (This prediction was not necessarily a reflection upon Scots law, for this Article, and this particular aspect of the guarantee, generate the bulk of applications to the European Court of Human Rights.) Some seventeen out of every twenty challenges involved fair trial issues, and matters of criminal process; of these cases, just under two in every five involved allegations of undue delay. This latter figure may indeed have been more striking were it not for the significant 'cluster' of cases on the issue of independent and impartial tribunals, a statistic attributable in large measure to the success of the challenge to the position of temporary sheriffs.[74] In civil cases, Article 6 also dominated but to a much lesser extent than in criminal cases. The other provisions which featured prominently included Article 8's guarantees of respect for private and family life (accounting for some one-fifth of these challenges), Article 3's prohibition of ill-treatment, and the protection of property under Article 1 of Protocol No 1.[75]

But how well founded were the arguments produced in these cases? Had there indeed been a 'field-day for crackpots', albeit only in particular localities? The research suggested that there probably had not been. It examined a sample of reported cases which indicated that remedies were only granted on human rights grounds (that is, where there was a specific indication that such arguments had been influential in a case) in a small but significant minority of cases: that is, in just under 17 per cent of reported cases, with remedies more frequently sought under SA than under HRA on account of the larger number of criminal cases.[76] But this is not the whole picture. Even if these arguments were plausible, how significant were they in the court's determination of the case? In many cases it was clear that human rights arguments were being advanced as supplementary to other submissions based upon existing legal principles and rules, and that courts, too, were in some instances prepared to avoid addressing Convention rights if the matter could be disposed of (favourably to the party raising the issue) on these alternative and existing grounds.[77] The research also suggested that weak or ill-informed arguments may have been advanced in certain reported cases. Insufficient data were available to

73 Greenhill, above n 72, pp 14–15.
74 *Starrs v Ruxton* 2000 JC 208.
75 That is, 19 per cent, 10 per cent and 8 per cent respectively: Greenhill et al, above n 72, pp 17–23. The main subject-matter headings for these challenges were asylum and immigration control (22 per cent), civil procedure (19 per cent), child law and property rights (both 10 per cent).
76 Above n 72, pp 23–26.
77 HRA, s 11 specifically provides that a person's reliance on a Convention right does not restrict any other right or freedom conferred on him by or under any law having effect in any part of the UK, or his right to make any claim or bring any proceedings which he could make or bring apart from the statute.

assess the quality of submissions in *unreported* cases, so it could not be ascertained whether spurious arguments were more frequently made in them than in reported cases.

A further question is the extent to which the opportunity to make a plausible human rights claim was being missed by litigants. The research identified this as an important issue but gave an understandable 'no comment' as only cases in which human rights arguments were actually made were examined. The report, though, did indicate several instances of potential areas for future challenge across several aspects of the Convention. Further, the phenomenon of human rights 'hot spots' (and therefore 'cold spots') remains a finding without an explanation.

The judicial response

The readiness of the courts to make a finding of violation of Convention rights was one aspect of the judicial response to the human rights legislation. The research also indicated that – in the volume of the case load – the legislation had not become a 'pain in the neck for judges'. But this is not to say that the intellectual issues posed by human rights legislation were negligible. As noted above, one of the key issues in HRA was the meaning to be given to 'public authority', and the lead in resolving this was very much assumed by the English courts. The problems facing the Scottish courts, as expected, focused more (though not exclusively) upon the implications of SA.

The co-existence of the two statutes posed some initial difficulty, for it was not inconceivable that the same issue could give rise to challenges under either or both statutes. Nor was the interplay between the two pieces of legislation always an obvious one. However, following cases such as *Starrs v Ruxton*[78] and *Brown v Stott*,[79] claims of violations of Convention rights in the context of criminal prosecutions were to be treated as raising devolution issues under SA (on account of the position of the Lord Advocate as both head of the public prosecution system and a member of the Scottish Executive) rather than as issues for disposal solely under HRA.[80] Further, how would constitutional sensitivities be resolved in the highest courts between Scottish and English judges? For example, there were some early suggestions that the Privy Council should be sensitive to its new role in determining issues of Scots criminal law and procedure.[81] And did the particular wording of SA, which bluntly stated that the Executive could not act contrary to Convention rights, really mean this? The issue came to a head over the question whether this statutory language

---

78 2000 JC 208.
79 2001 SC (PC) 43.
80 See further I Jamieson, 'Relationship between the Scotland Act and the Human Rights Act' 2001 SLT (News) 43, and 'Relationship between the Scotland Act and the Human Rights Act: recent developments' 2002 SLT (News) 33.
81 See, eg, *Mills v HM Advocate (No 2)* 2002 SLT 1359 at 1365C per Lord Hope: '[in disposing of questions affecting Scots criminal law], the Privy Council would be involved … in its role as a constitutional court and would doubtless approach any issues on that basis only, without entering further than necessary into questions of substantive law'; and earlier comments in *Montgomery v HM Advocate* 2001 SC (PC) 1 at 13: 'It follows that members of the Judicial Committee whose background is in English law must now exercise the intellectual discipline of thinking themselves into the Scottish system of criminal law when sitting on references or appeals from the High Court of Justiciary, as members of the committee whose background is in Scots law have always had to do of thinking themselves into the English system of criminal law when hearing appeals in criminal cases from the Commonwealth.'

had the consequence that the prosecutor was absolutely barred from proceeding with a prosecution in which there had been a breach of Article 6's guarantee of 'trial within a reasonable time'. In *R v HM Advocate,* the Privy Council decided by a majority of three to two (the members of the majority all being Scottish judges) that it did.[82] Subsequently, however, in *Attorney-General's Reference (No 2 of 2001)* [83] a specially convened panel of nine Law Lords (the two Scottish judges dissenting) decided in an English appeal that it would not be appropriate to stay proceedings on the ground of delay unless the delay made a fair hearing impossible, and went out of their way to emphasise that their conclusion was incompatible with that of the Privy Council in *R v HM Advocate.*[84]

Other issues have arisen. What approaches would the courts take in disposing of human rights challenges? In particular, would there simply be an attempt to follow Strasbourg jurisprudence wherever possible? Contempt of court is one clear area in which the Scottish criminal courts have relaxed their traditional stance. As Lord Rodger of Earlsferry put it:

> '[A]lthough a boundary has always existed between freedom of expression and the requirements of the due course of justice, Article 10 may have had the consequence of displacing that boundary from the familiar place where once it ran: the boundary may have been redrawn at a point which would not have been chosen by people looking at the matter primarily from the standpoint of the administration of justice. This is a useful reminder that, although the Convention gives expression to values which already infuse the law of Scotland, and may be regarded as commonplaces of all western legal systems, it does not always express or balance those values in the same way as Scots law has traditionally done'.[85]

Not all decisions of the domestic courts have, however, been as sympathetic to Strasbourg jurisprudence. The responsibility to 'give effect' to Convention rights by 'taking into account' (rather than being strictly bound by) relevant European case law can, of course, lead to divergence in opinion. While in the absence of some special circumstances, domestic courts should follow any clear and constant jurisprudence,[86] domestic courts may still on occasion adopt an approach which is arguably at odds with the thrust of Strasbourg case law. The Privy Council's decision in *Stott v Brown,*[87] which concerned a requirement placed upon a motorist to provide information to the authorities as to the driver of a vehicle when it was suspected that she had committed an offence, is difficult to reconcile with the approach of the European Court of Human Rights to self-incrimination.[88] The High Court of Justiciary's determination in *Unterschutz v HM Advocate,*[89] that an interview by Inland Revenue officials did not set the clock running in respect

82 *R v HM Advocate* 2003 SC (PC) 21.
83 [2004] 2 AC 72.
84 For discussion, see D Feldman, 'None, one or several? Perspectives on the UK's constitution(s)' (2005) 64 CLJ 329.
85 *Cox and Griffiths, Petitioners* 1998 SCCR 561 at 568.
86 *R (Alconbury Developments Ltd) v Secretary of State for the Environment, Transport and the Regions* [2001] 2 WLR 1389 at para 26 per Lord Slynn of Hadley.
87 2001 SC (PC) 43.
88 See, eg, S Di Rollo, 'Section 172 – an unconventional approach?' 2001 SLT (News) 13; and S Naismith, 'Self-incrimination: the case law of the European Court of Human Rights' (2001) HR&UK P 2.4(3). For a contrary view, see R Pillay, 'Self-incrimination and Article 6' [2001] EHRLR 78.
89 2003 JC 70.

of Article 6's right to a 'trial within a reasonable time' on the ground that such officials had no power themselves to bring a prosecution, is arguably similarly out of line with Strasbourg jurisprudence. On the other hand, a domestic court may rule in a manner which adopts a higher standard of protection than that strictly required by the Convention, particularly in a case where it is clear that the Strasbourg Court would most likely follow a similar approach in future. The approach in *Napier v Scottish Ministers*[90] was, at the time it was delivered, arguably in advance of what the Strasbourg Court would have decided in relation to prison conditions.

Another question was the extent to which the courts (and the legal profession) have responded to the potential for use of comparative materials in human rights litigation. Such use was expected. Application of new (or relatively so) approaches such as proportionality would be rendered easier if ready-made examples from other jurisdictions were to hand. In fact, reference to material from other jurisdictions has become common. For example, in *Karl Construction Ltd v Palisade Properties plc*[91] (a case concerning whether diligence in the form of inhibition on the dependence was contrary to Article 1 of Protocol No 1 of the ECHR) counsel for the pursuer referred the court to practice in a number of other European countries including Belgium, Denmark, France, Germany, Italy, Luxembourg and The Netherlands, to a leading decision of the US Supreme Court, and to the International Law Association's 'Helsinki Principles on Provisional and Protective Measures in International Litigation'. Similarly, in *Dyer v Watson*,[92] in considering the question whether two police officers facing charges of perjury were tried within a reasonable time, the court was asked to examine jurisprudence from England, the USA, Germany, Mauritius and New Zealand as well as from the Strasbourg organs. Comparative law thus has a new relevance.

Probably for linguistic (and thus practical) reasons, comparative material in human rights litigation in England and Wales and Scotland has in large part been drawn from Commonwealth jurisprudence. For example, in *Starrs v Ruxton* the court considered case law from Canada and Norway when examining the independence and impartiality of temporary judges.[93] Arguably, though, European domestic legal systems are of greater relevance, particularly where it may be important to consider whether there is an emerging European consensus upon a particular issue.

Nevertheless, borrowing from an increasingly defined package of values and solutions and transposing concepts and legal approaches, while helping emphasise the universality of human rights, carries with it the risk that judges are selective in their choice of sources, seeking to find a particular approach which fits with their own set of values or beliefs. A more fundamental objection is that domestic courts, in placing an over-reliance upon foreign decisions, are avoiding their own responsibilities to apply human rights principles in accordance with settled constitutional and legal traditions.[94]

---

90 2005 1 SC 229.
91 2002 SLT 312.
92 2002 SC (PC) 89.
93 1999 SCCR 1052.
94 See C McCrudden, 'A common law of human rights? Transnational judicial conversations on constitutional rights' (2000) 4 OJLS 499 at 507–508, discussing dicta of Lord Woolf in *Attorney-General of Hong Kong v Lee Kwong-kut* (1993) 3 HKPLR 72.

DEVELOPING A HUMAN RIGHTS 'CULTURE'

The ultimate aim behind the introduction of human rights legislation was to cement human rights values into government and society.[95] Litigation can clearly play a role in achieving this goal, but whether it alone is sufficient is open to some doubt, particularly if (as noted above) the very notion of 'human rights' is under constant attack by the populist press and by politicians. The talk is very much still about establishing a 'human rights culture'. But discussion of 'culture', if this is a shorthand reference to the extent to which human rights standards are generally respected by decision-makers and officials, does allow some further reflection as to whether additional nurturing through institutional means is required, for a second wave of legislative provisions concerning human rights is following the first, on this occasion specifically to deal with 'promotion' rather than protection through the courts.

The establishment of national human rights institutions (NHRIs) has become *de rigueur* in recent years. However labelled (ombudsperson, commission, commissioner, institute), the basic assumption is that a non-judicial but sufficiently independent authority charged with the promotion and protection of human rights can make a significant contribution to awareness and understanding of the public sector and of the public in general and thereby help improve compliance with human rights instruments. The current inspiration for such institutions can be directly attributed to the United Nations and its statement of guidance on its establishment (the 'Paris Principles'),[96] but earlier examples of such publicly-funded bodies abound. In the UK, the Commission for Racial Equality and the Equal Opportunities Commission are early examples of attempts by the Westminster Parliament to develop such public agencies, while the Disability Rights Commission is a third and later example. Arguably, their establishment has been motivated by the perceived need to render human rights principles effective rather than merely illusory.

At a Great Britain level, the decision to establish a new equality commission replacing these three bodies provided the opportunity for proponents of a British NHRI to advocate the introduction of such a body (and failing which, to press for the extension of the mandate of the proposed new equality body to include human rights more generally). The governmental response was rejection of the idea of a separate body but acceptance (possibly grudgingly) of a wider remit to include human rights. The new Commission for Equality and Human Rights (CEHR) established by the Equality Act 2006 is thus heralded as a body which will not only build on existing achievements of the three equality commissions already established but in addition will more generally promote equality (and in particular through tackling discrimination in relation to sexual orientation, religion or belief, and age) and 'a culture of respect for human rights' through such tasks as the provision of systematic advice and guidance to public bodies.[97]

As far as Scotland is concerned, the devolution settlement has resulted in a more complex situation. The commitment to establish a Scottish body formed part of the 2003 Partnership Agreement between the Labour and Liberal Democratic parties, and resulted in consultation exercises designed to test public support. But

---

95 See, eg, Lord Irvine of Lairg, Tom Sargant Memorial Lecture 1997.
96 See UN General Assembly Resolution 48/134 of 20 Dec 1993.
97 See Joint Committee on Human Rights, *The Case for A Human Rights Commission* (6th Report, Session 2002–03, HC 67–I/HL 489–I), para 13.

when the Scottish Commissioner for Human Rights Bill was finally published in 2005, it was clear that the Scottish body (in the form of a commissioner, with up to two deputy commissioners) would be a less imposing body than the CEHR. While many respondents stressed the positive outcomes that could be achieved by the establishment of the office (in general, proactively raising awareness of human rights, sharing of best practice in the public sector, giving advice and guidance, and highlighting deficiencies in current law and practice), others did so in the expectation that further powers would be made available in time (in particular, the authority to assist individuals to assert their human rights more effectively in court proceedings). The dominant response was positive: such an institution would be an indispensable necessity (or at least, of considerable assistance) in helping promote and establish a 'human rights culture' in Scottish society.[98] Other expressions of support stressed the anomalous situation which would arise were no such institution to be created: Scotland (or at least in respect of devolved issues) would be left as a human rights backwater as the CEHR will not have power to take action in respect of human rights in Scotland where 'the Scottish Parliament has legislative competence to enable a body to take action of that kind'.[99] In short, were the Scottish Parliament to decide not to create such an office, there would be a hiatus in protection.

Questions remain, however, as to how a Scottish institution will best dovetail with the CEHR to avoid confusion and duplication. And to what extent will a Scottish institution itself fit into existing devolved institutional arrangements? The Scottish Parliament quite properly sees itself as an institution charged with the responsibility of protecting human rights. It has also inherited a range of bodies at least indirectly charged with ensuring respect for human rights[100] as well as having created additional offices (such as the Children's Commissioner). A range of specific concerns became apparent at stage 1 of the parliamentary proceedings: need (was Scotland really in need of a human rights institution?); duplication (could an existing mechanism – most obviously, the Scottish Public Services Ombudsman – do the job?); co-ordination (how would the institution, if established, fit in with existing Scottish bodies such as the Children's Commissioner, the Prisons Inspectorate, and so on?); governance (can independence be squared with proper accountability to the Scottish Parliament?); resources (was the proposed level of funding – £1 million per annum – ever going to be sufficient?); and enforcement powers (why was the legal right of entry to places of detention so limited?); and did the institution require more effective powers to intervene in and/or in court proceedings?[101] These concerns led, in the light of the unprecedented lack of positive enthusiasm for a recommendation that the Bill's principles be accepted, to the subsequent making of certain concessions by the Executive.[102] At the time of

---

98 See further Scottish Commissioner for Human Rights Bill [SP Bill 48 Session 2 (2005)].
99 Equality Act 2006, s 7(1).
100 In particular, the Scottish Parliamentary and Health Service Ombudsman, the Local Government Ombudsman for Scotland and the Housing Association Ombudsman for Scotland. In 2002, these offices were amalgamated to form the Scottish Public Services Ombudsman, on which see Chapter 14 in this volume.
101 Justice I Committee (1st Report 2006, session 2, SP Paper 508), paras 150–166. The Scottish Executive argued that giving the Commissioner the right to raise proceedings in his or her own name would trespass on reserved matters as HRA s 7 limits the right to raise an action to a 'victim'.
102 See further *Response of the Scottish Executive*, available at *http://www.scottish.parliament.uk/ business/committees/justice1/reports–06/j1_SCHR_ExecutiveResponseStage1Report.pdf.*

writing, the Bill is still proceeding through the Scottish Parliament, but it seems likely that Scotland will shortly have two national human rights institutions. The result will be further complexity but – just as with the opportunities posed by the existence of two statutes 'transforming' the European Convention into domestic law – the wider promotion of a human rights 'culture' will doubtless benefit from an advance on two fronts. Double vision is unlikely to result in myopia.

CONCLUSION

The complexity of the overlapping legislative provisions concerning human rights has been tackled with sensitivity by the courts. Although SA has a narrower scope than HRA in that it does not apply to public bodies generally, it confers greater authority upon the judiciary to review the validity of legislation and executive action. In particular, while the courts cannot invalidate Acts of the Westminster Parliament, they can invalidate Acts of the Scottish Parliament. Further, there is no general proviso excusing Acts required to be done by primary legislation, and thus statutory authority is in general no defence to claims that Convention rights have been violated. Nevertheless, the fears of sceptics have not materialised. The workload of the courts has not increased to any significant degree, and the legal system certainly has not been swamped. Nor can it be convincingly argued that the legislation has led to the politicisation of the judiciary in Scotland. The courts have respected constitutional norms: the necessity for measures interfering with rights may primarily be a political one, but their proportionality is at least in part a judicial one. The danger of isolation by unfamiliarity (or through insularity) which Lord Hope warned against has been replaced by an awareness of the importance of human rights values in determining questions of statutory interpretation, in developing the common law, and in expanding the scope of judicial review. Scots law now has a real opportunity to ensure that the values inherent in the ECHR infuse domestic law and practice. With this has also come a widening appreciation of the importance of comparative legal analysis.

There is, though, an understandable concern that litigation may not be a sufficient bulwark of individual protection. Hence the more recent discussion surrounding the introduction of NHRIs in the UK. This development comes at an opportune time. Commentators increasingly argue that the most fundamental political challenges to the rule of law and to respect for human rights emanate from the same London administration which piloted the key legislation through Westminster. Its range of measures seeking to strengthen public security and safety under three broad agendas – 'respect', criminal activity (including, but not confined to, serious and organised crime) and immigration and asylum control – have included anti-social behaviour orders, strengthened anti-terrorist legislation, increased surveillance, the introduction of identity cards and additional restrictions upon free speech and public protest, while a sharp and significant increase in both the numbers of prisoners and the length of sentences of imprisonment complement the current policy picture. On another front, the administration's attempts (and those of the main opposition party) to portray the ECHR as an outdated instrument unable to accommodate necessary measures to address the challenges posed by twenty-first century threats to public safety, and its attacks on judicial decision-making, involve a significant campaign of attrition against constitutional and legal principles hitherto considered largely sacrosanct. That the years following the enactment of the HRA have been marked in this way is surprising, but does indicate the weakness of some of the arguments advanced by opponents of 'incorporation' who were more prepared to place their faith in the elected representatives of the people rather than in an unrepresentative judiciary to control the possible excesses of a government. They assumed that societal concerns as to safety and security would never be allowed (except in extreme cases of war or public emergency) to undermine due process or the substantive liberties of speech, association and conscience won over the centuries. It was inconceivable that a protestor would ever be arrested for simply reading out the names of military personnel who had been killed in conflict; it was impossible that the government would ever seek to argue in legal proceedings that the evidence obtained by the use of torture by non-state actors could in certain circumstances be admitted, or that a Home Secretary would seek to remove rights of appeal from those denied asylum and to rewrite the Geneva Convention on Refugees. Of course, neither 'incorporation' of the ECHR nor the establishment of an NHRI can ever ultimately prevent a society determining that collective interests outweigh individual rights, but each can ensure that the political debate is more informed and that its outcomes are more measured and proportionate.

Index